THE CAMBRIDGE HISTORY OF ENGLISH LITERATURE

VOLUME III

RENASCENCE AND REFORMATION

LONDON
Cambridge University Press
FETTER LANE

NEW YORK · TORONTO
BOMBAY · CALCUTTA · MADRAS
Macmillan

TOKYO
Maruzen Company Ltd

THE CAMBRIDGE HISTORY OF ENGLISH LITERATURE

EDITED
BY
SIR A. W. WARD
AND
A. R. WALLER

VOLUME III

RENASCENCE AND REFORMATION

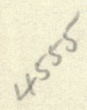

CAMBRIDGE
AT THE UNIVERSITY PRESS
1934

First edition 1908
Reprinted 1918, 1930
Cheap edition (text only) 1932
Reprinted 1934

PRINTED IN GREAT BRITAIN

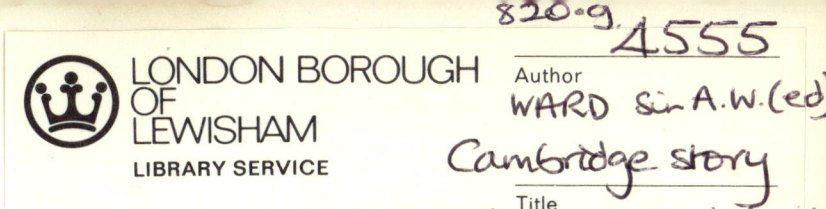

PREFATORY NOTE

The Cambridge History of English Literature was first published between the years 1907 and 1916. The General Index Volume was issued in 1927.

In the preface to Volume I the general editors explained their intentions. They proposed to give a connected account of the successive movements of English literature, to describe the work of writers both of primary and of secondary importance, and to discuss the interaction between English and foreign literatures. They included certain allied subjects such as oratory, scholarship, journalism and typography, and they did not neglect the literature of America and the British Dominions. The History was to unfold itself, "unfettered by any preconceived notions of artificial eras or controlling dates," and its judgments were not to be regarded as final.

This reprint of the text and general index of the *History* is issued in the hope that its low price may make it easily available to a wider circle of students and other readers who wish to have on their shelves the full story of English literature.

CAMBRIDGE
1932

CONTENTS

CHAPTER I

ENGLISHMEN AND THE CLASSICAL RENASCENCE

THE classical renascence implied a knowledge and imitation of the great literary artists of the golden past of classical antiquity, and, as a preliminary, a competent acquaintance with, and some power to use, the Latin and Greek languages. Italy gave it birth and it gradually spread beyond the Alps into Germany, France and England. In the end it created, almost imperceptibly, a cosmopolitan republic of which Guillaume Budé and Erasmus disputed the sovereignty, and where, latterly, Erasmus, by universal consent, ruled as chief. This republic established itself in a Europe almost savage, supremely warlike and comparatively untaught—in it and yet not of it. Its citizens were a select people who lived and worked in the midst of the tumult of arms, the conflict of politics and the war of creeds which went on around them. It spread widely and silently until it almost became the mark of a well-educated person to be able to read, write and converse fluently in Latin, and to know something of Greek. It refused to admit the limitations of sex. The learned lady (*erudita*) of the *Colloquia* of Erasmus easily discomfits the pretentious abbot. The prince of humanists himself, in no spirit of condescension, corresponded with the sisters of Pirkheimer and the daughters of More. At the celebrated reunions of Marguerite d'Angoulême, which were anticipations of the eighteenth century salon, Latin, Greek and even Hebrew were continually used. Her niece and grand-nieces were trained in the humanities. Mary of Scotland read Latin authors with George Buchanan. In England, well-born young ladies, towards the close of queen Mary's reign, were accomplished scholars. Elizabeth herself overwhelmed luckless ambassadors with floods of improvised Latinity. 'But this queen is extremely wise and has eyes that can flame,' wrote one who had, with difficulty, saved himself from the deluge.

The enthusiasts of the classical renascence, who had spent time and pains in mastering the secrets of style of the literary artists of antiquity, were somewhat disdainful of their mother tongues. They were inclined to believe that cultured thought could only find fit expression in the apt words, deft phrases and rhythmical cadences, of the revived language of ancient Rome. They preferred to write in Latin, and the use of the common speech of their cosmopolitan republic gave them an audience in all parts of educated Europe. Nevertheless, the classical renascence had a powerful effect in moulding the literary languages of modern Europe and in enriching them with graces of style and expression. Its influence was so pervading and impalpable that it worked like leaven, almost imperceptibly, yet really and potently.

The classical renascence recognised no one land in Europe as its own; it possessed all and belonged to all. Yet it is possible to describe its progress in Italy, Germany, France and even Spain, without introducing alien names. England is an exception. Erasmus belongs as much to the history of the classical renascence in our land as does Linacre, Colet, or More. The country received him when his fortunes were at a low ebb. He was about 33 years of age. The torments and temptations of Hertogenbosch, the midnight labours of Stein, the horrors of the Collège Montaigu and the penury of Paris had left their marks on his frail body. He had produced little or nothing. He was almost unknown and he had no sure prospects in life. In England he found friends, who gladly gave him hospitable welcome, whose cultured leisure enabled them to appreciate his learning, his humour, his untiring capacity for work and his ceaseless activity of mind. No wonder that the fortune-tossed wanderer was glad to fancy himself an Englishman and delighted in the men and women, the manners, the scholarship, even in the climate, of his new home—in everything English, in fact, save the beer and the draughty rooms.

He came, too, at the moment most fitting to make an impression. Scholasticism still reigned; but there were signs that its authority was waning. The honoured friend of English leading scholars, sought after by the educational reformer of one of its great universities, patronised by its archbishop, complimented by its young and popular king, Erasmus could not fail to make a deep impression on the country at a peculiarly impressionable time—an impression all the stronger because he appealed to the practical side of the English people in a way more directly than did any other humanist. They saw in him not a great classical specialist, but one who gathered the wisdom of the past to enrich and enlighten the present.

Erasmus visited England for the first time in the summer of 1499. He came in the company of young William Blount, lord Mountjoy, who had been one of his pupils in Paris. He seems to have resided, for a while, in London with Sir William Say, his pupil's father-in-law; then, at a country-house belonging to lord Mountjoy at Greenwich. He spent about two months at Oxford in the college of St Mary, an establishment for students of the Augustinian order presided over by prior Richard Charnock. He was back in London in the beginning of December; and, after a round-about journey by Dover, Calais and Tournehem, he arrived in Paris sometime about the end of January, 1500. His visit had been short, lasting about six months, just long enough to make him acquainted with the most prominent scholars in England; and his correspondence enables us to judge of the progress which the classical renascence had made there.

In a letter to Robert Fisher, 'the kyng's solicitor at Rome,' he instances four scholars whom he cannot praise too highly—John Colet, William Grocyn, Thomas Linacre and Thomas More. These men had learning neither hackneyed nor trivial, but deep, accurate, ancient Latin and Greek.

> When I hear my Colet, I seem to be listening to Plato himself. In Grocyn, who does not marvel at such a perfect round of learning? What can be more acute, profound and delicate than the judgment of Linacre? What has nature ever created more gentle, more sweet, more happy than the genius of Thomas More? I need not go through the list. It is marvellous how general and abundant is the harvest of ancient learning in this country[1].

The letters of Erasmus are, as a rule, more rhetorical than matter-of-fact; but, in this case, he seems to have been perfectly sincere. He believed that England was a specially favoured land, and that the classical renascence had made progress there in an exceptional way. Six years later, during his second visit, which lasted about fourteen months and was spent, for the most part, in London, he assured Servatius, the prior of the convent to which he was still nominally attached, that he had had intimate converse with five or six men in London who were as accurate scholars in Latin and Greek as Italy itself then possessed. His sincerity becomes manifest when it is remembered that these English scholars influenced his life as none of his innumerable

[1] *The Epistles of Erasmus*, F. M. Nichols, 1901, vol. I, p. 226, Ep. 110.

acquaintances was able to do. At his first visit he knew very little Greek. Their example and exhortations compelled him to study that language as soon as he returned to Paris. His pupil, lord Mountjoy, suggested to him his first book, *Adagia*; and prior Charnock encouraged him to undertake the task. It is scarcely too much to say that his first visit to England was the turning point in the career of Erasmus. Apart from it, he might have written *Adagia, Colloquia, Copia, Encomium Moriae*, but not *Novum Instrumentum* with the *Paraphrases, Enchiridion Militis Christiani, Institutio Principis Christiani*, nor his editions and commentaries on such early Fathers as Jerome and Chrysostom. He met men who, so far as the humanities were concerned, were riper scholars than himself and who, at the same time, were animated by lofty Christian aspirations; from them, Erasmus learnt to be a Christian humanist, with a real desire to see a reformation in life and morals in the church and in society, and a perception of the way in which the classical renascence might be made serviceable to that end.

Erasmus had never cared much for theology, although he had studied it in a somewhat perfunctory manner in order to qualify himself for the much esteemed degree of doctor of divinity. He had called himself *vetus theologus*, which meant one who accepted the teaching of Aquinas and cared little for the novelties introduced by John Duns Scotus. He had jeered at the Scotist theologians of the Sorbonne 'biting their nails and making all sorts of discoveries about *instances* and *quiddities* and *formalities*' and falling asleep at their task. Now, John Colet showed him that Aquinas was, perhaps, to be distrusted quite as much—a man who had taken upon himself to define *all* things, a man who had corrupted the teaching of Christ by mixing it with his profane philosophy. Colet made it plain, too, how the classical renascence could help in the work of reformation which all men then thought to be necessary. A scholar could edit the New Testament in Greek, and could translate the Scriptures into the vernaculars, so that the ploughman might repeat portions of them to himself as he followed the plough and the weaver might hum them to the tune of his shuttle. He could produce paraphrases of the more difficult portions. He could edit the writings of the earlier Fathers and show men what Christianity was before the schoolmen altered it. Such was the lesson which the English scholar impressed on the Dutch humanist, and Erasmus never forgot it. His intercourse with Colet gave a bent to his whole life.

The scholars whom Erasmus met in England during his earlier visits may be said to have been the pioneers of the classical renascence in this country. Before them, Englishmen had gone to Italy on business connected with the Holy See or to perfect themselves in canon law at the famous university of Bologna, and had used the opportunities given to study Latin and even Greek. We hear of Robert Flemming, afterwards dean of Lincoln, who studied Greek at Ferrara under Battista Guarino; of William Grey, who was taught by the famous Guarino, who brought Greek MSS to England and presented them to Balliol College; of John Gunthorpe; of William Tilly of Selling or Celling, who had travelled in Italy, had learned Greek and, most probably, taught it to his more promising pupils in the school of the monastery of Christ Church, Canterbury. These earliest English humanists are little more than names and the influence they exerted on their own land, however real it may have been, is obscure and scarcely discernible. The fact that they left their native land and studied under such a famous teacher as Guarino shows that there had arisen in England the beginnings of a desire to share in the classical renascence.

Thomas Linacre had been a pupil of William Tilly of Selling in the monastery school at Christ Church and, probably, had received his earliest aspirations towards scholarship from his master. He had gone to Oxford, where he had an opportunity of studying Greek under Cornelio Vitelli, who had been invited by the warden of New College, Thomas Chaundler, to act as praelector in his college, and who was the first to teach Greek publicly in England. His old teacher, William Tilly of Selling, was sent as ambassador by Henry VII to Innocent VIII; Linacre went with him and, spending some years in Italy, made the acquaintance of scholars and devoted himself to the humanities. At Bologna, he was introduced to Angelo Poliziano, and, at Florence, Lorenzo de' Medici permitted him to share the instructions given by that Italian humanist and by the learned Greek, Demetrius Chalcondylas, to his children Piero and Giovanni (afterwards pope Leo X). From Florence he went to Rome, where he became intimate with Hermolaus Barbarus, who, it is generally assumed, inspired him with the interest he afterwards displayed in the writings of Aristotle, Pliny, Galen and other medical writers among the ancients. In Venice, he made the acquaintance of Aldus Manutius Romanus, the great printer, and assisted him in the Aldine edition of Aristotle. In Padua, on the occasion of his graduating as M.D., he sustained a brilliant discussion against the senior physicians of that city. In Vicenza, he became the pupil of Nicolaus Leonides, equally famous as a humanist and as a physician. On Linacre's return to England he almost at once took the position which Leonides occupied in northern Italy. He was recognised as a distinguished physician and as the foremost scholar in his native land. He taught at Oxford, and Thomas More owed his knowledge of Greek to Linacre's instruction. He was tutor to prince Arthur. Later, he was one of the king's physicians to Henry VIII. He practised in London and was the founder of the Royal College of Physicians. He was appointed Latin tutor to princess Mary, then five years of age, and wrote for her use a grammar which afterwards became famous. This grammar was translated into Latin from the original English by George Buchanan, and, in this form, continued to be the standard Latin grammar in France for more than half a century. The rest of his writings were mainly medical translations from the works of Galen, the great Greek physician, whom he made known to European students of medicine.

William Grocyn was early distinguished by his knowledge of Greek and taught that language at Oxford before 1488. It is likely that he, as well as Linacre, owed his knowledge of Greek to Cornelio Vitelli. He followed Linacre to Italy, studied, like him, under Poliziano and Chalcondylas at Florence and, like him, made the acquaintance of the great Venetian printer. On his return to England, he taught Greek at Oxford, and his daily lectures were attended by the chief scholars of the time. Unlike most of the Italian humanists who were his contemporaries, Grocyn thought little of Plato and much of Aristotle. Yet he lectured on Pseudo-Dionysius at Oxford and for some time believed him to have been the convert of St Paul, but soon became convinced, either by independent study or by the criticism of Laurentius Valla, that the *Celestial Hierarchy* belonged to a much later age. He introduced Colet to the writings of Dionysius and also proved to him that the author could not have been the Areopagite. Grocyn resembled in many ways some of the older German humanists, who were content to spend their time in study and in directing and encouraging the work of younger scholars, without contributing to the store of learning by books of their own making.

With Grocyn and Linacre must be classed William Latimer, who had a great reputation for learning among his contemporaries,

English and continental. He had spent many years in Italy in acquiring a knowledge of the humanities, and his knowledge of Greek was highly esteemed by Erasmus. He was selected to be the tutor of young Reginald Pole, the future cardinal, whose scholarship, doubtless, was due to his early preceptor. The reasons he gave to Erasmus for refusing to act as teacher to John Fisher, bishop of Rochester, show the scorn of a scholar for the man who was content with a smattering of such a language as Greek and the preference of the humanist for classical Greek as compared with that of the New Testament.

Richard Pace and Cuthbert Tunstall are also to be classed among the English contemporaries of Erasmus who went to Italy to absorb the spirit of humanism in its peculiar home. The former studied at Padua, Ferrara and Bologna; the latter at Padua, where he made the acquaintance of Jerome Busleiden (Buslidianus), a scholar from the Netherlands and afterwards a friend both of More and of Erasmus. Both Pace and Tunstall were engaged in the diplomatic service of Henry VIII and received ecclesiastical preferment for their services. Tunstall was cardinal Wolsey's agent at the famous diet of Worms, and wrote to his master that he believed there were a hundred thousand Germans ready to lay down their lives in Luther's defence. Pace was employed in the vain endeavour to secure the imperial crown for Henry and the papacy for Wolsey.

The desire for classical learning spread widely. Students who could not go to Italy went to Paris, where teachers congregated. It was noticed there that the young Englishmen who came to the colleges in the French capital belonged, for the most part, to the aristocracy or to the moneyed classes. They were able to live in *pensionats* or boarding-houses, and did not share the hard life of the great majority of Parisian students, whose fate made them inmates of a college or drove them to highly-priced miserable garrets in the streets about the Place Maubert. In the *pensionats*, students lived under the care of a preceptor, and the best teachers the city afforded were hired to teach them the branches of learning they had come to acquire. Erasmus himself made the acquaintance of Englishmen by teaching in one of these boarding-houses. There he taught William Blount, lord Mountjoy, who brought him to England, Thomas Gray, Robert Fisher, cousin of John, afterwards bishop of Rochester, and the head of the boarding-house himself, who, most probably, was an Englishman of gentle birth from the Border (*Semi-Scotus*).

Royalty, even in the person of Henry VII, recognised the advantages of the classical renascence. Linacre, as has been said, was engaged to instruct the heir-apparent, Arthur, prince of Wales; the studious habits of young lord Mountjoy occasioned his selection to be elder companion to prince Henry. The part taken by Margaret, countess of Richmond and Derby, in establishing homes of the classical renascence in Cambridge has been discussed in a previous chapter of this work[1].

Among English scholars who were contemporaries of Erasmus, the first place must be given to John Colet, if precedence be determined not so much by the acquisition of exact scholarship as by the gifts of a commanding personality and the power to influence workers in a man's own and the succeeding generation. In another age, he might not have been the leader of men that he actually was; but, north of the Alps, during the close of the fifteenth and the earlier part of the sixteenth century, the moving force was religion, and Colet was the chief Christian humanist of England. Singularly enough, he seems to have been awakened to his vocation while in Italy. No evidence connects Colet with Florence, yet it is probable that his inspiration came from Savonarola. The probability is strengthened by his familiarity with the works of Marsilio Ficino, who, for a time, was completely under the influence of the great Florentine reformer, and of Giovanni Pico della Mirandola, who was his lifelong and ardent disciple. Colet began his work on his return to England. His was a typically English mind—conservative, practical, careless about exact definitions in theology—and the value of the classical learning for him was the use it could be put to in effecting the task which lay nearest his heart.

His sermon, preached before convocation (6 February 1511/12), was instinct with the sense of individuality, a new product of the renascence, and with a wise ecclesiastical conservatism. Everyone admitted the need of reformation: the question was how it could be effected. Colet argued that all reformation must begin within the individual soul, and that, if those in authority within the church set about reforming themselves, the movement would spread throughout the inferior clergy and the laity. No startling change was needed either in ecclesiastical constitution or in the enactment of new and drastic ecclesiastical laws. The existing laws could be made sufficient by the example of the bishops and their honest administration of their dioceses. The sermon was immediately

[1] See vol. II, chap. XV.

published, and has been frequently reprinted[1]. It was enlivened by pictures of the luxury, sloth and simony of the bishops and clergy of England, and, naturally, gave great offence. Colet's bishop, FitzJames of London, hastened to prefer charges of heresy against the dean of St Paul's, and extracts from his sermons, showing that he had at other times denounced the worship of images, large episcopal revenues and the practice of reading sermons, were laid before archbishop Warham with a view of procuring his condemnation. The charge was dismissed as frivolous.

Colet was more than careless of exact definitions in theology; he disliked them thoroughly. Most of those theologians who were at all tinged with the spirit of the renascence had turned from the later Scotist theology with its endless quibbles, but Colet went much further. He had a rooted dislike to Thomas Aquinas and had no sympathy with the reviving study of St Augustine. An examination of his various writings and of the reports of the lectures which he delivered in Oxford on his return from Italy suggests that he did not care for that use of legal terms and forms of thought which had been the characteristic of western theology from Tertullian to Aquinas and Ockham, to say nothing of post-reformation developments. The great men who built the western church and gradually formulated its elaborate constitution and its scheme of doctrine were almost all Roman lawyers, and their training influenced their ways of thinking on all matters ecclesiastical and theological. They inspired the medieval church with the conception of an intellectual imperialism, where a system of Christian thought, expressed in terms of legal precision, bound into a comprehensive unity the active intelligence of mankind. Dogmas thus expressed may become the instruments of a tyranny as galling as, and more penetrating than, that of an institution. In his revolt, Colet turned to the Christian thinkers who had lived before Gregory the Great, whose writings form the bridge between the earlier Latin Fathers and the schoolmen, to the Greek theologians who never exhibited the lawyer-like instincts of their western colleagues and, above all, to a thinker removed further than any other from the legal precision of statement which was distasteful to his practical English common-sense. It is probable that his intercourse with Christian humanists in Italy, and his introduction to the Christian Platonists and Neo-Platonists there, drew him to the writings of Pseudo-Dionysius, whom, at first, he

[1] In 1661, 1701 and 1708 (in the *Phoenix*, vol. II) in English, and in Knight's *Life of Colet* (1724, 1823).

believed to be the convert of St Paul and, therefore, able to tell what a Christian thinker taught during the first age of the church. After Grocyn had convinced him that these writings could not be of earlier date than the sixth century, he still held that, through them, he could recover a theology such as it had been before being subjected to the domination of the schoolmen. They led him to two things he was very willing to learn: that the human mind, however it may feel after, and apprehend, God, can never imprison His character and attributes in propositions—stereotyped aspects of thought—which can be fitted into syllogisms and built up into a compact and rigidly harmonious structure; and, also, that such things as hierarchy and sacraments are not to be prized because they are in themselves the active sources and centres of mysterious powers, but because they faintly symbolise the spiritual forces through which God works silently for the salvation of His people.

If the stress Colet laid on the worth of the individual soul, and his dislike of the puerilities and intricate definitions of medieval theology, were characteristic of the spirit of his age, striving to escape from the thickets of medieval thought and reach the open country, the lectures he delivered in Oxford after his return from Italy showed that he was strikingly original and in advance of his time in seeing how to apply classical learning to the requirements of Christian thought. His method of exposition, familiar enough after Calvin had introduced it in the reformed church, was then absolutely new. He discarded completely the idea, as old as Origen, indeed older, that the Scriptures may be understood in a variety of senses, and that the simple historical sense is the least valuable. He insisted on the unity of the meaning of Scripture, and that the one meaning was the plain historical sense of the words. An intimate acquaintance with the methods of exegesis common in the medieval church is necessary to enable us to understand not merely the originality but the daring involved in the thought and practice. Colet, however, went further. He believed that the aim of a true interpretation of Scripture was to discover the personal message which the individual writer meant to give; and this led him, in his lectures on the *Epistle to the Romans*, to seek for every trace which revealed the personality of St Paul. It was equally imperative, he believed, to know what were the surroundings of the men to whom the letter was addressed. This led him to study in Suetonius and other historians the conditions of the Roman populace during the first century. Colet was the first to introduce the historical method of interpreting Scripture, and, as such, was far in advance not merely of his own time but of many a succeeding generation. It is not surprising that his lectures were thronged by Oxford scholars and that the audience included such personages as Richard Charnock and Erasmus. They revealed a new world to men who had been accustomed to believe that the only method of interpreting Scripture was to string together quotations, appropriate and inappropriate, from the Fathers. Scholars like Cornelius Agrippa studied theology under the lecturer, and Erasmus wished to take part in his researches.

Colet continued his lectures at Oxford on the New Testament during six successive years. When he became dean of St Paul's, he was accustomed to preach courses of sermons which are said to have resembled his Oxford lectures and drew crowds of listeners to his church. *An Exposition of St Paul's Epistle to the Romans* and *An Exposition of St Paul's First Epistle to the Corinthians*[1], enable us to understand somewhat of Colet's lectures. Their merits must be judged by comparing them with contemporary attempts at exegesis.

Colet is now best remembered by his educational work. He resolved to set apart a large portion of his great private fortune to endow a school where boys could enjoy the privilege of an education in Latin and Greek. The buildings were erected on a site at the eastern end of St Paul's churchyard, and consisted of a school-house, a large school-room and houses for two masters. An estate in Buckinghamshire was transferred to the Mercers' company to provide for the salaries of the teachers. Other property was afterwards given to provide the salary of a chaplain to teach the boys divinity and for other school purposes. Colet's letters to Erasmus show how absorbed he was with his project and what pains he took to see that his ideals were carried out. He asked Linacre to write a Latin grammar for use in his school; but, not being satisfied with the book, he himself wrote a short accidence in English, and William Lily furnished a brief Latin syntax with the rules in the vernacular. This syntax was afterwards enlarged or re-written at Colet's request and, in this form, was revised by Erasmus. The book remained long in use and was revised and amended at various dates during two centuries. It was so highly valued that, in 1571, the upper house of convocation actually passed a canon making its use compulsory throughout England, and a bill was introduced in the House of Lords to give legal effect to the decision, but was

[1] Edited by J. H. Lupton from MSS in the Cambridge University Library (Latin text and English translation).

withdrawn. In 1758, after further emendation, it became the *Eton Latin Grammar.*

Colet wrote a short series of rules for the guidance of his teachers and scholars, and an English version of the creed and some prayers. They were printed at the beginning of the accidence. Erasmus, likewise, furnished some Latin prayers for the use of the scholars and wrote for the school his *Copia Verborum et Rerum*—a Latin phrase-book. In the last year of his life, Colet, after long thought, drew up a final set of statutes for his school. He formally appointed the Mercers' company to be the governing body and desired that the actual governors should be 'married men,' not ecclesiastics. The combination of religious education with the firm rejection of clerical control was very characteristic of the man. It indicated a trend of mind corresponding to that which was to be found in Germany at the same time.

From all the accounts that have come down to us, it is evident that Colet was a great personality, who impressed everyone with whom he came in contact by his incalculable force of character. He had not the scholarship of Grocyn, Linacre, Latimer, or even of More, yet he was the central figure in the group of English humanists who figure in the correspondence of Erasmus. He was, perhaps, the only man who exercised a commanding and abiding influence on the brilliant Dutch humanist. What his attitude would have been in the crisis which overwhelmed his friends More and Fisher, it is impossible to say. We may be sure that he could never have accepted in any complete way the Lutheran reformation. The revived Augustinianism of the German reformer would, certainly, have repelled him as it did Erasmus and many of the German humanists; but he held opinions which neither Fisher nor More ever shared.

He openly expressed his disbelief in the efficacy of relics, and ridiculed the credulity of the pilgrims when he made the famous journey to the shrine of Thomas à Becket at Canterbury which is recorded in *Peregrinatio Religionis ergo.* '*Viclevita quispiam opinor,*' was the remark made by the hearer when Colet's behaviour was described. He omitted the usual reference to the Blessed Virgin and the saints in his last will, and left no money to be expended on masses for the benefit of his soul. He delighted in the *Novum Instrumentum* of Erasmus, and would not have transmitted to him the criticisms and cautions which More thought proper to send. He was among the earliest Englishmen of his generation to believe that the Bible in the vernacular ought to be in the hands of the people, and he would not have indulged in the disparagement and angry comment with which More greeted the remarkably accurate translation of the New Testament by William Tindale. His refusal to permit ecclesiastical control over his school is very significant, and suggests that he shared the opinion which Cranmer came to hold, that the transference of power from the clergy to the laity was the only guarantee for a reformation of the evils he clearly saw infesting the church and society. He was passionately convinced of the degradation of the church of his day, and believed that, in order to effect its cure, Christians must revert to the thoughts and usages of primitive Christian society. It is scarcely too much to say that the process of the English reformation down to the publication of the *Ten Articles* and the *Bishop's Book* to a very large extent embodied the ideas of the dean of St Paul's.

His correspondence with Erasmus shows what time and thought Colet spent on the selection of the first teachers in his school. He finally made choice of William Lily, 'the grammarian,' for head-master, and John Ritwyse (Rightwise) for sur-master. Lily ranked with Grocyn and Linacre as one of the most erudite students of Greek that England possessed. After graduating in arts at Oxford, he went on a pilgrimage to Jerusalem, spent some time with the Knights of St John at Rhodes, and returning home by Italy studied there under Sulpitius and Pomponius Laetus. He became an intimate friend of Thomas More, and, in conjunction with him, published *Progymnasmata*, a series of translations from the Greek anthology into Latin elegiacs. For many generations the masters in St Paul's school maintained its reputation as the home of classical learning. It became the Deventer or Schlettstadt of England.

John Fisher, bishop of Rochester (1504), deserves a place among those scholars who belonged to the close of the reign of Henry VII, more from his sympathy with learning and his successful efforts to revive the intellectual activity of Cambridge university than from his actual attainments in scholarship. He was a Cambridge student, who graduated in 1487, and, by a singularly rapid promotion, became master of Michael house in 1497, and, in the end, chancellor of the university (1504, and elected for life in 1514). He early attracted the attention of Lady Margaret Tudor, countess of Richmond and mother of Henry VII, and became her confessor. He was the first holder of the Lady Margaret professorship of divinity (1502) founded by that lady to provide gratuitous instruction in theology. He was also employed by her to establish in the university her endowment for a preacher in the vernacular. The Lady Margaret foundation attempted to do what was being done all over Germany by endowments such as that of Peter Schott of Strassburg, which found a place for the celebrated John Geiler of Keisersberg.

Fisher was a patron, not a very highly appreciated one, of Erasmus. He was mainly instrumental, it is said, in procuring for him facilities for taking a divinity degree in Cambridge—facilities of which no use was made. On the accession of Henry VIII, lord Mountjoy, or Andreas Ammonius for him, wrote an extravagant letter to his old preceptor, telling him of the accession of a humanist prince and assuring him that Henry would make his fortune. The heavens were laughing, the earth exulting, all things full of milk, of honey and of nectar. Henry had assured the writer that he would foster and encourage learned men, without whom the rest of mankind would scarcely exist at all. 'Make up your mind that the last day of your wretchedness has dawned. You will come to a prince, who will say, "Accept our wealth and be our greatest sage."' Poor Erasmus hurried from Italy to find the king quite indifferent to his needs. It was then that Fisher, eager to promote learning in his university, induced the great humanist to lecture on Greek in Cambridge from August 1511 to January 1514. He used, first of all, the grammar of Chrysoloras and, later, that of Theodorus Gaza. He does not seem to have enjoyed his residence much and his letters are full of complaints about the scanty remuneration he received. He saw before him 'the footprints of Christian poverty' and believed that he would require to pay out a great deal more than he received. The university authorities, on the other hand, asked lord Mountjoy to assist them in paying the huge salary (*immensum stipendium*) they had promised their lecturer. Fisher very properly refused to make any advances from the money given him for the foundation of Christ's College, and sent him a private donation. The complaints of Erasmus must not be taken too seriously. His keen intelligence was enclosed in a sickly body whose frailty made continuous demands on the soul it imprisoned. It needed warm rooms free from draughts, stoves that sent forth no smell, an easy-going horse and a deft servant; and, to procure all these comforts, Erasmus wrote the daintiest of begging letters. We have but little certain information about the results of his work at Cambridge, but it must have been effective. He was a notable teacher, and Colet wished often that he could secure him for his school. He was at the university at the very time when it was in the act of changing from a medieval to a modern seat of learning; and Fisher congratulated himself on having induced the great scholar to remain a long time among its students.

Fisher's own writings were almost all controversial. He was the determined enemy of the Lutheran reformation, and the nature of his books is recognisable from their titles: *Confutatio Assertionis Lutheranae; De Eucharistia contra Johannem Oecolampadium libri quinque; Sacri Sacerdotii Defensio contra Lutherum*; a defence of Henry VIII's *Assertio septem Sacramentorum*; and so forth[1]. Fisher maintained his opinions loyally to the end. He resisted to the utmost of his ability Henry's claim to be considered the head of the church of England, and he refused to declare his belief in the invalidity of the marriage of Catharine of Aragon with the king. This resistance cost him his life. He was beheaded 22 June 1535.

Sir Thomas More, the associate with Fisher in his tragic death, the pupil of Linacre and Grocyn, the disciple of Colet and the beloved friend of Erasmus, was the one member of the band of English humanists who had a distinct gift of literary genius. The son of a well-known London lawyer, he was placed by his father in the household of archbishop Morton, who, recognising his precocious genius, sent him to Oxford. There he became a good Latinist and a fair scholar in Greek. His devotion to the study of law at Lincoln's Inn did not quench his ardour for classical learning. After he was called to the bar he delivered lectures in the church of St Lawrence, on St Augustine's *De Civitate Dei*, which were attended by 'all the chief learned citizens of London,' dwelling on the philosophy and history rather than on the theology of the book. He became reader at Furnival's Inn, was a member of parliament (1503—4) and there successfully withstood the exactions of the king. His subsequent withdrawal from public life, usually attributed to fear of the king, gave him opportunity to cultivate his acquaintance with Greek and Latin. Together with Lily, he translated epigrams from the Greek anthology into Latin elegiac verse, and, in company with Erasmus, he translated into Latin prose portions from Lucian. The former, largely added

[1] Of the place of Fisher's work in the history of English oratorical prose, see the later section on the work of divines in vol. IV of the present work.

to, were published in *Progymnasmata*[1] and the latter, in 1506, under the title *Luciani...compluria opuscula...ab Erasmo Roterodamo et Thoma Moro...traducta.*

More had gradually built up for himself an extensive and lucrative private practice, when he was drawn into the king's service. He was employed in the negociation of a commercial treaty with the Netherlands and, from the year 1516, he took office at court. He was made a privy councillor and was knighted in 1521. He became Master of Requests, under-treasurer, chancellor of the duchy of Lancaster (1525) and, finally, lord chancellor (25 October 1529). He held the office for two years and a half. The last years of his life were full of tragical suffering. Convocation and parliament had pronounced the marriage of Henry VIII with Catharine of Aragon invalid. The first act of succession (25 Henry VIII, c. 22), passed in the spring of 1534, had settled the succession in the children of Anne Boleyn, and all Englishmen were required to swear to maintain the act. More declared repeatedly that he accepted the act, but the oath which was afterwards prescribed went beyond the contents of the act and required a declaration about papal authority within the realm. This, More steadfastly refused to make. He was confined in the Tower in circumstances of great hardship, and, in the end, was condemned to suffer death under act 26 Henry VIII, cc. 1 and 13. The barbarous punishment devised for traitors was commuted by the king to beheading. More suffered on 6 July 1535. His execution, a judicial murder, and that of the bishop of Rochester, filled the world with horror. An interesting proof of the wide-spread character of this indignation has been furnished by the recently published (December 1906) process against George Buchanan before the Lisbon inquisition. The humanist confessed to the inquisitors that he had written his celebrated tragedy, *Baptistes*—a work translated into English, French, Dutch and German—with his eye fixed on the tyranny of Henry displayed in the trial and execution of Thomas More.

More was a voluminous writer both in Latin and in English. His fame rests chiefly on his Latin epigrams and *Utopia*; but his other work requires to be mentioned.

His verses, English and Latin, are, for the most part, mediocre, but contain some pieces of great merit. They are interesting because they reveal the character of the man, at once grave and gay, equally inclined to worldly pleasure and ascetic austerity; and they

[1] First edition 1518, second edition 1518, third, greatly enlarged, 1520.

are not free from that trait of whimsical pedantry which belonged to More all through his life, and which displayed itself when, being in love with the younger sister, he resolved to marry the elder because it was meet that she should be the first settled in life. He wrote of Venus and Cupid, of a soldier who wished to play the monk, of eternity, of fortune, its favours and its reverses, and a *Rueful Lamentation* on the death of Elizabeth, the queen of Henry VII. Many of his epigrams are full of sadness, of an uncertain fear of the future. They describe life as a path leading to death. They reveal a man who had seen and felt much suffering and who brooded over the uncertainties of life. They seem to anticipate the fate of one who fell almost at once from the throne of the lord chancellor into a cell in the Tower. His translation into English of the *Life of John Picus, Erle of Myrandula, a greate Lorde of Italy*, is an autobiography of ideals if not of facts. The young gifted Italian humanist, who was transformed by contact with Savonarola, with his refined culture, his longing for a monastic career, his deliberate choice of a lay life and his secret austerities, was repeated in his English admirer, who wore, almost continuously, a 'sharp shirt of hair,' who watched and fasted often, who slept frequently, 'either on the bare ground, or on some bench, or laid some log under his head.'

More's other prose writings[1], with the exception of *Utopia*, are controversial and devotional. The controversial include, besides those in Latin, *The Dialogue*, *The Supplication of Souls*[2], *A Confutation of Tindale's Answer*, *A Letter against Frith*, *The Apology*, *The Debellacyon of Salem and Bizance* and an *Answer to the 'Supper of the Lord.'* They form about three-fourths of the whole and deserve more consideration than they usually receive. They are by no means free from the scurrility which was characteristic of that age of controversy. His opponents are 'swine,' 'hell-hounds that the devil hath in his kennel,' 'apes that dance for the pleasure of Lucifer,' and so on. These writings are unusually prolix, but they show that the author was well read in theology and they manifest a great acquaintance with Scripture. More was no curialist or ultramontane, to use the modern word; but he was a man who felt the need of an external spiritual authority and clung to it. While Colet lived, he was More's director; during occasional absences, Grocyn supplied his place; after Colet's death, he felt increasingly the need for something external to rest on, and

[1] For the *History of King Richard III* attributed to him, see *post*, chap. XV.

[2] See *post*, chap. IV.

the thought of a historical church, which he defined to be 'all Christian people,' was necessary to sustain his faith. The style in all these English writings, their carefully constructed balanced sentences with modulated cadences, exhibit the scholar and the imitator of the Latin classics.

Utopia, the one work by More which still lives in all the freshness of youth, was written in Latin. The author was diffident about it. He showed the manuscript to friends, especially to Erasmus, and they were enthusiastic. The great French humanist Budé wrote the preface; Erasmus and Peter Giles (Aegidius) superintended the printing; the book took the learned world of Europe by storm in somewhat the same way as did *Moriae Encomium*; and the author was at once hailed as a member of the wide republic of letters. It was translated into most European languages; new editions appear continually; and it has become one of the world's classics. It may have been suggested by Plato's *Republic*—the names it contains are Greek—but the books have little in common. It borrows something from Augustine's *De Civitate Dei*, a favourite of the author. Yet the book is thoroughly original. The ground-plan had been suggested by the account of the voyages of Americo Vespucci; the sight of the wide, clean, well-paved streets of the towns in the Netherlands, refreshing after the crowded, narrow, filthy thoroughfares of London, the extent of garden ground within the walls of Bruges and Antwerp, suggested the 'commodious and handsome' streets and the gardens 'with all manner of fruit, herbs and flowers' of the city of Amaurote. The economic distress through which England was passing, the increase of sheep and the decay of agriculture, the destruction of farm steadings and of country towns, are all apparent in the book, and have produced many of its suggestions. The detestation of war shared by Colet, Erasmus and most of the humanists found utterance in the toleration of all religions and in conscription for agriculture but not for war. It is possible that Colet's well known opinions about priesthood appear in exaggerated form in *Utopia*. The book is full of allusions to the circumstances of the time during which the author lived; but critics are scarcely warranted in concluding, as many of them do, that they can find his practical remedies for the disorders of the age in the laws and usages of the imaginary state.

More lived long enough to see the maxims of *Utopia* applied in a way which must have horrified him, and which probably gave their sharp edge to his denunciations of the Peasants' war. He did not dream that, ten years after the publication of the book, and ten years before his own death, his *Utopia* would furnish texts for excited agitators on village greens or in the public-houses of German towns. But so it was. The *Moriae Encomium* of Erasmus and More's *Utopia* were made full use of in the future 'tumult' which they both dreaded.

It is not easy to say what influence this group of English humanists had in making the study of classical learning take root in their native land. Fisher's position as chancellor of the university secured the continuous study of Greek at Cambridge, and More is our authority for saying that its popularity there was so great that scholars who did not share the teaching were ready to con tribute to the support of the teacher. At Oxford, the struggle, evidently, was harder. Greek was denounced by obscurantist churchmen, and it was Sir Thomas More's task, while he was a power at court, to protect and encourage both lecturers and scholars. It may safely be said, however, that the example and writings of Erasmus were the most powerful stimulus to the desire to know something about, and to share in the revival of, classical learning.

Among the MSS preserved in the library of Corpus Christi college, Oxford, there is the ledger or day-book of an Oxford bookseller which records the books he sold during the year 1520. It gives us some indication of the reading of the period in a university city and enables us to see how far the classical renascence had become popular. John Dorne sold 2383 books during that year—some English, most of them Latin, one or two Greek. The English books were, for the most part, almanacs, ballads, Christmas carols, popular *Lives of Saints* and medieval romances, three copies of a book on cooking, three of one on carving, one on table etiquette, one on husbandry and three on the care of horses. One is a translation of Vergil into English—probably Caxton's *Aeneid* (Westminster, 1490).

Among the Latin books are breviaries, missals, *portiforiums*, a very large number of grammars and a few lexicons. A large part of the more important books represent the learning of the past, the scholastic theology and philosophy not yet displaced, and, as was to be expected, the Scotist greatly outnumber the Thomist theologians—John Duns Scotus himself being represented by twenty, and Thomas Aquinas and Augustine by four each. But the humanities, in the shape of Latin authors and Latin translations of Greek writers, are not much behind. Dorne sold that year thirty-seven copies of various works of Cicero, the same number of Terence, thirty of Aristotle, twenty-nine of Vergil, twenty-three of Ovid, fourteen of Lucan, twelve of Aristophanes (one being in Greek), nine of Lucian (one in Greek), eight of Horace, six of Sallust, eight of Pliny, three of Aulus Gellius and one of Tacitus and of Persius.

The names of the English humanists are only represented by one copy of Linacre's translation of Galen, and three of More's Latin letters to Edward Lee. The name of Lupset occurs, but only to record that that scholar took away a book without paying for it. The Italian teachers of these Englishmen appear on the list of sales—twenty-nine copies of various works of Sulpitius, twenty-two of Laurentius Valla and three of Angelo Poliziano. Budé, the greatest French humanist, is not represented, but Dorne sold thirty-three copies of works written or edited by his comrade, Jacques Lefèvre d'Étaples.

The outstanding feature of this list of sales of books, however, is the place occupied by the writings of Erasmus. One-ninth of the whole sales were of books written or edited by him. If the small primers, almanacs, ballads and so on and the grammars written by two popular Oxford grammar-school teachers be excluded, one customer out of every seven came to buy a book written by the great humanist. It is instructive, also, to notice what books of his command the largest sale. These are *Colloquia, De Constructione, Copia, Enchiridion Militis Christiani* and *Adagia*. The popularity of three of these writings occasions no surprise and conveys no information. The book entitled *Adagia* was a compendium of the wit and wisdom of antiquity, a collection of Greek and Latin proverbs which were made the text of short essays sparkling with the author's inimitable humour. Almost every one in that age wished to know something of ancient learning, and it was in this book served up to them in a way which made them feel able to comprehend it. *Colloquia* had grown gradually from being a collection of conversations on familiar subjects fitted for beginners in Latin until it had become a series of charming pictures of all sorts and conditions of men. It was the most popular book of the century and went through ninety-nine editions before 1546. It circulated everywhere. *Enchiridion* taught a simple piety of the heart and contained a calm and consistent appeal to the central standard of all Christian behaviour—the teaching and example of Jesus Christ. It was translated into English in 1518, into Czech in 1519, into German in 1524 and into Spanish in 1527. Seventy-five editions had been published before 1545. But *De Constructione* and *Copia* were books of an entirely different kind and appealed to a more limited class of readers. They were really text-books for advanced Latin students who wished to acquire a good style. In them the great literary artist disclosed the secrets of his art. The sale of many copies means the existence of circles of students, for, in those days, one book served many readers, who were trying to perfect themselves in the humanities, who were looking to Erasmus as their great teacher and who were taking pains to fashion themselves after his example. It shows the spread of the classical renascence among the students of England.

We do not find in England the extravagant adulation of the great Dutchman which meets us everywhere in Germany. There, he was the idol of every young scholar. They said that he was more than mortal, that his judgment was infallible and that his work was perfect. They made pilgrimages to visit him as to the shrine of a saint. An interview was an event to be talked about for years, and a letter from him was a precious treasure to be preserved as a heirloom. In England, they seized on one side of his work which specially appealed to their practical instincts, and tried to imitate it in their own way.

Among those who, following Erasmus, strove to make use of the writings of antiquity for the instruction and edification of their contemporaries were Sir Thomas Elyot and Thomas Wilson. The former is best known by his treatise, *The Boke named the Governour*, and the latter by his *Arte of Rhetorique.*

Elyot had no university training. He was educated at home and, at a comparatively early age, had acquired a good knowledge of Latin, Greek and Italian. He says that, before he was twenty, he had read Galen and other medical writings with a 'worshipful physician,' conjectured to have been Linacre.

His earliest work, *The Boke of the Governour*, the best known of his writings, made him famous and probably proved his introduction to the career as a diplomatic agent in which he spent the greater part of his life. It is a lengthy and exhaustive treatise on the education which those who are destined to govern ought to receive. It begins with a discussion of the various kinds of commonwealths, and sets forth the advantages of monarchy, aristocracy and democracy. The author decides that monarchy is the best form of government; but it demands the appointment of subordinate rulers over the various parts of the kingdom who are to be the eyes, ears, hands and legs of the supreme ruler. They ought to be taken from the 'estate called worshipful,' provided they have sufficient virtue and knowledge, but they must be carefully educated. It is the more necessary to insist upon this as education is not valued as it ought to be. Pride looks upon learning as a 'notable reproach to a great gentleman,' and lords are apt to ask the price of tutors as they demand the qualification of cooks.

The author then proceeds to map out what goes to make the thorough education of a gentleman fit to rule. He begins with his birth. Up to the age of seven, the child is to be under the charge of a nurse or governess. He is then to be handed over to a tutor or carefully selected master, and taught music and its uses, painting and carving, and is to be instructed in letters from such books as Aesop's *Fables*, 'quick and merrie dialogues' like those of Lucian, or the heroic poems of Homer. When he attains the age of fourteen he is to be taught logic, cosmography and 'histories,' and, although 'this age be not equal to antiquity' (the classics), he is, nevertheless, to make a beginning therein. His bodily frame is to be exercised in wrestling, hunting, swimming and, above all, in dancing, which profits much for the acquirement of moral virtues. Shooting with the crossbow is also to be practised and tennis, if not indulged in too frequently and if limited to brief periods of exercise, but football is to be 'put in perpetual silence' because 'therein is nothing but beastly furie and external violence, whereof procedeth hurte, and consequently rancour and malice do remaine with them that be wounded.' In his second and third books the author sets forth the lofty ideals which ought to inspire the governor and describes the way in which he can be trained to a virtuous life.

The whole book is full of classical reminiscences taken either directly from the authors of antiquity or borrowed from the humanists of Italy. It discourses on the methods of hunting practised among the Greeks and Romans, and the dances of the youths of Sparta are not forgotten. It is also interesting to notice that the education portrayed in the first book is almost exactly what had been given to the young Italian patrician for more than a generation; while the second and third books add those moral ideals which the more seriously minded northern nations demanded. It is the unfolding of a plan of education which Wilibald Pirkheimer, the friend of Erasmus, describes as having been his own, and it is the attempt to introduce into English life an ideal of the many-sided culture which the classical renascence had disclosed.

Elyot's reputation among his contemporaries rested on more than his *Boke of the Governour.* He wrote *The Castel of Helth,* full of prescriptions and remedies largely selected from Galen and other medical authorities of antiquity. His two tracts: *A swete and devoute sermon of Holy Saynt Ciprian, of Mortalitie of Man* and *The Rules of a Christian lyfe made by Picus, erle of Mirandula, both translated into Englyshe,* provided food for the soul. His translations from Latin and Greek into English, made at a time when all were anxious to share in classical learning, and only a few possessed a knowledge of the classical languages sufficient to enable them to share its benefits, were very popular and were reprinted over and over again. To this class belong: *The Doctrine of Princes, made by the noble oratour Isocrates, and translated out of Greke in to Englishe*; *The Bankette of Science* (a collection of sayings translated from the Fathers); *The Education or Bringinge up of Children, translated out of Plutarche*; *The Image of Governance, compiled of the actes and sentences notable of the moste noble Emperour Alexander Severus, late translated out of Greke into Englyshe* and others of a like kind. Henry VIII himself encouraged Elyot in the compilation of his Latin-English lexicon: *The Dictionary of Syr T. Eliot, knyght,* with its later title, *Bibliotheca Eliotae.* This dictionary and his translations continued to be appreciated in a wonderful manner for two generations at least. If Erasmus popularised the classical renascence for scholars, Elyot rendered it accessible to the mass of the people who had no acquaintance with the languages of antiquity.

Wilson's *Arte of Rhetorique* is almost exclusively drawn from such old masters as Aristotle, Cicero and Quintilian. The author discusses various kinds of composition, sets forth the rules which guided authors in the golden age of classical literature and applies them with considerable success to the art of writing in English. There is little or no originality in the volume, save, perhaps, the author's condemnation of the use of French and Italian phrases and idioms which he complains are 'counterfeiting the kinges Englishe.' The warnings of Wilson will not seem untimely if it be remembered that the earlier English poets of the period—Sir Thomas Wyatt the elder, and the earl of Surrey—drew their inspiration from Petrarch and Ariosto, that their earliest attempts at poetry were translations from Italian sonnets and that their maturer efforts were imitations of the sweet and stately measures and style of Italian poesie. The polish which men like Wyatt and Surrey were praised for giving to our 'rude and homely manner of vulgar poesie' might have led to some degeneration. Shakespeare himself is said to have studied Wilson and to have profited by his book.

Elyot made translation instruct his countrymen in the ethical and political wisdom of the ancients; Wilson used the same means to fire their patriotism. In a preface he drew a comparison between Athens and England and the danger which threatened the one from Philip of Macedon and the other from Philip II of Spain. Then followed *The Three Orations of Demosthenes, chiefe orator among the Grecians, in favour of the Olynthians, with those his four Orations against King Philip of Macedonie; most nedeful to be redde in these daungerous dayes of all them that love their countries libertie and desire to take warning for their better avayle* (1570).

It remains to note briefly another proof of the silent spread of the classical renascence. In all medieval universities and high schools, scholars delighted to act plays, especially during carnival time. As the classical renascence made progress, Scriptural subjects gave place to the comedies of Terence and Plautus and to school dramas[1] which, for the most part, were constructed for the purpose of incorporating in the text as many phrases as possible from Terence, Cicero and Vergil. The result of all this was that the great men of antiquity became known to the commonalty. Coriolanus and Julius Caesar were familiar names in England, and a Welsh soldier had at least heard of Alexander and of Macedon.

Thus, classical learning, at first the possession of a favoured few, then, by means of translations, the property of all people fairly educated, gradually permeated England so thoroughly that, though Shakespeare was not far distant from Chaucer by the measurement of time, when we pass from the one to the other it is as if we entered a new and entirely different world.

[1] See the chapter on the Academic drama in volume v of the present work.

CHAPTER II

REFORMATION LITERATURE IN ENGLAND

THE reformation left its mark upon the national literature, as upon the national life, but, beyond this abiding influence, there was, in this period, much literary activity of a mere passing interest. Yet even this was so significant of current thought, and helped so greatly to form public opinion, that it must not be forgotten. The appearance of the English Bible and the *Book of Common Prayer* must not hide from us the vigour of religious tracts and controversies, the number of sermons, of books of devotion and instruction, which seemed, to the age itself, of hardly less importance. Much of the religious literature which had appeared before had issued from definite local centres and, for the most part, reached merely local audiences. This was now ceasing to be the case, for the country was drawn more closely together, and the printing press, answering to the instincts of the day, gave writers a ready means of wider influence.

Lollard tracts and Lollard adaptations of orthodox works had long been current, especially in certain districts. Some of these, after a long life, were now printed, as, for instance, Wyclif's supposed work, *The Wicket*, which Coverdale edited. The question, therefore, arises how far the English reformation was either the outcome, or an indirect result, of the Lollard movement, and an answer may be given either from the literary, or from the purely historic, side. On the former, we gather that Lollard works were reprinted, partly, it may be, for their supposed value, but, also, to show that the opinions held by their editors had been taught in England long before. These reprints appeared, moreover, not in the early stages of the reformation, but when it was well under way. There is no need, therefore, to reckon these reprints among the causes of the reformation: their nature and the date of their appearance tend strongly against such an assumption. Approaching the question, however, from the purely historic side, we find that the Lollard movement had left behind it, in some localities, much religious discontent, and some revolutionary religious teaching. Such discontent and teaching would, doubtless, have come into being irrespective of Lollardy. When the reformation came, however, it found these influences already at work; no doubt it quickened them and drew them around itself. That is the utmost we can say.

This popular reformation literature, the successor, although hardly the descendant, of the Lollard literature, was, for the most part, printed abroad, and was, sometimes, prohibited by English bishops. But it would appear that probably Henry VIII, and certainly the protector Somerset, connived at its circulation, because they welcomed any help that made change seem desirable. The story of *The Supplication for the Beggars*, as told by Foxe, is an illustration of this.

Simon Fish, a gentleman of Gray's Inn, had to leave London, about the year 1525, for acting in a play which touched cardinal Wolsey; he, like Tindale, fled across the sea, and, while abroad, wrote *The Supplication for the Beggars*. This effectively written pamphlet urged the abolition of monasteries and the seizure of their lands; its incidental, and often coarse, abuse of ecclesiastics, and its many exaggerations, merely heightened the effect it produced. Either through Anne Boleyn or some royal servant the pamphlet reached the hands of Henry VIII, who is said to have studied it carefully and long kept it by him. Through the king's connivance, Fish was allowed to return from his banishment. By the time his pamphlet had appeared, the writings of Tindale, to whom Sir Thomas More replied in his *Dialogue*, were also current. Sir Thomas More, in his *Supplication of Souls*, replied to Fish, and the Cambridge student, John Frith, retorted upon More. The Lollard literature and controversies were thus swallowed up in the reformation, and, although a lower class of writings, such as that of Fish, still continued to be written and circulated, more literary interest belongs to a theological class that followed them. The new writings recalled, always in their exaggeration and sometimes in their violence, the old, but they were composed upon a larger scale; and the importance of single members of the class, and the numbers in which they were published, made this new movement more important than Lollardy had ever been.

This reformation movement was essentially academic in origin. The revival of letters had already shown its power at Oxford, where Colet, More and Erasmus had directed it into religious channels. The shares taken by these three in the classical renascence in England has already been discussed; and reference need only be made here to the impulse which Erasmus gave to religious thought and learning in Cambridge. Bishop Fisher had brought to the service of the university an enthusiasm for practical piety; he had revived the best side of medieval religious discipline; but he had placed the claims of practical life first, although that life was to be tempered with learning and purified by the Scriptures. Fisher gladly welcomed Erasmus, who was the fourth Lady Margaret Reader (1511); if Erasmus, as his works show, sympathised with Fisher's practical aim, he understood, as Fisher, who was not unreservedly a humanist, hardly did, the breadth of learning needed for effective preaching.

Thomas Bilney, whose friendship altered the life of Hugh Latimer, had for the first time (to use his own words, which should not be taken too literally) 'heard speak of Jesus, even then when the New Testament was first set forth by Erasmus.' William Tindale admired the great scholar and translated his *Enchiridion*, which Coverdale also summarised. Cranmer counted Erasmus among the authors he studied specially, and, when he gave himself up more exclusively to Biblical learning, he was still following the steps of his master. Erasmus was able, in a letter written later (1516), to his pupil, Henry Bullock of Queens', to speak with pride of the increased Biblical study at Cambridge as a result he had hoped for from his labours.

Robert Barnes, an Augustinian friar of Norfolk descent, had been educated at Louvain; and, on coming to Cambridge as prior of the Augustinian friars, he began to lecture, first on classics, and then on theology. George Stafford, a Fellow of Pembroke, was also a celebrated lecturer upon the Scriptures; the expositions with which he 'beatified the letters of blessed Paul' deeply affected Thomas Becon and others. This, like other great movements, had its distortions and its extremes; Skelton could ridicule the theologians who with a 'lytell ragge of rhetoricke,' a 'lesse lumpe of logicke,' a patch of philosophy, 'tumbled' in theology and were drowned in 'dregges of divinite,' posing as 'doctours of the chayre' at the taverns. Some of the young theologians were of 'whirling' spirits; some, like Robert Barnes, flew high and far into politics, and, by their indiscretion, brought danger upon themselves and their cause; some of them not infrequently dropped to the lower depths of controversy. But solid results remained. Richard Croke, who, after a distinguished career abroad, became Reader in Greek (1519), carried on the work already begun; he recognised the pre-eminent claim of the Bible upon theological students, and, when Wolsey (1527) formed his Cambridge colony at Oxford, the new and active school of thought entered upon a wider field. The English reformation began at Cambridge, and the Cambridge movement began with Erasmus, although he was not its sole author. For, both at Cambridge, and in the country at large, the general movement towards reform and the religious influence of the revival of learning formed a sympathetic atmosphere in which his influence easily spread.

The new movement—a quickening of religion and theology, upon the background of an awakened world—took many forms and turned in many ways. It was not always revolutionary, and, in one direction, it turned to older forms of devotion. Religion in England had enriched the church with the Sarum use, akin to other uses elsewhere and of wide importance, and with uses less popular in England, like those of Hereford and York; it had, further, formed the *Primers*, books of private devotion, translated in the fourteenth century from Latin into English, and printed at early dates and in many forms. Not only in England, but in other countries, the reformation concerned itself largely with these aids to devotion; everywhere appeared much needed revisions of liturgies and offices, everywhere attempts were made, more or less successfully, at altering them to meet popular needs, or to avoid abuses. In England, the great outcome was *The Book of Common Prayer*, which was essentially conservative, although its history showed much of revolution.

And, again, the reformation, owing both to the wishes of its academic founders and to the popular tendencies underlying it, concerned itself largely with popular preaching. It is a widespread error to assume that there was little popular preaching in the Middle Ages. It is true that there were many bishops and parish priests who shirked their canonical duties in this respect, but there was much popular instruction; there was, especially among the friars, much simple, at times even sensational, mission preaching. But the deepening of religious life that preceded the reformation led men to employ with greater diligence all means of helping others, and popular preaching was thus more widely used. Here again, both a conservative and a revolutionary tendency are observable. On the one hand, we can trace the fuller but continuous history of the older use of sermons. On the other hand, we find the tendency, seen at its strongest in Zwinglianism, to exalt the sermon above the sacraments, to put the pulpit in place of the altar. Both tendencies made the literature of sermons more popular, and more significant. But, in the literature thus revived, the academic and popular elements were closely mingled.

It would have been strange if, when interest in religion and religious questions was thus rising, religious controversies had not multiplied. The stir of newly felt needs and impulses to fresh devotion stimulated differences of opinion no less than did abuses calling loudly for reform. The English people had always been religious, and there had always been religious controversies; but now these were both multiplied and intensified. Some were of merely passing importance, although of much historic significance; but others represented real and solid endeavours to form public opinion. It is impossible to notice more than a few of them; some were caused by political relations and by the breach with Rome, and their existence has to be remembered, though they must not be taken for the chief religious interests of the time.

But, from the literary point of view, the most striking feature of the reformation is its connection with the English Bible, and that Bible itself is its greatest monument. Here, again, we might consider the production of the Bible as prepared by that more conservative movement, associated with the revival of learning and seen both in the Oxford reformers and in the Cambridge scholars already mentioned. But it was also connected with a more revolutionary school of thought, and was placed by many as the sole rule of life in sharp opposition to the teaching of the church. Thus, the history of the English Bible itself becomes mingled, strangely and sadly, with the history of religious strife. Beyond and above all that, however, its literary influence shows itself as uniquely as its power in giving an inspiration for life.

These general effects of the reformation upon the national literature must be examined in detail, although, even then, there will be many effects left unnoticed, and many results unaccounted for.

The history of *The Book of Common Prayer*, like many other parts of the English reformation, shows curious likenesses to the course of affairs abroad, mingled with features peculiar to itself. With the greater sharpness of national divisions and the stronger coherence of national languages, the use of the vernacular in the services of the church was more and more demanded. Not only among Lutherans and among Calvinists in France or Germany, but, also, among Catholics, the wish for it was felt. At the council of Trent, this concession was urged both by the emperor and by the king of France. Hymns, litanies and purely personal devotions such as *The Primer* provided, were insufficient; a widespread feeling existed that both the mass and the daily offices would be more serviceable and better appreciated in the vulgar tongue. This feeling gradually strengthened, and led to the evolution of the prayer-book. A Venetian ambassador, visiting England in 1500, was struck with the simple piety of the English people, and by their frequent attendance at church: not only at mass, but at the daily offices, they were very regular, and their deep-rooted love of the parish church with its services had marked effects upon the coming changes. In England, moreover, the course of revolution left the parish churches standing, although the monastic churches suffered; and this peculiarity of the English reformation made reform more conservative.

The changes were, at first, gradual. The wish for uniformity of service throughout the realm—felt elsewhere, but a necessity of the position of Henry VIII—was marked (1541) by a re-issue of the Sarum breviary, ordered by convocation (1542) to be used by the clergy throughout the province of Canterbury. There had been many struggles as to liturgical use in medieval days, and these were thus ended before the great struggle began. A chapter of the Bible was ordered to be read in English upon Sundays and holy days and (11 June 1544) the Litany was put forth in English. When, under Edward VI, the administration of the chalice to the people was adopted, again in sympathy with a demand widely made abroad, further change followed; the old Latin was retained but an English communion service for the people was added (Easter, 1548).

Under Henry, and under Edward, revision had begun with the *Primers*. Upon the side of purely popular and personal devotion, *Primers* had appeared with fresh matter, some of it revolutionary, some of it hortatory. Marshall's *Primer*, 1534 and 1535, was one of them; bishop Hilsey's (of Rochester) *Primer* (1539) was another, and was authorised by Cromwell for the king and by Cranmer as archbishop. King Henry's *Primer* (1545) was the last of a long series, and was intended to check the diversity which the printing press had intensified. The king had ordered Cranmer to turn certain prayers into English and to see that they were used in his province. This *King's Primer* embodied the English Litany, which, alike in its changes and in its incomparable prose, may be certainly ascribed to Cranmer. The same literary genius was now to work upon a larger field and with greater results. But it is necessary to note the popular tendencies that had helped to form the *Primers*. These books lay to Cranmer's hand, and, if much of the English prayer-book is to be ascribed to his fine workmanship, something was also due to the general literary excellence of the day. We have already seen how, in the case of Rolle and other devotional writers, the literary instinct arose from the union of popular feeling and intense personal devotion. The same process was seen at the reformation. Turns of expression in the *Primers*, due, sometimes, to unknown writers, rhythms in Tindale's Bible due to him alone, the vigour and pathos to be found in Frith and Latimer and other writers or sufferers—all these lead us to ascribe much to the age itself rather than to individuals. The reformation, like the Middle Ages, shows a fitting expression of devotion and religious thought, reached, as we might expect, more through schools and tendencies than through individual minds. The English Litany, and the stately Bidding prayer in its many forms, are good examples of this process of growth. And the same was the case with the English Bible itself. Nevertheless, much was also due to individual writers like Cranmer.

Together with this popular movement, shown in the *Primers*, a revision, by authority, of service-books had begun and slowly moved on. Under Henry, Cranmer had drafted the changes he proposed and a commission (1540) had drawn up a *rationale* which was more conservative than Cranmer's own scheme. Under Edward VI, both these were brought forward, and discussion of them went on. At Rome itself, cardinal Quignon had published (1535) a new breviary which gained great popularity and reached many editions. In its insertion of lessons and its omission of versicles, it aimed, in the spirit of the time, at edification rather than, as did the ancient offices, at devotion. But, as the conservative party gained power in Rome, a new ideal was formed, and the Roman breviary (1568), reformed in accordance with the wish of the council of Trent, more closely resembled the medieval form. On the other hand, in Germany, the *Consultation* (1543) of Hermann of Wied, archbishop of Cologne, was an attempt to combine the ancient type with the service-books of the Lutherans. Cranmer, who was himself a capable liturgical scholar, had studied both these liturgical schemes and was influenced by them.

This is not the place to deal with the difficult problems in the preparation of the Edwardine prayer-books of 1549 and 1552, the part played by convocation and the exact share of individual minds in their composition; nor do the complicated questions of theology or worship or rubrics belong to a literary history. It is enough to say that, while the earlier book may be regarded as the outcome of the influences already described, as a product of the ancient offices, of the wish for conservative reform and more popular instruction, of the need for unity in the realm and for the use of the national tongue, the second book went further in the way of change, doctrinal and ritual. Before its composition, foreign influence had grown stronger, and many minds in England had gone through phases which Cranmer illustrates in himself.

Born in Aslackton, Nottinghamshire (2 July 1489), he went as a boy to Jesus College, Cambridge, passed through the ordinary course of study and, when about twenty-two, turned to the study of Erasmus. Like other scholars, he came under the influence of the revived theological learning, and his library shows how deeply he received it. He gained a fellowship at Jesus College, which was soon lost by his marriage; a lectureship at Buckingham College (now Magdalene) was held during his short married life, but, on his wife's death, he was re-elected a Fellow of his old college. The temptation of a canonry at Cardinal College, Oxford, was not strong enough to remove him, as it did other Cambridge men, to the new field of work. As a priest and as a theological lecturer, with some fame as an examiner, he worked on in his old sphere, until the advice he gave to Henry VIII in the matter of his divorce brought him into royal favour and a larger world. He wrote a book embodying his views; a sojourn with the earl of Wiltshire, Anne Boleyn's father, was followed by a visit to Rome at the beginning of 1530, as one of his suite; he became archdeacon of Taunton (probably 1531); early in 1532 he was in Germany as ambassador to Charles V; and he was recalled from Germany to succeed Warham as archbishop of Canterbury (30 March 1533). In Germany, he had married a niece of Osiander; a connection which made his intercourse with German theologians easier, but which was awkward in view of his promotion. The step he had then taken marked a distinct breach with the ecclesiastical system of the day, although, in England, under Henry VIII, this was not, of necessity, a disqualification for office.

It is difficult to estimate fairly the character of Cranmer. Called from a quiet position to great scenes, forced to act a part beyond his strength, he showed weakness where it is rarely forgiven. He was pitifully compliant with Henry's wishes in the matter of his divorce; at the death of Edward, he let himself be hurried into a policy he did not wholly approve; his martyr's death lost something of its dignity, even if it gained in pathos, by his recantations. His instincts were conservative enough, his mind receptive enough, for the guidance of a great movement, but he failed in decision and power. And yet, no one who reads his letters and writings, or who traces his work upon the prayer-book, can doubt that he represents faithfully much of the mind of the English reformation. His feet stood upon the past, but his outlook was towards the future. He was skilled in all the older ecclesiastical learning, even in the canon law which many of his friends despised; and if, in some points, he would have changed beyond the limits reached, in others he would gladly have kept even more of the past. He had not only liturgical knowledge but also a liturgical interest which belonged rather to bygone times; he added to it an exquisite ear for a language that was just learning its strength. There is all the difference in the world between the crude bareness of the Litany as he found it, and its majestic rhythm when it left his pen. In other works, where he had no help from the past, as, for instance, in his theological writings, his style falls somewhat lower, but, even then, it is always nervous, simple and continuous. His chief writings deal with the Holy Eucharist, and their historical, as well as theological, interest is, therefore, great. His *Defence of the true and Catholic Doctrine of the Sacrament of the Body and Blood of Christ* (1550), to which he added while in prison and which was afterwards reprinted, shows his ample learning, and yet, even when dealing with intricate points, it is always simple in phrase and striking in its expressions. Learning was now coming down from its seclusion and addressing itself to a public anxious for enlightenment. Quickly as Cranmer could compose in Latin—his *Reply to the Three Articles* brought against him at his trial is an instance of his readiness—English came more naturally to him, and, in the continued debates of his trial, the disputants often forsook Latin for English.

The publication of the *Defence* brought upon him much controversy. Gardiner's *Explication and Assertion of the true Catholic Faith* (published in France, 1550) was an able criticism to which Cranmer replied in his *Answer* (October 1551). Richard Smyth, formerly professor at Oxford but deprived in favour of Vermigli (Peter Martyr), also attacked him in *A Confutation of the true and Catholic Doctrine* (1550), and Cranmer included him, too, in his reply to Gardiner.

Cranmer had the receptive mind which often goes with practical weakness; and thus he illustrated in himself the religious changes of his day, although he moved slowly to his final views. At Cambridge, books from Germany had been eagerly read by a little company that gathered at 'The White Horse,' and it was through him that German theologians, some of them fugitives because of the Augsburg Interim, were called to the English universities. Peter Martyr came to Oxford (May, 1549) and the more conservative Bucer (1549) with Fagius to Cambridge.

Foreign criticism had been exercised upon the prayer-book of 1549, and Cranmer's own mental changes worked along with the politics of the time to make its alteration seem desirable. The second prayer-book, therefore, while expressly sanctioning its predecessor as containing nothing but what was agreeable to the word of God and the primitive church, yet made many changes; some slight, others more important, the latter class mainly involving Eucharistic doctrine, upon which point, as upon that of vestments, controversy was most intense. Under Elizabeth, the vestiarian controversy reappeared, until it was swallowed up by the larger and more vital discussion upon church government. But, before that came, the Elizabethan prayer-book had been constructed (1559). The change from the medieval to the modern type had been really completed with the book of 1552, although under James I, as a result of the Millenary petition (24 March 1603) and the Hampton Court conference (14—18 January 1604), a few slight changes were made, but not in the direction of puritan complaints. After the Restoration, there was an attempt at closer agreement, but the Savoy conference (15 April 1661) did little towards attaining it. Parties were too clearly marked: between the puritan who claimed entire freedom for the minister and the bishop who wished to retain ancient use there could be little agreement. Nor, again, was it easy to satisfy at the same time those who believed in episcopacy, and those who maintained an exclusive presbyterianism. The formation of the English prayer-book in itself was now complete formally, as, practically, it had been complete long before. Its liturgical influence has been nearly as widespread as its literary example; it has become the parent of the Scots prayer-book, of the American and of the Irish, all with features of their own, but forming one great school after the English model.

It was the influence of Cranmer that restrained the English reformation from following more closely the extremes of foreign example. When Edward's reign was over, he regretted his compliance with regard to the change in the royal succession, but he was prepared to justify, with arguments that were forcible as well as learned, the theological position which he finally reached and which he had at least made possible under the second prayer-book. His martyrdom was a great incident in the reformation, and it added to his individual influence. To his friends and foes alike, the death-scene was both pathetic and important; eye-witnesses of very different sympathies have described it; and complicated questions, legal and canonical, have been asked concerning it. But the simple, self-distrusting mind of the scholar and writer wished to make no pose, and sought after no display. The cruelty shown him did little to check the movement. The leaders of the Elizabethan church were men of much his mould, but with an added touch of strength and effective purpose. They thankfully took as the basis of their work the prayer-book that had translated the devotion of the past into the language of the future. They followed Cranmer in his wish to learn from the church, as he had strongly expressed it in his *Appeal to a Council*; they followed him also in his love of the Scriptures.

One new feature in the prayer-book had been its exhortations. Edification and instruction were needed: not only, therefore, was much Scripture introduced, but short discourses or exhortations, Scriptural, pointed and, withal, majestic, were also added· some of them date from the order of communion issued in 1548, one, also in the communion service, was due to Peter Martyr. But the wish to instruct shown by these compositions found a larger field for itself in the *Homilies*. The first book of *Homilies* was issued (1547) when the policy of licensing a few preachers and silencing others was carried to an extreme. Cranmer, at an earlier date (1539—43), had been preparing homilies meant both to set the note of preaching and to provide sermons for those who preached with difficulty or not at all: he himself wrote for the first book the homilies of salvation, of faith and of good works, and, doubtless, he edited the whole volume. A later second book, issued under Elizabeth (before 1563), was lengthier, less interesting and feebler in style than the first book, in which Cranmer's own homilies have all the fine characteristics of his other works.

The *Homilies* were intended to make sure that instruction should be given and that it should be of a kind agreeable to the authorities; but they were not the only attempt in this direction: *The Institution of a Christian Man* (1537) had been meant as a guide for teaching, and in it, too, Cranmer had borne a large part.

But it was superseded by its free revision, *The Necessary Doctrine and Erudition of a Christian Man* (1543)—called *The King's Book* in contrast to its predecessor's popular name *The Bishops' Book*—made when the reaction of Henry's later years was at its height. The age was one of confessions and formulae of faith, and the English documents of this kind compare favourably with those of other lands. The English reformation is perhaps often judged exclusively by its political effects and not also by its literary history: if this second test were applied, our estimate of Cranmer and his influence might be even higher than it is at present.

The increasing stress laid upon edification made itself felt not only through the press, but even more through the pulpit literature of the day, which showed a great facility of expression and a command of genuine emotion not reached before. Medieval oratory, at its best, did not, and could not, equal it, because it was impossible, in the earlier days, to combine these two elements to the degree possible at the reformation. Even just before the reformation, bishop Fisher's sermons—perhaps the best of their time and delivered by a most saintly man—did not reach the same force and directness of speech, the vivid personal appeal, the command of an audience, to which many later sermons attained. In its sudden rise to excellence, the sermon of the day may, indeed, be compared with the drama: both were affected by the growth of the language, and also by a movement of thought able to wield that language with greater power; both suffered, at a later date, from an excess of fancy, beginning to appear even in Latimer's *Sermons on the Card* (December 1529). Among popular preachers, John Longland, bishop of Lincoln (1521—38) and chancellor of Oxford, had a great reputation; so, upon the other side, had John Hooper, afterwards bishop of Gloucester, whose sermons upon *Jonah*, before Edward VI, were vigorous in denunciation and fearless in reproof. But the reputation of all these capable preachers, speaking, as they did, to a generation tolerant, or even avaricious, of sermons, was overshadowed by the greater name of Hugh Latimer.

Latimer, the exact year of whose birth is uncertain (1485—91), took his bachelor's degree at Cambridge in 1510, and his bachelorship of divinity in 1524. As crossbearer (1522) to the university and as Fellow of Clare he had some academical position. Up to 1524, he had opposed the new teaching, and, in his 'act' for B.D., had attacked Melanchthon. But, after that discourse, Thomas Bilney, desiring to influence him, chose him as confessor and, as a penitent, gained him over to his own views. Together, they spent their days in works of mercy; in the evening, they, with Robert Barnes, Stafford and others, met at 'The White Horse' for reading and discussion. 'Little Germany,' as the place was called, became a centre of influence in the university, and remained so until an abusive sermon of Barnes, preached in St Edward's church on Christmas Eve 1525, brought danger upon the 'Germans.' Hitherto, Wolsey had been very tolerant and, although urged by the bishops to take steps against heresy at the universities, had refused to do so. But Barnes, who, like Latimer, had come under Bilney's spiritual influence, had not learnt reverence or discretion, and in this sermon he had attacked Wolsey with violence. Taken to London and examined before Wolsey, he agreed to recant; after this he was imprisoned for three years and then escaped to Germany. The incident scattered the band of Cambridge scholars and was a crisis in their history. It not only brought them into disrepute, but lent bitterness to their words and writings.

When Barnes preached this celebrated sermon, he had exchanged pulpits with Latimer, who, although he had just been inhibited by the bishop (West) of Ely, could still preach in the exempt chapel of the Augustinian priory. The trouble caused Latimer, also, to be called before Wolsey, who appreciated his good qualities and his sound old-fashioned learning, and allowed him to return to Cambridge with a general licence to preach, signed by the cardinal himself. The incident shows the attitude taken by those in high authority towards reform; but the bitterness of preachers like Barnes and the scurrility of some pamphleteers made it hard to maintain this attitude. Up to this time, the movement in England had been mainly based on learning and was distinctly English. In spite of the names of Lutherans and Germans loosely given to them, and of their sympathy for German writers, these Englishmen, as yet, owed little to foreign influence. But increasing intercourse gradually brought about a closer unity of opinion: few English theologians became Lutherans, but some became Zwinglians and others Calvinists. Latimer, however, may be taken as representing the earlier and more characteristic stage of the movement. He attacked specially those abuses which Erasmus had satirised—indulgences, pilgrimages, veneration of images; upon the positive side, he laid stress upon the life and example of Christ, and held up a high ideal of conduct. But he did not move of his own accord to any revolutionary conception of the church, to any assertion of individual liberty, or to an attack upon the doctrine of the sacraments, although that was the central topic of his examination at his trial (1555). Even then, however, he leaned mainly upon Cranmer's book, and confessed that he had only been of his final opinion for some seven years.

His boldness during the trial, and his determination, both for himself and in inspiring others, was a strange contrast to the timidity of some of his earlier Cambridge friends. His arguments were, however, less forceful than his example: he referred again and again to 'my lord of Canterbury's book' for proof of his assertions; and discussion of the one subject—that of the pope's supremacy—upon which he would have liked to enlarge, was refused him. The *Conferences* between him and Ridley (published in 1556) give a pathetic picture of their imprisonment.

> The number of the 'criers under the altar' must needs be fulfilled. Pardon me and pray for me: pray for me, I say: pray for me, I say. For I am sometimes so fearful, that I would creep into a mousehole; sometimes God doth visit me again with His comfort. So He cometh and goeth, to teach me to feel and to know mine infirmity, to the intent to give thanks to Him that is worthy, lest I should rob Him of His duty, as many do. Fare you well.

These were his words to Ridley. To another prisoner, wavering in the peril of death, he wrote:

> If any man perceive his faith not to abide the fire, let such an one with weeping buy his liberty, until he hath obtained more strength, lest the gospel by him sustain an offence of some shameful recantation. Let the dead bury their dead. Let us that be of the lively faith follow the Lamb wheresoever He goeth.

Clearly those were not mistaken who had seen in the great preacher an underlying strength of manliness, inspired by piety, as the foundation of his character.

The power of a preacher is hard to estimate, for much of it vanishes with the day itself. But the characteristics that draw us, even yet, to Latimer's sermons had their attraction then also. The homely anecdotes, the touches illustrative of social manners and habits, are valuable for us historically: at the time of their delivery they gave the sermons vividness and special force. Honesty and fearlessness, directness of appeal and allusions to matters of the day, showed the preacher's contact with life. They showed, moreover, how far he had departed from the previous conventionalities of the pulpit; almost the only trace of them is the frequent use (seen, also, in Longland's sermons) of Latin words that, to us, in no way deepen the impression. It was the nature of the man that spoke through all these things, and, because he was natural above all else, because he revealed himself to hearers whose natures he laid hold of by instinct, he gained great power. But minor points were not neglected: repetition, intolerable in writings, but declared, by masters of preaching, to be necessary in sermons meant for instruction, was a frequent feature. He grasped the attention, sometimes by what have been called 'antics,' and then he searched the conscience and touched the heart. It was an age that sought instruction, and he compelled it to listen. It would be hard to find sermons anywhere that show so plainly as do his the true relation between preacher and congregation. There was nothing in them of art, but there was the sense of a message driven home with sympathy and love. He preached because he must: the sermon was his natural expression. There had been nothing of the kind in English before; and not many years had passed before the technical scholastics of puritanism, the search after conceits of imagination and expression, made sermons such as his impossible.

A commission to investigate heretical books, upon which Latimer served, had been appointed (1530). Some restrictions were considered needful, but evasions of authoritative regulations were common: church and state had a common interest in checking the heresy and sedition which, often expressed with scurrility, was their common enemy. The control or licensing of books was, as a rule, assigned to the bishops; but the universities, not only in England but, also, on the continent, had been often appealed to. Henry (6 May 1530) summoned representatives of both universities to meet and examine suspected books. Their labours ended (24 May) in the condemnation of many works; some old, such as the writings of Wyclif and Hus, some new, such as those of Luther, Zwingli, Fish, Joye and Tindale. *The Parable of the Wicked Mammon, The Obedience of a Christian Man, The Revelation of Anti-Christ* and *The Sum of Scripture* were writings of Tindale and his school which produced great effect.

William Tindale is, to us, above all the translator of the Scriptures, but, to his own age, he was probably at least as much the theological pamphleteer. Of his early life, nothing is really known. He was born, probably about 1484, in Gloucestershire, and went to Oxford, where, under the name of Hichyns, he took his M.A. degree in 1515. He spent some time afterwards in Cambridge, and, about 1520, went as private tutor to Little Sodbury, in his native county. It was here that he formed his great design of translating the Bible into English, and the need of such a work was impressed upon him while preaching to the country people. His preaching in the villages and in Bristol first brought him into collision with the church authorities. He had to appear before the diocesan chancellor; but of the result of his summons—probably unimportant—nothing is known with certainty. Before long, Tindale went up to London with the special object of gaining protection for his work of translation (1523). From Tunstall, bishop of London, he received little encouragement; but Humphry Monmouth, an alderman and merchant, gave him shelter and friendship. Gradually, Tindale came to think that there was no place in England for his purpose, and he crossed over to Hamburg (1524). It was possible to print books abroad and send them into England by an evasion of the existing regulations; and the secret association of the Christian Brethren, who existed for the spread of this suspected literature, was specially active in East Anglia, in London and in other seaports. In Germany, Tindale came into contact with others who, for reasons as good as, or better than, his own, had left England; among these were William Roy, George Joye (with both of whom he afterwards quarrelled) and John Frith. Pamphlets which troubled the government became more numerous in England after Tindale's arrival on the continent; and yet, while their seizure was ordered, the king was reading them with pleasure. Tindale's theological opinions had, by this time, gone far beyond those of his original master, Erasmus, and he put them forth with confidence: he was now opposed to all ceremonies that were not perfectly understood; he questioned confirmation and baptism with arguments which were often expressed disrespectfully and sometimes irreverently; while his insistence upon the need of faith alone was accompanied by a dangerous depreciation of all good works. Some bitterness of expression may be allowed men who fear for their lives or are chafing under abuses they cannot remove, but the language of some pamphlets of the day passed all such allowance. Joye was even more violent than Tindale, whom More styled 'the captain of our English heretics'; but there were some who, like John Frith, argued out great issues in a becoming way. Frith's *Disputation of Purgatory* and *The Supper of the Lord*, which presented the Zwinglian view, led to controversy with Rastell and More. He first began the lengthy sacramental controversy, but the characteristic of his teaching was the assertion that purgatory and transubstantiation should be left open questions. This tolerance was impressed upon him by Tindale, whose associations with Marburg may have suggested to him the need of comprehensiveness. His advice to Frith, that he should go on preaching 'until the matter might be reasoned in peace at leisure of both parties,' was based upon expediency, but Frith soon raised the principle to a point of conscience. The *Articles whereof John Frith died* show us a writer and a martyr (1533) far above most theologians of the day in dignity and breadth. But Tindale's orders to him, that he should 'ever among thrust in that the Scripture may be in the mother-tongue and learning set up in the universities,' taken together with his letters to others, show the former as the leader of a wide-spread movement, directed by him with energy and zeal, but not always with knowledge or self-restraint. The typical misunderstanding of Wolsey displayed in *The Practice of Prelates* marks Tindale's limitations and defects. He was a scholar with something of a scholar's self-seclusion and ignorance of the world, and he is not the only scholar who, in writing upon theology or politics, has failed to calculate the effect of his language upon others. Furthermore, the circumstances of his life were unfavourable to his disposition. Publishers, like Froben at Basel, kept scholars, like Erasmus and Beatus Rhenanus, at work upon profitable tasks; the element of commercial speculation entered into all literary work; and thus, around Tindale with his great aim, were grouped others less lofty in mind and chiefly intent upon gain. His associates were often undesirable; his own absorption in his task and his curious love of self-assertion both tended to make him somewhat peevish in his dealings; and thus, partly because of himself, partly because of his friends, the story of his adventures abroad is a depressing one. The violence of these writers, the deceitful and underhand means by which they gained their influence, sometimes their treachery to each other, were certain to bring disaster upon themselves and others, and deprive them of much of the sympathy which might otherwise be theirs. But the main effect of Tindale's writings was to urge the private appeal to the sole authority of Scripture, secured by the unlimited power of the king, with his full power of reforming the church. Such teaching made him a useful ally to Henry VIII, and led to his being secretly encouraged. But his strong condemnation of Henry's divorce, creditable to him as it was, lessened his usefulness in Henry's eyes.

It is a relief to turn from the pamphlets to Tindale's Biblical translation. His scholarship was adequate and he was not dependent upon the *Vulgate* alone; his exposition of his methods—

like his love of the Scriptures, possibly derived from Erasmus—magnifies his conception of his task and its importance; he followed previous translators worthily, but with better weapons; and the improved style of his revised edition is, in itself, a testimony to his fitness for the work he undertook. It is impossible and unnecessary to follow his enforced travels closely; from Hamburg he passed (1525) to Cologne, and here the great scholar Cochlaeus frustrated his work. Tindale just contrived to escape to Worms, saving some sheets already printed. *St Matthew* and *St Mark* had already appeared separately, and now two editions of the New Testament in quarto and octavo, the former with prologue and glosses, were sent to England. The authorities were on the alert, and lists of prohibited books had been issued; but, in spite of this, a change of opinion was slowly coming.

Latimer joined his fellow commissioners (1530) in deprecating the publication of an English version; a letter to the king (December 1530) urging it has been wrongly ascribed to him. The scheme had been mooted long before, but archbishop Arundel's measures had put it off, and there were, of course, difficulties in the way. The king, in 1530, had hinted at the possibility of its realisation in the future, and convocation, in 1534, asked the king to appoint translators. But private enterprise, which did not stop to weigh conflicting dangers, 'prevented' the government in the matter.

It was to the glosses in Tindale's Testament that most objection was raised. His own theological views were extreme; convocation objected to his substitution of the words 'congregation,' 'elder' and 'penitence' for 'church,' 'priest' and 'penance'; and the glosses often conveyed extreme views in a petty form. To this, exception was, not unnaturally, taken. Lee, the old antagonist of Erasmus, urged the king to take steps against the introduction of such translations; and it is curious to notice that he assumes the English Bible itself to be prohibited. Tunstall preached against it and Henry decided that it should be 'brenned' (1527). But, in spite of the measures that were taken and the copies that were bought up, prohibition proved a failure. New editions were multiplied; the majority of English theologians were changing their views; an appeal to Scripture against their papal antagonists was gaining force; and, lastly, the king, especially in the days of Cromwell, saw some advantage to be gained from the forces he had tried to suppress. Bishop Nix of Norwich was not the only one who thought that the king favoured 'arroneous boks' (1530).

Other editions of Tindale's New Testament—one, of a poor character, pirated by his former helper George Joye—appeared, and (November 1534) Tindale published a revised edition of his own, to which he added not only slight marginal notes, but also those epistles in the Sarum use which came from the Old Testament or the *Apocrypha*. In the very year that Tindale was put to death (1536), an edition was printed in England. After many wanderings, to Marburg, to Hamburg and, finally, to Antwerp, he was treacherously seized (May 1535), not by English contrivance, and put to death at Vilvorde (6 October 1536). But his work was already done; copies of the New Testament, either his or founded upon his, were common, and he had made more than a beginning with the Old Testament; he had, moreover, fixed the character of the English translations for evermore. Instinctively he, like many writers or preachers of his day, had expressed himself in the popular style, not in the larger phrase affected by scholars, and, in that style, the Bible remained.

Miles Coverdale, afterwards bishop of Exeter, although inferior to Tindale in scholarship, was at least as closely connected with the English version. A Yorkshireman by birth, he became an Augustinian friar at Cambridge, where he had formed one of the band of reformers, and had been naturally influenced by his prior, Barnes; he had also early connections with Sir Thomas More and Thomas Cromwell. He soon left England, however, and probably (1529) met Tindale abroad. Not only did he thus enter the circle of translators, but he was urged by Cromwell to print an edition of his own, about which much correspondence took place between Cromwell and the editors and printers. The work, when it appeared (1535), was said to be translated from the Dutch (*i.e.* German) and Latin, and not to be for the maintenance of any sect; Coverdale recognised the previous labours of others, which he had, indeed, largely used, and he drew upon the Zurich Bible as well as upon Tindale's editions. He dedicated his work to Henry VIII, in the hope of receiving royal patronage, if not a royal licence; but this was not formally given. Cromwell's injunction (1536) that the Bible, in Latin and English, should be placed in churches was, doubtless, meant to refer to this edition, but the order was ineffective. Convocation, however, soon asked again for a new translation, and the second edition of Coverdale's work —published (1537) both in folio and quarto, and the first Bible printed in England—was licensed by the king. The edition of 1535, printed, probably, by Froschover at Zurich, had also been the first complete English Bible printed. Tindale had translated the *Pentateuch*, *Jonah* and some detached pieces, and may have left more in MS, but Coverdale now translated the whole. He did not claim any extensive scholarship, and his description of his work is modest; but his pains, nevertheless, had been great, and the prayer-book *Psalter*, still reminding us of his work, speaks of its literary merits to all.

The history of the English Bible had thus moved quickly; but the publicity, which Coverdale, perhaps even above Tindale, had aimed at, was gained even more largely by another edition. Thomas Matthew, or, rather, John Rogers, to give him his real name, formed another Bible by a combination of Tindale's Old Testament so far as it went and Coverdale's—the *Apocrypha* being included. This was printed abroad by R. Grafton (who was a fellow-worker with Coverdale) and T. Whitchurch (1537). It is usually thought that, in parts up to 2 *Chronicles*, where this edition differs from Coverdale's, it is indebted to remains left by Tindale, to which Rogers, Tindale's former assistant, probably had access. It was dedicated to Henry VIII, and Cranmer, who liked it better than all previous translations, was able to befriend it. The king gave leave for its sale, and thus it took a place not publicly gained before; its many notes, too, found it favour or disfavour according to the reader's opinions.

Coverdale began to prepare a new edition, for which he went abroad in the Lent of 1538; but, as the inquisition forbade its being printed in Paris, it was partly printed (1539) in England, after it (September 1538) had been ordered for use in churches. This edition is known as the Great Bible. Again, Coverdale's labours had turned more to other versions than to the text, and he had availed himself of some new continental versions. A second edition of it (April 1540) appeared with a preface by Cranmer, who saw, in an English Bible formally approved, his own great hope fulfilled; and this edition, therefore, became known as Cranmer's Bible, although he had done nothing for it beyond writing the preface. Then, at last, the English Bible was set up in churches (May 1540) and was in general use both public and private.

One more edition of the New Testament, significant from the place of its appearance, and destined from its doctrinal bias to be widely popular, was the Genevan New Testament of William Whittingham (1557), who had married a sister of Calvin's wife, and succeeded John Knox as English pastor at Geneva. The text was founded upon previous English versions, but Beza's Latin version, the rival of the *Vulgate*, was also used. The whole Bible appeared at Geneva (1560) with a dedication to queen Elizabeth and with more apparatus than had hitherto been added, the text being due to Whittingham, helped by Anthony Gilby and Thomas Sampson. As they were, respectively, the first Testament and Bible printed with verse-divisions and in roman type, they mark a distinct stage.

Convocation, the authority of which had been sometimes pushed aside, was not wholly satisfied with the Great Bible, and (1542) sought a revision of it by the *Vulgate*, but, although parts were assigned to various translators, nothing came of the proposal. Under Elizabeth, and upon the initiative of archbishop Parker, the Bishops' Bible was issued (1568); but, in the end, it was superseded by the *Authorised Version* (1611) prepared after the Hampton Court conference[1].

It should be noted that these Bibles varied in their treatment of the *Apocrypha*: Coverdale's, Matthew's and the Genevan Bible, following continental protestant usage, differentiated it from the Old Testament, and, after 1629, when we have the first example, editions of Bibles without the *Apocrypha* became common. Apart from any critical or theological views supposed to be involved, this omission was a serious literary loss, which is now being more understood.

It may seem curious that, with this activity in producing English versions, little was thought or said of the earliest English versions. They seem to have had but little effect, although one exception must be noted, in the Scots New Testament of Murdoch Nisbet (*c.* 1520). This was based upon Purvey's version, although the earlier Wyclifite version may, also, have been used: the adaptation of Luther's preface to the New Testament (1522), and the later addition of Tindale's prologue to *Romans*, indicate the use of these editions after the work had been begun. Nisbet belonged to Ayrshire, and had come under the influence of the Lollards of that district. He had not only been a fugitive for his religion, but, after his return home, had lived many years in hiding. His translation had, doubtless, been made for a help in his own ministry, but the importation into Scotland of Tindale's translation

[1] The position of the *Authorised Version* in English literature is discussed in a later chapter of the present work.

checked its use and so possibly prevented the publication of a linguistically and historically interesting version.

One further result of the liturgical changes and the growing use of the vulgar tongue calls for mention. The hymns in the daily offices had always been popular, and the tendency to replace them by English substitutes was natural and strong. The best example of devotional poetry was to be found in the *Psalms*, and, when religious and poetic interests were warmly felt, a rendering of the *Psalms* into English verse seemed a happy method of stirring up religious zeal. Clément Marot had set French psalms to popular tunes for the French court under Francis I; Calvin, whom many generations of puritans followed, kept Marot's words, although he rejected his tunes. An English courtier and poet attempted a like task in England. Thomas Sternhold, a Hampshire gentleman educated at Oxford, became groom of the robes to Henry VIII. He was in trouble for his religious views (1543), but kept his favour at court, and was there at a time when English was being largely used in Edward VI's chapel royal. Thinking to turn the minds of the nobles to higher things, he put some psalms into verse and (1548), a year before his death, published nineteen of them under the title of *Certayne Psalms.* A year later, John Hopkins, a clergyman of Suffolk, published thirty-seven psalms by Sternhold, with seven of his own. In later editions, he increased the number, and (1562) *The Whole Booke of Psalmes* by Sternhold, Hopkins, Thos. Norton and others, appeared in verse, and was added to the prayer-book. Not only was this done, but melodies, some of which are still in popular use, were also printed. Successive editions show traces of German influence, and a formidable rival appeared in the Genevan *Psalter*, due to Whittingham, Kethe and others. Its history is much like that of the older English version, with which it has much in common: fifty-one psalms were printed (1556) together with the form of prayer used by the English exiles, and, in later editions, more were added. The influence of Marot and Beza could be traced in it, and so reappears in its descendant, the *Scots Psalter* (1564). The growth of Calvinism made these versions more popular than that of Sternhold, but his compositions, which are marked by a concise and natural simplicity, are easy to distinguish. Metrical psalmody was in the air, and many writers, including archbishop Parker (*c.* 1555), tried their hands at it. Its popularity grew, but the growing separation between religion and all kinds of art, which marked the seventeenth century, lowered the literary quality of later editions. These earlier versions had been, however, deservedly popular, and opened a new channel for religious fervour. Their merits and their religious influence must not be judged by their later successors. They belonged to a time when religious feeling and literary taste were at a higher level, and they did something to replace a favourite part of the older service-books.

A general survey of the field teaches us how varied the religious impulses of the reformation were, and how vital they were for the national welfare, both upon their positive and negative sides. Party feeling and royal politics made the course of the movement sometimes slower, sometimes tumultuous. One change may be noted. In the lists of early printed books, a number of medieval manuals of devotion and instruction precede the controversial writings. At first, as in the Middle Ages, schools conceal individuals, the same material is re-used and authorship is difficult to settle. But, as in the cases of More and Tindale, the weight of well known names begins to be felt, and the printing press, fixing once for all the very words of a writer, put an end to processes which had often hidden authorship. The needs of controversy hastened the change, and individualism in literature began. An author was now face to face with his public. It is trite to call the reformation an age of transition, and its significance for creative thought is sometimes over-estimated. But, at its outset, the problems of its literature, its methods and its processes are medieval; at its end, they are those which we know to-day. If, in Germany, the revolution was heralded by medieval theses, in England, the reformation controversies sprang out of a literature purely medieval. But, at the close of the period we have dealt with, the translation of an English Bible, the formation of an English prayer-book, stand out as great religious and literary results, and each of them is due less to individual labourers than to the continuous work of schools. There may have been many who regretted much that had been lost; but to have preserved and adapted so much was no mean gain. Many of the absorbing controversies died away; but these results, which they had helped to produce, remained.

CHAPTER III

THE DISSOLUTION OF THE RELIGIOUS HOUSES

THE general wave of new thought breaking upon England in the first half of the sixteenth century swept away with it, among other things, the almost countless religious houses with which the country was covered. Their disappearance is more significant considered as an effect than as a cause; yet it cannot be doubted that, in its turn, it had an effect, both for good and for evil, on the movement in which it was an incident. And first let the losses to learning be estimated.

The destruction of books was almost incredibly enormous. Bale describes the use of them by bookbinders and by grocers and merchants for the packing of their goods. Maskell calculates the loss of liturgical books alone to have approached the total of a quarter of a million. An eye-witness describes the leaves of Duns Scotus as blown about by the wind even in the courts of Oxford, and their use for sporting and other purposes. Libraries that had been collected through centuries, such as those of Christ Church and St Albans, both classical and theological, vanished in a moment. It was not only the studious orders that gathered books; the friars, also, had libraries, though, as Leland relates of the Oxford Franciscans, they did not always know how to look after them. So late as 1535, a bequest was made by the bishop of St Asaph of five marks to buy books for the Grey Friars of Oxford. Nor can it be doubted that vast numbers of books less directly theological must have perished.

A second destruction was that of the homes of study which the religious houses, especially those of the Benedictines, provided for all who leaned that way. The classical renascence had not yet made sufficient way, except among the more advanced, to disturb the old system by which it was natural for the studious to enter the cloister and the rest to remain men of sport or war. The use of the word 'clerk' as denoting a man of education, apart from the question as to whether he were tonsured or not, indicates this tendency. Even Erasmus, it must be remembered, was once an Augustinian. Closely allied to the disappearance of this aid to learning was that of the influence of tradition which, if it held thinkers within narrow bounds, at the same time saved them the waste of energy that is the inevitable accompaniment of all new enterprise. There is abundant evidence to show that the religious houses were so used; at Durham, Gloucester and Canterbury, for example, there remain traces or records of the provision for making books accessible and for accommodating their readers; and the details of the life of Erasmus, as well as those of the life of Thomas More, show that the most advanced scholars of the age numbered among their equals and competent critics the students of the cloister. Such a man was prior Charnock of Oxford, Bere, abbot of Glastonbury, and Warham, archbishop of Canterbury. Further, it must be remembered, not only were monastic houses in themselves homes of study, but, from their religious unity with the continent, they afforded means of communication with scholars abroad. Not only were the great houses the natural centres to which scholars came, but from them there went out to the foreign universities of Bologna and Pisa such religious as were in any sense specialists. This, of course, practically ceased, not only because of the religious change, but because there were no longer rich corporations who could afford to send their promising pupils abroad. The proverbial poverty of scholars had, to a large extent, been mitigated by this provision. The lives of such men as Richard Pace show that among the religious were to be found generous patrons as well as professors of learning.

Next must be reckoned the direct and indirect loss to the education of children. To a vast number of religious houses, both of monks and nuns, were attached schools in which the children of both poor and rich received instruction. Richard Whiting, for example, the last abbot of Glastonbury, numbered among his 'family' three hundred boys whom he educated, supporting, besides, students at the university. Every great abbey, practically, was the centre of education for all the country round; even the Benedictine nuns kept schools attended by children of gentle birth, and, except in those rare cases where scholarly parents themselves supervised the education of their children, it may be said that, for girls, these were the only available teachers of even the simplest elements of learning. The grammar schools, which are popularly supposed to have sprouted in such profusion under Edward VI, may be held to have been, in nearly every case, remnants of the old monastic foundations, and, even so, were not one tithe of those which had previously existed. The rest fell with the monasteries, and, even in places of considerable importance, as at Evesham, practically no substitute was provided until nearly a century later. Signs of this decay of learning may be found to some extent in the records of the universities. The houses fell, for the most part, about the year 1538, but they had been seriously threatened for three or four years previously; and the effect may be seen in the fact that, at Oxford, in 1535, one hundred and eight men graduated, while, in 1536, only forty-four did so. Up to the end of Henry's reign, the average was but fifty-seven, in Edward's, thirty-three, while, during the revival of the old thought under Mary, it rose again as high as seventy. The decrease of students at Cambridge was not at first so formidable. This was natural, since that university was far more in sympathy with the new ideas than was her sister. But, ten years after the dissolution, a serious decrease showed itself. Fuller reports 'a general decay of students, no college having more scholars therein than hardly those of the foundation, no volunteers at all and only persons pressed in a manner by their places to reside.' He traces this directly to the fall of the religious houses. 'Indeed, at the fall of the abbeys fell the hearts of all scholars, fearing the ruin of learning. And those their jealousies they humbly represented in a bemoaning letter to king Henry VIII.' The king, whose dislike of the old canon law had abolished the degrees in that faculty, so that 'Gratian fared no better... than his brother Peter Lombard,' took steps to amend all this by the creation of Regius professors in Divinity, Law, Hebrew and Greek; but it was not until Mary was on the throne that the number of degrees taken yearly at Cambridge rose, once more, to their former minimum of eighty. Other details of the steps that Henry had taken to secure sound learning at Cambridge, shortly before the fall of the houses, while the university was yet 'very full of students,' will be found suggestive. Thus, scholars are urged in his injunctions to the 'study of tongues,' of Aristotle, Rodolphus Agricola, Melanchthon and Trapezuntius, while Scotus, Burleus, Anthony Trombet, Bricot and Bruliferius are forbidden.

Other causes, no doubt, contributed to the decrease of scholarship; the unrest of the age was largely inimical to serious study; but among these causes must be reckoned a further and more direct relation in which the monasteries stood towards the universities. At both Oxford and Cambridge were large establishments to which monks and friars came to finish their education; and, of these scholars, the numbers were so large that, in the century previous to the reformation, one in nine of all graduates seems to have been a religious. At Oxford, the Benedictines alone had four colleges, the Augustinians two and the Cistercians one. All this, then, after the first rush of the disbanded religious to Oxford, stopped with the dissolution, and the universities began to empty. In two years of Edward's reign, no student at all graduated at Oxford; in 1550, Latimer, a fierce advocate of the new movement, laments the fact that there seem 'ten thousand less students than within the last twenty years,' and remarks that 'it would pity a man's heart to hear that I hear of the state of Cambridge'; in Mary's reign, Roger Edgworth pleads for the poor students who have grievously suffered from the recent changes; the study of Greek, on Thomas Pope's evidence, had almost ceased to exist; Anthony Wood mourns over the record of the decline of the arts and the revival of ignorance; Edward VI rebukes the unscholarliness of his own bishops.

The estimation of the gain to learning and letters which followed the fall of the monasteries is more difficult to summarise, since the beginning of a new growth cannot be expected to produce the fruit of a mature tree. The effects must be more subtle and intangible, yet none the less real. And, even could it be accurately gauged by statistics, it would be impossible to place one against the other. We cannot set a pear and a peach in the same category. 'It is generally believed,' remarks Warton, 'that the reformation of religion in England...was immediately succeeded by a flourishing state of letters. But this was by no means the case.'

First, however, it may be stated confidently, that the breaking up of the old ground and the planting of it with new roots brings with it at least as much gain as loss. The scholastic method had done its work. From much concurrent testimony it is evident that there was no more progress to be made, at any rate for the present, along those lines. The deductive method was to yield more and more to the inductive; the rubbish generated by every system of thought carried to extremities must be swept away, and new principles enunciated. Against this inevitable movement, the religious houses, also inevitably, were the most formidable obstacle, since they focussed and protected a method of thought of which the learned world was growing weary. The old principles certainly had led up to fantastic conclusions and innumerable *culs-de-sac* in philosophy and science—conclusions which eminent men of the old party deplored as emphatically as their enemies. Sir Thomas More, who died in defence of the old faith, Erasmus, who clung as firmly as his friend to what he believed to be the divinely revealed centre of truth, and many others, protested as loudly as Latimer himself, and almost as contemptuously as Skelton, against the follies to which real learning had descended. With the fall of the monasteries, therefore, the strongholds of academic method were, for the time, shattered.

In the place of tradition, then, rose up enterprise. The same impulse of new life which drove Drake across the seas forty years later and burned in full blaze in the society of the brilliant Elizabethans, had begun to kindle, indeed, before the dissolution of the houses, but could not rise into flame until it had consumed them. In the world of letters it broke out in curious forms, showing a strange intermingling of the old and the new, few of them of intrinsic value and fewer yet, in any sense, final—always with the exception of the great leaders of humanist thought.

And the rich development that took place was furthered by the movement in which the fall of the religiou houses was a notable incident. They were obstacles, and they were removed. The monastic ideal was one of pruning the tree to the loss of luxuriance; the new ideal was that of more generous cultivation of the whole of human nature.

As regards education, although, as has been seen, the years immediately following the crisis were years of famine—of destruction rather than reconstruction—they were, at the same time, the almost necessary prelude to greater wideness of thought. It was not until three centuries later that the state, as distinguished from the church, took the responsibilities of education—for both schools and universities continued to remain, until nearly the present day, under clerical control—but, so soon as the confusion had passed, education did, to some extent, begin to recover its balance on a new basis. What had been, under the system of great monastic centres, the province of the more studious, began, more and more, to be diffused among the rest, or, at least, to be put into more favourable conditions for that dissemination. The fortunes of Greek scholarship show a curiously waving line. That branch of study was introduced, together with Greek manuscripts, by scholars such as prior William Tilly of Selling, who had become fascinated by Italian culture; but, with the general uprush of the classical renascence, it fell once more under suspicion and the pulpit began to be turned against it. With the fall of the monasteries, however, curiously enough, it nearly disappeared altogether—for example, at Oxford, though Wolsey himself had founded a chair for its study—and it was not until things were quiet that it again took its place among its fellows, and is to be found generally recommended for grammar schools along with the arts of 'good manners,' Latin, English, history, writing and even chess. Classics indeed, generally, when the confusion was over, found a fairer field than had been possible under clerical control. Pure Latin was, to a large extent, vitiated by its ecclesiastical rival; and Greek was associated vaguely in men's minds with the principles of Luther and the suspected new translations of the Scriptures, in spite of Fisher's zeal for its study at Cambridge, and the return of Wakefield from Tübingen in the same cause. 'Graeculus,' in fact, had become a colloquial synonym for 'heretic'; and both languages, as represented by such authors as Terence, Plautus and the Greek poets, were under grave suspicions as being vehicles for immoral sentiments. It is true that such men as prior Barnes lectured on Latin authors in his Augustinian house at Cambridge, yet it was not until a few years after the dissolution that even the classical historians began to be translated into English. Friars were reported actually to have destroyed books that in their opinion were harmful or even useless.

Another gain that compensated for the loss of the old kind of intercourse with Italy was, undoubtedly, to be found in the new connections of England with northern Europe as well as with the vigorous life of renascence Italy. The coming of such men as Bucer and Fagius to Cambridge at the invitation of the king, and a flood of others later, the intercourse with Geneva and Zurich, culminating in Mary's reign—these channels could hardly have been opened thus freely under the old conditions; and if this exchange of ideas was primarily on theological subjects, yet it was not to the exclusion of others. So long as the religious houses preserved their prestige in the country at large and in the universities in particular, every new idea or system that was antagonistic to their ideals had a weight of popular distrust to contend against: the average Englishman saw that ecclesiastics held the field, he heard tales of vast monastic libraries and of monkish prodigies of learning, he listened to pulpit thunderings and scholastic disputations, while all that came from Germany and the Low Countries was represented by single men who held no office and won but little hearing. When the houses were down and their prestige shattered, it was but between man and man that he had to decide.

And, further, in a yet more subtle way, the dissolution actually contributed to the prestige of the new methods of thought under whose predominance the fall had taken place and, under Elizabeth, these new methods were enforced with at least as much state pressure as the old system had enjoyed. There were, of course, other causes for the destruction—the affairs of the king, both domestic and political, religious differences, the bait of the houses' wealth—all these things conspired to weigh the balances down and to accomplish in England the iconoclasm which the renascence did not accomplish in southern Europe. It can hardly be said that the superior culture in England demanded a sacrifice which Italy did not demand; but, rather, that it found here a peculiar collocation of circumstances and produced, therefore, peculiar results. Yet in men's minds the revival of learning and the fall of the monasteries were inextricably associated; and the enthusiasm of Elizabeth's reign, with its countless achievements in art and literature and general effectiveness, was certainly enhanced by the memory of that with which the movement of thirty years before had been busily linked. Great things had been accomplished under a Tudor, an insular independence unheard of in the history of the country had been established; there were no limits then, it seemed, to what might be effected in the future. The triumphant tone in Elizabethan writers is, surely, partly traceable to this line of thought—they are full of an enthusiasm of freedom—and, in numberless passages, Shakespeare's plays served to keep the thought alight.

It can scarcely be reckoned as a gain that the dispersal of the libraries took place, except in one definite point, for it has been seen in what manner the books were usually treated. This gain was the founding of the school of English antiquaries under John Leland[1], and the concentration in their hands of certain kinds of manuscripts that, practically, had no existence except in the recesses of monastic libraries. In 1533, this priest was appointed king's antiquary. It was his office 'to peruse the libraries of all cathedrals, abbeys, colleges, etc.,' no doubt with a view to the coming dissolution; but for six years he travelled, and claims to have 'conserved many good authors, the which otherwise had been like to have

[1] See *post*, chap. xv.

perished, of the which part remain' in the royal libraries. That there was a slight degree of truth in this implied reproach we have already seen; and it is certain that access was now made possible to many copies of English and classical authors, the loss of which might have occurred under monastic complacency, and certainly would have occurred under reforming zeal. 'In turning over of the superstitious monasteries,' says Bale, Leland's friend and editor, 'little respect was had to their libraries.' Others followed Leland in his care for antiquities of literature and history. Matthew Parker, says Josselin his secretary, 'was very careful to seek out the monuments of former times.... Therefore in seeking up the chronicles of the Britons and English Saxons, which lay hidden everywhere, contemned and buried in forgetfulness,' as well as in editing and publishing them, Parker and his assistants did a good work which had scarcely been possible under the old system. Josselin himself helped, and Sir Robert Cotton's collection of Saxon charters and other manuscripts is one of the great founts of English history.

It is impossible, then, with any degree of justice, to set the gains and the losses, resultant from the dissolution, in parallel columns. The former were subtle, far-reaching, immature; the latter were concrete, verifiable and sentimental. Rather, until some definition of progress be agreed upon by all men, we are only safe in saying that, from the purely intellectual side, while the injury to the education of those who lived at the time, and the loss of innumerable books, antiquities and traditions for all time, are lamentable beyond controversy, yet, by the diffusion of general knowledge, by the widening of the limits of learning and philosophy, by the impetus given to independent research, art and literature, and by the removal of unjustifiable prejudice, we are the inheritors of a treasure that could hardly have been ours without the payment of a heavy price.

CHAPTER IV

BARCLAY AND SKELTON

Early German Influences on English Literature

Alexander Barclay was born about 1475. A Scotsman by descent, he probably came to England very early. He seems to have studied in Oxford, and, perhaps, also in Cambridge. In his *Ship of Fools* he states, with regret, that he has not always been an industrious student; but the title 'syr,' in his translation of *Bellum Jugurthinum*, implies that he took his degree, and in his will he styles himself doctor of divinity. He is said to have travelled in France and Italy; but whether he visited any foreign universities is rather doubtful. At all events, he strongly disapproves of this fashion of the time in *The Ship of Fools*. A fairly good scholar, he knew French and Latin well and seems to have been familiar, to a certain extent, even with German; but he probably did not know Greek.

Barclay started his literary career with a translation of Pierre Gringore's *Le chasteau de labour*, published by Antoine Verard (*c.* 1503) and reprinted by Pynson (*c.* 1505) and Wynkyn de Worde (1506 and *c.* 1510). Subsequently, in 1521, he wrote an *Introductory to write and to pronounce Frenche*, to which Palsgrave refers in his *Esclaircissement de la Langue Francoyse* (1530) in a by no means complimentary way. He even suggests that it was not an original work but was founded on an older treatise which Barclay may have found in the library of his monastery.

Barclay's connection with humanism is proved by his *Eclogues* (*c.* 1514) and a translation of *Bellum Jugurthinum*, published by Pynson (*c.* 1520) and re-edited five years after Barclay's death. Like the French primer, it was made at the suggestion of Thomas, duke of Norfolk, Barclay's patron. In earlier days he owed much to bishop Cornish, provost of Oriel College, Oxford, who made him chaplain of the college of Ottery St Mary, Devonshire. This living he probably held for some years, and, during this time, he completed his best known work, the translation of Brant's famous satirical allegory. *The Ship of Fools*, published first by Pynson in 1509, was dedicated, out of gratitude, to the said bishop. When he translated *The Myrrour of Good Maners*, about 1523, from the Latin of Dominicus Mancinus, Barclay was a monk at Ely. There he had probably written also his *Eclogues*, the *Introductory*, the *Sallust* and the lost *Life of St George*. The preface of *The Myrrour* not only shows that Barclay felt somewhat depressed at that time, but it also contains the interesting statement, that, 'the righte worshipfull Syr Giles Alington, Knight,' for whom the translation was made, had desired at first a modernised version of Gower's *Confessio Amantis*, a task Barclay declined as unsuitable to his age and profession. He must have been fairly well known at this time; for, according to a letter of Sir Nicholas Vaux to Wolsey, dated 10 April 1520, he is to be asked, 'to devise histoires and convenient raisons to florisshe the buildings and banquet house withal' at the meeting of Henry VIII and Francis I, known as the Field of the Cloth of Gold. In this letter, Barclay is spoken of as 'the black monk'; but, later, he left the Benedictines for the stricter order of the Franciscans in Canterbury. There he may have written the *Life of St Thomas of Canterbury*, attributed to him by Bale. Besides the works mentioned already, Barclay seems to have written other lives of saints, some sermons and a few other books to which reference will be made.

What became of him after the dissolution of the monasteries, in 1539, is not known. An ardent champion of the catholic faith, who had written a book *de fide orthodoxa*, as well as another on the oppression of the church by the French king, he probably found it hard to adapt himself to the altered circumstances of the times. But the years of adversity and hardship were followed at last by a short time of prosperity. In 1546, he was instituted to the vicarage of Great Baddow, in Essex, and, in the same year, also to that of St Matthew at Wokey, in Somerset. Both preferments, apparently, he held till his death. On 30 April 1552, he became rector of All Hallows, Lombard Street, in the city of London. Soon afterwards, he died at Croydon, where he had passed part of his youth, and there he was buried. His will was proved on the 10th of June in the same year.

As we have said before, Barclay's most important work is his translation of Sebastian Brant's *Narrenschiff*. What especially attracted him in the famous work of the Basel professor (first edition, Basel, 1494) was, undoubtedly, its moral tone. The idea of the whole was by no means new. Certain groups of fools had been ridiculed in German flying sheets and *Fastnachtsspiele* over and over again, and even the idea of the ship was not at all unfamiliar to Brant's readers. But, to combine the two, to summon all the different kinds of fools, and to send them on a voyage in a huge ship, or in many ships, was new and proved a great success. Not that Brant took much pains to work out the allegory adopted in the beginning; on the contrary, he was extremely careless in that respect, changing and even dropping it altogether in the course of the work. And, as to the classification of his fools, he proceeded quite unmethodically. They follow one another without any strict order, only occasionally connected by a very slight association of ideas. But it was just this somewhat loose arrangement that pleased Brant's readers; and, as his notion of folly was a very wide one, and comprised all sorts of personal and social vices and weaknesses, the book became an all-round satirical picture of the manners of the age. For the enjoyment of the scholar, Brant added to each chapter a great number of instances, taken from the Bible and from classical and medieval authors; for the more homely reader he put in many proverbs. When he called the whole a compilation, he did so, not out of sheer modesty, but because he knew well that this was the very best recommendation with his public, which loved authorities and desiderated them even for the most commonplace statements. As regards the spirit of the whole, it must be sought above all in the moral purpose of the work. Brant did not only blame people, but he wanted to induce them to mend their ways by demonstrating the absurdity or the evil consequences of their follies. His wit was not very striking, his satire rather innocent and tame, his morality somewhat shallow and his language not very eloquent. But he was in deadly earnest about his task and had a remarkable talent for observation. His pictures of contemporary life were always true, and often vivid and striking. Besides, there were the splendid woodcuts, done in a Hogarthian spirit, which helped to render the whole livelier and more dramatic, even where the words were a little dull. He thought, of course, mainly of his fellow-countrymen; but most of the follies and vices which he blamed and satirised were spread all over Europe, and the general feeling of discontent peculiar to that time of transition was extremely well expressed in the book. In spite of his learning, Brant was, decidedly, a son of the olden time. He does not insist upon reforms, but he tries to patch up. With all its reactionary spirit, *Das Narrenschiff* enjoyed a vast popularity and ran through many editions. Geiler von Kaisersberg made its matter the subject of 112 sermons, and it influenced the writings of such men as Murner and Erasmus. Within three years after its first appearance, it was translated into Latin by Brant's friend Locher, and then into almost every European language.

Barclay, probably, first became acquainted with it through the Latin version, which was soon as popular in England as everywhere else. His translation, published in 1509, was almost the last in verse to appear, and was followed in the same year by a prose translation by Henry Watson from the French version of Jehan Droyn. In the preface, Barclay states that he used Locher's translation as well as the French and German versions. In the original edition, Locher's text is printed in front of the English translation, and Cawood's edition of 1570 even puts on the title 'translated out of Latin into Englishe.' Careful comparison has shown that Barclay follows chiefly the Latin version, but that he made use of the French version by Pierre Rivière (Paris, 1497), which was founded on Locher also, and that he used at the same time, though in a much less degree, the German original. For one of the last chapters of his book he seems to be indebted to Jodocus Badius, whereas the ballad in honour of the Virgin Mary at the end is probably his own[1].

According to his prologue, he desired 'to redres the errours and vyces of this our royalme of Englande, as the foresayde composer and translatours hath done in theyr contrees.' Therefore, he followed his author 'in sentence' rather than word, and it is very interesting to see how he added here and abridged there, to suit his English public and his personal taste. On the whole, he was inclined to a certain diffuseness and wordiness. He tells us that Pynson, his publisher, who, apparently, knew him well, was afraid from the very beginning that the book might become rather bulky, and entreated him not to pack too many fools into his ship. As it is, Barclay's translation is two and a half times as long as his Latin original, namely fourteen thousand and thirty-four lines[2]. This is partly due to the metre, the heroic seven-lined stanza, which forms a curious contrast to the

[1] Cf. Fraustadt, *Über das Verhältnis von Barclay's 'Ship of Fools' zur lat., franz. u. deutschen Quelle.*

[2] Brant has 7034, Locher 5672 lines.

unpretending matter and is handled sometimes a little stiffly. The language is very plain and simple, as Barclay meant to write not for learned men but for the common people. A few Scots words betray the author's nationality. Whereas the learned Locher had obliterated the popular spirit of Brant's work, Barclay sought to intensify it by cutting out many classical references, exchanging unknown instances for such as were more familiar, introducing new comparisons and so on. He often makes remarks on the woodcuts, and tries still further to give character to the various kinds of fools. If Locher had endeavoured to work out the allegory of the ship a little better than Brant, Barclay, following English literary taste, went further in the same direction and tried to make the whole more coherent. He was very fond of philosophical and religious reflections and admonitions, which he added freely, particularly in the envoys to each chapter. Locher had left out many of Brant's proverbs; Barclay introduces a great many that are new.

There are a few personal touches in *The Ship of Fools.* Barclay, like Brant, twice describes himself as the steersman of his ship, which is bound for some English harbour, though it seems doubtful if she will ever arrive; once, he introduces himself as a humble passenger. Whereas he assigns a place in the ship to some people he apparently disliked, as stout Mansell of Ottery or twelve 'secondaries' of his college, he refuses to take in some of his friends as being too good. Once, he expresses his contempt of lighter poetry and speaks of his rival, John Skelton, in terms unusually strong[1]. Several times he alludes to the sinfulness of London or to the vices of English society, or he mentions English games and the bad influence of French fashions.

Sometimes, Barclay's additions are of a more general character, as when he speaks of vices that are not confined to any age or country in particular. The details which, in such instances, he introduces exhibit him at his best; he is then rather more lively than is usual with him, and often shows touches of real humour, as, for instance, in his satirical remarks on women.

Great stress is laid on the presumption and wrong-doings of officials, clerical and secular. On this head, Barclay, generally, has much more to say than Brant; and that he always had in his mind the conditions of his own country is proved, not only by his referring to English institutions and offices, but, also, by his express statement that some abuses are not so common in

[1] Sharper still is the attack on Skelton in the fourth *Eclogue*; cf. Dyce, p. xxxvi.

England as on the continent[1]. He complains of the bribery in vogue at Westminster Hall and he admonishes the 'yonge studentes of the Chancery' to rehabilitate justice. He always takes the part of the poor people against their oppressors. Bad secular officials are attacked as unsparingly as are haughty and greedy ecclesiastics. He is exceedingly severe on bad members of his own profession, blames artful friars and worldly priests and complains repeatedly of the promotion of ignorant and lazy people to offices for which they are not fit. He asserts quite frankly that unscrupulous prelates and bad priests are the main cause of the general muddle, and of the decay of the catholic faith, which he speaks of 'with wete chekes by teres thycke as hayle' (II, 193). But, like Brant, he does not advocate any thoroughgoing reforms and is extremely hard on heretics as well as on Turks and heathen.

As Brant admired the emperor Maximilian, so Barclay enthusiastically praises Henry VIII; and, when he expects him to start a crusade against the infidels, with James IV of Scotland as ally and commander-in-chief, this shows sufficiently that he is as bad a politician as the German professor who actually expected to see the imperial crown and the tiara united on the willing head of his romantic hero.

Barclay again shows himself at one with Brant, when he echoes his continual recommendation of the golden mean. He has not the slightest sympathy for people who, like Alexander, attempt more than they can accomplish, nor for those who neglect their own affairs by pushing those of others. Knowledge and learning he values only as instruments for the promotion of faith. As to discoveries, he tries to be up to date, but calls them useless, inasmuch as we shall never know the whole earth. So, in spite of his learning, his point of view is entirely medieval.

The literary influence of *The Ship of Fools* in England is noticeable, for instance, in *Cocke Lorell's bote* (*c.* 1510), with her crew of London craftsmen[2]. Perhaps, also, Skelton's lost *Nacyoun of Folys* (*G. of L.* 1470) was suggested by *The Ship of Fools*, the influence of which has also been traced in the same poet's *Bowge of Courte*[3]. The *Boke of Three Fooles*, ascribed to Skelton till quite recently, has turned out to be a mere reprint of some chapters of Watson's prose translation referred to above[4].

[1] Cf. Jamieson, I, p. 299. [2] See *post*, chap. V.

[3] Cf. Herford's *Literary Relations of England and Germany in the 16th century*, pp. 352 ff.; Rey, *Skelton's satirical poems in their relation to Lydgate's 'Order of Fools,' 'Cock Lorell's bote' and Barclay's 'Ship of Fools.'*

[4] Brie, *Engl. Stud.* XXXIII, p. 262; XXXVII, pp. 78 ff.

In both the cases mentioned we have to think of the Latin version rather than of Barclay's English translation. To the latter, however, Skelton may have been indebted for some traits in his *Magnyfycence*, written about 1516[1]. Copland's *Hye Way to the Spyttel Hous*, published after 1531, was certainly suggested by Barclay's chapter on beggars and vagabonds[2]. In the later Elizabethan time *The Ship of Fools* was of some influence on the development of emblem books by its woodcuts, and, even when its purely literary influence had faded, it was still liked as a collection of satirical types. There are frequent allusions to it in Elizabethan drama. Its greatest importance, perhaps, lies in the fact that, by substituting distinct types for the shadowy abstractions of fifteenth century allegory, it paved the way for a new kind of literature, which soon sprang up, and, in the Elizabethan time, found its highest expression in the drama of character[3].

Barclay's *Eclogues*, published about 1514, as we gather from several historical allusions, had a rather strange fate. Written by him in his youth, probably at different times, they were mislaid and lost for many years, until one day the author, then thirty-eight years of age, turning over some old books, lighted upon them unexpectedly. He looked them over, added some new touches and showed them to some friends, at whose request they were published. As the first specimens of English pastoral poetry they would possess some historical importance, even if there were nothing else to recommend them. But they are interesting enough in themselves to deserve our attention. The last of the five was, undoubtedly, written first, then, probably, followed the fourth and, finally, the three others, forming together a special group, were composed[4]. The matter for the fifth and fourth was taken from Mantuan, for the others from Aeneas Sylvius.

Johannes Baptista Spagnuoli, called Mantuanus, was, next to Petrarch, the most famous Italian writer of new Latin eclogues. In England, where, at that time, the Greek idyllic poet Theocritus was still quite unknown, Mantuan was valued even more than Vergil and was read in grammar schools to Shakespeare's time. This explains why Barclay followed him rather than the Roman

[1] Ramsay, *Magnificence*, pp. lxxii ff.

[2] For other poems related to *The Ship of Fools* see Herford, *The Literary Relations of England and Germany in the 16th Century*, chap. VI.

[3] Cf. Ward, A. W., *Dictionary of National Biography* on Barclay, and Herford, p. 325. Also Ramsay's introduction to his edition of Skelton's *Magnificence*, p. cxciv.

[4] Reissert, *Die Eclogen des Alexander Barclay*.

poet, whom, nevertheless, he knew quite well, as is proved by some reminiscences from the *Bucolics.*

The argument of the fifth *Eclogue*, called *The Cytezen and Uplondyshman*, is as follows. Amyntas, a shepherd, who, after a life of doubtful reputation and success in London, has been compelled to retire to the country, and Faustus, another shepherd, his poor but always contented comrade, who comes to town only on market days and prefers a simple village life, lie together in the warm straw on a cold winter day. They begin to talk 'of the dyversyte of rurall husbondes, and men of the cyte.' Faustus accuses and blames the townspeople, Amyntas the peasants. Amyntas, who counts himself the better man, begins with a description of winter with its disadvantages and pleasures. For poor people it is very bad, says Faustus, asserting that, whereas peasants have to suffer in winter for their improvidence, townspeople, luckier and wiser, live in abundance. Amyntas opposes him. Townsfolk are even more foolish than shepherds, only they are favoured by fortune. When Faustus suddenly turns ambitious and wants to become a great man, Amyntas reproves him and tells a story showing how God himself ordained the difference of ranks among men. One day, when Adam was afield and Eve sat at home among her children, God demanded to see them. Ashamed of there being so many, Eve hides some of them under hay and straw, in the chimney and in other unsavoury places. The others she shows to the Lord, who is very kind to them and presents them with various gifts. The eldest he makes an emperor, the second a king, the third a duke and so on. Full of joy, Eve now fetches the rest. But they look so dirty and are otherwise so disagreeable, that the Lord is disgusted and condemns them to live in drudgery and endless servitude. Thus began the difference of honour and bondage, of town and village.

Faustus, highly indignant, suspects that the story has been invented by malicious townspeople out of scorn for poor shepherds, and tells another story, showing that many well known people, from Abel to Jesus Christ, have been shepherds and that the Lord always held shepherds in particular favour. Then he denounces the town as the home of all wickedness and cause of all evils. Sometimes he is interrupted by Amyntas, who wonders whence he got all his knowledge, and charges him with exaggeration. In the end, Faustus congratulates himself on living in the country, untouched by the vices of townspeople.

The story in the beginning is taken from Mantuan's sixth

Eclogue, that of Faustus from the seventh. Barclay's translation is fairly good. He follows his model pretty closely, but shifts the names and sometimes makes the two speakers change their parts. As in *The Ship of Fools*, he is fond of making additions and amplifications. The chief interest is, of course, again moral and satirical. He tries to gain local colour by substituting English for classical names and by introducing situations taken from English town and country life. Thus, we have a lively description of football. He gives an admirable picture, full of striking realistic touches, of Eve amidst her children. In his characterisation of the two shepherds he is not always so successful.

In the fourth *Eclogue, Codrus and Minalcas*, treating of 'the behavour of riche men agaynst poetes,' the substance is taken from Mantuan's fifth *Eclogue*. This time, Barclay uses his source with much more freedom. Codrus, a well-to-do but stupid and stingy shepherd, perceiving Minalcas, a fellow of a poetic turn of mind but depressed by poverty, asks him why he has given up singing 'swete balades.' Minalcas answers that 'Enemie to muses is wretched poverty.' This Codrus declines to admit, but wishes to hear some old song; whereupon the other replies that a poet cannot thrive on idle flattery, and that he cannot look after his flock and write poetry at the same time. Everybody, retorts Codrus, ought to be content with his lot; for, if one man has the gift of riches, another has that of poetry; but he is by no means disposed to exchange the comforts of wealth for delight in song, and listens impatiently to the poet's complaints. By vague promises, Minalcas, at last, is induced to give some stanzas 'of fruitful clauses of noble Solomon.' As these are not to Codrus's liking, he recites a rather long 'wofull' elegy on the death of lord Edward Howard, high admiral, son of the duke of Norfolk, Barclay's patron, who lost his life in a daring attack on the French fleet before Brest, 25 April 1513. It is written in the usual style of this kind of poetry and contains a fairly good allegoric description of Labour, 'dreadfull of visage, a monster intreatable.' When Minalcas has finished, Codrus promises him some reward in the future; whereupon the disappointed poet swears at him and invokes on him the fate of Midas for his niggardliness.

The most interesting feature of the poem is the introduction of the two songs—a trick, however, used already by Mantuan in one of his eclogues. The style of the two songs is purely English.

In Barclay's first three *Eclogues*, the form only is taken from

Mantuan, the matter, as we have said above, from Aeneas Sylvius's *Tractatus de curialium miseriis*, a treatise in which the ambitious churchman expresses his disappointments. Nevertheless, here also Barclay owes a good deal to Mantuan in characterisation as well as in detail.

In the first, Coridon, a young shepherd, who wants to try his luck at court, is warned against doing so by his companion Cornix, who proves to him 'that all such courtiers do live in misery, which serve in the court for honour, laude or fame, and might or power.' A threatening storm compels the pair to break off their conversation.

In the second *Eclogue* it is taken up again. They speak of the court, and 'what pleasure is there sene with the fyve wittes, beginning at the eyne.' In a long dialogue on the discomforts of courtiers, it is shown that whosoever hopes for pleasure at court is certain to be disappointed. Barclay follows his source very closely here; and, if in the first *Eclogue* we do not quite see what a simple shepherd wants to do at the court, in the second we are as much surprised as is good Coridon himself to hear Cornix quote classical authors.

The third *Eclogue* completes the conversation with an exceedingly vivid description of the courtiers' undesirable and filthy dwellings. Bribery, in the case of influential officials and impudent servants, is mentioned, the evils of war and town life are dwelt upon, nepotism is blamed, and it is shown that court life spoils the character, and hinders a man from reading and studying. Coridon is convinced, at last, that he is much more comfortable in his present condition, and gives up his idea of going to court.

Whereas, in the translation of *The Ship of Fools*, Barclay often carefully tones down the strong language of the original, he is not so particular in his *Eclogues*. On the whole, their tone is that of renascence eclogues in general, *i.e.* satire on the times, under the veil of allegory. So we find it with Petrarch and Mantuan, so with Boccaccio and the other Italian writers of bucolic poetry, so in Spain and, later, in France in the case of Clément Marot, who, again, exercised a great influence on English pastoral poetry. But, besides these modern influences, we find throughout that of Vergil, who first introduced moral and satirical elements into bucolic poetry.

There are, also, some personal touches in Barclay's *Eclogues*. In the first, he excepts with due loyalty the court of Henry VII, 'which nowe departed late,' and that of Henry VIII, from all the miseries of which he is going to speak. There is, further, a moving passage describing how Barclay, on a fine May morning, visited Ely cathedral, where he laments the death of his patron, bishop Alcock. Another patron, bishop Morton, is mentioned in *Eclogues* III and IV. In the latter, he refers also to the 'Dean of Powles,' Colet, as a good preacher.

In spite of their interest and in spite of the fact that Cawood appended them to his edition of *The Ship of Fools*, in 1570, Barclay's *Eclogues* were soon forgotten. Spenser ignores them as he ignores other earlier attempts at pastoral poetry. In the dedication of *The Shepheards Calender*, 1579, we are simply told that the poet has chosen this poetical form 'to furnish our tongue with this kinde, wherein it faulteth.' Spenser's contemporaries, with whom pastoral poetry became fashionable under Italian influence, praised him as the father of the English eclogue, and had completely forgotten that, more than sixty years before, Barclay had sought for the first time to introduce the eclogue into English literature.

Barclay never wrote without a moral, didactic or satirical purpose, and his conception of literature was narrow. He was certainly not an original writer; but he was a steady and conscientious worker, who did some useful work as a translator of classical and other literature, and set out on some tracks never followed by English writers before him. In *The Ship of Fools* and, still more in his *Eclogues*, he handled his originals with remarkable freedom, and his attempts to meet the taste of his readers make these, his main works, exceedingly interesting as pictures of contemporary English life. As a scholar, he represents medieval, rather than renascence, ideals; as a man, he was modest and grateful to his friends and patrons; and his writings, as well as his will, prove him a kind-hearted friend of the poor.

Though Barclay was well known, there are few contemporary allusions to him. Bullein, perhaps a personal acquaintance, in his *Dialogue against the Fever Pestilence*, 1564, mentions him repeatedly; as does Bradshaw, in his *Life of Saynt Werburghe*, 1521. We find 'preignaunt' Barclay there in the distinguished company of Chaucer and Lydgate and, what would assuredly have been to him a great annoyance, also in that of 'inventive' Skelton, whom he seems to have greatly detested. As his book, *Contra Skeltonum*, is, unfortunately, lost, we cannot tell whether he had any special reason for his aversion to Skelton. The mere difference of character can hardly account for the extremely sharp attack on Skelton in *The Ship of Fools* as well as in the *Eclogues*, the less so, as Barclay usually expresses personal dislike in a tame, and unmalicious way.

John Skelton, born about 1460, probably at Diss in Norfolk, enjoyed a classical education like his younger rival. He studied at Cambridge, where the name Skelton is a Peterhouse name, and, perhaps, in Oxford. There, in 1489, he obtained the academical degree of *poeta laureatus*; this was also conferred on him in 1493 by the university of Louvain, and by his *alma mater Cantabrigiensis*. Somewhat late in life, he took holy orders. In 1498, when almost forty years old, he was ordained successively sub-deacon, deacon and priest, perhaps because he was to be tutor of young prince Henry, an appointment showing clearly that he was much thought of as a scholar. Even so early as 1490, Caxton mentions him in the introduction to his *Eneydos* as the translator of Cicero's *Epistolae familiares*, and of Diodorus Siculus, and appeals to him as an authority in that line. Later, in 1500, Erasmus, in an ode *De Laudibus Britanniae*, calls him *unum Britannicarum literarum lumen ac decus*, and congratulates the prince on having so splendid a teacher. On the other hand, Lily, the grammarian, with whom Skelton had a literary feud, did not think highly of him and said of him: *Doctrinam nec habes, nec es poeta.* Perhaps he did not like the poet's lost *New Gramer in Englysshe compylyd*, mentioned in the *Garlande of Laurell*, l. 1182. Skelton's Latin poems are rather bombastic, but smooth and polished. His *Speculum principis* (*G. of L.* 1226 ff.) is lost. He was well acquainted with French, and, in his *Garlande of Laurell*, he speaks of having translated *Of Mannes Lyfe the Peregrynacioun* in prose, out of the French, probably for Margaret, countess of Richmond and Derby, mother of Henry VII, on whose death, 29 June 1509, he wrote a Latin elegy. His knowledge of classical, particularly Latin, literature must have been very extensive. In his *Garlande of Laurell*, he mentions almost all the more important Latin and Greek authors, and, on the whole, shows a fair judgment of them. His knowledge of Greek was, perhaps, not deep[1]. Some passages in *Speke, Parrot* even indicate that he did not much approve of the study of Greek, then being energetically pursued at Oxford.

[1] His translation of Diodorus Siculus is done from the Latin version of Poggio, first printed 1472.

He there complains, also, of the decay of scholastic education and ridicules ignorant and pedantic philologists. He was particularly fond of the old satirists, and Juvenal seems to have been his special favourite. His poetry, however, does not betray any classical influences. With the Italian poets of the renascence he was, apparently, less familiar. He speaks of 'Johun Bochas with his volumys grete' (*G. of L.* 364), and mentions Petrarch and old Plutarch together as 'two famous clarkis' (*ibid.* 379).

English literature he knew best. In *Phyllyp Sparowe,* he judges Gower, Chaucer and Lydgate fairly well and lays stress particularly on Chaucer's mastership of the English language, whereas he calls Gower's English old-fashioned. On the other hand, he places Lydgate on the same level with the two older poets, finding fault only with the darkness of his language. He was extremely well versed in popular literature, and refers to it often. Guy of Warwick, Gawain, Lancelot, Tristram and all the other heroes of popular romance, were well known to him. We also find in his writings many allusions to popular songs, now partly unknown. He had himself written a Robin Hood pageant, to which Barclay alludes scornfully and which is also referred to later by Anthony Munday[1]. When, and how long, Skelton stayed at court, we cannot tell. In a special poem he boasts that he had a white and green garment embroidered with the name 'Calliope' given him by the king; but, as the official documents never mention his name, it is not likely that he ever stood in any closer relation to the court after his pupil had come to the throne. That he must have been there occasionally is proved by the poems against Garnesche. Skelton was rector of Diss in 1507, and held this office nominally till his death in 1529, when his successor is mentioned. Some of his poems certainly were written there; but, in others, particularly in his later satires, he shows himself so well acquainted with the sentiments of the London people that he must, at least, have visited the capital frequently. There is a tradition that Skelton was not very much liked by his parishioners on account of his erratic nature, and that he had quarrels with the Dominicans, who denounced him spitefully to the bishop of Norwich for being married[2].

Of Skelton's patrons, besides members of the royal family,

[1] Cf. Brie, 'Skelton-Studien,' in *Engl. Stud.* xxxvii, pp. 35 ff.; the figure of Skelton appears in Munday's *Downfall of Robert Earl of Huntingdon,* and in Ben Jonson's *Fortunate Isles.*

[2] Cf. *Merie Tales of Skelton* (1564).

the countess of Surrey, at whose castle, Sheriff Hutton, he wrote his *Garlande of Laurell* (*c.* 1520), may be mentioned. As the dedications of some of Skelton's works to cardinal Wolsey are later additions of the publishers[1], it is doubtful if the omnipotent minister of Henry VIII was his patron too. In any case, Skelton attacked him from about 1519[2], and so unsparingly that he was at last compelled to take sanctuary at Westminster with his friend abbot Islip. There he remained until his death, 21 June 1529. He was buried in St Margaret's Church, Westminster; but no trace is left of his tomb.

As a poet, Skelton is extremely versatile. He practised his pen in almost every kind of poetry. Unfortunately, many of his works are lost. We know them only from the enumeration in the *Garlande of Laurell* (1170 ff.); and even this is incomplete, as the author self-complacently states. In many cases the titles given there do not even enable us to draw any conclusions as to their contents or character. Even his extant works offer many difficulties—sometimes to be met by conjecture only—as regards interpretation and chronology. First editions are missing in most cases, and, owing probably to their personal and satirical character, some of the poems must have circulated in manuscript for a considerable time before they were printed[3].

Of Skelton's religious poems not many are extant, and, even of those ascribed to him, some, probably, are not his. From the titles in *The Garlande of Laurell* we must, however, conclude that he wrote many poems of this kind. Satires against the church, and even irreverence for her rites, are, with him, no signs of irreligiousness. He was as ardent a champion of the old faith as Barclay. In *Colyn Clout* he speaks contemptuously of Hus, Luther, and of Wyclif, whom he calls a 'develysshe dogmatist,' but the best proof of his keen hatred for heretics is the *Replycacion agaynst certayne yong scolers abjured of late*, written, probably, in 1526[4]. The poem is far too long to be impressive; but it is evidently dictated by strong conviction.

Skelton was not only a loyal son of the church, but, also, a patriotic Englishman, who hated his country's enemies and exulted when they were defeated. When Dundas charged the English with cowardice, Skelton wrote a very vigorous little poem in defence of

[1] Cf. Brie, pp. 11 ff.

[2] But cf. Ramsay, *Magnificence*, pp. cvi ff.

[3] Brie, p. 87, has attempted to date all Skelton's works, but admits himself that the results are not always satisfactory.

[4] Cf. Brie, pp. 64 ff.

his countrymen. A splendid opportunity for showing his patriotism presented itself to the poet when James IV was defeated and killed with a great number of Scots nobles, on Brankston moor and Flodden hills, in 1513. Immediately after the event, he wrote a ballad which he retouched later and called *Against the Scottes.* And, again, ten years later, when the duke of Albany, allied with the French, was beaten, Skelton celebrated the victory in a long and vigorous poem. On 22 September 1513, a choir at Diss recited an enthusiastic Latin hymn by Skelton on the victory of Flodden. A similar hymn was composed by him about the same time on the occasion of the conquest of Terouenne by Henry VIII and the battle of Spurs (16 August 1513).

As Skelton's authorship of an elegy *Of the death of the noble prince, Kynge Edwarde the Forth* seems a little doubtful[1], his first authentic court poem would seem to have been the lost *Prince Arturis Creacyoun,* 1489 (*G. of L.* 1178). In the same year he wrote a long elegy *Upon the doulourus dethe of the Erle of Northumberlande,* killed by Northumbrian rebels on 28 April 1489.

Skelton admired Henry VII, but he did not ignore his weaknesses. In a Latin epitaph he laments the king's death and praises him as a successful politician, but he alludes also to the avarice which made the first Tudor unpopular with his subjects. The general feeling of relief after Henry VII's death reveals itself in *Eulogium pro suorum temporum conditione,* written in the beginning of Henry VIII's reign. Skelton expected much of the young monarch, whom he praises in *A Lawde and Prayse made for our Sovereigne Lord the Kyng,* and especially at the end of the poem mentioned above on the victory over the duke of Albany.

Skelton knew, also, how to glorify noble ladies, especially when they patronised him and flattered his vanity. Most of his poems in this vein are inserted in *The Garlande of Laurell,* an allegorical poem, full of grotesque self-glorification, and telling how Skelton is summoned before lady Pallas, to prove himself worthy of his name's being 'regestred with lawreate tryumphe.' Among the crowd of all the great poets of the world he meets Gower, Chaucer and Lydgate, and is at last crowned with a 'cronell of lawrell' by the countess of Surrey and her ladies.

The Garlande of Laurell is a very long poem, of 1600 lines, built up with motives from Chaucer's *House of Fame* and the

[1] Brie, p. 27.

Prologue of the *Legend of Good Women*, and Skelton's self-conceit shown therein is not relieved by any touch of humour. The eleven little lyrics in praise of the poet's patroness and her ladies are somewhat monotonous; but they have a certain grace and are good examples of conventional poetry. Skelton's originality is more evident in *Phyllyp Sparowe*, a poem addressed to Jane Scroupe, a young lady who was a pupil of the black nuns at Carow, and whose pet sparrow had been killed by a cat. The bird is pictured at great length and its mistress's grief described in exaggerated language. All the birds under the sky are summoned to the burial, and each one there is appointed to its special office. Amongst the mourners we find our old friend Chaunteclere and his wife Pertelote from Chaucer's *Nun's Priest's Tale*, and the fabulous Phoenix, as described by Pliny. The sparrow's soul is recommended to God and Jupiter. To compose an epitaph for him proves too much for Jane, who, however, shows herself a well read young lady. The second part of the poem, connected rather loosely with the first, is a praise of the heroine in the typical manner. There is no clear design in the poem. Skelton seems quite unable, or unwilling, to stick to his theme. The whole is an odd medley of the most incongruous ideas, full of literary reminiscences and long digressions, which, very often, have no relation to the subject. But the short and lively metre is very effective and keeps up the attention throughout. The 'addition' shows that there were people who did not like this sort of poetry, especially as the ceremonial of the requiem is used for comic purposes in a manner that must have shocked pious souls. Barclay had mentioned the poem scornfully at the end of his *Ship of Fools* and the 'addition' seems to be Skelton's reply[1]. Barclay's allusion proves that *Phyllyp Sparowe* was written before 1508.

There are other poems of Skelton, written for ladies with whom he was acquainted, as conventional and insincere as are other productions of their kind. One of them even ends with the laconic remark: 'at the instance of a nobyll lady.' Who the lady was, we cannot tell; but another of Skelton's friends was 'mastres Anne, that farly swete, that wonnes at the Key in Temmys strete,' with whom the poet must once have been on very good terms. Of his 'pretty lines' to her[2], none are extant; but there are two poems in which he treats her in a different fashion, evidently because she had slighted him and had chosen a new

[1] Cf. also *G. of L.* 1257 f.

[2] *G. of L.* 1240 ff.

lover[1]. Another poem, caused by a similar disappointment, describes the once beloved lady at first very eloquently and then, all of a sudden, takes a sarcastic turn. The satirical poem 'My darlyng dere, my daysy floure' is very impressive and a most happy attempt to write in a popular vein.

As we have seen already, it was not advisable to rouse Skelton's anger. Vain and irritable, he was bent on quarrelling with everybody, especially when his pride in his knowledge or academic honours was hurt. Besides the quarrel with Lily, mentioned above, he had an encounter with the French historian Gaguin (*G. of L.* 374 ff., 1187)[2]. One of Skelton's satirical productions, now lost, *Apollo that whirrlyd up his chare* (*G. of L.* 1471 ff.), seems to have particularly annoyed certain people. Skelton himself, wonderful to relate, is sorry for having written it. The somewhat loosely constructed poem *Against venemous tongues* is worth mentioning only as the expression of personal experience.

There are other poems showing how dangerous it was to offend Skelton or to be disliked by him. When he was rector of Diss, he punished two 'knaves' of his parish who had shown disrespect to him and did not go to church (*G. of L.* 1247 ff.), by composing a very unflattering epitaph for them. In a similar strain is the epitaph *In Bedel.* In these poems, church rites are travestied as in *Phyllyp Sparowe.* In *Ware the Hauke*, Skelton censures a parson who had profaned his church by baiting a hawk in it. Except for its length and exaggerated language, the poem is not remarkable. Two other obscure poems, apparently directed against certain musicians or minstrels may also be mentioned.

All the poems referred to above show that Skelton had an amazingly large stock of abusive terms. But by far the best examples of his talent in this direction are his poems against the royal chamberlain Christopher Garnesche, who, at the king's command, had challenged him. Unfortunately, the poems of Skelton's adversary, which might have thrown some light on the poet's biography, especially on his relation to the court, are not extant. He abuses the chamberlain violently, using the strongest expressions imaginable and the most grotesque comparisons. That the whole was not a serious affair is repeatedly stated in the poems. It was nothing but an imitation of the *Flyting of Dunbar and Kennedy*, composed 1504—5, and printed in 1508, and, like its

[1] One of the two poems has been found only lately by Brie and is published in his *Skelton-Studien*, p. 29.

[2] Brie, p. 31.

model, is an interesting instance of the coarse vituperation common to the time.

Remarkable, also, for its coarseness is *The Tunnyng of Elynour Rummyng*, a fantastical description of an old ale-wife and her guests. Again, there is no plan to be discerned; but, sometimes, a sort of dramatic action is suggested, as the tipsy women come and go, misbehave themselves, chat and quarrel, or are turned out. There are some touches of humour in the poem; but it is drawn out too long and many accessories render it somewhat monotonous. The metre is the same short verse as in *Phyllyp Sparowe.*

The poems against Garnesche were not the only fruit of Skelton's sojourn at the court. As we have said before, it is not likely that he stayed there for any length of time after the accession of his former pupil; but, in any case, he must have seen a good deal of court life when he was the prince's tutor. Very soon after that time, probably, he set forth his unfavourable impressions in *The Bowge of Courte,* an allegorical poem, written in Chaucer's seven-lined stanza.

In a lengthy prologue, Skelton tells how he wanted to compete with the old poets, but was discouraged by Ignoraunce. He falls asleep in his host's house, 'Powers Keye' at 'Harwyche Port,' and has a strange dream. A stately ship enters the harbour and casts anchor. Merchants go aboard to examine the costly freight, and, with them, the poet, who does not perceive a single acquaintance among the noisy crowd. The name of the ship is 'Bowge of Courte' (free board at the king's table); her owner is the noble lady Sauncepere, rich and desirable is her merchandise, Favour, but also very dear. There is a general press to see the beautiful lady, who sits on a magnificent throne inscribed with the words '*Garder le fortune que est mauelz et bone.*' Addressed harshly by Daunger, the lady's chief waiting-woman, the poet, who introduces himself as Drede, feels crushed; but another gentlewoman, Desire, cheers him up and presents him with the helpful jewel Bone Aventure. She further advises him to make friends with Fortune, a somewhat capricious lady of great influence. Drede feels rather uneasy from the very beginning, but, like the rest, asks her favour, which she gives to them all.

The ship goes to sea with full sails. All seems well, until Drede notices aboard seven 'full subtyll persons,' all old friends of Fortune. They bluntly decline any communication with the stranger, whom, nevertheless, they approach, one after the other, trying, each in his own way, to deceive and to harm him. Most of them hide their hatred and jealousy under the mask of disinterested friendship, play the humble admirer of his superior scholarship, warn him against supposed foes, promise their help and prophesy for him a brilliant career. The only exception is Dysdayne, a haughty, objectionable fellow, who shows his aversion openly by picking a quarrel with him. Behind his back, they all join to ruin the inconvenient new-comer, who notices their whispering together with increasing misgivings. The last of the seven is still speaking to him, when, all of a sudden, he sees 'lewde felawes' rushing upon him from all sides with murderous purpose. In an agony of fear, he seizes the ship-board to leap into the water, wakes up and writes his 'lytyll boke.' In a concluding stanza, the poet affirms his good intention. What he has written was a dream—but sometimes there is some truth in dreams!

The poem may have been written a little before 1509. At all events it is one of Skelton's earlier productions, for he would not have used the allegorical framework for satirical purposes at a later time. His handling of the traditional form is here highly original. The seven figures are not of the usual bloodless kind of personified abstractions, but more like types taken from real life; and, even if one is not inclined to admit the direct influence of Brant on Skelton in this poem, their strong resemblance to the courtiers in *The Ship of Fools* is not to be denied. The characterisation shows a powerful imagination, combined with a strong talent for description. Even the recurrence of the same motives does not impair the strong impression of the whole, and there are none of the tiresome digressions here of which Skelton seems enamoured in other poems. Almost dramatic life pervades the whole poem, which is called by Warton, very appropriately, a poem 'in the manner of a pageant.' With all its personal or traditional features, *The Bowge of Courte* is a classic satire on court life.

In *Colyn Clout*, written about 1519, we are told by Colyn, the roaming vagabond, that everything is wrong in England and that the clergy are to blame for it. The bishops do not look after their flocks, but strive after worldly honours and promotion by every means. Haughty, covetous and ignorant, they set a bad example to all the rest, are fond of hunting and hawking and live in luxury, whereas the poor people starve. The worst are the upstart prelates, whose former poor lives Colyn describes with grim humour. They should beware of God's punishment and mend their ways, for 'after *gloria*, *laus*, may come a soure sauce.' There is, however, little hope; for, blinded by flatterers, they are incorrigible. Like 'prynces aquilonis' they sit on their thrones, live in great palaces and erect costly tombs for themselves. They vex the poor people with arbitrary jurisdiction and take away from them the little they have with high taxes. For many other things they are also to blame. 'Bestiall and untaught' men, who are not able to read or to spell their names, they appoint as priests, preferring habitual drunkards that lead disorderly lives to worthy candidates. Monks and nuns are seen roving about everywhere, their monasteries being dissolved. Swarming all over the country, also, are glosing friars, flattering the people, especially silly women, to get a scanty living, and cheating poor parish-priests of their small revenues. Partly the lay-folk, especially noblemen, are also to blame. For, if they tried to become better educated and cared more for politics than for pleasure, they would not be compelled to leave the rule of the country to the clergy. The most dangerous thing seems to Colyn—or the poet—that one man has all the power. This, of course, is a hint at the omnipotent minister-cardinal Wolsey, who, towards the end of the poem, appears more and more as the representative of the higher clergy.

Skelton's heavy charges against the clergy, and especially against prelates, are the same as Barclay's, only put forward with far greater energy and passion. They are not arranged after a fixed plan. His method is, as ten Brink has put it, 'concentric.' The same reproaches recur again and again, intensified continually by the addition of new instances, until we get an all-round picture of the general corruption. The idea of putting the whole into the mouth of a representative of the people is extremely happy. With increasing interest we follow the arguments of Colyn, who tells only what he has heard the people say. We even see the effect on the stubborn prelates, who declare that they will go on in their wickedness in spite of all attacks. The idea, however, is not kept up to the end. The personality of the poet comes forth more and more till, at last, he throws off the mask altogether. But, for all that, the poem appears throughout as the expression of popular sentiment. The lively metre adds considerably to the vivacity of the whole and is much more developed and refined than, for instance, in *Phyllyp Sparowe.*

At the end of *Colyn Clout*, Skelton had declared the intention to let his pen rest. Nevertheless, he began his next satire, *Speke, Parrot,* a very short time afterwards. Written down, probably, at intervals, and preserved in a greatly mutilated condition[1], it is the most incoherent of all his poems and, in parts, absolutely unintelligible. Parrot, the pet bird of a noble lady, of fabulous origin and a wonderfully clever linguist, after some other satirical remarks, says unpleasant things about Wolsey, who had been the object of the poet's satire at the end of *Colyn Clout.* He is characterised as the all-powerful favourite, who rules even the king, his master. Many of the satirical hints are incomprehensible; but they seem to bear some relation to certain of Wolsey's political missions (in 1521?). He is called 'a malyncoly mastyf' and 'mangye curre dog,' because he was said to be the son of a butcher at Ipswich, and appears as a senseless busybody, undertaking too much and spending large sums of money to no effect. The king is warned emphatically against him. 'His woluys hede, wanne, bloo as lede, gapythe over the crowne' says the poet. The poem ends in a general satire on the time.

Skelton's invectives against Wolsey in *Colyn Clout* and *Speke, Parrot* were strong enough, but there was more in store. Between November 1522 and January 1523, he wrote another 'lytell boke' against Wolsey, called *Why come ye nat to courte,* by far the most pungent and most daring satire he ever composed. It is a crushing judgment upon Wolsey's whole life and character. Again the poet asserts how dangerous it is to leave the rule of a whole realm to one man, and shows the fatal effect of that measure in Wolsey's special case. Everything is wrong now in England. The old trustworthy men have withdrawn from court, where the wilful upstart reigns despotically, bullying the nobles and respecting not even the orders of the king, who trusts him blindly. The failures in foreign policy, the general poverty, caused by heavy taxation, the reigning injustice—all are Wolsey's doing. There is a striking picture of the cardinal's haughty behaviour in the Starchamber, where nobody dares contradict him. At last, the poet comes to the conclusion that the most appropriate place for Wolsey would be in Hell, on Lucifer's throne. He even appears as 'Of Jeremy the whyskynge rod the flayle, scourge of almighty God' (1160), and, finally, is dismissed with a hearty: 'God sende him sorowe for his sinnes!' Skelton's method is the same here as in *Colyn Clout.* There are some tiresome digressions in the poem; but, on the other hand, there are passages of really dramatic vivacity.

All Skelton's poems against Wolsey are full of exaggerations and

[1] Cf. *G. of L.* l. 1188.

unjust imputations. Wolsey's statesmanship, his learning and the services he rendered to his country, are grossly underrated; but, here again, Skelton expresses not only his personal opinion but that of a large portion of the nation, which hated the omnipotent minister and held him responsible for many things, not all of which could be laid to his charge. In any case, we must admire the poet's courage. For, even if *Why come ye nat to courte* was not printed then, the poem must have circulated in numerous copies. Wolsey must have heard of it pretty soon, if he did not even get a sight of it himself, and Skelton must have been well aware of the consequences. As has been seen, he had a very narrow escape from the cardinal's revenge.

We have not yet spoken of Skelton's extant dramatic production. The lost Robin Hood pageant, mentioned above, was not his only attempt in that direction. In the *Garlande of Laurell* he mentions '*of Vertu the soverayne enterlude*' (1177) and '*the commedy, Achademios callyd by name*' (1184). Neither has been preserved, and the loss of the latter is to be regretted particularly, because, probably, it would have shown Skelton's views on educational questions, whereas now we have only a few dark passages in *Speke, Parrot* for information on that point. Another of Skelton's comedies, *De bono ordine*, is mentioned by Bale; and Warton relates the plot of a play called *Negromansir*, which treated of a lawsuit against Simony and Avarice, with the devil as judge and a public notary as barrister or scribe. Warton's account is somewhat mysterious[1] but the subject would have been truly Skeltonic. The poet is said to have used all sorts of metres and to have interspersed the English text with numerous scraps of Latin and French. What the 'paiauntes that were played in Joyows Garde' (*G. of L.* 1583) were like, it is impossible to say. The *Enterlude of Godly Queene Hester* is probably not by Skelton[2]

The morality *Magnyfycence*, written about 1516[3], is the only specimen of the poet's dramatic production that has come down to us. The hero, Magnyfycence, is brought to ruin by the joint efforts of Fancy, Counterfet Countenaunce, Crafty Conveyaunce, Clokyd Colusyon, Courtly Abusyon, Lyberte and Folly. Left alone after his fall, 'naked as an asse,' he is visited by Adversyte, Poverte, Dyspare and Myschefe, and is just about to slay himself, when Goodhope, Redresse, Sad Cyrcumspeccyon and Perseveraunce save

[1] Cf. Greg, *Queene Hester*, pp. viii ff.; Brie, p. 33; Ramsay, pp. xix.
[2] Brie, p. 33; Ramsay, pp. cxvi.
[3] Ramsay, pp. xxii, cviii.

him and restore him to his former prosperity. There is a good deal of tedious moralising in the play. Especially at the end, Magnyfycence, whose change of mind is somewhat sudden, is simply drowned in good lessons. His grandiloquence before his fall, reminding one of Herod in the miracle-play, is as exaggerated as are his pitiful lamentations after it. The intrigue is rather cheap and by no means new; and the allegorical characters, except, perhaps, Poverty, are not so well drawn as in *The Bowge of Courte*, where Skelton had treated a similar subject. The length of the play is out of proportion to its meagre contents, and the whole is somewhat monotonous and lifeless, except for a few comic scenes, written in the short verse Skelton favoured. There are many satirical hints all through the play, and it has been suggested that it was meant as a warning to Henry VIII and as a first veiled attack on Wolsey[1]. In construction and plan, *Magnyfycence* is very much like the older moralities, and there are analogies even in single traits. In one respect, however, it is entirely different. Whereas, in the others, the subject is always very much the same, namely, the struggle of good and evil in human nature, we find here, for the first time, an attempt to treat a special case. Magnyfycence is not man in general, who falls, repents and is forgiven, but he is the type of a noble-minded prince who is ruined by misapplied liberality. So, in spite of its obvious shortcomings, the play holds an important place in the history of English drama. It marks the transition from the older purely religious moralities to the secular allegorical drama[2].

Skelton has often been judged too severely for the coarseness of some of his poems. Pope was particularly hard on him. On the other hand, such men as Southey and the elder Disraeli liked his 'ragged' rime and found some pith in it. His poetic production shows an extraordinary variety. He moves with ease, sometimes even with mastership, in all the traditional forms of poetry. In his longer poems he is very original, particularly where he uses his characteristic style, the short 'breathless rimes,' not unknown before him, but never used so largely and effectively as by him. Sometimes they literally chase along, and the reader is carried away by them. A good specimen of Skeltonic verse is the beginning of *Colyn Clout*:

> What can it avayle
> To dryve forth a snayle,
> Or to make a sayle
> Of an herynges tayle,
> To ryme or to rayle,

[1] Ramsay, pp. cvi ff.

[2] *Ibid.* pp. x ff., lxxi ff.

To wryte or to indyte,
Eyther for delyte
Or elles for despyte;
Or bokes to compyle
Of dyvers maner style,
Vyce to revyle
And synne to exyle;
To teche or to preche,
As reason wyll reche?

Lack of constructive power often spoils the impression of Skelton's poems; but this deficiency is made up for in many cases by an immense vivacity and by the originality of the ideas. His satires against the clergy in general, and, particularly, those against Wolsey, are remarkable for their boldness. Of all the poetical successors of Chaucer in England Skelton is by far the most original.

Compared with *The Ship of Fools*, most of the other contributions of German to English literature in the beginning of the sixteenth century seem insignificant[1]. That German influence should be felt in England at the time was only natural. In Germany, the reformation had its chief seat, many publications of a reformatory character were printed there or in Holland, and it became a second home to many refugees, who became acquainted with German literature and adopted what they found useful for their purpose. But, as most of these men were not great writers, and, as Germany was very soon left behind by Elizabethan England, this influence, in most cases, was not lasting.

Of German popular poetry, next to nothing became known in England, and it is not before 1593 that we find the titles of a few stray German ballads mentioned in the Stationers' Register. Miles Coverdale tried to introduce the protestant hymn into England about 1540. His *Goostly Psalmes and Spiritual Songes* are a fair selection of the first period of protestant hymnology (1527—31), and might have been effective under more favourable conditions. But the translation was too poor; moreover, Italian influence was so strong just at that time that the attempt proved a failure.

From Germany, the English reformers learned how to use the dialogue as a weapon in the religious struggle. A great many polemical dialogues were written in Germany by advocates of either side, with a decided balance in favour of the protestant, in number as well as in literary value. The most distinguished

[1] Fuller information concerning the subjects treated in the remaining paragraphs of this chapter will be found in Herford's *Studies*, and Brie's *Eulenspiegel in England*. See also the chapter that follows this.

names in the beginning of the movement were those of Erasmus and Hutten, who were followed by a host of more or less capable men. The strain of these 'discussions' varies very much, according to the individuality of the authors. Learned and popular elements were blended in various ways; and sometimes we have miniature dramas, especially when the writers, to illustrate their point, used the background of contemporary life.

In England, the number of controversial dialogues is comparatively small; and there is no such continuous tradition as in Germany. One of the first is *Rede me and be not wrothe*, composed by two converted Greenwich friars, William Roy and Jerome Barlow, in Strassburg, in 1528. The framework is suggested by Niclas Manuel's famous *Krankheit der Messe*[1], of which the dialogue is simply a continuation; the contents are English—a violent attack on the English clergy and its highest representative, cardinal Wolsey. Numerous striking parallels to Skelton's satires occur; but the tone of the whole is emphatically protestant. Compared with Manuel's spirited production, the English imitation seems dull, and it is far too long to be impressive. Wolsey's agents bought up all copies obtainable almost instantly, and, in 1531, it was proscribed and soon forgotten. According to Tindale, Roy had translated another reformatory work, *Dialogus inter patrem christianum et filium contumacem*; but the translation, as well as the original, are lost. Barlow recanted in 1533 and wrote, probably very soon after, a somewhat feeble *Dialogue upon the origin of the protestant fashions.* Purely English in spirit is the *Proper Dyalogue betwene a Gentillman and a Husbandman*, complaining of the oppression of the lay people by the clergy after a fashion which would have been impossible in Germany.

The Catholic side is represented at that time by no writer of distinction. Skelton, who, apparently, had written the interlude, *Negromansir*, alluded to above, in the favourite form of a trial, was dead, and More's somewhat lifeless dialogue against Tindale's book on the mass is of an entirely different type.

Under Edward VI, protestant dialogue flourished with the official sanction of the government, dealing particularly with the mass, which was ridiculed under various names as 'Round Robin,' 'Jack in the Box,' 'Jack of Lent' and so on. Among the translations of German dialogues we find Hans Sachs's *Goodly disputacion between a christian shoemaker and a Popysshe Parson*, printed by one Anthony Skoloker, in 1547. In 1548, Day

[1] See *post*, p. 86.

printed *John Bon and Mast Parson,* a disputation on Corpus Christi by L. Shepherd. *Robin Conscience* is a good English example of the well known 'son against father' type, showing strong influence of the morality play. The excellent translations of two of Erasmus's dialogues, published about 1550, are absolutely un-English.

The more elaborate form of the trial, used largely in Germany already in the *Fastnachtsspiele,* was adopted in England particularly by William Turner, a Northumbrian man of science and theologian and a disciple of Latimer, who travelled in Germany between 1530 and 1540. His *Hunting of the Fox* (Basel, 1573), answered by Gardiner's *Contra Turneri vulpem,* was followed by the much better *Hunting of the Wolf* and, in 1547, by the *Examination of the Mass.* Still more elaborate than this specimen of the 'drama of debate' is the *Endightment against Mother Messe.* The last dialogue of Edward's reign, a *dialogus duarum sororum,* mentioned by Bale, is a translation of one of Wolfgang Resch's dialogues, by Walter Lynne, of very little literary value. Under Mary, only very few protestant dialogues were written; under Elizabeth, German influence was dead, and the form was applied to all sorts of secular subjects. Six dialogues by Wingfield, printed 1566, *Contra Expugnatores Missae,* taking the Catholic side, are rather weak and tame[1].

Towards the end of the century, translations of sensational German news sheets occur sporadically in the Stationers' register. These details of strange occurrences, explained by protestant pessimists as signs of doom, became extremely popular in England, as is seen, for instance, in Ben Jonson's *The Staple of News.* A ballad of *bishop Hatto* was entered in the Stationers' register in 1586, and the story of the greedy ecclesiastic occurs again in *The Costlie Whore,* while *The Piper of Hamelin* is mentioned in Verstegen's *Restitution of Decayed Intelligence* in 1605. Of the numerous German collections of amusing stories, compiled by learned and unlearned authors in the sixteenth century, sometimes without method, sometimes attached to certain personalities, and illustrating with coarse humour the low life of the time without much pretension to literary distinction, only a very few became known in England. Strange to say, of the most interesting figure of all, Markolf, we have only a few traces[2]. The *Pfaffe Amis,* in

[1] German influence is also to be seen in the English drama at the time of the reformation; but of this some account is given in a later volume of this *History.*

[2] Cf. Herford, pp. 267 ff.; Brie, *Eulenspiegel,* p. 72.

spite of his being called a native of England, seems quite unknown. In *The Parson of Kalenborowe* (*Der Pfarrer von Kalenberg*), *c.* 1510 (?), we have a very free prose version of a South German original, but taken, probably, from a more copious Dutch prose narrative. Of *Howleglass,* something is said in the chapter which follows this. Copland's versions of the feats of Eulenspiegel, the best known representative of German low life of the time, printed between 1559 and 1563, were thought the oldest ones, until, a few years ago, there was found a short fragment of a much older one, printed by John of Doesborch 1516—20. It is a very clumsy translation, full of misunderstandings, taken not from one of the High German versions but from a lost Low German original[1].

Exposing the coarseness of his time, Brant, in *Das Narrenschiff,* created a new saint, Grobianus, who soon became the typical representative of rude and indecent behaviour, particularly at table. He must have been a very popular figure when, in 1549, a young student of Wittenberg, F. Dedekind, wrote his Latin *Grobianus,* which was translated (1551) by Caspar Scheidt into German with considerable additions. A new version by Dedekind, *Grobianus et Grobiana,* in which the hero has a female companion, followed in 1552. The book enjoyed a vast popularity, not only in Germany, but also in France and England. In 1605, *Grobianus* was translated into English as *The Schoole of Slovenrie.* Traces of grobianism can be found in Dekker's *Gul's Hornbooke* (1609). The figure of Grobianus appears utterly transformed in the interlude *Grobiana's Nuptials,* where it has become the type of the Oxford man of Jacobean time with his affectation of simplicity. Dedekind's book was appreciated in England even so late as the eighteenth century, and it was certainly not by chance that a new translation of it, which appeared in 1739, was dedicated to Swift.

[1] Cp. Brie, 'Eulenspiegel in England,' *Palaestra,* XXVII.

CHAPTER V

THE PROGRESS OF SOCIAL LITERATURE IN TUDOR TIMES

THE popular literature of each nation does not begin or end: it evolves. One generation hands down to the next a store of sentiment, humour and worldly wisdom which, together with a spirit of investigation and ridicule, slowly change their form and scope with every stage of civilisation. But it is almost impossible definitely to mark out an epoch of popular thought. The middle classes entered on the sixteenth century with the same tastes as their forefathers; a love of romantic ballads and fables, together with the satirical humour and practical sagacity which had always found expression in a literature quite separate from monastic culture and the civilisation of the court. The invention of printing greatly multiplied the production of tracts and, all through the century, the commons continued to demand their own kind of books. This literature remained practically untouched by the renascence, but gathered new depth and meaning from the throes of transition which the people underwent during the reign of the Tudors.

One of the most important influences was the growth of city life, which always develops a curiosity in the eccentricities of commonplace character, and leads men to take an increasing interest in their neighbours' lives. A striking example of this development is *Cocke Lorell's bote*. The tract is a burlesque rhapsody on the lower middle classes; they are grouped under the classification of a crew which takes ship and sails through England. The idea of satirising the follies of mankind under the heading of a mock order or fraternity comes from the Middle Ages, and, as has been seen, a new impulse was given to this conception by Brant's *Narrenschiff*. But *Cocke Lorell's bote* is not a mere imitation of the German school. Its author does not portray moral perversity; nor has he a touch of the German's pedantic wealth of classical allusion. His sentiment is medieval and goes back to the traditional satires on shopkeepers, bakers and millers, which had been a commonplace since the days of Joannes de Garlandia. But, above all, we can trace the long conflict between immemorial paganism and the institutions of a civilised Christianity. This was still an age of blasphemous and saturnalian parody, when feasts of the ass, the bull and the Innocents were celebrated before cathedral altars. The spirit of the children of Thor appears again and again in sixteenth century literature; in the glorification of drunkenness[1], the ferocious conflicts between husband and wife[2]; the buffoonery and bestiality of the jest-books and the superstitions displayed in the witch-controversy. In *Cocke Lorell's bote* we have the parody of the pope's bull and the grant of privileges. Besides, the author is not a reformer or a moralist. His tradesfolk are knaves rather than fools. He shows the spirit of the time by being in thorough sympathy with their roguery, ruffianism and immorality. The captain of his 'bote' is the notorious Cocke Lorell, a tinker after Overbury's own heart (probably a historical personage), who was a byeword as late as Jacobean times. And yet the tone is not that of a preacher or a satirist: the ship comes to no misfortune. It is a sermon on the text:

Mery it is wan knaves done mete[3].

The conception of the 'bote' and the fraternity is mere literary conventionality. But the style of portraying low-class character is full of interest. The writer delights in curriers and cobblers, whose only possession is a bleaching-pot; in a shoeman who quarrels with them for a piece of leather; a farmer whose odour makes the crew sick; a miller who substitutes chalk for flour. Personal peculiarities also appeal to him. We heard of 'goggle-eyed Thompson,' 'Kate with the crooked foot' and 'Alys Esy, a gay

[1] *Jyl of Breyntford's Testament; Colin Blowbol's Testament.*

[2] *Schole-house of women; Curste Wyfe lapped in Morrelles skin*, etc.

[3] Compare one of the *King Henry's Mirth or Freemen's Songs*, in *Deuteromelia*, in which the freedom and irresponsibility of the humbler walks of life are extolled over the anxieties of more exigent occupations. The ballad ends with:

Who liveth so merry and maketh such sport
As those that be of the poorest sort?
Chorus. The poorest sort, wheresoever they be,
They gather together by one, two and three
And every man will spend his penny,
What makes such a shot among a great many.

story-teller,' in fact a crew not unlike Harman's list of vagabonds. Thus, the butcher:

> All begored in reed blode;
> In his hande he bare a flap for flyes,
> His hosen gresy upon his thyes,
> That place for magottes was very good;
> On his necke he bare a cole tre logge,
> He had as moche pyte as a dogge.

It has already been shown that Brant and Barclay substituted the type for the abstraction which was a familiar feature of medieval literature. *Cocke Lorell's bote* marks a further advance. Its crew are no longer types; they are almost individuals. Moreover, their personality is not elaborately described, but merely indicated by a few suggestive traits, thus illustrating how literary impressionism was finding its way in the coarse, doggerel verse of the people.

This spirit of character-study found expression through another inherited literary form. The fifteenth century had produced devotional and sentimental documents in the form of a will or testament[1], and these were borrowed from by ribald humorists who grouped the objects of their satire under the heading of a legacy instead of a ship or fraternity. The idea originated among the Romans of the decadence and was developed by French writers of the fifteenth century, especially by Villon in his half serious, half ribald will, *Le Grant et le petit Testament* (two separate poems), 1489. The first English imitation is *Jyl of Breyntford's Testament*, in which Jyl bequeaths an unsavoury and opprobrious legacy to certain typical fools, being particularly careful to bring the number of her legatees up to a quartern. Those for whom she expresses her contempt are either the people who cannot take their place in life—who quarrel without cause, who borrow without paying back, who trample needlessly on their fellows in advancing their own interests—or those who neglect their own interests to serve others.

The Testament of Mr Andro Kennedy, 1508, to which reference has been made in a previous volume[2], was possibly influenced by *Le Testament de Taste Vin* (*c.* 1488), or both were influenced by earlier drinking songs; just as Taste Vin decrees his body to be buried under the floor of a tavern, Kennedy leaves his soul to his lord's wine-cellar. The poem is an interesting

[1] *E.g.* Lansdowne MS, reprinted in *Reliquiae Antiquae*, p. 260, and Robert Henryson's *Testament of Cresseid*.

[2] See vol. II, p. 256.

specimen of macaronic verse devoted to personal satire. But the most important production of this class is *Colin Blowbol's Testament.* Colin, just recovering from an appalling surfeit, and looking 'pale of hew like a drowned rat,' espies an equivocal confessor, through whose agency a will is finally composed, in which the drunkard bequeaths his soul to Diana (as goddess of the salt seas, in which he expects to do penance for his unflagging indulgence in sweet wine); his lands to the notorious district of 'Southwerke'; six marks of spruce to his secretary, 'registered a brother in the order of folly'; and a sum to defray a Gargantuan burial feast to be held in a labyrinth such as Daedalus built (this part of the description is reminiscent of Ovid and Apollodorus). A sense of discrimination in character is shown by the provision of a dais for those who wax boastfully loquacious in liquor, a lower table for those who become maudlin and foolish and a third for brawlers over their cups. Just as *Cocke Lorell* contains a list of sixteenth century trades, so this tract enumerates thirty-two kinds of wines anciently in vogue. Blowbol means a drunkard, and the tract is a parody of more serious things in honour of drink. The original manuscript, as we have it, is badly written and the composition shows traces of confusion or carelessness. Yet the production is worth notice because of the unmistakable evidence it bears to the growing interest in character and in discrimination of types.

This fashion of writing mock testaments appears to have become popular. Evidence of its influence on the new court poetry is found in such love complaints as *The Testament of the Hawthorne*[1]. But the most interesting of later testaments is *The Wyll of the Devyll*, printed and composed about 1550 by Humphrey Powell. The tract was probably inspired by Manuel's *Krankheit der Messe*[2], and the greater part is taken up with savage invective against the Roman Catholic church, the devil, on his death-bed, bequeathing his vices and superstitions to papists and priests. But the booklet has a popular side. The devil, in disposing of his treasures and worldly experience, does not forget others who are likely to appreciate them; men of law receive two right hands to take money of both parties; with Shakespearian insight into vice, lechers are presented with 'a crafty wytte to wrest the Scriptures and to make them serve for filthy purposes'; idle housewives are given more of the same society to keep them company; dicers receive a thousand pair of false dice;

[1] 2nd ed. of *Tottel's Miscellany*, 1557.

[2] See *ante*, p. 80.

butchers are supplied with fresh blood to sprinkle on their stale meat, and other tradesmen with other means of deception. The book is most significant. Its range covers the great religious controversy of the century and penetrates with singular felicity into the minor abuses of society. Yet it appears in an essentially popular literary form, and shows how considerable a part of the reading public was found among the common people.

Except in its form, *The Wyll of the Devyll* belongs mostly to the attack on social and occasional evils which figured largely in the works of Brinkelow, Crowley, Awdeley, Harman, Bullein and others. Meanwhile, the literature of classified character continued its own development uncoloured by contemporary events. To this type belong several broadsides, such as the *XX Orders of Callettes or Drabbys* and its counterpart the *XX Orders of Fooles*, registered in 1569—70, and *A New Ballad against Unthrifts. The Galley late come into Englande from Terra Nova, laden with Phisitiens, Apothecaries and Chirurgians* is now lost. In 1575, Awdeley printed the *XXV Orders of Knaves*, in which 'brief and sarcastic catchwords out of the immemorial bill of charges against those that serve[1]' are worked into condensed portraits of remarkable distinctness. But the French *Danses Macabres* of the fifteenth century had already shown that subjection to death was the most effective classification of human types. The song of *The Shaking of the Sheets*, first alluded to in *Misogonus* (*c.* 1560), exposes, with malicious felicity, the futility of life's different pursuits in the face of death. These verses were meant to accompany a symbolic 'jigge' or masquerade, which seems to have been a common practice since the performance of a *danse macabre* in the Parisian cemetery of the Innocents in 1424. The subject was even more frequently represented by woodcuts with explanatory verses. One of the most curious is a broadside without title or date containing a representation of Death pursuing the Priest, the King, the Harlot, the Lawyer, the Clown (*i.e.* countryman), followed by ten stanzas in which each type boasts of the power he or she holds over the others, and Death of his power over them all. Another early broadside entitled *The Daunce and Song of Death* has four engravings of the Miser, the Prisoner, the Judge and two Lovers, with a moral verse under each, the whole concluding with an apologue. This spirit of type-satire continued till the Civil War. Its last and most striking development is the Theophrastian character, in which the sixteenth century

[1] Herford, C. H., *Literary Relations of England and Germany*, p. 363.

view of society reappears in a form inspired by the fashionable classicism of the Jacobean age.

As in previous centuries, the ale-house continued to figure in popular literature as the scene where character, especially female character, revealed itself in amusing and grotesque colours. Jyl herself was

> A widow of a homely sort,
> Honest in substaunce and full of sport.

The out-of-door life which the middle-class husband led and the primitive nature of the home drove the wife to seek the society of her associates at the tavern. The fifteenth century had produced some amusing scenes[1] in these headquarters of female conspiracy against men, and the sixteenth century followed its lead. Skelton's *Tunnyng of Elynour Rummyng* contains a coarse, graphic picture of the manners and morals of the low-class women who frequented that lady's establishment near Leatherhead. Higher in the social scale, we find the traditional character[2] (possibly suggested by the 'woman of Samaria') who has married and cheerfully buried five husbands in quick succession. An anonymous satirist has cleverly crowded all the vices of the middle-class wife into a career of this type in a half moral, half burlesque poem *The boke of Mayd Emlyn.* Emlyn's character is vigorously portrayed. She is one of those women who dress gaily, get drunk at taverns, dally with gallants and fling the nearest articles at their husbands when they remonstrate. She is a female Bluebeard, driving her husbands to suicide or disposing of them by direct murder and, between each bereavement, she goes into deep mourning, on one occasion keeping an onion in her handkerchief to stimulate tears. One of her intrigues leads her and her paramour to the stocks, where, true to her character, she immensely enjoys her publicity. Emlyn finally takes up her residence at the stews, and the story closes with a glimpse of the wretched woman begging her bread in her old age.

Sometimes the career of the ale-house adventuress throws light on the different types of society, as in the *Widow Edith.* In twelve 'mery gestys' this ingenious personage imposes on all

[1] See vol. II, chap. XVI.

[2] The grief of newly bereaved wives and their readiness to be consoled was a commonplace as early as Gautier Le Long's *La Veuve* (twelfth or thirteenth century), and may, perhaps, help to explain the scene between the duke of Gloster and lady Anne in *Richard III* (Act I, sc. 2). Cf., also, *The Wife of Bath.*

classes by appearing to be in temporary distress and announcing that she is a lady of considerable wealth. The tale was evidently written to please the commons, and it is full of the character drawing they love. Edith lodges with poor people and we see something of their homely cheer and good nature. She encounters a doctor of divinity who holds forth on the covetousness of men and most willingly absolves her when he hears of her wealth. She meets two pilgrims; the satirist discloses their weakness, which is not love of money but vainglorying in good works, so Edith attempts suicide and gives them the satisfaction of saving her. The career of the adventuress leads her into the households of great men, where the head servants fall in love with her alleged fortune. There are admirable touches of character in the scene in which the earl of Arundel's yeomen escort her to her home and improve the occasion by courting her wealth. The tract purports to be the disclosure of an adventuress actually alive; but the author is far more interested in the humour and dramatic interest of his narrative and has borrowed largely, in treatment and spirit, from the jest-books. Each of Edith's victims has his own individuality, which is developed by action as well as by appropriate speeches. There is true narrative power in the succession of events which, in the case of each imposture, lead up to a disillusionment.

The literature of the Middle Ages is prolific in warnings[1] against marriage and in tales of domestic discord. Germany began the sixteenth century with a number of learned indictments against female character. But the English literature of this period was mostly influenced by a large number of French tracts, such as *Les souhaits des hommes, et les souhaiz et beautés des dames*, and *Les quinze joyes de mariage.* These poems accept the traditional views held concerning women, but begin to penetrate more deeply into the problems of domestic life and show a keener appreciation of its dramatic humour. A large number of English tracts are obviously inspired from these and similar sources. In every case we see how the readers who still delight in coarse allusions and horseplay are also attracted by character drawing and the creation of situations. One of the most representative is *The Schole-house of women.* The author begins with a prolix disquisition on the character of women. He comes to the conclusion that the majority are fastidious, sharp tongued, quick tempered, disputatious, fond of double dealing, and, when married, querulous and more inclined to gossip

[1] See vol. II, chap. XVI.

than to mind the house. The writer then shows the real school of women by means of an admirable dialogue in which a young wife is drawn out by an experienced gossip to disclose the cruelty and selfishness of her husband at home. The elder, out of the storehouse of her experience, counsels the younger the best way to domesticate her consort, especially when he takes to beating. Then the writer continues to expatiate on the subtlety, loquacity, hypocrisy and versatility of the female mind, borrowing freely from the *Quinze joyes* and the *C. Mery Talys.* After this comes a list of Biblical and historical characters, all women and all bad, supported by quotations from Solomon and Cicero. The tract was written to please, and its author's object was attained: his pamphlet was twice reprinted.

This popularity proved that the public were ready for two new types of literature: the comedy of character, foreshadowed in the dialogue of the old and young gossip, and the essay, with its discursive appeals to ancient literature. So lively was the interest taken in this type of popular reading that the *Schole-house* raised a small controversy after the manner of medieval French literature[1]. Edward Gosynhyll published in 1541 *The Prayse of all women, called Mulierum paean*, and, a few years later, Edward More published *The Defence of Women.* Kynge eventually published the *Paean* and the *Schole-house* side by side in the same volume.

Another satire on women, which combined the dialogue with the street ballad, is *The Proude Wyves Paternoster.* The idea of giving piquancy to worldly sentiments by associating them with divine service came from France. Thus, in *La Paternostre à l'userier* and in *La Credo à l'userier*, the money-lender interweaves the Latin of the missal with worldly reflections on wealth and business. In the English tract, the scene opens at church on a feast day, and amongst the women, all in their best clothes, is one who intermingles each phrase of the Paternoster with secret prayers to gain ascendancy over her husband and to rival her neighbours' finery. An accident leads her into conversation with another gossip, and their chatter lasts till the end of the service. But the wife has absorbed venomous counsels from her companion. She returns home, asks her husband for some money, is refused, breaks out into recriminations and

[1] In the fourteenth century, Jean Le Fèvre had translated Matheolus and then refuted him. Christine de Pisan had attacked Jean de Meun. In the fifteenth, the disputants became far more numerous, but both factions are dominated by Martin de Franc.

leaves his presence with vague threats. The husband, in great uneasiness, goes to consult the curate, who bids him trust in God's grace. The man returns home comforted, only to find his house rifled and his wife gone. There is here no poetic sentiment; but the dramatic humour of the conversations, the characters of the two women and especially those of the men, are admirable.

In the Middle Ages, domestic anarchy often took the form of a fight for the breeches[1]. In Germany, the city magistrates even recognised and sanctioned a duel between the partners for life. The *Towneley* and *Chester Mysteries* represented brawls between Noah and his wife. In the sixteenth century, this view of the relationship between husband and wife took the form of a *Merry Jeste of a Shrewde and Curste Wyfe lapped in Morelles skin*, compiled out of various sources, including *The Geystes of Skoggan*[2] and two French *fabliaux*. This version of the domestic battle tells how a young farmer, apparently kind-hearted and honourable, marries the elder daughter of a man of substance. The bride soon shows that she intends to rule her new home, but the yeoman strips her, flogs her till she faints and sews her up in the salted hide of an old horse. In this plight she capitulates, and peace reigns in place of discord.

This view of the perversity, garrulousness and vanity of women continued long after our period to influence those who preferred satire to sentiment. It forms the basis of the Theophrastians' conception of female character, and underlies much of the polite humour of the eighteenth century essayists.

But the shrewd, ironical spirit of the sixteenth century required something more than unchivalrous satire. The love of learning was growing apace, but with the enthusiasm for scholarship came depression from over-study. The melancholy which was conspicuous in Elizabethan and Jacobean times[3] was already beginning to puzzle thoughtful men, and it was not without specific earnestness that physicians recommended gaiety as a tonic for an exhausted body[4]. Scholars found the surest relaxation then, as now, in conversation. And their conversation took the form we should expect from men

[1] *Vide* Wright, T., *History of Caricature and Grotesque*, chap. VIII. Cf. *De la Dame qui fut corrigée*.

[2] Cf. 'How Scoggin caused his wife to be let blood.' *De la femme qui voulut éprouver, son mari*. Cf. also, *The Taming of a Shrew*.

[3] *Vide* Andrew Boorde, *Dyetary of Helth*, 1542; Bright, T., *Treatise of Melancholie*, 1586; T(homas) W(alkington), *The Opticke Glasse of Humors*, 1605.

[4] *Epistulae obscurorum Virorum*, 1st series, *Magister Conradus ad magistrum Ortuinum Gratium*.

in sympathy with Plutarch, Plautus and Cicero: that is to say, of jokes, witticisms, repartees and clinches. Thus, a large number of Latin *Facetiae* appeared in print from the pens of fifteenth and sixteenth century scholars. The style of narrative is strikingly similar to the collections of *Exempla*, with which the Latinists, thanks to their semi-ecclesiastical education, would be familiar. These *bons-mots* and anecdotes diverted the student and the controversialist by touches of common life or, at the most, by flashes of classical wit. Their triviality ensured relaxation, but the scholar's attention was held by an appeal to his sense of paradox and epigram.

This interest in witticisms and anecdotes soon spread to the middle classes, whose habit of mind had for centuries been formed by story-telling. The *jongleurs* and *trouvères* had preserved 'those popular tales, which from time immemorial had circulated among nations of Indo-European descent[1]' and which continued to find a place in all subsequent miscellanies down to the eighteenth century. Ever since the Franciscans and Dominicans had used apologues to enforce their exhortations, collections of *Exempla* had been compiled from such sources as *Vitae Patrum* and the *Legends of the Saints*. *Gesta Romanorum* had supplied tales, mostly romantic, from obsolete Latin chronicles and German legends. The sixteenth century still encouraged the medieval love of the marvellous and heroic, but it also gave great impulse to the half cynical, half amused indulgence which had always greeted the triumphs of the knave, the blunders of the fool, the flashes of the quick-witted and the innumerable touches of often undignified nature which make the whole world kin. This increased interest in the vagaries of one's neighbour was partly due to the spread of education, which brought into clearer relief the different grades of intelligence and stupidity. It also arose from the growth of the city population, where legal maladministration often reduced daily intercourse to a trial of wits. Moreover, the townsman felt, though in a less degree than the scholar, the need for the relaxation of social intercourse. The minstrel and jester made a livelihood and sometimes rose to fame[2] by gratifying this unromantic curiosity in life; but the publication of Latin *Facetiae* had shown how their place could be taken by jest-books printed in the native tongue.

These jest-books, in Italy, France, England and Germany, drew largely on each other and even more on the inexhaustible stores of the past, eschewing romantic and religious sentiment and

[1] Courthope, *History of English Poetry*, vol. I, p. 63.
[2] *E.g.* Scogan, Tarlton and Archie.

reproducing only wit, ribaldry, satire and realism. The earliest English jest-book, previous to most of the German miscellanies, was in print by about 1526 under the title of *A C. Mery Talys.* This miscellany covers practically the same ground as the *Fabliaux,* treating of the profligacy of married women, the meanness and voluptuousness of the priesthood, the superstition and crassitude of the peasant, the standing jokes against feminine loquacity and obstinacy, the resources of untutored ingenuity and the comedy of the fool outwitted by the knave. All the tales are narrated with a pointedness and simplicity which show how well English narrative prose had learnt its lesson from Latin. Some of the anecdotes, to modern taste, are merely silly or obscene. But a certain number, following in the footsteps of the Latin *Facetiae,* harbour a sense of wit and subtlety beneath apparent crudity. A more pronounced leaning towards the new humanism is seen in *Mery Tales and Quicke Answeres* (1535). The compiler draws less on medieval stories and puts some of Poggio's *facetiae* and the tales of Erasmus's *Convivium Fabulosum* and a selection from his *Apophthegmata*[1] within reach of English readers. Latin quotations illustrate some of the anecdotes, and the reflections, with which 'jests' are frequently concluded (probably in imitation of *Exempla*) are, in some cases, more discursive. The twenty-eighth story ends with a disquisition on dreams which already anticipates the essay.

Anecdotes and repartees, closely related to conversation and practical jokes, tended to be associated with a personality. *Joci et Sales... ab Ottomaro Luscinio* had appeared in 1529, and *Facetie et motti arguti di alcuni eccellentissimi ingegni et nobilissimi signori,* collected by Lodovico Dominichi, was published in 1548. Following the example of the continent, English compilers soon found it advantageous to put their jests and cranks on the market associated with some character famous for humour or knavery. Thus, we have the *Merie Tales of Master Skelton,* in which a collection of extravagant anecdotes, associated with the laureate's personality and his rectorship of Diss, is used to introduce clerical burlesque such as the people loved. But the most perfect type of biographical jest-book was registered in 1565—6, under the title *The Geystes of Skoggan.* The kind of exploit which the *Fabliaux* attributed to the '*clerc*' is now attributed to the household jester. Amazing tales of dishonesty, insolence, and knavery are collected from native and foreign sources, including two from

[1] *Vide* De Vocht, H., *De Invloed van Erasmus op de Engelsche Tooneelliteratur der XVIe en XVIIe eeuwen.* Ghent, 1908.

the Markolf legend and one (in later editions) from Brantôme. Several had already appeared in *Mery Tales and Quicke Answeres.* These are skilfully woven into a continuous narrative, marking definite progress in the scamp's career from his student days at Oxford to a position at the courts of two monarchs, and thence to his death. These licentious antics were probably not acceptable, even in the rude and profligate court of Edward IV, in whose reign the historic Scogan lived. But the jest-book was becoming more democratic under German influence and pictured the priesthood and the nobility only as accessories to the buffoonery of low life. So welcome was this coarser, more plebeian humour that German jest-books were put on the market in English translations. *Der Pfarrer von Kalenberg* was translated and adapted to English ideas about 1510 and *Eulenspiegel*[1] was translated from an abridged Antwerp edition by William Copland under the title of *Howleglass,* while the same printer produced an English version of the old Danish tale of Rausch as *Friar Rush.* Such tales as *Skoggan's* and *Howleglass* are a link between the jester and the adventurer whose career was becoming a part of the people's reading. Contempt for the routine of daily life is unmistakable. Howleglass's biographer goes so far as to say: 'Men let alone and take no hede of cunning men yt dwel bi them; but prefer them a litle or nought for ther labour nor be beloved: but rural persones and vacabundes have all their desyre.' In such a sentiment, the levelling tendency of democracy has already grown into sympathy with the *picaro.* But these *gestes* have no literary kinship with *Lazarillo de Tormes.* Neither *Howleglass, The Parson of Kalenborowe, Skoggan* nor *Skelton* has the individuality which suggests the novel. Moreover, they still move in the distorted world of caricature, where the stupid are incredibly stupid, and the lucky unnaturally lucky. In France, the jest-book became a vehicle for all the wisdom and satire at Rabelais's command. But in England, the fermentation of the age found expression through other channels, and the jest-books only helped to prepare the way for the detached literature of the seventeenth century by appealing to a sense of humour, wit and verbal subtlety.

This sense found its fullest scope in criticism and ridicule. Again, the literature of the sixteenth century, not yet conscious of itself, had recourse to the past. Satires against certain localities are among the features of the Middle Ages, when decentralisation

[1] See *ante*, p. 82. On the *Eulenspiegel* cycle, see Herford, C. H., *op. cit.* chap. v.

gave counties and even towns the isolation of a separate country. A monk of Peterborough in the twelfth or thirteenth century satirised the inhabitants of Norfolk[1]; while satires are also found concerning the people of Stockton and Rochester, and, at a later period, on the inhabitants of Pevensey. 'Merry tales' were composed or compiled on these lines for readers sufficiently intellectual to laugh at folly. Germany set the example by producing, in the sixteenth century, a collection of witticisms on Schildburg: the inhabitants of this famous town are represented as experiencing so much inconvenience from their far-famed wisdom that they determine to establish a reputation for folly, a reputation which still lives. A similar method of unifying anecdotes of stupidity was adopted by the English in the reign of Henry VIII, when *Merie Tales of the Mad Men of Gotam* appeared. The same type of humour took a slightly different form in *The Sack-Full of News*, a collection, mostly of bucolic ineptitudes, compiled for city readers in an age when Barclay could say to the countryman: 'even the townsmen shall laugh you to scorn.'

Jest-books did not efface a kindred form of miscellany—books of riddles. Wynkyn de Worde printed *Demaundes joyous*, which was chiefly an abridgment of *Les demandes joyeuses*; and the *Booke of Merry Riddles* probably appeared before the earliest known edition of 1600. These questions and answers enjoyed no mean consideration as a mental training[2], and, undoubtedly, helped to form the standard of wit and conceit in later Elizabethan and Jacobean times. The riddle books are full of such questions as: 'What is that that shineth bright of day and at night is raked up in its own dirt?'—'The fire'; 'What is it that getteth his living backward?'—'The ropemaker'; 'Of what faculty be they that every night turn the skins of dead beasts?'—'The friars.' In the character writers, we meet with the same type of wit, only, in them, it is reversed. Thus, in the Overbury collection, we read that a serving man is a creature who, though he be not drunk, yet is not his own man, and that the daily labour of a waterman teaches him the art of dissembling because he goes not the way he looks. In *Micrologia*, 'a player... is much like a counter in arithmetic and may stand one while for a king, another while a beggar, many times as a mute or cipher.' In Butler, 'a melancholy man is one that keeps the worst company in the world, that is, his own.'

[1] Cf. Wright, T., *Early Mysteries and other Latin Poems*, 1838.

[2] This tendency begins to be marked before the sixteenth century by such books as *Mensa philosophica* and *Liber Faceti*.

The primary object of these anecdotes, *facetiae* and riddles was to occupy idle hours. The English miscellanies are always 'merry'; and the foreign jest-books have even more suggestive titles. This natural inclination for amusement, in which even elderly students took refuge from over-work, had come down to the sixteenth century with a love of singing and dancing[1]. By 1510, Erasmus declared that *Britanni, praeter alia, formam, musicam et lautas mensas, proprie sibi vindicent*[2]. Miles Coverdale[3], in 1538, testifies that the taste for singing was universal among carters, ploughmen and women 'at the rockes' and spinning wheel. Words in metre were composed to give a fuller zest to music and dancing, but the conditions of their production were quite different from those which evolved the folk-lore ballad[4]. The change was inevitable from the time the minstrel left the baronial hall for the city square. The transformation became complete so soon as the invention of printing made it more profitable to sell ballads than to sing them. These fly-leaves and broadsides, specially produced for the occasion and sold for a penny, have nearly all perished. Popular ones were pasted on the wall and the less valued were devoted to more ephemeral purposes. Both destinies led to annihilation, but the demand for them must have grown rapidly, for, in the second decade of the sixteenth century, the author of the *Interlude of the Nature of the Four Elements* complains of 'the toys and trifles' printed in his time; so that, while in English there were scarcely 'any works of connynge,' the most 'pregnant wits' were employed in compiling 'ballads and other matters not worth a mite.' Henry VIII encouraged such productions in the early part of his reign but suppressed them wholesale when any part of his policy was attacked. In 1533, a proclamation was issued to suppress 'fond books, ballads, rimes and other lewd treatises in the English tongue.' In 1543, an act of parliament was passed to put a stop to the circulation of 'printed ballads, plays, rimes, songs and other fantasies.' At the beginning of Mary's reign, an edict was made against 'books, ballads, rimes and treatises' which had been 'set out by printers and stationers, of an evil zeal for lucre and covetous of vile gain.' These suppressions, added to the perishable nature of the product, have destroyed all but about fifty-six ballads of the reigns from Henry VIII to Elizabeth. But, by 1556, the Stationers' company was incorporated and the development and nature of this primitive

[1] See Chappell, W., *Popular Music of the Olden Time*, vol. I, p. 253.

[2] *Encomium Moriae.*

[3] *Address unto the Christian reader.*

[4] See vol. II, chap. XVII.

journalism is more easily traceable. From about 1560 to 1570, about forty ballad-printers are registered, but, here again, the bulk of their output has perished. The vast number of broadsides that have come down to us belong to later periods, and owe their existence to the labours of private collectors such as Selden, Harley, Bagford and Pepys. Some of those still extant, which date from the first two decades of Elizabeth's reign, continue the spirit of the jest-books or reflect the sentiment of the 'botes' and 'fraternityes,' but the greater number are akin to the new spirit of Elizabethan and Jacobean times[1].

We have seen in the foregoing summary how large a reading public still remained untouched by the renascence, and continued to enjoy medieval literature, borrowing freely from France and Germany. But, at the same time, the great social changes of the sixteenth century were inspiring a large number of quite different tracts. Trade was encouraged by both the Henrys, and the growing taste for luxury, which ruined the gentry, enriched the commercial classes. Moreover, the discovery of the New World added immensely to the opportunities of making money. This commercial activity seemed, to the moralists of the age, to be a rupture with the good traditions of the past. In 1540—50, was printed Charles Bansley's *Pryde and Abuse of Women*, which belongs to quite a different world of satire from that of *The Schole-house of Women* or *The Proude Wyves Paternoster*. The coarse, picturesque narrative is gone and, with it, the rough humour and caricature. Bansley's invective is a sermon in verse. He views female failings in the light of the Seven Deadly Sins, and lashes their ostentation and vanity as Romish and inspired by the Devil. At about the same time, a dialogue called *The Booke in Meeter of Robin Conscience* was printed, in which Conscience remonstrates first with his father, whose aim is to have abundance of worldly treasure, then with his mother Neugise, who follows French fashions and dresses like one nobly born, whereas the wife of the previous century would never have ventured to rival the gentlewoman's finery, and, lastly, with his sister, Proud Beauty, who has mastered the essentials of cosmetics and delights to 'colly and kis.'

A class which increases in wealth and importance does not

[1] Broadside ballads are still sung in the streets of Paris during public holidays, and can be heard any night at *Les quat-z-arts* and *Le Grillon*. As in former times, they are the best indication of popular sentiment. The same survival is found in London in the nineteenth century. *Vide* Hindley, C., *History of the Catnach Press*, 1886.

stand still. Burghers began to marry their sons and daughters to insolvent nobility, and Henry, who aimed at creating an aristocracy dependent on himself, frequently recruited the diminished ranks of the old peers from among burghers, lawyers and borough magistrates. This growth of the royal court at the expense of the feudal castle filled London with raw courtiers[1], drawn from all classes, who attached themselves to men of influence, partly to see the world, and partly to advance their own fortunes under shelter of a great name. Such a suddenly enriched or ennobled society was not likely to be reconciled to the simple, rough life of their forefathers. Luxury and excitement became necessities and received their comment in contemporary literature. In 1530, the *Address in verse to new-fanglers* was prefixed to Chaucer's *Assembly of Fowls.* Wynkyn de Worde issued three editions of *A Treatise of a Gallant,* which laments the pride, avarice and ambition of the new fledged courtier and his love of quarrel. The tract deplores the influx of foreigners, whose phraseology was corrupting the purity of the English idiom, and censures the Englishman's admiration for French customs and French vices. At this time, the example of Henry VIII and his sister Margaret made dice and card-playing fashionable and the pleasures of gambling gave great opportunities to the gentleman thief, who now became a perpetual menace to society, and, in 1532, apparently, was printed a *Manifest detection of the most vyle and detestable use of dice play and other practices like the same.* This tract is one of the first great exposures of the age, throwing into relief the practices and resources of those who fall 'from the hardness of virtuous living to the delicacy and boldness of uncareful idleness and gainfull deceit.' We learn how the provincial is met at Paul's by a gentleman with three or four servants in gay liveries, an acquaintance is cleverly established, the 'couzin' is unwittingly introduced to the gaming-house and, eventually, he is fleeced. Elaborate tricks to entice the 'couzin' with different kinds of cogged dice, even the name of the most reliable maker, canting terms, the mode of making cards and other forms of imposture and thievery, are all made public. These disclosures are presented in a lively dialogue, in clear, simple English. The sixteenth century love of anecdote is gratified and the conversation is carried on between two well-defined characters, the one a raw courtier, the other an experienced man of the world.

[1] Cf. a poem by Richard Edwards in *The Paradyse of Daynty Devises,* beginning

> In Youthfull yeares when first my young desires began
> To pricke me forth to serve in court.

The triumph of the reformation under Henry VIII and the suppression of the monasteries had raised great hopes in those churchmen who looked on Rome as the root of all evil. But the disorganisation of society always brings abuses to the surface and the venality of judges, the chicanery and delays of law-suits, the tyranny of the powerful and the oppression of the poor and defenceless now became doubly apparent. The prevailing clear-sightedness as to the evils of both past and present found vigorous expression in Brinkelow's *Complaynt of Roderyck Mors.* Brinkelow's sectarian hatred of popery precludes the slightest regret for the abolition of the old religion; in fact, he laments that the 'body and tayle of the pope is not banisshed with his name.' At the same time, his sense of justice and righteousness keeps his eyes open to the fact that ecclesiastical and state administration[1] are no better under the new order and that the social conditions are a great deal worse. A marked feature of the tract is the constant appeal to the king's divine authority to rectify social and legal abuses. Henry's practice differed greatly from the ideas of his conscientious supporters. The riches he appropriated from the monasteries were not devoted to the relief of the economic situation, as Brinkelow urged him to use them (chap. XXII). Part went to the king's middle class favourites, who now availed themselves of the fall of noble families and the eviction of abbey-lands, to speculate in agriculture and buy country estates. This upstart squirearchy knew nothing of the old baronial practice of hospitality, and the passing away of the ancient ideal added, in some measure, to the pessimism of the times. Some ballads have come down to us lamenting the new order, such as John Barker's, printed 1561, with the burden:

> Neibourhed nor love is none,
> Treu dealyng now is fled and gone.

Besides neglecting the claims of good fellowship, the *nouveau riche* introduced methods of commercial competition into land speculation. The rearing of cattle was found to be more profitable than the leasing of farms[2]. Thus, neither the lords of the manor nor freehold tenants hesitated, when it was advantageous, to abolish the small homesteads that had supported the yeomanry

[1] Chap. XII, *That kynges and lordes of presons should fynd their presoners suffycyent fode at their charge: and of men that have lyen long in preson, &cete*, is one of the first signs of a literature which, in the next century, was to include *The Blacke Dogge of Newgate* (c. 1600), *The Compters Common-Wealth* (1617), *Essayes and Characters of a Prison and Prisoners* (1618), by Mynshul, and *Wil Bagnal's Ghost* (1655).

[2] Traill, *Social England*, vol. III, chap. IX.

of baronial England. Evicted tenants were forced to become vagabonds or seek a livelihood in manufacturing industries, thus further disorganising the labour market; and, all this while, the reckless extravagance of the court raised the general cost of living, and the debasement of the currency and increase of taxation made poverty more acute.

Amid such disorder and suffering the modern spirit of competition was ushered into the world, and contemporary literature could see little but evil in the period of transition. It was especially the spectacle of men trampling on one another in the struggle for wealth which roused Robert Crowley from the production of controversial and religious tracts. Crowley was a printer, a puritan and a famous preacher. Most of his pamphlets, sermons and answers are composed for theologians; but the reading public was sufficiently large and the influence of the press sufficiently universal to make it worth his while to address the whole commons of the realm in five popular tracts. In 1550, he boldly exposed the more glaring social and moral abuses of the time in a series of short verse essays, arranged in alphabetical order and entitled *The one and thirty epigrams.* But, in spite of these devices, his standpoint remains that of a Hebrew prophet and his style that of a preacher. In *The Voice of the Last Trumpet,* which appeared in the same year, he shows even more clearly how far his sectarian training had unfitted him to handle problems of progress or social reform. The tract is a methodical appeal to the different classes to lay aside their peculiar sins; his view is still that of the Middle Ages, and God is supposed to have placed barriers between the classes[1] which no individual can cross without sin. Crowley warns his readers not to stray from their class, but to let the gentry cultivate learning, the commons obedience, and all will be well. In 1550, he also printed *The way to wealth,* a graphic and searching enquiry into the mutual hatred and distrust which existed between the rich and the poor, showing how peasants attribute the late seditions to farmers, graziers, lawyers, merchants, gentlemen, knights and lords, while the upper classes—'the gredie cormerauntes'—point to the wealth and insolence of the peasantry. But he sternly warns the lower classes against disobedience and covetousness, bidding them be patient and not usurp the functions of their rulers. He rebukes the clergy—'the shephardes of thys church'—for their lust of wealth,

[1] Even in Dances of Death, such as that painted on the wall of the church of La Chaise Dieu in Auvergne, and that at Basel, each individual takes precedence according to his class. Wright, T., *History of Caricature and Grotesque*, chap. XIII.

but reserves his sharpest censure for the rich men who tyrannise over the commons. In the following year he produced *Pleasure and pain, heaven and hell,* an even more direct protest against competition or, as Crowley calls it, 'the gredy rakeyng togyther of the treasures of this vayne worlde,' which was widening the gulf between rich and poor. Still writing for the large reading public, he couched his expostulation in the attractive form of a poem representing Christ's address to the world on the Last Judgment Day. But the most interesting of Crowley's tracts is the *Informacion and Peticion agaynst the oppressours of the pore commons of this realme.* In this address to the parliament of Edward VI, the preacher fulminates against the rich in the language of the *Psalms* and *Isaiah.* He draws a powerful picture of the misery caused by the aggressions of the wealthy: how poverty makes slaves of men and drudges or prostitutes of women, how youths are reduced to beggary and, in the end, 'garnysh the galowe trees.'

Crowley had neither the intellectual equipment nor the literary talent necessary to illuminate the perplexity and suffering of his age. His five tracts simply give voice to the thoughts of those who looked backward and cried 'order,' when they felt that the times were out of joint.

In these and similar pamphlets one thing particularly arrests the attention—the continual references to the ever increasing class of beggars and vagabonds. As early as 1528, Simon Fish begins his *Supplication* with these tremendous words:

> Most lamentably compleyneth theyre wofull mysery unto youre highnes youre poore daily bedemen, the wretched hidous monstres (on whome scarcely for horror any yie dare loke), the foule unhappy sorte of lepres and other sore people, nedy, impotent, blinde, lame and sike, that live onely by almesse, howe that theyre nombre is daily so sore encreased that all the almesse of all the weldisposed people of this youre realme is not halfe ynough for to susteine theim.

The historic class of outlaws, vagabonds and pilgrims had been enormously increased by the victims of falling prices and decaying guilds. The phenomenon forces itself on the attention of Robert Copland, who printed and probably composed *The Hye Way to the Spyttel Hous,* after 1531. No work more clearly illustrates the transitional state of English literature. Copland describes himself as taking shelter from the rain in the porch of a spyttel house and interrogates the porter on the inmates. The author really wishes to describe the different types of fools and knaves; but, instead of grouping them under a fraternity, boat or testament, he chooses the spyttel house to serve as a frame, the picture containing those who knock for entrance. Under this heading, nearly all the lower types of humanity are classed, not only the idle and the lascivious, but busybodies and those who refuse to forgive their neighbours or discipline their servants; even idle and domineering wives are also among those who visit the hospital. Thus, in its main conception, the book belongs to the general body of early sixteenth century satire. But the tract is profoundly coloured by the element of beggary. A hospital would not have been chosen as a substitute for the traditional background unless poverty was a very general curse, and we have a ghastly picture of the destitute wretches who crave admission. In the first part of the dialogue, the porter gives some amusing and graphic anecdotes of the tricks of sham beggars, thus showing that Copland had caught a glimpse of the boundless fields of comedy and humour which form part of the realm of roguery.

Such was the state of the poor while the religious houses still stood, but the suppression of the monasteries added to the army of the unemployed and, at the same time, deprived the destitute of the alms which had been expressly given in trust for them. Those who had formerly looked to the religious houses for help were now thrown upon society; mendicancy became a recognised fact; and legislation, while suppressing vagabondism, instituted compulsory relief for the poor and needy. Such a system, badly administered in a time of social disorganisation, led to inevitable abuse. Pauperism became a profession exercised by ingenious impostors, who perverted the administration of charity and, when occasion offered, robbed travellers, stole horses out of pastures and hooked linen out of house windows.

Vagabondism was a menace to society, and the curiosity which people feel in anything alarming was satisfied in 1561 by Awdeley's *Fraternitye of vacabones.* Again we see the power of literary tradition. Awdeley, apparently, found no more appropriate title than one as old as Wireker; but those who expected a satire on social types assembled under this denomination were disappointed. Under an old name, he followed up the idea of the German *Liber Vagatorum,* and produced an anatomy of vagabond life and vagrancy. The tract is divided into two parts; the first consists of a series of concise definitions of thieves' cant and contains startling revelations, how the 'Abraham man' walks this earth feigning madness and calling himself Poor Tom[1], how the 'washman' lies in the highway with artificial sores produced by

[1] Compare *King Lear,* Act III, sc. 4.

spickwort or ratsbane and how these and suchlike impostors have not only their own language but are organised into an independent community with the 'upright man' at their head, who domineers over the society and takes the lion's share of the booty.

The most jejune of descriptions would be welcome when accompanied, as these were, by sensational disclosures of a mysterious and dangerous class. But, in the second part—the company of 'cousoners' and shifters—Awdeley deals with three types of the gentleman thief. Here, the definitions which reveal the insidious refinements of the well dressed adventurer necessarily expand into narrative; but Awdeley was quite unconscious that he had found a vein of humour and episode which has not even yet been exhausted. His tales are concise explanations of a process of deception; his only object is to give information.

All the opportunities which Awdeley missed are turned to the fullest account by Thomas Harman. The writer, who describes himself as a 'poore gentleman,' sought to supply the place of the suppressed monasteries by keeping open house for mendicants. In this charitable spirit, he came into personal contact with almost every type of pauper, and gradually discovered that his compassion was generally lavished on professional impostors. Having penetrated 'their depe dissimulation and detestable dealynge, beinge marvellous suttle and craftye in their kynde,' he gave his discoveries to the world in *A Caveat or Warening for Commen Corsetors, vulgarely called Vagabones.* The book is put forward as an 'alarum' to forewarn honest citizens; but, in reality, it contains the researches of a sociologist. Harman alludes rather ungratefully to Awdeley's superficial outline as 'A small breefe... that made a lytle shewe of there names and usage, and gave a glymsinge lyghte, not sufficient to perswade of their pevishe peltinge.' In twenty-four chapters, varying in length from a few lines to several pages, Harman accumulated important data out of which the character of the sixteenth century thief may be constructed. We learn something as to their dress, food, origin, training and sexual relations. The different departments of a highly specialised profession are explained. Their complicated frauds are fully investigated, and we catch glimpses of the dark shallows of their private life. With the instinct of a scientist, the author appends a list of the chief thieves then living, and gives specimens and translations of their slang.

This spirit of philosophical enquiry is the first sign of modern thought in a popular tract. But, in other respects, Harman's work has the characteristics of his own age. He was writing for the public which read *A C. Mery Tales* and *The Geystes of Skoggan*; so his book is enlivened with curious stories in illustration of thieves' practices. The principle of recommending exposures to the masses has been formulated by Erasmus *quoniam autem rudis ac simplex aetas huiusmodi fraudibus potissimum est obnoxia, visum est exemplo non inamoeno depingere modum imposturae*[1]. But Harman has his full share of sympathy for a piece of successful knavery, and he loves an episode which hinges on a trial of wits. His anecdotes mark a pronounced advance on the stories of the jest-books. The actors are no longer chessmen, who automatically bring about a situation; they are living characters, and the author adds to the interest of his book by interweaving personal experiences with his pictures of mendicant life. In such stories as that of the 'Roge' (cap. IV) and the 'Walking Morte' (cap. XIX), his curiosity as to the eccentricities and humour of villainy effaces his mission as an exposer of abuses.

Awdeley's and Harman's books, together with *Liber Vagatorum*, have influenced a whole class of literature, from Greene's 'conny-catching pamphlets' to *The Prince and the Pauper*. And yet the *Caveat* does not anticipate the spirit of the picaresque novel. Though attracted by knavery, Harman has no toleration for the knave. 'Lewtering Luskes, lasy Lorells, rowsey ragged rabblement of rakehells' are amongst his designations for this class, and his only methods for 'reforming the criminal' are the stocks and the whip.

It is worth noticing that this work, a pamphlet of unquestioned merit, is free from the literary ideals of the court. Harman alludes contemptuously to 'this delycat age,' and disclaims all pretensions to eloquence, declaring that he has set forth his work 'symplye and truelye, with such usual words and termes as is among us wel known and frequented.'

While the social miseries of England were inspiring a whole literature of narrative and exposure, the sixteenth century spirit of cosmopolitanism was also finding popular expression. Curiosity with regard to other countries was by no means a creation of the age. The thirteenth and fourteenth centuries produced short Latin descriptions of the characteristics of different nations, and a series of pen and ink caricatures of the Irish, Welsh and Gascons are found in the margin of a document of the time of Edward I. But popular interest in the continent received a new impulse during the sixteenth century. The immigration of foreigners had, by 1517, become a marked feature of English commercial life, and the period from 1512

[1] Preface to *Colloquia familiaria*.

to 1558 is one of tentative exploration, which, though it produced no startling mercantile discoveries, accustomed England to the idea of the expansion of Europe, and helped to produce a revolt against insularity. As early as *The Nature of the Four Elements*, 'declaringe many proper poynts of philosophy naturall and of dyvers strange landys and of dyvers straunge effects and causes,' we have a conception of cosmography serving as a basis for a morality play. The production, apparently, found no imitators. But the broadening of the national outlook is proved by the ever-increasing number of allusions to foreign countries, in the tracts of the time[1].

The growth of cosmopolitan ideas found its expression in a collection of essays on the chief nationalities and kingdoms of Europe composed by the traveller and physician Andrew Boorde. This work was finished by 1542, but was not published until 1547, under the significant title of *The Fyrste Boke of the Introduction of Knowledge.* Again we find a work of considerable merit probably intended to preface a universal encyclopaedia and yet produced for a public which had not completely dissociated popular literature from the grotesqueries of the former age. Each chapter begins with a prologue in doggerel verse, spoken by a typical member of the country under discussion, and illustrated by one of Copland's stock woodcuts. These verses are intended to portray, and, in some cases, to caricature, what is typical of each nation. Thus, the Englishman stands naked, musing on what clothes he shall wear; the Fleming cheerfully admits that he is sometimes 'drunken as a rat'; the Cornishman expresses himself in half intelligible English; the Bohemian stands by Wyclif and cares nothing for the pope; the Venetian is represented with money to pacify the Turks and the Jews. But the *Introduction* is not merely a forerunner of the modern cartoon. Verse and prose are intermingled as in Thomas's *Historye of Italye*; the doggerel prologues are followed by prose descriptions in which the author discusses the geographical situation, the produce and the 'naturall dysposicion,' that is to say, the culture, religion and customs, of the inhabitants. He ends each enquiry with information on the coinage, sometimes with a few specimens of the language, and, in one or two cases, with directions for travel. Like much of the popular literature of the sixteenth century, the

[1] Such as *Supplication for the Beggars, Complaynt of Roderyck Mors, Dialogue between Cardinal Pole and Thomas Lupset* (n.d.), *Rede me and be not wrothe* (1528), *The Boke named the Governour* (1531), etc., etc.

Introduction stands between two ages; it still retains the coarse laughter and credulity of the past. Boorde believes that Merlin built Stonehenge, and gravely records the legend of the White Cock and Hen of St Domingo. But, at the same time, he has the observation of an age conscious of progress. He notices the advance of civilisation in different lands, and he understands the importance of a country's natural resources. The economical situation interests him; he observes that England is the land of capital, and that Spain depends on her sea trade for wealth. He has an eye for the poverty of people who, like the Welsh, are still sunk in the squalor and ignorance of the Middle Ages. Anything striking about the government attracts him, and the religious situation frequently receives comment. And yet he has the individualist's love of peculiarities. He notices the Irishman's device for cooking, he reads that the Flemings eat frogs' legs and that the Genoese are high in the instep.

Besides satisfying men's curiosity in foreign lands, Boorde put his medical knowledge and experience within reach of the uninitiated, by *A Compendyous Regyment or a Dyetary of Helth.* This treatise on the cultivation of health, one of the earliest composed in English, shows how quickly knowledge was spreading through the middle classes. It was an age when the government insisted on quarantine but neglected sanitation, and when Harrison believed that the soot and smoke of chimneyless houses hardened the constitution. Boorde was one of the first to see how greatly sanitation influenced the well-being of man. The first part of his *Dyetary,* really a separate treatise, shows how the secret of health is to choose a convenient site for one's house. But the most striking feature of his system deals with the reaction of the mind on the body[1]. In placing his house, a man should choose a congenial prospect,

> for and the eye be not satysfyed, the mynde cannot be contented. And the mynde cannot be contented the herte cannot be pleased: if the herte and mynde be not pleased nature doth abhor. And yf nature do abhor, mortyfycacyon of the vytall and anymall and spyrytuall powers do consequently folowe.

In the second part of his treatise, Boorde gives practical advice on such matters as sleeping, exercise and dress. He includes an exhaustive examination of diet; but most of his purely medical knowledge is still traditional. Yet, in scope and method,

[1] Cf. *Medici dicunt etiam quod sanum est quando aliquis est laetus. Epistolae Obscurorum Virorum,* vol. I, ep. 9. Magister Conradus de Zuiccavia.

the book is an effort to shake off the ignorance of the past and apply to practical life the learning gathered in universities.

Boorde was not the only physician who advanced the culture of his age. In those days, chirurgeons and doctors were men of general knowledge. Thomas Vicary insists that, besides his professional training, a chirurgeon should be versed in natural philosophy, grammar, rhetoric and abstract science. John Halle adds astronomy, natural history and botany to the list. These sciences were needed to equip the practitioner with the skill and ability to put his own art to the fullest use. And thus the physician kept in touch with the knowledge of his time. Robert Recorde, said to have been physician to Edward VI and Mary, wrote dialogues on arithmetic, geography, mensuration, astrology, astronomy and algebra. But no writer has embodied so much sentiment, learning, eloquence and dramatic power in his scientific treatises as William Bullein. In his first book, *The Gouvernement of Healthe*, we find a reflection generally considered the property of Shakespeare:

> In dede the poore sylly shepehard doth pleasantly pipe with his shepe, whan mighty princes do fight amonge their subjectes, and breake manye slepes in golden beds, whan bakers in bags and brewers in bottels, do snorte upon hard strawe, fearing no sodaine mishappe.

In 1562, he produced *Bullein's Bulwarke of Defence againste Sicknes, Sorues, etc.*, obviously modelling his title on Elyot's successful *Castel of Helth*. Bullein's attitude to his subject can best be expressed in the words of his own dedication:

> I beyng a child of the Commonwealthe am bounde unto my mother, that is, the lande, in whom I am borne: to pleasure it with any good gift that it hath pleased God to bestowe upon me, not to this ende to instructe the learned but to helpe the ignoraunt, that thei maie resort to this little Bulwarke.

The book is divided into four separate treatises, the second in the form of a dialogue, and it contains what he had learnt from travel and study about herbs, surgery, the cultivation of health and the practical part of a physician's work. But the scholars who were carrying on this work of enlightenment had many other things of which to tell the people besides remedies for their bodies. Although the College of Physicians had been incorporated as early as 1518, the position of medical men was far from established. Bullein ascribes their low estate to the impostures and frauds of empirics and mountebanks[1]. Here, again, the curtain is lifted which hides the low life of

[1] Cf. *Ep. Obsc. Virorum*, vol. I, epp. 33 and 34.

the Middle Ages, and, in a passage of bitter eloquence[1], we hear of the escaped criminals, idle labourers and runaway serving-men that sell worthless or poisonous drugs, practise witchcraft and necromancy, doing more harm, according to Bullein, than limitours, pardoners or vagabonds. The whole work has many digressions and touches of autobiography. But the personal note is sounded to most effect when the physician who had undergone the insult of a prosecution for murder and was then languishing in prison for debt, utters the lament[2] beginning: 'Truely there is none other purgyng place or purgatorie but this'—not only in bodily suffering but in anguish of soul,

continuall thought, sometyme wishyng that Death might conquere life, broken hart and vexed spirite, full of sondrie inwarde affections and alteracions of minde, small rest or quietnes, sorowful for the death of kindred, or frendes, being changed into bitter enemies, whiche is a greate plague.

The most important of Bullein's works, from a literary point of view, is *A Dialogue both pleasaunte and pietifull wherein is a goodly regiment against the fever Pestilence with a Consolacion and Comfort against death*, of which the earliest extant copy is dated 1564. Although no great plague had visited England for many years, the congestion of the poor in cities made smaller visitations a frequent occurrence. Yet none of the great physicians before Gilbert Skene wrote anything that has come down to us on the epidemics. But Bullein's tract is a great deal more than one of the earliest treatises to suggest remedies for the plague. In his hands, the *Dialogue* is hardly less than a drama of death. He sketches twelve types of society as a physician would satirise them in an age when death was rampant. The action is twofold. At the beginning, the interest centres round the grasping money maker Antonius, who is sinking fast, but keeps off the thought of death by attaching Medicus to his person. Antonius, heretofore, had contented himself with an otiose observance of religion, but is now troubled by visions of hell. Medicus, unlike Halle's ideal physician, is a cynical atheist, but, like Chaucer's prototype, makes a fortune by attending the wealthy and neglecting the poor. Between these two, the causes and cures of the fever are discussed. This part of the *Dialogue* illustrates the transitional stage of the science, which attributes fever to infected air and the ill health of the patient, but also accepts eclipses of the moon as a probable

[1] *A Dialogue betwene Sores and Chyrurgi*, fol. vi.

[2] *Booke of Compoundes*, fol. liiij. (Both the *Dialogue* and the *Booke of Compoundes* are sections of the *Bulwarke*.)

cause, and varies such practical safeguards as cleanliness, gaiety and avoidance of emotion[1] with the most extravagant quackeries. Two lawyers, Avarus and Ambodexter, hover round the fortune of Antonius, speculating on his death and scheming to influence his will. The scene then shifts to the home of a prosperous, self-satisfied burgher, who with his wife and servant Roger are travelling into the country to escape from the plague stricken city, with its ringing bells and sounds of woe. The tedium of the journey is beguiled by discussions on portents and comments on the dishonesty of lawyers. Roger, a country wit, with the liberty of the household jester, full of rustic wisdom and folklore, contributes quaint stories and anecdotes after the manner of *A C. Mery Talys.* They reach an inn where the wife's admiration for the wall-paintings discloses a series of emblems passing in review the abuses and evils of the age. Another traveller, Mendax, joins them at dinner, and, through his extravagant accounts of foreign lands, Bullein satirises not only *Utopia* but books of travel and legend from Pliny, Isidore and Strabo to Sebastian Münster and Boiastuau. They proceed on their journey, but black clouds gather, thunder is heard, Roger flees, the wife hides and Mors appears. Civis is warned in terrible words that his last hour has come, and, after fruitless parleyings, is left with a mortal thrust to write his will and, with the help of Theologus, to prepare his soul for death. When the danger is past, Roger reappears, infinitely disgusted that his own name does not appear in his master's will. As the household is now broken up, he thinks of joining the cozeners and vagabonds, but fears the gallows. If only he had Civis's money he would soon make a sumptuous living by usury. Thus, in one episode, Bullein satirises moneylenders and points out the vagabonds' recruiting ground.

No summary can give an idea of the learning contained in the *Dialogue.* The discussions range from Aristotle's theory of the elemental forces to symbolic sketches of the chief English poets[2]. Its satire reaches nearly every abuse of the age, and there are passages of unmistakable eloquence and power. The influence of the morality plays is obvious, but the true historical significance of the tract consists in the fact that the thought has outgrown the literary form. The dialogue was a medieval device to convey

[1] This idea was far older than Bullein. Cf. the maxim of the school of Salernum:

Si tibi deficiant Medici, Medici tibi fiant
Haec tria: mens hilaris, requies, moderata dieta.

[2] Cf. *Bowge of Courte*, in which Skelton represents the poets laureate (*i.e.* learned men) both ancient and modern assembled by Pallas.

instruction in an attractive form, and, as the reading public increased during the sixteenth century, this means of sugaring the pill was constantly resorted to. But the exchange of argument between two or more persons loses its effectiveness unless confined to the discussion of a single thesis, or the conflict of two characters. The detached essay and the Theophrastian character are needed to supersede the dialogue when ideas become more varied and the picture of life less simple.

We have seen how the great changes of the sixteenth century—the increase of luxury, the rise of the middle class, the growth of competition, the suppression of the monasteries, the expansion of Europe, the frequency of pestilence—inspired a vigorous literature, quite distinct from the theological and aesthetic movements of the time. But, while the popular printing presses were thus exposing fraud and enlightening ignorance, the superstitions of an earlier age were reappearing in an aggravated form. The belief in fetishes, totems, the evil eye, luck-bones, folk-remedies, love charms and nefarious magic was rampant in England. Christianity and paganism were, among the unthinking and untaught peasantry, inextricably mingled. Jugglery and legerdemain had still the glamour of the miraculous, and magic was used to discover lost things, bring back wayward lovers and cure disease. Astrologers still foretold events by studying the position of the stars, and sold information as to the auspicious hour for all kinds of human enterprise, from the founding of cities to the taking of medicine. Waldegrave, in 1580, published an attack on prognostications in the *Foure Great Lyers, Striving who shall win the Silver Whetstone.* The writer quotes the Biblical injunction against taking thought for the morrow, and appends a list of the 'absurd, unknowne and insolent wordes' used by prognosticators to impress the inexperienced. But he still admits, on the authority of Scripture, that national benefits or calamities are foreshadowed in the heavens, and will not definitely deny that stars influence the fortunes of the individual. Mankind had not yet given up the search for the philosopher's stone, and the debasement of coinage during Henry's and Edward's reigns was an additional inducement to search for wealth by means of alchemy. Such superstition offered limitless opportunities for 'alcumysticall cousenages,' in which the unwary, beguiled by a specious manner and by the tricks of the trade, invested money in experiments, or entrusted it to be multiplied. These practices were exposed from time to time and added to the general sense of corruption and wickedness which oppressed mankind. The temper of the age is illustrated by the belief that the heresies, vanities and worldliness of the nation would shortly cause some awful manifestation of divine anger.

No sooner was this vague terror established than the old heathen belief in portents and prodigies made itself felt. Conrad Lycosthenes closed his *Prodigiorum ac Ostentorum Chronicon*, in 1557, with the warning that these miracles and strange sights 'were the certain prognostications of changes, revolutions, and calamities and the veritable tokens of God's wrath.' The popular presses were already making a profitable business out of news sheets, in verse or prose, publishing sensational reports from all the world. They now profited by this religious terror to publish broadsides announcing prodigies and portents. We read of children born without arms and legs, a monstrous pig with a dolphin's head, a child born with ruffs, and another having 'the mouth slitted on the right side like a libarde's (leopard's) mouth, terrible to beholde.' These fly-leaves, beginning with a most circumstantial description of the portent, end with an exhortation to the people of England to take warning at the manifestations of God's wrath and to repent. Many of them relate to the year 1562, which Holinshed and Stow record as especially fertile in monsters.

But the superstitious excitability of the people reached its most harmful phase in the revival of witch persecutions. To the medieval mind, heaven and hell were two tremendous powers fighting for the supremacy of man. The church was, indeed, master, but the devil was not destroyed. From time to time, his influence was felt, and now, in this age of pestilence, blasphemous controversy and schism, men thought that the Evil One was re-asserting his power. His activity was most clearly discovered in witchcraft. All sorcery was a voluntary alliance with the powers of evil. In the case of witches, a carnal union with the devil was supposed to have taken place. Men who believed themselves at war with the invisible fiend would not be long in assailing his confederates on earth. In 1541, Henry VIII passed the first act against sorcery and magic; in 1562, the law was revived; and, in 1575 and 1576, persecutions were renewed. Terror was increased by the diseases of insanity and hypochondria being misunderstood. It was an age of monstrous hallucinations; men believed that they were wolves and fled to the mountains; nuns imagined they were cats and began to mew; maidens vomited pins; men believed they had snakes in their vitals. Remedies were no less monstrous. People rubbed themselves with magic ointment to produce dreams and cured diseases by drinking water out of a murdered man's skull. This 'nightmare of superstition' did not obsess everybody; there were enough readers to call for three editions of a burlesque rhapsody which ridiculed sorcery, spells and cat-legends under the title *Beware the Cat.* The tract, with its new fashioned artificialities of style, was, probably, designed for the rapidly increasing class of exquisites, and it did not appeal to the majority of Englishmen, whose minds were unsettled by the momentous changes of the age.

This species of fanaticism was now no longer confined to the vulgar and uneducated. The theology and science of Germany had already been brought to bear on the subject. As early as 1487, *Malleus Maleficarum,* which established such fantasies as the *incubus* and *succubus,* the initiation of magicians, the black art and the counter-charms of the church, had received the sanction of the theological faculty and a patent from Maximilian I. Johannes Trithemius produced, in 1508, *Antiphonus Maleficiorum,* which accepted witchcraft as a fact, and taught the Christian how to defend himself against it. Cornelius Agrippa, on the other hand, argued against the persecution of witches in his *De Occulta Philosophia,* and his pupil, the physician Johann Weier, exposed the superstition and cruelty of that practice in *De Praestigiis Demonum et Incantationibus ac Beneficiis.* Weier still believed in a certain magic worked by the devil, but he discovered how much the imagination had to do with witchcraft, and how much of sorcery can be explained by a knowledge of natural phenomena. The book provoked the keenest opposition, especially from Jean Bodin, who put all his experience as a judge in witch trials and all his theoretic knowledge of magic and sorcery into his *Traité de la Démonomie des Sorciers.*

Reginald Scot's *Discoverie of Witchcraft,* in 1584, is the first great English contribution to this European controversy. He had already given proof of the qualities of foresight, reflectiveness and common sense in a work on hops, designed to improve one of the industries of his country. The *Discoverie,* also, was primarily intended as a humanitarian protest—'A Travell in the behalfe of the poore, the aged and the simple.' But the primitive belief in magic and witchcraft had now become a matter for academic discussion, and Scot's work is inevitably coloured by continual restatement of Agrippa's and Weier's arguments, and by counterblasts to *Malleus* and Jean Bodin.

It is essentially a work of investigation and exposition. In that uncritical and pedantic age, the great sources of knowledge seemed to confirm man's natural belief in magic and sorcery. It was argued that *Deuteronomy*, the Twelve Tables, the Justinian code, recognised the existence of witches. Among profane literature, no lesser authorities than Manilius, Vergil, Horace, Ovid, Tibullus and Lucan had given credence to sorcery. A refutation of such contentions hinged on the interpretation of texts. Thus, much of the *Discoverie* is devoted to an academic examination of Hebrew and Latin words. But Scot was not only a scholar. In the administration of his inherited estates, he came into contact with the unprogressive population of rural districts, and he also seems to have acquired at Oxford a sound knowledge of law. He boldly criticises the legal methods of procedure with accused witches, and shows how melancholy and old age often cause women to incur the suspicion of sorcery. One feature of his book is its thoroughness. Witchcraft was involved in other forms of credulity; to believe in one manifestation of supernatural power was to admit all to be possible. So Scot explains the legerdemain which beguiled the simple; he detects the frauds and impostures of friars and priests who encouraged the belief in invisible spirits. Borrowing from the keen humour and intelligence of Erasmus, he exposes the tricks of alchemists, and discredits the practice of incantation and devil-conjuring by merely enumerating at full length the ludicrously elaborate charms then in use. With admirable skill he attributes the superstitions of witch-mongers to the influence of the Roman Catholic religion. He sums up the conclusions of his work in these words:

Witchcraft is in truth a cousening art, wherin the name of God is abused, prophaned and blasphemed, and his power attributed to a vile creature. In estimation of the Vulgar people it is a supernaturall worke, contrived betweene a Corporall old woman and a spirituall divell. The maner thereof is so secret, mysticall and strange, that to this daie there hath never beene any credible witnes thereof. It is incomprehensible to the wise, learned or faithfull, a probable matter to children, fooles, melancholike persons and papists.

But Scot's *Discoverie* produced no permanent effect on the beliefs of his time. The treatise is too diffuse and ill-constructed to be read with pleasure. Furthermore, science was not sufficiently advanced to substitute reason for superstition. Melanchthon's *Initia Doctrinae physicae* was based on a belief that the devil bore sway over natural phenomena. Paracelsus was infected with the same error; Reuchlin believed in witches. Cardanus contended that certain complaints and affections must be the result of magic and 'the workyng of cursed sciences,' since physic and chirurgery knew of no remedy. Scot, also, had the limitations of his contemporaries. He still believed in a 'naturall magicke' and he accepted many of the legends of classic lore, such as the belief that a certain river in Thrace makes white sheep produce black lambs, and a large number of folk-remedies, such as the belief that the bone of a carp's head staunches blood.

We have seen how prominent a part the middle classes played in forming the literature of the sixteenth century. While accepting the stories, satire and learning of the Middle Ages, they created a demand for English books that should reflect the tendencies of the present and embody the humour and wisdom of the past. One feature of their reading is its assimilation of French, Italian and German thought; another, its attractiveness for 'clerks' and 'gentlemen' as well as for 'the commons.' This popular literature was not obscured by the 'melodious bursts' of Elizabeth's reign. On the contrary, social and fugitive tracts continued to develop along the same lines till the Civil War. Satires on folly and domestic discord, character studies, jest-books, broadside ballads, beggar books, treatises on cosmography, the cultivation of health, universal knowledge and witchcraft continued to flourish throughout the Jacobean period, and the great work of exposing abuses was bequeathed to not incompetent hands. Nevertheless, a change in the temper of the people begins to be noticeable during the last twenty years of the sixteenth century. Puritanism, which had long made itself felt, now became prominent; national sentiment took possession of the people; the conceits of pseudo-classicism became an almost universal fashion; style preoccupied readers and writers; the essay was developed; the gulf between popular and court literature began to widen; above all, London grew into a centre—or, rather, a hotbed—of professional writers. These changes were felt at once in the people's literature. The tracts of Churchyard, Gilbert, Greene, Nashe, Gifford, Lodge, Chettle, Dekker, Thynne, Overbury, Jonson, Earle, Parrot, Wye Saltonstall, Breton, Brathwait, Peacham, Parker and Rowlands belong to a different era. Reginald Scot has been classed with Tudor writers because his work is a *résumé* of the thoughts of that time and his treatment has the rather clumsy earnestness of an earlier period. But the others mark a subsequent stage in popular English literature and are dealt with in later chapters of the present work.

CHAPTER VI

SIR DAVID LYNDSAY

AND THE LATER SCOTTISH 'MAKARIS'

ALTHOUGH Sir David Lyndsay, properly the last inheritor in Scotland of the Chaucerian tradition, was, evidently, well read in the great English master and his successors, and was influenced both in his poetic form and method by Dunbar and Douglas, his verse is informed by a spirit radically different from that of previous 'makaris.' Like Dunbar, he was largely a satirist; he was a satirist of the political, social and ecclesiastical corruptions of his age, just as Dunbar was of those of the previous age. But, in Lyndsay's time, the sentiment against social and ecclesiastical corruptions had become much stronger. It was rapidly becoming national; and its more absorbing character was ultimately to have a fatal effect on poetry. The character of Lyndsay's verse was symptomatic of the approach of a period of poetic decline. The artistic purpose is not so supreme in him as in Dunbar. He is less poetical and more didactic. While by no means so polished and trenchant, he is much more special and precise. The gilded coarseness of gentlewomen, the hypocrisy and worldliness of churchmen, the greedy covetousness of courtiers, were to Dunbar, according to his mood, subjects for bitter or humorous mirth. To his mirth, blended with humour, or wrath or contempt, he gave expression in biting and brilliant verse, without any very definite purpose beyond that of finding vent for his emotions and scope for his art. To Lyndsay, on the contrary, the definite purpose was almost everything; he was, primarily, less a poet than a political and social reformer; and he made use of the literary medium that would best achieve his moral purpose. Had he lived in modern times, he might have been either a prominent and successful statesman, or a brilliant writer on the burning questions of the hour; and, had the period of his literary activity fallen only a few years later than it did—when the advantages of the invention of printing were more utilised, and had begun to create a demand for vernacular prose—he might have indulged in admonitions, exhortations and blasts, somewhat after the manner of Knox: he had no mastery, like Buchanan, of either Latin verse or prose, even had his particular purpose not been better served by utilising different forms of vernacular verse.

Sometimes, like Douglas, Lyndsay employed allegory, and he, also, employed it for a moral purpose; but, unlike Douglas, he was not content to deal with the virtues and vices in the abstract, or merely in meditatively pictorial fashion; his primary aim was to point out, and hold up to scorn, the definite political, social and moral scandals of the time. In his early manhood he may have written a variety of verse with a merely artistic purpose, but the earliest of his poetical pieces which has come down to us is *The Dreme*, which internal evidence seems to show was written shortly after the escape of the young king, James V, from the tutorship of the Douglases in 1528. From the time of the birth of James V, in 1512, Lyndsay had been, as he records in the introductory *Epistil to the Kingis Grace*, the king's personal attendant—his sewer (arranger of his table), cupbearer, carver, treasurer, usher and cubicular. Being the king's chief companion in his more solitary hours, he had been accustomed to entertain him with all kinds of ancient tales; and, now that James had come to years of discretion, and had personally to undertake the responsibilities of government, Lyndsay proposed to show him 'a new story'—one of a different kind from any told to him before, and more suited to the graver character of his new circumstances. The poem was intended for the king's perusal, and thus the pill had to be gilded in order that it might be accepted. This accounts for the introductory display of the poet's accomplishments as a master of terms aureate, and for his resolve to make known his revelations in the elaborate allegorical fashion that was a poetic convention of the time.

The Dreme of Lyndsay may have been suggested by *The Dreme* of Dunbar; but it is about ten times as long, and it has nothing in common with it beyond the name and the description of a dream for its theme. Certain stanzas in Lyndsay's prologue are, however, very similar in manner and substance to some of the introductory stanzas of Dunbar's *The Thrissil and the Rois*, and, like the latter poem, it is written in the rime royal of Chaucer, all except the epilogue, which is in the nine-lined stave used by Dunbar in *The Goldyn Targe*, by Chaucer in *Anelida and*

Arcite and by Gavin Douglas in part of *The Palice of Honour.* The general form of Lyndsay's poem seems to have been suggested rather by *The Palice of Honour* than by any poem of Dunbar, who did not intermeddle with extended allegory. Like *The Palice of Honour*, it records an adventurous journey, but of a less purely imaginative or allegorical character, for Lyndsay is made to visit what he regards as actual realities—the lowest hell, purgatory, the seven planets, heaven and paradise. The character of the journey may have been suggested to him by Chaucer's *House of Fame*; but other-world scenes had, generally, much attraction for the imagination of medieval poets. This portion of the poem was, also, largely a conventional excrescence. It was chiefly introductory to his main theme. He was here intent partly on displaying his poetic paces with a view to arouse the literary interests of the king and secure his attention, partly on putting him in such a frame of mind as would induce him to give serious consideration to the succeeding exposure of the poverty, wrongs and miseries of his subjects.

As revealed to Lyndsay by Dame Remembrance, Scotland is described as possessing within itself all that is needful for the highest prosperity: abundant rivers and lochs for fish, many lusty vales for corn, fruitful hills and green meadows for the pasturage of sheep and cattle, forests swarming with deer and other animals of the chase, various rich metals and precious stones, and, if none of the finer fruits of the warmer climates, from which spices and wines are made, various sorts of fruit of a thoroughly good and wholesome kind. This description tallies with actual fact; in the Scotland of Lyndsay's time, there was an abundant supply of food for the limited number of its inhabitants. It possessed all the essential resources for comfort and prosperity, and it was inhabited, as Dame Remembrance points out, by a strong, ingenious and courageous people. Why, then, he asks, has there come to be such evident poverty, such great unhappiness, such a lack of virtuous well-doing? And the answer of Dame Remembrance is that the cause is lack of policy, lack of proper administration of justice and lack of peace. This is further revealed in detail by John the Commoun Weill, whose arrival as he is hastening to leave the country, and whose ragged costume, lean looks and dejected bearing are described with vivid picturesqueness. In reply to Lyndsay's query as to the cause of the miserable and poverty-stricken appearance of one whose life was exemplary, and whose aims high and honourable, John the Commoun Weill informs him of the banishment from the country of all his best friends, of the unrighteous triumph of his enemies and of his evil treatment in every part of the country where he sought refuge—the borders rampant with theft and murder and mischief; the highlands peopled by lazy sluggards; the islands and the western regions a prey to unthrift, laziness, falsehood and strife; and the more civilised portions of the lowlands, from which 'singular profit' (selfish greed), after doing him great injury and offence, expelled him with opprobrious epithets. He then proceeds to describe in detail, and with much terse vigour, the corruptions and inefficiency both of the civil and spiritual rule during the king's minority, and intimates his determination not again to give Scotland the comfort of his presence, until she is guided by the wisdom of 'ane gude and prudent Kyng.'

With the departure of John the Commoun Weill, the visions vouchsafed to the poet come to a close. He is brought again by Dame Remembrance to the cove where he had laid him down to sleep; and, after being awakened by the shot of a cannon from a ship in the offing, he proceeds to his home, where, after a good dinner, he sits himself down to record the events of his vision. To this record he finally appends an epilogue entitled *An Exhortation to the King*, which takes the form of shrewd advice, and serious and solemn warning.

The Complaynt—in the octosyllabic couplet, and of rather later date—records, in a brisk, mocking fashion, the methods adopted by the Douglases to enrich themselves at the king's expense, and to make him the passive instrument of their ambition; describes the generally scandalous condition both of church and state under their rule; and congratulates him on his escape from the clutches of such false friends, and on the marked improvement in social order and general well-being throughout the kingdom, except as regards the 'spiritualitie.' On the doings of the ecclesiastics he advises him to keep a watchful eye, and see that they preach with 'unfeyneit intentis,' use the sacraments as Christ intended and leave such vain traditions as superstitious pilgrimages and praying to images. Finally, Lyndsay—as poets were then accustomed to do—ventures to suggest that the king, now that his affairs were prosperous, might do worse than bestow on him some token of his regard, either by way of loan or gift. Should he be so good as to lend him one or two thousand pounds, then Lyndsay jocosely undertakes, with 'seelit obligations,' to promise repayment as soon as any of several equally unlikely things should come to pass: when kirkmen cease to crave dignities, or when wives no longer desire sovereignty over their husbands, or as soon as a winter happens without frost, snow, wind or rain; or he will repay him after the Day of Judgment; or, if none of these conditions please him, then he hopes that, out of his sovereign bounty, he will bestow on him some definite reward.

The humorous hint of Lyndsay was successful, for, shortly afterwards, in 1530, he was made Lyon King of Arms. His promotion did not, however, tend to silence his reformatory zeal, but, on the contrary, made him more anxious to do what he could to promote the success of the young king's sovereignty. In *The Testament and Complaynt of our Soverane Lordis Papyngo* (parrot) he exposed more particularly the corruptions and worldliness of the spirituality, and this in a more comprehensive and scathing fashion than in his two previous pieces, while the versification is, in parts, more elaborately polished. It opens with a prologue—in one of the nine-lined staves, *aab, aab, bcc,* used by Douglas in *The Palice of Honour*—in which, after a glowing and finely expressed tribute to his poetic predecessors from Chaucer, and various polite allusions to his poetic contemporaries, he affirms that even if he had 'ingyne' (genius), as he has none, the 'polleit terms' had been already pulled, and there was nothing left in all 'the garth of eloquence' but 'barren stok and stone.' For lack, therefore, both of a novel poetic theme and a novel poetic method, he had been reduced to record the complaint of a wounded papyngo.

In this ingenious and humorous apology he partly followed conventional models. Yet, in all likelihood, he was conscious of his own lack of high poetic inspiration, of his unworthiness to be named alongside of Chaucer and other English masters, or the 'aureate' Kennedy, or Dunbar, who 'language had at large,' or the more recent Gavin Douglas, whose death he laments, and whose translation of Vergil he specially celebrates; and his apology must also be taken as a kind of intimation that, in recording the complaint of the papyngo, he was influenced less by poetical ambition than by the desire to render service to the higher interests of his country.

The introductory stanzas of the poem dealing with the accident that befel the papyngo—which, with the remainder of the poem, are in rime royal—are modelled on the aureate methods of Chaucer and Dunbar, blended with the more profuse classical imagery of

Douglas. Of the animal fable, the chief exponent was, of course, Henryson, but, in the more modified form adopted by Lyndsay, it is made use of both by Chaucer and Dunbar. In the case of Dunbar, it is, in *The Thrissil and the Rois* and the *Petition of the Grey Horse*, utilised more indirectly and with more subtle art. Truth to tell, there is little or no art in Lyndsay's use of the expedient, so far as regards the counsel of the dying bird either to the king or to the 'brether of the courte.' In both cases, the voice is the voice of Lyndsay, without any attempt to disguise it. The counsel to the king—or the first epistle—consists of a series of plain and definite advices, couched, practically, in the language of prose, as how best to discharge his multifarious and difficult duties; and the second epistle gives a terse and striking summary of the great tragedies of Scottish history from the time of the duke of Rothesay, with a view to impress on the courtiers both the uncertainties of kingly favour, and the evil consequences of unscrupulous personal ambition. This second part concludes with the dying bird's touching words of farewell to the chief scenes of her former happiness: Edinburgh, the 'heych tryumphant toun,' fair 'Snawdoun' (Stirling) with its 'touris hie' and 'Falkland! the fortrace of Fyfe.'

In the concluding section of the poem, the fable form is much more strictly observed. Here, also, all is pure satire—much of it of a very clever and trenchant character, although some of the scenes are rather too prolonged. It relates the communing of the wise bird with its 'holy executors,' who appear in the form of a pyot (representing a canon regular), a raven (a black monk) and a ged or hawk (a holy friar). The disposition and aims of these ghostly counsellors are sufficiently manifest; and they act entirely in keeping with their reputed character. The poor parrot would have much preferred to have, at her death-bed, attendants of a less grovelling type of character, such as the nightingale, the jay, the mavis, the goldfinch, the lark, etc.; but, since none of them has come, she has to be content with the disreputable birds who have offered her their services. After a piquant discussion with them on the growth of ecclesiastical sensuality and greed, she thereupon proceeds to dispose of her personality—her 'galbarte of grene' to the owl, her eyes to the bat, her beak to the pelican, her music to the cuckoo, her 'toung rhetoricall' to the goose and her bones to the phoenix. Her heart she bequeaths to the king; and she leaves merely her entrails, including her liver and lungs, to her executors who, however, immediately on her death, proceed to devour her whole body, after which the ged flies away with her heart, pursued by the two other birds of prey.

The king, who practised verse, though no piece definitely known to be his has been preserved, had, it would appear, replied in a rather mocking and scurrilous fashion to certain of Lyndsay's hints as to his amatory inclinations; and to this Lyndsay wrote an *Answer* in rime royal, after the coarsely plain-spoken fashion of his time, which casts, directly and indirectly, a vivid light on the gross character of contemporary morals and manners. Another piece, meant as a satire on the king's courtiers, is *Ane Publict Confessioun of the Kingis auld Hound callit Bagsche*, written in the French octavo, and describing, in light, amusing fashion, the evil doings, and the consequent narrow escapes from condign punishment, of an inveterately wicked old hound, as related by the hound itself to the present pet dogs of the king, with the view of warning them to live a quieter, more exemplary and less spiteful life than had the old hound. Another satire, *Kitteis Confessioun*, written in couplets, records with bitter irony the unedifying particulars of a lady's interview with a priest on the occasion of her auricular confession. Here he deprecates the custom of minute and systematic confession as injurious rather than beneficial to the morals and the self-control of the supposed penitent. Confession, he thinks, should be made to a preacher only when the person is in dire distress or desperation and in need of special advice. A second satire, but much less serious in tone, on female folly, is *Ane Supplicatioun againis Syde Taillis*—in the octosyllabic couplet—a witty and amazingly coarse description of the various evils resulting from the inconvenient fashion of wearing long trains, which had infected not merely the ladies of the court, but women of all ranks and classes, including even nuns and female farm servants. *Ane Description of Pedder Coffeis*—in the octave of three rimes—deals with quite another phase of contemporary manners; it is a satirical account of the wiles of seven varieties of the peddling merchant, of which one is a lewd parish priest, and another an avaricious cathedral dignitary. Another satirical piece is *The Justing betwix James Watson and Johne Barbour*—in the heroic couplet—written for the entertainment of the king on the occasion of his marriage, in 1538, to Mary of Lorraine. Modelled on Dunbar's *Joustis of the Tailȝeour and the Sowtar*, it is quite good-natured and not so grotesquely extravagant as Dunbar's piece, although, at the conclusion, he borrows some of Dunbar's grossness.

But by far the most searching and scorching of Lyndsay's satires is, of course, the long and elaborate drama entitled *Ane Pleasant Satyre of the Thrie Estaitis in commendatioun of Vertew and Vituperatioun of Vyce.* Our information on the early history of the drama in Scotland is very scanty; but the lack of information does not imply a lack of plays. The absence of reference to morality and mystery plays in the High Treasurer's accounts may be explained by the fact that they were, primarily, popular amusements. On the other hand, such information as we possess regarding morality plays in Scotland in the fifteenth and sixteenth centuries seems to suggest that, while their character was analogous rather to the morality play of France than to that of England, they were a very common diversion. Adjoining the principal towns were playfields with elevations forming a kind of amphitheatre. The earliest play of which we have mention is one entitled *The Halyblude*, which was acted on the Windmill hill at Aberdeen, in 1445; and there is also mention of two others having been acted there in later years. More definite is the reference by Knox to 'a play againis the Papists' by friar Kyllour, performed before James V at Stirling, on Good Friday morning, 1535. 'Diverse comedies and tragedies,' by John Wedderburn, wherein 'he nipped the abuses and superstitions of the time,' were, also, played at Dundee, in 1540, among them *The History of Dionysius the Tyrant*, in the form of a comedy which was acted in the playfields. Neither Knox nor Calderwood conveys the slightest impression that performances of extended plays were uncommon; but they had no reason for alluding to other plays than those used for satirising the ecclesiastics. Later, in 1568, there is mention of a play by Robert Sempill, performed before the Lord Regent, and, a few years afterwards, Knox was present at the performance of a play, by John Davidson, one of the regents of St Andrews university, in which was represented the capture of Edinburgh Castle—then held for queen Mary—and the execution in effigy of its defenders. Further, an act of the kirk in 1575, for the censorship of 'comedies, tragedies and other profane plays,' is a sufficient indication of the popularity of the diversion. Nevertheless, Lyndsay's *Pleasant Satyre* is the only surviving example of a sixteenth century Scottish play, though an anonymous play entitled *Philotus* was published in 1603, and there is an early graphic fragment—probably by Dunbar—in the Bannatyne MS, entitled *The Interlude of the Droichis Part of the Play*[1].

[1] See vol. II of the present work, pp. 253, 255.

In his official capacity of Lyon King of Arms, Lyndsay, doubtless, acquired considerable dramatic experience, for he had the general superintendence of the pageantry and diversions on the occasion of royal fêtes, and, probably, devised the farces, masques and mummeries. Indeed, there is evidence that, at an earlier period of his life, he was accustomed to act in such entertainments or in more elaborate plays. *Ane Pleasant Satyre* is not the work of a dramatic novice. It is specially notable for its dramatic quality: it manifests a fine instinct for telling dramatic situations and dramatic contrasts and a complete comprehension of the method both of impressing and tickling a popular audience. In construction, in variety of dramatic interest, in vividness of presentation, in keenness of satire, in liveliness of wit—though the liveliness is apt to degenerate into grossness—and in what is termed stage 'business,' it is immensely superior to any contemporary English play. The nearest approach to it in dramatic development is Bale's *King John*, which is of later date—probably about 1548. Lyndsay's play was performed before James V at Linlithgow in 1540, and it may have been performed elsewhere at an earlier date. It was performed, at some unknown date, at Cupar-Fife, and, in 1554, at Greenside (at the foot of the Calton hill), Edinburgh. Not improbably, it was written at the instance of the king, who, about the same time, was encouraging Buchanan to satirise the Franciscans. Henry Charteris, the first publisher of Lyndsay's *Works*, could attribute Lyndsay's escape from persecution only to the special intervention and mercy of heaven; but it is to be remembered that Lyndsay did not, like Buchanan, direct his attacks against any special religious order, that he enjoyed the intimate friendship of the king and, it may be, of Mary of Lorraine as well, and that he was not a preacher, nor even a full-blown reformer. He was neither Calvinist nor puritan, and was less interested in disputes about doctrines and forms of church polity than in the social and political well-being of the people.

Ane Pleasant Satyre is a morality play, but it is also something more. It is a blend of secular and sacred drama, and embodies something of the French morality farce. It introduces real, as well as allegorical, personages, and it lightens the action of the play by comic devices borrowed from French models. In parts, it manifests the special characteristics of modern comedy. It inevitably does so by reason of the very specific character of its satirical representation of contemporary manners. Though hampered as a comedy by its morality conventions, it is a morality play of a very advanced type: a morality play aided in its dramatic action and relieved in its dramatic seriousness by a strong infusion of comedy, and by the intermixture of interludes of a strikingly realistic character. The strictly morality portions are superior to the morality plays of Bale; and the interludes are much more elaborate and finished specimens of comedy than the interludes of Heywood. Lyndsay's knowledge of the ways of the world and of the temper and characteristics of the crowd, and the minute character of his zeal as a reformer, were important elements contributing to his dramatic success. Neither in this nor in other satires was he content with generalities. His desire was to scourge the definite social evils of his time, and he had therefore to represent them in living form, as manifested in the speech, manner and bearing of individual persons.

For this reason, the play is of unique interest as a mirror of the Scotland of Lyndsay's time—when Catholicism was tottering to its fall. It is an excessively long play, its representation occupying a whole day, from nine in the morning until six in the evening; but its length enables the playwright to present a pretty comprehensive epitome of contemporary abuses and of contemporary manners and morals. The flagrant frailties of the ecclesiastics are portrayed with sufficient vividness in the speeches of representative types and in the amusing exposition of their relations with allegorical personages, good and bad; but it is in the tone of Lyndsay's wit, in the character of the horseplay by which he seeks to tickle his audience, in his method of pandering to their grosser tastes, in the farcical proceedings of such persons as the soutar, the tailor and their two wives, in the interviews between Pauper and Pardoner, in the dealings of Pardoner with the soutar and the soutar's wife and in the doings and speeches of Folly, that the peculiar social atmosphere of the time is most graphically revealed.

The play is divided into two parts, and part I, which represents the temptation of Rex Humanitas by Sensualitie, is divided into two acts, with an interlude between them. Sensualitie is introduced to the king by Wantonness, Placebo and Solace, in whose company he then passes to a private apartment, after which Gude Counsell makes his appearance. Gude Counsell declares his intention to 'repois sometime in this place,' but is immediately followed by Flatterie and Falset, who, shortly after they have congratulated each other on their happy meeting, are joined by their indispensable companion Dissait; whereupon, the three resolve to introduce themselves to the king under the guise respectively of Devotion, Sapience and Discretion. Shortly afterwards, the king returns to the stage and calls for Wantonness, who introduces him to the three vices; and, after a conversation with him in their feigned characters, in the course of which their proficiency in their several methods of guile is admirably indicated, he gives them welcome as 'three men of gude.' Here the king, observing Gude Counsell standing dejectedly at a distance, sends his new friends to bring him to his presence; but, when they discover who he is, they hustle him out of the place, threatening him with death should he dare to return. They then inform the king that the person he saw was a house-breaker whom they had ordered to be sent to the thieves' hole. Gude Counsell having been expelled, the king is now entirely in the hands of his evil companions, and sits down amongst the ladies, who sing to him a song, led by Sensualitie. Here Veritie makes her appearance carrying a New Testament, but is speedily followed by the Spiritualitie—including the abbot and the parson—who, at the instance of Flatterie, put Veritie in the stocks, after she had offered up an impressive prayer, beginning:

> Get up, thou sleepis all too long, O Lord!
> And mak sum ressonibill reformatioun.

Veritie being disposed of, Chastitie makes her appearance, whom, on her asking for 'harberie,' Diligence recommends to go to a 'prioress of renown,' sitting amongst the rest of the Spiritualitie. The prioress, however, asks her to keep her distance, the Spiritualitie tell her to pass on, for they know her not, and even Temporalitie informs her that, if his wives knew she were here, they would 'mak all this town on steir.' With the sorrowful departure of Chastitie from the company, act I ends. It is admirably conceived and written, the terseness and point of the satire being accentuated by the very skilful management of the dramatic situations.

Act I is followed by an interlude, relating the adventures of Chastitie after her expulsion from high society. On introducing herself to a tailor and soutar, she is cordially welcomed by these worthies; but, while they are entertaining her, their wives enter, and, after a boisterous scene, during which the wives set on their husbands in savage fashion both with tongue and hand, Chastitie is driven away; whereupon, after further 'dinging' of their 'gudemen,' the wives resolve to have a feast in celebration of their victory, the tailor's wife sitting down to make 'ane paist,' and the soutar's wife kilting up her clothes above her waist, that she may cross the river on her way to the town to fetch a quart of wine.

Diligence (the master of the ceremonies), who had found Chastitie wandering houseless, late at night, at the beginning of act II introduces her to the king; but, Sensualitie objecting to her presence, she is put in the stocks by the three disguised vices. She is, however, comforted by Veritie with the news that Divyne Correctioun is 'new landit,' and might be expected very soon. Hereupon, Correctioun's varlet (or messenger) enters, on hearing whose message Flatterie resolves to take refuge with the Spiritualitie or hide himself in some cloister. He therefore bids adieu to his two friends, who, before leaving, resolve to steal the king's box, but quarrel over the division of the spoil and Dissait runs away with the box through the water, just as Divyne Correctioun enters. At the instance of Correctioun, Gude Counsell and Veritie are set free from the stocks, and, accompanied by Veritie, Gude Counsell and Chastitie pass to the king. On the advice of Correctioun, the king then consents to the expulsion of Sensualitie, who, on seeking the protection of the Spiritualitie, is warmly welcomed by them as their 'dayis darling.' By further advice of Correctioun, the king then receives into his society Gude Counsell, Veritie and Chastitie; and, on their confessing their faults and promising to have no further dealings with Sensualitie, Correctioun also pardons Wantonness, Placebo and Solace. Then, after a speech by Gude Counsell, Diligence, by order of the king, warns all members of parliament, both the Spiritualitie and the Temporalitie, to appear speedily at court. He then intimates that the first part of the play is ended, and that there will be a short interval —which he recommends them to employ in refreshing themselves and in other ways not now mentioned in ordinary company.

Between the first part and the second there is an interlude, while the 'king, bishops and principal players are out of their places.' It introduces us to a pauper, who is really a small farmer reduced to poverty by ecclesiastical oppression, and on his way to St Andrews to seek redress. When Diligence endeavours to drive him away as 'ane vilde begger carle,' he climbs up to the king's chair and seeks to seat himself in it. With some difficulty Diligence succeeds in making him vacate it, but, struck by his sad and respectable demeanour, asks him where he comes from and what is his errand. Pauper then recites to him in moving terms the story of his wrongs at the hands of the ecclesiastics, who have brought him to utter poverty by their greedy extortions on the death of his father, his mother and his wife, which had successively occasioned him the loss of his mare and his three cows; while even the clothes of the deceased persons have been seized as perquisites by the vicar's clerk. After telling his pitiable story, Pauper, with the consent of Diligence, lays him down to rest; and there enters Pardoner, who, unchallenged by Diligence, proceeds to make a speech in which he rails at the 'wicket New Testament,' which has greatly injured his trade, and exposed the craft which he had been taught by a friar called Hypocrisy; bans Martin Luther, Black Bullinger and Melanchthon; and expresses the wish that Paul had never been born, or his books never read except by friars. Then, placing his wares on a board, he proceeds to dilate on their several merits, the picturesque recital being, on Lyndsay's part, a masterpiece of mocking irony, full of grotesque allusions admirably adapted to provoke the amused mirth of the rude crowd. The soutar, who, meanwhile, has entered and listened to the recital, now resolves to take advantage of Pardoner's arrival to obtain a dispensation for separation from his wife. While he is in conference with the holy man for this purpose, his wife appears, just in time to hear his very plain-spoken description of her character and doings; but, although furiously angry with him for libelling her as he has done, she, in answer to Pardoner's query, affirms that she is content with all her heart to be separated from him; and, thereupon, Pardoner, on condition that they perform a mutual ceremony too coarse for description, sends them away uncoupled, 'with Belial's best blessing.' Then, after an interview between Pardoner and his boy-servant Willikin, during which we obtain the information that village middens are the chief hunting grounds for Pardoner's holy relics, Pauper awakes from sleep. On Pauper handing to the holy man his solitary groat, Pardoner guarantees him in return a thousand years of pardons; but, since Pauper cannot see the pardons and has no evidence that he has obtained anything, he comes to the conclusion that he is merely being robbed; and the interlude ends with a grotesque encounter between the two, during which Pauper pitches both board and relics into the water.

Part II deals more specifically with the evils of the time than part I. The three estates, in response to the previous summons, now appear before the king; but they are shown us walking backwards, led by their vices—Spiritualitie by Covetousness and Sensualitie, Temporalitie (the Lords) by Publick Oppression and

Merchant (the representatives of the burghs) by Falset and Dissait. On Diligence, however, summoning all who are oppressed to come and make their complaint to the king, John the Commoun Weill makes his appearance, and, after a piquant conversation with the king, denounces the vices of the three estates in no measured terms, and requires that such scandalous persons should be put in the stocks, which, at the instance of Correctioun, is immediately done, Spiritualitie bidding Covetousness and Sensualitie a farewell, the sadness of which is mitigated by the hope of soon meeting them again. Then, at the instance of John the Commoun Weill, who delivers an impressive address on the abuses of the administration, the Temporal Estates repent of their conduct, promise amendment and embrace John the Commoun Weill. The Spiritualitie, however, not only remain impenitent, but impudently seek to represent their doings as in the highest degree exemplary; the abbot, the parson and the lady prioress, each in characteristic fashion, seeking to show that their violation of their vows, so far from being dishonourable, is rather to their credit than not, and that their sins of omission are really condoned by the character of what are usually deemed their sins of commission. This leads to a long debate, during which Pauper, and also the soutar, the tailor, a scribe and Common Thift, all add liveliness and point to the discussion. Then Common Thift—who had no other resource but to steal—is induced by Oppressioun to go into the stocks in Oppressioun's stead, on condition that Oppressioun will come again soon and relieve him; but Oppressioun slinks away from the scene, leaving Common Thift unsuccoured. Doctor, then, at the instance of Correctioun, mounts the pulpit, and delivers a sermon amid ill-mannered interruptions from the abbot and the parson. During its delivery, Diligence spies a friar whispering with the abbot, and, suspecting that he intends to 'set the town on steir' against the preacher, has him apprehended; and, on his being brought in by the sergeant and stripped of his habit, he is seen to be no other than Flatterie. The lady prioress is then spoiled of her habit, and, on being discovered to have been wearing under it a kirtle of silk, gives her malison to her parents for compelling her to be a nun, and not permitting her to marry. Flatterie is then put in the stocks, and the three prelates are stripped of their habits, which are put upon three sapient, cunning clerks. The prelates seek to find comfort from Covetousness and Sensualitie; but these former friends now renounce them, and they depart to earn an honest living in secular occupations. Thereafter, John the Commoun

Weill, clothed in gorgeous apparel, takes his place in the parliament, and, after acts have been passed for the reform of clamant abuses, the malefactors in the stocks are led to the gallows. Flatterie saves himself by undertaking the office of executioner; and with their characteristic last speeches and Flatterie's cynical self-congratulation, the drama proper is brought to a close.

This latter portion, which is a good deal longer and more complicated in its action than part I, is, at the same time, more diversely and elaborately clever. It is enlivened by a great variety of picturesque incidents, and the satire is so pointed and so topical, and the various *dénouements* are led up to with such admirable wit, that the audience must have been kept throughout in a high state of amused excitement, mingled with righteous expectation, and must, at the close, have been not less seriously impressed with the lessons of the play, than enthusiastic over its dramatic merits.

The play proper is followed, for the diversion of the multitude, by a farcical interlude, after the manner of the French monologues, a comic sermon being delivered by a buffoon dressed up as Follie, in which shrewd advice is mingled with an extremely coarse display of low wit.

If the glamour of poetry be absent from *The Pleasant Satyre*, its sententiousness and wit are occasionally varied by strains of lofty eloquence; and, if its moralising seems to us a little tedious and commonplace, it would have a different aspect to Lyndsay's contemporaries. Moreover, the more serious portions of the play are relieved by an unfailing flow of witty satire, which is all the more irresistible in that the special idiosyncrasy of each wicked or foolish character is revealed with admirable consistency, and that each is unconsciously made the exponent of his own wickedness or folly. Viewed as literature, the merit of the play is of a high order: the style is always clear, terse and pointed, even when neither witty nor eloquent. Though rather rough and careless in his rhythm, Lyndsay shows an easy command of rime as well as some skill in varying his metres to suit his subject. The dialogues are, for the most part, in an eight-lined stave in the rime *couée* used in early English plays, or in the octosyllabic couplet; but, for various recitals in character, he has recourse to a rimed alliterative stave used in several old romances, to the heroic couplet, to the French octave and the *kyrielle*; and to various forms of the six-lined stave in rime *couée*, including that which was a favourite of Burns.

The satirical *Tragedie of the Cardinal*, written shortly after the death of cardinal Beaton, and printed, probably, in 1547, a kind of parody of the lives in Boccaccio's *De Casibus Virorum Illustrium*, offers a detailed account of the cardinal's errors in conduct and policy, which his ghostly personality is supposed to relate as a warning to prelates and princes; but the dejection of the disembodied individuality seems to affect the poem, which is one of the least sprightly of Lyndsay's poetic efforts. Even so, however, it compares favourably with the long *Dialog betuix Experience and Ane Courteour*, which seems to have been suggested by Lyndsay's epitome. Opening with a discussion of the moral reasons for human suffering and misery, it includes an argument for the circulation of the Bible in the vernacular, an account of the creation of Adam and Eve, a prelection on man's first sin, an explanation and description of the Flood, an account of the rise and fall of the four great monarchies—which, according to the author, were the Assyrian, the Persian, the Grecian and the Roman—a reference to the first spiritual or papal monarchy with a description of the court of Rome and a dissertation on death, Anti-Christ and the general Judgment.

Only two other of Lyndsay's pieces remain to be mentioned, and they are of an entirely non-didactic nature: *The Deploratioun of the Death of Queen Magdalene* and *The Historie of the Squyer Meldrum*. The former, in rime royal, is modelled on the aureate method adopted by Dunbar in his more ceremonial pieces, but lacks the imposing musical melody of Dunbar's verse, and jolts along in a rather rough and uneven fashion. In couplets, Lyndsay was more at his ease, and in this medium he has related the varied and surprising adventures of a Fife neighbour, Squire William Meldrum, umwhile laird of Cleish and Binns, with unfailing spirit and with a point and graphic particularity that, to the modern reader, is sometimes a little disconcerting. Modelled after the *Squire's Tale* of Chaucer, Lyndsay's narrative, though in substance relating the actual experiences and achievements of Meldrum, reproduces them with a gloss which makes the poem assume the form of a kind of burlesque of the old romances. Apart from its special merits, it is of interest as revealing Lyndsay's enjoyment of mere merriment devoid of satire.

Of James V, Lyndsay's royal patron, no verses that can be authenticated survive; for he can as little be credited with the authorship of *Peblis* and *Christis Kirk*, as of *The Gaberlunzie Man* and *The Jolly Beggars.* For an account of Lyndsay's other poetic contemporaries and a summary of their individual merits we are indebted to Lyndsay's prologue to *The Complaynt of the Papyngo.*

Of the poetry of Sir James Inglis, whom he commends as without a superior 'in ballatis, farces and in plesant playis,' and who is credited by some with the authorship of *The Complaynt of Scotland,* no examples remain that are definitely known to be his. John Bellenden, the translator of Boethius and Livy, prefixed to his translations moral 'prohemiums' ornamented with classical allusions, and is also the author of 'a godly and lernit work callit *The Banner of Pietie,*' contained in the Bannatyne MS; but these specimens of his art far from justify Lyndsay's eulogy of him as 'ane plant of poetis.' To Kyd, the Bannatyne MS ascribes *The Richt Fontane of hailfull Sapience,* which may well enough have been the production of one who Lyndsay affirms was 'in cunnyng and practick rycht prudent,' for it is admirable rather as advice than as poetry. Stewarte, who, while Lyndsay wrote, was daily compiling 'full ornate werkis,' and who, in Rolland's *Seven Sages,* is referred to as a court poet, is represented in the Bannatyne MS by several pieces very much in the style of Dunbar, including a ribald *Flyting betwix the Sowtar and the Tailyour,* and an aureate love poem—in the French octave with refrain—*For to declare the hie Magnificence of Ladies*—which he does with more ardour than inspiration. Stewarte of Lorne, also referred to by Lyndsay, may possibly be the W. Stewarte whose name is attached in the Bannatyne MS to a short allegorical piece entitled *This Hinder Nycht neir by the Hour of Nine.* John Rolland, a Dalkeith notary who, about 1560, wrote *The Sevin Sages,* was also the author of a long and dull allegorical piece, entitled *The Court of Venus.* Among poetry of later date than 1530, in the Bannatyne MS, is *Gife Langour makis men licht,* attributed to lord Darnley, but, we must suppose, written by some unknown poet as an imaginary representation of Darnley's sentiments; a humorous love-song *O Gallandis All I cry and call,* signed 'Balnaves'; two love-songs, signed 'Fethy,' and, probably, the production of Sir John Futhy, a priest and organist, who is also credited, by the MS of Thomas Wode in Dublin university, with the authorship of a sacred song *O God abufe* set to music by himself, but of which no copy is known to survive; a song *Be Merry Brethren,* signed 'Fleming,' and consisting of a series of advices to husbands as to how to deal with unruly wives; a short humorous piece, *Brother Beware, I red you now,* attributed to Sir John Moffat, to whom another than Bannatyne attributes that humorous rural tale *The Wyf of Auchtirmuchty*; two love poems *The Lanterne of Lufe* and *Absent,* attributed to Steill, who is also the author of a romance in the Maitland MS, entitled *The Ring of the Roy Robert.* In quite a different vein is the lament of one Clapperton, in the Maitland MS, *In Bowdin on blak Monanday.* In the Bannatyne MS are three grossly witty ballads on notorious courtesans of the time, written by Robert Sempill, the author of powerfully satirical reformation broadsides, including *The Legend and Discourse of the life of the Tulchene Bischope of St Andrews.* Most of the verses of these and other decidedly more minor poets in the Bannatyne and Maitland MSS manifest considerable technical skill; but both in subject and manner they are largely imitative, and, though their wit is occasionally clever, they generally lack the distinctive qualities of poetry. Most of the anonymous verse in the Bannatyne and Maitland MSS, belongs, evidently, to an earlier period than that of Lyndsay and has been discussed in an earlier chapter of the present work; indeed, there is definite proof of early date in regard to many pieces, including some of the finest songs; but there are a few, such as *My Hart is quhyt,* which are probably of the time of Alexander Scott, if not even by Scott himself.

A satirical piece of about Lyndsay's time, and preserved by Knox in his *Historie of the reformatioun,* is the earl of Glencairn's *Epistle direct from the Holy hermit of Allarit to his Brethren the Gray Freiris*; and a later versifier, who manifests something of Lyndsay's spirit and method, though little of his vigour or skill, is William Lauder, afterwards minister of Forgandenny, who wrote in octosyllabic couplets *Ane Compendious and breve Tractate concernyng the office and dewtie of Kyngis, Spirituall Pastoris, and Temporall Jugis* (1556) and is the author of several minor poems of somewhat similar intent.

A social satirist of a much milder type than Lyndsay was Sir Richard Maitland, who was not very much Lyndsay's senior in years, though most of his verse was written after Lyndsay's death. A descendant of the Richard de Matelant who defended the family keep of Thirlestane against Edward I, and whose deeds were celebrated in ancient song and story, Maitland belonged to that class of Scottish gentry from which government and court officials were chiefly drawn, and held the office of judge from the time of James V until 1584. Having, about his sixtieth year, lost his sight, he, partly to divert his mind from the troubles of the time, partly to occupy the now duller hours of his leisure, devoted them, with the aid of his daughter, to literature; and, besides compiling *A Chronicle and Historie of the House and Surname of Seatone*, and composing a good many poetical pieces, he set himself to gather the collection of Scottish MS poetry, which, copied out by his daughter, is now preserved in the Pepysian library of Magdalene College, Cambridge. In his poetry, as well as otherwise, he is a survival of the ante-reformation period. As regards both the form and spirit of his verse, he is a disciple of Dunbar, though his satire lacks Dunbar's boisterous humour and keenness of wit, and his reflective pieces Dunbar's emotional pungency. He has nothing in common with Lyndsay; though quite alive to the evils of the old *régime*, he did not, while it existed, make them the object of his satire; nor, when the new *régime* was established, was he by any means persuaded of that *régime's* perfection. In *Quhair is the Blytheness that has been* he laments the decay of the old merry customs, and in his *Miseries of the Tyme* he bewails the lack of any real amendment either in church or state. Like his famous son, William the secretary, he was more an enlightened patriot and a shrewd man of the world than either an ecclesiastical or political partisan. The evils of internal dissension and strife are set forth by him in the poems *Of the Assemblie of the Congregation*, 1559, and *On the New Yeir*, 1560; and, at a later period, he advocated a reconciliation of the two parties in *Againis the Division of the Lordis*, *On Union among the Lordis*, *Againis Discord among the Lordis* and *Lament for the Disorders of the Cuntrie*. He brought to the consideration of social, political and religious questions much of the impartiality and practical worldly wisdom of the judge; and his satire is severest when he deals with social disorders or violations of the law, as in *The Satire of the Aige* and *Againis the Theivis of Liddisdaill*, the latter of which has something of the denunciatory rush of Dunbar's *Donald Owre*, on which it is modelled. In *The Satire of the Toun Ladeis*, an amusing recital of the extravagant caprices of contemporary female fashions, his tone is mainly that of half cynical, half good-humoured mockery, while his verses on the *Folye of Ane auld man maryand ane Young Woman*, are shrewdly sententious and mildly witty in the suggestive fashion characteristic of the time. The *Ballat of the Greatness of the World*, prompted, it may be, like Lyndsay's *Dialog*, by a perusal of the translation of the Scriptures, and written in the stave of *The Cherrie and the Slae*, indicates his acceptance of the conventional beliefs of his time; but the poem is a very uninspired performance; and much more of his real self appears in the half humorous, half melancholy musings of such pieces as *Na Kyndes without Siller*, *Gude Counseillis*, *Advyce to lesum Merynes* and *Solace of Aige.* Maitland was hardly a poet, nor is he of much account as a satirist; but his verse is of considerable interest as a record of the ingenuous sentiments of a highly accomplished and upright man, who, at this troubled and critical period of Scottish history, kept, in a manner, aloof from both parties.

Alexander Scott, almost the only lyrist, except such as are anonymous, of importance amongst the old Scottish poets, stands still more aloof in spirit than Maitland from the emotional and fervent zeal of the reformers. His poetry is entirely secular in theme and manner, with the exception of a translation of two psalms, the first and the fiftieth, which, though cleverly rimed, are both of them rather frigid and mechanical. Seeing Montgomerie refers to him, in 1584, as 'old Scott,' he was probably born not later than towards the close of the first quarter of the sixteenth century. If, again, his supposed *Lament of the Master of Erskine* be properly named, he most likely began to write not later than 1547, for the master, who is reported to have been the lover of the queen dowager, was slain at Pinkie in that year, and the poem is credited with embodying his imaginary farewell to her. *Of May* must, also, have been written before the act of parliament passed in 1555 against the old May celebrations; and, although the only other poem of his that can be dated is his *New Yeir Gift to Queen Mary*, 1562, none of his verses that has been preserved is of later date than 1568.

Of the thirty-six pieces of which Scott is known to be the author, thirty are of an amatory character, and the majority of them seem to have been greatly influenced in style and spirit by the love lyrics in *Tottel's Miscellany*, 1557, whether Scott had an acquaintance with such pieces before they were published or not. To Scott's verse there thus attaches a certain special interest, as suggesting the possibility of a new school of Scottish poetry, which, while retaining certain northern characteristics, would gradually become more and more assimilated to the English school; but this possibility had already been made futile by the triumph of a puritanic reformation. Scott was a creation of the ante-reformation period; and, although his themes and his method of treatment are partly suggested by the lyrical school of England, he may still be regarded as, primarily, the pupil of Dunbar. The influence of the English school is modified by characteristics that are distinctly Scottish. While the *Miscellany* seems to have suggested to him the appropriateness of short staves for certain forms of the love lyric, he was not content to confine himself to the staves that were there represented; as a metrist he belongs properly to the school of the old Scottish 'makaris.' Besides utilising several of Dunbar's staves he had recourse to a variety of earlier staves in rime *couée*; and in the use of these medieval forms he shows a consummate mastery. His distinct poetic gift is shown in the facility, the grace and the musical melody of his verse, and his power of mirroring sentiment and emotion in sound and rhythm; and there are also qualities in the tone and spirit of his verse that individualise it and distinguish it from the lyrical school of England. It is not so much imitative, as representative of his own characteristic personality. He is terser, more pungent, more aphoristic than the English lyrists. In most of his lyrics, the emotional note vibrates more strongly—in the utterance of joy, as in *Up Helsum Hairt*; in the expression of sorrowful resignation, as in *The Lament of the Master of Erskine*, and *Oppressit Hairt Indure*; or in the record of his amatory experiences, as in *Lo Quhat it is to Lufe*; and it may further be added that when, as in the *Ballad maid to the Derisioun and Scorne of Wantoun Wemen*, he is indecorous, he evinces a grossness that his English contemporaries cannot rival. Apart from his lyrics and his translation of two psalms, the only other pieces of Scott are *The New Yeir Gift*, and *The Justing and Debait*. In the former, after complimenting the queen in the aureate fashion of Dunbar, he devotes himself to a recital of the social evils of the time, more after the manner of Maitland than of Lyndsay; and he concludes with an envoy in which he gives an elaborate display of his accomplishments in alliteration and internal rime. *The Justing and Debait*, written in the *Christis Kirk* stave, is a mock tournament piece after the fashion of Dunbar's *Turnament* and Lyndsay's *Justing*, but less an uproarious burlesque than a lightly witty narrative.

Alexander Montgomerie, the last of the Scottish 'makaris,' probably held some office at the court of James VI, and, most likely, was the king's chief instructor in the art of verse. He has a good deal in common with Scott, of whom he may be reckoned a kind of disciple. His temperament was, however, less poetical; he lacked Scott's geniality as well as artistic grace; he was more varied and voluminous; he was a still greater, if a less successful, experimenter in curious metres, and, as might be supposed from his later date, he was, in some respects, still more influenced by the English school. Still, like Scott, as a metrist, he belongs to the Scottish school, the metres which he invents being merely modified reconstructions and combinations of the old ones, while what staves, as the 'ballade,' he borrows from the English lyric school, have a certain similarity to the old staves, the only difference in the 'ballade' stave being the modern lilt of the double refrain. Even in the sonnet, of which he left no fewer than seventy examples, he has a certain non-English individuality; for while, in some instances, he adopted the sonnet forms of *Tottel's Miscellany*, he also translated several of Ronsard's sonnets in the Ronsard form, and wrote a Ronsard variation. Further, his connection with the old Scottish school is seen in his use of the old rimed alliterative stave of the romances in *Ane Answer to ane Helandmanis Invective* and in the *Flyting* between him and Sir Patrick Hume of Polwarth.

The most popular of Montgomerie's pieces was, apparently, *The Cherrie and the Slae*; but its popularity had only an indirect connection with its poetic merits. These are not remarkable and are not superior to those of *The Bankis of Helicon*, which is in the same measure. But, in *The Cherrie and the Slae*, Montgomerie does not, as in *The Bankis of Helicon*, have recourse to aureate terms or classical imagery. Though somewhat dull and archaic as an allegory, the piece as regards its language is perfectly simple and unaffected; in the descriptions of nature there are no attempts at meretricious ornaments; they represent the fresh and quite unsophisticated pleasure and admiration of the average person; while the general drift of the poem is obscure, it is pervaded by the maxims of that homely and commonplace philosophy, of the repetition of which the average uneducated person never tires; and, finally, the quatorzain in which the piece is written, was, with the peculiar jingle of its wheels, well adapted to catch the popular ear, although the full capabilities of the stave were only revealed by Burns in the recitativos of *The Jolly Beggars*. As a very varied metrist in what James VI termed 'cuttit and broken verse,' Montgomerie showed both remarkable ingenuity and a good musical ear; but he was not a poetic melodist—partly from his despondent views of life and deficiency in animal spirits, his verses are, for the most part, lacking in poetic flow. His reflective pieces are too lowspirited to be effective; his amatory verse is not animated by much lyrical fervour; and his religious pieces and versions of psalms, sometimes written to special tunes, while characterised by apt phrasing and considerable metrical felicity, do not manifest much fervour or depth of conviction. Yet *The Night is near Gone* has the true accent of poetry, and, in several other pieces, he has poetic moments.

With Montgomerie, the school of the old 'makaris' properly ends. While James VI, who, in 1585, published *Essayes of a Prentise*, and, in 1591, *Poeticall Exercises*, remained in Scotland, poetry was practised by a few poets under his immediate patronage. William Fowler translated *The Triumphs of Petrarch*, and Stewart of Baldines presented the king with *Ane Abbregement of Roland Furious translated out of Aroist*; but both works are preserved only in manuscript, the one in the Edinburgh university library and the other in the Advocates' library. In 1590, John Burel wrote a *Descriptioun* of the queen's entry into Edinburgh, and an allegorical piece *The Passage of the Pilgrim*, but neither has much merit. Poetry, except of a religious kind, now came under taboo, and the religious verse was of a very mediocre character. Alexander Arbuthnot, principal of Aberdeen university, amused his leisure hours by cultivating the secular muse, but, as he relates, in secret, and with fear and trembling, lest 'with rascal rymours I sall raknit be.' On the other hand, Alexander Hume, minister of Logie and younger brother of the Hume of Montgomerie's *Flyting*, sought to substitute 'for prophane sonnets and vain ballads of love' a series of *Hymns and Sacred Songs*, in which are discernible an assimilation in form of Scottish to English verse, and, equally so, the fatal decay in Scotland of poetic inspiration. In the succeeding century, the writing of verse, mostly in the English language and form, was practised by certain of the Scottish gentry; but, as regards the bulk of the people, secular poetry remained for nearly two centuries under an ecclesiastical ban.

CHAPTER VII

REFORMATION AND RENASCENCE IN SCOTLAND

In the year 1528, three events occurred in Scotland, which, as the near future was to prove, were fraught with pregnant consequences alike for the state and for the national religion and national literature. In that year, James V, after a long tutelage, became master of his kingdom; Patrick Hamilton, the "protomartyr" of the Scottish reformation, was burnt; and Sir David Lyndsay published his first work, *The Dreme.* Taken together, these three events point to the fact that Scotland was entering on a new phase of her national life, and at the same time indicate the character of the coming revolution. From the transformation thus to be wrought in the national aims and ideals the chief Scottish literature of the period received its distinctive stamp, and we have but to recall its representative productions—those of the anonymous authors of *The Gude and Godlie Ballatis*, of John Knox and of George Buchanan—to realise the gulf that separates it from the period immediately preceding.

From James I to Gavin Douglas, Scottish literature had been mainly imitative, borrowing its spirit, its models and its themes from Chaucer and other sources. The characteristic aim of this literature had, on the whole, been pleasure and amusement; and, if it touched on evils in the state, in the church or in society, it had no direct and conscious purpose of assailing the institutions under which the nation had lived since the beginning of the Middle Ages. Totally different were the character and aim of the representative literature of the period which may be dated from the publication of Lyndsay's *Dreme* in 1528 to the union of the crowns in 1603. The literature of this period was in the closest touch with the national life, and was the direct expression of the convictions and passions of that section of the nation which was eventually to control its destinies and to inform the national spirit. Not pleasure or amusement but strenuous purpose directed to practical results was the motive and note of this later period; its aim was to reach the heart of the people, and the forms which it assumed were exclusively determined by the consideration of this end.

Between the years 1520 and 1530, there were already indications that a crisis was approaching in the national history which would involve a fundamental change in traditional modes of thought on all the great questions concerning human life. The problem which the nation had to face was whether it would abide by its ancient religion or adopt the teaching of Luther, the writings of whose followers were finding their way into the country at every convenient port. But this question involved another of almost equally far reaching importance—was France or England to be Scotland's future ally? Should the old alliance with France be maintained, the country must hold fast to existing institutions; there would be no change of religion and no essential change in hereditary habits of thought and sentiment. Throughout the period now opening, these were the great issues that preoccupied the nation, and it was from the conflict between them that the most important literary productions of the age received their impulse, their tone and their characteristic forms.

The literature produced under these conditions was essentially a reformation literature, and its relation to the movement of the reformation is its predominating characteristic. Nevertheless, though Scotland received her most powerful impulse from the reformation, the renascence did not leave her wholly untouched, though conditions peculiar to herself prevented her from deriving the full benefit of that movement. Her scanty population and her limited resources were in themselves impediments to the expansion of the spirit which was the main result of the revival of learning. The total population of Scotland in the sixteenth century cannot have been much over 500,000, of whom only about half used a Teutonic form of speech. Out of such a total there could be but a small proportion who, by natural aptitude and by fortunate circumstances, were in a position to profit by the new current that was quickening the other nations of western Europe. The poverty of the country, due to the nature of the soil rather than to any lack of strenuousness on the part of its people, equally hindered the development of a rich and various national life. Scotland now possessed three universities; but to equip these in accordance with the new ideals of the time was beyond her resources, and the same difficulty stood in the way of maintaining great schools such as the renascence had originated in other countries. Finally, the renascence was checked in Scotland, more than in any other country, by the special conditions under which the reformation was here accomplished. From the beginning to the end of the struggle, the Scottish reformers had to contend against the consistent opposition of the crown, and it was only as the result of civil war that the victory of their cause was at length assured. Thus, at the period when the renascence was in full tide, Scotland was spending her energies in a contest which absorbed the best minds of the country; and a variety of causes debarred her from an adequate participation in that humanism which, in other countries, was widening the scope of thought and action, and enriching literature with new forms and new ideas. Nevertheless, though the renascence failed in any marked degree to affect the general national life, it found, both in literature and in action, distinguished representatives who had fully imbibed its spirit.

It is from the preaching of Patrick Hamilton in 1527, followed by his execution in 1528, that Knox dates the beginning of the reformation in Scotland; and it is a production of Hamilton, *Patrikes Places*, that he adduces as the first specimen of its literature. 'Literature,' however, this document can hardly be called, as it is merely a brief and bald statement of the Lutheran doctrine of justification by faith, originally written in Latin, and translated into Scoto-English by John Frith. Associated with Hamilton in the beginnings of the Scottish reformation is a more voluminous writer, Alexander Alane (for this and not *Aless* was his real name, as appears from the registers of the university of St Andrews), but better known by his Latin designation, Alesius. Born in Edinburgh in 1500, Alesius was trained for the church in the university of St Andrews. In an attempt to convince Hamilton of the error of his ways, he was shaken in his own faith, and suspicions soon arose regarding his own orthodoxy. A Latin oration delivered against the vices of the clergy left no room for doubt regarding his religious sympathies, and he was thrown into prison, whence, with the aid of friends, he escaped to the continent (1532). Alesius never returned to Scotland, but, both in England and Germany, he played an important part in forwarding the cause of the reformation. He is the author of at least twenty-eight works, all written in Latin, partly consisting of commentaries on Scripture, but mainly of tracts and treatises on the theological controversies of the time. Of his controversial writings, three have special reference to religious opinion in Scotland—*Epistola contra Decretum quoddam Episcoporum in Scotia, quod prohibet legere Novi Testamenti Libros lingua vernacula* (1533); *Responsio ad Cochlaei Calumnias* (1533); and *Cohortatio ad Concordiam* (1544). The question discussed in all these productions is the liberty of reading the Scriptures in the original—a liberty which was first granted by the Scottish parliament in 1543, and to which Alesius may have materially contributed. To Alesius, also, we owe the earliest known description of his native city of Edinburgh, which he contributed to the *Cosmographia* of Sebastian Münster (1550).

More interesting for the literary history of the period is Knox's mention of Kyllour's play, *The History of Christ's Passion*, to which reference has already been made[1]. Of Kyllour and his play we know nothing beyond the casual reference of Knox. It is matter for greater regret that two plays, mentioned by the church historian, Calderwood, have not come down to us. The subjects of the two plays point to the preoccupations of the age—the one being a tragedy on John the Baptist, a favourite handle for satirical attacks on the evils of church and state, and the other a comedy on Dionysius the Tyrant. Scanty as these references are, they lead to the conclusion that dramatic representations furnished the means by which the champions of the new religion first sought to communicate their teaching to the people. But scenic displays were not the most effectual vehicles for spreading their tenets throughout the nation; only a comparatively small public could be reached by them, and the state had it always in its power to prohibit them, when they overstepped the limits prescribed by the law. Another form of literature, therefore, was required, at once less overt and of wider appeal, if the new teaching was to reach the masses of the people; and such a vehicle was now to be found.

It was about the year 1546 that there appeared a little volume which, after the Bible itself, did more for the spread of reformation doctrines than any other book published in Scotland. As no copy of this edition has been preserved, we can only conjecture its contents from the first edition of which we possess a specimen—that of 1567, apparently an enlarged edition of the original. The book generally known in Scotland as *The Gude and Godlie Ballatis* is, next to Knox's *Historie of the reformatioun*, the most memorable literary monument of the period in vernacular Scots. The chief share in the production of this volume, also known as *The Dundee Book*, may, almost with certainty, be assigned to three brothers, James, John and Robert Wedderburn, sons of a rich

[1] See *ante*, p. 122.

Dundee merchant, all of whom had studied at the university of St Andrews, and were for a time exiled for their attachment to the reformed doctrines. Besides a metrical translation of the *Psalms*, the book contained a number of *Spirituall Sangis* and *Plesand Ballatis*, the object of which was to convey instruction in points of faith, to stimulate devotion and to stigmatise the iniquities and errors of the Roman church. Of both songs and ballads, fully one half are more or less close translations from the popular German productions which had their origin in the Lutheran movement. But the most remarkable pieces in the book are those which adapt current secular songs and ballads to spiritual uses, appropriating the airs, measures, initial lines or choruses of the originals. This consecration of profane effusions was not unknown in the medieval church, and for the immediate object in view a more effective literary form could not have been devised. At a time when books were dear and were, in general, little read, these *Godly Ballads*, set to popular tunes, served at once the purpose of a pamphlet and a sermon, conveying instruction, while, at the same time, they roused to battle. What amazes the reader of the present day in these compositions is the grotesque blending of religion with all the coarseness and scurrility of the age. Yet this incongruity is only a proof of the intense conviction of their authors: in the message they had to proclaim they believed there was an effectual safeguard against all evil consequences, and that in the contrast between the flesh and the spirit the truth would only be made more manifest. Moreover, there is an accent and a strain in the *Ballads* which is not to be found in Lyndsay even in his highest mood. Even when he is most in earnest, Lyndsay never passes beyond the zeal of the social reformer. In the *Ballads*, on the other hand, there is often present a yearning pathos as of soul speaking to soul, which transmutes and purifies their coarsest elements, and transfuses the whole with a spiritual rapture. And the influence that the *Ballads* exercised—mainly on the inhabitants of the towns, which almost universally declared for the reformation—proves that the writers had not misjudged their readers. For fully half a century, though unsanctioned by ecclesiastical authority, the *Ballads* held their place as the spiritual songs of the reformation church.

To the year 1548 belongs the first production of John Knox who was to be at once the chief leader of the Scottish reformation and its chief literary exponent. The work is entitled ***An Epistle to the Congregation of the Castle of St***

Andrews: with a Brief Summary of Balnaves on Justification by Faith, and, as its author informs us, was written in Rouen, while he was 'lying in irons and sore troubled by corporall infirmitie, in a galley named Nostre Dame.' Like all the other works of Knox, it was prompted by an immediate occasion and was directed to an immediate practical purpose. So closely linked, indeed, are the six volumes of his writings to his public career, that they are virtually its running commentary. From first to last his one concern was to secure the triumph of reformation doctrine, as he conceived it, and it would be difficult to find a sentence in his writings which does not bear more or less directly on this object. To all secular interests, except so far as they touched religion, he displays the indifference of an apostle; though, like the reformers of every type, he had a profound conviction, as his action was notably to prove, that education was the true handmaid of piety. His eulogy on his countryman, the humanist George Buchanan, shows that a *pietas literata* was no less his ideal than it was that of Melanchthon. 'That notable man Mr George Buchanan,' he writes, 'remains to this day, the year of God, 1566 years, to the glory of God, to the great honour of the nation and to the comfort of them that delight in letters and virtue.' A religion based on the Bible, as he understood it, and a national system of education which should provide for every grade of study and utilise every special gift for the general well-being—such were the aims of Knox's public action and the burden of his testimony in literature.

With one great exception, no productions of Knox possess more than a historical interest as the expression of his own mind and temper and of the type of religion of which he was the unflinching exponent. Mainly controversial in character, neither by their literary quality nor by their substance were they found of permanent value even by those to whom they made special appeal. The long list of his writings, which had begun with *The Epistle on Justification,* was continued in England, where, for five years, we find him acting as an officially commissioned preacher of the reformation as it was sanctioned by the government of Edward VI. The titles of the pieces which he threw off during this period sufficiently indicate their nature and scope: *A Vindication of the Doctrine that the Sacrifice of the Mass is Idolatry* (1550), *A Summary according to the Holy Scriptures of the Sacrament of the Lord's Supper* (1550), *A Declaration of the True Nature and Object of Prayer* (1553) and *The Exposition upon the Sixth*

Psalm of David (1554). The accession of Mary Tudor in July, 1553, made England an impossible place for protestants like Knox, and his next five years, with the exception of a brief visit to Scotland, were spent on the continent, mainly in Geneva, where Calvin had already established his supremacy.

Knox's exile on the continent gave occasion to another series of productions, all prompted by some pressing question of the moment. The protestants in England had to be comforted and encouraged during their trying experiences under the government of Mary Tudor, and this end he sought to accomplish in his *Two comfortable Epistles to his afflicted Brethren in England* (1554) and in his *Faithful Admonition to the Professors of God's Truth in England* (1554)—the latter of which, however, by its ill-timed attack on the existing authorities in England, did not improve the position of those for whose good it was intended. In 1554, Knox was appointed to the charge of a congregation of English exiles in Frankfort-on-the-Main, but, within a year, there arose such a storm of controversy on points of doctrine and ceremonies that he was fain to demit his charge and retire to Geneva. In his *Narrative of the Proceedings and Troubles of the English Congregation at Frankfurt on the Maine*, 1554—5, Knox gave his story of the controversy, the historical interest of which is that out of it grew the two parties which were eventually to divide the Church of England—the party of puritanism (of which Knox is to be regarded as one of the chief founders), and the party which accepted Elizabeth's policy of compromise.

The condition of the protestants in Scotland under the regency of Mary of Lorraine evoked another series of long epistles, the burden of which was an arraignment of the policy of the government and an exhortation to the faithful to look confidently forward to a day fast coming when the true religion would prevail. From 1555 to 1559, with the exception of a visit to Scotland during part of the years 1555 and 1556, Knox made his home in Geneva, where he acted, for a time, as co-pastor to a congregation of English exiles, more in harmony with his own opinions than that of Frankfort. His passionate desire, however, was to preach his gospel in England and Scotland, but this desire he saw thwarted by the two female rulers who now governed these countries. It was out of the indignation of his baffled hopes, therefore, that, in 1558, he published his *First Blast of the Trumpet against the Monstruous Regiment of Women*, which of all his works had the widest notoriety in his own day. From the classical writers, the

Roman law, the Bible and the Fathers, he supports the argument for which he vehemently contends—that 'to promote a Woman to beare rule, superioritie, dominion, or empire above any Realme, Nation or Citie is repugnant to nature, contumelie to God, a thing most contrarious to his reveled will and approved ordinance.' In his main contention, Knox was at one with the most influential writers of the sixteenth century, Jean Bodin among others, but, even by divines of his own way of thinking, his pamphlet was generally regarded as a hasty and ill-considered performance. In 1559, it was answered by John Aylmer, one of the Marian exiles, subsequently bishop of London, in his *Harborowe for Faithfull and Trewe Subjectes agaynst the late blowne Blaste concerning the Government of Women*, in which the most effective point made is that, as a limited monarchy, England is specially guarded from the drawbacks incident to female sovereignty. But the course of public events proved to be the most stringent commentary on the contention of the *Blast*. At the close of the very year of its publication Mary Tudor died and the protestant Elizabeth succeeded to the throne of England—an event which Knox was bound to recognise as the happiest dispensation for the welfare of his own cause.

While still in Geneva, Knox produced another work, of less resounding notoriety than the *Blast*, but a more solid and careful performance. This was his *Answer to a great Nomber of blasphemous cavillations written by an Anabaptist and adversarie to God's eternal Predestination*. Like all his more important works, it was prompted by the circumstances of the moment. The dogma of predestination was the foundation of the theological system of Calvin, to whom Knox looked as his spiritual father, but the doctrine had been impugned by many, and notably by Sebastian Castalio, who had been expelled from Geneva for the general heterodoxy of his opinions. From the protestants in England, also, there came a request to their brethren in Geneva that they would prepare a reply to a book which had recently been written against the same dogma, and to Knox was assigned the task. The result was his lengthy treatise on predestination which fills one volume of the six that comprise his published works. It is Knox's most elaborate effort in constructive theology, but, strenuous and dexterous though he is in meeting the arguments of his adversary, he possessed neither the self-control nor the systematising genius which made his master, Calvin, the lawgiver of reformed doctrine. It is to Calvin's *Institutes of the*

Christian Religion, and not to Knox's treatise, that the followers of both must have recourse for the magistral statement of the constitutive dogma of their theological system.

The triumph of the reforming party in Scotland in 1559 at length restored Knox to his native country, where his presence was to be the dominating fact in the political and religious situation, and where he was to produce the work which is the great literary monument of the time. As the immediate result of the victory of protestantism, appeared the *First Book of Discipline*, of which Knox was not, indeed, the sole author, but which bears his imprint on every page, and is the brief summary of his ideals in religion and education. Here, as directly connected with the literary history of Scotland, we are only concerned with the scheme of national instruction which the book sets forth with detailed precision. In every parish there was to be a school and in every important town a college, from which the aptest scholars were to be sent to the three universities—attendance in all three grades being exacted by state and church. The poverty of the country and protracted civil commotions prevented the scheme from being realised; but an ideal had been set forth which never passed out of sight, and, during successive centuries, the parish schools of Scotland were the nursing-homes of her most vigorous intellectual life.

Like all his other works, Knox's *Historie of the reformatioun in Scotland* was suggested by an immediate occasion and was written to serve a special purpose. Its express aim was to justify the proceedings of the protestant leaders who had been the chief instruments in overthrowing the ancient religion, and it was at their desire that he undertook the task. His book, therefore, is essentially that of an apologist and not of a historian; and he makes no disguise of the fact. That right and justice were all on one side and that those who opposed the reformation were blinded either by folly or iniquity, is his unflinching contention from the first sentence to the last. So transparent is this assumption, however, that it hardly misleads the reader; and through what he may consider the perversion of characters and events he cannot fail to discern their salient and essential traits. Thus, in the most remarkable parts of Knox's book, his interviews with queen Mary, the weak points in his own cause and in his own personal character are as manifest as those of his adversary. The *History* consists of five books, the last of which, however, is so inferior in vigour to the others that its materials must have been put together by another hand. It is in the first book, which traces the beginning and progress of the reformation in Scotland, that Knox displays his most striking gifts as a writer—such passages as those describing the rout of Solway Moss, the mission and death of George Wishart and the battle of Pinkie being the nearest anticipation of Carlyle to be found in English literature. In the second and third books, we have one of the earliest examples of an appeal to historical documents as vouchers for the truth of the narrative: fully three-fourths of these books consisting of papers supplied by the leaders of the reformation in Scotland and England. But it is the fourth book that has made the most vivid impression on the national memory, and may be said to have created the prevalent conception of the Scottish reformation. The theme of this book is the return of Mary to Scotland, and the compromise that followed between her and the reforming leaders. Here we have the reports of the dramatic interviews between Mary and Knox, and of his fulminations from the pulpit in the church of St Giles, and here, also, those characterisations of Mary and other leading personages which are written for all time. What Sainte-Beuve said of the *Memoirs* of Saint-Simon may be said with even greater truth of Knox's *History*: the periods before and after that which he describes are dim and obscure by comparison. And it is a further tribute to the literary interest and importance of the book, that it is the first original work in prose which Scotland had yet produced. There had been translations and compilations in prose, but there had not, as yet, been any work which bore the stamp of individual genius and which might serve as a model for Knox's undertaking. In this fact, and in his long residence in England and association with Englishmen abroad, we have the explanation of the diction—the anglicised Scots—which was made a reproach to him by his Catholic adversaries.

Knox's *History* is the chief literary monument of the Scottish reformation; but to the same period belong a number of works, more or less of a historical character, which prove that prose had now become an accredited vehicle of expression as well as verse. Next in literary quality to the work of Knox is *The Historie and Cronicles of Scotland* by Robert Lindesay of Pitscottie—one of the few productions of the time which can be read with interest at the present day. Lindesay was an ardent protestant, and, in the parts of his *History* where he deals with the change of the national religion, he is a thoroughgoing partisan. With religion, however, he is not primarily concerned, and his aim is not controversial like that of Knox. What mainly interested him in the past were picturesque episodes illustrating the manners of the times and the characters of the leading actors; and it is to him that we owe some of the most lively pictures in the national history. As his easy credulity as well as the structure of his book shows, Lindesay had no very severe criterion of historic accuracy. His account of the reign of James II (1436—60), with which his *History* begins, is merely a translation of Hector Boece's Latin *History of Scotland*—a work of inventive imagination in which the wildest fables are recorded as ascertained facts. From 1542 onwards, he drew upon his own observation or on the testimony of eye-witnesses; but it is precisely in this portion of his work that he exhibits in least degree that gift of vivid narrative which made him the delight of Sir Walter Scott as the nearest approach to a Scottish Froissart.

Of a different order is the work of Sir James Melville of Halhill, who, first as page to queen Mary and, afterwards, as her ambassador, played a subordinate part in the transactions of his time. His *Memoirs*, in which he records his own observations of what he had seen and heard in the course of his public life, still retain their value as one of the historical sources for the period. Though a protestant in religion, he possessed the confidence of Mary; and his sympathies are with her and not with her rival, Elizabeth. Melville's point of view is that of the courtier and the diplomatist, and in his decorous and sober pages there is little indication of the seething passions of the time. In the *Memorials of Transactions in Scotland* (1569—73) of Richard Bannatyne, Knox's secretary, we have another example of the stimulus given to historical narrative by the events of the reformation. In the form of a diary, Bannatyne records the events that he saw passing before his eyes in those momentous years when the victory of protestantism was definitely assured by the surrender of Edinburgh Castle by the last champions of Mary. But the most memorable passages in the book are those which record the last days of his master, from whose hand there are some entries written in the most vigorous style of his *History*. Another example of the general interest in contemporary events is the *Diary of Mr James Melville, Minister of Kilrenny in Fife* (1566—1601). Of the nature of an autobiography rather than of a diary, this is one of the most delightful books of the kind in the language. In the author himself, we have the most attractive type of the Presbyterian pastor, and his account of his home life and of his education at school and university is of high value as a picture of the life of the time. As a specimen of the Scottish language of the period, and as one of the best known passages in early Scottish literature, his description of Knox preaching at St Andrews in his last days may hardly be passed over:

I saw him everie day go hulie and fear (slowly and warily) with a furring of martricks (martens) about his neck, a staff in the an hand, and guid godly Richart Ballanden [Bannatyne] his servand, holdin upe the other oxter (arm-pit) from the Abbaye to the paroche Kirk, and be the said Richart and another servent lifted upe to the pulpit, whar he behovit to lean at his first entrie; bot or he haid done with his sermont he was sa active and vigorus, that he was lyk to ding that pulpit in blads (break the pulpit in pieces) and flie out of it.

A few other works, also of the nature of annals, though not attaining to the dignity of literature, may be noted as illustrating the interest in history which had been mainly occasioned by the revolutionary events of the period. The *Diurnal of remarkable Occurents*, a work by different hands, notes events from the time of James V till the year 1575; the period from 1566 to 1596 is dealt with in *The Historie and Life of James the Sext*, briefly continued till 1617; and, further, we have the *Memoirs of the Affairs of Scotland* (1577—1603) by David Moysie, and the *Diary of Robert Birrel* (1532—1605).

The cultivation of prose was the most important literary result of the reformation, but it did not check the tendency to versifying which had been assiduously practised throughout the reigns of the Jameses. In verse, however, there was produced no work comparable to Knox's *History* in prose. However we may explain the fact, from the reformation dates a period of barrenness in imaginative literature, similar to that which in England followed the death of Chaucer, and it lasted to the poetic revival in the beginning of the eighteenth century. With few exceptions, the verse written during the reformation struggle was prompted by the occasion of the hour—its principal themes being the sensational events on which the destinies of the nation appeared to hang. Printed in black letter on one side of a leaf of paper, ballads of this character issued in a constant stream from the press of Robert Lekprevik, the Edinburgh printer. Almost all of them were written by supporters of the reformation, and are mainly coarse and virulent attacks on Mary and such conspicuous persons as were known to be her friends.

The principal authors to whom the ballads have been ascribed are Robert Sempill, Sir John Maitland of Thirlstane, the Rev.

John Davidson and Sir William Kirkcaldy of Grange. Of Sempill, the most prolific writer of his class, little is known beyond the fact that he was an ardent supporter of the reformation and an uncompromising enemy of queen Mary, and that he lived in the thick of the sensational events of his time. His two best pieces are the *Sege of the Castel of Edinburgh* and *The Legend of a Lymaris Lyfe*, the coarse vigour of which sufficiently explains his temporary popularity; but in none of his work does Sempill rise to the dignity of poetic satire which ensures permanent literary interest. Sir John Maitland—better known in political than in literary history as the framer of the act of 1592 which has been called the Magna Charta of the Church of Scotland—strikes a higher note than Sempill. In the three poems that have been attributed to him, *Ane Admonition to my Lord Regentis Grace, Ane Schort Invectyve aganis the Delyverance of the Erle of Northumberland*, and *Aganis Sklanderous Tungis*, there is a restraint, a good sense and dignity, which became one who filled successively the offices of a senator of the College of Justice, of secretary of state and of lord high chancellor of Scotland. To Sir William Kirkcaldy of Grange only one piece is assigned—*Ane Ballat of the Captane of the Castell*—that is, of Edinburgh, the last stronghold held for queen Mary, of which Kirkcaldy himself was the captain. Of little poetic merit, this ballad has at least the distinction of being one of the few in which loyalty to Mary is expressed with chivalrous and heartfelt devotion—a devotion which he expiated with his life on the capture of the castle in 1573. The reformation in Scotland had no more strenuous adherent than the Rev. John Davidson, and, as he lived till 1603, his uncompromising opinions brought him into frequent trouble with James VI in his policy of suppressing presbyterianism and introducing episcopacy. A personal friend and admiring disciple of Knox, Davidson has extolled his virtues and, at the same time, sketched the main events of his career in *Ane Brief Commendation of Uprichtness*—a valuable document for Knox's biographers. To the eulogy of Knox is also devoted a second of the three poems known to be the work of Davidson—*Ane Schort Discurs of the Estaitis quha hes caus to deploir the Deith of this excellent Servand of God*, the closing lines of which may be quoted as a specimen of the general level of his style:

> Lyke as himself is unto gloir,
> So sall all ages ay recyte
> Johne Knoxis Name with greit decoir.

The writers who have been mentioned all belonged to the reforming party, but, throughout the whole period, the ancient church had also its representatives in literature, one of whom, at least, had a European reputation in his own day. This was John Mair or Major, who has been called 'the last of the schoolmen,' and who is the one eminent thinker whom we can with certainty say that Scotland gave to scholasticism. Born in Haddingtonshire in 1479, and dying in 1549 or 1550, Major lived to see the beginnings of the reformation in Scotland, but, though in many respects a liberal thinker both in religion and politics, he continued to the end a steady adherent of the communion in which he was reared. After a year's study (1493) at the university of Cambridge, Major passed to the university of Paris, where, till 1518, with the exception of a brief visit to Scotland, he was successively student, regent in arts, and doctor in theology. From 1518 to 1525, he lectured on logic and theology, first in the university of Glasgow and afterwards in the university of St Andrews, where he had George Buchanan as one of his pupils. Between 1525 and 1531, he was again in Paris, where he was now regarded by all the learned world as the most distinguished champion of medievalism in its opposition to the new studies. He had attained this reputation through the long series of his publications, begun in 1503, of which the most notable was his *Commentary on the Four Books of the Sentences of Peter Lombard* (1509). In all these works, Major is the schoolman pure and simple; the subjects he treats, his manner of handling them, are those of the medieval logician when scholasticism had become an exhausted movement. For the men of the new order, therefore, Major was an obscurantist against whom ridicule was the only appropriate weapon. Melanchthon selected him as the special object of attack in his reply to the condemnation of Luther by the Sorbonne. 'I have seen John Major's *Commentaries on Peter Lombard*,' he writes; 'he is now, I am told, the prince of the Paris divines. Good heavens! What wagon-loads of trifling.... If he is a specimen of the Parisian, no wonder they have so little stomach for Luther.' A shaft was aimed at Major by a still greater hand; in the wonderful library of St Victor in Paris, Pantagruel found a book entitled *The Art of Making Puddings* by John Major. Despite the mockery of the humanists, however, there are ideas and suggestions to be found in his voluminous disquisitions which prove that he was a shrewd and independent thinker when he addressed himself to practical questions. No reformer saw more clearly or denounced more stringently the corruptions and abuses of the church as it existed in Scotland; he held as liberal opinions as his pupil Buchanan regarding the relations of rulers and subjects; and a suggestion which he threw out as to the most effective method of dealing with mendicancy was adopted with fruitful results in Germany and the Low Countries. But his good sense and independent judgment are best exemplified in his one book which is not a scholastic treatise—his *Historia Majoris Britanniae tam Angliae quam Scotiae.* The Latin in which the *History* is written shows no trace of the influence of the revival of letters; it is the Latin of the schoolmen, impure, inharmonious and difficult. On the other hand, Major as a historian stands on a far higher level than that of the medieval chronicler. His work bears no evidence of great research, but he carefully selects the significant facts that were accessible to him, and judges men and events, if not with philosophic grasp, yet with a genial shrewdness which gives piquancy to his narrative. In six books he relates the history of the two countries from the earliest times till the reigns of Henry VII and James IV. What is noteworthy in his narrative is his rejection of the legendary origins of Scotland which had been invented to rebut the English claims of paramountcy, and which continued to be retailed by Scottish historians into the eighteenth century. But the most signal illustration of Major's insight and originality is his attitude regarding the political relations of the two kingdoms whose histories he relates. Almost alone among his countrymen, and at a period when the hereditary animosities of England and Scotland were never more intense, he counselled political union as the natural consummation of their respective destinies and in the best interest of both peoples.

One of the most notable specimens of the vernacular prose of the period is the singular production entitled *The Complaynt of Scotland*, the anonymous author of which was an adherent of the ancient church, and an ardent opponent of the English alliance. Primarily a political pamphlet, it was prompted by the miseries of the country that followed the defeat of the Scots at Pinkie by the duke of Somerset in 1547; and the object of its author is to point out to his countrymen the various evils to which their misfortunes were due. Till within recent years, the *Complaynt* was regarded as an original work, but it is now known to be, in great part, an adaptation of *Le Quadrilogue Invectif* of Alain Chartier (1422). The object of Chartier's work was to encourage his countrymen in their effort to expel the English, and, as the same situation now existed in Scotland, the author of the *Complaynt* found material in Chartier ready to his hand. After an introduction, consisting of an epistle to queen Mary and an epistle to the reader, the book opens with a succession of chapters (the first mainly a translation of Chartier), in which the author discourses on such themes as the 'mutations of monarches,' the wrath of God against wicked peoples, and the approaching end of the world—all with more or less direct bearing on the miseries of Scotland. In chapter VI, we have what the author calls 'ane monologue recreative,' in which, with curious irrelevancy, a shepherd is made to expound the Ptolemaic system. Then follows what is to be considered the main portion of the book—the vision of Dame Scotia and her indictment of the iniquities of nobles, clergy and commons, which have produced the existing miseries of their country. Here, again, the author is indebted to Chartier, from whom he has appropriated the conception of the vision, besides certain portions of his text. Such is the general plan of this fantastic production, which may have been drawn from other sources not yet discovered. Regarded merely as a specimen of early Scottish prose, however, the book has an interest of its own. The author himself assures us that he uses the 'domestic scottis language'—a statement which he modifies by the further remark that he found it necessary 'til myxt oure langage vitht part of termis dreuyn [derived] fra Lateen.' Another source of interest in the book is the multitude of curious details regarding the life of the time which are not to be found elsewhere. Of its author nothing is known, though he has been variously identified with Sir James Inglis, abbot of Cambuskenneth, Sir James Inglis, abbot of Culross, Sir David Lyndsay and one of the three Wedderburns. From the book itself, we gather that he was a Catholic and an enemy of England; and the recent discovery that he had read a manuscript of Octavien St Gelais, bishop of Angoulême, suggests that he may have been in the suite of queen Mary in France, and strengthens the conjecture that the work was printed in Paris in 1548 or 1549.

A notable volume was archbishop Hamilton's *Catechism* (1552), so called because it was issued by his authority after receiving the sanction of a provincial council. Written in the purest Scots of the time, the *Catechism* presents the fundamental Catholic doctrines in the simplest and most attractive form, though in the tumultuous period that followed its publication it had little influence in furthering the cause of its promoters. The most eminent defender of the old church was Quintin

Kennedy, a son of the second earl of Cassillis, who, in 1558, published *The Compendius Tractive*, which stated the case against protestantism with such persuasiveness and ability that, by the admission of an opponent, it perceptibly affected the progress of the new opinions. Better known than his *Tractive*, however, is the *Ressoning* between him and Knox: the record of an oral controversy that took place at Maybole in 1562, and lasted for three days.

A larger amount of work was produced by Ninian Winzet, another Catholic controversialist, who, in his *Certain Tractatis for Reformatioun of Doctryne and Manneris* (1562), frankly admitted the corruptions of the Catholic church in Scotland, but contended that they afforded no rational ground for changing the national religion. It is noteworthy in Winzet and other Roman Catholic writers of the time that they claimed to be the upholders of the national tradition not only in religion but in policy. In the alliance with England, but for whose intervention the reformation in Scotland would not have been accomplished, they saw the ruin of their country; and all things English were the objects of their special detestation. For this reason it was that they resented the intrusion of English words into the Scottish vocabulary, and regarded it as a patriotic duty to write in what they considered the purest Scots. In a well known sentence, Winzet caustically upbraids Knox (who, in point of fact, wrote for England as well as for Scotland) for his use of English modes of expression. 'Gif you,' he writes, 'throw curiositie of novations has forget our auld plane Scottis quhilk your mother lerit you: in tymes cuming I sall write to you my mynd in Latin; for I am not acquynted with your Southeroun.'

The highest place among the Catholic writers of the period undoubtedly belongs to John Leslie, bishop of Ross, the friend, adviser and most distinguished champion of Mary, whom he attended during her imprisonment in England. Like many others of his Scottish contemporaries, Leslie chose history as his special province, and, like all the historians and chroniclers who have already been mentioned, he chose as his theme the history of his own country. His first work, written during his residence in England, took up the national history from the death of James I, where Hector Boece had stopped, and continued it to the year 1561. This fragment, composed in the vernacular, was followed up by a more ambitious performance in Latin (*De Origine, Moribus et Rebus Scotorum*), published at Rome in 1578, in which he narrated the national history from its origins. In 1596, this was translated into Scots by Father James Dalrymple, a Scottish monk at Ratisbon, but the manuscript was not published till 1888. The first seven books of Leslie's Latin history are mainly an epitome of Hector Boece, and he is as credulous as Boece himself regarding freaks of nature and his country's legends. In the later portions of his work, however, he writes with seriousness and moderation, and his narrative of events during the reign of Mary is one of the valuable sources for the period. Writing as a dignitary of the church, he has his own point of view; but his natural equability of temper saved him from the explosions of Knox, while his mediocre gifts rendered his work commonplace compared with that of his great rival.

The works that have been enumerated belong, for the most part, to the main stream of the reformation literature, which may be regarded as the distinctive product of the period. Parallel with this main stream, however, there was another class of writings which, in greater or less degree, and more or less directly, proceeded from the secular movement of the renascence. It is a noteworthy fact in the history of Scotland from the earliest Middle Ages, that, sooner or later, she came under the influence of every new development in western Christendom. Especially since the war of independence against England, which had thrown her into the arms of France, her intercourse with the continent had been close and continuous. From the middle of the fourteenth century, there had been a constant stream of Scottish students to the university of Paris and to other universities of France, with the result that every novelty in the spheres of thought or action speedily found its way into Scotland. It was to be expected, therefore, that the revival of learning would not leave Scotsmen untouched, and in one distinguished Scot its influence is manifest. This was Hector Boece, a native of Dundee, and subsequently the first principal of the newly founded university of Aberdeen. Boece was a member of the university of Paris during the greater part of the last two decades of the fifteenth century, and was the esteemed fellow student and friend of Erasmus—a fact which, in itself, suggests that Boece's sympathies were with the new ideals of the time. And the character of his two published works, his *Vitae Episcoporum Murthlacensium et Aberdonensium* (1522), and his *Historia Gentis Scotorum* (1527), show conclusively that he had studied the classical writers in the new spirit. While his contemporary, John Major, who also studied at Paris, wrote his *History of Greater*

Britain in the traditional style of the medieval chroniclers, Boece deliberately made Livy his model and endeavoured to reproduce his manner and method. His sole concern, indeed, was to present his subject in the most attractive form of which it was capable, and his one aim to prove to the world that Scotland and her people had a history which surpassed that of every other country in point of interest and antiquity. His name is now a byeword for the inventive chronicler; but he was not so regarded by his contemporaries, and, even so late as the eighteenth century, his astounding narrative of fabulous kings and natural wonders was seriously accepted by the majority of his countrymen. Translated into French by Nicolas d'Arfeville, cosmographer to Henri II, Boece found wide currency on the continent, and in France, to the present day, many prevalent impressions of Scotland are traceable to his lively fancy. In England, Boece had still greater good fortune; his tale of Macbeth and Duncan, taken from him by Holinshed, supplied Shakespeare with the plot of his great tragedy, as well as with those vivid touches of local colour which abound in the play.

But Boece's *History* is memorable for another reason besides its wide currency and its audacious fictions: it gave occasion to the first book in Scottish prose which has come down to us. At the instance of James V, who thus followed the example of other princes of the renascence, it was translated into Scots (1536) by John Bellenden, archdeacon of Moray, one of the many versifiers who haunted the court. Bellenden proved an admirable translator —his flowing and picturesque style doing full justice to his original, while he added so much in Boece's own manner that he further adapted it to the tastes of the time. Also by the command of James—another illustration of the influence of the renascence in Scotland—Bellenden undertook a Scottish translation of all the existing books of Livy, though only five were actually completed. Besides being a translator, Bellenden has claims as a poet on the strength of the versified prologues to his Livy and Boece's *History* and other pieces, and it is specially for his skill in verse that his contemporary, Sir David Lyndsay, commends him as

> The cunnying clark, quhilk writith craftelie,
> The plant of poetis, callit Ballendyne,
> Quhose ornat warkis my wit can nocht defyne.

In the works of Boece and Bellenden, the influence of the revival of learning is distinctly apparent, but it is in George

Buchanan that Scotland has its pre-eminent representative of the movement known as humanism. By his contemporaries, both in England and on the continent, Buchanan's mastery of Latin, equally in prose and verse, was acknowledged with emphatic unanimity. *Poetarum nostri saeculi facile princeps*—so he was described by Henri Estienne, and the eulogy, approvingly repeated by Camden, was generally regarded as just by the scholars of every country. And for fully two centuries after his death his fame suffered little diminution. In the seventeenth century, Saumaise speaks of him as 'the greatest man of his age,' and Grotius calls him *Scotiae illud numen*. As a writer of history, Dryden declared that Buchanan was 'comparable to any of the moderns and excelled by few of the ancients.' In the eighteenth century, according to Warton, he was still 'a popular modern classic,' and Dr Johnson, not a genial critic of Scotsmen in general, conceded that 'Buchanan not only had great knowledge of the Latin, but was a great poetical genius.' As pre-eminently, therefore, as Knox represents the reformation in Scotland, Buchanan represents the revival of letters.

Born in 1506 or 1507, at Killearn in Stirlingshire, Buchanan was sent in his fifteenth year to the university of Paris, where, during two years, he was assiduously trained in the composition of Latin verse. Returning to Scotland, he attended the lectures of John Major in the university of St Andrews, whom, in the true spirit of humanism, he describes as 'teaching the art of sophistry rather than dialectics.' A second sojourn in Paris (1525—35?), extending to about ten years, decided his future career; thenceforward, his life was to be that of the typical scholar of the renascence—a life devoted to the study of the classical writers and the interpretation of them to his contemporaries as a consecrated vocation. It was Buchanan's lifelong conviction, which he shared with most scholars of his time, that Latin must eventually become the literary language of Christendom, and that it would be disastrous to literature should it prove otherwise. What his new reading of the Bible was to Knox, *pura oratio*, the language of Cicero or of Vergil was to Buchanan.

With few exceptions, the writings of Buchanan were prompted by some immediate occasion of the moment. As far as we know, it was during his second residence in Paris that he began to throw off those shorter poems mainly directed against idle and dissolute monks and priests, or against opponents of the new studies which had resulted from the revival of learning. At this period, the struggle between the champions of the old and the new studies was at its height in the schools of Paris, and it was in the teeth of the most vehement opposition on the part of the university that Francis I, in 1530, founded the Collège Royal for the study of Greek, Latin and Hebrew. With all the energy of his ardent temper, Buchanan threw himself on the side of the reformers. In caustic epigrams he denounced the obscurantism of those who opposed the study of the classical writers as these were now interpreted through the labours, of the Italian humanists. But his most effectual contribution to the cause of the new studies at this time was his translation into Latin of Linacre's *Grammar*, published in Paris in 1533, which ran through seven editions before the close of the century. In the dedication of the book to his pupil the earl of Cassillis, he takes the opportunity of stating the reasons for its publication, and his words deserve to be quoted as illustrating the ideals to which his life was dedicated and as clearly defining the position of the adversaries with whom he waged a lifelong battle.

> 'But I am perfectly aware,' he says, 'that in translating this book many will think that I have given myself quite unnecessary trouble. We have already too many of such books, these persons will say, and, moreover, they add, can anything be said worth the saying which is not to be found in authors who have long enjoyed the approval of the schools? As for the novelties which make a large portion of this book, such as the remarks on the declensions of nouns, of relatives, and certain moods and tenses of verbs, they think them mere useless trifling. Such criticism can only come of sheer ignorance or the blindest prejudice, that will listen only to its own suggestions, and gravely maintains that departure from tradition in such matters is to be regarded as a proof not so much of foolish self-confidence as of actual impiety. From these persons, so wise in their own conceit, I appeal to all men of real learning and sincere love of letters, confident that to all such Linacre will generally commend himself.'

To the same period of his second residence in Paris belongs a poem, the first in his *Book of Elegies*, which calls for special mention as a valuable historical document of the time. The poem is entitled, *Quam misera sit conditio docentium literas humaniores Lutetiae.* In vivid terms it describes the round of the daily duties of a regent in a Paris college, the squalid conditions of the class-rooms, the behaviour of the pupils, the insubordination of the chance comers (*errones, galoches*) who are permitted to attend the lessons and the grumbling of parents 'that their sons learn nothing and that fees must still be paid.'

Another migration in Buchanan's wandering career gave rise to three poems which had a determining influence on the future course of his life. In 1535, he returned to Scotland with his pupil, the earl of Cassillis, and, during his residence in the country with that nobleman, he translated into Latin verse a pasquinade of Dunbar, *How Dumbar wes desyrd to be ane freir*, but which Buchanan entitled simply *Somnium.* In this poem, a pungent attack on the Franciscan order, St Francis, its founder, appears in a dream, and beseeches him to don the habit. The reply of the poet is that he can be an honester man as he is, though, if St Francis could promise him a bishopric, he would gladly listen to his proposals. It was Buchanan's first declaration of war against the great order—the worst enemies, as he considered them, of reform in religion and learning. His engagement with Cassillis having expired, Buchanan was on the point of returning to France, when an offer came to him from James V to become tutor to the lord James Stewart, one of James's natural sons, not to be confounded with another natural son of the same name, afterwards the regent Moray. Like his immediate predecessors, James was a patron of poets, and took pleasure in their effusions. As James's public policy showed, he was a true son of the church, but he happened to have a personal grudge against the Franciscans, and he charged Buchanan to sharpen his pen against the order. Against his own inclination, for, by his previous satire, he had already provoked that formidable body, he wrote the piece entitled *Palinodia*, in which, according to his own account, he sought to express himself with such ambiguity as at once to satisfy the king and not to give further offence to the Franciscans. In point of fact, the satire is a more deadly attack than the *Somnium* on the vices and obscurantism of the order. But even this scathing satire did not satisfy James, and he demanded another 'which should not only prick the skin, but probe the vitals.' The result was *Franciscanus*, the longest and most elaborate of all Buchanan's satires. All the charges that were then generally brought against that body, their contempt of their own rules, their rapacity, their frauds on the public—are here set forth with a far keener purpose to wound than appears in the contemporary satire of Lyndsay. The poem was not completed at this time, and it was not till Buchanan's final return to Scotland, in 1560, that he put the finishing touches to it, and published it with a dedication to the regent Moray. Though it was not now printed, however, the Franciscans were aware of its existence, and not even the authority of the king could secure him from their vengeance. Supported by cardinal Beaton, the most powerful churchman in the country, they accused him of heretical opinions, and James was constrained to commit him to prison, from which, however, by James's own connivance, he escaped across the Border into England.

Arrived in London, Buchanan, according to his own account, found Henry VIII 'burning Protestant and Catholic alike, on the same day and in the same fire,' though, in a poem addressed to Henry at this time, he ascribes to him all the virtues of an Alfred or a St Louis. In another set of verses, accompanied with a collection of his poems, he sought to commend himself to Henry's minister, Thomas Cromwell, then all powerful, and gives a pitiful account of his own fortunes as one

Qui vagus, exul, inops, terra jactatur et unda
Per mala quae fallax omnia mundus habet.

As Cromwell made no response to his appeal, and as England was hardly a safe place for one of his opinions, under the pretence of proceeding to Germany he took ship for France, but only to find his arch enemy Beaton in Paris. An invitation to become a professor in the newly founded Collège de Guyenne at Bordeaux relieved him from immediate want and danger, and there, for the next three years, we find him as one of the *précepteurs domestiques* attached to the college. Expressly founded for instruction in the new studies, this institution had already gained the repute of being the best of its kind in France, and among other pupils attracted to it was Montaigne, who himself tells us that he had Buchanan '*ce grand poète escossois*' as one of his *précepteurs de chambre.*

Now in surroundings that were congenial to him, and in association with colleagues of tastes kindred to his own, Buchanan was stimulated to productions on a more ambitious scale than anything he had hitherto attempted. As his poetic gifts and his command of Latin were regarded as unrivalled, to him was entrusted the task of being the spokesman of the college on all public occasions. When the emperor Charles V passed through Bordeaux on his memorable visit to Francis I, it was Buchanan who was commissioned to hail the illustrious guest in a congratulatory ode—a task which he brilliantly accomplished in one of his *Sylvae—Ad Carolum V Imperatorem, Burdegalae hospitio publico susceptum, nomine Scholae Burdegalensis.* By a rule of the college, each professor was expected to compose a Latin play every year, to be acted by the pupils under his charge, and, in the performance of this duty, Buchanan produced four plays during his residence in Bordeaux. Two of these were translations of the *Medea* and *Alcestis* of Euripides, primarily undertaken, Buchanan himself tells us, to improve his scholarship in Greek, for in Greek, it is significant Buchanan was self taught. The other two plays, *Jephthes* and *Baptistes*, are original compositions, modelled on the classical examples, and expressly written to enforce that *pietas literata* which was the ideal of all the schools that, like the Collège de Guyenne, had recently been founded in France. In Buchanan's judgment, the former, founded on the story of Jephthah's vow, is the better drama, and in none of his productions has he risen to a higher strain of moral intensity and elevation of thought and expression. It is in the *Baptistes*, however, that we find the fullest and hardiest expression of the convictions which, frequently at his own peril, he consistently proclaimed throughout his whole career. The principal character, John the Baptist, is the fiery apostle of precisely those doctrines of political and religious liberty which were then perturbing Christendom, and his death at the hands of Herod is pointed as the moral of all religious and political tyranny.

Buchanan must have known that it was at his own risk that he expressed these opinions in such a city as Bordeaux—where heresy had, indeed, lately appeared, and where, about the date of the appearance of *Baptistes*, a heretic had actually been burned. It was doubtless, therefore, for reasons connected with his personal safety, that he left Bordeaux in 1542—3, between which date and 1547 we all but lose sight of him. To this period, however, belongs a poem which deserves special attention as being the most minutely personal of his productions and as illustrating what is notable throughout his life—the affection and regard in which he was held by the most distinguished scholars of the time. The poem, entitled *Ad Ptolemaeum Luxium Tastaeum et Jacobum Taevium cum articulari morbo laboravit*, was written on his sick bed, where he had lain for a year between life and death, and its burden is that his sufferings had been made light by the tender attention of friends, whose names and special services he enumerates in glowing remembrance.

In 1547, Buchanan received an invitation which was to lead to the most eventful experience in his chequered career and to the production of the most memorable of all his works. The invitation was to join a band of scholars, intended to complete the staff of teachers in the university of Coimbra in Portugal, which had been remodelled by king John III. Buchanan accepted the offer, but, within a year, the Jesuits, then supreme in Portugal, obtained control over the university, and Buchanan and others were accused of heresy and conveyed to the Inquisition in Lisbon. During a year and a half, Buchanan was repeatedly under examination by the inquisitors, mainly on the charge of eating meat in Lent and of satirising the Franciscans. Convinced at length that, though he had been an erring son of the church, he was no heretic, they allowed him his liberty, but on the condition that he should spend six months in a neighbouring monastery in some penitential exercise. The penance which he chose, or which was imposed upon him, was his *Psalmorum Davidis Paraphrasis Poetica*—the work which more than any other has secured to him his eminent place among modern Latin poets. Buchanan's translation of the *Psalms* may fairly be considered one of the representative books of the sixteenth century, expressing, as it does, in consummate form, the conjunction of piety and learning which was the ideal of the best type of humanist. Versified translations of the *Psalms* were the favourite exercise of the scholars of every country, but, by general consent, Buchanan was acknowledged to have surpassed all competitors in the felicity of his rendering, and it was on the title-page of their editions of his translation that Henri and Robert Estienne assigned him the distinction above referred to, of being *poetarum nostri saeculi facile princeps.* As a manual at once of piety and scholarship, it was received with universal acclamation. In Buchanan's own lifetime it was introduced into the schools of Germany and an edition, set to music, was published in 1595. Till within recent years, it was read in every school in Scotland where Latin was taught, and among educated Scotsmen of every shade of opinion it became their treasured companion, to which they had recourse for religious edification and solace.

On the expiry of his time of penance in the monastery, Buchanan was at liberty to leave Portugal, and his first thought was to seek a home in England, now a protestant country under the rule of Edward VI. The distracted state of England, however, as he tells us, offered little prospect of peaceful employment to scholars, and, once more, he sought a haven in France—his second home, as he always considered it. In one of his most beautiful poems, *Adventus in Galliam*, he expresses his delight on finding himself again on its hospitable soil. 'Buchanan,' says de Thou, 'was born by the banks of the Blane in the country of the Lennox, but he was of us by adoption,' and, in the glowing tributes he pays in these lines to the French and their country, Buchanan fully justified the statement. To the same period, also, belong his odes on the capture of Calais from the English and of Metz from Germany, in which he speaks with all the fervour and pride of a Frenchman in his country's triumph. In 1555, Buchanan had been appointed tutor to Timoleon du Cossé, son of Charles du Cossé, comte de Brissac, one of the marshals of France, and the connection gave occasion to the most elaborate of all his poems—the poem entitled *De Sphaera*. All Buchanan's more serious productions are informed by a strenuous didactic purpose, and it was primarily for the instruction of his pupil that *De Sphaera* was undertaken. Its theme is the exposition of the Ptolemaic cosmogony in opposition to the system which had recently been promulgated by Copernicus, and which, with few exceptions, had been rejected by learned and unlearned as impious and irrational. The poem was intended as its author's greatest stroke for durable fame, and in its execution he has lavished all his learning and all the poetic art at his command. As we have it, it consists of five books, the last two of which are unfinished; and it remains as a curious memorial of a literary ambition which strangely mistook the course of the world's thought, equally regarding its theme and the language in which it is written.

Towards the year 1560, there came a change in Buchanan's opinions which divides his life in twain. Hitherto, though he had spoken freely of monks and priests, he had remained a member of the church of Rome, but, from a special study of the Bible, as he tells us, he now became convinced that the truth was to be found in protestant teaching. As Scotland adopted protestantism as its national religion in 1560, after an exile of more than twenty years he returned to his native country. Now, as always, his new associations prompted him to renewed production. During the first six years after his return to Scotland, it was queen Mary who was the chief inspirer of his muse. Before he left France, he had already celebrated her marriage with Francis I in an *Epithalamium* containing the famous description of his countrymen beginning

Illa pharetratis est propria gloria Scotis,

which are among the best known lines he has written. To Mary, also, he now dedicated the second edition of his translation of the *Psalms* in the most admired of all his shorter poems, the epigram beginning

> *Nympha, Caledoniae quae nunc feliciter orae*
> *Missa per innumeros sceptra tueris avos.*

Till 1567, he remained in close connection with the court, reading the classics with Mary in her leisure hours, composing a masque on the occasion of her marriage with Darnley, and celebrating the birth of her son, afterwards James VI, in a *Genethliacon* in which he did not conceal his opinions regarding the duties of rulers to their subjects.

The murder of Darnley, the head, be it noted, of Buchanan's own clan, converted him into a bitter enemy of Mary, as, like all protestants, he believed that she was accessory to the crime. Henceforward, therefore, he identified himself with the political and religious party which drove her from the throne, and it was in the interests of that party that his subsequent writings were mainly produced. In his *Detectio*, written at the request of the protestant lords, he has presented their case against Mary with a vehemence of statement which can only be understood and justified by comparison with the polemical writings of contemporary scholars. In the service of the same cause, he produced the only two pieces which he wrote in vernacular Scots—*Chamaeleon*, a satire on Maitland of Lethington, and the *Admonition to the trew Lordis*, a warning to the protestant lords themselves regarding their past and future policy. What is noteworthy in these two pamphlets is that Buchanan shows the same mastery of the Scottish language as he does of Latin, and their periodic sentences are an exact reproduction of his Latin models. But Buchanan's greatest literary achievement of this period was his *Rerum Scoticarum Historia*, published in 1582, the year of his death, in which he related the history of Scotland from its origin till the death of the regent Lennox in 1571. Dedicated to James VI, with whose education he had been entrusted, the underlying object of the book is the inculcation of those principles of political and religious liberty of which Buchanan had been the consistent champion throughout his career. By the leading scholars of Europe it was adjudged to be a work of transcendent merit, and even in the eighteenth century it was seriously debated whether Caesar, Livy, or Sallust had been his model. In this *History*, which for fully two centuries kept its place as a standard authority,

Buchanan had appealed both to scholars and protestant theologians, and in another work, *De Jure Regni apud Scotos* (1579), he made a still wider appeal on questions which were then agitating every country in Christendom. Written in the form of a dialogue (between Thomas Maitland and Buchanan) this treatise is, virtually, an apology for the Scottish reformation, and, as a classic exposition of protestant political theory, it found wide acceptance both in Britain and on the continent—Dryden in the following century even accusing Milton of having embodied it in his *Defence of the People of England.*

'No man,' says archbishop Spottiswoode, 'did better merit of his nation for learning, nor thereby did bring it to more glory,' and this is Buchanan's specific and pre-eminent claim to the regard of his countrymen. Read as classics by all educated Scotsmen, his works, prose and verse, perpetuated the study of Latin, which, to the comparative neglect of Greek, remained a rooted tradition in the curriculum of a learned education in Scotland. Scotland, as has already been said, owing to conditions peculiar to itself, was more powerfully affected by the reformation than by the renascence, yet, through the work of Buchanan, and of others of kindred tastes, though less distinguished than himself, one result, at least, was secured from both movements: religion has ever been associated with learning in the mind of the Scottish people.

CHAPTER VIII

THE NEW ENGLISH POETRY

THE reign of Henry VIII was not, as students of history know, a period of unbroken internal peace. Nevertheless, when the wars of the Roses were over and a feeling of security had been induced by the establishment of a strong dynasty, a social and intellectual life became possible in England which the troubles of the reigns of Henry VIII and his two successors were sufficient to check but not to destroy. More important still, England, having more or less settled her internal troubles by a judicious application of the balancing system, became a power to be reckoned with in European politics. This brought her into touch with the kingdoms of the continent, and so, for the first time in a more than incidental way, submitted her intellectual life to the influences of the renascence. The inspiration of the new poetry, we shall find, was almost entirely foreign. It was upon French, and, especially, upon Italian, models that the courtiers of Henry VIII founded the poems which now began to be written in large numbers. The extent to which the practice of versifying prevailed cannot now be gauged; but modern investigation shows it to have been very wide. To make poems was one of the recognised accomplishments of the knight as conceived in the last phase of chivalry, the days with which we are, for the moment, concerned; and it is not, perhaps, too much to say that every educated man made poems, which, if approved, were copied out by his friends and circulated in manuscript, or included in song-books. It was not, however, till 1557 that some few were, for the first time, put into print by Richard Tottel, in the volume, *Songes and Sonettes, written by the ryght honorable Lorde Henry Haward late Earle of Surrey, and other*, commonly known as *Tottel's Miscellany.*

This volume tends to prove that the movement had one pioneer and two leaders. The pioneer was Sir Thomas Wyatt, who was joined in the leadership by Henry Howard, known as earl of Surrey. A sketch of their lives, especially of that of the former, may be of interest as helping to show the extent to which England was brought into touch with European influences.

Thomas Wyatt was born in or about 1503, and was educated at Cambridge, possibly, also, at Oxford. In 1511, his father was joint constable with Sir Thomas Boleyn of Norwich Castle, and, as a boy, he made the acquaintance of a lady—Sir Thomas's daughter Anne—with whose name report was to link his own very closely. In 1525, after holding certain offices about the person of the king, Thomas Wyatt accompanied Sir Thomas Cheney on a diplomatic mission to France. In 1526—7, he was sent with Sir John Russell, the English ambassador, to the papal court; and visited Venice, Ferrara, Bologna and Florence. On his return, he was captured by the imperial forces under the constable of Bourbon, but escaped. In 1529—30, he was high marshal at Calais. In 1537, he went as ambassador to the emperor, and remained abroad, mainly in Spain, till 1539; in the April of that year he was recalled, in consequence of the intrigues of his fellow-ambassador, Bonner. At the end of the same year he was despatched to Flanders to see the emperor and followed him to Paris, returning in 1540. On the fall of Cromwell, who had supported Wyatt, Bonner succeeded in obtaining Wyatt's imprisonment in the Tower; whence, having either denied the accusation or pleaded for mercy, he was afterwards released. He retired to his house at Allington, in Kent, and employed his leisure in writing his satires and his paraphrase of the penitential psalms. In 1542, we find him knight of the shire for Kent; and, in the summer of that year, hastening in ill health on a mission to conduct the imperial ambassador to London, he caught a fever, and died on the road, at Sherborne, on 11 October. One other episode of his life remains to be mentioned. He was commonly regarded as, in youth, the lover of Anne Boleyn; and it was reported that, when the king wished to make that lady his wife, Wyatt informed him of his previous relations with her. Whatever the truth of an obscure matter, Wyatt was chief ewerer at the coronation of Henry's second queen in 1533; and, though we find him committed to the Tower in May 1536, the period of her downfall, it was probably only as a witness. One of his sonnets, *Whoso list to hunt,* has clear reference to Anne Boleyn, ending, as it does, with the line: '*Noli me tangere*; for Caesar's I am'; for, though it is imitated from Romanello[1] or Petrarch (157, *Una candida cerva*), it may yet be of personal application. There is also an epigram

[1] According to Nott, p. 571.

Of His Love called Anna, and another reference to Anne has been found by some in the sonnet *Though I myself be bridled of my mind.* His confinement in May 1536 was, undoubtedly, one of the facts in his life which induced him to regard May as his unlucky month[1].

It will be seen that Wyatt frequently travelled abroad, and that he spent a period of some months in Italy. And it was from Italy that he drew the ideas and the form by means of which English poetry was rejuvenated. The changes which English versification passed through in the period between Chaucer and the Elizabethans are described elsewhere[2]. Neither the principles of rhythm and accent, it would seem, nor even the grammar of Chaucer were fully understood by his followers, Lydgate, Occleve and Hawes. In place of Chaucer's care in arranging the stress and pause of his line, there is chaotic carelessness; and the diction is redundant, feeble and awkward. Meanwhile, the articulate final *-e*, of which Chaucer made cunning use, had been dropping out of common speech, and the accent on the final syllable of words derived from the French, such as *favour*, *virtue*, *travail*, had begun to move back to the first syllable, with the result of producing still further prosodical confusion and irregularity. It was the mission of Wyatt and his junior contemporary, Surrey, to substitute order for confusion, especially by means of the Italian influence which they brought to bear on English poetry, an influence afterwards united by Spenser (Gabriel Harvey assisting) with the classical influence.

Wyatt's chief instrument was the sonnet, a form which he was the first English writer to use. Of all forms, the sonnet is that in which it is most difficult to be obscure, turgid, or irregular. Its small size and precise structure force on the writer compression, point and intensity, for a feeble sonnet proclaims itself feeble at a glance. No better corrective could have been found for vague thought, loose expression and irregular metre; and the introduction of the sonnet stands as the head and front of Wyatt's benefaction to English poetry. His model—in thought, and, up to a certain point, in form—was the sonnet of Petrarch, of whom he was a close student. Wyatt's sonnets number about thirty: ten of them are translations of Petrarch, and two others show a debt to the same author. But either he did not apprehend, or he deliberately decided not to imitate, the strict Petrarchian form; and the great majority of the English sonneteers before Milton followed his example. The main difference is this: that, whereas the

[1] Cf. the sonnet: *Ye that in love finde luck.*

[2] See *post*, chap. XIII.

sextett of the strict Petrarchian sonnet never ends with a couplet, the sonnets of Sir Thomas Wyatt, and Elizabethan sonnets in general, nearly always do. The effect produced, that of a forcible ending, is opposed to the strict principles of the sonnet, which should rise to its fullest height at the conclusion of the octave, to sink to rest gradually in the sextett. But the final couplet has been used so freely and to such noble ends by English writers that objection is out of place. Wyatt was possibly induced to adopt this form partly by the existence of the favourite Chaucerian rime royal stanza of seven lines, riming *ababbcc.* Of Wyatt's sonnets, two or three (*e.g. Was never file; Some fowles there be; How oft have I*) do actually, by their sense, fall into two divisions of seven lines; but it is plain that this was not the principle on which he constructed his sonnets. For the most part, the separation of octave and sextett is clearly marked, and the rimes of the former are arranged in Petrarchian fashion, *abbaabba*, with occasional variations, of which *abbaacca* is a not uncommon form. The effect of the sonnet-form on Wyatt's thought and diction we shall examine presently; for the moment, we are concerned with his metrical reforms. He was a pioneer, and perfection was not to be expected of him. He has been described as a man stumbling over obstacles, continually falling but always pressing forward. Perhaps the best way of illustrating his merits and his shortcomings is to quote one of his sonnets in full; and it will be convenient for the purpose to take his version of a sonnet of Petrarch which was also translated by Surrey, in order to compare later the advance made by the younger writer.

> The longe love, that in my thought I harber,
> And in my hart doth kepe his residence,
> Into my face preaseth with bold pretence,
> And there campeth, displaying his banner.
> She that me learns to love, and to suffer,
> And willes that my trust, and lustes negligence
> Be reined by reason, shame, and reverence,
> With his hardinesse takes displeasure.
> Wherwith love to the hartes forest he fleeth,
> Leavyng his enterprise with paine and crye,
> And there him hideth and not appeareth.
> What may I do? when my maister feareth,
> But in the field with him to live and dye,
> For good is the life, endyng faithfully.

The author of this sonnet clearly has much to learn. The scanning of *harber, banner, suffer, campeth, preaseth, forest* as iambics is comprehensible; but, in line 6, we have to choose between a heavy stress on the unimportant word *my*, or an articulated final *-e* in *lustes*; while, in line 8, we can hardly escape *hardìnesse*, and must have either *takës* again, or *dis-plè-a-sùre* (a possibility which receives some very doubtful support from line 8 of the sonnet, *Love, Fortune, and my minde*, in the almost certainly corrupt version in the first edition of *Tottel's Miscellany*). In lines 11 and 12, we find the curious fact that *appeareth* is rimed with *feareth*, not on the double rime but on the last syllable only; while the last line throws a heavy emphasis on *the*. The author, in fact, seems to have mastered the necessity of having ten syllables in a decasyllabic line, but to be very uncertain still in questions of accent and rhythm. Some of the lines irresistibly suggest a man counting the syllables on his fingers, as, indeed, the reader is often compelled to do on a first acquaintance; on the other hand, we find a beautiful line like the tenth, which proves the author, however unskilled as yet, to be a poet. The use of the caesura is feeble and often pointless, and the total impression is that of a man struggling with difficulties too great for him. But it is fair to remember two things: first, that pronunciation was then in a state of flux (in one of his satires we find Wyatt scanning *honour* as an iambic and as a trochee in the same line); secondly, that he made great advance in technique, and that some of the ruggedness of his work (not including this sonnet), as it appears in the first edition of *Tottel's Miscellany*, is due to a faulty text, partly corrected in the second edition. Nott, who published the original MS in 1816, discovered that Wyatt had occasionally marked the caesura with his own hand, and sometimes indicated the mode of disposing of a redundant syllable. There are sonnets (for instance, *Unstable dream*) which run perfectly smoothly—to say no more—showing that mastery came with practice, and that errors were not due to want of correct aim and comprehension.

This, then—the introduction of the sonnet with its chastening and strengthening influence on metre and diction—is Wyatt's great service to English poetry; but his service did not end there. His close study of Petrarch and other Italian authors resulted in an innovation quite as important, the introduction of the personal note. The conventionality of character, sentiment and machinery inherited from the *Roman de la Rose* disappeared; and, in its place, came poetry professedly and intentionally personal, and, within limits, actually introspective. Following Petrarch, Wyatt sang, in his love-poetry, almost exclusively of his own sufferings at the cruelty, much more rarely of his own joy in the kindness, of his mistress. To say that many of the sonnets are translations and, therefore, cannot represent the actual feelings of the translator, is to question the sincerity of almost every Elizabethan sonneteer. The pleasures and pains of love are the same in all ages; it is the convention of expression which changes. The new convention, of which the existence must be recognised in Wyatt, is a convention of personal emotion, in which the poet at least pretends to be singing of his own heart. And in Wyatt we meet with constant proof that he is so singing. In imitating Petrarch, he frequently adopted to the full the Petrarchian scheme for the content of a sonnet—the selection of an image which is then elaborated with as many cognate and subsidiary metaphors as may be. Take, for instance, Wyatt's sonnet *My galley charged with forgetfulnesse,* which is copied from Petrarch's *Passa la nave mia colma d'obblio.* His heart is a ship, steered cruelly through a winter sea by his foe, who is his lord; the oars are thoughts; the winds are sighs and fearfulness; the rain is tears; the clouds are disdain; the cords are twisted with error and ignorance; while reason, that should be his consort (or comfort), is drowned. If there were nothing of superior matter to this in Wyatt, his achievement would almost be limited to his metrical reforms; but the genuineness and originality of the poet are shown in other sonnets in which he either alters his original, modifying some more than usually strained conceit into something in better taste, or writes with no original but his own heart. See lines 5—8 in his sonnet, *Yet was I never of your love agreved,* in which he flatly contradicts the sentiment of Petrarch. And, more than once, he flies in the face of the slavery to the mistress prescribed in the code of chivalric love from which he drew much of his inspiration; declaring roundly (*e.g.* in the sonnet, *My love to skorn*) that,

> As there is a certayn time to rage:
> So is there time such madnes to aswage;

and bids his cruel mistress a manly farewell. It is not fanciful, perhaps, to find such a sentiment characteristically English. The chivalric ideal, codified in Castiglione's *Il Cortegiano,* was, as we shall see further in discussing Surrey, of great weight in this, the last century of chivalry in England; but there is, perhaps, something in our temperament that forbade its complete acceptance in the matter of the servitude of love.

The same sentiment appears even more clearly in Wyatt's lyrics not in sonnet form, and especially in those composed of short lines. A delightful song in three quatrains of octosyllabic lines, *Madame, withouten many wordes*, is as brave and cavalier a way of demanding a 'yes' or 'no' as Suckling himself could have uttered; and *What should I say! Since Faith is dead*, a little song of tetrasyllabic lines with a refrain, is a resolute if graceful farewell. It is in these lighter lyrics that some of Wyatt's finest work is to be found. *Forget not yet the tried intent* is known to all readers of poetry. It is marked, with other poems, by two things: the use of the refrain and the unmistakable impression it conveys of having been written to be sung. The refrain is a valuable means of knitting a poem together, helping Wyatt almost as much as the practice of the short poem—in a metre imitated, as a rule, from Italian or French—towards being clear, exact and musical. Of the influence of music on the writing of poetry more will be said elsewhere. It would be rash to state that in the reign of Henry VIII music so far followed the rhythm of poetry as to exert a good influence on its form. Still, a lyric was, in those days, written, as a matter of course, to be sung, and when poems sing themselves it may be safe to give to music a share in the good work. We do not find in Wyatt the elaborate metrical harmonies that grew up in Elizabeth's days. His stanzas are always short, and simple in construction, without much involution of rime, and they have a sweetness, a dignity and a sincerity that make them strongly attractive. But their place in the history of English poetry is more important than their intrinsic qualities. Here, for the first time, we find deliberately studied and worked upon by the poetic imagination that cry of the heart, which, beginning with the recognised pains of the chivalric lover, became the subject, in a thousand moods and forms, of what may not unfairly be considered the finest achievement of English poetry.

Besides sonnets and other lyrics, Wyatt's work falls under three heads: epigrams, satires and devotional pieces. Epigram means, with Wyatt, not a stinging stave of wit, but a single conceit or paradox vividly expressed—for instance: *The lover compareth his hart to the over-charged gonne* (which may be specially noticed because a later use of the same idea will help to show the deterioration of the school of Wyatt); *Comparison of love to a streame falling from the Alpes; How by a kisse he found both his life and death*; and so forth. The epigrams, indeed, differ little in matter from the more metaphysical of the sonnets; though, here and there, we find the form used for the strong expression of personal feeling, as in *Wiat, being in prison, to Brian* (written, probably, during his incarceration in 1540, to his friend Sir Francis Bryan, also a poet), and in *The Lover professeth himself constant.* For the matter of a few of the epigrams, and for the construction of all, Wyatt's model is the *Strambotti* of Serafino; the form throughout is a decasyllabic octave riming *abababcc,* and, for his ideas, the writer generally sought far and wide through such foreign and classical learning as he possessed. Seneca, Josephus and Ausonius (possibly following Plato) are among the authors on whom he draws. Of greater interest, both intrinsic and technical, are his satires, which were written in his retirement at Allington towards the close of his active and chequered life. They are three in number. The first, *Of the meane and sure estate written to John Poins,* tells the fable of the town and country mouse, which he adapts from Horace (*Sat.* II, vi), being, possibly, acquainted also with Henryson's poem *The Uponlandis Mous and the Burges Mous,* though that poem was not yet printed; while the conclusion is enlarged from Persius, *Sat.* III. The second, *Of the courtiers life written to John Poins,* is an adaptation of a satire of Luigi Alamanni, and explains that the author, scorning the obsequiousness and deceit demanded of courtiers, finds it better to live in retirement; the third, *How to use the court and him selfe therin, written to syr Fraunces Bryan,* takes its general ideas from Horace's advice to Tiresias (*Sat.* II, v), and preaches ironically the doctrine, 'Put money in thy purse.' The adaptations are free, and ideas are drawn from more than one author. There are several references, for instance, to Chaucer, and the references are, in general, modernised. Adaptations though they be, these satires have every mark of sincerity. The evils of court life and the blessings of honest retirement are a common theme with the authors collected in *Tottel's Miscellany*; no other contributor writes with such convincing fervour, such manly rectitude, as Wyatt. His personality and his strong feeling are more patent in the satires than in any other of his poems; and their very ruggedness of form seems—as in the later case of Donne or Marston—to be adopted for the better expression of honest indignation. Fifty years afterwards, Hall, the author of the *Virgidemiarum,* believed himself to be the first English satirist, and from the fact that Wyatt's satires were not previously imitated it is clear that he was in advance of his time. The metre adopted by Wyatt is that of Alamanni, the *terza rima,* decasyllabic lines with 'linked' rimes *ababcbcdcded*, etc. This, too, is the scheme of rime he uses in his versions of the seven penitential psalms, which were probably composed during the same period of his life as the satires. Each psalm is introduced by a fanciful narrative, modelled on Beza's *Praefatio Poetica*, of the moods in which David wrote it. The versions themselves are very free; the psalms, in fact, are used rather as pretexts for the expression of the poet's own feelings than as originals for rendering anew. He is appalled by the sense of his sinfulness, fretted 'to the bones' with remorse, and full of apprehensions of the Judgment. Wyatt also translated other psalms. Warton's statement that he translated the whole *Psalter* is, apparently, erroneous; and the only other surviving version is that of *Psalm* 37.

Enough has been said to show that Wyatt was, for his time, a well-read man in French, Italian and classical literature. He knew something, too, of Chaucer, as the frequent references to, or quotations from, his works show; but his almost exclusive use of French and Italian models indicates that he did not study Chaucer for his versification[1]. His poetry conveys the charm of a brave and strong spirit; his technical faults are those of a pioneer; but his great claim to recognition, like that of his contemporary and follower, Surrey, lies in his successful effort to raise his native tongue to dignity by making it the vehicle of 'polite' and courtly poetry, an effort which his model, Petrarch, had himself made in his time. For this purpose, both Wyatt and Surrey use, according to the prescription of Castiglione, the ordinary diction of their day, free from affectation of archaism and from vulgarity; and it is rare for the modern reader to encounter unfamiliar words in their poetry.

The exact relation of Surrey to Wyatt has been a matter of dispute. The accident of birth, no doubt, led to Surrey's poems being placed before those of Wyatt in *Tottel's Miscellany*, and this accident may have induced commentators to regard Surrey as the master of Wyatt, rather than to take the probably more truthful view, that each influenced the other, but that Wyatt was the pioneer. He was, at any rate, an older man than Surrey, who was born in 1516 (?). Henry Howard was the eldest son of lord Thomas Howard, son of Thomas, earl of Surrey and duke of Norfolk, and himself became, by courtesy, earl of Surrey in 1524, on his father's succeeding to the dukedom. From a poem to which reference will be made later it seems possible that he was educated with the duke of Richmond,

[1] [See addenda.]

Henry VII's natural son, who, later, married his sister. At any rate, he was brought up in all the virtues and practices of chivalry, which find a large place in his poems. He visited the Field of the Cloth of Gold with the duke of Richmond, possibly accompanied him thence to Paris to study and lived with him, later, at Windsor. In 1536, the duke died, and the same year saw the execution of Surrey's cousin, Anne Boleyn. In 1540, we find him a leader in the tournament held at the marriage of Anne of Cleves, and, after a mission to Guisnes, he was appointed, in 1541, steward of Cambridge university. Part of the next year he spent in the Fleet prison, on a charge of having sent a challenge; but, being soon released on payment of a heavy fine, he began his military career by joining his father in an expedition against the Scots. The next episode in his life is difficult of explanation: he was brought before the privy council on a charge of eating meat in Lent and of breaking windows in the city with a cross-bow. His own explanation was (cf. *London! hast thou accusèd me*) that it was an access of protestant fervour: he regarded himself as 'a figure of the Lord's behest,' sent to warn the sinful city of her doom. In this connection, it is fair to remember that, later, he was accused of being inimical to the new religion. The obvious explanation was that the proceeding was a piece of Mohockism on the part of a (possibly intoxicated) man of twenty-seven. At any rate, Surrey had to suffer for the excess. He was again shut up in the Fleet, where, probably, he paraphrased one or more of the psalms. On his release, he was sent, in October 1543, to join the English troops then assisting the emperor in the siege of Landrecy; and, in 1544, he won further military honour by his defence of Boulogne. On his return, he was thrown into prison at Windsor, owing to the intrigues of his father's enemy, Jane Seymour's brother, the earl of Hertford; was released, again imprisoned, and beheaded in January 1546/7.

In his military prowess, his scholarship, his position at court, his poetry and his mastery in chivalric exercises, Surrey is almost as perfect a knight as Sidney himself. And what strikes the reader most forcibly in the love poems which form the bulk of his work is their adherence to the code of the chivalric courts of love. There is not to be found in Surrey the independence, the manliness or the sincerity of Wyatt. In his love poems, he is an accomplished gentleman playing a graceful game, with what good effect on English poetry will be seen shortly. Surrey was formally married at 16; but the subject of many of his poems was not his wife, but his 'lady' in the chivalric sense, the mistress whose 'man' he had become by a vow of fealty. Setting aside the legends that have grown up about this fair Geraldine, from their root in Nashe's fiction, *The Unfortunate Traveller* (1594), to the sober 'biography' of Anthony à Wood and others, the pertinent facts that may be regarded as true are no more than these: that Elizabeth Fitz-Gerald was a daughter of the ninth earl of Kildare, and, on her father's death in the Tower, was brought up in the household of princess Mary, becoming one of her ladies of the chamber. That she was a mere child when Surrey first began to address poems to her confirms the impression received by the candid reader: these poems, in fact, are the result, not of a sincere passion, but of the rules of the game of chivalry as played in its decrepitude and Surrey's youth. Like Wyatt, he takes his ideas from Petrarch, of whose sonnets he translates four completely, while Ariosto provides another; and his whole body of poetry contains innumerable ideas and images drawn from Petrarch, but assimilated and used in fresh settings. *The frailtie and hurtfulnesse of beautie; Vow to love faithfully howsoever he be rewarded; Complaint that his ladie after she knew of his love kept her face alway hidden from him; Description of Spring, wherin eche thing renewes, save onelie the lover; Complaint of a lover, that defied love, and was by love after the more tormented; Complaint of a diyng lover refused upon his ladies injust mistaking of his writyng*—such are the stock subjects, as they may almost be called, of the Petrarchists which Surrey reproduces. But he reproduces them in every case with an ease and finish that prove him to have mastered his material, and his graceful fancies are admirably expressed. Earlier in the chapter we quoted Wyatt's translation of a sonnet by Petrarch. Let us compare with it Surrey's version of the same:

Love that liveth, and reigneth in my thought,
That built his seat within my captive brest,
Clad in the armes, wherin with me he fought,
Oft in my face he doth his banner rest.
She, that me taught to love, and suffer payne,
My doutfull hope, and eke my hote desyre,
With shamefast cloke to shadowe and refraine,
Her smilyng grace converteth straight to yre.
And cowarde Love then to the hart apace
Taketh his flight, whereas he lurkes, and plaines
His purpose lost, and dare not shewe his face.
For my lordes gilt thus faultlesse byde I paynes.
Yet from my lorde shall not my foote remove,
Swete is his death, that takes his end by love.

The advance in workmanship is obvious at a glance. There is no need to count Surrey's syllables on the fingers, and the caesuras are arranged with variety and skill. The first line contains one of the very few examples in Surrey's poems of an accented weak syllable (*livèth*), and there, as in nearly all the other cases, in the first two feet of the line. It will be noticed, however, that, whereas Wyatt was content with two rimes for his octave, in Petrarchian fashion, Surrey frankly makes up his sonnet of three quatrains and a couplet, which was the form the sonnet mainly took in the hands of his Elizabethan followers. Once or twice, Surrey runs the same pair of rimes right through his first twelve lines; but gains, on the whole, littlo advantage thus. Whichever plan he follows, the result is the same: that, improving on Wyatt's efforts, he makes of the sonnet—what had never existed before in English poetry—a single symphonic effect. It is worth noting, too, that, though his references to Chaucer are even more frequent than Wyatt's, Surrey polishes and refines, never leaving unaltered the archaisms which Wyatt sometimes incorporated with his own language.

A favourite metre of Surrey—a metre used now and then by Wyatt, too—is one of which the student of this period may grow tired as he traces its decadence through Turbervile, Googe and others, to its brief restoration to honour in the hands of Southwell. It was of English origin, being, probably, a development of the ballad quatrain, and was commonly called 'poulter's measure,' from the dozen of eggs that varies, or varied then, between twelve and fourteen. An example will explain the name:

> Suche waiward waies hath love, that most part in discord
> Our willes do stand, whereby our hartes but seldom doe accord.
> Disceit is his delight, and to begile, and mock
> The simple hartes whom he doth strike with froward divers strok.

It is, as the reader will see, the 'common time' of the hymn-book; a combination of two sixes with a fourteener; or, as later writers preferred to have it printed, a stanza of 6686, only the second and fourth lines riming. It is easy to write, because there is no doubt about the accent, and because it saves rimes; and while, in feeble hands, it can become a monotonous jog-trot, it is lyrical in quality, and has in Wyatt's hands a strength, in Surrey's, an elegance, and in Southwell's, a brilliance, which should redeem it from total condemnation. One of Surrey's most delightful poems, *Complaint of the absence of her lover being upon the sea*, is written in this metre, in the management of which, as in that of all the others he attempts, he shows himself a born poet, with a good ear and a knowledge of the necessity of relating line to line and cadence to cadence, so that a poem may become a symphonic whole.

His clearest title to fame, however, rests on his translations from the *Aeneid* of Vergil into blank verse. There is unrimed verse even in Chaucer (*Tale of Melibeus*); and the movement against rime as a piece of medieval barbarity, which was supported, later, by Gabriel Harvey and even by Campion and found its greatest exponent in Milton, had already begun. Still, it is most likely that it was from Italian poetry (possibly Molza's translation of Vergil[1], 1541) that Surrey immediately drew the idea. The merits of the translation do not very much concern us; the merit of having introduced to England the metre of *Tamburlaine the Great*, *The Tempest*, *Paradise Lost* and *The Excursion* is one that can hardly be overrated. Surrey's own use of the metre, if a little stiff and too much inclined to make a break at the end of each line, is a wonderful achievement for his time, and a further proof of his genuine poetical ability.

We have referred to Surrey as a perfect knight; and, in one of his poems, which all readers will possibly agree in thinking his best and sincerest, he gives a picture of his youth which shows in little all the elements of the courtier-knight. This is the *Elegy on the duke of Richmond*, as it has been called (*So cruell prison how coulde betide, alas*), which he wrote early in 1546 during his imprisonment in 'proude Windsor,' the scene of his earlier and happier days. In this, he draws a picture of the life led by himself and his friend. We hear, first of all, of the large green courts whence the youths were wont to look up, sighing, to the ladies in the Maidens' Tower; then of the dances, the tales of chivalry and love; the tennis-court, where the ball was often missed because the player was looking at the ladies in the gallery; the knightly exercises on horseback and on foot; the love-confidences exchanged; the stag-hunt in the forest; the vows of friendship, the bright honour. Here is as clear and complete a picture of the standard of knighthood as any that exists; and chivalry, decaying and mainly reminiscent as it may even then have been, was the inspiration of Surrey's life and of his poetry. It must be noted of him, too, that he shows a fresh and original delight in nature, and was probably the author (as stated in *England's Helicon*) of the famous pastoral *Phylida was a fayer mayde*[2].

[1] Published under the name of cardinal Ippolito de' Medici.

[2] See the chapter on *Song-books* in volume IV.

Of the other contributors to *Tottel's Miscellany*, only four are known by name: Nicholas Grimald, Thomas lord Vaux, John Heywood and Edward Somerset. Of these, the nearest to Wyatt and Surrey is lord Vaux, like them a courtier and trained in the spirit of chivalry. Only two of his poems appear in *Tottel's Miscellany*: *Thassault of Cupid upon the fort*, which was probably suggested by Dunbar, and *The aged lover renounceth love*, the song of which the grave-digger in *Hamlet* is singing a corrupt version as he digs Ophelia's grave. *The Paradyse of Daynty Devises*, which will be noticed later, contains the bulk of his surviving poetry; this falls into two main divisions: poetry of love and chivalry, and religious poetry. A brave, simple and musical writer, Vaux is among the best of the poets of his day. He is by no means free from the Petrarchian conceits favoured by his two forerunners; but his reflections on the brevity of life show a serious and devout mind, and possibly his best poem is *When I look back*, in which he craves the forgiveness of God for the faults and follies of youth. John Heywood is better known as a playwright than as a lyrical poet; the single poem which appears in *Tottel's Miscellany* is a not unpleasing description of the physical and moral charms of his lady, in a style which became exceedingly common. For chastity, she is Diana, for truth, Penelope; after making her, nature lost the mould, and so forth. But the freshness has not yet worn off such statements, and the poem not only has a natural sweetness about it, but contains one of the few simple references to country things which are to be found in the volume. Somerset's contribution is entitled *The pore estate to be holden for best*, and merely states, in two septets of rimed twelve-syllabled lines, a favourite commonplace with these authors. The fact that the first letters of the lines with the last letter of the last line make up the author's name, is significant of artificiality.

From one point of view, Grimald is a very interesting poet. About Wyatt, Surrey and Vaux there is no trace of the professional author. Their poetry was partly the accomplishment of their class, partly the natural expression of feelings aroused by their own lives and the life of their day. Grimald was no courtier, and his literary work was that of the professed man of letters. Educated at Cambridge and Oxford, he became chaplain to bishop Ridley, under whom he translated a work of Aeneas Sylvius and Laurentius Valla's book against the donation of Constantine. Early in Mary's reign, he was imprisoned for heresy, but recanted, and is said to have become a spy during the Marian persecutions. In 1556,

Tottel had published Grimald's translation of Cicero *De Officiis*; and it has been supposed, not without possibility, that he was associated with Tottel, perhaps as editor, in the publication of the *Miscellany*. The first edition (June 1557) contained forty of his poems, and gives his name in full. In the second edition, published a month later, at least thirty of these poems have disappeared, and the author's name has shrunk to N. G. The facts have never been explained. Grimald is particularly fond of 'poulter's measure' and long lines, which, mainly by good use of his learning, he succeeds in keeping above the level of doggerel. He excels in complimentary and elegiac verse; and has left at least two delightful poems: the *Funerall song, upon the deceas of Annes his mother*, which is not only a quaint mixture of learning and homeliness, but a golden tribute to the subject of the elegy, and *The Garden*, which celebrates, with unquestionable enjoyment, the pleasures and profit to be drawn from nature. In another of his poems, *The Lover asketh pardon of his dere, for fleeyng from her*, in which he plays upon his lady's name of Day, Courthope finds the Petrarchian convention replaced by 'the earliest notes in English poetry of that manner which culminated in the "metaphysical" style.' The value of Grimald, however, lies not so much in his matter or his music, as in his attempt to be distinct and terse through the application of his knowledge of the classics to English poetry. He studied and translated Latin epigrams, and, to some extent, was a forerunner of the later classical influence on English diction and construction.

That the remainder of the authors in *Tottel's Miscellany* are declared 'uncertain' does not, necessarily, mean that they were unknown. Men, and sometimes women, wrote for the amusement of themselves and their friends, not for publication. Their verses were handed round, copied out into the manuscript books, of which many survive in public and private libraries, and admired in a small circle. Puttenham (*The Arte of English Poesie*, 1589) speaks of

> notable Gentlemen in the Court that have written commendably and suppressed it agayne, or els suffred it to be publisht without their owne names to it: as if it were a discredit for a Gentleman to seeme learned, and to shew him selfe amourous of any good Art.

Tottel's Miscellany is the first symptom of the breaking down of this bashful exclusiveness, under the desire for poetry felt by lovers and by those outside the court circle who had begun to share in the spread of knowledge and taste due to the renascence. It was the 'book of songs and sonnets' the absence of which Master

Slender lamented in *The Merry Wives of Windsor* (I, 1). Reading had gone some way towards taking the place of listening to the bard or *jongleur*, and Tottel was enterprising enough to attempt to satisfy the new demand. But the authors—living and dead—remained, in many cases, anonymous. One of the poets of the *Miscellany* was, probably, Wyatt's friend, Sir Francis Bryan, though his pieces have not been identified. The range of subjects among these 'uncertain' authors is limited. Of the love-poems, some continue the Petrarchian style of Wyatt and Surrey; others complain in more native fashion of the fickleness and frailty of woman. Praises of the mean estate and warnings of the uncertainty of life and the vanity of human wishes are very numerous. We find here the ideas introduced by Wyatt and Surrey repeated a hundred times; and certain conceits and ideas (*e.g.* that of nature losing, or breaking, the mould, the uncertain state of a lover, 'That all thing sometime finde ease of their paine, save onely the lover,' and so forth) are common to all. One or two poems raise an impression of something more than fashion. In particular, the author of a set of 'poulter's' called *Of the wretchednes of this world* seems to speak from his heart. In complaining of the lapse of good laws and the increase of evil customs and wicked men, he expresses, perhaps only more forcibly, and not more sincerely, than his fellows, the feelings roused in all by the decay of the old feudal order before the new England of Elizabeth came to restore security and an ideal. The reigns of Edward VI and Mary, and, to a great extent, the latter part of that of Henry VIII, were not favourable to the growth of poetry; and we find the fellows and successors of Wyatt and Surrey content to carry on their tradition without improving on the versification of the latter (one of them is guilty of the line: 'Of Henry, sonne to sir John Williams knight') or adding to the stock of subjects and ideas. Some of the authors, clearly, were familiar with the work of Boccaccio—the story of Troilus and Cressida is a favourite reference—and one poem contains the earliest English translation of a passage of Ovid, the letter of Penelope to Ulysses. As regards the metres, 'poulter's measure' is the most prominent; decasyllables and eights are common, and the rimes are often on the scheme of the rime royal stanza. Alliteration, which Grimald favoured to some extent, is more common among the 'uncertain' authors than in Wyatt and Surrey[1].

[1] Courthope, *Hist. Eng. Poet.* II. p. 165, points out that *Piers Plowman* had recently been reprinted and may have encouraged alliteration by its example.

One of those 'uncertain' authors, according to his own account, was Thomas Churchyard. The son of a farmer and born near Shrewsbury, Churchyard gave some part of his long life to war, the rest to poetry. He served under the emperor and other famous captains in Scotland, in Ireland, in the Low Countries and in France, where he was taken prisoner and escaped. He was, in fact, a soldier of fortune, and, on laying down his arms, he continued to look to fortune for a maintenance. That fortune played him false till he was over seventy, denying him the court place he desired and rewarding him then only with a pension from the queen, was not the whole secret of his frequent reflections on the vanity of human wishes, for that was a trick of the times. And beneath his complaints lay a poetic bravery which goes far to atone for the monotony of his style and the poverty of his thought. Soldier-like, he ruffles it in a glittering display of similes and comparisons. His ingenuity in this field is inexhaustible, and one little commonplace is decked out in a hundred guises till the brain is dazzled. The display covers very little substance, and his fondness for alliteration and the monotony of his stress (which he seems to drive home by his practice of marking his caesuras with a blank space in the printed line) make his valiant 'fourteeners' and 'common-time' stanzas prized rather for the rarity of his editions than for the merit of his poetry. At the same time, Churchyard was, for his period, a smooth and accomplished versifier, who had taken to heart the lesson taught by Wyatt and Surrey, and who did his share of the work of restoring form and order to English poetry.

His earliest publication seems to have been a three-leaved poem, *The myrrour of man*[1]. Early in his career he is found in controversy, and employing a weapon which he always found useful, the broadside. In 1563 came his best work, the long 'tragedy' of *Shore's Wife* in *A Mirror for Magistrates.* In 1575, he published the first of the books with the alliterative titles or sub-titles which he liked—*Churchyardes Chippes.* In 1578, he began to make use of matter which served him well, his military experiences: the *Wofull Warres in Flaunders* of that year was followed by the *Generall Rehearsall of Warres* (*Churchyard's Choise*), which reviews the deeds of the soldiers and sailors of England from the time of Henry VIII, and his descriptions of the sieges of Leith and Edinburgh are among the best of his narrative

[1] A. H. Bullen in the *D. of N. B.*, *s.v.* The notice contains a good deal of bibliographical information which it is difficult to obtain elsewhere.

poems. In the next year, 1579, he appears in a new light as devising and describing 'shows' for the queen on her progresses. Others of his principal works were *The Praise of Poetrie* (1595), in which he attempted to do in verse what Sidney's *Apologie* had done in prose, and *The Worthines of Wales* (1587), a vigorous book which, to some extent, anticipates the *Poly-Olbion* of Michael Drayton. He translated three books of Ovid's *Tristia* and began a translation of Pliny which he destroyed. Grumbling, hoping, quarrelling and making friends again, with Nashe (who realised his merit) and others, paying fine homage to the great men of his day, he continued writing till his voice sounded strange in the new era, long after Colin Clout had described him as 'old Palaemon that sung so long untill quite hoarse he grew.'

The decadence of the school of Wyatt and Surrey may be seen in other miscellanies, which will soon be considered; but, for the moment, we must turn aside to a poet who felt none of the Italian influence—Thomas Tusser.

Tusser, who was born in Essex about 1525, became a singing boy at St Paul's, was at Eton under Nicholas Udall, who, he records, flogged him, and went on to King's College and Trinity Hall, Cambridge. Leaving the university for reasons of ill-health, he entered, as a musician, the service of William lord Paget, who, later, was privy seal to Mary. Of lord Paget and his two sons, Henry and Thomas, in succession, he considered himself ever afterwards the retainer. In 1553, or thereabouts, he left London for a farm near Brantham, in Suffolk, where he introduced into England the culture of barley. In 1557, he published his *Hundreth good pointes of husbandrie,* which was enlarged in 1570, or earlier, by *A hundreth good poynts of huswifery,* again, in 1573, to *Five hundreth pointes of good husbandry,* and again in 1577 and 1580—to run through five more editions before the end of the century. His life was restless. At one time we find him a lay-clerk in Norwich cathedral, thanks to Sir Robert Southwell, of the family of Southwell the poet; later, he is quarrelling over tithes near Witham, in Essex, then in London, and again in Cambridge, possibly as a choirman at Trinity Hall. In 1580, he died in the parish of St Mildred, Poultry, where he is buried.

The *Hundreth* and *Five Hundreth* points are an extraordinary, but most entertaining, collection of maxims on farming, weather-lore, forestry, agriculture, thrift, virtue, religion and life in general. The title-pages given in the bibliography to this chapter are in the spirit of the work itself, which is full of a shrewd and kindly humour, and a ripe, if pedestrian, wisdom. The book gives a complete picture of the farmer's life of the day; and, for two centuries at least, it was read far and wide as a practical manual of farming. The year is divided into months; and the duties of each month in farm, garden and house, together with many of its customs, superstitions and observances, not without their value for the antiquary and the student of manners, are set forth in rimed four-foot anapaestic couplets (the metre of *Bonnie Dundee*), that carry the modern reader along at a hand-gallop till he is ready to drop, but must have proved very easy reading to the country gentlemen and farmers of the sixteenth and seventeenth centuries. And, the better to fix the precepts in the mind, each month has its epitome in verse which could be learned by heart. The greater part of Tusser's work is in the metre mentioned above; but the prefatory poems, of which there are many, offer a more interesting variety of metrical experiment than any work of the same date. In the 'Epistle to Lord William Paget' he uses a stanza of six lines of eight, rimed *ababcc*; the 'Epistle to Lord Thomas Paget' is an example of metre which Swinburne was afterwards to use with wonderful effect in combination with another: it is the 7776, riming *aaab*, with double-rimes at *a*, which forms the last part of the stanza of *Proserpine*, only Tusser doubles it into *aaabcccb*. 'To the Reader' is written in 'Skeltonics,' a long (and, in Tusser's case, regular) stanza of four-syllabled iambic lines riming *aabbccdeeffggd*. The other metres need not be mentioned in detail, but two must be singled out. The *Conditions of Husbandrie* consists of stanzas, of which the last two lines are Tusser's favourite four-foot anapaests; while the first two are either among the rare examples of the use of the amphibrach (⏑ – ⏑), or, more probably, are two-foot anapaests with a double rime. The 'Preface to the Buyer' is interesting, as the first example of the three-foot anapaestic line which was used, later, by Shenstone and Prior, and which is familiar to all as the metre of Cowper's 'I am monarch of all I survey.' Tusser's ingenuity leads him into many faults; he affects acrostics and alliteration (in his *Things Thriftie* there are twelve couplets in which every word begins with a T; every line but the last two of his *Ladder to Thrift* ends in *ie* or *y*); but these things are easily pardoned to a man who was writing, not to please the literary circles of the town, but to fix his maxims in the heads of the country; and the same ingenuity stood him in good stead in the matter of metre. He was too good a scholar, with too good an ear, to leave things as irregular as they had been in the hands of Skelton. Taking measures and feet that were English and familiar, he polished and combined them with no contemptible skill, uniting an ease in movement with a terseness and exactness of expression that were new in this field; though he lies outside the main stream of development and has, on that account, been too much neglected, his achievement and influence were valuable. He has been accused of carelessness and wilfulness in rime, perhaps unfairly. Many of the cases that have been cited might, if studied patiently and systematically, prove to be documents for the provincial or common pronunciation of the day. Certain of Tusser's compressions and elisions (*e.g.* his frequent use of an ablative absolute) found no imitator till Browning.

We have seen the influence of the classics on the form of English poetry beginning feebly to make itself felt with Grimald. That influence must not be confounded with the study and translation of classical authors, which had begun earlier, with Barclay, Gavin Douglas and Surrey; for, while Surrey, for instance, had translated from the *Aeneid*, the influence moulding his own work was almost entirely Italian. But the study of the classics was soon to exercise its own influence; and, six years after the first publication of *Tottel's Miscellany*, we find Barnabe Googe introducing in his *Eglogs, Epytaphes and Sonettes* (1563) the form of the pastoral, which, doubtless, he had learned from Barclay's adaptations of the eclogues of Mantuan. Barnabe Googe, the son of a recorder of Lincoln, was born about 1540, educated at Cambridge and Oxford and, after travelling in France and Spain (see his poems written on starting and returning), taken into the service of Sir William Cecil. His earliest literary work was a translation of a satirical allegory, the *Zodiacus Vitae* of Marcellus Palingenius. His original poems appear to have been written before 1561, when he started for the continent, for they were then left in the hands of his friend, Blundeston, who took them 'all togyther unpolyshed,' to the printer. Googe returned in time to correct them and to finish one of the poems, *Cupido Conquered*. The eclogues, epitaphs and sonnets (*i.e.* songs, for he has left no sonnets proper) were his last original work. He died in or about 1594. His eclogues are eight in number, and are interesting, partly because of the influence they must have exerted on Spenser, and partly from the manner of their treatment. Googe was an earnest protestant; and he combines with the pastoral of the classical idyllists some horror at their views of love, much devout thought and considerable indignation against Bonner and his works. His eclogues, indeed, are a curious mixture; for, while the talk is chiefly of love, the poet rarely fails to improve the occasion. In eclogue II, for instance—one of the most beautiful of the set in structure and rhythm—we have the death-song of Damoetas as he dies for love of a cruel mistress. In eclogue IV, the ghost of Damoetas visits Meliboeus and warns him to avoid love, which not only makes men wretched in life but dooms them after death. The eclogue is aimed against the pagan view both of love and heroism. In the sixth eclogue, as elsewhere in Googe, we hear that idleness is the root of love, a complaint which can be cured by exercise and work. In the eighth, Cornix sums up in a religious discourse. We have noticed in *Tottel's Miscellany* the evidence of a troubled time of transition in politics and social life. The same evidence occurs in Googe. 'Nobylitie begins to fade, and Carters up do sprynge,' he cries; the chief estate is in the hands of Sir John Straw and Sir John Cur, who, though they think themselves noble, are but fish which, 'bred up in durtye Pooles, wyll ever stynke of mudde.' The fifth and sixth of the eclogues are borrowed from the *Diana* of Montemayor, and, possibly, are the first traces in English poetry of the influence of the Spanish romances.

The pastoral, then, with Googe, is not a refuge from the life of his times, but a means of giving vent to his thoughts about it; and the third eclogue, from which we have quoted, goes some way towards explaining why the revival initiated by Wyatt and Surrey was not carried on with more fervour. As a metrist, Googe is careless and often feeble. The metre of his eclogues is the fourteener line; he cuts it into two on his page; but, even so, is not always certain how many feet it should contain. This practice of division, when applied, as in his epitaphs, to decasyllabic lines, results in a monotonous fall of the caesura after the second foot. His songs are largely moral in tone, like his eclogues. Their limited range of metre shows a lack of invention; and, though the movement is free, we miss the genuine lyrical note which less learned poets were then achieving.

In Turbervile, Googe's friend and fellow-worker, the school of Wyatt and Surrey comes perilously near its nadir. George Turbervile was born of a good Dorset family, and was educated at Winchester and New College. Later, he became secretary to Thomas Randolph, and accompanied him on his embassy to Russia, whence he wrote 'certain letters in verse,' which may be found in the first volume of Hakluyt. Like Googe, he composed very little original poetry, though he was an energetic translator. Ovid's *Heroical Epistles,* Mantuan's *Eclogues* and Mancinus's *Plaine Path to Perfect Vertue* were all translated by him between 1567 and 1568, and the first had run through five editions by 1605. That Turbervile was a man of taste is proved by his lines to Surrey (in the last of which, by the way, he scans *Earle's,* as he always does, as a dissyllable); praising him because 'our mother tongue by him hath got such light, As ruder speech thereby is banished quite,' and because he puts 'each word in place.' The refining influence of Surrey was what Turbervile admired and attempted, with some success, to carry on in his *Epitaphs, Epigrams, Songs and Sonets* (1567), his only volume of original poetry. The praise of Surrey shows no little skill in managing the heroic couplet with ease and point; but the inevitable double-six-and-fourteener had a fatal attraction for him, and becomes in his hands little better than doggerel. The reason was partly, no doubt, that his stock of ideas was small. He fell back very largely on Wyatt for his matter, and, in attempting to refine Wyatt, he waters him down sadly. Of Wyatt's eight-line adaptation of Serafino, *The furious goone,* Turbervile makes eighteen lines. Of the famous epigram about the two men, the noose and the gold, which Plato (if he were the author of the Greek version) wrote in two lines, Ausonius in four and Wyatt in eight (*For shamefast harm of great, and hatefull nede*) Turbervile makes twelve; Wyatt's *Complaint upon Love to Reason* is imitated in 'poulter's measure' and enlarged to allow Plato, Tullie, Plutarch, Sense and Reason herself all to speak against Love; Turbervile's *Pretie epigram of a scholer, that having read Vergil's* Aenidos, *maried a curst wife,* takes seven stanzas to say what a writer in *Tottel's Miscellany,* whom Warton is inclined to believe to be Sir Thomas More, had said in two; and instances could be multiplied. Turbervile's satire addressed *To the Rayling Rout of Sycophants* (by which he means critics) throws an interesting side-light on the literary activity of the age; at least one of his poems, *The green that you would wish me wear,* is deservedly well known for its beauty and spirit, while his *Lover* is a good example of an airy and delicate use of very short lines which Googe never accomplished.

Thomas Howell, the author of *The Arbor of Amitie* (1568)

Newe Sonets, and pretie Pamphlets (1568) and the better known *Devises* (1581), is a poet of greater variety than either Googe or Turbervile. Two points of detail should secure his memory from oblivion: first, that his *Devises* contains a poem beginning *Goe learned booke, and unto Pallas sing,* believed to contain the earliest extant reference in literature to Sidney's *Arcadia,* which Howell must have seen in manuscript; and, next, that *A Dreame,* in the same volume, is written in the fourteen-lined stanza, possibly of Scots origin, which was used, later, by Montgomerie and is best known through *The Jolly Beggars* of Burns. For the rest, Howell, of whose life little is known beyond that he was born possibly at Dunster in Somerset, educated possibly at Oxford, and was certainly gentleman-retainer in the related families of the earls of Pembroke and of Shrewsbury, was a close student of *Tottel's Miscellany* and reproduced, in all sincerity, but with no spark of genius, the thoughts and the characteristics of the school of Wyatt and Surrey. He knew his Petrarch, and he knew his Chaucer; and he devoted himself to repeating in the approved style of the time the approved truths about the sorrows of love, the uncertainty of fortune and the briefness of life. To Howell, as to his contemporaries, the fourteen-syllabled line offered irresistible attractions; but he wins interest by the variety of metres he attempts, and by giving, perhaps, a foretaste of the flexibility which was shortly to constitute one of the greatest charms of lyrical poetry.

Of Humfrey Gifford, whose *Posie of Gilloflowers* was published in 1580, and of Matthew Grove, whose *Historie of Pelops and Hippodamia* with the *Epigrams, songes and sonnettes* that follow it, was published in 1587, little need be said. Gifford, who was a friend of the Stafford family, was a translator from the French and Italian and a versifier of small merit, who writes, mainly, in decasyllabic lines, but employs, also, the popular fourteeners. He is not above riddles, anagrams and so forth. One of his poems, however, entitled *For Souldiers,* is a brave and spirited piece in a complicated but easy-moving, swinging metre; and the prose epistle to the reader may be mentioned as containing a sentence which, possibly, suggested to Shakespeare Iago's speech in *Othello* (III, 3): 'Who steals my purse, steals trash,' etc. Of Matthew Grove, even his publisher knew practically nothing. Unless his poems, too, were published (as was probably the case) some time after they were written, his was a belated voice singing on the eve of the Armada much as men had sung under Henry VIII, and as if Sidney and Spenser had never been.

To return now to the miscellanies. The earliest to follow

Tottel's Miscellany was *The Paradyse of Daynty Devises* (1576) 'devised and written for the most part' by Richard Edwards but not, apparently, published till ten years after his death. Edwards was master of the children of the queen's chapel, and is best known not by his lyrics, but by his plays. He was a poet, however, of no small merit, and of his own poems in this volume one, at least, rises to a high level: *In going to my naked bed,* with its refrain on *amantium irae,* 'The falling out of faithful friends renewing is of love.' The tone of the collection (which opens with a translation from St Bernard) is, on the whole, very serious and didactic; the motives of love and honour that had inspired Wyatt and Surrey have dropped out of use, and in their place we find but few signs of any joy in life. The pleasant woes of the lover have given place to apprehensions of the shortness and vanity of life and the need of preparing for death and judgment, themes familiar to the poets of two centuries earlier. The contributors to the volume, in its first (1576) and second (1578) editions, number, in all, twenty-three, with two anonymous poems. The author who signs himself 'My luke is losse' is an ingenious contriver of metrical patterns and repetitions, though a monotonous poet; William Hunnis, Edwards's successor in office and, like him, a dramatist, is over-ingenious, too, but one of the best of the company; among the others are Jasper Heywood, the translator of Seneca; M. Yloop (?Pooly); Richard Edwards himself; Thomas lord Vaux (see above); Francis Kinwelmersh, a writer of sincere religious poems, whose contributions include a delightful song by *A Vertuous Gentlewoman in the praise of her love* and his carol *From Virgin's wombe,* which was deservedly popular with the musicians; W. R., who, possibly, is Ralegh, though the attribution of the single poem signed with these initials was changed in the second edition; Richard Hill; D. S. (Dr Edwyn Sandys); Churchyard; F. G., who is probably young Fulke Greville; Lodowick Lloyd (of whose epitaph on Sir Edward Saunders the quotation of two lines will be a sufficient criticism: 'Who welnigh thirtie yeeres was Judge, before a Judge dyd fall, A judged by that mighty Judge, which Judge shal judge us all'); E. O. (Edward Vere, earl of Oxford); M. Bew; George Whetstone (in the second edition only); and M. Thom. Fulke Greville, lord Brooke (if, indeed, he be author of the poem signed with his initials), will be discussed in a later chapter; Edward Vere is, perhaps, more famous for his quarrel with Sidney and for his lyric *If women would be fair and yet not fond* than for all the rest of his work. This volume contains more of his poetry than any later collection; but it is early work, written before he had taken his place as the champion of the literary party that opposed Sidney and Gabriel Harvey, or before he had developed his special epigrammatic vein. In *The Paradyse of Daynty Devises,* his work partakes of the devotional character of the miscellany.

The next miscellany to be published was the least meritorious of all. In *A Gorgious Gallery of Gallant Inventions* (1578), the faults that developed in the school after the death of Surrey became more pronounced. Alliteration is almost incessant, and the metre which we have found constantly gaining in favour and deteriorating in quality here runs wild. The book was edited, or, rather, 'joyned together and builded up,' by one T. P. (Thomas Proctor), who contributes *Pretie Pamphlets or Proctor's Precepts* and other poems. Another contributor is Owen Roydon, who complains of the 'sicophantes,' by which, like Turbervile, he intends the critics. Short gnomic verses on the virtues are common; Troilus and Cressida are constantly to the front; loving letters (from beyond the seas and elsewhere) are frequent; subject, indeed, and method show a complete lack of freshness and conviction, and we are treated to the dregs of a school. One poem, however, *Though Fortune cannot favor,* is, at least, manly and downright; *The glyttering showes of Floras dames* has lyrical quality; and certain *Prety parables and proverbes of love* are interesting by their use of anapaests. The *Gorgious Gallery,* too, contains the popular and famous song, *Sing all of green willow.*

The next miscellany, which is the last book to be mentioned here, was *A Handefull of pleasant delites,* by Clement Robinson and others, of which the only copy known, that in the British Museum, was published, in 1584, by Richard Jones, a publisher of ballads. The Stationers' register, however, shows that, in 1566, a licence was issued to Clement Robinson for 'a boke of very pleasaunte Sonettes and storyes in myter.' The 1584 volume, therefore, has been thought to be a later edition of the book of 1566, into which were incorporated poems written since that date. It may be noted that every poem in the *Handefull* has its tune assigned it by name. This practice was not unknown in earlier anthologies—in the *Gorgious Gallery,* for instance. In the *Handefull,* it is consistently followed. The tunes assigned are, sometimes, those of well known dances, 'the new Rogero,' the 'Quarter Brailes,' the 'Black Almaine'; or of popular ballads, such as 'Greensleeves.' Of the influence of music on the lyrical poetry of the age more will be said in a later chapter. So far as the *Handefull* is concerned, though by no means free from doggerel, its contents have often an honest life and spirit about them, which are welcome after the resuscitated, ghostly air of the *Gorgious Gallery.* Still, the book belongs, by subject and treatment, to the poetical age which was closing. Twenty-five of the poems are anonymous, and, among them, those of the editor, Clement Robinson. The named contributors are Leon Gibson, the author of a lively *Tantara* ; G. Mannington, whose *Sorrowful sonet made at Cambridge Castle* is parodied at length in Chapman, Marston and Jonson's *Eastward Hoe* (1603); R. Picks; Thomas Richardson; and I. Thomson—the last of whom contributes a *New Sonet of Pyramus and Thisbie,* which it is hard to believe Shakespeare had not seen. He certainly had seen the song on flowers, which contains the line: 'Rosemarie is for remembrance, betweene us daie and night.'

CHAPTER IX

A MIRROR FOR MAGISTRATES

A Mirror for Magistrates constitutes an important link between medieval and modern literature. It is a monument of industry, extending, in its most recent edition, to more than 1400 closely printed pages, and retailing stories of misfortune and wickedness in high places, stretching from the time of Albanact (B.C. 1085) to that of queen Elizabeth. Its very title recalls a large class of earlier works, of which Gower's *Speculum Meditantis* or *Mirour de l'Omme* is a conspicuous example. Its aim is medieval, whether we take the statement of its editor, Baldwin, in the address to the nobility—'here as in a loking glass, you shal se if any vice be in you, how the like hath ben punished in other heretofore, wherby admonished, I trust it will be a good occasione to move to the amendment'—or that in the address to the reader—'which might be as a mirour for al men as well nobles as others to shewe the slipery deceiptes of the wavering lady, and the due rewarde of all kinde of vices.' Its plan of stringing together a number of 'tragedies' is medieval in its monotony—so much so that Chaucer put into the mouth of both Knight and Host a vigorous protest against it as adopted by himself in *The Monk's Tale.* The scheme of the *Mirror*, with its medieval device of an interlocutor, was taken over directly from Lydgate's translation (through Premierfait) of Boccaccio's *De Casibus Virorum Illustrium,* of which, indeed, the *Mirror* is a continuation: originally, it was intended to be bound up in one volume with *The Fall of Princes,* and the first 'tragedy,' in all the earlier editions, is entitled *The Falle of Robert Tresilian.* On the other hand, the *Mirror* had a large share in the development of historical poems and history plays in the Elizabethan period, and Sackville's *Induction* is known to all who care for English poetry.

Warton's ascription of the original design of the *Mirror* to Sackville still passes current, and even later historians leave the issue somewhat obscure. The assertion that Sackville was the originator of the whole work was not made by Niccols (editor of the 1610 version of the *Mirror*); Warton was misled by more recent authorities—that of Mrs Cooper, perhaps, in the *Muses Library* (1738). It seems worth while to make the matter clear by quoting what Niccols actually says in his edition as to Sackville's connection with the undertaking:

> This worthie president of learning, intending to perfect all this storie himselfe from the Conquest, being called to a more serious expence of his time in the great state affaires of his most royall ladie and soveraigne, left the dispose thereof to *M. Baldwine*, *M. Ferrers* and others, the composers of these tragedies, who continuing their methode which was by way of dialogue or interlocution betwixt every tragedie, gave it onely place before the duke of *Buckingham's* complaint.

There is nothing here ascribing to Sackville the original design. Indeed, the words 'perfect' and 'continuing' imply that Sackville's undertaking was preceded by that of Baldwin, Ferrers and others; and this is plainly stated in Baldwin's preface of 1563. When he proposed to read Sackville's *Induction*—

> 'Hath hee made a preface,' sayd one, 'what meaneth hee thereby, seeing none other hath used the like order?' 'I will tell you the cause thereof,' sayd I, 'which is this; after that hee understoode that some of the counsayl would not suffer the booke to bee printed in such order as wee had agreede and determined, hee purposed to have gotten at my handes all the tragedies that were before the duke of *Buckingham's*, which hee would have preserved in one volume. And from that time backward, even to the time of William the Conquerour, he determined to continue and perfect all the story him selfe, in such order as *Lydgate* (following *Bochas*) had already used. And therefore to make a meete induction into the matter, hee devised this poesie.'

Stanzas 76 and 77 of the *Induction* and stanza 2 of *The Complaynt of Henry Duke of Buckingham* show that Sackville intended to write other 'complaints,' and there is some probability in Courthope's suggestion that 'when the Council prohibited the publication of the book, probably on account of its modern instances, he resolved to begin with ancient history.' According to the testimony of both Baldwin and Niccols, he intended to begin at the Conquest and to fill the gap between 1066 and 1388, which, as a matter of fact, was not filled until 1610. But that Sackville was one of the partners in the original design is doubtful, as he was only eighteen years of age when the first edition of the *Mirror* was being printed.

Baldwin says in his 'Epistle dedicatory' (1559): 'The wurke was begun, and part of it printed .iiii. years agoe,' and this statement is borne out by a curious circumstance pointed out by W. F. Trench. The title-page of the first edition has survived at the end of a few copies of Wayland's edition of Lydgate's *Fall of Princes*, and, on the reverse, Wayland printed his licence, dated 20 October 1553, and beginning: 'Mary by the grace of God, Quene of Englande, Fraunce, and Ireland, *defendour of the faith and in earth of the Churche of Englande, and also of Ireland, the supreme head.*' Mary was relieved of the title 'head of the church' by a statute passed 4 January, 1555, and it was informally dropped some months before that time. In the letter of John Elder to the bishop of Caithness, dated 1 January 1555, and printed by Wayland, the letters patent are reproduced with the omission of the words italicised above. Wayland was a good Catholic and a printer of (mainly) religious books, and, naturally, he would make haste to conform with the law. Elder's letter, printed in 1555, shows that he did so, and *A memorial of suche Princes as since the tyme of King Richard the Seconde have been unfortunate in the Realme of England* (so runs the original title-page) must have been printed in 1554.

Wayland, however, was not the printer who originated the undertaking, and his attempt to carry it into execution was hindered by the lord chancellor, Stephen Gardiner. By the time that a licence had been procured through the influence of lord Stafford, Wayland had gone out of business, and the first editions issued to the public were printed by Thomas Marsh. The first editor of the *Mirror*, William Baldwin, apparently began his connection with the work of publishing as servant to Edward Whitchurch, who published his *Treatise of Moral Philosophy* (1547) and *The Canticles* (1549). On the accession of queen Mary, Whitchurch, who was a zealous protestant, apparently gave up business, and sold his stock-in-trade to Wayland and Tottel. Baldwin then entered the service of Wayland, who had taken over Whitchurch's office at the sign of the Sun in Fleet street; and from his presses were issued Baldwin's *Brief Memorial* (1554) and a new edition of the *Moral Philosophy* (1555). Whitchurch had in hand an edition of Lydgate's *Fall of Princes*, and this was taken up by both Wayland and Tottel. Tottel's edition bore a title-page including one of Whitchurch's ornamental borders, marked with his initials; Wayland's was issued from Whitchurch's former office. Whitchurch, therefore, as Trench has shown, was the printer referred to in the extract from Baldwin's address 'To the Reader' given below (1559); and this conclusion is borne out by the fact that those concerned in the enterprise were, with the exception of Wayland, all protestants. It leads to the further inference that the book was first planned in the reign of Edward VI.

The origin of the enterprise is best set forth in Baldwin's own words in the following extract from his address 'To the Reader' (1559):

When the printer had purposed with hym selfe to printe *Lidgate's* booke of the fall of Princes, and had made privye thereto, many both honourable and worshipfull, he was counsailed by dyvers of them, to procure to have the storye contynewed from where as *Bochas* lefte, unto this presente time, chiefly of such as Fortune had dalyed with here in this ylande... which advice liked him so well, that hee requyred mee to take paynes therein.

Baldwin refused to undertake the task without assistance, and the printer, presumably still Whitchurch, persuaded divers learned men to take upon them part of the work.

And when certayne of them to the numbre of seaven, were through a generall assent at one apoynted time and place, gathered together to devise thereupon I resorted unto them, bearing with mee the booke of *Bochas*, translated by *Dan Lidgate*, for the better observation of his order: which although wee liked well yet would it not conveniently serve, seeing that both *Bochas* and *Lidgate* were deade, neyther were there any alive that medled with like argument, to whome the unfortunate might make theyr mone. To make therefore a state meete for the matter, they all agreede that I shoulde usurpe *Bochas*' rome, and the wretched princes complayne unto mee: and tooke upon themselves, every man for his part to be sundry personages, and in theyr behalfes to bewaile unto mee theyr greevous chaunces, heavy destenies, and woefull misfortunes.

Ferrers marvelled that Bochas had forgotten, among his miserable princes, those of our own nation—Britons, Danes, Saxons and English down to his own time.

It were therefore a goodly and notable matter, to searche and discourse our whole story from the first beginning of the inhabiting of the isle. But seeing the printer's mind is to have us followe where *Lidgate* left, wee will leave that greate laboure to other that maye entende it, and (as one being bold first to breake the yse) I will begin at the time of *Richarde* the second, a time as unfortunate as the ruler therein.

The original design was, therefore, suggested to Whitchurch, and by him committed to Baldwin and his associates. Ferrers thought of beginning from the time of the ancient Britons, and it was the printer who decided that they should 'follow where Lidgate left.' Baldwin intended to continue the story to queen Mary's time, but he was fain to end it much sooner. 'Whan I first tooke it in hand, I had the help of many graunted and offred of sum, but of few perfourmed, skarce of any' ('To the Nobilitie,' 1559). The original design of the *Mirror* was not carried out in its entirety until 1610; all the later contributions to it were contemplated in the plans of the original authors, and were, as we shall see, accomplished in consequence of their suggestions.

What were to have been the contents of the original issue in folio, we do not know, except that they included the tragedies of Richard II and Owen Glendower, and, probably, most of those of part I (1559) and some of part II (1563).

It appears from the end-links of Clarence (Quarto 1) and Shore's Wife (Q 2) that Baldwin planned three parts or volumes: first to the end of Edward IV's reign; then, to the end of Richard III; and, lastly, 'to the ende of this King and Queene's reigne' (Philip and Mary). It further appears, from a reference to 'our queene because she is a woman, and our king because he is a straunger' in the Blacksmith's end-link, that this tragedy was written at the same time, although it was not given to the public until 1563. In the Shore's Wife end-link (Q 2), the tragedy of Somerset was also mentioned, and, presumably, that also was in existence in the reign of Philip and Mary, for a place was left for it in the first quarto, although it was not published until the second quarto. As actually given to the public, part I contained nineteen tragedies—those of Tresilian, Mortimer, Gloucester, Mowbray, Richard II, Owen Glendower, Northumberland, Cambridge, Salisbury, James I (of Scotland), Suffolk, Cade, York, Clifford, Worcester, Warwick, Henry VI, Clarence, Edward IV; in the prose links, mention is made of three others—those of the duchess Eleanor and duke Humphrey of Gloucester (printed in 1578) and that of Somerset (printed 1563). Part II contained only eight tragedies—those of Woodville, Hastings, Buckingham, Collingbourne, Richard III, Shore's Wife, Somerset and the Blacksmith[1].

In 1574, Marsh issued *The First parte of the Mirour for Magistrates, containing the falles of the first unfortunate Princes of this lande. From the comming of Brute to the incarnation of our saviour and redemer Jesu Christe.* John Higgins, the editor, says he was moved to the work by the words of Baldwin in his address 'To the Reader': 'the like infortunate princes offered themselves unto me as matter very meete for imitation, the like admonition, miter, and phrase.' He, accordingly, took the earliest period, up to the birth of Christ, and was inclined with time and leisure 't'accomplish the residue til I came to the Conquest.' His first edition included the lives of Albanact (B.C. 1085), Humber, Locrinus, Elstride, Sabrine, Madan, Malin, Mempricius, Bladud,

[1] As to the authorship of parts I and II, see table in bibliography.

Cordila, Morgan, Forrex, Porrex, Kimarus, Morindus, Nennius, and (in some copies) Irenglas (B.C. 51). These were all written by himself and were reprinted in 1575 without noteworthy change. Baldwin's first and second parts were now combined as the last part and published by Marsh under that title in 1574 (Q 4) and, again, in 1575 (Q 5). The sixth quarto (1578) is a reprint of the fifth, except that it includes the long promised tragedies of Eleanor Cobham and Humphrey, duke of Gloucester, by Ferrers.

The first and last parts were united in an edition published by Marsh in 1587, and edited by Higgins, who had rewritten his own legends of Bladud, Forrex and Porrex, and added to his list Iago, Pinnar, Stater, Rudacke, Brennus, Emerianus, Chirinnus, Varianus, Julius Caesar, Tiberius, Caligula, Guiderius, Hamo, Claudius, Nero, Galba, Otho, Vitellius, Londricus, Severus, Fulgentius, Geta, Caracalla, making forty lives in all, and bringing his part of the work down to A.D. 209. To the last part he added Sir Nicholas Burdet (1441), written by himself; two poems, 'pende above fifty yeares agone,' by Francis Dingley of Munston—*The Lamentation of James IV* and *Flodden Field*—and Cardinal Wolsey, by Churchyard.

Meanwhile, Thomas Blenerhasset had set to work to fill the gap left by Higgins after B.C. 51, and published in 1578 the following tragedies, extending from A.D. 44 to 1066: Guidericus, Carassus, Helena, Vortiger, Uther Pendragon, Cadwallader, Sigebert, Lady Ebbe, Alurede, Egelrede, Edric, Harold. These were issued by a different printer (Richard Webster) and, therefore, were not included by Marsh in his edition of 1587, Higgins covering part of the same ground, and having promised in his address 'To the Reader,' in 1574, to come down to the same point—the Conquest—that Blenerhasset actually reached.

The next editor, Niccols (1610) adopted the plan suggested by Sackville, and omitted the prose links. For the first part, he took Higgins's *Induction*; for the second, Sackville's; and, for the third, one of his own composition. The first part included the forty tragedies by Higgins and ten of Blenerhasset's—omitting Guidericus (supplied, since Blenerhasset wrote, by Higgins) and Alurede (supplied by Niccols himself); for the latter reason, he omits Richard III in part II and he also leaves out James I, James IV and the Battle of Flodden, apparently out of consideration for the Scots; part III contains ten tragedies of his own—Arthur, Edmund Ironside, Alfred, Godwin, Robert Curthose, Richard I, John, Edward II, Edward V, Richard III. England's Eliza, also his own, with a separate *Induction*, describes the reign of queen

Elizabeth. Thus, the original design, projected in the reign of Edward VI, was completed in the reign of James; but the day of the *Mirror* had gone by. The new and complete edition did not sell, and the sheets were re-issued under fresh titles in 1619, 1620 and 1621.

As to the popularity and influence of the successive editions of *A Mirror for Magistrates* in the sixteenth century there can be no doubt. Besides obvious imitations in title and method[1], many other works were published similar in plan, though not in title. Some of these, such as George Cavendish's *Metrical Visions*, were, evidently, due to the example of Boccaccio's *De Casibus* through Lydgate; others, such as *A Poor Man's Pittance*, are either avowed or obvious imitations of the *Mirror*. In the last decade of the century, isolated legends came into vogue, apparently through the success of Churchyard's *Jane Shore* (Q 2), which, probably, suggested Daniel's *Rosamond* (1592) and this, in turn, Shakespeare's *Rape of Lucrece*[2]. Drayton's *Cromwell* (1607) was actually included by Niccols in his edition of the *Mirror*, but, together with his *Legends of Robert Duke of Normandy*, *Matilda the Chaste* and *Piers Gaveston* (1596), Lodge's *Tragical Complaynt of Elstred* (1593) and Fletcher's *Richard III* (1593), it belongs to the class of poems suggested by the *Mirror* rather than to the cycle proper. Probably, the influence of the *Mirror* on the public mind through the interest it aroused in the national history did as much for literature as the direct imitations. In this way, the *Mirror* contributed to the production of Daniel's *Civil Wars*, Drayton's *Barons' Wars*, *England's Heroicall Epistles* and Warner's *Albion's England*, though there is little evidence of direct connection. As to the influence of the *Mirror* upon the history plays, fuller investigation only serves to confirm Schelling's summary of the probabilities:

> Upwards of thirty historical plays exist, the subjects of which are treated in *The Mirour for Magistrates*. And, although from its meditative and elegiac character it is unlikely that it was often employed as an immediate source, the influence of such a work in choice of subject and, at times, in manner of treatment cannot but have been exceedingly great.

In critical esteem, the *Mirror* hardly survived the period of its popular influence. No sooner had the book been given to the public, than Jasper Heywood proclaimed the 'eternall fame' of its first editor, Baldwin (prefatory verses to Seneca's *Thyestes*, 1560);

[1] The following may be noted: the *Mirror of Madness* (1576), *Mirror of Mutabilitie* (1579), *Mirror of Modesty* (1579), *Mirror of Martinists* (1589), *Mirror of Magnanimity* (1599), *Mirror of Martyrs* (1601).

[2] Sidney Lee's *Life of Shakespeare*, p. 77.

Sidney, in his *Apologie*, praised the *Mirror* more discreetly as 'meetly furnished of beautiful parts'; Hake, in 1588, commended it as 'penned by the choicest learned wits, which, for the stately proportioned vein of the heroic style, and good meetly proportion of verse, may challenge the best of Lydgate, and all our late rhymers[1]'; and Harington, in his *Ariosto* (1591), praised the tragedies without reserve as 'very well set downe, and in a good verse.' After this date, the fame of the *Mirror* became less certain, and the modern reader will hardly feel surprise at the fate which has overtaken it. The moralising is insufferably trite, and unrelieved by a single spark of humour. Seldom does the style rise to the dignity and pathos of subject and situation; the jog-trot of the metre is indescribably monotonous, and one welcomes the interruption of the connective passages in prose, with their quaint phrases and no less quaint devices. Joseph Hall ridiculed its 'branded whining ghosts' and curses on the fates and fortune; and, though Marston tried to turn the tables on Hall on this point, his *Reactio* does not appear to have succeeded in impressing the public. Chapman, in *May Day* (1611), makes fun of Lorenzo as 'an old Senator, one that has read Marcus Aurelius, *Gesta Romanorum, Mirror of Magistrates*, etc.' Edmund Bolton[2] and Anthony à Wood[3] imply that the *Mirror* had been rivalled, if not superseded, in popular favour by Warner's *Albion's England*. Both refer to it as belonging to a past age.

In the eighteenth century, when the *Mirror* was recalled to notice in Mrs Cooper's *Muses Library*, it was to direct special attention to the work of Sackville, but appreciation of the poetic quality of Sackville was no new thing. It was the prevailing opinion of his contemporaries that, if he had not been called to the duties of statesmanship, he would have achieved great things in poetry. Spenser gave expression to this view with his usual courtly grace and in his own 'golden verse' in the sonnet addressed to Sackville in 1590, commending *The Faerie Queene* to his protection:

In vain I thinke, right honourable Lord,
By this rude rime to memorize thy name,
Whose learned Muse hath writ her owne record
In golden verse, worthy immortal fame:
Thou much more fit (were leasure to the same)
Thy gracious Soverains praises to compile,
And her imperiall Majestie to frame
In loftie numbers and heroicke stile.

Some of Spenser's praise might be set down to the desire

[1] Warton, ed. 1841, vol. IV, pp. 203—4. [2] *Hypercritica*, written *c.* 1620.
[3] Ed. 1813, vol. II, p. 166.

to conciliate an influential patron, for lord Buckhurst had just been installed at Windsor as a knight companion of the order of the Garter; and, in the following year, by the direct interposition of the queen, he was elected chancellor of the university of Oxford. But, when all temptation to flattery had long passed away, Pope chose him out for special commendation among the writers of his age as distinguished by 'a propriety in sentiments, a dignity in the sentences, an unaffected perspicuity of style, and an easy flow of numbers; in a word, that chastity, correctness, and gravity of style which are so essential to tragedy; and which all the tragic poets who followed, not excepting Shakespeare himself, either little understood or perpetually neglected.'

Only the small extent of Sackville's poetical work has prevented him from inclusion among the masters of the grand style. This distinction is the more remarkable because the occasion of which he took advantage, and the material he used, were not particularly favourable. He evidently felt that the vast design of Baldwin and his fellows was inadequately introduced by the bald and almost childish prose preface, with its frank acceptance of medieval machinery, which had seemed sufficient to them. He turned to the great examples of antiquity, Vergil and Dante; indeed, apparently, he had intended to produce a *Paradiso* as well as an *Inferno.* Sorrow says:

> I shall thee guide first to the grisly lake,
> And thence unto the blissful place of rest,
> Where thou shall see, and hear, the plaint they make
> That whilom here bare swing among the best:
> This shalt thou see: but great is the unrest
> That thou must bide, before thou canst attain
> Unto the dreadful place where these remain.

The astonishing thing is that Sackville is not overwhelmed by the models he has adopted. His command of his material is free and masterful, although he has to vivify such shadowy medieval abstractions as Remorse of Conscience, Dread, Revenge, Misery, Care, Sleep, Old Age, Malady, Famine, Death and War. It is not merely that his choice of phrase is adequate and his verse easy and varied. He conceives greatly, and handles his great conceptions with a sureness of touch which belongs only to the few. He was undoubtedly indebted to Chaucer and Gavin Douglas, and, in his turn, he influenced Spenser; but his verse bears the stamp of his own individuality. The *Induction* has not Spenser's sensuous melody; and it is far removed from Chaucer's ingenuous subtlety and wayward charm; but it has an impassioned dignity and grave majesty which are all its own.

CHAPTER X

GEORGE GASCOIGNE

GASCOIGNE, like the writers of *A Mirror for Magistrates*, belongs to a period of literary transition; his work is superior to theirs as a whole, though nowhere does he rise to the full and heightened style of Sackville's *Induction*. Like them, he was highly esteemed in his own time, and made notable contributions to the development of poetry, but his work soon came to be spoken of with an air of condescension, as possessing antiquarian rather than actual interest. Gabriel Harvey added highly appreciative notes to his copy of *The Posies*, still preserved in the Bodleian library, and bearing in his handwriting the date *Cal. Sept.* 1577; and, in *Gratulationes Valdinenses* (1578) he mentions Gascoigne among the poets to be included in every lady's library[1]. Harvey, further, wrote a Latin elegy and an English epitaph on Gascoigne at his death[2], and made complimentary references to the poet in his earlier correspondence[3]. But, in 1592, he adopted a patronising tone: 'I once bemoned the decayed and blasted estate of M. Gascoigne: who wanted not some commendable parts of conceit and endeavour[4]'; and, in 1593, he mentioned Gascoigne with Elderton, Turbervile, Drant and Tarleton as belonging to an age outgrown: 'the winde is chaunged, and their is a busier pageant upon the stage[5].' About a year later, Sir John Davies gives point to one of his *Epigrammes*[6], by an allusion to 'olde Gascoines rimes' as hopelessly out of date. Edmund Bolton, in his *Hypercritica* (*c.* 1620), says: 'Among the lesser late poets George Gascoigne's Works may be endured'; and Drayton in his epistle *Of Poets and Poesy* tells the truth even more bluntly. After speaking of Surrey and Wyatt, he continues:

> Gascoigne and Churchyard after them again
> In the beginning of Eliza's reign,
> Accounted were great meterers many a day,
> But not inspired with brave fire, had they
> Liv'd but a little longer, they had seen
> Their works before them to have buried been.

[1] *Liber IV. De Aulica.*
[2] Sloane MSS, British Museum.
[3] *Harvey's Letter Book,* Camden Society.
[4] *Foure Letters.*
[5] *Pierce's Supererogation.*
[6] *In Ciprium,* 22.

In his attitude towards his work, Gascoigne further illustrates this transition spirit. He took up poetry as an amusement, and, somewhat unwillingly, came to acknowledge it as a profession. Lack of resolution combined with the unfavourable conditions of the time to prevent his attaining eminence. Gabriel Harvey, in his somewhat pedantic fashion, remarks, in a *Censura critica* written on a blank half page of *Weedes,* on the personal defects of the author.

> Sum vanity; and more levity; his special faultes, and the continual causes of his misfortunes. Many other have maintained themselves gallantly upon some one of his qualities: nothing fadgeth with him, for want of Resolution, and Constancy to any one kind. He shall never thrive with any thing that can brooke no crosses: or hath not learned to make the best of the worst, in his profession. It is no marvel, though he had cold success in his actions, that in his studdies, and Looves, thought upon the warres; in the warres, mused upon his studdies, and Looves. The right floorishing man, in studdy, is nothing but studdy; in Loove, nothing but Loove; in warr, nothing but warr.

Gascoigne himself, in the poem on his 'woodmanship' addressed to lord Grey of Wilton[1], admits that he tried without success the professions of a philosopher, a lawyer, a courtier and a soldier. He was born of a good Bedfordshire family, and educated at Trinity College, Cambridge, as appears from his references to the university in *The Steele Glas* and the dedication of *The Tale of Hemetes the heremyte,* and in *Dulce bellum inexpertis*[2] to his 'master' Nevynson[3]. He left the university without a degree, entered Gray's Inn in 1555 and represented the county of Bedford in parliament 1557—9. His youthful extravagances led to debt, disgrace and disinheritance by his father, Sir John Gascoigne.

> 'In myddest of his youth' he tells us (I. 62) he 'determined to abandone all vaine delightes and to returne unto Greyes Inne, there to undertake againe the studdie of the common Lawes. And being required by five sundry Gentlemen to write in verse somewhat worthye to bee remembred, before he entered into their fellowshippe, hee compiled these five sundrie sortes of metre uppon five sundrye theames, whiche they delivered unto him.'

Gascoigne's ingenuous use of the word 'compiled' disarms criticism, but it makes the whole incident only the more significant of the attitude of himself and his companions towards his verse. It was occasional and perfunctory, the work neither of an inspired artist on the one hand, nor of a professional craftsman on the other. However, Gascoigne not only wrote the versified exercises

[1] Cambridge edition, ed. Cunliffe, J. W., vol. I, p. 348.
[2] Stanza 199, vol. I, p. 180 *u.s.*
[3] Stephen Nevynson was a fellow of Trinity and proceeded M.A. in 1548.

demanded of him: he paid the fines for his neglected terms, was called 'ancient' in 1565, and translated *Supposes* and (together with Francis Kinwelmersh) *Jocasta*, which were presented at Gray's Inn in 1566. He took a further step towards reform by marrying a rich widow, whose children by her first marriage brought a suit in 1568 for the protection of their interests. The action seems to have been amicably settled, and he remained on good terms with his stepson, Nicholas Breton, who was himself a poet of some note. But it is to be feared that, as 'a man of middle age,' Gascoigne returned to the evil courses of his youth, if we are to accept the evidence of his autobiographical poem *Dan Bartholmew of Bathe*. The last stanza but three (I, 136) makes the personal character of the poem obvious, and this is probably one of the 'slaunderous Pasquelles against divers personnes of greate callinge' laid to his charge in the following petition, which, in May 1572, prevented him from taking his seat in parliament:

Firste, he is indebted to a great nomber of personnes for the which cause he hath absented him selfe from the Citie and hath lurked at Villages neere unto the same Citie by a longe time, and nowe beinge returned for a Burgesse of Midehurste in the Countie of Sussex doethe shewe his face openlie in the despite of all his creditors.

Item he is a defamed person and noted as well for manslaughter as for other greate cryemes.

Item he is a common Rymer and a deviser of slaunderous Pasquelles against divers personnes of greate callinge.

Item he is a notorious Ruffianne and especiallie noted to be bothe a Spie, an Atheist and Godles personne.

The obvious intention of the petition was to prevent Gascoigne from pleading privilege against his creditors and securing immunity from arrest, so the charges need not be taken as proving more against him than he admitted in his autobiographical poems; in any case, the document interests us only so far as it affected his literary career. In the *Councell given to Master Bartholmew Withipoll* (I, 347), written in 1572, Gascoigne expressed his intention of joining his friend in the Low Countries in the August of that year; and his *Voyage into Hollande* (I, 355) shows that he actually sailed from Gravesend to Brill in March 1573. During his absence (probably in the same year) there appeared the first edition of his works, undated, and professedly piratical, though Gascoigne afterwards acknowledged that it was published with his knowledge and consent.

Of this edition, very few copies remain, and much interesting matter which appeared only in it has been but lately put within the reach of the ordinary student[1]. Unusual precautions were taken, even for that day, to free the real author of the enterprise from responsibility. An anonymous H. W. delivers to an anonymous A. B. to print a written book given to him by his friend G. T. 'wherin he had collected divers discourses and verses, invented uppon sundrie occasions, by sundrie gentlemen' (I, 490). G. T. (who might be Gascoigne's friend George Turbervile, but is much more likely to be Gascoigne himself) thus takes the place of the editor of the volume, although he protests that, after having 'with no small entreatie obteyned of Master *F. J.* and sundry other toward young gentlemen, the sundry copies of these sundry matters,' he gives them to H. W. for his private recreation only, and not for publication. G. T. does not even know 'who wrote the greatest part of' the verses, 'for they are unto me but a posie presented out of sundry gardens' (I, 499). But, when the second edition appears in 1575 under the poet's own name, A. B., G. T., H. W. and F. J. all dissolve into Gascoigne himself. The 'divers discourses and verses ... by sundrie gentlemen' all now appear as the 'Posies of George Gascoigne,' G. T.'s comment on the verses of Master F. J. is printed as from Gascoigne's own hand, Gascoigne admits that the original publication was by his consent and a close examination of the two editions leads to the conclusion that the first was prepared for the press and written from beginning to end by Gascoigne himself, printer's preface and all. The following sentence in 'The Printer to the Reader' (I, 476)

> And as the venemous spider wil sucke poison out of the most holesome herbe, and the industrious Bee can gather hony out of the most stinking weede

is characteristic of Gascoigne's early euphuistic style, of which we have several examples inserted by him in his translation of Ariosto's *Suppositi* (I, 197). And when Gascoigne comes to write in his own name an epistle 'To the reverende Divines' for the second edition, from which the printer's address to the reader is omitted, he repeats this very simile (I, 6):

> I had alledged of late by a right reverende father, that although in deede out of everie floure the industrious Bee may gather honie, yet by proofe the Spider thereout also sucks mischeevous poyson.

He also adopts with the slightest possible emendations the introductory prefaces to the various poems for which G. T. took the responsibility in the edition of 1573. All this is very characteristic of the time and of the man. His eagerness for publication belongs

[1] Ed. Cunliffe, J. W., Cambridge English Classics.

to the age to come, his anxiety first to disown it and then to excuse it is of his own and an earlier time.

Even in 1575, Gascoigne is still most anxious to preserve what a modern athlete would call his 'amateur standing.' He protests that he 'never receyved of the Printer, or of anye other, one grote or pennie for the first Copyes of these Posyes' (I, 4) and he describes himself, not as an author, but as 'George Gascoigne Esquire professing armes in the defence of Gods truth.' In commemoration of his exploits in the Low Countries, he adopted a new motto, *Tam Marti quam Mercurio*, and this double profession of arms and letters is also indicated in the device which adorns the *Steele Glas* portrait of 1576—an arquebuss with powder and shot on one side, and books with pen and ink on the other. In the frontispiece to *The Tale of Hemetes the heremyte*, Gascoigne is pictured with a pen in his ear and a sword by his side, a book in his right hand and a spear in his left.

The *Hundreth sundrie Flowers* gave offence, Gascoigne himself tells us, first by reason of 'sundrie wanton speeches and lascivious phrases' and, secondly, by doubtful construction and scandal (I, 3). The author professed that he had amended these defects in the edition of 1575. A comparison of the two texts shows that only a few minor poems were omitted completely (I, 500—2) and some of these, apparently, by accident; while certain objectionable passages and phrases in *The Adventures of Master F. J.* were struck out. It was evidently this prose tale which gave the chief offence, on both the grounds stated. Gascoigne protested 'that there is no living creature touched or to be noted therby' (I, 7); but his protest is not convincing. According to G. T. 'it was in the first beginning of his writings, as then he was no writer of any long continuaunce' (I, 495) and the story apparently recounts an intrigue of Gascoigne's youth, as *Dan Bartholmew of Bathe* one of his 'middle age.' In the second edition, the prose story is ascribed to an unknown Italian writer Bartello, and in some new stanzas added to *Dan Bartholmew* at the end the following occurs:

Bartello he which writeth ryding tales,
Bringes in a Knight which cladde was all in greene,
That sighed sore amidde his greevous gales,
And was in hold as *Bartholmew* hath beene.
But (for a placke) it maye therein be seene,
That, that same Knight which there his griefes begonne,
Is *Batts* owne Fathers Sisters brothers Sonne.

In this roundabout fashion, quite characteristic of Gascoigne (cf. I, 405), he lets the reader know that Bartello and Bartholmew are the same as the green knight; and the green knight, as we know from *The fruite of Fetters*, in which Bartello is again given as authority, is Gascoigne himself. He did not improve matters in this respect by the addition to the second issue of marginal notes, evidently intended rather to heighten curiosity than to allay it. With reference to his rival in *Dan Bartholmew*, he notes at the side 'These thinges are mistical and not to bee understoode but by Thaucthour him selfe,' and, after this, the entry 'Another misterie' frequently occurs. Fleay has disregarded the author's warning, and has endeavoured to identify the persons indicated, not very satisfactorily. The fact is that by a 'misterie' Gascoigne simply means something scandalous. When in his *Voyage into Hollande* he casts reflections on the chastity of the Dutch nuns, he pulls himself up with the remark 'that is a misterie'; and the husband in *The Adventures of Master F. J.*, who catches his wife *in flagrante delicto*, forbids the handmaid to speak any word 'of this mistery.'

The edition of 1573 is of further interest because it gives a list of the author's works up to that date (I, 475) apparently arranged in chronological order, beginning with *Supposes*, *Jocasta* and *The Adventures of Master F. J.*, all known to be early works, and ending with the *Voyage into Hollande*, written in 1573, and *Dan Bartholmew*, which is left unfinished. The edition of 1575 completes this poem, and adds *Dulce bellum inexpertis* and *The fruite of Fetters*, recounting Gascoigne's experiences of war and imprisonment in Holland. *Die groene Hopman*, as the Dutch called him, was not well regarded by the burghers, and the dislike was mutual. Gascoigne ascribes the distrust of those to whom, according to his own account, he rendered valiant and repeated service, to a love affair with a lady in the Spanish camp; but it was, perhaps, also due to his eagerness to make himself acquainted with the burghers' affairs and to the 'Cartes ... Mappes ... and Models' which he offers to lay before lord Grey of Wilton in explanation of '*Hollandes* State' (I, 363). Gascoigne's poems on his adventures in the Low Countries throw some remarkable sidelights on the relations between the burghers and their English allies.

Certayne notes of Instruction concerning the making of verse or ryme in English[1], appended to the edition of 1575, apparently as an afterthought, for it is lacking in some copies, was, like many of Gascoigne's works, the first attempt in English of its kind, and it was soon followed by the more elaborate treatises of Webbe

[1] See *post*, chap. XIV.

and Puttenham. The *Notes* have the occasional character common to much of Gascoigne's work; yet they mark, perhaps, the division between his amateur and his professional career. He now directed his literary activities to the two ends of winning powerful patronage and establishing himself in public esteem. He was employed by Leicester in this same year, 1575, to furnish complimentary verses to the queen on her famous visit to Kenilworth castle; his most elaborate effort on this occasion, the 'shew' of Zabeta, was not presented, perhaps because it pressed on Elizabeth somewhat too insistently the advantages of marriage. At Woodstock, he 'pronounced' *The Tale of Hemetes the heremyte* before her majesty, and, in the following January, presented versions of it in French, Latin and Italian to her as a New Year's gift, with a request for employment. The request was evidently granted, for his next New Year's gift, *The Grief of Joye*, is offered as witness 'how the interims and vacant hours of those daies which I spent this somer in your service have byn bestowed.'

Though Gascoigne hardly attained the dignity of a literary artist, he certainly succeeded in laying aside the frivolity of his youth and became a portentous moralist. In the dedication of his last acknowledged publication, *A Delicate Diet, for daintie mouthde Droonkardes*, dated 10 August 1576, he contrasted the wanton poems of his youth with the serious works of his maturity:

> When my wanton (and worse smelling) Poesies, presumed fyrst to peark abroade, they came forth sooner than I wyshed, and much before they deserved to be lyked. So that (as you maye sithens perceyve) I was more combred with correction of them, then comforted in the constructions whereunto they were subject. And too make amendes for the lost time which I misbestowed in wryting so wantonlie: I have of latter dayes used al my travaile in matters both serious and Morall. I wrote first a tragicall commedie called *The Glasse of Government*: and now this last spring, I translated and collected a worthy peece of worke, called *The Droomme of Doomes daie*, and dedicated the same to my Lord and Maister: And I invented a *Satyre*, and an *Ellegie*, called *The Steele glasse*: and *The Complaint of Phylomene*. Both which I dedicated to your good Lord and myne, *The Lord Greye of Wylton*: These works or Pamphlets, I esteeme both Morall and Godly.

So, indeed, they are, but they are not of great literary importance. *The Steele Glas* has, perhaps, received more than its due meed of critical appreciation. It has none of the qualities of the great Latin satirists imitated a generation later by Hall and Marston: perhaps its greatest claim to distinction is the sympathy with the hard lot of the labouring poor, shown also by Gascoigne in some of his earlier work (cf. *A gloze upon this text, Dominus iis opus habet*). *The Droomme of Doomesday* is, in part, a translation of Innocent III's *De Contemptu Mundi sive de Miseria Humanae Conditionis*, and *A Delicate Diet, for daintie mouthde Droonkardes* has nothing to distinguish it from the religious tracts of the time.

In the dedication of *The Droomme of Doomesday*, Gascoigne wrote (2 May 1576) that he was 'in weake plight for health as your good L. well knoweth,' and he was unable, through illness, to correct the proofs. He was again ill for some months before his death on 7 October 1577. But, between these two illnesses he evidently recovered sufficiently to be sent on a mission from the privy council to the English merchant adventurers in Antwerp. He wrote to the lord treasurer from Paris on his way on 15 September 1576 and again on 7 October, and in November he received twenty pounds for 'bringinge of Letters in for her Majesties affaires frome Andwarpe to Hampton Court.' In the same month, his printer issued anonymously, although 'seene and allowed,' *The Spoyle of Antwerp Faithfully reported by a true Englishman, who was present at the same.* Recent events in Belgium lend the pamphlet a special interest, but, apart from these painful associations, it is a craftsman-like piece of reporting, giving Gascoigne an additional claim to our attention as the first English war correspondent. His authorship of the pamphlet, which was for a long time held doubtful, was recently established beyond question by a comparison of the signatures of the letters preserved in the Record office with that of George Gascoigne in the manuscript of *Hemetes the heremyte*; they are undoubtedly identical[1].

In many departments of literature Gascoigne wrote the first work of its kind that has come down to us—the first prose tale of modern life, the first prose comedy, the first tragedy translated from the Italian, the first maske, the first regular satire, the first treatise on poetry in English. He was a pioneer, and, as a pioneer, he must be judged. Two of his contemporaries and immediate successors passed upon him just and yet considerate verdicts. Tom Nashe in his prefatory address in Greene's *Menaphon*, 'to the Gentlemen Students of both Universities,' writes

> Maister Gascoigne is not to bee abridged of his deserved esteeme, who first beate the path to that perfection which our best Poets have aspired to since his departure; whereto he did ascend by comparing the Italian with the English as *Tully* did *Graeca cum Latinis*[2].

[1] See the facsimiles published in *Mod. Lang. Rev.* vol. VI p. 90 (January 1911).

[2] R. B. McKerrow, *Works of Thos. Nashe*, vol. III, p. 319.

and R. Tofte says 'To the Courteous Reader' of *The Blazon of Jealousie* (1615):

> This nice Age, wherein wee now live, hath brought more neate and teirse Wits, into the world; yet must not old George Gascoigne, and Turbervill, with such others, be altogether rejected, since they first brake the Ice for our quainter Poets, that now write, that they might the more safer swimme in the maine Ocean of sweet Poesie.

These moderate estimates of Gascoigne's achievements have stood the test of time, and the recent trend of criticism has been in his favour. His poems give the impression of a distinct, though not altogether pleasing, personality. He is the *homme moyen sensuel* of the time, with added touches of reckless debauchery in his youth, and of too insistent puritanism in his later days of ill-health and repentance; even in his 'middle age' he is too much inclined to recount his amatory adventures with a suggestive air of mystery, bound to excite the curiosity of his readers and make things uncomfortable for the ears of the ladies; his manners in this respect are as bad as his morals. He was probably a better soldier than lover, but one has a suspicion that his own account of his exploits in the Netherlands does not tell the whole truth; he was obviously intolerant of discipline and little inclined to conciliate the burghers whose cause he had come to serve. As a writer, he was distinguished among the men of his own time by his versatility. N. R., writing in commendation of the author of *The Steele Glas*, after running over a list of the great poets of antiquity, says:

> Thus divers men, with divers vaines did write,
> But Gascoigne doth, in every vaine indite.

This dissipation of his energies over different fields of literature prevented him from attaining excellence in any one kind, for he had only moderate ability: the surprising thing is that he was able to do many things well—most of them better than they had been done by his predecessors, though in all he was easily outstripped by the writers of the age that followed. His prose style is easy and generally free from affectation, though he indulges now and again in the curious similes and balanced alliteration which, later, became characteristic of euphuism. As a metrist, he has a facility which extends over a wide range, but his fluency is mechanical, the regular beat of his verse often giving the effect of water coming out of a bottle. His long poems, whether in blank verse or rimed measures, soon become monotonous and tedious. The caesura in *The Steele Glas* occurs almost invariably after the fourth syllable, and is regularly marked by Gascoigne with a comma :

> When vintners mix, no water with their wine,
> When printers passe, none errours in their bookes,
> When hatters use, to bye none olde cast robes[1],

and so on. In *Dan Bartholmew of Bathe*, in spite of a variety of stanza forms, some of them elaborate enough, the general effect is still monotonous. Gascoigne is seen at his best in trifles—short poems which do not call for great depth of thought or sustained interest, and in which his excessive fluency is kept within bounds. Even in these he rarely hit upon a pregnant thought or striking phrase ; but he succeeded in introducing into English poetry from the Italian models whom he studied (Ariosto seems to have been his especial favourite) a greater ease and smoothness than had been attained by Wyatt and Surrey. The following sonnet is a good example of his characteristic virtues :

> That selfe same tonge which first did thee entreat
> To linke thy liking with my lucky love:
> That trustie tonge must nowe these wordes repeate,
> *I love thee still*, my fancie cannot move.
> That dreadlesse hart which durst attempt the thought
> To win thy will with mine for to consent,
> Maintaines that vow which love in me first wrought,
> *I love thee still*, and never shall repent.
> That happie hande which hardely did touch,
> Thy tender body to my deepe delight:
> Shall serve with sword to prove my passion such
> *As loves thee still*, much more than it can write.
> Thus love I still with tongue, hand, hart and all,
> And when I chaunge, let vengeance on me fall[2].

Next to his love poetry, his verses in compliment to the queen are perhaps most worthy of attention, especially those which he wrote for 'the princely pleasures at Kenelworth Castle.' He directed his muse, with amazing ingenuousness, to the goal of professional advancement, and this combined with other reasons to prevent any lofty flight or permanent achievement; but, as the first of the Elizabethan court poets, he is notable as the precursor of an important movement.

[1] Cambridge edition, vol. II, p. 171.
[2] *Ibid.*, vol. I, p. 92.

CHAPTER XI

THE POETRY OF SPENSER

THE life of Spenser extended from the years 1552 to 1599, a period which experienced a conflict of elementary intellectual forces more stimulating to the emotions and imagination than, perhaps, any other in the history of England. Throughout Europe, the time-honoured system of society which had endured since the age of Charles the Great was undergoing a complete transformation. In Christendom, so far as it was still Catholic, the ancient doctrines of the church and the scholastic methods of interpreting them held their ground in general education; but the weakening of the central basis of authority caused them everywhere to be applied in different ethical senses. A change of equal importance had been wrought in the feudal order of which the emperor was the recognised, but now only nominal, chief, since this universal constitution of things had long been reduced to insignificance by the rise of great independent nations, and the consequent beginning of wars occasioned by the necessities of the balance of power. Feudalism, undermined partly by the decay in its own spirit, partly by its anarchical tendencies, was giving way before the advancing tide of commercial intercourse, and, in every kingdom of western Europe, the central authority of the monarch had suppressed, in different degrees, the action of local liberty. In a larger measure, perhaps, than any country, English society was the stage of religious and political conflict. As the leader of the protestant nations, England was surrounded by dangers that presently culminated in the sending of the Spanish armada. Her ancient nobility, almost destroyed by the wars of the Roses, had been supplanted by a race of statesmen and courtiers called into existence by the crown, and, though the continuity of Catholic tradition was still preserved, the sovereign, as head of the church, exerted almost absolute power in the regulation of public worship. The conscience of the nation wavered in this struggle between old ecclesiasticofeudal forms and the infant ideas of civil life; and confusion was itself confounded by the influence of art and letters imported from the more advanced, but corrupt, culture of modern Italy. To the difficulty of forming a reasonable view of life out of these chaotic conditions was added the problem of expressing it in a language as yet hardly mature enough to be the vehicle of philosophical thought. Wyatt and Surrey had, indeed, accomplished a remarkable feat in adapting to Italian models the metrical inheritance transmitted to them by Chaucer; but a loftier and larger imagination than theirs was required to create poetic forms for national aspirations which had so little in common as those of England with the spirit of Italy in the sixteenth century.

The poet whose name is rightly taken as representative of the general movement of literature in the first half of Elizabeth's reign was well fitted by nature to reflect the character of this spiritual conflict. A modest and sympathetic disposition, an intelligence philosophic and acute, learned industry, a brilliant fancy, an exquisite ear, enabled Spenser's genius to respond like a musical instrument to each of the separate influences by which it was stirred. His mind was rather receptive than creative. All the great movements of the time are mirrored in his work. In it is to be found a reverence for Catholic tradition modified by the moral earnestness of the reforming protestant. His imagination is full of feudal ideas, warmed into life by his association with men of action like Sidney, Grey, Ralegh and Essex, but coloured by a contrary stream of thought derived from the philosophers of the Italian renascence. Theological conceptions, originating with the Christian Fathers, lie side by side in his poetry with images drawn from pagan mythology, and with incidents of magic copied from the medieval chroniclers. These imaginative materials are, with him, not fused and assimilated in a form of direct poetic action, as is the case in the poetry of Chaucer, Shakespeare and Milton; but, rather, are given an appearance of unity by an allegory, proceeding from the mind of the poet himself, in a mould of metrical language which combines native words, fallen out of common use, with a syntax imitated from the great authors of Greece and Rome. An attempt will be made in the following pages to trace the correspondence in the work of Spenser between this conflict of external elements and his own poetic genius, reflecting the spirit of his age.

In respect of what was contributed to the art of Spenser by his personal life and character, it is often difficult to penetrate to the reality of things beneath the veil of allegory with which he chooses to conceal his thoughts. We know that he was born in London in (probably) 1552, the son of a clothier whose descent was derived from the same stock as the Spencers of Althorp. To this connection the poet alludes in his pastoral poem *Colin Clout's Come Home Again*, when, praising the three daughters of Sir John Spencer, he speaks of

> The honor of the noble familie:
> Of which I meanest boast my selfe to be.

We know, also, that he was one of the first scholars of the recently founded Merchant Taylors' school, from which he passed as a sizar to Pembroke Hall, Cambridge, on 20 May 1569. Furthermore, it is evident, from the sonnets contributed, in 1569, to *A Theatre for Worldlings*[1], that he must have begun early to write poetry.

At Cambridge, he came under three influences, each of which powerfully affected his opinions and imagination. The first was his friendship with Gabriel Harvey. This man, the son of a rope-maker at Saffron Walden, was a person of considerable intellectual force, but intolerably arrogant and conceited, and with a taste vitiated by all the affectations of the decadent Italian humanism. He entered Pembroke Hall as Fellow the year after Spenser matriculated, and soon secured a strong hold over the modest and diffident mind of the young undergraduate. His tone in the published correspondence with Spenser is that of an intellectual bully; and so much did the poet defer to the elder man's judgment, that, at one time, he not only attempted to follow Harvey's foolish experiment of anglicising the hexameter, but was in danger of being discouraged by him from proceeding with *The Faerie Queene.*

Again, Spenser was strongly influenced by the religious atmosphere of his college. Cambridge protestantism was, at this time, sharply divided by the dispute between the strict disciplinarians in the matter of church ritual, headed by Whitgift, master of Trinity, afterwards archbishop of Canterbury, and those followers of Cartwright, Lady Margaret professor of Divinity, from whom, in course of time, came forth the Martin Marprelate faction. Pembroke Hall seems to have occupied a middle position in this conflict. Its traditions were emphatically Calvinistic. Ridley, bishop of London, one of the most conspicuous of the Marian martyrs, had been master of the college; he was succeeded by his pupil Grindal,

[1] See *post*, chap. XII.

afterwards archbishop of Canterbury; and the headship, when Spenser matriculated, had passed to Young, at a later date bishop of Rochester, whose Calvinism was no less marked than that of his predecessors. Spenser, moved by the *esprit de corps* of his college, eulogised both his old master and Grindal, when their mild treatment of the nonconformists brought them into discredit with the queen. It may, perhaps, be inferred from a letter of Gabriel Harvey to Spenser, that the college did not side with Cartwright in opposing the prescribed ritual; but many allusions in *The Shepheards Calender* show that Spenser himself disapproved of the relics of the Roman system that disguised themselves under the garb of conformity.

But, however staunchly he held to the principles of the reformed faith, his protestantism was modified and softened by another powerful movement of the time, namely, the study of Platonic philosophy. The revival of Platonism which began with the renascence was, of course, the natural antithesis to the system of Aristotelian logic, as caricatured by the late schoolmen; but it was also distinct from the Christianised Neo-Platonism which culminated in the ninth century, when Joannes Scotus (Erigena) popularised the doctrines of the so-called Dionysius the Areopagite, embodied in his book *The Celestial Hierarchy.* Modern Platonism implied an interpretation of the Scriptures in the light of Plato's philosophy studied, generally, at the fountain head, and particularly in the dialogues of *The Republic, Timaeus* and the *Symposium.* Originated in the Platonic academy at Florence by Ficino and Pico della Mirandola, it was taken up by the reforming party throughout Europe, and was especially favoured in the universities of Paris and Cambridge. To the imagination of Spenser, it proved exceedingly congenial, and confirmed him in that allegorical habit of conception and expression which characterises alike his love poems, his pastoral poems and his romance.

Among these, Platonism, as was natural, shows itself most crudely in his youthful love poetry. After taking his B.A. degree in 1573, and proceeding to his M.A. degree in 1576, he seems to have left the university, and to have paid a visit of some length to his relatives in Lancashire. There, he probably made the acquaintance of the unknown lady who, in his correspondence with Gabriel Harvey, in *The Shepheards Calender* and in *Colin Clout's Come Home Again*, is celebrated under the name of Rosalind. There is nothing in the pastoral allusions to her indicating that Spenser's attachment involved feelings deeper than were required for literary panegyric. Since the time of Petrarch, every woman commemorated by Italian or English poets had been of one type, beautiful as Laura, and 'cruel' enough to satisfy the standing regulations prescribed by the old courts of love. In the lyrics of the troubadours, and even in the sonnets of Petrarch, there is genuine ardour, but these were the fruit of days when it was still possible to breathe in society the chivalrous atmosphere of the crusades. The fall in the temperature of love poetry in the sixteenth century reveals itself unmistakably in the art of Spenser. His *Amoretti* or sonnets, written in praise of the lady whom he married towards the close of his life, are no better than the average compositions of the class then fashionable[1]. The 'cruelty' of Rosalind, probably not much more really painful to the poet than that caused in his later years by 'Elisabeth,' was recorded in a more original form, in so far as it gave him an opportunity of turning his training in Platonic philosophy to the purposes of poetical composition. His two *Hymnes in honour of Love and Beautie*, though not published till 1596, were, he tells us, the product of his 'green youth,' and it may reasonably be concluded that they were among the earliest of his surviving works. They show no novelty of invention, being, from first to last, merely the versification of ideas taken from Plato's *Symposium*, read in the light of Ficino's commentary. The poet, however, by showing how truly he himself comprehended the philosophy of Love and felt his power, conveyed an ingenious compliment to his mistress:

> Love, that long since hast to thy mighty powre
> Perforce subdude my poor captivëd hart,
> And, raging now therein with restlesse stowre,
> Doest tyrannize in everie weaker part;
> Faine would I seeke to ease my bitter smart
> By any service I might do to thee,
> Or ought that else might to thee pleasing bee.

Love, he thinks, would doubtless be best pleased with an exposition of the doctrines of true love: hence his elaborate analysis of the passion, in which he follows, step by step, the *Symposium* of Plato, or, rather, Ficino's commentary on that dialogue. Ficino himself had not sought originality any more than Spenser. Like all the men of the early renascence, he submitted his own opinions to those of the authors of antiquity as if these were inspired. Whatever

[1] See *post*, chap. XII.

was written in the *Symposium* he accepted as revealed truth; and, since the views of Plato's imaginary speakers were often at variance with each other, he took pains to reconcile them. He had studied Plato in the light of ideas propagated through the teaching of the Neo-Platonists, who had absorbed into their philosophy many elements of oriental magic: accordingly, the process of reconciliation ended in a new development of Plato's original theory by Ficino, whom Spenser followed, with as little desire to question his authority as the Italian philosopher had shown in his interpretation of the Greek text. In the *Symposium*, for example, where the whole texture of the dialogue is humorous and dramatic, Phaedrus, whose theory is, of course, quite opposed to that of Socrates, speaks of Love as the eldest of the gods, and is contradicted by Agathon, who calls Love the youngest god. Ficino tries to harmonise these two ideas by introducing into the theory a Christian element derived from the Neo-Platonism of the pseudo-Dionysius. He says that the Love, guiding the Creator, was, indeed, older than the creation of the universe; but that God afterwards created the order of angels, and that Love turned the angelic intelligences towards God; so that Love may be called at once the youngest, and the eldest, of the divine powers[1]. Spenser, taking up Ficino's reasoning about the two ages of Love, combines it with the mythological account of Love's birth reported by Socrates from Diotima in the *Symposium*.

> Great God of Might, that reignest in the mynd,
> And all the bodie to thy hest doest frame,
> Victor of gods, subduer of mankynd,
> That doest the Lions and fell Tigers tame,
> Making their cruell rage thy scornefull game,
> And in their roring taking great delight;
> Who can express the glorie of thy might?
>
> Or who alive can perfectly declare
> The wondrous cradle of thine infancie,
> When thy great mother Venus first thee bare,
> Begot of Plentie and of Penurie,
> Though elder then thine owne nativitie,
> And yet a chyld, renewing still thy yeares,
> And yet the eldest of the heavenly Peares?

Ficino is followed with equal closeness in the *Hymne in honour of Beautie.* Like him, Spenser describes the blending of the soul with corporeal matter, and, like him, refutes the doctrine that beauty is

[1] Ficino, *In Platonis Libros Argumenta et Commentaria. Symposium. Oratio Quinta*, 10.

merely proportion of parts and harmony of colour[1]; he imitates the Italian in describing the descent of the soul from heaven to form the body, and the correspondence between the beautiful soul and the beautiful body[2]; the reason why a beautiful soul sometimes forms only an ugly body[3]; the attraction of one beautiful soul to another by means of celestial influences[4]; the mode in which the passion of love begins[5]. To show that the whole is intended as a compliment to Rosalind, he breathes the hope:

> It may so please, that she at length will streame
> Some deaw of grace into my withered hart,
> After long sorrow and consuming smart.

As the foundations of Spenser's imaginative thought were thus laid in Platonic philosophy, it was almost inevitable that, when his genius expanded, he should also look to Plato for his instrument of poetic expression, and should illustrate his abstract doctrine by the aid of concrete myths.

After spending some time in Lancashire, he was brought south, through the influence of his friend Harvey, and employed in the service of the earl of Leicester. In this capacity, he made the acquaintance of Leicester's nephew, Philip Sidney, whose ardent imagination and lofty spirit greatly stimulated him in the prosecution of his poetical designs. The poet's correspondence with Gabriel Harvey, at this period, throws much light on the ambiguities and fluctuations of his literary motives. He tells Harvey, whom he knew to be likely to sympathise with him, how he has become one of an 'Areopagus,' in which Sidney and Dyer were the leading spirits, and the prime object of which was to naturalise in the language a system of versification based on quantity. He himself ventures on some experiments in this direction, so wretched in execution as to remove all grounds for wonder at the poor quality of his compositions in Latin verse. At the same time, his letters make it evident that he was engaged in writing, in metres constructed with accent and rime, on subjects much better suited to the turn of his genius. Feeling that the power of poetry lay chiefly in imagery, he began, after his philosophical exposition of Platonic doctrine in the *Hymnes in honour of Love and Beautie*, to consider under what artistic forms he might make his thought more intelligible to the general reader.

[1] Ficino, *Symposium, Argumenta. Oratio Quinta*, 3. 6; *Hymne in Honour of Beautie*, 67—73.

[2] Ficino, *ibid.* 6; *Hymne*, 109—136. [3] Ficino, *ibid.* 5; *Hymne*, 144—150.

[4] Ficino, *Oratio Sexta*, 6; *Hymne*, 200—213.

[5] Ficino, *ibid.* 6; *Hymne*, 214—234.

Two images were at once ready to his hand in the shepherd and the knight—the heroes, so to speak, of two widely popular forms of poetry, pastoralism and romance. Both of these seem to have suggested themselves to him about the same time as fitting subjects for poetical allegory, for, before the publication of *The Shepheards Calender*, he had forwarded to Harvey specimens of his workmanship in *The Faerie Queene*. The pastoral, however, as a style more easy of execution for a poet wanting in experience, attracted him first, as may be inferred from the quaintly conceited account of his motives prefixed by his commentator E. K. to *The Shepheards Calender*:

> And also appeareth by the basenesse of the name, wherein it semeth he chose rather to unfold great matter of argument covertly then, professing it, not suffice thereto accordingly. Which moved him rather in Æglogues then other wise to write, doubting perhaps his habilitie, which he little needed, or mynding to furnish our tongue with this kinde, wherein it faulteth; or following the example of the best and most auncient Poetes, which devised this kind of wryting, being both so base for the matter, and homely for the manner, at the first to trye theyr habilities; and as young birdes, that be newly crept out of the nest, by little first to prove theyr tender wyngs, before they make a greater flyght.

Whatever were the precise reasons that determined Spenser to make his first poetical venture in the region of pastoral poetry, there can be no doubt that he must have perceived the opportunities afforded to invention by the practice of his literary predecessors. In the first place, the eclogue gave great scope for allegory. Even in Theocritus, the poet is presented under the guise of a shepherd, and in Moschus's lament for Bion this dress takes a distinctly personal character. From such a beginning it was but a step for Vergil to make the shepherd a mouthpiece for compliments addressed to statesmen in the city; and, with equal readiness, the eclogue, in the Middle Ages, passed from civil into ecclesiastical allegory for the purposes of flattery or satire. A certain convenient obscurity thus began to cover all pastoral utterances, so that, to quote the words of Petrarch, 'it is the nature of this class of literature that, if the author does not provide a commentary, its meaning may, perhaps, be guessed, but can never be fully understood.'

The eclogue, again, recommended itself to Spenser on account of the great variety of matter that had come to be treated in it. In its most elementary conditions, it was used to represent either a contest in singing between two shepherds, a lover's complaint, or a dirge for some dead acquaintance. Transported into the region of allegory, the singing dialogue might be turned into a channel for discoursing on the contemporary state of poetry; love might be treated in its Platonic character; the dirge might be developed into a court panegyric. All these modes of application were of use to a poet in Spenser's position. He also saw that it was possible for him to invest the eclogue with a certain novelty of appearance. Till the dawn of the renascence, all pastoral poetry had been written in Latin, the last author of this kind being Baptista Mantuanus, a Carmelite friar (1448—1516); but Jacopo Sanazzaro, of Naples, in 1490, broke new ground in his *Arcadia*, a kind of romance, interspersed with eclogues, written in Italian. Clément Marot, in France, before the middle of the sixteenth century, naturalised the form of the Latin eclogue in the French vernacular. His *Complaincte d'un Pastoureau Chrestien*, his *Eglogue au Roy* and his *Elegie sur Mme Loise de Savoye*, furnished models of which Spenser freely availed himself. In England, Barnabe Googe moved along the same protestant and humanist lines as Marot, importing, also, into his pastoral dialogues, romantic elements borrowed from *Diana*, which he had probably read during his travels in Spain. Traces of acquaintance with all these compositions are visible in *The Shepheards Calender*, lightly imprinted on a form of the eclogue which is the invention of Spenser himself.

The Shepheards Calender was published in 1579. It was dedicated to 'The Noble and Vertuous Gentleman, worthy of all titles both of Learning and Chevalrie, M. Philip Sidney.' With characteristic diffidence, the poet hesitated in giving his work to the world, partly from the fear, as he confesses in a letter to Harvey, of 'cloying the noble ears' of his patron, and thus incurring his contempt, partly because the poem itself was written in honour of a private person, and so might be thought 'too base for his excellent Lordship.' Sidney hastened to show that these apprehensions were groundless, by bestowing high praise on *The Shepheards Calender*, in his *Defence of Poesie*, qualified, indeed, by one important censure: 'That same framing of his style to an olde rusticke language, I dare not allow: since neither Theocritus in Greeke, Virgill in Latine, nor Sanazara in Italian, did affect it.' The objection is of historical interest, as illustrating the extent to which the men of the early renascence in England submitted themselves to the authority of the ancients, and to the Aristotelian criticism of the Italian academies: the remark itself touches merely the superficial question of style, and does not attempt to penetrate the deeper question how far the traditional form of the pastoral can be taken as a proper vehicle for modern thought and feeling. For the age of Elizabeth it bore immediate fruit. On the one hand, Sidney's praise gave a vogue to the pastoral style; on the other, his censure of rusticity in language warned those who attempted the pastoral manner off Spenser's example. Drayton, in his *Eclogues,* while preserving the clownish nomenclature of *The Shepheards Calender,* takes care to make his speakers discourse in the language of polished literature.

The Shepheards Calender was introduced to the notice of the public by a commentator signing himself E. K., who is conjectured, with every probability, to have been Spenser's fellow-collegian and contemporary, Edward Kirke. E. K.'s preface, addressed to Gabriel Harvey, and written in the contorted style approved by him, was divided into two portions, one being a defence of Spenser's practice in respect of diction, the other a description of his design. Of the latter, E. K. says:

> Now, as touching the generall dryft and purpose of his Æglogues, I mind not to say much, him selfe labouring to conceale it. Onely this appeareth, that his unstayed yougth had long wandred in the common Labyrinth of Love, in which time to mitigate and allay the heate of his passion, or els to warne (as he sayth) the young shepheards, his equalls and companions, of his unfortunate folly, he compiled these XII Æglogues, which, for that they be proportioned to the state of the XII monethes, he termeth the *Shepheards Calendar,* applying an olde name to a new worke.

Had the design of *The Shepheards Calender* been so simple as E. K. suggests, the work would have had unity, but little variety. Spenser would have confined himself to a rendering of the traditional idea of pastoral love adapted to the changes of the different seasons; but, as a matter of fact, the unity of the design lies solely in an allegorical calendar, treated ethically, in agreement with the physical characteristics of the different months. The idea of love is presented prominently only in four of the eclogues, viz. those for January, March, June and December: of the rest, four, those for February, May, July and September, deal with matters relating to morality or religion; two are complimentary or elegiac, those for April and November; one, that for August, describes a singing match pure and simple; and one, that for October, is devoted to a lament for the neglect of poetry. Hence, it appears that Spenser, without making much account of the singleness of purpose ascribed to him by his commentator, contrives to include within the plan of the pastoral calendar a large number of those traditional motives which had been employed by his predecessors in this class of poetry. And, from this fact, we may safely make two inferences, which apply to all Spenser's allegories, philosophical, pastoral, or romantic. In the first place, it is misleading to gather the sense of the allegory from the apparent nature of his theme. His mind did not energise within its professed subject, like that of Bunyan in *The Pilgrim's Progress,* where the plan, action and characters of the story are plainly evolved directly from the inherent spiritual thought. In the second place, the true significance of Spenser's allegorical matter can only be discovered by tracking the sources of his allegorical forms. His motives are artistic rather than ethical, and he is concerned less with matter of thought than manner of expression. This is the case even with those classes of his compositions in which his motive appears to be primarily philosophical. If, for example, the Platonism in his *Hymnes* be compared with that of Wordsworth in the *Ode on the Intimations of Immortality,* a striking difference of conception is at once observable. Wordsworth's poetical inspiration comes immediately from within: the speculations of Plato, no doubt, set his imagination to work, but his imaginative reasoning is his own; whereas, in the *Hymnes,* as has been already shown, Spenser merely expounds, without alteration, the theory of beauty which he has derived from the commentary of Ficino on Plato's *Symposium*; his sole original contribution to the poetry is the beautiful and harmonious form of English verse which he makes the vehicle of the thought.

If we look away from the authorised account of Spenser's design in *The Shepheards Calender* to the actual gestation of the poem in his imagination, it is plain that, before constructing his general idea, he had carefully studied the pastoral practice of Theocritus, Bion, Vergil, Mantuan and Marot. His sympathetic intelligence had been impressed by many imaginative passages in these authors, and he desired to reproduce them in a novel form. For this purpose, he chose, as the basis of his entire work, an allegory founded on the widely popular *Kalendrier des Bergers* —an almanac describing the tasks of shepherds in the different months of the year—and resolved to include within his poetical edifice the various subjects hitherto handled in the eclogue. In dealing with the subject of love, he naturally took as his models the Greek and Latin idyllists, who had preceded him with many complaints of shepherds unfortunate in their wooing. But the direct expression of passion by these pagan poets had to be harmonised with the sub-tone of Platonism imported into amorous verse by the troubadours and Petrarch. Colin Clout, the love-lorn shepherd, whose lamentations run, more or less, through all seasons of the year, has been treated by Rosalind, 'the widowe's daughter of the glenne,' with the 'cruelty' prescribed to ladies in the conventional rules of the courts of love and utters his despair in the winter months of January and December. His feelings are much more complex than those ascribed, for example, by Theocritus to the lover of Amaryllis, and, in the following stanza, it is plain that the pastoral sentiment has been transferred from the fields to the artificial atmosphere of court life:

> A thousand sithes I curse that carefull hower
> Wherein I longd the neighbour towne to see,
> And eke tenne thousand sithes I blesse the stoure
> Wherein I sawe so fayre a sight as shee:
> Yet all for naught: such sight hath bred my bane.
> Ah, God! that love should breede both joy and payne!

Again, in the complaint of Colin in December, the essential motive is distinctly literary: it lies much less in the lover's pain than in the recollections of his untroubled youth, that is to say, in a passage of this character in Marot's *Eglogue au Roy*, which Spenser has very closely imitated. So, also, in the March eclogue, where the dialogue is carried on between two shepherds called Thomalin and Willie, the real motive is to imitate Bion's second idyll—containing a purely pagan conception of love—in the rustic style specially devised by Spenser for his speakers. The result is not very happy. Bion's idyll is, really, an epigram. It describes how a boy fowler spied Love sitting like a bird on a tree, and how he vainly endeavoured to ensnare him with all the arts he had lately learned. The boy relates his want of success to an old bird-catcher who had taught him, and is bidden to give over the chase, since, when he attains to man's estate, instead of trying to catch Love, he will regret being caught by him. Spenser's imitation of this is comparatively clumsy. He represents two young shepherds talking together in a manner befitting the spring season. Thomalin tells his friend how he recently startled from the bushes a 'naked swayne' (so Moschus describes Love) and how he shot at him with his arrows till he had emptied his quiver, when he ran away in a fright, and the creature shot at him and hit him in the heel. Willie explains to his friend that the swain was Love, a fact with which he is acquainted because his father had once caught him in a fowling net, fortunately without his bow and arrows. The eclogue concludes, as usual, with 'emblems' chosen by the two speakers. The epigrammatic terseness of Bion, whose idyll is contained in sixteen lines, is lost in Spenser's diffuse description, which runs to one hundred and seventeen.

In the eclogues of a religious turn, the primary inspiration is seen to be no less traditional and literary. Here, the main suggestion is, generally, furnished by Mantuan. Mantuan, in his eighth eclogue, introduces two shepherds, Candidus and Alphus, discussing the respective advantages of life in the mountains and on the plains. The treatment is simple enough. Candidus, who represents the former, praises the mountains, chiefly on account of the monasteries built in them. He also mentions the earthly paradise and the fall of man, at once with the *naïveté* characteristic of a rustic mind and with the pagan imagery proper to Latin verse:

> *Esse locum memorant, ubi surgit ab aequore Titan,*
> *Qui, nisi dedidici, contingit vertice Lunam,*
> *Et vixisse illic hominem, sed postea abactum*
> *Improbitate gulae, quod scilicet omnia poma*
> *Manderet, et magno servasset nulla Tonanti.*

Spenser, in his eclogue for July, imitates this passage in imagery scarcely less formally pagan:

> Besyde, as holy fathers sayne,
> There is a hyllye place,
> Where Titan ryseth from the mayne
> To renne hys dayly race,
> Upon whose toppe the starres bene stayed,
> And all the skie doth leane;
> There is the cave where Phoebe layed
> The shepheard long to dreame.
> Whilome there used shepheards all
> To feede theyr flocks at will,
> Till by his foly one did fall,
> That all the rest did spill.

Mantuan contents himself with clothing theological allusions in classical imagery; his mountains and plains are really mountains and plains; Spenser, in his eclogue, extends his allegory to all the images suggested to him by Mantuan: his mountains become types of ecclesiastical pride and luxury, his plains, of the humility required by true religion.

In the eclogue for September, he follows more closely Mantuan's steps in the pastoral called *Religio*. Mantuan himself had built his poem allegorically on Vergil's first eclogue, in which Tityrus describes to his friend Meliboeus—a shepherd driven from his farm—the glories of the city of Rome, whither he had gone, when his lands were lost to him by his ruinous love for Galatea, and had had them restored by the bounty of a divine youth, who now enabled him to live with comfort in the country. The medieval poet, satirically inverting the idea, represents Candidus, a shepherd from the north of Italy, arriving in the neighbourhood of Rome, where he hopes to find rich pasture for his flock. Bitterly disappointed with the climate of that barren place, he bewails his lot to his friend Faustulus, who explains to him all the evils that arise from the character of the shepherds of the neighbourhood and the dogs that devour the sheep. Here, the sense is, of course, allegorical. Spenser takes up Mantuan's idea, with certain modifications, making Diggon Davie, his chief speaker, return to his native district, after wandering abroad with his flock, and relate to Hobbinol his sad experiences. The satire, which reflects on the worldliness of the Anglican clergy, is more particular than that of Mantuan, and contains many personal allusions.

Two eclogues, those for April and November, are devoted, respectively, to courtly compliment and courtly elegy. Here, Spenser found his models both in Vergil and Marot. The first eclogue of Vergil is intended to convey a compliment to Octavianus: his last is an imaginary elegy in honour of his friend Gallus. Marot, in his *Eglogue au Roy*, under cover of pastoral imagery, returns thanks to his sovereign, Francis I, for the relief given him in his old age; while, in his *Elegie sur Mme Loise de Savoye*, he adapts the traditional manner to courtly purposes on the principle applied by Vergil in his tenth eclogue. Spenser, following closely in the track of Marot, nevertheless diverges, as usual, slightly from his model, partly for the sake of being original, partly to preserve the air of greater rusticity affected in his own eclogues. In April, the praises of Elizabeth are recited by Hobbinol from a lay made by Colin, who has left his daily work for love of Rosalind: in November, Dido, 'the great shepherd's daughter,' is lamented by Colin himself, in lyrical strophes which replace the uniform stanza employed by Marot throughout his elegy on Loise de Savoye.

Finally, Spenser uses the eclogue for the allegorical purpose of discoursing on the contemporary state of poetry. Here, again, a lead had been given him by Mantuan in his fifth eclogue, *De Consuetudine Divitum erga Poetas*; but Mantuan himself had an original in the sixteenth idyll of Theocritus, in which the poet, addressing Hiero, tyrant of Syracuse, complains of the meagre patronage extended to the poets of the time, and claims generous assistance. Spenser, in his October eclogue, adheres closely to the framework of Mantuan's poem. Like Candidus, in that composition, Cuddie, the poet, appealed to by his companion Piers, maintains that his

> poore Muse hath spent her spared store,
> Yet little good hath got, and much lesse gayne;

like Sylvanus, Piers exhorts his friend to sing to the country folk, for glory, if not for gain; and, if he will not do this, to try his fortune at court. But, when Cuddie still resists his friend's appeal, Piers, who is of a more exalted spirit than Sylvanus, cries:

> Then make thee winges of thine aspyring wit,
> And, whence thou camst, flye backe to heaven apace.

Cuddie, however, is dejected by unsuccessful love, and, though Piers maintains that love (in Plato's sense) should lift him 'above the starry skie,' Cuddie persists in declaring that

> All otherwise the state of Poet stands;
> For lordly love is such a Tyranne fell,
> That where he rules all power he doth expell;
> The vaunted verse a vacant head demaundes.

If he is to sing of lofty themes, his imagination must be heated to them by the material goods of life:

> For Bacchus fruite is frend to Phœbus wise;
> And, when with Wine the braine begins to sweate,
> The nombers flowe as fast as spring doth ryse.

The characteristics of Spenser's pastoral style, then, make it plain that, if we would estimate aright the value of his allegory, we must consider the form of his eclogues apart from their matter. As regards the latter, the eclectic treatment which he bestowed upon his materials is a sign—as eclecticism is in all the arts—of exhaustion in the natural sources of inspiration. Spenser may be regarded as, in one sense, the last master in a cosmopolitan style of poetical composition, and, in another, as the pioneer of a new departure in the art of English poetry. The atmosphere of *The Shepheards Calender* is thoroughly artificial. As treated by its inventor, Theocritus, the essence of the idyll was truth to nature. His beautiful and lucid rendering of the pains and pleasures of shepherd life, the musical simplicity of the verse, in which he calls up images of whispering pine-trees, falling waters, climbing flocks and flowering hills, are as charming to the English mind to-day as they were to his Greek audience more than two thousand years ago. But, when Spenser took up the eclogue, it was as heir to a long line of ancestors, each of whom had added to it some imaginative element disguising the simplicity of the fundamental style; pastoral poetry, in fact, had now reached a stage where allegory was believed to be essential to it, and when Petrarch could say of it that, 'if the author does not provide a commentary, its meaning may, perhaps, be guessed, but can never be fully understood.' Every one can fully understand the naïve and passionate despair of Theocritus's goatherd after his vain appeal to Amaryllis in the third idyll; but there is little appearance of genuine emotion in the allegorical grief of Colin Clout, timed to suit the wintry season. Nature, again, speaks in each line of the idyll called *The Adoniazusae*, where Gorgo and Praxinoe chatter to each other precisely after the fashion of Englishwomen going to look on at a public spectacle. But, in Spenser's eclogues for May, July and September, we have to accustom ourselves to an exotic atmosphere before we realise the propriety of transferring the pastoral image from the rural to the ecclesiastical flock; nor can we at all reconcile the theological refinements in the discourse of Piers and Palinode to the actual simplicity of the bucolic mind. Whatever authority Spenser could have cited from Vergil and Marot for the compliment he paid to Elizabeth, as 'queene of shepheardes all,' it is surely an anomaly in nature to associate the pastoral image with one that inevitably calls up a vision of 'ruffs, and cuffs, and farthingales, and things.'

If, however, Spenser's practice in bucolic poetry be viewed mainly on the technical side, *The Shepheards Calender* appears as a most important monument in the history of English poetry. Every reader must admire the skill displayed by the poet in providing a suitable form for the great variety of his matter. His selection of the *Kalendrier des Bergers*, as the foundation of his allegory, is an excellent piece of invention, and the judgment with which he distributes his materials over the various seasons, the consistency with which he preserves the characters of his shepherds, the propriety of the rural images employed for the ornament of discourse, all show the hand of a great poetical artist. His achievements in the sphere of verbal harmony are the more admirable when the immature state of the language before the publication of this poem is taken into account.

E. K. devotes the larger part of his prolegomena to defending the mode of diction afterwards blamed by Sir Philip Sidney:

And firste of the wordes to speake, I graunt they be something hard, and of most men unused, yet both English, and also used of most excellent Authors, and most famous Poetes. In whom, wheneas this our Poet hath bene much traveiled and throughly redd, how could it be, (as that worthy Oratour sayde) but that walking in the sonne, although for other cause he walked, yet needes he mought be sunburnt; and, having the sound of those auncient Poetes still ringing in his eares, he mought needes, in singing, hit out some of theyr tunes. But whether he useth them by such casualtye and custome, or of set purpose and choyse, as thinking them fittest for such rusticall rudenesse of shepheards, eyther for that theyr rude sounde would make his rymes more ragged and rustical, or els because such olde and obsolete wordes are most used of country folke, sure I think, and think I think not amisse, that they bring great grace, and, as one would say, auctoritie to the verse.... For, if my memory faile not, Tullie, in that booke wherein he endevoureth to set forth the paterne of a perfect Oratour, sayth that ofttimes an auncient worde maketh the style seeme grave, and as it were reverend, no otherwise then we honour and reverence gray heares, for a certein religious regard, which we have of old age.

Spenser may very well have meant to emulate the neologising tendency of the almost contemporary *Pléiade*; in which case, it is interesting to observe the opposite principle on which he proceeded; for, while the French reformers aimed mainly at coining new words from Latin and Greek, the English poet sought, in the first place, to revive old standard words which had fallen out of colloquial use. But, on the whole, it seems probable that, above all things, he was anxious to treat language as entering into his allegory, and to frame a mode of diction which should appear to be in keeping with his pastoral characters. For this purpose, he, in the first place, turned, as E. K. says, to the monuments of ruder antiquity, and revived obsolete words from the writings of Chaucer and Lydgate. Wyatt and Surrey had also founded themselves on Chaucer, but with a different motive, their aim being, rather, to make a selection of such old literary words as should seem to be not uncongenial to courtly speech; Spenser, on the contrary, was deliberately archaic. With his literary archaisms he blended many peculiarities of dialect, turning from the southern dialect, which had become the basis of literary composition and polite conversation, to the midland or northern varieties of the tongue, which were held to be rustic and uncourtly. And, besides these two recognised sources of vocabulary, he drew considerably on his own invention, from which he often coined a word conformable to the style of his verse, but unauthorised by precedent in speech or writing. The result of this procedure was, on the one hand, as Ben Jonson says, that 'Spenser, in affecting the obsolete, writ no language'; on the other, that he constructed a style singularly appropriate to the multiform character of his pastoral allegory. When he thought that the situation demanded it, he could be clownish to the point of doggerel, as in September, where two shepherds, Hobbinol and Diggon Davie, discourse about religion. But in many other eclogues the rustic dialect is thrown aside, and it is evident that the poet means to make use of his pastoral subject mainly for the purpose of metrical experiment. In this sphere, he displays the genius of a great poet-musician. We have only to compare the rhythms of *The Shepheards Calender* with those of *A Mirror for Magistrates* in general, and even with that of Sackville's *Induction* in particular, to see that a metrical writer had arisen who excelled all his predecessors in his sense of the capacity of the English language for harmonious combinations of sound: whether he takes an irregular lyrical flight, or employs the iambic rhythm in uniform stanzas, he shows that he can use the courtly style of diction to the utmost advantage. Nothing can be more beautiful, for example, than the versification of the two following stanzas:

Colin, to heare thy rymes and roundelayes,
Which thou wert wont on wastfull hylls to singe,
I more delight then larke in Sommer dayes;
Whose Echo made the neyghbour groves to ring,
And taught the byrds, which in the lower spring
Did shroude in shady leaves from sonny rayes,
Frame to thy songe their chereful cheriping,
Or hold theyr peace, for shame of thy swete layes.
I sawe Calliope wyth Muses moe,
Soone as thy oaten pype began to sound,
Theyr yvory Luyts and Tamburins forgoe,
And from the fountaine, where they sat around,
Renne after hastely thy silver sound;
But, when they came where thou thy skill didst showe,
They drewe abacke, as halfe with shame confound
Shepheard to see them in theyr art outgoe.

No less melodious are the lyrical songs which, in the eclogues for April and November, he turns to the purposes of compliment or elegy, and which anticipate the still more exquisite music of the *Prothalamion* and *Epithalamion*, the work of his later years.

In *The Faerie Queene*, Spenser applies the allegorical method of composition on the same principle as in *The Shepheards Calender*, but, owing to the nature of the theme, with great difference in the character of the results. He had taken up the idea of allegorising romance almost at the same time as he contemplated the pastoral, and had submitted specimens of his work on it to the pedantic judgment of Harvey, who thought little of the performance in comparison with other poems by his friend, written, probably, more in accordance with his own affected taste. These latter, as Spenser informed Harvey, comprised *Dreames, Stemmata Dudleiana, The Dying Pelican* and *Nine Comedies* in imitation of Ariosto; none of them survive. He may have been discouraged by Harvey's want of appreciation of *The Faerie Queene*; but, at any rate, he was soon called away to more practical work by accepting, in 1580, the position of secretary to lord Grey, who had been appointed lord deputy in Ireland. Public duties and the turbulent state of the country, doubtless, only allowed him intervals of leisure for excursions into the 'delightful land of Faerie,' but we know that he continued to develop his design—of which he had completed the first, and a portion of the second, book before leaving England—for the work is mentioned by his friend Lodowick Bryskett as being in progress in 1583. Spenser's name appears as one of the 'undertakers' for the colonisation of Munster, in 1586, when he obtained possession of Kilcolman castle, the scenery in the neighbourhood of which he often mentions in *The Faerie Queene.* Here, in 1589, he was visited by Ralegh and read to him the three books of the poem which were all that he had then completed. Ralegh, delighted with what he heard, persuaded Spenser to accompany him to England, no doubt holding out to him prospects of preferment at court, whither the two friends proceeded in the winter of 1589. The first portion of *The Faerie Queene* was published in 1590.

In estimating the artistic value of this poem, we ought to consider not only what the poet himself tells us about the design, but the motives actually in his mind, so far as these discover themselves in the execution of the work. Allegory, no doubt, is its leading feature. The book, says Spenser, is 'a continued allegory or darke conceit.' But he goes on to explain the manner in which his main intention is to be carried out:

> The generall end therefore of all the booke (he says in his letter to Ralegh) is to fashion a gentleman or noble person in vertuous and gentle discipline: Which for that I conceived shoulde be most plausible and pleasing, being coloured with an historicall fiction, the which the most part of men delight to read, rather for variety of matter then for profite of the ensample, I chose the historye of King Arthure, as most fitte for the excellency of his person, being made famous by many mens former workes, and also furthest from the daunger of envy, and suspition of present time. In which I have followed all the antique Poets historicall; first Homere, who in

the Persons of Agamemnon and Ulysses hath ensampled a good governour and a vertuous man, the one in his Ilias, the other in his Odysseis: then Virgil, whose like intention was to doe in the person of Aeneas: after him Ariosto comprised them both in his Orlando: and lately Tasso dissevered them againe, and formed both parts in two persons, namely that part which they in Philosophy call *Ethice*, or vertues of a private man, coloured in his Rinaldo; the other named *Politice* in his Godfredo.

A certain ambiguity and confusion is here visible, showing that Spenser had not clearly thought out his design according to the fundamental principles of his art. It is possible to please, as well as teach, by an allegory of action, if the conduct of the story be kept as clear and consistent as it is in *The Pilgrim's Progress*. It is possible to teach, as well as please, by epic example, because the imagination may be lifted into a heroic atmosphere of valour and virtue; but, in order to achieve such a result, the poet must charm the reader, as Homer does, into a belief in the reality of his narrative. A history like that in *The Faerie Queene*, which, *ex hypothesi*, is allegorical, and, therefore, cannot be real, destroys the possibility of illusion. Spenser was confronted by a difficulty which, in a less formidable shape, had presented itself even to Tasso, when devising the structure of *Gerusalemme Liberata*, one of the poems which Spenser selects as a proof that it is possible to teach in poetry by means of the historical 'ensample.' The Italian poet sought to solve the problem by combining with the real action of history the marvellous machinery of romance, which Ariosto had employed in *Orlando Furioso*, and which was demanded, as an indispensable element in medieval epic poetry, by the public taste. It cannot be said that his solution was entirely successful. It is impossible to persuade the average reader of the reality of an action in which the historical personages of Godfrey and Bohemund are blended with the romantic figures of Herminia and Clorinda, and in which we have to travel in fancy from actual battles under the walls of Jerusalem to the fabulous gardens of the enchantress Armida. Professed history and obvious fiction cannot be harmonised so as to produce a completely credible effect; and credibility is out of the question when romance itself is proclaimed, as it is by Spenser, to be only symbolical. How, for example, can we believe that the historical prince Arthur ever came to the allegorical house of Pride, or really fought with the abstract personage, Disdain?

When we turn from the poet's description of his design to the method of his execution, we see that this exactly resembled his procedure in *The Shepheards Calender*. As, in that work, he consulted the practice of all his pastoral predecessors, so, in the structure of *The Faerie Queene,* he followed the lines of the great romantic poets of Italy, and particularly those of the author of *Orlando Furioso.* At an early date after taking his degree, he had confided to his correspondent Gabriel Harvey his hope of being able to emulate or even 'overgo' Ariosto, and the whole of *The Faerie Queene*—particularly the first three books—bears witness to the frequency with which Spenser props his invention on that of his great Italian model. Not only did he transform many characters in *Orlando Furioso,* such as Atlante, Alcina, Bradamante, into his own Archimago, Duessa and Britomart, but he borrowed whole episodes from Ariosto's poem for the purposes of his story. To mention only a few, the search of Britomart for Artegall is imitated from the search of Bradamante for Ruggiero; as the latter heroine comes to the cave of the fairy Melissa to be informed of her destiny, so does Britomart to the dungeon of Merlin; the courtship of Britomart by Artegall exactly resembles the love-making between Ruggiero and Bradamante; Britomart's male attire occasions the same mistake about her sex to Malecasta, as in the parallel case of Bradamante and Fiordespina; the same relations exist between Britomart and Radigund as between Bradamante and Marfisa; while the transformation of the witch Duessa is directly copied from that of the Fay Alcina. Added to all this, Spenser imitates the narrative of Ariosto in the constant change of person, scene and action. He evidently hoped that while thus 'emulating' Ariosto in 'variety of matter' he might 'overgo' him in 'profite of ensample'; nor does his expectation seem unnatural, when we remember that Harington, the first translator of *Orlando Furioso,* was obliged to disguise the want of moral purpose in his original by insisting—it can hardly be supposed with much sincerity—that all Ariosto's marvellous fictions are to be construed allegorically. To Spenser, it seemed possible, by blending with the romantic manner of Ariosto the varied religious, philosophical and patriotic materials of which he could avail himself, to produce a finer poem in the romantic class than any that had yet appeared. But he did not reckon with all the difficulties in his way.

Orlando Furioso embodies the quintessence of knight errantry. Its virtue lies entirely in its spirit of action. Without any well defined subject, like the consequences of the wrath of Achilles or the loss of Eden, without any single hero on whose fortunes the conduct of the poem turns, Ariosto contrived to include in a connected work an infinity of persons, incidents, marvels, descriptions and emotions, which sustains without weariness the interest of any reader who chooses to surrender his imagination entirely to the poet's guidance. In *Orlando Furioso,* there is no progress from point to point towards a well discerned end; the character of the poem is proclaimed in the two opening lines,

> *Le donne, i cavalier, l' arme, gli amori,*
> *Le cortesie, l' audaci impresi, io canto,*

which form the prelude to a varied spectacle of human action and passion. The sole unity in this ever changing scene lies in the imagination of the poet himself, who acts as the interpreter of his puppet show, and enlists our interest on behalf of his fictitious creatures by the lively sympathy with which he accompanies them in every marvellous, humorous, or pathetic adventure. Numerous as are his personages, he never loses sight of one of them, and will break off, at the climax of a thrilling situation, to transport the reader into a different quarter of the globe, where, a few cantos back, a valorous knight or hapless lover has been left in circumstances of seemingly irremediable misfortune. His effects are produced entirely by the realistic power of his fancy; and perhaps no poet in the world has ever approached, in this respect, so nearly as Ariosto to the standard of Horace:

> *Ille per extentum funem mihi posse videtur*
> *Ire poeta, meum qui pectus inaniter angit,*
> *Irritat, mulcet, falsis terroribus implet,*
> *Ut magus, et modo me Thebis, modo ponit Athenis.*

The feat is accomplished simply and solely by the vivid representation of action and character. The images are complete in themselves; and to attempt to add anything to them, in the shape of reason or moral, would destroy the reality of their airy being. Ariosto, as Aristotle says of Homer, 'tells lies as he ought'; he cheats the imagination into a belief in what would be probable in a really impossible situation.

While adopting the form of the romantic epic as the basis of allegory throughout his entire poem, Spenser seems soon to have discovered that he could only travel easily by this path for a short distance. In his first two books, indeed, it was open to him to represent chivalrous action of an allegorical character, which might be readily understood as a probation undergone by the hero, prince Arthur, in the moral virtues of holiness and temperance. The first book shows the militant Christian, in the person of the Red Cross Knight, travelling in company with Una, the lady of his love, personifying wisdom or the highest form of beauty, on an enterprise, of which the end is to free the kingdom of Una's parents from the ravages of a great dragon, the evil one. The various adventures in which the actors in the story are involved are well conceived, as setting forth the different temptations to which the Christian character is exposed; and this idea is still more forcibly worked out in the second book, which illustrates the exercise of temperance; for, here, the poet can appropriately ally the treatment of this virtue in Greek philosophy with the many allusions to it in the New Testament. In the allegories of the house of Mammon, the house of Alma and the bower of Bliss, the beauty of the imagery is equalled by the propriety with which treasures of learning are employed to bring the moral into due relief. At this point, however, the capacities of the moral design, as announced by the poet, were exhausted. 'To fashion a gentleman or noble person' in the discipline of chastity, the subject of the third book, would have involved an allegory too closely resembling the one already completed; and it is significant that a female knight is now brought upon the scene; while, both in the third and in the fourth book, the moral is scarcely at all enforced by allegory, but almost always by 'ensample,' or adventure. Justice, the virtue exemplified in the fifth book, is not, as would be anticipated from the preface, an inward disposition of the knightly soul, but an external condition of things, produced by the course of politics—scarcely allegorised at all—in real countries such as Ireland, France and the Netherlands; on the other hand, the peculiarly knightly virtue of courtesy is, in the sixth book, illustrated, also with very little attempt at allegory, by means of episodes of adventure borrowed, almost directly, from the romantic narrative of the *Morte d'Arthur*.

The absence of depth in Spenser's moral allegory is further shown by the multiplicity of his aims. He explains in his letter to Ralegh why his poem is called *The Faerie Queene*.

In that Faery Queene I meane glory in my generall intention, but in my particular I conceive the most excellent and glorious person of our soveraine the Queene, and her kingdome in Faery land. And yet, in some places els, I doe otherwise shadow her. For considering she beareth two persons, the one of a most royall Queene or Empresse, the other of a most vertuous and beautifull Lady, this latter part in some places I do expresse in Belphœbe, fashioning her name according to your owne excellent conceipt of Cynthia, (Phoebe and Cynthia being both names of Diana.) So in the person of Prince Arthure I sette forth magnificence in particular; which vertue, for that (according to Aristotle and the rest) it is the perfection of all the rest, and conteineth in it them all, therefore in the whole course I mention the deedes of Arthure

applyable to that vertue, which I write of in that booke. But of the XII. other vertues I make XII. other knights the patrones, for the more variety of the history: Of which these three bookes contayn three.

The attention of the reader is thus withdrawn from the purely ideal figure of the perfect knight, to unriddle, sometimes compliments addressed to great persons at court (*e.g.* queen Elizabeth, who, as occasion requires, is Gloriana, or Belphoebe, or Britomart; lord Grey, who is Artegall; Sir Walter Ralegh who is Timias), and sometimes invectives against the queen's enemies, in the person of Duessa, who, when she is not Theological Falsehood, is Mary, queen of Scots.

This ambiguity of meaning is intensified by the mixture of Christian with pagan imagery, and by the blending of classical mythology, both with local antiquarian learning and with the fictions of romance. In the fifth canto of the first book, for example, Duessa, or Papal Falsehood, goes down to hell, under the guidance of Night, to procure aid from Aesculapius for the wounded paynim Sansfoy, or Infidelity; and her mission gives an opening for a description of many of the torments mentioned in Vergil's 'Inferno.' On her return to the upper air, she goes to the 'stately pallace of Dame Pryde,' in whose dungeons are confined many of the proud men mentioned in the Old Testament, or in Greek and Roman history. Shortly afterwards, prince Arthur relates to Una his nurture by the supposed historic Merlin; and the latter, in the third book, discloses to Britomart the line of British kings, as recorded by Geoffrey of Monmouth, and prophesies the reign of Elizabeth.

Such profusion of material and multiplicity of motive, while it gives to *The Faerie Queene* an unequalled appearance of richness and splendour, invalidates the profession of Spenser that the poem is 'a continued allegory.' Allegory cannot be here interpreted as it may be, for example, in Plato's *Phaedrus*, where the myth is avowedly used to relieve and illuminate the obscurities of abstract thought. It cannot be interpreted in Dante's meaning, when he makes Beatrice say: 'thus it is fitting to speak to your mind, seeing it is only from an object of sense that it apprehends what it afterwards makes worthy of the understanding.' Nor does it approach in moral depth the simple allegory of *The Pilgrim's Progress*, in which the author evidently employs the form of a story merely as the vehicle for the truth of Christian doctrine. In other words, the sense of Spenser's allegory does not lie in its external truth: its value is to be found in its relation to the beauty of his own thought, and in the fidelity with which it reflects the intellectual temper of his time.

The main difficulty that Spenser had to encounter in treating the subject of *The Faerie Queene* lay in the conduct of the action. His design was at once ethical and practical, namely 'to fashion a gentleman or noble person in vertuous and gentle discipline'; and this he proposed to do by portraying 'in Arthure, before he was King, the image of a brave Knight, perfected in the twelve private Morall Vertues, as Aristotle hath devised.' But the knight, as such, no longer, in any real sense, formed part of the social organism. He had been rapidly vanishing from it since the epoch of the crusades, and almost the last glimpse of him in English poetry is in the fine and dignified person of the Canterbury pilgrim, the 'verray parfit, gentil knyght,' who is represented as having warred against the infidel on behalf of Christendom in Prussia and Lithuania. So long as it was possible to believe in his existence, men pleased their imaginations with reading of the knight's ideal deeds in the romances; but the time was close at hand when the romances themselves were, necessarily, to be made the subject of just satire. Absolutism had everywhere crushed the energies of feudalism; the knight had been transformed into the courtier; and the 'vertuous and gentle discipline,' deemed requisite for him in his new sphere, was, for the most part, to be found in such regulations for external behaviour as are laid down in Castiglione's *Il Cortegiano*. Long before the close of the eighteenth century, it would have been possible to write, *mutatis mutandis,* the epitaph of feudalism in the glowing words of Burke:

> The age of Chivalry is gone. That of sophisters, economists, and calculators has succeeded; and the glory of Europe is extinguished for ever. Never, never more, shall we behold that generous loyalty to rank and sex, that proud submission, that dignified obedience, that subordination of the heart, which kept alive, even in servitude itself, the spirit of an exalted freedom. The unbought grace of life, the cheap defence of nations, the nurse of manly sentiment and heroick enterprise is gone! It is gone, that sensibility of principle, that chastity of honour, which felt a stain like a wound, which inspired courage whilst it mitigated ferocity, which ennobled whatever it touched, and under which vice itself lost half its evil by losing all its grossness.

Spenser himself felt that he was dealing with a vanished state of things:

> So oft as I with state of present time
> The image of the antique world compare,
> When as mans age was in his freshest prime,
> And the first blossome of faire vertue bare;

Such oddes I finde twixt those, and these which are,
As that, through long continuance of his course,
Me seemes the world is runne quite out of square
From the first point of his appointed sourse;
And being once amisse growes daily wourse and wourse.

Under these altered conditions, it would be unreasonable to look in *The Faerie Queene* for a 'continued allegory' of action. What we do find there is the chivalrous spirit, such as still survived in the soul of Sidney and a few others, uttering itself, when opportunity offers, in short bursts of enthusiastic and sublime sentiment, as in the following stanza on Honour:

In woods, in waves, in warres, she wonts to dwell,
And wil be found with perill and with paine;
Ne can the man that moulds in ydle cell
Unto her happy mansion attaine:
Before her gate high God did Sweate ordaine,
And wakefull watches ever to abide;
But easy is the way and passage plaine
To pleasures pallace: it may soon be spide,
And day and night her dores to all stand open wide[1].

There is nothing in *Orlando Furioso* so lofty as this; nor can the great poet of Italian romance for a moment compare with Spenser in 'that generous loyalty to rank and sex . . . that subordination of the heart,' which, as Burke observes, is one of the noblest characteristics of chivalry. Not only does the ancient tendency to woman-worship, common to the Teutonic race, survive in the figure of Gloriana, *The Faerie Queene*, but in all Spenser's treatment of female character there is a purity and elevation worthy of his chivalrous subject. His Una and Amoret are figures of singular beauty, and his handling of delicate situations, involving mistakes about sex or descriptions of female jealousy, contrasts finely with that of Ariosto. The gross realism in the painting of Bradamante's feelings, when suspicious of Ruggiero's relations with Marfisa, set side by side with the imitation of that passage in the episode of Britomart, Radigund and Artegall, shows how wide a gulf of sentiment separated the still knightly spirit of England from the materialism of the Italian renascence.

Finally, the genius of heroic action which, in the romances of chivalry—as became the decentralised character of feudal institutions—is diffused over a great variety of actors, places and situations, tends, in *The Faerie Queene*, to concentrate itself in the person of the sovereign, as representing the greatness of the English nation. The patriotic spirit of the times constantly breaks

[1] Book II, canto III, stanza 41.

forth in emotional utterance, as in the stanza describing the enthusiasm with which prince Arthur reads the books of 'Briton documents.'

> At last, quite ravisht with delight to heare
> The royall Ofspring of his native land,
> Cryde out; Deare countrey! O how dearely deare
> Ought thy remembraunce and perpetuall band
> Be to thy foster Childe, that from thy hand
> Did commun breath and nouriture receave.
> How brutish is it not to understand
> How much to her we owe, that all us gave;
> That gave unto us all what ever good we have[1].

With the glorification of a patriot queen, Spenser was able, appropriately, to link all the legendary lore handed down to him by Geoffrey of Monmouth, together with the fables of the *Morte d'Arthur*, and with that local antiquarianism which, in the historical researches of men like Camden and Holinshed, had done much to kindle the English imagination. Contemporary politics and personal association also furnished him with a large part of the material in his fifth book.

The medium of allegory through which he viewed the institution of knighthood, while it deprived *The Faerie Queene* of human interest and unity of action, gave fine scope for the exercise of the imaginative powers peculiar to the poet. As a poetical painter, using words and rhythms in the place of external form and colour, he is, perhaps, unrivalled. We pass through his scenes, laid in the 'delightful land of Faerie,' as through an enchanted landscape, in which a dream-like succession of pageants, and dissolving views of forests, lakes, castles, caves and palaces, each suggesting some spiritual meaning, and, at the same time, raising in the fancy a concrete image, relieve the tedium of the journey. 'An ampler ether a diviner air,' diffused by his imagination over the whole prospect, blends the most dissimilar objects in a general effect of harmony; and so exquisite is the *chiaroscuro* of the composition that no sense of discord is felt in the transition from the celestial hierarchy to 'Cupido on the Idaean hill,' from woodland satyrs to the mount of heavenly contemplation, from Una, the abstract symbol of Christian truth, to Belphoebe, the half-pagan anti-type of the chaste Elizabeth. At the same time, each portion of the picture is brought into relief by the firmness of the outlines and the richness of the colouring, fine examples of which are the cave of Despair and the masque of the Seven Deadly Sins, in the first book, the house of Mammon and the bower of Bliss in

[1] Book II, canto X, stanza 69.

the second. In these two books, as the spiritual sense is more emphatic, the allegorical imagery abounds: with the progress of the poem, the allegory dwindles, and adventures become proportionately more frequent; but, even in the third and fourth books, the poet always seems to diverge with pleasure into picturesque descriptions, such as that of the witch's cottage, in canto VII of book III, or the marriage of the Thames and the Medway, in canto XI of book IV. As a specimen of the mingled propriety and sublimity of allegorical painting, nothing finer can be found than the description, in the fragmentary legend of Constancy, of the Titaness Mutability in the moon—an image well fitted to exhibit the truths of Christian doctrine under the veil of pagan mythology:

And now, when all the earth she thus had brought
To her behest, and thralled to her might,
She gan to cast in her ambitious thought
T' attempt the empire of the heavens hight,
And Jove himselfe to shoulder from his right.
And first, she past the region of the ayre
And of the fire, whose substance thin and slight,
Made no resistance, ne could her contraire,
But ready passage to her pleasure did prepaire.

Thence to the Circle of the Moone she clambe,
Where Cynthia raignes in everlasting glory,
To whose bright shining palace straight she came,
All fairely deckt with heavens goodly storie;
Whose silver gates (by which there sat an hory
Old aged Sire, with hower-glasse in hand,
Hight Time) she entred, were he liefe or sory;
Ne staide till she the highest stage had scand,
Where Cynthia did sit, that never still did stand.

Her sitting on an Ivory throne shee found,
Drawne of two steeds, th' one black, the other white,
Environd with tenne thousand starres around
That duly her attended day and night;
And by her side there ran her Page, that hight
Vesper, whom we the Evening-starre intend;
That with his Torche, still twinkling like twylight,
Her lightened all the way where she should wend,
And joy to weary wandring travailers did lend.

Besides the imagination of a great word-painter, Spenser brought to the expression of his allegory the gifts of a skilful metrical musician. As in *The Shepheards Calender*, so in *The Faerie Queene*, it was his object to invent a kind of poetical dialect suitable to the unreal nature of his subject. Effects of strangeness and antiquity, mingled with modern elegance, are produced, in the later poem, partly by the revival of old words and the importation of foreign ones, partly by the musical disposition of words in the line, partly by combinations of rime, in a stanza of his own invention, constructed, by the addition of an alexandrine verse, out of the ten-syllabled eight-lined stanza used by Chaucer. The character of his vocabulary and of his syntax may be exemplified in the following stanza:

> And therewithall he fiersly at him flew,
> And with importune outrage him assayld;
> Who, soone prepared to field, his sword forth drew,
> And him with equall valew countervayld:
> Their mightie strokes their haberjeons dismayld,
> And naked made each others manly spalles;
> The mortall steele despiteously entayld
> Deepe in their flesh, quite through the yron walles,
> That a large purple streame adowne their giambeux falles[1].

The idea of simplicity mingled with archaism here aimed at is also raised by the avoidance of anything like a precise search for epithets in those classical combinations of adjective and substantive which he frequently employs. His epithets are generally of the conventional kind—'busy care,' 'bloody might,' 'huge great balance,' etc. He also uses deliberately archaic forms, such as 'to achieven' for 'to achieve,' 'worldës' for 'world's,' and the like. The frequent use of inversions, such as 'him assayld,' 'his sword forth drew,' is, in part, the result of conscious archaism; but it is also the natural consequence of the recurrence of rime. This recurrence, again, suggested to Spenser many characteristic effects of sound: he saw, for example, that the immediate sequence of rime in the fourth and fifth lines provided a natural half-way house for a turn in the rhetoric of the sentence; so that the fifth line is used, generally, either as the close of the first stage in the stanza, or the beginning of the second; but he is very skilful in avoiding monotony, and will often run a single sentence through the stanza, or will break up the stanza into as many parts as there are lines, *e.g.*

> Behinde him was Reproch, Repentaunce, Shame;
> Reproch the first, Shame next, Repent behinde:
> Repentaunce feeble, sorrowfull, and lame;
> Reproch despightfull, carelesse, and unkinde;
> Shame most ill-favourd, bestiall, and blinde:
> Shame lowrd, Repentaunce sighd, Reproch did scould;
> Reproch sharpe stings, Repentaunce whips entwinde,
> Shame burning brond-yrons in her hand did hold:
> All three to each unlike, yet all made in one mould[2].

[1] Book II, canto VI, stanza 29. [2] Book III, canto XII, stanza 24.

These metrical combinations and permutations are often employed very beautifully in pathetic passages:

> Ye Gods of seas, if any Gods at all
> Have care of right, or ruth of wretches wrong,
> By one or other way me, woefull thrall,
> Deliver hence out of this dungeon strong,
> In which I daily dying am too long:
> And if ye deeme me death for loving one
> That loves not me, then doe it not prolong,
> But let me die and end my days attone,
> And let him live unlov'd, or love him selfe alone.
>
> But if that life ye unto me decree,
> Then let mee live as lovers ought to do,
> And of my lifes deare love beloved be:
> And if he should through pride your doome undo,
> Do you by duresse him compell thereto,
> And in this prison put him here with me;
> One prison fittest is to hold us two.
> So had I rather to be thrall then free;
> Such thraldome or such freedome let it surely be.
>
> But O vaine judgement, and conditions vaine,
> The which the prisoner points unto the free!
> The whiles I him condemne, and deeme his paine,
> He where he list goes loose, and laughes at me.
> So ever loose, so ever happy be!
> But where so loose or happy that thou art,
> Know, Marinell, that all this is for thee[1].

Throughout the various examples here given, it will be noticed that alliteration plays an important part in the composition of the general effect. Spenser would not have deigned to include himself among those whom his commentator E. K. calls 'the rakehelly rout of our ragged rymers (for so themselves use to hunt the letter)'; but he knew that alliteration was in the genius of the English language, and he was the first to show its capacities for those liquid sequences of labial letters, carried through a rhythmical sentence, by means of which Milton afterwards produced his effects of verbal harmony.

As his years advanced, Spenser seems to have felt more and more that his allegorical conception of court chivalry, founded on Platonism, protestantism and romance, had little correspondence with the actual movement of things. First of all, in 1586 died Philip Sidney, the 'president of nobleness and chivalrie,' an irreparable loss to the cause of knighthood in high places, which is lamented in the pastoral elegy, *Astrophel.* Besides this, the poet's expectations of his own preferment at court had been sadly disappointed: the queen had favoured his suit, but the way was

[1] Book IV, canto XII, stanzas 9—11.

barred by Burghley, who seems to have borne him a grudge, probably on account of his early connection with Burghley's rival, Leicester. In 1591, a volume of his collected poems was published with the significant title *Complaints.* An air of deep melancholy runs through most of the contents. In *The Ruines of Time,* dedicated to the countess of Pembroke, he makes the female genius of the ruined city Verulam lament, in touching stanzas, the death of Sidney, from which he passes to indignant reflections on the neglect of poetry by the great, in evident allusion to his own treatment by Burghley:

O griefe of griefes! O gall of all good heartes!
To see that vertue should dispised bee
Of him, that first was raisde for vertuous parts,
And now, broad spreading like an aged tree,
Lets none shoot up that nigh him planted bee:
O let the man, of whom the Muse is scorned,
Nor alive nor dead be of the Muse adorned!

The same strain is taken up in *The Tears of the Muses,* where the nine sisters are made in turn to bewail the degraded state of the stage and the different forms of literary poetry. Of their laments, the most characteristic, as showing Spenser's lack of sympathy with the development of the English drama, is that of Thalia:

And him beside sits ugly Barbarisme,
And brutish Ignorance, ycrept of late
Out of dredd darknes of the deepe Abysme,
Where being bredd, he light and heaven does hate:
They in the mindes of men now tyrannize,
And the faire Scene with rudenes foule disguize.
All places they with follie have possest,
And with vaine toyes the vulgare entertaine;
But me have banished, with all the rest
That whilome wont to wait upon my traine,
Fine Counterfesaunce, and unhurtfull Sport,
Delight, and Laughter, deckt in seemly sort.

Here, doubtless, he alludes to the growing popularity of the plays of Greene and Marlowe, as compared with the classical 'court comedies' of 'pleasant Willy' (Lyly), who ceased to write for the stage about 1590, and who, therefore, is spoken of as 'dead of late.' But the most direct utterance of Spenser's spleen against the time is to be found in his *Prosopopoia or Mother Hubberd's Tale,* which, in its groundwork, he calls 'the raw conceipt of my youth,' but which, in its existing form, must have been polished and altered to suit the change of circumstances. Founded on the precedent of *The Nun's Priest's Tale,* in the Canterbury pilgrimage, it contains, in the story of the ape and the fox, a bitter attack on the customs of the court. Besides the famous lines, beginning 'How little knowest thou that has not tried'—which we may well suppose were added, in 1590, to the first cast of the poem—we have the picture of the 'brave courtier,' evidently intended for a portrait of Philip Sidney, and its striking contrast in the description of the ape, whose manners are copied from all the corruptions of Italy. Once more, the poet employs his invective against the great men (personified by the ape) who disdain learning.

> And whenso love of letters did inspire
> Their gentle wits, and kindle wise desire,
> That chieflie doth each noble minde adorne,
> Then he would scoffe at learning, and eke scorne
> The Sectaries thereof, as people base
> And simple men, which never came in place
> Of worlds affaires, but, in darke corners mewd,
> Muttred of matters as their bookes them shewd,
> Ne other knowledge ever did attaine,
> But with their gownes their gravitie maintaine.

In all this he seems to be aiming at Burghley, the type of the newly risen courtier, who is unfavourably contrasted with the older nobility. The latter, he says,

> for povertie,
> Were forst their auncient houses to let lie,
> And their olde Castles to the ground to fall,
> Which their forefathers, famous over-all,
> Had founded for the Kingdomes ornament,
> And for their memories long moniment.

Language of this kind seems to show plainly that the poet's advancement at court was barred by political obstacles. But he also had to encounter a certain opposition in the change of taste. In 1591, after a year spent with the English court, he returned to what he considered exile in Ireland, and there, in the form of an allegorical pastoral, called *Colin Clout's Come Home Again*, he gave expression to his views about the contemporary state of manners and poetry. While exalting the person of the queen, with imagery never surpassed in richness, and paying noble compliments to those of her courtiers who had duly appreciated the beauties of *The Faerie Queene*, he reflects severely, through the mouth of Colin Clout, on the general state of courtly taste, especially in respect of love poetry:

> Not so, (quoth he) Love most aboundeth there.
> For all the walls and windows there are writ,
> All full of love, and love, and love my deare,
> And all their talke and studie is of it.

Ne any there doth brave or valiant seeme
Unlesse that some gay Mistresse badge he beares:

. . . . . .

For with lewd speeches, and licentious deedes,
His mightie mysteries they do prophane,
And use his ydle name to other needs.
But as a complement for courting vaine.

These strokes seem to be aimed partly at the degraded vein of Petrarchism, manifested abundantly in the sonnets of this period, and partly at the style of Italian romance, brought into fashion by Greene and his disciples. Spenser himself yielded not a jot to the fashion of the times. It is true that his *Amoretti,* written in honour of the lady to whom he was married in 1594, are conceived in the most conventional Petrarchian spirit, as what we may suppose he thought most likely to please his 'Elisabeth.' But the description of 'perfect love,' and the praises of Rosalind in *Colin Clout's Come Home Again*, breathe the same heroic Platonism as his *Hymnes to Love and Beautie*; while, in his *Prothalamion*, and, still more, in his *Epithalamion*, he carries the lyrical style, first attempted in *The Shepheards Calender*, to an unequalled height of harmony, splendour and enthusiasm. In 1595, he again came over to England, bringing with him the second part of *The Faerie Queene*, which was licensed for publication in January 1595—6. While at court on this occasion, he seems to have resolved to oppose his influence, as far as he might, to the prevailing current of taste in poetry, by publishing his youthful *Hymnes in honour of Love and Beautie.* Lofty and Platonic as these were in their conception, he protests, in his dedication of them to 'The Right Honorable and Most Vertuous Ladies, the Ladie Margaret, Countesse of Cumberland, and the Ladie Marie, Countesse of Warwicke,' that he desires, 'by way of retractation, to reforme them, making, instead of those two Hymnes of earthly or naturall love and beautie, two others of heavenly and celestiall. In the later *Hymnes*, he identifies the doctrine of Platonic love, in its highest form, with the dogma of Trinity in Unity:

Before this worlds great frame, in which al things
Are now containd, found any being-place,
Ere flitting Time could wag his eyas wings
About that mightie bound which doth embrace
The rolling Spheres, and parts their houres by space,
That High Eternall Powre, which now doth move
In all these things, mov'd in it selfe by love.

It lov'd it selfe, because it selfe was faire;
(For faire is lov'd;) and of it self begot,
Like to it selfe his eldest sonne and heire,

Eternall, pure, and voide of sinfull blot,
The firstling of his joy, in whom no jot
Of loves dislike or pride was to be found,
Whom he therefore with equall honour crownd.

With him he raignd, before all time prescribed,
In endlesse glorie and immortall might,
Together with that third from them derived,
Most wise, most holy, most almightie Spright!
Whose kingdomes throne no thought of earthly wight
Can comprehend, much lesse my trembling verse
With equall words can hope it to reherse.

Finding still no opening for himself at court, Spenser returned, once more, to Ireland, in 1597, where, in September 1598, he was appointed sheriff of Cork, as a man fitted to deal with the rebels of Munster. These, however, proved too strong for him, and, at the rising under Hugh O'Neile, earl of Tyrone, his castle of Kilcolman was taken and burned in October 1598. He himself, escaping with difficulty, was sent by the lord deputy to London with despatches about the rebellion. His calamities seem to have broken his spirit. In spite of the favour extended to him by influential courtiers like Essex, he is said to have been oppressed by poverty; and, very soon after his arrival in London, he died in King street, Westminster, on 16 January 1599.

To sum up the foregoing sketch of the poetry of Spenser, it will be seen that he differed from the great European poets who preceded or immediately succeeded him, in that he made no attempt to represent in his verse the dominant moving spirit in the world about him. Chaucer and Shakespeare, the one in the *fabliau*, the other in the romantic drama, held 'the mirror up to nature' and showed 'the very age and body of the time his form and pressure.' Ariosto, by blending the opposite forms of the *fabliau* and the *roman*, reflected the genius of knight errantry as it appeared to the sceptical onlooker in courts. Milton succeeded in telling the Christian story of the loss of Eden in the form of the pagan epic. While Dante, like Spenser, made allegory the basis of his poetical conception, no more vivid picture can be found of contemporary life and manners in Italian cities under the Holy Roman Empire than in *The Divine Comedy*. But, in the conduct of his story, Spenser never seems to be in direct touch with his times: his personages, knights or shepherds, wear plainly the dress of literary masquerade; and, though the fifth book of *The Faerie Queene*, published in 1596, deals allegorically with such matters as the revolt of the Netherlands and the recantation of protestantism by Henri IV of France, it contains no allusion to the Spanish armada.

But the very absence of clear drift and purpose in the allegory of *The Faerie Queene* made it a faithful mirror of the spirit of the age. Through all the early portion of Elizabeth's reign, in which the poetical genius of Spenser formed itself, the nation, in its most influential elements, showed the doubt and hesitancy always characteristic of times of transition. A clergy, halting between catholic tradition and the doctrines of the reformers; a semi-absolute queen, coquetting in her foreign policy between a rival monarch and his revolted subjects; a court, in which the chivalrous manners of the old nobility were neutralised by the Machiavelian statecraft of the new courtiers; a commercial enterprise, always tending to break through the limits of ancient and stable custom: these were the conditions which made it difficult for an English poet, in the middle of the sixteenth century, to form a view, at once clear and comprehensive, of life and action.

Spenser himself evidently sympathised strongly with the old order that was passing away. He loved the time-honoured institutions of chivalry, closely allied to catholic ritual; he reverenced its ideals of honour and courtesy, its exalted woman-worship, its compassion for the poor and suffering. But, at the same time, he was strongly impelled by two counter-movements tending to undermine the ancient fabric whose foundations had been laid by Charles the Great: the zeal of the protestant reformer, and the enthusiasm for letters of the European humanist. The poetical problem he had to solve was, how to present the action of these antagonistic forces in an ideal form, with such an appearance of unity as should satisfy the primary requirements of his art.

To fuse irreconcilable principles in a directly epic or dramatic mould was impossible; but it was possible to disguise the essential oppositions of things by covering them with the veil of allegory. This was the method that Spenser adopted. The unity of his poetical creations lies entirely in the imaginative medium through which he views them. His poetical procedure is closely analogous to that of the first Neo-Platonists in philosophy. Just as these sought to evolve out of the decayed forms of polytheism, by means of Plato's dialectic, a new religious philosophy, so, in the sphere of poetry, Spenser attempted to create, for the English court and the circles immediately connected with it, from the perishing institution of chivalry, an ideal of knightly conduct. Glimpses of real objects give an air of actuality to his conception; his allegory, as he himself declares in his preface to *The Faerie Queene*, has reference to 'the most excellent and glorious person of our

Soveraine the Queen.' Viewed in the crude light of fact, the court of Elizabeth might be, as the poet himself describes it in *Mother Hubberd's Tale*, full of petty intrigue, low ambitions, corrupt dealings, Machiavelian statecraft, shameless licence; but, exalted into the kingdom of Gloriana, clothed with the purple atmosphere of romance and the phantasms of the golden age, the harsh realities of life were veiled in a visionary scene of knights and shepherds, sylvan nymphs and satyrs, pagan pageants and Christian symbols; the ruling society of England was transformed into the 'delightful land of Faerie.'

The diction and the versification of Spenser correspond felicitously with the ideal character of his thought. As in the later case of *Paradise Lost*, what has been justly called the 'out-of-the-world' nature of the subject required, in *The Faerie Queene*, a peculiar vehicle of expression. Though it be true that, in affecting the obsolete, Spenser 'writ no language'; though, that is to say, he did not attempt to amplify and polish the living language of the court, yet his mixture of Old English words with classical syntax, in metres adapted from those used by Chaucer, produces a remarkably beautiful effect. Native oppositions of style disappear in the harmonising art of the poet. Though ill-qualified to be the vehicle of epical narrative, the Spenserian stanza has firmly established itself in the language, as a metre of admirable capacity for any kind of descriptive or reflective poetry; and it is a striking illustration of what has been said in the foregoing pages that it has been the instrument generally chosen by poets whose genius has approached nearest to the art of the painter, or who have sought to put forward ideas opposed to the existing condition of things. It is employed by Thomson in *The Castle of Indolence*, by Keats in *The Eve of St Agnes*, by Shelley in *The Revolt of Islam* and by Byron in *Childe Harold's Pilgrimage*. To have been the poetical ancestor of the poetry of these illustrious writers shows how deeply the art of Spenser is rooted in the imaginative genius of his country, and he needs no better monument than the stanza in his own *Ruines of Time*:

> For deeds doe die, however noblie donne,
> And thoughts of men do as themselves decay;
> But wise wordes, taught in numbers for to runne,
> Recorded by the Muses, live for ay;
> Ne may with storming showers be washt away,
> Ne bitter-breathing windes with harmfull blast,
> Nor age, nor envie, shall them ever wast.

CHAPTER XII

THE ELIZABETHAN SONNET

THE sonnet, which, for practical purposes, may be regarded as an invention of thirteenth century Italy, slowly won the favour of English poets. Neither the word nor the thing reached England till the third decade of the sixteenth century, when English sonnets were first written, in imitation of the Italian, by Sir Thomas Wyatt and the earl of Surrey. But these primary efforts form an isolated episode in English literary history; they began no vogue. A whole generation—more than a quarter of a century—separated the final sonneteering efforts of Surrey and Wyatt from the birth of the Elizabethan sonnet. At first, the Elizabethan growth was sparse; nor did it acquire luxuriance until queen Elizabeth's reign was nearing its last decade. Then, sonneteering became an imperious and universal habit, a conventional recreation, a modish artifice of gallantry and compliment. No poetic aspirant between 1590 and 1600 failed to try his skill on this poetic instrument. During those ten years, more sonnets were penned in England than in any other decade.

The harvest of Elizabethan sonneteering is a strange medley of splendour and dulness. The workers in the field included Sidney, Spenser and Shakespeare, who, in varying degrees, invested this poetic form with unquestionable beauty. Shakespeare, above all, breathed into the sonnet a lyric melody and a meditative energy which no writer of any country has surpassed. It is the value attaching to the sonneteering efforts of this great trio of Elizabethan poets, and to some rare and isolated triumphs of their contemporaries, Daniel, Drayton and Constable, which lends to the Elizabethan sonnet aesthetic interest. The profuse experiments of other Elizabethans lack critical importance and add nothing to the lasting fruits of poetic achievement. Few in the crowded rank and file of Elizabethan sonneteers reached high levels of poetic performance. Fewer still were capable of sustained flight in the loftiest regions of poetry. Most of the fertile producers betrayed a crudeness and a clumsiness of thought and language which invited and justified ridicule.

None the less does the average Elizabethan sonnet illustrate the temper of the time. It bears graphic witness to the Elizabethan tendency to borrow from foreign literary effort. Even the greatest of Elizabethan sonneteers did not disdain occasional transcription of the language and sentiment of popular French or Italian poetry. The rank and file almost entirely depended for inspiration on their foreign reading. The full story of the Elizabethan sonnet is, for the most part, a suggestive chapter in the literary records of plagiarism, a testimony to the frequency of communication between literary Englishmen and literary Frenchmen and Italians, an illustration of the community of literary feeling which linked the three nations to one another.

The influence which Wyatt and Surrey, the English pioneers of the sonnet, exerted on the Elizabethan sonneteers is shadowy and indeterminate. Their experiments, as has been seen[1], were first published posthumously in 1557 in *Tottel's Miscellany*, which included verse from many other pens. The sixty sonnets contained in Tottel's volume—for the most part primitive reflections of Petrarch—represent, so far as is known, all the English sonneteering work which was in being when queen Elizabeth's reign opened.

George Gascoigne, in his treatise on poetic composition, which appeared as early as 1575, accurately described the normal construction of the sonnet in sixteenth century England when he wrote:

> Sonnets are of fouretene lynes, every line conteyning tenne syllables. The firste twelve do ryme in staves of foure lines by crosse meetre, and the last two ryming togither do conclude the whole.

Though *Tottel's Miscellany* was reprinted seven times between 1557 and 1584, and acquired general popularity, little endeavour was made during those seven and twenty years to emulate its sonneteering experiments. In the earliest poetic miscellanies which followed *Tottel's Miscellany*, sonnets are rare. Only three quatorzains figure in *The Paradyse of Daynty Devises*, 1576. Of these, only one pays any regard to metrical rules. The two others are carelessly formed of seven riming couplets, and the lines are not of ten but of twelve or fourteen syllables. In the succeeding miscellany, *A Gorgious Gallery of Gallant Inventions*, 1578, the quatorzains number no more than four.

Despite Wyatt and Surrey's efforts, it was by slow degrees

[1] See *ante*, chap. VIII.

that the sonnet came to be recognised in Elizabethan England as a definite species of verse inviting compliance with fixed metrical laws. George Gascoigne, although he himself made some fifteen experiments in the true quatorzain, accurately diagnosed contemporary practice when he noted, in 1575, how 'some thinke that all Poemes (being short) may be called Sonets, as in deede it is a diminutive worde derived of *Sonare*.' This view held its ground more stubbornly than is often recognised. When Clement Robinson, in 1584, published his *Handefull of pleasant delites*, he described the volume as containing 'sundrie new sonets' with 'everie sonet orderly pointed to its proper tune,' and he headed many of his poems with such titles as 'A proper sonet,' or 'A sorrowful sonet.' Yet Robinson's sonnets are all lyric poems of varied length, usually in four- or six-lined stanzas. No sonnet in the technical sense came from his pen. The tradition of this inaccurate nomenclature survived, indeed, to a far later generation; and writers like Thomas Lodge and Nicholas Breton, who made many experiments in the true sonnet form, had no hesitation in applying the term to lyric efforts of varied metre and in stanzas of varied length, which bore no relation to the quatorzain. As late as 1604, Nicholas Breton brought out a miscellany of poetry under the general title, *The Passionate Shepheard*; the second part bore the designation 'Sundry sweet sonnets and passionated Poems,' each of which is separately headed 'Sonet I,' and so forth; but two only of the poems are quatorzains and those in rambling lines of fourteen syllables. Breton's 'Sonet I' is in thirty-four stanzas of four lines each, with one stanza of six lines. His 'Sonet II' is in thirty-two stanzas of six lines each. The long continued misuse of the word illustrates the reluctance of the Elizabethans to accept the sonnet's distinctive principles.

It was contemporary French, rather than older Italian, influences which first stirred in the Elizabethan mind a fruitful interest in the genuine sonnet. The first inspiration came from Clément Marot, the protestant French poet of the early years of the sixteenth century, who was a contemporary of Wyatt and Surrey. He studied Petrarch with ardour, translated into French some of his sonnets and odes and made two or three original experiments in the sonnet-form under the title of 'Epigrammes.' Although it was only after Marot's death that the reign of the sonnet was definitely inaugurated in France, his tentative ventures impressed some of his English readers. But Marot's influence was fugitive; it was quickly eclipsed. The sonnet was not naturalised in France until Marot's successors, Pierre de Ronsard and his friends, deliberately resolved to adapt to the French language the finest fruit of foreign literature. Ronsard and his companions assumed the corporate title of *La Pléiade,* and the sonnet became the rallying flag of their school. In Italy, Petrarch's sonneteering disciples multiplied greatly at the end of the fifteenth and the beginning of the sixteenth century; and the French innovators detected in the rejuvenated Italian sonnet a potent influence of domestic regeneration. The manifesto of the new movement in French poetry was written by Joachim du Bellay, one of its ablest champions. He solemnly urged Frenchmen to write sonnets after the manner of Petrarch and the more modern Italians. While pointing out to the French nation the avenues to literary culture which the ancient classics offered them, Du Bellay was especially emphatic in his commendation of the Italian sonnet as a main source of culture: *Sonne-moi ces beaux sonnets,* he adjured his fellow-countrymen, *non moins docte que plaisante invention italienne, pour lesquels tu as Pétrarque et quelques modernes Italiens.*

The primary debt that the Elizabethan sonnet owed to the French development of literary energy is attested by the first-fruits of Spenser's muse—first-fruits which constitute him the virtual father of the Elizabethan sonnet. There seems little question that Spenser, as early as 1569, when a boy of seventeen, contributed some twenty-six sonnets, anonymously, to a pious tract rendered, by another hand, from Flemish into English, under the title of *A Theatre for Worldlings.* There, Spenser made his first entry on the literary stage. With some changes, these youthful poems were reprinted, twenty-two years later, in an acknowledged collection of Spenser's minor verse, called *Complaints,* for the whole of which the poet's responsibility goes unquestioned. Spenser's early ventures in the sonnet form were divided into two categories, the one entitled *The Visions of Bellay,* the other *The Visions of Petrarch.* The latter title is misleading. Both sets of sonnets were drawn directly from the French—the first from Joachim du Bellay and the second from Clément Marot.

Du Bellay's sonnets were rendered by Spenser literally, though without rime. This embellishment he only added to his revised version. He also undertook, later, the translation of a longer series of Du Bellay's sonnets, *Les Antiquités de Rome,* which the English poet rechristened *The Ruins of Rome.* Elsewhere, in his mature work, a close study of Du Bellay is apparent, and he openly acknowledged his indebtedness to Du Bellay's delicate muse in a laudatory sonnet which includes these lines:

> Bellay, first garland of free Poësie,
> That France brought forth, though fruitfull of brave wits,
> Well worthie thou of immortalitie. . . .

The second set of sonnets, which, under the name of *The Visions of Petrarch,* Spenser penned in his early days, were drawn, not from the Italian, but from Marot's French poem, in twelve-lined stanzas, entitled *Les Visions de Petrarque.* There, Marot reproduces canzone XLII in Petrarch's collection of sonnets to Laura. The French title, which conforms with the subject-matter, is Marot's invention; Petrarch gave his canzone no specific heading. Spenser's first draft of 1569 (which was largely recast in the re-issue of 1591) slavishly adhered to the French, as may be seen from the 'envoy,' which, in Marot's verse, runs thus:

> *O chanson mienne, en tes conclusions*
> *Dy hardiment: Ces six grand visions,*
> *A mon seigneur donnent un doulx desir*
> *De briefvement soubz la terre gesir.*

Spenser first rendered these lines thus:

> My song thus now in thy Conclusions,
> Say boldly that these same six visions
> Do yelde unto thy lorde a sweete request,
> Ere it be long within the earth to rest.

The text of the original Italian differs from both the French and the English, and is of superior point and quality.

These youthful ventures of Spenser herald the French influence on Elizabethan sonneteering. But, among French sonneteers, neither the veteran Marot nor his junior Du Bellay, to whom Spenser offered his boyish homage, was to play the foremost part in the Elizabethan arena. Du Bellay, though a writer of sonnets on a very generous scale, fell below his leader Ronsard alike in productivity and in charm. Some, too, of Ronsard's humbler followers, notably Philippe Desportes, were as sonneteers scarcely less voluminous and popular than their master. Ronsard and Desportes were the chief French tutors of English poets at the end of the sixteenth century, and Desportes, for a season, took precedence of Ronsard. 'Few men,' wrote Lodge of Desportes, in 1590, 'are able to second the sweet conceits of Philippe Desportes whose poetical writings are ordinarily in everybody's hand[1].'

At the same time, Petrarch and many of his Italian imitators were rediscovered by the Elizabethans, and Petrarch's sway was

[1] *Margarite,* p. 79.

ultimately re-established, so that he and his Italian disciples exerted, at the close of queen Elizabeth's reign, the most powerful spell of all on English sonneteers. Elizabethan critics failed to detect in the Elizabethan sonnet much appreciable deviation from its Petrarchian archetype. 'In his sweete-mourning sonets,' wrote Sir John Harington, a typical Elizabethan, in 1591, 'the dolefull Petrarke...seemes to have comprehended all the passions that all men of that humour have felt.' Gabriel Harvey, in his *Pierces Supererogation* (1593, p. 61), after enthusiastic commendation of Petrarch's sonnets ('Petrarch's invention is pure love itself: Petrarch's elocution pure beauty itself'), justifies the common English practice of imitating them on the ground that

all the noblest Italian, French and Spanish poets have in their several veins Petrarchized; and it is no dishonour for the daintiest or divinest muse to be his scholar, whom the amiablest invention and beautifullest elocution acknowledge their master.

Spenser's youthful experiments attracted little attention. Thomas Watson was the earliest Elizabethan to make a reputation as a sonneteer. Steevens, the Shakespearean commentator, echoing, with characteristic perversity, the pedantic view of some Elizabethan scholars, declared Watson to be 'a much more elegant' writer of sonnets than Shakespeare. Watson, in truth, was a frigid scholiast, who was characteristically indifferent to strict metrical law. Yet his work is historically of great value as marking the progress and scope of foreign influences. In early life, Watson translated all Petrarch's sonnets into Latin; but only two specimens of his rendering survive. This laborious undertaking formed the prelude to his sonneteering efforts in English. In 1582, he published, at the earnest entreaty of his friends, according to his own account, one hundred 'passions' or poems of love, which contemporaries invariably described as sonnets, though, with rare exceptions, they were each eighteen lines long. The book was entitled: *The* ΕΚΑΤΟΜΠΑΘΙΑ *or Passionate Centurie of Love.* Congratulatory quatorzains prefaced the volume. One friend greeted Watson as the successor of Petrarch, the inheritor of that vein which glorified Madonna Laura. Another admirer, writing in Latin, credited Watson with the power of achieving for English poetry what Ronsard had done for French.

The most curious fact about this first collection of so-called sonnets by Watson is the care with which the writer disclaims originality. To each poem he prefaces a prose introduction, in which he frankly indicates, usually with ample quotations, the

French, Italian or classical poem which was the source of his inspiration. He aims at little more than paraphrasing sonnets and lyrics by Petrarch and Ronsard, or by Petrarch's disciples, Serafino dell' Aquila (1466—1500), Ercole Strozza (1471—1508) or Agnolo Firenzuola (1493—1548), together with passages from the chief writers of Greece and Rome. As a rule, his rendering is quite literal, though, now and then, he inverts a line or two of his original, or inserts a new sentence. In the conventional appeals to his wayward mistress, and in his expressions of amorous emotions, there is no pretence of a revelation of personal experience. Watson's endeavour won almost universal applause from contemporaries, but it is wholly a literary exercise, which appeals for approval, not on the ground of sincerity of emotion, but, rather, by reason of its skill in dovetailing together fragments of foreign poetry.

The welcome offered Watson's first published collection of sonnet-poems induced him to prepare a second, which, however, was not issued till 1593, a year after his death. Watson's second venture bore the title *The Tears of Fancie, or Love Disdained*; it differed from the first in respecting the primary law which confined the sonnet within a limit of fourteen lines. Although no *apparatus criticus* was incorporated with it, the influence of France and Italy was no better concealed from the seeing eye in Watson's final sonneteering essay than in its predecessor. Watson's *Tears of Fancie* were, once more, drops of water from Petrarch's and Ronsard's fountains.

Watson's example largely encouraged the vogue of the Elizabethan sonnet, and crystallised its imitative temper. The majority of Elizabethan sonneteers were loyal to his artificial method of construction. Some of his successors were gifted with poetic powers to which he was a stranger, and interwove the borrowed conceits with individual feeling, which, at times, lifted their verse to the plane of genuine poetry. Yet even from those sonnets which bear to Watson's tame achievement the relation which gold bears to lead, signs of his imitative process are rarely obliterated altogether.

Sidney entered the field very soon after Watson set foot there; for some years both were at work simultaneously; yet Watson's influence is discernible in much of Sidney's effort. Sidney, admittedly, is a prince among Elizabethan lyric poets and sonneteers. He loiters far behind Shakespeare in either capacity. But Shakespeare, as a sonneteer, should, of right, be considered apart[1]. With

[1] See the chapter on Shakespeare's poetry, in volume v.

that reservation, Sidney may fairly be credited as marching at the head of the contemporary army of sonneteers.

Although the date cannot be stated with certainty, it is probable that Sir Philip Sidney's ample collection of sonnets, which is known by the general title of *Astrophel and Stella*, was written between the years 1580 and 1584. Widely circulated in manuscript before and after Sidney's death in 1586, they were not printed till 1591, and then surreptitiously by an enterprising publisher, who had no authority from Sidney's representatives to undertake the task. It was not until 1598 that a fully authorised version came from the press.

Sidney's sonnets, like those of Petrarch and Ronsard, form a more or less connected sequence. The poet, under the name of Astrophel, professes to narrate the course of his passion for a lady to whom he gives the name of Stella. The relations between Astrophel and Stella closely resemble those between Petrarch and his poetic mistress Laura, in the first series of the Italian poet's sonnets, which were written in the lifetime of Laura. There is no question that Sidney, like Petrarch, was, to a certain extent, inspired by an episode in his own career. Stella was Penelope, the wayward daughter of Walter Devereux, first earl of Essex, and sister of Robert Devereux, second earl of Essex, queen Elizabeth's favourite. When she was about fourteen years old, her father destined her for Sidney's hand in marriage; but that project came to nothing. In 1581, when about nineteen, she married Robert, second lord Rich, and became the mother of a large family of children. The greater number of Sidney's sonnets were, doubtless, addressed to her after she had become lady Rich. In sonnet XXIV, Sidney plays upon her husband's name of Rich in something of the same artificial way in which Petrarch, in his sonnet V, plays upon the name of Laura his poetic mistress, who, also, was another's wife. Sidney himself married on 20 September 1583, and lived on the best terms with his wife, who long survived him. But Sidney's poetic courtship of lady Rich was continued till near the end of his days.

Astrophel's sonneteering worship of Stella enjoyed a popularity only second to that of Petrarch's poetic worship of Laura. It is the main theme of the collection of elegies which was written immediately after the tragically premature close of Sidney's life. The elegiac volume bore the title *Astrophel*; it was dedicated to Sidney's widow; his sister, the countess of Pembroke, wrote a poem for it; Spenser was the chief contributor. Throughout the work, Sidney's lover-like celebration of Stella is accounted his most glorious achievement in life or literature.

Sidney's sonnets rehearse a poetic passion, to which the verse of Petrarch and his disciples supplied the leading cue. The dedication to Sidney's wife of *Astrophel*, that tribute of eulogy which acclaims his mastery of the sonnet, seems to deprive his sonnet-story of the full assurance of sincerity. Wife and sister would scarcely avow enthusiastic pride in a husband's and a brother's poetic declaration of illicit love, were it literally true. Sidney, as a sonneteer, was an artist rather than an autobiographer. No mere transcript of personal sensation won him the laurels of an English Petrarch.

Charles Lamb detected in Sidney's glorious vanities and graceful hyperboles 'signs of love in its very heyday,' a 'transcendent passion pervading and illuminating' his life and conduct. Hazlitt, on the other hand, condemned Sidney's sonnets as jejune, frigid, stiff and cumbrous. The truth probably lies between these judgments. Felicitous phrases abound in Sidney's sonnets, but he never wastes his genius on a mere diet of dainty words. He was profoundly touched by lyric emotion. He was endowed with the lyric power of creating at will the illusion of a personal confession. He is capable of the true poetic effect. None the less, his poetic story of passion is out of harmony with the facts of his biography, and it is reminiscent of foreign models. Yet neither the interval between the fiction and the fact, nor the indebtedness to French or Italian masters could dull the vivacious strength of Sidney's poetic power.

None who is widely read in the sonnets of Petrarch or Ronsard fails to perceive the foreign echoes in Sidney's sonnets. The appeals to sleep, to the nightingale, to the moon, to his bed, to his mistress's dog, which form the staple of much of Sidney's poetry, resemble the apostrophes of the foreign sonneteers far too closely to entitle them to the unqualified credit of originality.

Both in his *Apologie for Poetrie* and in his sonnets, Sidney describes with scorn the lack of sincerity and the borrowed artifices of diction, which were inherent in the sonneteering habit. He complained that his English contemporaries sang

> poor Petrarch's long deceasëd woes
> With new-born sighs and denizenëd wit. (*Sonnet* xv.)

Echoing Persius, he professes to follow a different method:

> I never drank of Agannipe's well . . .
> I am no pickpurse of another's wit. (*Sonnet* LXXIV.)

Yet the form, no less than the spirit, of Sidney's sonnets renders his protest of doubtful significance. Sidney showed a higher respect than any of his native contemporaries for the metrical constitution of the Italian and French sonnet. As a rule, he observed the orthodox Petrarchian scheme of the double quatrain riming thus: *abbaabba.* In the first eight lines of Sidney's sonnets, only two rimes were permitted. In the last six lines, his practice was less orthodox. Four lines, which were alternately rimed, were often followed by a couplet. But, in more than twenty sonnets, he introduced into the concluding sizain such variations of rime as *ccdeed,* which brought his work into closer relation with the continental scheme than that of any other Elizabethan.

Although Sidney's professions of originality cannot be accepted quite literally, he may justly be reckoned the first Englishman to indicate the lyric capacity of the sonnet. His supremacy in that regard was at once frankly and justly acknowledged by his contemporaries. On the first appearance of his effort in print, his admirer, Thomas Nashe, addressed contemporary practitioners this warning apostrophe: 'Put out your rushlights, you poets and rhymers! and bequeath your crazed quatorzains to the chandlers! for lo, here he cometh that hath broken your legs.'

Sidney's example, far from discouraging competition, proved a new, and a very powerful, stimulus to sonneteering endeavour. It was, indeed, with the posthumous publication of Sidney's sonnet-sequence, *Astrophel and Stella,* in 1591, that a sonneteering rage began in Elizabethan England. Each of the six following years saw the birth of many volumes of sonnet-sequences, which owed much to the incentive of *Astrophel and Stella.* Samuel Daniel's *Delia* and Henry Constable's *Diana* first appeared in 1592, both to be revised and enlarged two years later. Three ample collections followed in 1593; they came from the pens respectively of Barnabe Barnes, Thomas Lodge and Giles Fletcher, while Watson's second venture was then published posthumously and for the first time. Three more volumes, in addition to the revised editions of Daniel's *Delia* and Constable's *Diana,* appeared in 1594, viz.: William Percy's *Coelia,* an anonymous writer's *Zepheria* and Michael Drayton's *Idea* (in its first shape). E. C.'s *Emaricdulfe,* Edmund Spenser's *Amoretti* and Richard Barnfield's *Cynthia, with certaine Sonnets,* came out in 1595. Griffin's *Fidessa,* Linche's *Diella* and William Smith's *Chloris* appeared in 1596. Finally, in 1597, the procession was joined by Robert Tofte's

Laura, a pale reflection of Petrarch's effort (as the name implied), although travelling far from the metrical principles of the genuine form of sonnet. To the same period belong the composition, although the publication was long delayed, of the Scottish poet, Sir William Alexander's *Aurora* and of the *Caelica* of Sidney's friend, Sir Fulke Greville.

All these collections were sequences of amorous sonnets. The Elizabethan sonnet was not exclusively applied to themes of love. Religious meditation and friendly adulation frequently commanded the attention of sonneteers. But the amorous sequence is the dominant feature of the history of the Elizabethan sonnet. The spiritual and adulatory quatorzains fill a subsidiary place in the picture. The amorous sequences incline, for the most part, to Watson's level rather than to Sidney's, and, while they respect the English metrical form, they generously illustrate the prevailing tendency to more or less literal transcription from foreign masters.

The sonneteering work of Spenser in his maturity is to be linked with Sidney. But even his metrical versatility and genuine poetic force did not preserve him altogether from the injurious influence of the imitative tendency. Only a small proportion of his sonnets embody original ideas or betray complete freedom in handling old conceits. In his metre alone, did Spenser follow a line of his own devising; his prosody diverged alike from the ordinary English, and the ordinary foreign, model. Most of his sonnets consisted of three quatrains, each alternately rimed, with a riming couplet. Alternate rimes and the couplet were unknown to sonnets abroad. Yet Spenser followed the foreign fashion in restricting the total number of rimes in a single sonnet to five instead of extending it to seven as in the normal English pattern. He made the last lines of his first and second quatrains rime respectively with the first lines of his second and third quatrains, thus *abab bcbc cdcd*. Spenser approached no nearer the prosody of Italy or France. In three instances, he invests the concluding riming couplet with a wholly original effect by making the final line an alexandrine.

Spenser bestowed on his sequence of eighty-eight sonnets the Italian name of *Amoretti*. His heroine, his 'sweet warrior' (sonnet LVII), is the child of Petrarch's '*dolce guerriera*.' His imagery is, at times, assimilated with little change from the sonnets of his contemporary Tasso, while Ronsard and Desportes give him numerous suggestions, although he rarely stoops to mere verbal translation of foreign verse. Spenser's *Amoretti* were addressed to the lady who became his wife, and a strand of autobiography was woven into the borrowed threads. Yet it is very occasionally that he escaped altogether from the fetters of current convention, and gave free play in his sonnets to his poetic faculty.

Spenser's sentiment professedly ranges itself with continental and classical idealism. In two sonnets he identifies his heroine with the Petrarchian (or Neo-Platonic) *ἰδέα* of beauty, which had lately played a prominent part in numberless French sonnets by Du Bellay, Desportes, Pontus de Tyard, Claude de Pontoux and others. Many Elizabethan sonneteers marched under the same banner. Drayton, in conferring on his sonnets the title *Idea*, claimed to rank with the Italian and French Platonists. But Spenser sounds the idealistic note far more clearly than any contemporary. He writes in sonnet XLV:

> Within my heart (though hardly it can shew
> Thing so divine to view of earthly eye),
> The fair Idea of your celestial hew,
> And every part remains immortally.

This reflects the familiar French strain:

> *Sur le plus belle Idée au ciel vous fustes faite,*
> *Voulant nature un jour monstrer tout son pouvoir;*
> *Depuis vous luy servez de forme et de miroir,*
> *Et toute autre beauté sur la vostre est portraite.*
> (Desportes, *Diane*, II, lxvii.)

Like the French writers, Spenser ultimately (in sonnet LXXXVII) disclaims any mortal object of adoration in ecstatic recognition of the superior fascination of the *ἰδέα*:

> Ne ought I see, though in the clearest day,
> When others gaze upon their shadows vain,
> But th'onely image of that heavenly ray,
> Whereof some glance doth in mine eye remain.
> Of which beholding the Idaea plain,
> Through contemplation of my purest part,
> With light thereof I do myself sustain,
> And thereon feed my love affamish'd heart.

Pontus de Tyard had already closed the last book of his *Les Erreurs Amoureuses* on the identical note:

> *Mon esprit a heureusement porté,*
> *Au plus beau ciel sa force outrecuidée,*
> *Pour s'abbreuuer en la plus belle Idée*
> *D'où le pourtrait i'ay pris de la beauté.* (bk. III, xxxiii.)

Spenser's sonnets similarly helped to familiarise the Elizabethan reader with a poetic conceit, which, although not of French origin, was assimilated with fervour by the sonneteers of *La Pléiade*. The notion that poets not merely achieved immortality through their verse, but had the power of conferring immortality on those to whom their poetry was addressed, was a classical conceit of great antiquity, which Pindar among the Greeks, and Horace and Ovid among the Latins, had notably glorified. The Italians of the renascence had been attracted by the fancy. But Ronsard and his disciples had developed it with a complacency that gave it new life. From France it spread to Elizabethan England, where it was quickly welcomed. Sir Philip Sidney, in his *Apologie for Poetrie* (1595), wrote that it was the common habit of poets 'to tell you that they will make you immortal by their verses.' 'Men of great calling,' wrote Nashe, in his *Pierce Pennilesse* (1593), 'take it of merit to have their names eternised by poets.'

Spenser was among the Elizabethan sonneteers who conspicuously adapted the conceit to English verse. Shakespeare, alone excepted, no sonneteer repeated the poetic vaunt with greater emphasis than Spenser. He describes his sonnets as

> This verse that never shall expire. . . .
> Fair be no longer proud of that shall perish.
> But that, which shall you make immortal, cherish.
>
> (*Sonnet* XXVII.)

He tells his mistress

> My verse your virtues rare shall eternise,
> And in the heavens write your glorious name.
>
> (*Sonnet* LXXV.)

With unbounded confidence he asserts:

> Even this verse, vow'd to eternity,
> Shall be thereof immortal moniment;
> And tell her praise to all posterity,
> That may admire such world's rare wonderment.
>
> (*Sonnet* LXIX.)

Through all such passages Spenser speaks in the voice of Ronsard. It was Ronsard who had, just before Spenser wrote, promised his patron that his lute

> *Par cest hymne solennel*
> *Respandra dessus ta race*
> *Je ne sçay quoy de sa grace*
> *Qui te doit faire éternel.* (*Odes*, I, vii);

who had declared of his mistress

> *Victorieuse des peuples et des Rois*
> *S'en voleroit sus l'aile de ma ryme.* (*Amours*, I, lxxii);

who had foretold

> *Longtemps après la mort je vous feray revivre.*
> *Vous vivrez et croistrez comme Laure en grandeur,*
> *Au moins tant que vivront les plumes et le livre.*
>
> (*Sonnets pour Hélène*, II.)

In the hands of Elizabethan sonneteers, the 'eternising' faculty of their verse became a staple, and, indeed, an inevitable, topic. Especially did Drayton and Daniel vie with Spenser in reiterating the conceit. Drayton, who spoke of his sonnets as 'my immortal song' (*Idea*, VI, 14) and 'my world-out-wearing rhymes' (XLIV, 7), embodied the boast in such lines as

> While thus my pen strives to eternize thee.
> (*Idea*, XLIV, 1.)
> Ensuing ages yet my rhymes shall cherish. (XLIV, 11.)
> My name shall mount unto eternity. (XLIV, 14.)
> All that I seek is to eternize thee. (XLVII, 14.)

Daniel was no less explicit

> This [*sc.* verse] may remain thy lasting monument.
> (*Delia*, XXXVII, 9.)
> Thou mayst in after ages live esteemed
> Unburied in these lines. (XXXIX, 9, 10.)
> These [*sc.* my verses] are the arks, the trophies I erect
> That fortify thy name against old age;
> And these [*sc.* verses] thy sacred virtues must protect
> Against the dark and time's consuming rage. (L, 9–12.)

Shakespeare, in his reference to his 'eternal lines' (XVIII, 12), and in the assurances which he gives to the subject of his addresses that his sonnets are, in Spenser's and in Daniel's exact phrase, his hero's 'monument,' merely accommodated himself to the prevailing taste, even if he invested the topic with a splendour that none else approached. But had Shakespeare never joined the ranks of Elizabethan sonneteers, the example of Spenser, Daniel and Drayton would have identified the Elizabethan sonnet with the proud conceit.

It was not Spenser's work as a sonneteer which gave him his enduring place on the heights of Parnassus: he owes his immortality to other poetic achievement, which lent itself to larger and freer development. Some of Spenser's contemporaries, who, although endowed with a more modest measure of poetic power, did not lack poetic feeling, unluckily confined their effort, in obedience to the prevailing vogue, almost entirely to the sonnet. The result was that the dominant imitative tendencies almost succeeded in stifling in them all original utterance. Such an one was Henry Constable, master of a tuneful note, who drank too deep of the Franco-Italian wells to give his muse full liberty of expansion. Like Desportes, he christened his sonnet-sequence by the name of *Diana*, and Italian words *sonetto primo*, *sonetto secondo* and so forth formed the head lines of each of his quatorzains. He was a writer on a restricted scale. Only twenty-three poems figure in the original edition of his volume, which he christened *Diana, The praises of his Mistres, In certaine sweete Sonnets* (1592). 'Augmented with divers quatorzains of honourable and learned personages,' the book reappeared in 1594. The poems there numbered seventy-six; but many of the added pieces were from other pens. At least eight were the work of Sir Philip Sidney. The second edition of *Diana* was a typical venture of an enterprising publisher, and was devised to catch the passing breeze of popular interest in sonnet-sequences. Its claim to homogeneity lies in its reiterated echo of Italian and French voices. Such of the added poems as can be confidently assigned to Constable himself show a growing dependence on Desportes. Very often he translates without modification some of the Frenchman's baldest efforts. His method may be judged by the following example. The tenth sonnet in the sixth decade of Constable's *Diana*, 1594, opens thus:

My God, my God, how much I love my goddess!
Whose virtues rare, unto the heavens arise.
My God, my God, how much I love her eyes!
One shining bright, the other full of hardness.

The *Diane* of Desportes (I, xxvi) supplies the original:

Mon dieu! mon dieu! que j'aime ma deesse
Et de son chef les tresors precieux!
Mon dieu! mon dieu! que j'aime ses beaux yeux,
Dont l'un m'est doux, l'autre plein de rudesse.

Both Daniel and Lodge deservedly made a higher literary reputation than Constable. But each exemplified in even more remarkable fashion the practice of literal translation. Daniel had lyric gifts of a brilliant order. But he had no hesitation in seeking both the language and the imagery of numerous lyrics as well as of numerous sonnets in foreign collections. Like Spenser, he was well read in Tasso; and much of his inspiration came direct from Tasso's sonnets. The fine pastoral poem beginning 'O happy golden Age,' which he appended to his sonnet-sequence *Delia*, is a felicitous, though literal, rendering of a song in Tasso's pastoral play *Aminta*, Atto I, sc. 2 (*O bella età de 'l oro*). Many of Daniel's happiest quatorzains bear the same relation to preceding efforts of the same poet; and, in several cases, where Daniel's English text wanders somewhat from the Italian, the explanation is to be found, not in the free expansiveness of Daniel's genius, but in the depressing circumstance that Daniel was following the

French rendering of Tasso by Desportes instead of making direct recourse to the Italian text. Tasso was only one of Daniel's many foreign tutors. It was probably on Desportes that he most relied, and the servility of his renderings from the French is startling.

Thomas Lodge, whose sonnet-sequence *Phillis* appeared in 1593, improves on Daniel's example as a borrower of foreign work. In fact, he merits the first place among Elizabethan plagiarists. Of thirty-four poems in strict sonnet form which were included, without hint of any indebtedness, in his volume *Phillis*, as many as eighteen have been tracked to foreign sources. These eighteen sonnets, which were published by Lodge as the fruits of his own invention, are shown on investigation to be literal transcripts from the French and Italian. Further investigation is likely to extend the range of his loans.

It is worth while to analyse the proofs that are at present accessible of Lodge's obligations. Lodge did not confine his borrowings to the great writers of France and Italy. He laid hands on work of second and third rate pens, which never acquired widespread fame. That six of the eighteen sonnets under examination should be paraphrases of Ronsard, or that five should translate Ariosto, is far less surprising than that three should come direct from an obscure Italian author, Lodovico Paschale, whose sonnet-sequence appeared at Venice in 1549. Paschale was an undistinguished native of Cattaro, in Dalmatia, and his work has only once been reprinted since its first appearance, and that nearly two hundred years after original publication. From Paschale comes one of the best known of Lodge's sonnets, which opens thus:

> It is not death, which wretched men call dying,
> But that is very death which I endure,
> When my coy-looking nymph, her grace envying,
> By fatal frowns my domage doth procure.

Paschale's sonnet began thus (1549 edition, p. 40 *verso*)

> *Morte non é quel che morir s' appella,*
> *Ma quella é uera morte ch' io supporto,*
> *Quando Madonna di pietá rubella,*
> *A me riuolge il guardo acerbo e torto.*

Other foreign poets on whom Lodge silently levied his heavy loans were Petrarch, Sanazzaro and Bembo among Italians, and Desportes among Frenchmen.

The only other Elizabethan of high poetic rank, apart from

Shakespeare, who prominently associated himself with the sonneteering movement, was Michael Drayton. In one effort, Drayton reached the highest level of poetic feeling and expression. His familiar quatorzain opening 'Since there's no help, come let us kiss and part' is the one sonnet by a contemporary which deserves to rank with some of Shakespeare's best. It is curious to note that Drayton's triumphant poem was first printed in 1619, just a quarter of a century after he first sought the suffrages of the Elizabethan public as a sonneteer. The *editio princeps* of his sonnet-sequence, called *Ideas Mirrour. Amours in Quatorzains*, included fifty-two sonnets, and was reprinted no less than eight times, with much revision, omission and addition, before the final version came forth in 1619.

Drayton's sonneteering labours constitute a microcosm of the whole sonneteering movement in Elizabethan England. He borrows ideas and speech from all available sources at home and abroad. Yet, like many contemporary offenders, he deprecates the charge that he is 'a thief' of the 'wit' of Petrarch or Desportes. With equal vigour of language he disclaims pretensions to tell the story of his own heart:

> Into these loves who but for passion looks:
>   At this first sight, here let him lay them by!
> And seek elsewhere in turning other books,
>   Which better may his labour satisfy.

For the most part, Drayton is a sonneteer on the normal Elizabethan pattern, and his sonnets are rarely distinguished by poetic elevation. Occasionally, a thin rivulet of natural sentiment winds its way through the fantastic conceits which his wide reading suggests to him. But only in his famous sonnet did his genius find in that poetic form full scope.

The title of Drayton's sonnet-sequence, *Idea*, gives a valuable clue to one source of his inspiration. The title was directly borrowed from an extensive sonnet-sequence in French called *L'Idée*, by Claude de Pontoux, a poetic physician of Chalon. The name symbolises the Platonic ἰδέα of beauty, which was notably familiar to Du Bellay and Pontus de Tyard in France and to Spenser in England. Drayton's 'soul-shrined saint,' his 'divine Idea,' his 'fair Idea,' is the child of de Pontoux's *Céleste Idée, Fille de Dieu* (sonnet x). But Drayton by no means confined his sonneteering studies to the volume whence he took his shadowy mistress's name. Drayton's imitative appeals to night, to his lady's fair eyes, to rivers; his classical allusions, his insistence that his verse is eternal—all these themes recall expressions of Ronsard, and Desportes, or of their humble disciples. A little is usually added and a little taken away; but such slight substance as the sentiments possess is, with rare exception, a foreign invention. Doubtless, Drayton was more conscious than his companions of the triviality of the sonneteering conventions. No precise foreign origin seems accessible for his sonnet (xv) entitled *His Remedy for Love*, in which he describes a potion concocted of the powder of a dead woman's heart, moistened with another woman's tears, boiled in a widow's sighs and breathed upon by an old maid. The satire is clearly intended to apply to the strained simples out of which the conventional type of sonnet was, too often, compounded.

Like Sidney, Spenser and Daniel, Drayton, despite his warning, added fuel to the fire of the sonneteering craze. His work inspired younger men with the ambition to win the fame of sonneteer.

The most accomplished of Drayton's disciples was Richard Barnfield, who dubs Drayton, 'Rowland my professed friend.' His endeavours are noteworthy because they aim at a variation of the ordinary sonneteering motive. The series of twenty sonnets which Barnfield, in 1595, appended to his *Cynthia*, a panegyric on queen Elizabeth, are in a vein which differentiates them from those of all the poets of the day save Shakespeare's sonnets. Barnfield's sonnets profess to be addressed, not to the poet's mistress, but to a lad Ganymede to whom the poet makes profession of love. But the manner in which Barnfield develops his theme does not remove his work very far from the imitative products of his fellow sonneteers. As he himself confessed, his sonnets for the most part adapt Vergil's second *Eclogue*, in which the shepherd Corydon declares his affection for the shepherd boy, Alexis. Barnfield had true power of fervid expression, which removes him from the ranks of the poetasters. But his habit of mind was parasitic. He loved to play with classical conceits. His sonnets, despite divergences from the beaten path in theme, pay tribute in style and construction to the imitative convention.

The collections of sonnets by Barnabe Barnes, and by Giles Fletcher, by William Percy, William Smith, Bartholomew Griffin and Robert Tofte merit briefer notice. They reflect, with fewer compensations than their better known contemporaries, the tendencies to servility. All but Fletcher were young men courting the muse for the first time, who did not pursue her favours in their adult years. They avowed discipleship to Sidney or to Spenser, to Daniel, or to Drayton, and took pleasure in diluting their master's words with clumsy verbiage drawn from the classics or from contemporary poetry of the continent. Rarely did they show facility or individuality, and, still more rarely, poetic feeling.

Barnabe Barnes, who made his reputation as a sonneteer in the same year as Lodge, was more voluminous than any English contemporary. He gave some promise of lyric power which he never fulfilled. As a whole, his work is crude and lacks restraint. At times, he sinks to meaningless doggerel, and some of his grotesque conceits are offensive. His collection of amorous sonnets bore the title of *Parthenophil and Parthenophe. Sonnets, Madrigals, Elegies and Odes.* Here, one hundred and five sonnets are interspersed with twenty-six madrigals, five sestines, twenty-one elegies, three 'canzons,' twenty odes (one in sonnet form) and what purports to be a translation of Moschus's first *Eidullion.*

Many of Barnes's poems are echoes of Sidney's verse, both in *Arcadia* and in *Astrophel and Stella.* His canzon II is a spirited tribute to Sidney under his poetic name of Astrophel. The first stanza runs:

> Sing! sing Parthenophil! sing! pipe! and play!
> The feast is kept upon this plain,
> Among th'Arcadian shepherds everywhere,
> For Astrophel's birthday! Sweet Astrophel!
> Arcadia's honour! mighty Paris' chief pride!
> Where be the nymphs? The Nymphs all gathered be,
> To sing sweet Astrophel's sweet praise.

Barnes also boasted of his debt to

> That sweet Tuscan Petrarch, which did pierce
> His Laura with love sonnets.

But Barnes's volume is a spacious miscellany of echoes of many other foreign voices. He often emulates the anacreontic vein of *La Pléiade*, and had obviously studied much Latin and Greek poetry of post-classical times. There is a likelihood that Shakespeare knew his work well, and resented the unaccountable esteem which it enjoyed on its first publication.

Giles Fletcher, a former fellow of King's College, Cambridge, was of maturer age than most contemporary sonneteers, when he brought out his sonnet-sequence of *Licia*, for he was then 44 years old. On his title-page, he boldly announces that his 'poems of love' were written 'to the imitation of the best Latin poets and others.' In an address to his patroness, the wife of Sir Richard Molineux, he deprecates the notion that his book enshrines any episode in his own experience. He merely claims to follow the fashion, and to imitate the 'men of learning and great parts' of Italy, France and England, who have already written 'poems and sonnets of love.' He regrets the English poets' proclivities to borrow their 'best and choice conceits' from Italy, Spain and France, and expresses a pious preference for English homespun; but this is a counsel of perfection, and he makes no pretence to personal independence of foreign models.

A definite, if slender, interest attaches to Bartholomew Griffin's *Fidessa,* a conventional sequence of sixty-two sonnets. Griffin was exceptionally bold in imitating home products, and borrowed much from Daniel and Drayton's recent volumes. But it is worthier of remembrance that one of his sonnets, on the theme of *Venus and Adonis,* was transferred with alterations to Jaggard's piratical miscellany of 1599, *The Passionate Pilgrim,* all the contents of which were assigned to Shakespeare on the title-page.

Only the worst features of the Elizabethan passion for sonneteering—its clumsy inanity and slavish mimicry—are visible in the remaining sequences which were published in the last decade of the sixteenth century. William Percy, in his *Sonnets to the fairest Coelia,* 1593, bade his lute 'rehearse the songs of Rowland's (*i.e.* Drayton's) rage,' and found, with Ronsard, 'a Gorgon shadowed under Venus' face.' The anonymous poetaster who published, in 1594, a collection of forty sonnets under the title *Zepheria* took his own measure when he confessed

> My slubbering pencil casts too gross a matter,
> Thy beauty's pure divinity to blaze.

'R. L. Gentleman,' doubtless Richard Linche, published thirty-nine sonnets, in 1596, under the title *Diella,* a crude anagram on Delia. He freely plagiarised phrases and imagery of well known sonneteers at home and abroad.

William Smith, a sycophantic disciple of Spenser, who published fifty-one sonnets under the title *Chloris,* in 1596, and Robert Tofte, who 'conceived in Italy' a sequence of forty sonnets in irregular metres, entitled *Laura* (1597), merely give additional proof of the plagiarising habit of the day.

But, as the queen's reign closed, there were signs that the literary standard of the sonnet-sequence of love was rising above such sordid levels as these. The old paths of imitation were not forsaken, but the spirit of adaptation showed to higher advantage in the work of a few writers who, for the time, withheld their efforts from the press. Chief among these was the courtly Scottish poet, Sir William Alexander, afterwards earl of Stirling, who deferred the publication of his sonneteering experiment—'the first fancies of his youth'—till 1604. Then he issued, under the title *Aurora*, one hundred and six sonnets, interspersed, on the Italian and French pattern, with a few songs and elegies. Alexander is not a poet of deep feeling. But he has gifts of style which raise him above the Elizabethan hacks. Another Scottish poet, whose muse developed in the next generation, William Drummond of Hawthornden, began his literary career as a sonneteer on the Elizabethan pattern just before queen Elizabeth died. In early youth, he made himself familiar with the most recent literary effort of Italy, and reproduced with great energy numerous Italian sonnets of comparatively recent date. But he impregnated his adaptations with a native fire which places him in an altogether different category from that of the juvenile scribblers of Elizabethan London. With these two Scotsmen, Alexander and Drummond, may be classed Sidney's friend, Fulke Greville, afterwards lord Brooke, who wrote (but did not publish) at the end of the sixteenth century a miscellaneous collection of poems called *Caelica*. The collection consisted of one hundred and nine short poems, on each of which the author bestowed the title of sonnet. Only thirty-seven, however, are quatorzains. The remaining seventy-two so-called 'sonnets' are lyrics of all lengths and in all metres. There is little internal connection among Brooke's poems, and they deserve to be treated as a series of independent lyrics. Nor is there any sign of real passion. Lord Brooke's poetic mistresses, Caelica and Myra, are poetic figments of his brain, and he varies his addresses to them with invocation of queen Elizabeth under the poetic title of Cynthia, and with reflective musings on metaphysical themes. The style is less complicated than is habitual to Brooke's other literary work, and the medley sounds a melodious note. Greville emulated the example of Sir Philip Sidney; but the imagery often associates itself, more closely than was suffered by Sidney's aims, with the anacreontic vein of the Greek anthologists and of the French sonneteers. The series was published for the first time as late as 1633, in a collection of lord Brooke's poetical writings. It may be reckoned the latest example of the Elizabethan sonnet-sequence.

The pertinacity with which the crude artificialities and plagiarisms of the sonnet-sequence of love were cultivated in the last years of queen Elizabeth's reign involved the sonnet as a form of poetic art in a storm of critical censure before the vogue expired. The rage for amorous sonneteering came to excite an almost overwhelming ridicule. The basest charges were brought against the professional sonneteer. Sir John Harington, whose epigrams embody much criticism of current literary practices, plainly states that poets were in the habit of writing sonnets for sale to purchasers who paraded them as their own. He mentions the price as two crowns a sonnet, and asserts:

> Verses are now such merchantable ware,
> That now for sonnets sellers are and buyers.

There is, indeed, other evidence that suitors were in the habit of pleading their cause with their mistresses by means of sonnets which had been bought for hard cash from professional producers. In sonnet XXI, Drayton narrates how he was employed by a 'witless gallant' to write a sonnet to the wench whom the young man wooed, with the result that his suit was successful. Other grounds of offence were discovered in the sentimental insincerity of the conventional type of sonnet, which sanctioned the sickly practice of 'oiling a saint with supple sonneting.' The adjective 'sugared' was scornfully held to be the epithet best fitted for the conventional sonnet. Sir John Harington, in an epigram 'comparing the sonnet and the epigram' (Bk. I, No. 37), condemns the sonnet's 'sugared taste,' and prays that his verse may have salt to make it last.

Sir John Davies was one of those who protested with vehemence against the 'bastard sonnets' which 'base rhymers' daily begot 'to their own shame and poetry's disgrace.' To expose the futility of the vogue, he circulated, in manuscript, a series of nine 'gulling sonnets' or parodies of the artificial vices of the current fashion. In one of his parodies he effectively reduces to absurdity the application of law terms to affairs of the heart. The popular prejudice against the sonnet found expression in most unlikely places. Echoes of the critical hostility are even heard in Shakespeare's plays. In *The Two Gentlemen of Verona* (III, 2. 68 ff.) there is a satiric touch in the recipe for the conventional love-sonnet which Proteus offers the amorous duke:

> You must lay lime to tangle her desires,
> By wailful sonnets, whose composëd rime
> Should be full fraught with serviceable vows. . . .
> Say that upon the altar of her beauty
> You sacrifice your tears, your sighs, your heart.

Mercutio treats Elizabethan sonneteers somewhat equivocally when alluding to them in his flouts at Romeo:

> Now is he for the numbers that Petrarch flowed in: Laura to his lady was but a kitchen wench; marry, she had a better love to be-rhyme her.
> (*Romeo and Juliet*, II, 4. 41—44.)

When the sonnet-sequence of love was yielding to the loud protests of the critics, Ben Jonson, in *Volpone* (Act III, sc. 2) struck at it a belated blow in a contemptuous reference to the past 'days of sonneting' and to the debt that its votaries owed to 'passionate Petrarch.' Elsewhere, Jonson condemned, root and branch, the artificial principles of the sonnet. He told Drummond of Hawthornden that

he cursed Petrarch for redacting verses to sonnets, which he said were like that tyrant's bed, where some who were too short were racked, others too long cut short. (Jonson's *Conversation*, p. 4.)

Jonson was here silently appropriating a depreciatory simile, which had been invented by a well known Italian critic of the sonnet, but there is no question that the English dramatist viewed the vogue of the Elizabethan sonnet as, for the most part, a discredit to the age.

To what extent the critics of the Elizabethan sonnet were moved to hostility by resentment of the practice of clandestine translation from the foreigner offers room for discussion. A close study of the criticism to which many sonneteers were subjected leaves little doubt that plagiarism was out of harmony with the standard of literary ethics in Elizabethan England. The publication, in the avowed guise of an original production, of a literal rendering, not merely an adaptation, of a poem by a foreign contemporary exposed the offender on discovery to a severe censure. It has been suggested that foreign poetry was so widely known in Elizabethan England as to render specific acknowledgment of indebtedness superfluous. But the poetic work which was tacitly translated by Elizabethan sonneteers often came, not from the most popular work of great authors of France and Italy, but either from the obscurer publications of the leading poets or from the books of men whose repute was very restricted. In comparatively few cases would the average Elizabethan reader be aware that Elizabethan sonnets were translations of foreign poets unless the information were directly given him. Moreover, whenever plagiarism was detected or even suspected, critics condemned in no halting terms the plagiarist's endeavour to ignore his obligation. Of one who published without acknowledgment renderings of Ronsard's far-famed and popular verse (although, as a matter of fact, the borrower was too incompetent to be very literal), Puttenham wrote thus in his *Arte of English Poesie* (1589):

This man deserves to be endited of pety *larceny* for pilfering other mens devises from them and converting them to his own use, for in deede as

I would wish every inventour, which is the very Poet, to receave the prayses of his invention, so would I not have a translatour to be ashamed to be acknowen of his translation.

The word 'larceny' is italicised in the original edition. Michael Drayton, in the dedication to his sonnets, in 1594, charged the literal borrowers with 'filching.' Again, Daniel, a sonneteer who, despite his great gifts, depended largely on the literal inspiration of foreign verse, was forcibly rebuked by a discerning contemporary for yielding to a practice which was declared, without any qualification, to be 'base.' In the play *The Returne from Parnassus* (part II, act II, sc. 2), the following warning is addressed to Daniel:

> **Only let him more sparingly make use**
> **Of others' wit, and use his own the more,**
> **That well may scorn base imitation.**

To the same effect was Sir John Harington's ironical epigram, 1618 (II, 30), headed, 'Of honest theft. To my good friend Master Samuel Daniel,' which concludes thus:

> **Then, fellow-Thiefe, let's shake together hands,**
> **Sith both our wares are filcht from forren lands.**

The extravagant character of the denunciation in which some contemporary critics of the plagiarising habit indulged is illustrated by another of Harington's *Epigrams* (II, 77), which is headed, 'Of a censurer of English writers.' It opens thus:

> **That Englishmen have small or no invention,**
> **Old Guillam saith, and all our works are barren,**
> **But for the stuffe we get from authors forren.**

Elizabethan sonneteers who coloured, in their verse, the fruits of their foreign reading with their own individuality deserve only congratulation. The intellectual assimilation of poetic ideas and even poetic phraseology conforms with a law of literature which is not open to censure. But literal translation, without acknowledgment, from foreign contemporary poetry was, with little qualification, justly condemned by contemporary critics.

Although the sonnet in Elizabethan England, as in France and Italy, was mainly devoted to the theme of love, it was never exclusively confined to amorous purposes. Petrarch occasionally made religion or politics the subject of his sonnets and, very frequently, enshrined in this poetic form the praises of a friend or patron. As a vehicle of spiritual meditation or of political exhortation or of friendly adulation, the sonnet long enjoyed an established vogue in foreign literature. When the sonnet-sequence of love was in its heyday in Elizabethan England, the application of the sonnet to purposes of piety or professional compliment acquired popularity. The art of the sonnet, when it was enlisted in such service, largely escaped the storm of censure which its amorous extravagances excited.

Barnes and Constable, in close conformity with foreign practice, each supplemented their amorous experiments with an extended sequence of spiritual sonnets. Barnes's volume of 'spiritual sonnets' was printed in 1595; Constable's religious sonnets only circulated in manuscript. In 1597, too, a humbler writer, Henry Lok, sent forth a swollen collection of three hundred and twenty-eight sonnets on religious topics, which he entitled, *Sundrie sonets of Christian Passions with other affectionate sonets of a feeling conscience.* Lok paraphrases many passages from the Scriptures, and was well read in the book of *Ecclesiastes.* His piety is unquestionable. But there is little poetic quality in his ample effort.

Sonnets inscribed by poets in the way of compliment to their friends or patrons abound in Elizabethan literature. James I, in his *Treatise of poetry,* 1584, ignores all uses of the sonnet save for the 'compendious praising' of books or their authors and for the prefatory presentation in brief summary of the topic of any long treatise. The latter usage was rare in England, though Shakespeare experimented with it by casting into sonnet form the prologues before the first two acts of *Romeo and Juliet.* But, before, during and after Shakespeare's day, the English author was wont to clothe in the sonnet shape much professional intercourse with his patron. Few writers were guiltless of this mode of address. Not infrequently, a long series of adulatory sonnets forms the prelude or epilogue of an Elizabethan book. Spenser's *Faerie Queene* and Chapman's translation of Homer's *Iliad* are both examples of literary work of repute which was ushered into the world with substantial supplement of adulatory sonnets. Both Spenser and Chapman sought the favour of a long procession of influential patrons or patronesses in a series of quatorzains. Even those self-reliant writers of the day who contemned the sonnet-sequence of love, and declined to make trial of it with their own pens—men like Ben Jonson and Chapman—were always ready to salute a friend or patron in sonnet-metre. Of sonnets addressed in the way of friendship by men of letters to colleagues of their calling, a good example is the fine sonnet addressed by the poet Spenser to Gabriel Harvey, 'his singular good friend.'

Some of these occasional sonnets of eulogy or compliment reach a high poetic level, and are free from most of the monotonous defects which disfigured the conventional sonnet of love. To the first book of Spenser's *Faerie Queene*, Sir Walter Ralegh, the poet's friend, prefixed two sonnets, the first of which was characterised by rare stateliness of diction. No better illustration is to be found of the characteristic merits of the Elizabethan vogue. Ralegh's sonnet was written in 1595, when the sonneteering rage was at its height; and, while it attests the predominant influence of Petrarch, it shows, at the same time, how dependence on a foreign model may be justified by the spirit of the adaptation. Ralegh's sonnet runs as follows:

A Vision upon this conceit of the Faery Queene.

Methought I saw the grave where Laura lay,
Within that Temple where the vestal flame
Was wont to burn; and passing by that way
To see that buried dust of living fame,
Whose tomb fair love, and fairer virtue kept,
All suddenly I saw the Fairy Queene:
At whose approach the soul of Petrarch wept,
And from thenceforth those graces were not seen;
For they this Queen attended, in whose stead
Oblivion laid him down on Laura's hearse.
Hereat the hardest stones were seen to bleed,
And groans of buried ghosts the heavens did pierce:
Where Homer's sprite did tremble all for grief,
And cursed th' access of that celestial thief.

'Celestial thief' is a weak ending, and crudely presents Ralegh's eulogistic suggestion that Spenser, by virtue of his great poem, had dethroned the older poetic deities. Ralegh's prophecy, too, that oblivion had, at length, 'laid him down on Laura's hearse' was premature. The tide of Petrarchian inspiration flowed on long after the publication of *The Faerie Queene*. But Ralegh's sonnet, viewed as a whole, illustrates how fruitfully foreign imagery could work in Elizabethan minds, and how advantageously it could be applied to new purposes by the inventiveness of poetic genius.

CHAPTER XIII

PROSODY FROM CHAUCER TO SPENSER

In the short summary or survey of the progress of English prosody which was given towards the end of the first volume of this history, we reached the period of the alliterative revival, in or about the early days of Chaucer. In the second and third volumes, the actual record of poetry has been carried, approximately, to the death of Spenser; and incidental notices of the prosody of nearly three centuries have, necessarily, been included. But it has been judged proper to continue here the retrospect, in connected fashion, of the general history of English versification.

The prosody of the fourteenth century, after its very earliest periods, is a subject of very complex interest as well as of extreme importance; and its complexity is not really difficult to disentangle. It is from the neglect to study it as a whole, more, perhaps, than from any other cause, that general views of English prosody, in the not very numerous cases in which they have been taken at all, have been both haphazard and confused. Yet the facts, if only a little trouble be taken with them, offer their own explanation most obligingly, and illustrate themselves in a striking and, indeed, almost unique manner. The contemporary existence of such poets as Chaucer, Gower and whosoever may have written the *Piers Plowman* poems would be remarkable in any literature, at any time and from any point of view. In relation to English prosody it points, formulates, illuminates the lesson which ought to be learnt, in a manner which makes it surprising that this lesson should ever have been mistaken. The 'foreign' element—the tendency to strict syllabic uniformity of the line and to further uniformity in its metrical subdivisions—receives special, and, for a long time, almost final, expression in the hands of Gower. The 'native' reaction to alliterative accentual rhythm finds its greatest exposition—exposition which seems to disdain formally all transaction with metre and rime, though it cannot altogether avoid metrical colour—in the lines of *Piers Plowman*. And the middle way—the continuation of the process which has produced Middle

English prosody out of the shaping of the Old English lump by the pressure of the Franco-Latin mould—is trodden by the greatest of the three, with results that show him to be the greatest. The verse of *Piers Plowman* does all that it can with the method—it makes it clear that no other knight on any other day of the tournament is likely to do better on that side—but it also shows the limits of the method and the weakness of the side itself. Gower does not quite do this, partly because he is weaker, and partly because he has a better instrument—but he shows that this instrument itself needs improvement. Chaucer shows, not only that he is best of all, not only that his instrument is better than the others, but that this instrument, good as it is, has not done nearly all that it can do—that there is infinite future in it. He experiments until he achieves; but his achievement still leaves room for further experiment.

But, for real prosodic information, it is necessary to fall back upon the predecessors of these famous poets, in order to perceive how they reached their actual position. Naturally, when one comes to think of it, the predecessors of the right and left hand representatives are of less importance than those of the central protagonist. The attempts in more or less pure alliteration before *Piers Plowman* hardly deserve study here, for *Piers Plowman* 'puts them all down': the practitioners of the octosyllable, more or less precisely written, are of even less account prosodically. But with the great mass of verse writers, in scores of varying forms, who are the active forerunners of Chaucer (whether he directly studied them or not is beside the question) it is very different. In the huge body of mostly anonymous verse which is contained in a series of manuscripts beginning with the Harleian 2253 and ending with the Vernon, and which includes the work of named writers like Hampole, William of Shoreham and Laurence Minot, we find endless experiment, in almost every instance of which the action and reaction of mould and mass continue to develop the main process often referred to. It is, of course, possible, by keeping the eye wholly to one side, to lump all or most of these things under general categories of 'so many [generally *four*] stress lines,' or, by directing it mainly to the other, to discover Latin or French originals more or less clumsily imitated. But if the examples are first carefully considered as individuals and the common features which they present are then patiently extracted in connection, it will go hard but the *nisus* towards new forms, familiar to us later, will emerge. And, to some students at any rate, the presence of foot-arrangement and its results—inchoate and imperfect as they may be—will pretty certainly manifest itself.

The most important, if the most disputed, of these results is the actual attainment, whether by deliberate intention or not, of what was to become the great staple of English poetry, the 'decasyllabic' 'five-stress' or 'five-foot' line. The older statements (not quite obsolete yet) that this line does not appear before Chaucer—that Chaucer 'introduced' it—are certainly false; while the attempts sometimes made to assign its invention, and its first employment in couplets, to Hampole are not very well founded. Something, at least, very like it appears as early as the *Orison of Our Lady*, and frequently reappears in later poems, especially in *The Pricke of Conscience*, but also in other poems of the Vernon and other MSS which, probably, are later than Richard Rolle. But it is, in this particular place, less proper to establish this point by detailed argument than to draw attention to the fact that it is only one result of a whole multitude—the result of the ceaseless and resistless action and reaction of 'mould and mass.' If the English decasyllable or heroic and the English alexandrine (which appears in many places, sporadically, from Mannyng to *Piers Plowman*), and combinations of them, with or without shorter lines, were merely imitations of French, they must have been more regular: their very irregularity shows that something was forcing or cramping (for either metaphor may be used) the hands of the practitioners.

The greatest of these practitioners naturally get their hands most free, but in different ways: in *Piers Plowman*, by shirking the full problem on one side, in Gower, by shirking it on the other. How Chaucer meets it has been told in detail in the proper place. Here, we need only consider his results in the couplet and in rime royal—the octosyllable, for all his excellent practice in it, must be regarded as a vehicle which he definitely relinquished; and his stanzas, other than the septet with final couplet, are of minor importance. But he left the two great combinations of the decasyllabic line in such a condition that, given the existing literary language (largely his work) and the existing pronunciation of it, hardly anything further could be achieved or expected. The stanza exhibited—except, perhaps, in respect of *pause*—a severer standard of uniformity than the couplet; five hundred years of subsequent practice have shown that, in all cases, this is desirable, since too great a variety in the individual line interferes with the concerted effect of the group. But the couplet itself exhibits an amount of freedom which has been denied rather because the deniers think it ought not to be there than because they can prove its absence[1]. It certainly admits of either single (masculine) or double (feminine) rime; it certainly admits of extension in sense from line to line and from couplet to couplet; the pause, though hovering somewhere about the middle, by no means always definitely or necessarily alights there, or anywhere; and the lines are certainly not of invariable syllabic length. Here, perhaps, agreement ceases. But even those who, though they allow that Chaucer sometimes used nine syllables only, and often (with the double rime) eleven, would elsewhere crumple up an apparent hendecasyllable or dodecasyllable into ten, leave an opening to the other side. Call the means of crumpling 'slur,' 'elision,' 'synaloepha,' or what you will, the actual fact remains that some lines are crumpled and some not; and will permit *un*crumpling to those who choose. Those who do choose see in Chaucer, and have no mind to alter or disguise what they see, 'feet'—monosyllabic, dissyllabic and trisyllabic of various composition—and lines—'acephalous,' heroic or alexandrine, as the case may be. In other words, they see what, in different degrees, has existed in English prosody ever since. And both parties, however much they may differ on this point, agree, each on its own system, that the prosody and versification of Chaucer are as accomplished, as orderly, as reducible to general rule and system, as the prosody and versification of any poet in the world, at any time. That a different opinion was once and long held is universally admitted to have been the result of sheer and almost excusable ignorance of certain facts affecting pronunciation, especially the pronunciation of the final *-e*.

Thus, the prosody of the fourteenth century proceeds, as has been said above, in a manner perfectly intelligible and even surprisingly logical. The processes of adjustment of mould and mass certainly are at work in the thirteenth century; probably, if not quite certainly, in the twelfth; and they continue, not merely unhindered to any important degree by the alliterative-accentual revival, but, in a certain fashion, assisted, and, as it were, clarified, by it, in the fourteenth. The more disorderly elements, the rougher matters, are drawn off into this alliterative direction. No very great poet shows himself to be a danger in the other direction of excessive smoothness and syllabic limitation; while a very great

[1] Attempts have been made at various times to argue direct and extensive copying of contemporary French prosody by Chaucer. I have been for years pretty well acquainted with that prosody, and can pronounce it quite different from his.

poet does show himself capable of conducting prosodic development on the combined principles of freedom and order. And, what is more, this is not only a great poet, but one recognised as great by his own contemporaries; and his reputation continues at its highest for more than another century. It might seem impossible that so favourable a state of things should turn to anything but good; that standards, at once so finished and so flexible as those of the heroic couplet and the rime royal of Chaucer, should be corrupted or lost. A stationary condition might seem to be the worst that could reasonably be feared; and there would not seem to be anything very terrible in a stationary state of Chaucerian verse.

But the fifteenth century was fated to show that, in prosody, as in everything else, something unexpected is the only safe thing to expect. The actual versification of the successors of Chaucer has been discussed in the chapters appertaining to it; and it has there been pointed out that some authorities do not take so low a view of it as seems necessary to the present writer[1]. But the fact remains that, in order to get the verses of Lydgate, Occleve and the rest into any kind of rhythmical system, satisfactory at once to calculation and to audition, enormous liberties have to be taken with the text; complicated arrangements of licence and exception have to be devised; and, in some cases, even these failing, the franker vindicators have to fall back on the supposition that mere accent, with unaccented syllables thrown in almost at pleasure, is the basis of Lydgatian and other prosody. Now, it may be so; but, in that case, the other fact remains that very small liberties, if any, need be taken with the text of Chaucer; that necessary exceptions and licences in his case are extremely few; and that, whether his metre be accentual or not, it is most certainly not *merely* accentual, in the sense that unaccented syllables may be peppered down at pleasure as a seasoning, still less in the sense that the number of accents itself may be altered at pleasure. In rime royal especially, Chaucer's line-length and line-arrangement are almost meticulously correct. In his followers, examples of from seven to seventeen syllables, and of from four to seven apparent accents, are not merely occasionally, but constantly, found. And yet we know that almost all these writers had Chaucer constantly before them and regarded him

[1] Professor Max Förster of Würzburg has been good enough to favour me with a communication to the effect that some MSS of Burgh, at any rate, are much less disorderly than the printed editions.

with the highest admiration; and we know, further, that his followers in Scotland managed to imitate him with very considerable precision.

No real or full explanation of this singular decadence has ever yet been given; probably none is possible. But, in two respects, at least, something like an approach may be made to such an explanation. The first of these is that Chaucer, assisted by Genius but somewhat neglecting Time, 'standardised' the language rather too soon. We know that, in his own day, the management of the final *-e* was far less uniform and systematic in the case of others than in his own; that it was, in fact, changing into something like its modern value. This, of itself, would suffice, with its consequent alternate use and disuse, forgetfulness and remembrance—nay, its positive temptation to make a convenience and licence of the thing—to dislocate and corrupt the metre. And there were certainly some, probably many, other changes which would help to produce a similar effect. Nor is it probable that many, if any, poets had a distinct theoretic understanding of the metres that they used—the best part of two hundred years had to pass after 1400 before we find trace of any such thing. They were 'fingering' at Chaucer's measures by 'rule of thumb,' and with hands furnished with more thumbs than fingers.

But there was probably another cause which, while less certain, is highly probable, though it needs careful study and application to its possible result. The alliterative-accentual revival had not only spread very far and taken great hold, but it had, as has been shown, exhibited a singular tendency to combine itself even with very elaborate metrical arrangements. Nor is there anything improbable in the supposition that this tendency spread itself much more widely than such unmistakable instances as the *Awntyrs of Arthure*, or the *Epistill of Swete Susane*, or even Gavin Douglas's eighth prologue would, of themselves, indicate. Nay, it is probable that the admixture was not so much an 'adultery of art' as an unconscious process.

Its results, however, were (except in one important respect to be noted later) rather unfortunate, and even in not a few cases very ugly. For exactly how much the combination counted in the degradation of rime royal and, in a less degree, of the decasyllabic couplet—the octosyllabic, always an easy-going form, escaped better—it would be rash to attempt to determine. But, almost indisputably, it counted for a great deal—for next to everything—in the rise of the curious phenomenon called 'doggerel' which we perceive during this century, and which, towards the close of it, and at the beginning of the next, usurps a very great position in the realm of verse.

Chaucer applies the term 'doggerel' to undistinguished and unpoetic verse or rime, apparently of any kind; and the widest modern use of it is not dissimilar. But, at the time of which we are speaking—the whole (probably) of the fifteenth century and the beginning of the sixteenth—the word is wanted for a peculiar kind of verse, rimed, indeed, all but invariably, and deriving almost its whole poetical claim from rime, but possessing characteristics in some respects approaching, on one side, unrimed accentual structure of various lengths, and, on the other, the rimed 'fourteener' or its offspring, the common measure.

We saw, in treating of *Gamelyn* (which is pretty certainly older than the fifteenth century, though it is impossible to say how much), that the metre of that remarkable piece is the fourteener of Robert of Gloucester, 'fingered' in a peculiar way—first by freely lengthening and shortening the iambic constituents and, secondly, by utilising the middle pause in such a fashion as to make of the line two counter-running halves, rather than one uniform current with only a slight centre-halt. It is from the neglect of fingering in this process, and from the increase of attention to occasional accent only, that the 'doggerel' of which we are speaking, which is dominant in the Middle Drama, very frequent elsewhere and, perhaps, actually present in not a little literary rime royal verse, takes its rise. It varies greatly in length; but most writers group their doggerel, roughly, in passages, if not in whole pieces. The shortest form (except the pure Skeltonics) vaguely represents octosyllabic or 'four-accent' verse; the middle, decasyllables; the longest, alexandrines or fourteeners, though, in many instances, this telescopes itself out to sixteen or seventeen syllables, if not more, and tempts the reader or reciter to 'patter,' to take them or even four 'short' syllables in the stride from one 'long' to another[1]. The effect is sometimes suitable

[1] Some examples may be desirable:

Skeltonic:

And as full of good wyll
As faire Isaphyll:
Coryaunder.
Swete pomaunder,
Goode Cassaunder.

Pseudo-octosyllabic:

Very common—a fair sample is in Heywood's *Husband, Wife and Priest*,

But by my soul I never go to Sir John
But I find him like a holy man,

enough for the lower kind of comic verse; but, for the higher kind, even of that, it is utterly unsuitable; while, for anything passionate or serious, it is fatal. It is the prevalence of it, in combination with the similar but even worse welter in serious verse, which has given the fifteenth century in English poetry so bad a name that some native historians have often said little about it, and that some famous foreign critics have dismissed it, almost or altogether, with a kind of contemptuous kick.

The result, however, if of doubtful beauty in itself, was probably necessary, and can be shown to be a beneficent chapter in the history of English verse. For, in the first place, the Chaucerian 'standardising,' as has been shown, had been attempted a little too early; and, in the second, there was a danger that it might have been carried yet further into a French uniformity and regularity which would have caused the abortion of most of the special beauties of English verse. And, though the main literary versification lacked music—even when, as, for instance, in Occleve, it had a certain mechanical correctness—while the doggerel was not so much poetry as jog-trot, or capering prose, there was a third division of verse which, until lately, has received very little attention, but which far exceeded the other two in poetical beauty and also in real prosodic interest. This is the great body of mostly, if not wholly, anonymous ballads, carols, nursery rimes, folk songs and miscellaneous popular lyrics generally—much of our oldest supply of which probably comes from this century—as *Chevy Chace*, *The Nut Brown Maid*, the exquisite carol *I sing of a maiden* certainly do.

The note of all these productions is that they were composed, in many cases, for definite musical accompaniment—in all, to be 'sung or said,' in some sort of audible measure and rhythm, from musical arrangement itself down to the reciter's drone, or the nurse's sing-song. One general result of this is that a merely

where the very next lines slide into *pseudo-heroics*:

> For either he is saying his devotion,
> Or else he is going in procession.

Pseudo-alexandrine: Bale's *Kyng Johan*:

> Monkes, chanons and nones in dyvers colours and shape,
> Both whyte, blacke, and pyed, God send their increase yll happe.

Pseudo-fourteeners: *Thersites*:

> To augment their joy and the commons felicity,
> Fare ye well, sweet audience God grant you prosperity.

But it is important to observe that by 'pattering' or dwelling, these kinds may be run into one another to a great extent.

prosaic effect is almost impossible—that there must be some sort of rhythmical division and system, and that this must be marked. Another particular result of the greatest value is that 'triple time' will not be gainsaid—or, in other words, that trisyllabic feet force their way in. The influence of music has not always been of unmitigated benefit to prosody; but, at this time, it could hardly, by any possibility, do harm, and might do infinite good. From the rough but still perfectly rhythmical verse of 'The Percy out of Northumberland,' through the somewhat more regular and complicated, but equally unartificial 'For I will to the greenwood go, alone, a banished man,' to the delicately modulated melody of the carol above referred to, everything is equally opposed to the heartbreaking prose of the staple rime royal and the mere disorder of the doggerel. And what these now famous things show, dozens, scores, hundreds of others, less famous, show likewise. As the simpler and more uniform English line of which the iambic foot forms the staple—the line suitable for poems of length and bulk and weight—has been hammered into shape during the thirteenth and fourteenth centuries, so the varieties of mixed cadence, suitable for lyric, are now being got ready; and, by a curious dispensation, exactly while the staple line is being not so much hammered as blunderingly knocked and bulged out of shape.

This lyric adjustment—which, in its turn, was to have important effects later on the staple line itself—went on continuously till it developed and refined itself, by steps which may be noticed presently, into the unsurpassed composition of 1580—1660. But, meanwhile, however slowly and tardily, the disorder of the staple line itself was reformed in two directions. The literary line—which had aimed at following Chaucer or Gower, and had wandered off into formless prose—girt itself up again (something over tightly) into octosyllables and decasyllables, pure fourteeners or 'poulter's measure.' The loose forms recognised their real basis and became anapaestic—regular, though unmusical, at first—as in Tusser. The documents of the first change, so far as practice goes, are to be found in the *corpus* of English verse during the middle of the sixteenth century, beginning with Wyatt and Surrey. As concerns theory, Gascoigne's *Notes of Instruction*, though a little late, shows us the completed process. Earlier, less explicit, but not less really cogent evidence of discontent and desire to reform may be found in the craze for classical metres, the true source of which was by no means merely an idle desire to imitate the classics, but a very worthy, though mistaken, longing to get rid of the anarchy with which rimed English metres were associated, and to substitute a well tried and approved order. But perhaps most noteworthy of all is a piece of prose discussion in *A Mirror for Magistrates*, where examples of the broken fifteenth century rhythm, which had been prevalent from Lydgate to Hawes, are produced, 'misliked' and excused on the ground of their being suitable to the time of their subject—the reign of Richard III. This appears in almost the oldest part of that curiously composite book; and, in a part a little later, but still before Spenser, there is a deliberate description of English alexandrines as written in agreement with 'the Roman verse called iambics.'

In the two famous writers in whom the reformation of English verse first distinctly appears, the reforming influences—or, to speak with stricter correctness, the models chosen in order to help the achievement of reform—are, without doubt, Italian, though French may have had some subsidiary or go-between influence. Sonnet and *terza rima* in Wyatt, and the same with the addition of blank verse in Surrey (putting aside lyrics), tell the tale unmistakably. And it is to be noticed that sonnet, *terza rima* and blank verse—the first two by their actually strict and rigid outline and the third through the fear and caution imposed on the writer by the absence of his usual mentor, rime, act almost automatically. But (and it is a precious piece of evidence in regard to their erring predecessors as well as to their penitent and reformed selves) it is quite clear that even they still have great difficulty in adjusting rhythm to pronunciation. They 'wrench accent' in the fashion which Gascoigne was to rebuke in the next (almost in the same) generation; they dislocate rime; they have occasional recourse to the valued *-e* which we know to have been long obsolete, and even to have turned in some cases to the *-y* form in adjectives.

Whatever their shortcomings, however (and, in fact, their shortcomings were much less than might have been expected), there is no doubt that the two poets whose names have long been and must always be inseparable deserve, in prosody even more than in poetry generally, the credit of a 'great instauration'—of showing how the old patterns of Chaucer and others, adjusted to the new pronunciation, could be got out of the disarray into which they had fallen, by reference (immediately) to Italian models. Nor is it superfluous to point out that Italian, though apparently a language most different in vocalisation and cadence from English, has the very point in common with us which French lacks—the combination, that is to say, of strict, elaborate and most various external conformation of stanza with a good deal of syllabic liberty inside the line. These two things were exactly what wanted encouragement in English: and Italian gave them together.

For the moment, however, and naturally, the stricter side of the teaching was more attended to than the looser. The older prosody, at an exceedingly uncertain time but, most probably, on the bridge of the fourteenth and fifteenth centuries, had produced some very lovely things: not only the three above mentioned (of which only *The Nut Brown Maid* can be later than the middle of the fifteenth century, and that may not be) but others certainly early, such as *E. I. O.*, *Quia amore langueo* and many less known pieces. But doggerel had invaded lyric too, and sunk it to merely popular uses; and it would be difficult to pick out a really beautiful lyric that is certainly of the last generation of the fifteenth or the first of the sixteenth century. Here, therefore, as elsewhere, the reform had to be rather in the precise direction; and for at least fifty years from Wyatt (who must have begun writing as early as 1530) to Spenser, English lyric, like English poetry generally, is 'on its good behaviour': careful of syllabic exactness within and correspondence without; afraid of trisyllabic liberty; obviously nervous and 'keeping its foot,' lest it slip back into the quicksand of doggerel or the quagmire of scarcely rhythmed prose.

To say this is by no means (as some seem rather uncritically to interpret it) to speak disobligingly of the lesser contributors to *Tottel's Miscellany*, of Turbervile, of Gascoigne, or even of Googe, though in all these (especially in the first mentioned group and the last mentioned individual) exactness is too often secured by sing-song and jog-trot. Certainly it is not to belittle the work of Wyatt and Surrey and Sackville, though, in the first two of these, especially in their 'poulter's measure,' sing-song and jog-trot do appear. The fact is that the business of this generation—almost of these two generations—was to get things ready for their successors—to make a new raising of English prosody to its highest power possible in the hands of Spenser and Shakespeare, by once more thoroughly stamping it with rhythm. Chaucer had done this, but the material had given way; and, in doing so, it had cast an obsolete air on the forms themselves. Thus, even the magnificent rime royal of Sackville, full of the new and truly Elizabethan spirit as it is, has a sort of archaic and artificial air at times, the air of something that, if it were less magnificent, might be called *pastiche*. And nobody until

Spenser himself—and not the earliest Spenser—writes good 'riding rime.' But they exercise themselves in the regular fourteener, split and coupleted or sandwiched with alexandrines, as if this return to almost the oldest of English metres was instinctively felt to have some exercising and energising quality. And they practise, sometimes, very prettily and always very carefully, divers lyrical measures of good gymnastic power. The sonnet is too high for most of them, after the original adventurers: it will have to wait a little. But blank verse, handled in a stiff and gingerly manner, is still now and then practised, especially by that great experimenter and systematic prosodist Gascoigne. Some of them, especially Turbervile, can get a good deal of sweetness out of variegated rime.

In one department only, by a singular contrast, does anarchy hold its ground almost to the last: and that is the drama. The fact can hardly be quite unconnected with the other fact that the pure medieval drama had been rather remarkable for prosodic elaboration and correctness, its vehicles being, in the main, either fair octosyllabic couplets or more or less complicated lyrical stanzas—often quite exact in construction and correspondence. But doggerel had broken in early and was, no doubt, encouraged by the matter of moralities and interludes, when these came to take the place of the miracle plays. At any rate, by the end of the fifteenth century and throughout the first two-thirds, if not the first three-fourths, of the sixteenth, the drama was simply overrun with doggerel—doggerel of all sorts and shapes and sizes. Yet, even here, the tendency to get out of the welter at last made itself felt. First, the doggerel tried to collect and solidify itself back into the fourteener from which it had, in a manner, 'deliquesced.' Then it tried couplet or stanza in decasyllables. And then, the stern standard of the *Gorboduc* blanks at last reared itself, too stern and too stiff to draw many followers round it at first, but destined to undergo transformation till it became one of the most wonderful of metres past, present, or even, perhaps, to come—the rimeless, rhythmful, Protean-Herculean blank verse of Shakespeare.

But we are less concerned here with the fortunes of particular metres, or particular styles, than with the general progress of English prosody. This—at a period the signpost to which is the publication of *The Shepheards Calender* but the influences and attainments of which are not, of course, limited to a single book or a single person—had reached one of its most important stages, a stage unparalleled in importance except by those similarly indicated in *The Canterbury Tales* and *Paradise Lost.* During the fifteenth century, it had been almost unmade from some points of view; but invaluable assistances for the remaking had been accumulated in all sorts of byeways. In the two middle quarters of the sixteenth, it had been almost remade—in the sense that the presence of general rhythm had been restored in accordance with actual pronunciation; and that, as one school of prosodists would say, stressed and unstressed, accented and unaccented syllables, had been taught to observe more orderly and proportional arrangement: as another, that metrical scansion by feet had been once more vindicated and regimented. But, during these two generations of reforming experiment, there had been comparatively few poets of distinguished genius: of those who possessed it, Wyatt and Surrey came a little too early, Sackville practised on too small a scale and in too few varieties. Nay, the very fact of reforming and innovating experiment necessitated a period of go-cart and then, as it were, one of marking time.

But, by 1580, or a little earlier, both these periods were over, and the flock of singers of the great Elizabethan time found that they had been relieved of the preliminary drill. Even the classical metre craze—threatening as it might seem to be to English poetry and prosody—did good, not merely by showing what is not the way, but by emphasising the most important characteristic of what is: that is to say, the composition of the line, not by a muddle of promiscuous syllables, but by constituents themselves regularly and systematically composed and constituted. Even the 'woodenness' of blank verse at first forces the ear to attend to the order and position of the stresses, to the existence and conformation of the feet. The jog-trot of the fourteeners and the 'poulter's measure' says the same thing heavily, as do the varied lyrical forms of Gascoigne and Turbervile not so heavily; nay, the so-called doggerel of Tusser (which is only doggerel in phrase and subject and spirit, for its form is quite regular) says nothing else. Whether it canters or trots, it may now seem to some ears to run 'mind your feet' and, to others, 'mind your stress'; but the difference is here merely logomachic. They heard it then—into whatever words they translated it—and they went and did it.

It may seem that the selection of Spenser to show exactly what this stage signifies is unjust to others. Certainly, if misunderstood, it would be so. It is as nearly certain as anything can be that Sidney and others did not learn their prosody from

Spenser, and that even Drayton and other men, who lived and wrote far into the seventeenth century, were, in a sense, rather his junior schoolfellows than his pupils. But his direct influence soon became immense and all-pervading, and, as an early and masterly representative of influences that others were feeling, there is no one to match him. The prosodic lessons of *The Shepheards Calender* are all but unmistakable. On one point only is difference of opinion of an important kind possible—whether the famous loose metre of *February* and two other months is definite *Genesis and Exodus* or *Christabel* (to look before and after)—'four-stress' or 'iambic' with trisyllabic substitution permitted—or whether it is an attempt at Chaucerian '*five*-stress' or 'heroic.' The present writer has not the slightest doubt on the subject: but others have. Omitting this, every metre in the *Calender*, and every one subsequently tried by its author, though it may be differently named by different systems, is, with the proper translations of terminology, unmistakable. In the various forms of identical stanza, from the sizain through the septet and octave to his own special creation; in the sonnet; in the still larger strophes of his odes; in the more variegated lyrical outlines of some of the *Calender* poems; in the riding rime (here quite unmistakable) of *Mother Hubberd's Tale*—the exact and regular accentuation or quantification of each scheme is unerringly observed. That great bone of contention, the 'trisyllabic foot,' in metre not based trisyllabically, makes comparatively rare appearance in him; the believers in 'slur' or 'elision' seldom have to resort to either expedient. There are a very few possible alexandrines (outside the last line) in *The Faerie Queene*; but they are probably, or certainly, oversights. He fingers this regularly rhythmical line, whatever its length, into the widest variety by altering the pauses and weighting or lightening special places with chosen phrase. He runs the lines into one another, or holds them apart within the stanza, inexhaustibly. But, on the whole, despite his great variety of outline and combined form, he is once more a prophet and a practitioner of regularity—of order—of unbroken, uneccentric, music and rhythm. This is his mission in prosody—to make, so far as his example can reach, a gallimaufry and jumble of mixed and jolting cadences impossible or intolerable in English. His very abandonment of the promising, and, as it afterwards turned out, inestimable, 'Oak and Brier' measure, is, on one theory of that measure, just as much as on another, evidence of a final dislike to even the possibility of such jumble and jolt.

To, and with, one great measure, Spenser (except doubtfully and in his earliest youth) did nothing; and it was as well that he did nothing. Nor is this yet the place in which to take any general survey of the features and progress of blank verse; for, though they had, by the end of the queen's reign, reached almost, or quite, their highest, it was as part of a movement which was still moving and which certainly could not yet be said to be moving downward. But the reason why it was well that Spenser took no part in this is that his mission was, as has been said, essentially a mission, though not of cramp or fetter, of order and regularity. Now, blank verse did not require such a missioner then. It had started, in the first ardour of the movement against doggerel, with severe practice and example on the part of Surrey and, later, of Sackville. What it wanted, and what it received, was experiment and exploration of the most varied and daring kind, in all its own possible licences and transformations. Spenser, be it repeated, was not the man to do anything of that kind for it; and the two wisely let each other alone.

Even in regard to blank verse, however, the Spenserian lesson must have been of inestimable service. It is hardly excessive or fanciful to regard him, not merely as one of the greatest and one of the very first of Elizabethan composers, but as the greatest and the first of Elizabethan conductors, an impeccable master of rhythm, time and tune. This was what English poetry had wanted for nearly two hundred years and had now got. The ear was taught and the correspondence between ear and tongue was established. Nor—with a pretty large exception in regard to blank verse, where Spenser's baton was quiet, in the mid-seventeenth century, and something of one in regard to the looser form of heroic couplet about the same time—were these great gains ever let slip. Their exercise, indeed, was, later, confined and hampered unduly; but its principle was not controverted. In Edward VI's time, this general system of rhythm, time and tune had but just been tentatively and imperfectly attained by Wyatt and Surrey; there has not been any general change in it from Spenser's period to the time of Edward VII. A few words have changed their usual accent and Spenser's peculiar system of 'eye-rime' has made it desirable to keep his spelling, lest we destroy an effect which he wished to produce. But, whatever you do with the spelling, you will not alter the rhythm; whereas, if you modernise Chaucer, you must either put continual new patches and pieces into the verse or lose the rhythm altogether. Words may fall out, and words may come in, but the latter find, as the former leave, a fixed system of prosodic arrangement to which they have but to adjust themselves. Ben Jonson may have been right or wrong in saying that Spenser 'writ no language,' while he certainly was wrong in assigning mere 'imitation of the ancients' as the cause thereof. But, though he did not—it is said—like the Spenserian stanza, his own more authentic and half-casual selection of Spenser as the antithesis to 'the Water poet' shows us that he did not go wrong on his poetic powers. Amongst the evidences of those powers it would be ridiculous to say to-day that Spenser discovered the rhythmical-metrical system of English poetry; and it would be unjust to say that he alone rediscovered and adjusted it to existing circumstances. But he was among the rediscoverers: and the greatest of them up to his own time. In all matters of English prosody, except blank verse and the trisyllabically based measures, we may go back to Spenser and to his generation for example and practical precept; and it will always be possible so to go back until the language undergoes some transformation of which there is not at present even the faintest symptom.

CHAPTER XIV

ELIZABETHAN CRITICISM

It is, perhaps, only after long and thorough reading of Middle English literature that the student becomes aware how completely absent from it is the spirit of literary criticism. Not, of course, that, in this respect, it differs very much from its continental contemporaries, but that the absence is, perhaps, more complete—at any rate longer lasting—than with any of them. Almost the first utterance that belongs even to the precincts and outskirts of the critical province is Robert Mannyng's statement (in the prologue of his *Chronicle, c.* 1330) of his reason for preferring one metre to another, which is merely that it was more likely to be appreciated. The unknown annotator who observed that *Cursor Mundi* is 'the best book of all' was certainly not thinking of its literary merits. Here, as elsewhere, the first real signs of advance are found in Chaucer; but Chaucer's criticism, though, probably, no one was ever born with more of the critical spirit, is mainly implicit and undeveloped. Yet the presence of it is unmistakable, not merely in his remarks on his own prosody, not merely in the host's on *Sir Thopas,* not merely in *Sir Thopas* itself and in the way in which the company fall upon the luckless monk, but in many slighter symptoms. Indeed, it may be said that the first definite sign of the awakening of the critical instinct in English writers, other than Chaucer, is in their admiration for Chaucer himself. It is true that this admiration had singular yokefellows; but that is quite natural. Even as you must walk before you run, and totter before you walk, so must criticism itself, at the first, be uncritical.

The first body of critical observations in English is, probably, to be found in the prefaces of Caxton; and a very interesting, though a rather infantine, body it is. His very earliest work, the translation of the *Recuyell,* is dictated to him by his sense of 'the fair language of French, which was in prose so well and compendiously set and written.' He afterwards 'remembers himself of his simpleness and unperfectness' in both languages. He perceives, in reference to the *Dictes of the Philosophers,* that lord

Rivers's translation is 'right well and cunningly made.' He sees that, though Boethius was 'an excellent author of divers books craftily and curiously made in prose and metre,' yet the style of *De Consolatione* is 'hard and difficult,' so that Chaucer deserved 'perpetual laud' for translating it. Benet Burgh has 'full craftily made' *Cato* in 'ballad royal.' And the praises of *The Canterbury Tales* and of the *Morte d'Arthur*, more elaborate than these, but also much better known, might be called the first real 'appreciations' in English.

These elementary and half unconscious critical exercises of Caxton, as a moment's thought will show, must have had a great influence, exercised, no doubt, as unconsciously as it was generated, on the new readers of these new printed books. Yet it was long before the seed fell into a soil where it could germinate. Even when, at the beginning of the next century, regular *Rhetorics* began to be written at first hand in imitation of the ancients, or through modern humanists like Melanchthon (the earliest instance, apparently, is that of Leonard Coxe of Reading, in 1524), the temptation to stray from strictly formal rhetoric into criticism was not much felt until there arose at Cambridge, towards the middle of the century, that remarkable school of friends who are represented in the history of English prose by Ascham, Cheke and Wilson, and whose share in the revival of letters is dealt with elsewhere in the present volume[1]. Even then, on the eve of Elizabeth's reign, and with the new burst of Italian critical writing begun by Trissino, Daniello and Vida, the critical utterances are scanty, quite unsystematic and shot (as one of the three would have said) 'at rovers.' The really best work of the trio in this kind is Cheke's, who, if he was mistaken in his caution to Sir Thomas Hoby against the practice of borrowing from ancient tongues in modern[2], has left us, in the criticism on Sallust quoted by Ascham, a really solid exercise in the art: not, of course, absolutely right—few things are that in criticism—but putting one side of rightness forcibly and well, in his depreciation (as Quintilian, doubtless his inspirer, has put it) of 'wishing to write better than you can.' It may, however, be noted that all the three set themselves against over-elaboration of style in this way or that. It was this which provoked Thomas Wilson (whom we may not now, it seems, call 'Sir' Thomas) to diverge from the usual course of rhetorical precept, not merely into some illustrative tales, but into a definite onslaught on 'ink-horn' terms—foreign, archaic, technical or what not. It is not

[1] See chaps. I and XIX. [2] See chap. XIX.

known exactly who first hit on this phrase, the metaphor of which is sufficiently obvious; but it is freely used about this time. And we can quite easily see how the 'aureate' phraseology of the fifteenth century—the heavy bedisenment of Latinised phrase, which we find not merely in poetry but in such books as the early English version of Thomas à Kempis—must have challenged opposition on the part of those who were anxious, indeed, to follow the classics for good, but desirous, at the same time, that 'our English' should be written 'pure.' And the contemporary jealousy and contempt of the medieval appears not less clearly in Wilson's objection to the Chaucerising which Thynne's edition, evidently, had made fashionable.

The strengthening power of the critical sense, however, and, at the same time, its lack of education and direction, are best shown in Ascham. It is something, but not much, that he exhibits to the full that curious confusion of aesthetic and ethic which, essentially Platonic and patristic, cannot be said to have been wholly discouraged by Aristotle, and which the period, uniting, for once, the three tendencies, maintained, almost in the teeth of its own humanism, more strenuously than ever. This confusion, or—to adopt a less question-begging word—this combination, has always had, has and, no doubt, always will have, its defenders: nor is it a bad thing that they should exist, as protesters against the too absolute doctrine of 'art for art only.' But Ascham's inability to apply the strictly critical *distinguo* extends far beyond the condemnation of romance as suggesting the violation of the sixth and seventh commandments, or the discouragement of the importation of foreign literature as involving that of foreign immorality, or (this is Cheke, not Ascham, but Ascham approves it) the urging of Sallust's laxity of conduct as an argument against his literary competence. It is not shown in the unceasing opposition of the whole trio to 'aureate' and 'inkhorn' terms, an opposition which may, indeed, have been excessive, but which cannot be said to have been misplaced, when such a man as Hawes, not so many years earlier, could be guilty of two such consecutive lines as

> Degouted vapoure most aromatyke,
> And made conversyon of complacence.

It appears mainly, and most dangerously, in Ascham's doctrine of Imitation. Of this imitation, he distinguishes two kinds (literally, three, but, as he himself says, 'the third belongeth to the second'). The first of these is the original *mimesis* of Aristotle:

'a fair lively painted picture of the life of every degree of man.' The second is 'to follow, for learning of tongues and sciences, the best authors.' But he expressly limits the first kind to comedy and tragedy, and says that 'it doth not much belong at this time to our purpose.' It is the second kind, not so much the representation of nature as the actual copying of the existing art of man, to which he devotes his whole attention, in which he obviously feels his whole interest. If he does not, like Vida, say, in so many words, 'steal from' the ancients, he has, practically, nothing more to urge than 'follow' them, and 'borrow from' them. In some respects, and to some extent, he could, of course, have said nothing better. But, in respect of one point, and that the chief one which gives him a position in English criticism, his following was most corrupt. After the matter had long remained in some obscurity, it has been shown pretty exactly how the idea came about that English verse needed reforming on classical patterns. Chaucerian prosody, to some extent in the hands of Chaucer's own contemporaries like Lydgate and Occleve, but, still more, in those of his and their successors, had fallen into such utter disarray that, in many cases, little but the rime ('and that's not much') remained to distinguish verse from prose. In Ascham's own day, the very worst of this tyranny was, indeed, past; and the apparent reorganising of pronunciation on the basis of dropping the value of the final *-e*, and other changes, had restored a certain order to verse. But the favourite 'fourteener' (Ascham expressly smites 'the rash ignorant heads that can easily reckon up *fourteen* syllables') was still, for the most part, a shambling, slovenly, sing-song, with nothing of the fire which Chapman afterwards infused into its unbroken form, or of the ineffable sweetness which the seventeenth century lyrists extracted from the divided couplet. On the other hand, the euphony of Greek and Latin metres was universally recognised. Why not imitate them also? The possibility and propriety of this imitation (recommended, no doubt, by the fact that, dangerous error though, on the whole, it was, it had more than a grain of truth at the bottom of it, as regards feet, though not as regards metres) seems to have arisen at Cambridge, likewise, and at St John's College, but not with one of the three scholars just mentioned. The chief begetter of it appears to have been Thomas Watson, master of the college, afterwards bishop of Lincoln, and a man who did not succeed in playing the difficult game between papist and protestant with such success as Ascham and Wilson. Ascham himself has preserved with approval the remarkably, but not extraordinarily, bad hexameters in which Watson puts into English the first two lines of the *Odyssey,*

> All travellers do gladly report great praise of Ulysses
> For that he knew many mens manners and saw many cities,

and, in more places than one, he denounces 'rude beggarly riming' not (as he might have done with some colour) in favour of the new blank verse actually started by Surrey long before he wrote, but in favour of classical 'versing.' From his time this became, with another less technical one, the main question of Elizabethan criticism, and we may despatch it before turning to the less technical question, and to others. We do not know exactly at what time Watson began to recommend and attempt English hexameters; but it must have been almost certainly before 1554, when both he and Ascham left Cambridge. And it may have been any time earlier, as far back as 1535, which seems to have been the first year that he, Ascham and Cheke (to whose conversations on this subject, and on others connected with it, Ascham often refers) were at the university together. It is more likely to have been late than early. At any rate, the idea took root in St John's and, somewhat later still (probably between 1561 and 1569), produced the celebrated and mysterious rules of Thomas Drant, another fellow of the college. These rules[1] are repeatedly referred to in the correspondence beween Harvey and Spenser to be noticed presently, though Harvey, with his usual bluster, disclaims all knowledge of them. Ascham himself is really our earliest authority on the subject, and seems (from Nashe's references, for instance) to have been practically recognised as such even then.

To do him justice, however, his affection for 'versing' appears to have been much more lukewarm than his dislike of rime. If, when he cites Watson's doggerel, he commits himself to the statement that 'our English tongue may as well receive right quantity of syllables and true order of versifying as either Greek or Latin,' he makes exceedingly damaging admissions afterwards, as that 'our English tongue doth not well receive the nature of *Carmen Heroicum* because the *dactylus,* the aptest foot for that verse, is seldom found,' and that the said *carmen* 'doth rather trot and hobble than run smoothly in English.' He makes himself amends, however, by scolding rime with a curious pedantic pettishness; and by advancing the notable argument that, whosoever is

[1] Not now known to be extant, and nowhere stated with any precision by Spenser himself.

angry with him for misliking rime may be angry with Quintilian for misliking it. This remark is, of course, of the highest value as showing how far from any true critical point of view a man, always a good scholar and, generally, a man of good sense, could find himself at this time. Nor is there less instruction in the other fact that, while he is aware of Surrey's blank verse, and though it discards his bugbear rime, he is not in the least satisfied with it, because it has not 'true quantity.' Now, as Surrey's blank verse, though not very free or flexible, is, as a rule, correct enough in accent-quantity, it is clear that Ascham was woolgathering after a system of 'quantity by position,' quantity, as opposed to accent, and the like, which never has been, and is never likely to be, established in English. This 'true' quantity is, in fact, the key of the whole position, and the quest for it occupies all the acuter minds among the earlier disputants on the subject. Ascham, while hopeful, makes no serious effort to discover it, though his confession about Watson's hexameters and those of others amounts to a confession that it had not been discovered. Spenser and Harvey, in their correspondence, do not so much quarrel as amicably 'wrangle,' in the technical sense, over the difficulties of quantity by position. Can you possibly pronounce or, without pronouncing, value for prosodic purposes 'carpenter' as 'carpēnter'? May you, while retaining the short pronunciation, but availing yourself of the long accent of 'mother' in its first syllable, make the short second syllable long before a consonant in the next word? Although Spenser, in his letters, nowhere acknowledges the impossibility of these tricks with words, his entire abandonment of this kind of versing in his mature work speaks more eloquently than any formal abjuration. As for Harvey, the sort of boisterous pedantry with which he seems to think it proper to suffuse his writing makes it very difficult to judge how far he is serious. But the verse (of which, apparently, he thought well enough to repeat it three times)

> O blessëd Virtue! blessëd Fame! blessed Abundance!

is sufficient to show that he did believe in quantity by position, inasmuch as 'blessed,' in the first two cases, before consonants, becomes 'blessëd,' and in the third, before a vowel, remains 'blessed.' But he is simply grotesque in many of his examples; and it is difficult not to believe them caricatures or partly so, though it is true that Spenser himself, master of harmony as he was in the true measures, and a very serious person, is nearly as much a doggerelist as others in these false measures.

Webbe, Puttenham and others to be mentioned presently engage in this question—Puttenham slightly, Webbe with a blundering eagerness—and it continues to be discussed at intervals till it is fought out by Campion and Daniel. But the most intelligent and the most illuminative of the earlier remarks on it come from one of the wildest of the practitioners, Richard Stanyhurst. For his wildness lies not so much in his prosody, as in his diction, where he wilfully hampers himself by making it his principle to use no word that had been used by his predecessor Phaer. As a critic of prosody, he is a curious mixture of sense and crotchet. He sees, and insists upon, the undoubted, and generally overlooked, truth that many important monosyllables in English, 'me,' 'my,' 'the,' 'and,' etc., are common: but he wishes to indicate the double pronunciation which, in effect, proves this, by spelling 'mee' and 'thee,' in the latter case introducing a gratuitous confusion with the pronoun. He follows, as a rule, Latin quantity in English, thus making 'honour' short, in spite of the accent, and 'mother' (which he spells 'm*oo*ther') long, because of *mater*. He admits quantity by position, but, apparently, not in middle syllables; and, properly recognising the English tendency to carry back the accent, wants to make this uniform to the extent of 'ímperative' and 'órthography.' Lastly, he has a most singular system of deciding the quantity of final syllables, not by the last vowel, but by the last consonant, whereby he is driven to make endless exceptions, and a large number of 'common' endings. In fact, the main value of Stanyhurst is that the prevalence of the common syllable in English is, really, at the bottom of all his theory. But the question could never be properly cleared up on these lines, and it remained in a state of theoretical unsettlement, and of occasional tentative, but always unsuccessful, practice till it was settled in the way mentioned above, and to be described below. It is curious that Milton makes no reference to it in the afterthought outburst against rime which he subjoined to the later copies of *Paradise Lost*. It would have been extremely interesting to have heard his deliberate opinion, at any rate of Campion.

The other main question, or, rather, group of questions, to which the criticism of what we have yet to speak of was devoted, concerns the general character and status of poetry at large, or, at least, the general rules of certain important poetical kinds. These matters had been eagerly and constantly discussed abroad during the middle of the century, in fact during nearly the whole of its two inner quarters, when most of the authors mentioned in the present chapter began to write. There was even a considerable stock of Italian and Latin critical writing on the question, which was soon to be supplemented in French, when Ascham himself turned his attention to the matter. These discussions turned, on one side, on the Platonic distrust, largely altered and dosed with the puritan dislike, of poetry, as such, and especially of dramatic poetry; and, on another side, on the proper laws, more particularly of the drama, but also of other poetic kinds. As for real historical criticism, for the examination of English poetry as it was, in order to discover what it ought to be, circumstances were not favourable; but some attempts were made even in this line. On the whole, it will be most profitable, having thus given the general conditions and directions, to consider in order the actual exponents and documents of the subject. Of Ascham and his group it is probably not necessary to say more. The direction to the subject which they gave was invaluable, but their actual utterances on it could not but be somewhat sporadic and haphazard. In particular, few of them were, or could even be expected to be, devoted to English literature as it was. General principles of a pedagogic kind, almost always coming round to the imitation of the ancients, were what they could give, and, perhaps, what it was best for them to give.

The first remarks of a critical kind upon English verse may be found, unexpectedly enough, in the dry desert of *A Mirror for Magistrates*[1], among the intermixed conversations of the earlier part. And, some years later, the first wholly and really critical tractate devoted to English letters is again prosodic. This is the somewhat famous *Certayne notes of Instruction concerning the making of verse or ryme in English,* written at the request of Master Eduardo Donati by George Gascoigne. It may have been, to some extent, suggested by Ronsard's ten years earlier *Abrégé de l'art Poëtique Français,* but, if so, there is nothing in it of the awkward and irrelevant transference to one matter of observations originally made on matter quite different, which sometimes occurs in such cases. Indeed, the first point of likeness—that both insist upon 'some fine invention' (*le principal point est l'invention*)—is *publica materies* from the ancients. And Gascoigne's genuine absorption in his actual subject appears by his early reference to alliterative poetry in the very words of Chaucer's parson: 'to thunder in *Rym, Ram, Ruff,* by letter (quoth my master *Chaucer*).' Nor does he

[1] See the previous chapter.

waste much time in generalities, though those which he has are well to the point, as in the remark 'If I should undertake to write in praise of a gentlewoman, I would neither praise her crystal eye nor her cherry lip, etc. For these are *trita et obvia*.' Nay, he even anticipates Wordsworth's heroic *petitio principii* by saying that invention 'being found, pleasant words will follow well enough and fast enough.' A brief caution against obscurity leads to an advice to keep just measure, 'hold the same measure wherwith you begin,' for the apparent obviousness of which he apologises, observing, with only too much reason, that it was constantly neglected. A further caution, equally obvious and equally necessary, follows, on keeping natural emphasis or sound, using every word as it is commonly pronounced or used—a caution which, it is hardly necessary to say, was needed even by such a poet as Wyatt, was not quite superfluous long after Gascoigne's time and would, if observed, have killed the classical 'versing,' which Gascoigne nowhere notices save by innuendo, in its cradle.

But it is immediately after, and in connection with, this, that the most interesting and important point in the whole treatise appears, in a statement which helps us to understand, if not to accept, an impression which evidently held its ground in English poetical theory for the best part of two centuries and more. It is that 'commonly now a dayes in English rimes' (for, though he does not recommend 'versing,' he 'dare not call them English verses') 'we use none other order but a foot of two syllables, whereof the first is depressed or made short, and the second is elevate or made long,' *i.e.* the iamb. 'We have,' he says, 'used in times past other kinds of metres,' quoting an anapaestic line; and he makes the very remarkable statement that 'our father *Chaucer* hath used the same liberty in feet and measures that the Latinists do use.' He, apparently, laments the limitation, but says we must 'take the ford as we find it,' and again insists that no word is to be wrested 'from his natural and usual sound,' illustrating his position. He deprecates the use of polysyllables as un-English and unpleasant; of rime without reason; of unusual words, save with 'discretion,' in order to 'draw attentive reading'; of too great insecurity and too great facility; of unnatural inversion. But he allows that 'shrewd fellow . . . poetical license.' These things, though in most, but not all, cases right and sensible and quite novel from an English pen, are almost trivial. Not so his pronouncement on pauses—'rests' or 'ceasures.' He admits these to be 'at discretion,' especially in rime royal, but again exhibits the stream of tendency in the most invaluable manner, by prescribing, as best, the middle syllable in octosyllables and alexandrines, the fourth in decasyllables and the eighth in fourteeners. The term rime royal reminds him that he should explain it and other technicalities, which he proceeds to do, including in his explanation the somewhat famous term 'poulter's measure' for the couplet of alexandrine and fourteener popular in the mid-sixteenth century. And he had forgotten 'a notable kind of ryme, called ryding ryme, such as our Mayster and Father *Chaucer* used in his Canterburie tales.' It is, he thinks, most apt for a merry tale, rime royal for a grave discourse. And so, judiciously relegating 'poulter's measure' by a kind of afterthought to psalms and hymns, he ends the first, one of the shortest but, taking it altogether, one of the most sensible and soundest, of all tractates on prosody in English and one of our first documents in criticism generally. Incidentally, it supplies us with some important historical facts as to language, such as that 'treasure' was not pronounced 'treasùre,' that to make a dissyllable of 'Heaven' was a licence—Mitford, two centuries later, thought the monosyllabic pronunciation vulgar and almost impossible—and the like.

It is very difficult to exaggerate the importance of the appearance in this work—the first prosodic treatise in English, and one written just on the eve of the great Elizabethan period—of the distinct admission, all the more distinct because of its obvious reluctance, that the iamb is the only foot in English serious rime, and of the preference for middle caesuras. As symptoms, these things show us the not unnatural recoil and reaction from the prosodic disorderliness of the fifteenth century and the earliest part of the sixteenth, just as Gascoigne's protests against wrenching accent show the sense of dissatisfaction even with the much improved rhythm of Wyatt and Surrey. But they also forecast, in the most noteworthy fashion, the whole tendency towards a closely restricted syllabic and rhythmical uniformity which, after several breakings-away, resulted in the long supremacy of the stopped, centrally divided, decasyllabic couplet as *the* metre of metres, from which, or compared with which, all others were declensions and licences. The reader may be reminded that, even before Gascoigne, there are interesting, and not much noticed, evidences of the same revulsion from irregular metres in the prose inter-chapters of *A Mirror for Magistrates.*

Gascoigne, however, had been purely prosodic; the current of Elizabethan criticism, increasing very largely in volume shortly after his time, took a different direction, except in so far as it still now and then dealt with the delusion of classical 'versing.' George Whetstone, in his dedication of *Promos and Cassandra* (1578), touched, briefly, on the disorderliness of the English stage, and its contempt alike of unity and probability. But, immediately after this, a quarrel, half critical, half ethical, arose over the subject of drama and poetry generally, a quarrel which is the first thing of the kind in English literary history and which enriched English criticism with its first work of distinct literary importance for authorship, range and quality. The challenge of this quarrel was Stephen Gosson's famous *School of Abuse* (1579) with its appendix of pamphlets; the chief feat of arms in it was Sir Philip Sidney's *Apologie for Poetrie* or *Defence of Poesie* (not printed till 1595 but certainly written before 1583). Gosson had dedicated his work to Sidney; and Sir Philip, showing a sense of literary manners which, unfortunately, has never been too common, abstains from replying directly to his dedicator, though his whole argument is destructive of Gosson's. Others were less scrupulous, and, indeed, had less reason for scruple; and Thomas Lodge, in a pamphlet the exact title of which is lost, takes up the cudgel in all but the full tone of Elizabethan 'flyting.' This reply, however, as well as Gosson's original attack and its sequels, has very little really literary criticism in it. Gosson, himself a playwright for some time, seems to have been suddenly convinced, probably by a conversion to puritanism, of the sinfulness of poetry generally, and the line of stricture which he takes is almost wholly moral; while, not unnaturally, he is followed, for the most part, in this line, by Lodge who, however, indulges in a certain amount of rather confused comment and eulogium on the classics. In the time and circumstances it was certain that Sidney would, to some extent, do the same; his strain, however, is not only of a much higher mood but also of a wider and a more varied.

Beginning, with a touch of humour, on the tendency of everybody to extol his own vocation, he plunges, almost at once, into the stock defence of poetry: from its age and the wonders ascribed to it of old; its connection with philosophy; the way in which Plato is poetical even in his onslaughts upon it; its time-honoured and world-spread vogue; the high and incomparable titles of '*poietes*,' '*vates*,' 'maker'; its command of every kind of subject, vying with nature in something like creation; its connection with Divinity itself. Then he sketches its kinds, and insists upon the poet's nobleness as against all competitors, setting him above both philosopher and historian. Examples of excellence for imitation, and of misdoing for avoidance, are given. The poet has all, 'from Dante his heven to his hell,' under the authority of his pen. After much on this, he returns to the kinds—examining and dismissing objections to pastoral, elegy and what not. At this point, he makes a sweep towards his special subject of drama, but touches it lightly and goes off to the heroic, whence, his preamble or exposition being finished, he comes to 'poet-haters,' the name, and even the person, of Gosson being carefully left in obscurity. He examines and dismisses once more the stock objections—waste of time, lying, encouragement of evil desires, etc. and, of course, sets the excellence of use against the possibility of abuse. And so, all generalities done (the famous commendation of *Chevy Chace*, 'Percy and Duglas,' has occurred long before), he shapes his concluding course towards English poetry, to find out why England has 'growne so hard a stepmother' towards poets; why there is such a cold welcome for poetry here. And, at this point, both the most strictly genuine criticism and the most piquant oddity of the piece begin, though it would be very unfair to Sidney not to remember that he is writing just after *The Shepheards Calender* had appeared, in the mere overture of the great Elizabethan concert.

'The verie true cause,' he thinks, 'of our wanting estimation, is want of desert, taking uppon us to be poets, in despite of Pallas.' Art, imitation and exercise, as well as mother-wit, are necessary for poetry, and English poets use neither art nor imitation rightly. Chaucer 'did excellently' but had 'great wants,' a sentence which surprises the reader less when he finds that *A Mirror for Magistrates* is 'meetly furnished of bewtiful partes.' *The Shepheards Calender* 'hath much Poetrie in his Egloges, indeed woorthie the reading.' But Sidney 'dare not allow' the framing of even his own familiar friend's language to a rustic style, 'since neither Theocritus in Greeke, Virgill in Latine, nor Sanazara in Italian, did affect it.' Besides these (he had duly praised Surrey), he 'remembers to have seen few printed that had poetical sinews in them' and, looking back from 1580 to 1530, as he is evidently doing, one cannot much wonder. Then he accumulates wrath on the infant drama—again, be it remembered, before Peele, before Lyly, before Marlowe, or just when their earliest work was appearing. But his wrath is bestowed upon it for the very things that were to make the greatness, not only of these three, but of Shakespeare and all the rest. Our tragedies and comedies observe rules 'neither of honest civilitie nor skilfull Poetrie,' excepting *Gorboduc*, which itself is not faultless. It is faulty in place and time: all the rest are faulty not only in these but in action. And then we have the often quoted passage satirising the 'free' drama in all these respects, with a further censure of the mixture of tragedy and comedy, and an aspiration after the limiting of comedy to Terentian-Plautine types and of tragedy to the 'divine admiration' excited by the tragedies of Buchanan. 'Our Songs and Sonets' are frigid, etc., etc. He insinuates, rather than definitely advances, a suggestion that English should use both riming and 'versing.' And he ends with a half-enthusiastic, half-satirical peroration on 'the Planet-like Music of Poetrie.'

The quaint perversity of all this, and the still quainter revenge which time took on it by making the next fifty years and more a flourishing time of English poetry in almost direct consequence of the neglect of Sidney's censures, is a commonplace. It ought to be as much a commonplace to repeat the sufficient explanation of it—that he lacked the basis and *sine qua non* of all sound criticism, to wit, a sufficient quantity of precedent good poetry. But, of late, considerable interest has been taken in the question whether he got his principles from specific or general sources; and there has been a tendency to regard him as specially echoing not merely Scaliger but the Italian critic Minturno. There are, no doubt, coincidences with these two, and, especially, with Minturno; but it is the opinion of the present writer that Sidney was rather familiar with the general drift of Italian criticism than following any special authority.

The *Discourse of English Poetrie* which William Webbe, a Cambridge graduate and private tutor in the house of an Essex squire, published in 1586, is far below Sidney's in learning, in literary skill and, above all, in high sympathy with the poetic spirit. But Webbe is enthusiastic for poetry according to his lights; he has the advantage of writing later; and his dealings with his subject are considerably less 'in the air.' He even attempts a historical survey—the first thing that ought to have been done and the last that actually was done—but deficiency of information and confusion of view are wofully evident in this. Gower is the first English poet that he has heard of; though he admits that Chaucer may have been equal in time. But it does not seem that he had read anything of Gower's, though that poet was easily accessible in print. He admires Chaucer, but in a rather suspiciously general way; thinks Lydgate 'comparable with him for meetly good proportion of verse' and 'supposes that Piers Ploughman was next.' Of the supposed author of this poem, he makes the strange, but very informing, remark that he is 'the first who observed the quantity of our verse without the curiosity of rhyme.' He knows Skelton; does not, apparently, know Wyatt; speaks again strangely of 'the *old* earl of Surrey'; but, from Gascoigne onwards, seems fairly acquainted with the first Elizabethans, especially commending Phaer, Golding and Googe, and thinking Anthony Munday's work 'very rare poetry' in giving 'the sweet sobs of Shepherds,' an estimate which has had much to do with the identification of Munday and 'Shepherd Tony.' But Webbe's judgment is too uncertain to be much relied on.

Still, it must be to his eternal honour that he admires Spenser, lavishly and ungrudgingly, while not certain that the author of *The Shepheards Calender* is Spenser. He is deeply bitten with the mania for 'versing'; and a great part of the tractate is occupied with advice and experiments in relation to it and with abuse of rime. He actually tries to 'verse' some of the most beautiful lines of the *Calender* itself, and hopes that Spenser and Harvey (whom he evidently thinks Spenser's equal) will 'further that reformed kind of poetry.' So that, once more, though Webbe is not to be compared with Sidney in any other way, we find a strange and almost laughable similarity in their inability to 'orientate' themselves—to put themselves at the real English point of view. If one had had his way, we should have had no Shakespeare; if the other had had his, we should never have had the true Spenser.

Somewhat earlier than Webbe's little book there had, apparently, been written, and, somewhat later (1589), there was published, a much more elaborate *Arte of English Poesie*, which is a sort of combination of a *Poetic* and a *Rhetoric* especially copious on the subject of figures. It appeared anonymously, the printer even saying (but this was not a very uncommon trick) that it 'came into his hands without any author's name.' That of Puttenham was not attached to it for another quarter of a century. Until quite recently, it has been usual to identify the author with a certain George Puttenham. Arguments for preferring his brother Richard were put forward so long ago as 1883, by Croft, in his edition of *The Governour* of Sir Thomas Elyot, a relation of the Puttenhams; but little notice was taken of them for a time. Of late, Richard Puttenham has been the favourite, without, in the present writer's judgment, much cause.

The fact is that there are arguments against both the Puttenhams, and there is little more than presumption in favour of either. The authorship, however, is of little or no importance; the book is a remarkable one. It is quite evidently written by a courtier, a man of some age, who represents all but the earliest Elizabethan generation, but one who has survived to witness the advent of Spenser, and who is well acquainted with the as yet unpublished work of Sidney. He has pretty wide reading, and is something of a scholar—the extraordinary names of some of his figures are, probably, a printer's blunder. He knows rather more about English poetry than Webbe, for he does not omit Wyatt; but he includes the chronicler Harding in a fashion which raises suspicions. Still, that 'Piers Plowman's verse is but loose metre' is a distinct improvement. Contemporaries, with the inclusion of 'the Queene our Sovereign Lady,' who, of course, 'easily surmounteth all the rest,' are judged not unhappily—Sidney and 'that other gentleman who wrote the late *Shepherds Calendar*' being praised for eclogue and pastoral; Ralegh's verse receiving the memorable phrase 'most lofty, insolent and passionate,' while the attribution of 'sweet solemn and high conceit' to Dyer, of 'a good metre and a plentiful vein' to Gascoigne and of 'learned and well corrected' verse to Phaer and Golding, is, in none of these instances, unhappy. And the distinct recognition of Surrey and Wyatt as 'the two chief lanterns of light to all others that have since employed their pens in English poesy' deserves the highest praise. It is, in fact, except the traditional and parrot-like *encomia* on Chaucer, the first *jalon*—the first clear and firm staking out of English poetical history. Puttenham, however, is chiefly busy, as his title justified him in being, with the most strictly formal side of poetry—with its art. He will not allow feet, for a reason which, at any rate in his own statement of it, is far from clear, but seems to have a confused idea that individual English words are seldom complete feet of any kind, and that we have too many monosyllables. But he is exact in the enumeration of 'measures' by syllables, and of 'staffs' by lines, pushing his care, in this respect, so far as to give careful diagrams of the syllabic outline, and the rime-connection of these latter. In fact, Puttenham is nothing if not diagrammatic; and his leaning in this direction makes him very complacent towards the purely artificial forms—eggs, altars, lozenges, rhombi—which were to be the object of much ridicule. He is also copious (though he regards it with lukewarm approval) on classical 'versifying'; and, in fact, spares no pains to make his work a manual of practical directions for manufacturers of verse. These directions occupy the whole of his second book—'of proportion' as he calls it. The third—'of ornament'—is almost wholly occupied by the elaborate list of figures above referred to. His fourth, 'of Poets and Poesy,' contains the history also mentioned, and a good deal of stock matter as to the kinds of poetry, its ethical position and purport, an enquiry into the origin and history of rime (much less prejudiced and much better informed than the strictures of the 'versers') and several other things. Puttenham, it is clear, is, to some extent, hampered and led astray by the common form and commonplace of the school rhetorics which he is trying to adjust to English poetic; and he has the enormous disadvantage of writing twenty years too soon. If his *Arte of Poesie* could have been informed by the spirit, and enriched by the experience, of Daniel's *Defence of Ryme*, or if Daniel had cared to extend and particularise this latter in the manner, though not quite on the principles, of Puttenham, we should possess a book on English prosody such as we do not yet possess and perhaps never shall. As it is, there is a great deal of 'dead wood' in the *Arte*. But it is none the less a document of the highest value and interest historically, as showing the seriousness with which the formal and theoretical side of poetry was, at last and after almost utter neglect, being taken in England. It may owe something to Sidney—Gregory Smith has well observed that all these critical writers, long before Sidney's tract was published, evidently knew it in MS. But by far the greater part of it is devoted to exactly the matters that Sidney did not touch.

Sir John Harington, in that preface to his *Ariosto* which he rightly calls, rather, a brief apology of poetry and of the author and translator, refers directly to Sidney and, indeed, travels over much the same ground in the general part of his paper; but he acquires independent interest when he comes to deal with his special subject. Indeed, one may, perhaps, say that his is the first 'critical introduction' in English, if we except 'E.K.'s' to the *Calender*. It is interesting to find him at once striking out for the rope which, down to Addison, if not still later, the critic who felt himself out of his depth in pure appreciation always tried to seize—the tracing of resemblances in his author to the ancients, in this case to Vergil. One might, indeed, be inclined to think that, except in point of adventure, no two poets could possibly be more unlike than the author of the *Aeneid* and the author of

Orlando. But Sir John does not consider so curiously. There is *arma* in the first line of the one and *arme* in the first line of the other; one ends with the death of Turnus and the other with that of Rodomont; there is glorification of the Julian house in one and glorification of the house of Este in the other. In fact, 'there is nothing of any special observation in Vergil but my author hath with great felicity imitated it.' Now, if you imitate Vergil, you must be right. Did not 'that excellent Italian poet, Dant' profess that, when he wandered out of the right way, Vergil reclaimed him? Moreover, Ariosto 'hath followed Aristotle's rules very strictly' and, though this assertion may almost take the reader's breath away, Harington manages to show some case for it in the same Fluellinian fashion of argument which has just been set forth in relation to Vergil. Nor ought we to regard this with any contempt. Defensible or indefensible, it was the method of criticism which was to be preferred for the greater part of at least two centuries. And Harington has a few remarks of interest in regard to his own metre, rime, and such matters.

The illiberal, and, to some tastes, at any rate, rather wearisome, 'flyting' between Harvey and Nashe over the dead body of Greene necessarily contains a large number of passages which are critical after a fashion—indeed, the names of most writers of the strictly Elizabethan period will be found with critical epithets or phrases attached to them. But the whole is so thoroughly subdued to the general tone of wrangling that any pure critical spirit is, necessarily, absent. Nashe, with his usual faculty of hard hitting, says to his foe, 'You will never leave your old tricks of drawing Master Spenser into every piebald thing you do.' But the fact is that both merely use other men of letters as offensive or defensive weapons for their own purposes.

A few, but only a few, fragments of criticism strictly or approximately Elizabethan may now be noticed. These are *The Excellency of the English Tongue* by Richard Carew (1595—6 ?), a piece in which patriotism reinforces itself with a good amount of knowledge; the critical prefatory matter of Chapman's *Iliad* (or, rather, its first instalments in 1598), which contains a vigorous onslaught on Scaliger for his 'soulblind impalsied diminuation' of Homer; Drayton's interesting prosodic note (1603) on his own change of metre, etc., when he rehandled *Mortimeriados* into *The Barons Wars* (his still more interesting verse epistle to Reynolds is much later); Meres's famous catalogue of contemporary wits (1598), known to everyone for its references to Shakespeare, but in no part or respect discovering much critical ability; passages of William Vaughan (1600), Edmund Bolton and a few others. But the last of all strictly Elizabethan discussion of matters literary, and almost the most valuable part of it, is the notable duel between Thomas Campion and Samuel Daniel on the question of rime.

These two tractates, entitled, respectively, *Observations in the Art of English Poesy* and *A defence of Ryme*, appeared in the second and, probably, the third years of the new century, and both the attack and the defence exhibit a most noteworthy alteration when we compare them with the disquisitions on 'versing' from fifty to ten years earlier. 'Nothing keeps the same,' except Campion's abuse of the rime that he had used, was using and was to use with such charm. The earlier discussions could hardly be called controversies, because there was practically nothing said on behalf of rime—unless the silent consensus of all good poets in continuing to practise it may be allowed to be more eloquent than any positive advocacy. And nearly (not quite) the whole energy of the attack had been employed, not merely to dethrone rime, but to instal directly classical metres, especially hexameters and elegiacs, in the place of it. Campion still despises rime; but he throws the English hexameter overboard with perfect coolness, without the slightest compunction and, indeed, with nearly as much contempt as he shows towards rime itself. 'The Heroical verse that is distinguished by the dactyl hath oftentimes been attempted in our English tongue but with passing pitiful success,' and no wonder, seeing that it is 'an attempt altogether against the nature of our language.' Accordingly, in the 'reformed unrhymed numbers' which he himself proceeds to set forth, he relies, in the main, on iambs and trochees, though (and this is his distinguishing characteristic and his saving merit) he admits not merely spondees but dactyls, anapaests (rarely) and even tribrachs as substitutes. By the aid of these he works out eight kinds of verse: the 'pure iambic' or decasyllabic[1], the 'iambic dimeter or English march,' which, in strict classical terminology, is an iambic (or trochaic) monometer hypercatalectic[2], the English trochaic, a trochaic decasyllable[3], the English elegiac,

[1] The more secure the more the stroke we feel.
(*With licence of substitution.*)

[2] Raving war, begot
In the thirsty sands.

[3] Kate can only fancy beardless husbands.

an eccentric and not very harmonious combination of an ordinary iambic decasyllable and of two of his 'dimeters' run together[1], the English sapphic[2], a shortened form of this[3], a peculiar quintet[4] and the English anacreontic[5].

He ends with an attempt, as arbitrary and as unsuccessful as Stanyhurst's, to determine the quantity of English syllables on a general system: *e.g.* the last syllables of plurals, with two or more vowels before the *s*, are long, etc.

The *Defence of Ryme* with which Daniel replied is, time and circumstance being duly allowed for, one of the most admirable things of its kind in English literature. It is perfectly polite—a merit not too common in criticism at any time, and particularly rare in the sixteenth and the seventeenth centuries. Indeed, Daniel, though it would not appear that there was personal acquaintance between him and Campion, has the combined good taste and good sense (for it is a powerful argument on his own side) to compliment his adversary on his own success with rime. His erudition is not impeccable; but it is sufficient. He devotes some, but not much, attention to the 'eight kinds of verses,' making the perfectly true, and very damaging, observation that they are all perfectly consonant with the admitted practice of English poetry, and that they wantonly divest themselves of the additional charm that they might derive from the rime usual in it. But, with true critical sense, he sticks in the main to the chief point—the unreason of the objection to rime, and the futility of the arguments or no-arguments by which it had been supported. 'Our understandings are not all to be built by the square of Greece and Italy.' 'Ill customs are to be left,' but what have we save bare assertion to prove that rime is an ill custom? Let the ancients have done well without it;

[1] Constant to none but ever false to me,
Traitor still to love through thy faint desires.

[2] Faith's pure shield, the Christian Diana,
England's glory crowned with all divineness,
Live long with triumphs to bless thy people
At thy sight triumphing.

[3] Rose-cheeked Laura, come,
Sing thou smoothly with thy beauty's
Silent music, either other
Sweetly gracing.

[4] Just beguiler,
Kindest love yet only chastest,
Royal in thy smooth denials,
Frowning or demurely smiling
Still my pure delight.

[5] Follow, follow
Though with mischief.

is that any reason why we should be forbidden to do well with it? Let us 'tend to perfection' by 'going on in the course we are in.' He admits blank verse freely in drama and allows, not less freely, that rime may be abused. But he will defend the 'sacred monuments of English,' the 'best power of our speech, that wherein so many honourable spirits have sacrificed to Memory their dearest passions,' the 'kind and natural attire of Rhyme,' which 'adds more grace and hath more delight than ever bare numbers can yield.' And so, with no bombast or slop of rhetoric, but with that quiet enthusiasm which is the inspiration of his own best poetry, and that simple propriety of style which distinguishes him both in poetry and prose, Daniel lays down, almost or quite for the first time in English, the great principle that 'the Dorians may speak Doric,' that each language and each literature is entitled to its own ways and its own fashions. It is curious enough that Ascham, who, long before, had begun by the sturdy determination to write English matters in the English tongue for Englishmen, should, also, have been the first to be false to this principle in the prosodic direction. Daniel, two generations after *Toxophilus*, establishes the principle in this department also.

The critical work of two of the greatest of Elizabethans, Bacon and Ben Jonson, falls, both logically and chronologically, into other chapters, and represents, wholly in Bacon's case, almost wholly in Jonson's, a different and more advanced stage of criticism. Yet something of what we are about to say applies to them also, and it may be of hardly less use as a preliminary to the study of them than as a summary and criticism of the positive results which have been presented in historical survey by the foregoing pages.

Until the provision of increased facilities for study which has been given during the last thirty years or so by the labours of many scholars, there was some excuse for want of clear comprehension of the importance of Elizabethan criticism. But there is no such excuse now; though it is doubtful whether, even yet, the subject has generally received from students the attention that it deserves. The episode—if the term may be applied to a passage at the beginning of an action—is an interesting, and almost entirely normal, example of the peculiar English way of proceeding in such matters, the way which is euphemistically described as that of tentative experiment, but which has received from political plain speaking the description of 'muddling through.' After such purely preliminary attitudes to criticism as those of Chaucer and Caxton, men, about the second quarter of the sixteenth century, perceive that some theory of English writing, and some regular adjustment of practice to that theory, is advisable, if not positively necessary; and that the advisability, if not even the necessity, is more especially applicable to verse-writing. But, so far as regards English itself, they have absolutely no precedent; they have a century of very dubious practice immediately behind them, and hardly any knowledge of what is beyond that century, except in regard to one very great writer, and one or two smaller ones, who are separated from them by a great gulf in pronunciation, vocabulary and thought. On the other hand, in the ancient languages and literatures they have not merely models of practice universally accepted as peerless, but theoretical treatises, numerous and elaborate; while the more accomplished modern languages, also, offer something in precept and more in practice. It is almost inevitable that they should do what they do do—should apply ancient and foreign-modern principles to English without sufficient consideration whether application is possible and desirable. Hence, the too famous English 'heroic'; hence, the cumbering and lumbering of the new English rhetoric with matter which may have been not at all cumbrous or lumbering in its original place. Hence, the ready adoption of the interesting, but, to a great extent, irrelevant and otiose, discussions about the abstract virtue of poetry. Hence, the undue haste to teach the infant, or hardly adolescent, drama the way it should go, without waiting to see what would come of the way in which it was going.

It was a partial misfortune—but partial only because the efforts made were far better than none at all—that the chief and most abundant modern critical treatises available were either mere echoes of the classics or devoted to a modern language—Italian—which has but small affinities with English. The Spanish critics began just too late to give much assistance, even had English writers been disposed to take lessons from Spain; and, in their own country, their voices were soon whelmed. The French required very careful reading not to do more harm than good. And, above all, behind the whole of at least poetical, and especially prosodic, criticism, there was easily perceivable, though, perhaps, not consciously perceived, the dread of relapse into doggerel—the aspiration after order, civility, accomplishment, as contrasted with 'barbarous and balductoom' vernacularity. And, outside the strictly literary sphere, numerous influences determined or affected some, at least, of the issues of criticism: the puritan distrust of poetry and, specially, of the stage; the Anglican dislike of possible

Roman influences in foreign literature, the contempt of the whole period for medieval things.

Yet it is remarkable how, from the very first and throughout, there is a glimmering sense that, after all, English must 'do for itself'—that 'the kingdom is within,' here as elsewhere. In the act of abusing rime and recommending 'verse,' Ascham admits more than a misgiving as to whether the English hexameter is possible. In the act of limiting English poetry as a matter of actual observation to dissyllabic feet, Gascoigne is careful to remark that 'we have had' others, and, apparently, rather wishes that we may have them again; while it is remarkable how directly he goes to the positive material of actual poetry for the source of his rules. Sidney, classiciser as he is, practically assures us, by that famous confession as to *Chevy Chace*, that we need be under no apprehension but that English verse will always appeal to the Englishman as no other can. A rather sapless formalist like Puttenham does adopt, and with not so very scanty knowledge, that historical method in which all salvation lies; and so, in his more blundering way, does even an enthusiast for innovation like Webbe. Finally, we find Daniel striking into and striking out in the full stream of truth. 'We shall best tend to perfection by going on in the course we are in.' *Tu contra audentior ito!*

Yet, at the same time, the critical literature of the period not less distinctly avoids the mistake, too well known elsewhere, of neglecting the comparative study of other languages and literatures, ancient as well as modern. Indeed, half the mistakes that it does make may be said to come from overdoing this comparison. At the particular stage, however, this mattered very little. It was, undoubtedly, up to this period, a defect of English that, though constantly translating and imitating, it had translated and imitated, if not quite unintelligently, yet with no conscious and critical intelligence—in a blind and instinctive sort of way. This is now altered. Sidney's not daring to allow Spenser's 'framing of his style to an olde rusticke language ... since neither Theocritus ... Virgill ... nor Sanazara ... did affect it,' is, indeed, altogether wrong. It is wrong, as a matter of fact, to some extent, as regards Theocritus; it is inconsistent as ranking a mere modern like Sanazzaro, of certainly no more authority than Spenser himself, with Theocritus and Vergil; and it is a *petitio principii* in its assumption that Greeks, or Latins, or Italians, can serve as prohibitory precedents —as forbidders, merely by the fact of not having done a thing— to Englishmen. But the process is literary and critical, if the procedure and application are erroneous. English, so to speak, is, at least, 'entered' in the general academy of literatures; it submits itself to competition and to co-examination; it is no longer content to go on—not, indeed, as Ascham vainly says, 'in a foul wrong way' but—in an uncultivated and thoughtless way. It is taking stock and making audit of itself, investigating what has been done and prospecting for what is to be done. Nor should it be forgotten that there is such work as Mulcaster's, which, though not strictly literary criticism, is linguistic and scholastic criticism of no unliterary kind. Mulcaster[1], in his *Positions* and *Elementary*, following Thynne and others, almost founds the examination of the language itself; as does that part of Ascham's *Scholemaster* which has hitherto been passed over and which concerns the teaching of the classical tongue by means of English—a process which, as all sound thinking on education has seen since, involves, and carries with it, the teaching of English by means of the classical tongues. The whole body of effort in this kind is one great overhauling of the literary and linguistic resources of the nation—a thing urgently required, long neglected, yet, perhaps, not possible to have been attempted with any real prospect of benefit until this particular time.

Nor would it be wise to over-estimate the futility of the futilities, the mistake of the mistakes, that were committed. The worst and most prominent of them all—the craze for 'versing'—sprang from a just sense of the disorderliness of much recent English poetry, and led almost directly to the introduction of a new and better order. As for what may seem to us the idle expatiations on the virtues of poetry in the abstract, or the superfluous defences of it, these were things which, according to all precedent, had to be gone through, and to be got over. Even on the side where there was still most to seek—the diligent and complete exploring of the actual possessions of English in a really historical spirit—more must have been done than is obvious on the surface, or we should not be able to find, a few years after Elizabeth's death, a man like William Browne acquainted with the poems of Occleve, who had never been favoured by the early printers, and actually reproducing Occleve's work among his own. That there was even some study of Old English is well known. On the whole, therefore, though these various efforts were not well co-ordinated, and, in many cases, not even well directed to their immediate objects, it would be the grossest of errors to belittle or misprise them; and

[1] See also chap. XIX.

it is only a pity that the taste for critical enquiry was not better represented in the first two generations of the seventeenth century itself. For, in that case, Dryden, who actually availed himself of what he could get from Jonson, would have found far more to go upon; and, with his own openness of mind and catholicity of appreciation, would have done even more than he did to keep his successors in turn from falling into that pit of ignorant contempt for older literature which engulfed too many of them. Even as it was, the Elizabethan critics did something to give pause to the hasty generalisation that periods of criticism and periods of creation cannot coincide. If they did not lay much of a foundation, Gascoigne, Sidney and Daniel, in their different ways, did something even in this way; they did a good deal towards clearing the ground and a good deal more towards surveying it. It is unfortunate, and it is a little curious, that they did not devote more attention to prose, especially as their guides, the ancients, had left them considerable assistance; but they were, no doubt, misled (as, for that matter, the ancients themselves were, to a great extent) by the exclusively rhetorical determination of ancient criticism in this respect. For poetry, however, they did not a little; and, after all, there are those who say that by 'literature' most people mean poetry.

CHAPTER XV

CHRONICLERS AND ANTIQUARIES

THE chroniclers and antiquaries of the Tudor period, various as they were in style and talent, shared the same sentiment, the same ambition. There breathed in each one of them the spirit of nationality. They recognised that the most brilliant discovery of a brilliant age was the discovery of their own country. With a full voice and a fervent heart they sang the praise of England. They celebrated with what eloquence they possessed her gracious climate, her fruitful soil, her brave men and her beautiful women. Both by precept and by example they did honour to their native tongue. 'Our English tongue,' said Camden, 'is as fluent as the Latin, as courteous as the Spanish, as Court-like as the French, and as amorous as the Italian.' Camden praised by precept alone, and composed all his works, save one, in Latin. The other chroniclers, discarding Latin and writing in their own English, paid the language a far higher tribute—the tribute of example. All agreed with Plutarch that 'a part of the Elisian Fields is to be found in Britain.' And, as they regarded these fair fields with enthusiasm, so they looked back with pride upon Britain's legendary history and the exploits of her kings. Steadfast in observation, tireless in panegyric, they thought no toil, no paean, outran the desert of England. Topographers, such as Camden and Leland, travelled the length and breadth of England, marking high road, village and township, collecting antiquities, copying inscriptions and painting with what fidelity they might the face of the country. The ingenuity of Norden and Speed designed the maps which have acquired with time an unexpected value and importance. The popular historians, gentle and simple, gathered the truth and falsehood of the past with indiscriminate hand, content if they might restore to the world the forgotten splendour of England, and add a new lustre to England's ancient fame.

Their good will and patriotism were limited only by their talent.

Zealous in intention, they were not always equal to the task they set themselves. The most of them had but a vague sense of history. They were as little able to sift and weigh evidence as to discern the true sequence and meaning of events. Few of them were even dimly interested in the conflict of policies or in the science of government. What they best understood were the plain facts of battle and death, of plague and famine, of sudden comets and strange monsters. The most of their works are the anecdotage of history, and not to be wholly despised on that account, since an anecdote false in itself is often the symbol of the truth, and since, in defiance of research, it is from the anecdotes of the Tudor chroniclers that we derive our knowledge of English history. For that which had been said by others they professed an exaggerated respect. They accepted the bare word of their predecessors with a touching credulity. In patient submission and without criticism they followed the same authorities. There is no chronicler that did not use such poor light as Matthew Paris and Roger Hoveden, Geoffrey of Monmouth and Gildas, Giraldus Cambrensis and Polydore Vergil could afford. Each one of them borrowed his description of Agincourt from Titus Livius, and, with a wisdom which deserves the highest applause, they all adapted to their purpose the account of Richard III's reign attributed to Sir Thomas More. With one or two exceptions, then, the *Chronicles* are not so much separate works as variations of the same legend. Their authors pillaged from one another with a light heart and an unsparing hand, and, at times, did what they could to belittle their robberies by abusing the victims.

If their sense of history was small, small also was their tact of selection. They looked upon the world with the eye of the modern reporter. They were hot upon the discovery of strange 'stories.' They loved freaks of nature and were never so happy as when a new star flashed into their ken. Their works, indeed, hold a place midway between history and what we should now call journalism. Stow, for instance, tells us that, in 1505, 'on S. Thomas Day at night, afore Christmas was a bakers house in Warwike Lane brent, with the Mistres of the House, ii women servants, and iii others'; and he brings his *Chronicle* to an end, not upon the praise of England or of queen Elizabeth but upon a monstrous birth. 'The XVII day of June last past,' he writes, in the year 1580, 'in the parish of Blamsdon, in Yorkshire, after a great tempest of lightning and thunder, a woman of foure score years old named Ales Perin, was delivered of a straunge and hideous Monster, whose heade was like unto a sallet or heade-peece.... Which Monster,' adds Stow, devoutly, 'brought into the world no other news, but an admiration of the devine works of God.' Not even Camden, scholar though he was, rose always superior to the prevailing habit of gossip. 'I know not,' he writes, under the year 1572, 'whether it be materiall or no, here to make mention, as all the Historiographers of our time have done, how in the moneth of November was seene a strange starre.' And, presently, he interrupts his account of a mission to Russia, in 1583, with this comment upon Sir Hierome Bowes, the ambassador:

> Hee was the first that brought into England, where the like was never seene (if an Historian may with good leave make mention of so small a thing) a beast called *Maclis*, which is a creature likest to an Alçe, very swift, and without joynts.

Camden at least apologised for his amiable irrelevancy, and it is not for modern readers to regret a practice which has preserved for them the foolish trivial excitements of the moment. But it is a truth not without significance that the chroniclers, who might have kept before their eyes the example of the classics, and who might have studied the two masters of what was then modern history—Macchiavelli and Commines—should have preferred to follow in the footsteps of the medieval gossips and of the ambling Fabyan. And, as they thought no facts too light to be recorded, so they considered no age too dark for their investigation. They penetrated, with a simple faith, 'the backward and abysm of time.' The most of them begin their histories with Brute, who, they say, was born 1108 B.C., and thus prove that, for all their large interests and their love of life, they were not without a spice of that pedantry which delights to be thought encyclopaedic.

The chroniclers, then, share the same faults and the same virtues. But beyond these similarities of character there is room enough for the display of different temperaments and personal talents. Each one will be found to possess a quality or an interest which the others lack, and it is by their differences rather than by their resemblances that they must be judged. The first of them, Edward Hall, holds a place apart. Of the man himself we know little. Of gentle parentage, he was educated at Eton and King's College, Cambridge. He entered Gray's Inn in due course, was appointed common serjeant of the city of London in 1532 and was afterwards a judge in the sheriff's court. The first edition of his *Chronicle* was printed by Berthelet, in 1542, and was so effectively burnt by the orders of queen

Mary that it exists only in fragments. Reprinted by Grafton, in 1548 and 1550, it won and deserved esteem and is now commonly regarded, for one reign at least, as an authority at first hand. The truth is, Hall wrote as an eye-witness as well as a chronicler, and his work is naturally divided into two parts, far distant from one another both in style and substance. The title of the book gives an instant clue to this natural division. 'The Union of the two noble and illustrate famelies of Lancastre and Yorke,' thus Hall describes it in his grandiloquent language,

> beeyng long in continual discension for the croune of this noble realme, with all the actes done in bothe the tymes of the Princes, both of the one linage, and of the other, beginnyng at the tyme of Kyng Henry the Fowerth, the first aucthor of this devision, and so successively proceadyng to the reigne of the high and prudent prince, King Henry the Eight, the indubitate flower and very heire of both the sayd linages.

So far as the death of Henry VII, Hall is a chronicler after the fashion of Holinshed and Stow. He accepted the common authorities, and translated them into his own ornate English, or embellished them with new words and strange images. With the accession of Henry VIII he began a fresh and original work. Henceforth, he wrote only of what he saw and thought from day to day. And, in thus writing, he revealed most clearly what manner of man he was. His patriotism equalled his loyal worship of king Henry VIII, the greatest monarch, in Hall's eyes, who had sat upon the English throne. The reformation had his full sympathy, and he looked upon the see of Rome with protestant suspicion. When the king was proclaimed supreme head of the church, Hall's enthusiasm was unbounded. Hereafter, he says, 'the Pope with all his college of Cardinalles with all their Pardons and Indulgences was utterly abolished out of this realme. God be everlastyngly praysed therefore.' And, if he was a patriotic Englishman first, he was, in the second place, a proud and faithful Londoner. He championed the interests of his fellow-citizens with a watchful eloquence. When, in 1513, the fields about Islington, Hoxton and Shoreditch were enclosed by hedges and ditches, that youth might not shoot nor old age walk abroad for its pleasure, Hall triumphantly records that a mob of citizens, armed with shovels and spades, levelled the hedges and filled the ditches with so diligent a speed that the mayor bowed in submission, and that the hateful restraints were never afterwards set in the way of young or old. He was, moreover, the first to raise the cry of 'London for the Londoners.' He hated the alien with a constant heart, and in the many quarrels which arose between the citizens and the French artificers, Hall was always on the side of the citizens. And it was this feeling for London which intensified Hall's dislike of the proud cardinal. A student rather of the world than of politics, he could not appreciate at their proper worth the grandeur of Wolsey's schemes. He knew only that Wolsey was extortionate, that, whenever he was in need of money, he came to the city, and he echoed the cry of the aldermen: 'For Goddes sake, remembre this, that riche merchauntes in ware be bare of money.'

It has been thrown at Hall for a reproach by some of his critics that he was too keenly interested in the pomp of the court, in the shows and sights of the streets. One of his editors has gone so far in misunderstanding as to expunge or curtail many of his characteristic descriptions. This perversity seems the stranger, because a love of display was in Hall's blood. He lived in an age, and a city, of pageants. King and cardinal vied with one another in splendour and ingenuity. They found a daily excuse for some piece of well-ordered magnificence. May Day, Christmas and Twelfth Night each had its appointed festival. The king and his friends lived in a perpetual masquerade, and Hall found the right words for their every extravagance. No writer ever employed a more variously coloured vocabulary. Turn his pages where you will, and you will find brave pictures of banquets and disguises. And his style rises with the occasion. The Field of the Cloth of Gold inspires his masterpiece. The pages dedicated to this royal meeting-place are brilliant with jewels and the precious metals. Gold and the cloth of gold, tissue and hangings of cramosyn, sackbuts and clarions flash and re-echo like the refrain of a ballade,[1] and everywhere 'Bacchus birls the wine,' which 'by the conduyctes in therth ranne, to all people plentiously with red, white, and claret wyne, over whose hedde was writen in letters of Romayn in gold, *faicte bonne chere quy vouldra.*'

I have said that Hall's *Chronicle* is made up of two separate works. With a wise sense of propriety he employs two separate styles. If this distinction be not made, it is not easy to admit the justice of Ascham's famous criticism. Now, Ascham, in urging the use of epitomes, illustrates his argument thus from Hall's *Chronicle*:

As if a wise man would take Halles Cronicle, where moch good matter is quite marde with Indenture Englishe, and first change strange and inkhorne tearmes into proper, and commonlie used wordes: next, specially to wede out

> that, that is superfluous and idle, not onelie where wordes be vainlie heaped one upon an other, but also where many sentences, of one meaning, be so clowted up together, as though M. Hall had bene, not writing the storie of England, but varying a sentence in Hitching schole.

The censure implied in this passage is amply justified by the first part of Hall's *Chronicle.* Where he is adapting the words of other writers, he does not check his love of 'Indenture Englishe'; he exults in 'inkhorne tearmes'; and he 'clowtes' up his sentences with superfluous variations. But no sooner does he describe what he sees, no sooner do his brain and hand respond to his eye, than he forgets the lessons of 'Hitching schole,' and writes with a direct simplicity which in no sense deserves the reproach of Ascham. Though it is true that the simplicity of his time was not the simplicity of ours, Hall employs with excellent effect the words of familiar discourse, and records that of which he was an eye witness with an intimate sincerity, which separates him, on the one hand, from journeymen like Stow, and, on the other, from scholars like Camden and Hayward, whose ambition it was to give a classic shape and form to their prose.

Raphael Holinshed's *Chronicles of England, Scotland and Ireland* are wider in scope and more ambitious in design than the work of Hall. Though they are not more keenly critical, they are, at least, more widely comprehensive than any of their rivals. They begin with Noah and the Flood, and the history of the British Isles descends well-nigh to the day of publication. And, if Richard Stanyhurst may speak for them all, the industrious compilers took a lofty view of their craft. 'The learned,' says Stanyhurst,

> have adjudged an historie to be the marrow of reason, the cream of sapience, the sap of wisdome, the pith of judgment, the librarie of knowledge, the kernell of policie, the unfoldresse of treacherie, the kalendar of time, the lanterne of truth, the life of memorie, the doctresse of behaviour, the register of antiquitie, the trumpet of chivalrie.

If Holinshed's history were all these, it is not surprising that it was fashioned by many hands, and in nothing did the editor prove his wisdom more clearly than in the selection of his staff. Of Holinshed himself little is recorded. He came of a Cheshire family, and is said by Anthony à Wood to have been educated at Cambridge and to have been 'a minister of God's word.' All that is certain is that he took service with Wolfe, the publisher, to whom, says he, he was 'singularly beholden,' and under whose auspices he planned the *Chronicles* which bear his name. The death of Wolfe, in 1573, was no interruption to the work, and in 1578 appeared the first edition, dedicated, in the familiar terms of adulation, to Sir William Cecil, baron of Burghley. Each portion of the *Chronicles* is assigned to its author with peculiar care. The *Description of England* is William Harrison's. It is Holinshed himself who compiled the *Historie of England* from the accustomed sources. The *Description of Scotland* is a 'simple translation' made by William Harrison. His vocation, he tells us, calls him to a far other kind of study, 'and this is the cause,' he writes,

wherefore I have chosen rather, onlie with the loss of three or foure daies to translate Hector out of the Scotish (a toong verie like unto ours) than with more expence of time to devise a new, or follow the Latine copie.... How excellentlie if you consider the art, Boetius hath penned it,... the skilfull are not ignorant, but how profitablie and compendiouslie John Bellenden Archdeacon of Murrey his interpretor hath turned him from the Latine into the Scotish toong, there are verie few Englishmen that know.

From the same Hector Boece, together with Johannes Major and 'Jovian Ferreri Piedmontese,' 'interlaced sometimes with other authors,' Holinshed digested his *Historie of Scotland.* The *Description of Ireland* was the work of Richard Stanyhurst and Edmund Campion, his 'first friend and inward companion,' and Richard Hooker provided the translation of Giraldus Cambrensis, which served Ireland for a chronicle.

The work, done by many hands, preserves a uniformity of character. Holinshed, it is true, made the apology which his age seems to have demanded. 'The histories,' he says, 'I have gathered according to my skill... having had more regard to the manner than the apt penning.' Again, declaring that his speech is plain, he disclaimed any rhetorical show of elegance. Thus the Elizabethans deceived themselves. Plainness was the one virtue beyond their reach. They delighted in fine phrases and far-sought images. Even while they proclaimed their devotion to truth unadorned, they were curious in the selection of 'decking words,' and Holinshed and his colleagues wrote with the colour and dignity which were then within the reach of all. The history which was of his own compiling is of a better scholarship than we expect of the time. He cites his authorities at first hand, though he still accepts them without question; he avoids the trivialities which tempt too many of the chroniclers; and he concludes the reign of each king with a deftly drawn character. The popularity which the work achieved is not surprising. The simple citizen found in its pages the panegyric of England which was grateful to his patriotism. The poet sought therein, and sought not in vain, a present inspiration. 'Master Holinshed,' said

Spenser, 'hath much furthered and advantaged me.' Shakespeare borrowed from his pages the substance of his historical plays, and, paying him the same compliment which he paid to North, did not disdain to turn his rugged prose into matchless verse—a compliment which, of itself, is sufficient for immortality.

As Hall's *Chronicle* is memorable chiefly for the vivid sketch it affords of life as it was lived in the reign of Henry VIII, so it is Harrison's *Description of England* which gives a separate distinction to the history of Raphael Holinshed. No work of the time contains so vivid and picturesque a sketch. In his first book, Harrison makes the customary concession to the encyclopaedic habit of the Elizabethans. He begins with a description of the whole earth, accepts with a simple credulity the familiar legends and wonders gravely whether the land was ever inhabited by giants. But no sooner does he leave the province of fairy-stories for the province of fact, than he displays a knowledge as wide as his interest is deep. His is a very vigilant treatise. His theme is whatever was done or thought in the England of his day. Nothing comes amiss to him. He is as learned in the history of the church as in the speech and rascality of the Egyptian rogues, his account of whom closely follows Harman's *Caveat or Warening for Commen Corsetors.* He is eloquent concerning either university, as in duty bound, since he belonged to both. For fine and excellent workmanship he praises 'the moold of the king's chapell in Cambridge,' next to which in beauty he sets the divinity school at Oxford. For the rest, he finds perfect equality between them; they are the body of one well ordered commonwealth, divided only by distance; in brief 'they are both so deere unto me,' says he, 'as that I can not readilie tell unto whether of them I owe the most good will.' Thereafter, he discusses the food and diet of the English, approving 'our tables plentifully garnished,' and deploring the cooks of the nobility, who are 'for the most part musicall headed Frenchmen and strangers.' Our apparel and attire suggest to him a chapter of fine invective. He is the resolute enemy of foreign fashions. He cannot bear the fantastical folly of our nation more easily than Shakespeare. He is at pains to prove that nothing is more constant in England than inconstancy of attire. 'Such is our mutabilitie,' he writes

that today there is none to the Spanish guise, to morrow the French toies are most fine and delectable, ere long no such apparell as that which is after the High Almaine fashion, by and by the Turkish maner is generallie best liked of, otherwise the Morisco gounes and the Barbarian sleeves make such a comelie vesture that except it were a dog in a doublet, you shall not see anie so disguised, as are my countrie men of England.

In the same spirit he describes the building and furniture of Englishmen, their cities and towns, their fairs and markets, their gardens and orchards, their woods and marishes, their dogs, especially the mastiff or banddog, 'stubbourne, ougly, eagre, burthenous of body (and therefore but of little swiftnesse), terrible and feareful to behold, and more fearse and fell than any Archadien curre.' And to all things animate and inanimate he brings the criticism of an active and humorous mind, which not even patriotism can warp to a false judgment.

And, in describing England, he has half knowingly described himself. It is our own fault if this amiable, shrewd and scholarly parson be not our familiar friend. Born in London, in 1534, he was educated at Westminster school and (as has been said) took his degrees at both universities. Henceforth, he lived the tranquil life of a country clergyman, endowed with forty pounds a year, which, *computatis computandis*, he thought no great thing. He was household chaplain to Sir William Brooke and rector of Radwinter in Essex, and, wherever he sojourned, he pursued most zealously the calling of scholar and antiquary. He devised the chronology which served as a guide to Holinshed. He collected coins, he examined monuments; in brief, he neglected nothing which could throw a light upon the history of his country. While his wife and her maids brewed his beer with such skill and economy 'that for my twentie shillings I have ten score gallons of beere or more,' he boasted of his garden, whose whole area was little above 300 foot of ground, and which yet contained three hundred simples, 'no one of them being common or usuallie to be had.' An untravelled man, he wrote often of what he knew only by hearsay. 'Untill nowe of late,' he confesses to Sir W. Brooke,

> except it were from the parish where I dwell, unto your Honour in Kent; or out of London where I was borne, unto Oxford and Cambridge where I have bene brought up, I never travelled 40 miles foorthright and at one journey in all my life.

And not only was he something of a recluse, but he wrote his *Description* when his books and he 'were parted by fourtie miles in sunder.' Nevertheless, he managed to consult the best authorities. He was one of the unnumbered scholars who owed a debt to Leland's famous notes. Stow and Camden were of his friends, and, doubtless, lent him their aid, and he acknowledges a debt to 'letters and pamphlets, from sundrie places and shires of England.' Yet, if we leave his first book out of our count, he was far less beholden than the most of his contemporaries. He had the skill of making the facts of others his own. And as the substance, so the style, of the book belongs to him. Though he proffers the same apology as Holinshed, he proffers it with far less excuse. He protests that he never made any choice of words, 'thinking it sufficient truelie and plainlie to set foorth such things as I minded to treat of, rather than with vaine affectation of eloquence to paint out a rotten sepulchre.' And then straightway he belies himself by describing his book as 'this foule frizeled Treatise of mine,' which single phrase is enough to prove his keen interest, and lively habit, in the use of words.

In love of country he yielded to no man of his age. Herein, also, he was a true Elizabethan. The situation of the island, its soil, its husbandry ('my time fellows can reape at this present great commoditie in a little roome'), the profusion of its hops, 'which industrie God continue,' the stature of its men, the comeliness of its women—all these he celebrates in his dithyrambic prose. He is one of the first to exalt the English navy. 'Certes,' says he, 'there is no prince in Europe that hath a more beautifull and gallant sort of ships than the queenes majestie of England at this present.' And, like many other patriots, he fears the encroachment of softer manners and of growing luxury. Comfort he holds the foe of hardihood. The times, in his view, were not what they were. When, indeed, have they been? He contemplates the comely houses and the splendid palaces which made a paradise of Tudor England with a kind of regret. He sadly (and unreasonably) recalls the past, when men's houses were builded of willow, plum, hornbeam and elm, when oak was dedicated to churches, palaces and navigation. 'And yet see the change,' says he, in a characteristic passage,

> for when our houses were builded of willow, then had we oken men; but now that our houses are come to be made of oke, our men are not onlie become willow, but a great manie, through Persian delicacie crept in among us, altogither of straw, which is a sore alteration.

Harrison's lament was ill-founded. In less than a score of years, the men of willow, or of straw, defended their oaken ships with oaken hearts against the armada.

Withal, Harrison was of an ingenious mind and simple character. When he had wandered, in fancy, the length and breadth of England, he wrote down in all gravity the four marvels of his country. And they were: a strong wind, which issueth out of the hills called the Peak; Stonehenge; Cheddar Hole; and 'Westward upon certeine hilles'—this may be cited only in his own words—

'a man shall see the clouds gather togither in faire weather unto a certeine thicknesse, and by and by to spread themselves abroad and water their fields about them, as it were upon the sudden.' These wonders surprise by their simplicity. Simple, also, are Harrison's wishes, yet all save one are still ungratified. 'I could wish,' he wrote,

that I might live no longer than to see foure things in this land reformed, that is: (1) the want of discipline in the church: (2) the covetous dealing of most of our merchants in the preferment of the commodities of other countries, and hinderence of their own: (3) the holding of faires and markets upon the sundaie to be abolished, and referred to the wednesdaies: (4) and that everie man, in whatsoever part of the champaine soile enjoieth fortie acres of land and upwards, after that rote, either by free deed, copie hold, or fee farme, might plant one acre of wood, or sow the same with oke mast, hasell, beech and sufficient provision be made that it may be cherished and kept.

Thus, in his wishes as in his life, Harrison was a wise patriot. He sought nothing else than a knowledge of his country, and her advantage. A scholar and a man of letters, he was master of a style from which the wind of heaven has blown the last grain of pedantry. Best of all, he painted an intimate portrait of himself, in painting also the truest picture that has come down to us of the England that Shakespeare knew and sang.

John Stow and John Speed were chroniclers of a like fashion and a like ambition. They were good citizens, as well as sound antiquaries, and, by a strange chance, they followed the same craft. 'We are beholding to Mr Speed and Stow,' writes Aubrey, echoing Sir Henry Spelman, 'for *stitching* up for us our English history. It seems they were both tailors—quod N.B.' And if Speed found a pleasanter employ, a tailor Stow remained unto the end of his days. One in their pursuits, they were one, also, in disinterestedness. The love of England and of letters brought neither of them any profit. Stow 'made no gain by his travail,' and died poor. With a sort of pathos, he pleads that men who 'have brought hidden Histories from duskie darkness to the sight of the world' deserve thanks for their pains, and should not be misrepresented. 'I write not this,' says he, 'to complain of some men's ingratitude towards me (although justly I might).' There is the pith of the matter enclosed within parentheses, and Stow, may be, was thinking of Grafton's reckless animadversion on 'the memories of superstitious foundacions, fables and lyes foolishly stowed together.' Speed lags not behind in reproach of the world, and felicitation of himself. He describes his work as 'this large Edifice of Great Britain's Theatre,' and likens himself to the silkworm, that ends her life in her long-wrought clue. 'So I in this Theatre have built my owne grave,' he writes; 'whose Architecture howsoever defective it may be said to be, yet the project is good, and the cost great, though my selfe have freely bestowed this paines to the Presse, without pressing a penny from any man's purse.' Yet neither the one nor the other complained justly of neglect. Stow won all the honour, both in his lifetime and after, which belongs to the lettered citizen. He grew into a superstition of homely wit and genial humour. Henry Holland, Philemon's son, calls him 'the merry old man,' and Fuller celebrates his virtues as Stow himself would have them celebrated. He admits that he reported toys and trifles, *res in se minutas*, that he was a smell-feast, who could not pass by Guildhall without giving his pen a taste of the good cheer, and he excuses this on the ground that 'it is hard for a citizen to write history, but that the fire of his gun may be felt therein.' So much may be truly said in dispraise. For the rest, Fuller has nothing but applause. He declares that our most elegant historians have thrown away the basket and taken the fruit—even Sir Francis Bacon and Master Camden. And 'let me add of John Stow,' he concludes, 'that (however he kept tune) he kept time very well, no author being more accurate in the notation thereof.' And Speed, even if he pressed no penny from any man's purse, did not ask the aid of any scholar in vain. Sir Robert Cotton opened his library and his collections to the chronicler's eye. Master John Barkham gave such help as he alone could give, while Master William Smith, Rouge Dragon, was ever at hand to solve the problems of heraldry. Surely no citizen ever found better encouragement, especially in the telling of a thrice-told tale.

Stow was the more industrious of the two. In 1561, he published an edition of Chaucer's works. Four years later came his *Summarie of Englyshe Chronicles*, and then, in 1580, he dedicated to Robert Dudley, earl of Leicester, a far better book, *The Chronicles of England from Brute until this present yeare of Christ* 1580. His purpose it is to celebrate 'the worthie exploits of our Kings and governors,' and of that purpose he takes a lofty view. He regards himself not only as a historian, but as an inculcator of sound morals. 'It is as hard a matter,' he says in pride,

> for the Recorder of Chronicles, in my fansie, to passe without some colours of wisedome, invitements to vertue, and loathing of naughtie factes, as it is for a welfavoured man to walk up and downe in the hot parching Sunne, and not to be therewith sunburned.

His knowledge is not often better than that of his predecessors. He believes in the same fairy-tales; he accepts without question the same rumours. But, in one respect, he differs from all his rivals: he possesses an interest in literature which they lack. Under the year 1341, he records the death of John Malvern, fellow of Oriel College, and author of the book entitled *The Visions of Pierce Plowman*, and, in due course, he laments Geoffrey Chaucer, 'the most excellent poet of Englande, deceased the XXV of October, 1400.' His knowledge of literature did not give him a lettered style. His prose is the plainest and most straightforward of his time, and he deserves whatever praise may be given to the diligent and conscientious journeyman.

John Speed, on the other hand, was a born rhetorician. His love of words outstripped his taste. When Richard I dies, 'now ensued,' says he, 'the fatall accident, which drew the blacke cloud of death over this triumphal and bright shining Starre of Chevalrie.' The battle of Agincourt inspires him to such a piece of coloured writing as Hall would not have disdained. Whatever the occasion be, he is determined to attain what he thinks is a brilliant effect, and his *Historie of Great Britaine* is marred by a monstrous ingenuity. One virtue he has which must not be passed over: he supports his narrative more often than the others from unpublished documents. He quotes the *Life of Woolsey*, which Stow had quoted before him without acknowledgment, and ascribes it honourably to George Cavendish. His character of Henry VII is borrowed, with some verbal differences, from the manuscript of Sir Francis Bacon, 'a learned, eloquent knight, and principall lawyer of our time.' In brief, truth and patriotism are his aims. Like all the chroniclers, and with an unrestrained eloquence, he hymns the glory of England, 'the Court of Queene Ceres, the Granary of the Western world, the fortunate Island, the Paradise of Pleasure and Garden of God.'

With William Camden, the chronicle reached its zenith. His *Rerum Anglicarum et Hibernicarum Annales, regnante Elizabetha* is by far the best example of its kind. Though it is 'digested into annals,' according to the practice of the time, though its author bundles marriages, deaths, embassies and successions together, like the common 'stitchers of history,' though he does not disdain strange stars and frozen rivers, it is informed throughout with a sense of history and with a keen perception of conflicting policies. Old-fashioned in design alone, the work is a genuine piece of modern history, in which events are set in a proper perspective, and a wise proportion is kept of great and small. Its faults are the faults inherent in the chronicle: no sure plan of selection, a rigid division into years, an interspersion of the text with documents. Its virtues are its own: clearness of expression, catholicity of interest, a proud consciousness of the great events, whereof Camden was at once the partaker and the historian.

He declares in his preface that William Cecil, baron Burghley, 'opened unto him first some memorials of state of his own,' and that afterwards he

> sought all manner of help on every side ... for most of which (as I ought) I hold myself chiefly bound to Sir R. Cotton, who with great expense and happy labour hath gathered most choice variety of Histories and antiquity; for at his torch he willingly suffered me to light my taper.

He learned much, also, by his own observation and by converse with those who had played their part in affairs, and, heedless of himself, he made no sacrifice save to truth. Nor does he vaunt his achievement in any lofty terms. He will be content, he says, with professional modesty, to be 'ranked amongst the lowest writers of great things.' He would have been placed far higher in the general esteem, if he had not, by an unhappy accident, composed his book in Latin. This misfortune, the greater because he was one of the last to inflict so grave an injustice upon himself, was mitigated by the skill and loyalty of his translators. The first part of his *Annales*, the substance of which had already been communicated to Thuanus, was published in 1615, and, ten years later, translated out of the French into English by Abraham Darcie, who gave his own flourishing title to the book: *The True and Royall History of the famous Empresse Elizabeth, Queene of England France and Ireland &c. True Faith's defendresse of Divine renowne and happy Memory.* The second part, which describes the affairs of the kingdom from 1589 to the queen's death, was printed posthumously in 1627, and translated into English by Thomas Browne, student of Christ Church, under the title of *Tomus Idem et Alter* (1629).

Such is the history of the book. Its purpose and motive are apparent upon every page: to applaud the virtues of the queen and to uphold the protestant faith. In devising fitting titles for Elizabeth, Camden exhausts his ingenuity. She is the Queen of the Sea, the North Star, the restorer of our naval glory. He defends her actions with the quiet subtlety which suggests that defence is seldom necessary. His comment upon the death of Mary of

Scotland is characteristic. Thus were achieved, he thinks, the two things which Mary and Elizabeth always kept nearest their hearts: the union of England and Scotland was assured in Mary's son, and the true religion, together with the safety of the English people, was effectively maintained. But Camden was not wholly engrossed in the glory and wisdom of the queen. He looked beyond her excellences to the larger movements of the time. None understood better than he the spirit of enterprise which was founding a new England across the sea. He pays a just tribute of honour to Drake and Hawkins, he celebrates the prowess of John Davis and William Sanderson and he hails the rising colony of Virginia. Of Shakespeare and the drama he has not a word to say. The peculiar glory of his age escaped him. The death of Ascham, it is true, tempts him to a digression, and persuades him to deplore that so fine a scholar should have lived and died a poor man through love of dicing and cock-fighting. And he fires a salute over the grave of Edmund Spenser, who surpassed all English poets, not excepting Chaucer, and into whose tomb the other poets cast mournful elegies and the pens wherewith they wrote them. But, in the end, he returns to his starting-place, and concludes, as he began, on a note of panegyric. 'No oblivion,' he says,

> shall ever dim the glory of her Name: for her happy and renowned memory still lives, and shall for ever live in the Minds of Man to all posterity, as of one who (to use no other than her successor's expression) in Wisedome and Felicitie of goverment surpassed (without envy be it spoken) all the Princes since the days of Augustus.

Master Camden, as his contemporaries call him with respect, was well fitted for his task by nature and education. He was a man of the world as well as a scholar. Born in 1551, he was brought up at the Blue Coat school, and sent thence, as chorister or servitor, to Magdalen College, Oxford. Presently, he migrated to Broadgate's Hostel, now Pembroke College, and, afterwards, to Christ Church. In 1582, he took his famous journey through England, the result of which was his *Britannia*; ten years later, he was made headmaster of Westminster school; and, in 1597, was appointed, successively, Richmond Herald, and Clarencieux King of Arms. His life was full and varied; his character, as all his biographers testify, candid and amiable. The works he left behind speak eloquently of his learning and industry. To our age, he is best known as the historian of Elizabeth. To his own age, he was eminent as an antiquary, and it was his *Britannia*, published in 1582, and rescued from Latin by the incomparable Philemon Holland in 1610, which gave him his greatest glory. Anthony à Wood calls him 'the Pausanias of the British Isles.' Fuller, not to be outdone in praise, says that 'he restored Britain to herself.' Like all the other topographers of his century, he made use of Leland's notes, but the works of the two men are leagues apart. Camden's *Britannia* is, in effect, a real piece of literature. It is not intimate, like Harrison's *England*. It is not a thing of shreds and patches, like the celebrated *Itinerary*. Wisely planned, nobly written and deliberately composed, it is the fruit of deep and diligent research. Camden loved England and loved to embellish her with his phrases. He carried his readers along the high-roads, through the towns and cities of his native country, revealing, as he went, her natural scenery, her antiquities, her learning and her strength. And if, to-day, we shared his pride in England, we should still echo, with all sincerity, the praises lavished upon his work by his contemporaries.

Ralph Brooke, with more malice than discretion, charged Camden with making an unacknowledged use of Leland's *Collectanea*. The acknowledgment was generously given, and Leland's *Collections* were made but to be used. Camden, in fact, was only following the general practice of his age. There was no topographer who did not take what he wanted from Leland, and there was none who did not improve what he took. If Leland's inchoate notes were of service to Harrison and Camden, they did all that could be expected of them. The truth is, Leland was a superstition. He received the inordinate praise which is easily given to those of whom it is said that they might achieve wonders if they would. The weight of learning which he carried was thought to be so great that he could not disburden it in books. He aroused great expectations, and never lessened them by performance. His erudition was inarticulate; his powers were paralysed by ambition; he knew so much that he feared to give expression to his knowledge; and he won the greater glory because the masterpiece never achieved was enveloped in an atmosphere of mystery. His career, however, the career of the silent scholar, is not without its interest and tragedy. Born in 1506, he studied both at Christ's College, Cambridge, and at All Souls, Oxford, and, after some years spent in Paris, where he was the friend of Budé, and may, through his mediation, have encountered Rabelais, he was appointed chaplain and librarian to Henry VIII, and rector of Pepeling in the marches of Calais. In 1533, his great opportunity came, for, in that year, he was given a commission, under the broad seal, to travel in search of England's antiquities, to examine whatever records were to be found and to read in the libraries of cathedrals, colleges, priories and abbeys. For some six years he gave himself to this toil with tireless diligence, and, in 1546, presented to the king the only finished piece of his writing that exists in English: *The laboriouse Journey and Serche of Johan Leylande, for Englandes Antiquities, geven of hym as a newe yeares gyfte to kyng Henry the VIII in the XXXVII yeare of his raigne.* In this somewhat ornate pamphlet, Leland extols the reformation, reproves the usurped authority of the bishop of Rome and his complicos and sets forth the extent and result of his many journeys. In no spirit of pride, but with a simple truth, he describes his peragration. 'I have so traveled in your domynions,' he writes,

both by the see coastes and the myddle partes, sparynge neyther labour nor costes by the space of these VI yeares past, that there is almost neyther cape nor baye, haven, creke or pere, ryver or confluence of ryvers, breches, washes, lakes, meres, fenny waters, mountaynes, valleys, mores, hethes, forestes, woodes, cyties, burges, castels, pryncypall manor places, monasterys, and colleges, but I have seane them, and noted in so doynge a whole worlde of thynges verye memorable.

It is a formidable list, and we may well believe that this old pedant on the tramp omitted nothing in his survey. Whatever he saw or heard he committed to his note-book, and carried back with him the vast undigested mass of facts from which many wiser heads are said to have pilfered. His ambition was commensurate with his industry. He trusted shortly to see the time when the king should have his 'worlde and impery of Englande set forthe in a quadrate table of sylver,' and, knowing that silver or brass is impermanent, he intended, as he told the king,

by the leave of God, within the space of XII moneths folowyng, such a descripcion to make of the realme in wryttinge, that it shall be no mastery after, for the graver or painter to make the lyke by a perfect example.

Nor would his work end here. He determined to restore the ancient names which Caesar, Tacitus and others employed. In brief, said he,

I trust so to open the wyndow, that the lyght shal be seane, so long, that is to say by the space of a whole thousand yeares, stopped up, and the glory of your renoumed Britain to reflorish through the worlde.

Alas for the vanity of human hopes! It is easy to travel; it is not easy to convert a traveller's note-book into literature;

and John Leland, elegant poet though he was in the Latin tongue, found the work of arrangement and composition beyond his powers. Unhappily, he seems to have known the limit of his talent. He complains that 'except truth be delycately clothed in purpure her written veryties can scant fynde a reader.' This purple vesture it was not his to give, and the world looked in vain for his expected masterpiece. When, at last, he recognised that it was for others he had gathered the honey of his knowledge, he went mad, 'upon a foresight,' said Wood, 'that he was not able to perform his promise.' Some charged him with pride and vain-glory without justice. He was not proud, merely inarticulate. The work he designed for himself was done by Camden. And, now that his *Itinerary* is printed, it is difficult to understand the enthusiasm of his contemporaries. It makes no pretence to be written. It is the perfection of dryasdust, and the only writer with whom Leland may profitably be compared is the author of Bradshaw's *Guide*. Here are two specimens of his lore, chosen at random:

Mr Pye dwellit at . . . a litle from Chippenham, but in Chippenham Paroche.

One told me that there was no notable Bridge on Avon betwixt Malmesbyri and Chippenham. I passed over 2 Bekkes betwixt Malmesbyri and Chippenham.

The statements are superbly irrelevant, and it is clear that the old tailors had the better of the vaunted scholar.

As a topographer, indeed, it is Stow who takes his place by Camden's side. The *Survey of the Cities of London and Westminster* (1598 and 1603) is a diligent and valuable piece of work, at once faithful and enthusiastic. For Stow, London was the fairest, largest, richest and best inhabited city in the world, and he gave it all the care and study which he thought it deserved. Other travellers went further afield. To Richard Carew, we owe *A Survey of Cornwall* (1602); and John Norden cherished the wider ambition of composing a series of county histories. Only a fragment of his vast design, which he would have entitled *Speculum Britanniae*, has come down to us—a 'preparative' to the whole work, together with brief sketches of Middlesex and Hertford (1593). The failure is more to be regretted because Norden himself was a man of parts. He came of a 'gentile family,' says Wood, was authorised, in 1593, by a privy council order to travel through England and Wales, 'to make more perfect descriptions, charts and maps' and was a very deft cartographer, as is shown to all in Camden's *Britannia*. The liveliest of his works, the *Surveyor's Dialogue* (1608), may still be read with pleasure. Therein, Norden deplores, like many another, the luxury which had come upon the country under the rule of the Tudors; he observes, with sorrow, the enhanced prices of all commodities, the smoke of many chimneys, which 'hinders the heate and light of the Sunne from earthly creatures,' and the many acres of deforested land. The farmers, he says, are not content unless they are gentry, and 'gentlemen have sunke themselves by rowing in vanities boate.' In brief, he sees about him the signs of ruin and desolation, and his treatise may aptly be compared with some passages of Harrison's *Description of England*.

What the travellers did for their country, Sir Thomas Smith, in his *Common Wealth of England* (written in 1565, printed in 1583), did for its law and government. No treatise ever written owed less to ornament. As the author himself says, he has 'declared summarily as it were in a Chart or Map' the form and manner of government and the policy of England. His is no feigned commonwealth such as never was nor shall be, no vain imagination, no fantasy of philosophers, but England as she

> standeth and is governed at this day the eight and twentie of March, Anno 1565, in the seventh yeere of the Raigne and Administration thereof by the most religious, virtuous, and noble Queene Elizabeth.

In style and in substance the book is as concise as a classic. It wastes no words and betrays few emotions. Only once or twice does Sir Thomas Smith permit himself a touch of humanity or a hint of observation. The yeomen of England, the good Archers, 'the stable troupe of Footmen that affraid all France,' arouse him to a fitful enthusiasm, and, in the discussion of England's malefactors, he reveals a flash of real insight, namely that Englishmen, while they neglect death, will not endure torture. 'The nature of our Nation is free, stout, hault, prodigall of life and blood,' says he, 'but contumely, beating, servitude, and servile torment, and punishment it will not abide.' The popularity of the book is easily intelligible. It appealed to a people hungry for knowledge of itself, but it gives no hint of the erudite Greek professor, the adroit ambassador, the wise secretary of state, the curious astrologer, all whose parts Sir Thomas Smith played with distinction and success.

An encyclopaedic method claims for John Foxe, the martyrologist, a place among the chroniclers. Not that his aim and purpose resembled theirs. It was not for him to exalt his country, or to celebrate the triumphs of her past. His was the gloomier task of recounting the torments suffered by the martyrs of all ages, and he performed it with so keen a zest that it was not his fault if one single victim escaped his purview. In other words, he was content only with universality, and how well he succeeded let Fuller tell: 'In good earnest, as to the particular subject of our English martyrs, Mr Foxe hath done everything, leaving posterity nothing to work upon.' And so he goes back to the beginning, describing the martyrdoms of the early church, and of those who suffered in England under king Lucius. As he passes by, he pours contempt upon Becket, proving that he, at least, was no true martyr, being the open and avowed friend of the pope. But it is when he arrives within measurable distance of his own time that he finds the best food for his eloquence. The prowess of Henry VIII, the exploits of Thomas Cromwell, his prime hero, the magnanimity of Anne Boleyn, 'who, without controversy, was a special comforter and aider of all the professors of Christ's gospel,' tempt him to enthusiasm, and he rises to the highest pitch of his frenzy when he recounts the tortures of those who suffered death in the reign of queen Mary. He is no sifter of authorities; he is as credulous as the simplest chronicler; he gathers his facts where Grafton and Stow gathered theirs, and he makes no attempt to test their accuracy. His sin is the greater because he is not writing to amuse or to enlighten his readers, but to prove a point in controversy. He is, in brief, a violent partisan. His book is the longest pamphlet ever composed by the hand of man. It is said to be twice as long as Gibbon's *Decline and Fall*, and never for one moment does it waver from its purpose, which is to expose the wickedness of 'the persecutors of God's truth, commonly called Papists.' It is idle, therefore, to expect accuracy or a quiet statement from Foxe. If anyone belong to the other side, Foxe can credit him neither with honesty nor with intelligence. Those only are martyrs who die for the protestant cause. The spilt blood of such men as Fisher and More does not distress him. For the author of *Utopia*, indeed, he has a profound contempt. He summarily dismisses him as 'a bitter persecutor of good men, and a wretched enemy against the truth of the gospel.' It follows, therefore, that Foxe's mind also was enchained. It was not liberty of opinion which seemed good in his eyes, but the vanquishing of the other side. Though he interceded for certain anabaptists condemned by queen Elizabeth, it was his object to rescue them not from punishment but from the flames, which was, he thought, in accord with a Roman rather than with a Christian custom. However, the success of his *Actes and Monuments* was immediate. It was universally read, it aroused a storm of argument, it was ordered to be chained in churches for the general edification of the people. The temper in which it is written, the inflexible judgment which, throughout, distorts the truth with the best motive, have rendered the book less valuable in modern than in contemporary eyes. If we read it to-day, we read it not for its matter or for its good counsel, but for its design. As a mere performance, the *Actes and Monuments* is without parallel. Foxe was an astounding virtuoso, whose movement and energy never flag. With a fever of excitement he sustains his own interest (and sometimes yours) in his strange medley of gossip, document and exhortation. The mere style of the work—homely, quick and appropriate—is sufficient to account for its favour. The dramatic turn which Foxe gives to his dialogues, the vitality of the innumerable men and women, tortured and torturers, who throng his pages—these are qualities which do not fade with years. Even the spirit of bitter raillery which breathes through his pages amazes, while it exasperates, the reader. From the point of view of presentation, the work's worst fault is monotony. Page after page, the martyrologist revels in the terms of suffering. He spares you nothing, neither the creeping flames, nor the chained limb, until you begin to believe that he himself had a love of blood and fire.

The man was just such a one as you would expect from his book. Born in 1517, to parents 'reputed of good estate,' sent to Oxford, in 1533, by friends who approved his 'good inclination and towardness to learning,' and elected fellow of Magdalen College, he was presently accused of heresy and expelled from Oxford. He was of those who can neither brook opposition nor accept argument. Henceforth, though he never stood at the stake, he suffered the martyrdom of penury and distress. Now tutor in a gentleman's house, now in flight for the sake of his opinions, he passed some years at Basel reading for the press, and, in 1559, he published at Strassburg the first edition of his masterpiece, in Latin. In 1563, it was printed in English by John Day, with the title *Actes and Monuments of these latter and perilous times touching matters of the Church.* With characteristic ingenuity, he composed four dedications: to Jesus Christ, to the queen, to the learned reader and to the persecutors of God's truth, commonly called papists. The last is a fine example of savage abuse, and, as Foxe wrote in safety and under the protection of a protestant queen, its purpose is not evident. No more can be said than that rage and fury are in his heart and on his tongue, that he possessed a genius of indignation which he had neither wish nor power to check and that he bequeathed to us a larger mass of invective than any writer in any age has been able to achieve.

The most of the writers hitherto discussed have been intent either to amuse or to inform. They have composed their works, for the most part, in sound and living English, because they spoke and wrote a language that had not yet been attenuated by the formality of pedants and grammarians. Few, if any, of them were sensible of an artistic impulse. They began at the beginning and pursued their task patiently unto the end, unconscious of what the next page would bring forth. But there are three writers, the author of *The history of King Richard the thirde*, George Cavendish and Sir John Hayward, who are separated from the chroniclers, even from Camden himself, both by ambition and by talent. Each of them set before him a consistent and harmonious design; each of them produced, in his own fashion, a deliberately artistic effect. *The history of Richard the thirde* has been generally ascribed to Sir Thomas More, on hazardous authority. An incomplete manuscript of the book was found among his papers, and printed as his both in Hall's *Chronicle* and in Grafton's edition of Hardyng. Some have attributed to More no more than the translation, giving to cardinal Morton the credit of a Latin original. Sir George Buck, in his *History of the Life and Reigne of Richard III*, printed in 1646, but written many years earlier, declares that 'Doctor Morton (acting the part of Histiaeus) made the Booke, and Master Moore like Aristagoras set it forth, amplifying and glossing it.' Where the evidence is thus scanty, dogmatism is inapposite, and no more can be said than that the book itself does not chime with the character and temper of More. It is marked throughout by an asperity of tone, an eager partisanship, which belong more obviously to Morton than to the humane author of *Utopia*.

From beginning to end, Richard III is painted in the blackest colours. No gossip is overlooked which may throw a sinister light upon the actions of the prince. It is hinted, not only that he slew Henry VI, but that he was privy to Clarence's death. The most is made of his deformed body and cunning mind, the least of his policy. If accuracy be sacrificed, the artistic effect is enhanced. The oneness of Richard's character gives a unity and concentration to the portrait which cannot be overpraised. For the first time in English literature, we come upon a history which is not a mere collection of facts, but a deliberately designed and carefully finished whole. The author has followed the ancient models. He knows how fine an effect is produced by the putting of appropriate speeches in the mouths of his characters. The value of such maxims as sum up a situation and point a moral does not escape him. 'Slipper youth must be underpropped with elder counsayle,' says he. And, again: 'The desire of a kingdome knoweth no kinred. The brother hath bene the brother's bane.' Here we have the brevity and the wise commonplace of the Greek chorus. Above all, he proves the finest economy in preparing his effects. The great scene in which Richard arrests lord Hastings opens in a spirit of gentle courtesy. 'My Lord,' says the protector to the bishop of Ely,

you have very good strawberries at your gardayne in Holberne, I request you let us have a messe of them. Gladly my lord, quod he, woulde God I had some better thing as redy to your pleasure as that.

And then the storm breaks. In brief, the author's sense of what is picturesque never slumbers. The sketches of the queen and Shore's wife are drawn by a master. The persistence with which Richard tightens his grasp upon the throne is rendered with the utmost skill. Nor is the sense of proportion ever at fault. You are given the very essence of the tragedy, and so subtle is the design that, at the first reading, it may escape you. The style is marked by a strict economy of words and a constant preference of English before Latin. From beginning to end, there is no trace of flamboyancy or repetition, and, while we applaud the wisdom of the chroniclers who made this history of Richard their own, we cannot but wonder that one and all failed to profit by so fine an example of artistry and restraint.

Few books have had a stranger fate than George Cavendish's *Life and Death of Thomas Woolsey*. Written when queen Mary was on the throne, it achieved a secret and furtive success. It was passed in manuscript from hand to hand. Shakespeare knew it and used it. As I have said, both Stow and Speed leaned upon its authority. First printed in 1641, it was then so defaced by interpolations and excisions as to be scarce recognisable, and it was not until 1667 that a perfect text was given to the world. And then, for no visible reason, it was ascribed to William, not to

George, Cavendish. The uncertainty had no other excuse save that William, the better known of the two, was the founder of a great family. Speed gives the credit where it was due, to George —and Speed's word was worth more than surmise. However, all doubt was long since removed, and to George Cavendish, a simple gentleman of the cardinal's household, belongs the glory of having given to English literature the first specimen of artistic biography. Steadfast in devotion, plain in character, Cavendish left all to follow the fortunes of the cardinal. He was witness of his master's pomp and splendour; he was witness of his ruin and his death. He embellished his narrative with Wolsey's own eloquence; he recorded the speech of Cromwell, Northumberland and others; and he imparts to his pages a sense of reality which only a partaker of Wolsey's fortunes could impart. But he was not a Boswell, attempting to produce a large effect by a multiplicity of details. His book has a definite plan and purpose. Consciously or unconsciously, Cavendish was an artist. His theme is the theme of many a Greek tragedy, and he handles it with Greek austerity. He sets out to show how Nemesis descends upon the haughty and overbold, how the mighty are suddenly cast down from their seats, how the hair-shirt lurks ever beneath the scarlet robes of the cardinal. This is the confessed end and aim of his work. He is not compiling a 'life and times.' He discards as irrelevant many events which seem important in the eye of history. The famous words which he puts in the mouth of Wolsey dying might serve as a text for the whole work: 'If I had served God as diligently as I have done the king, he would not have given me over in my grey hairs.'

That his readers may feel the full pathos of Wolsey's fall, he paints the magnificence of his life in glowing colours. Titles are heaped upon titles. The boy bachelor grows to the man of affairs, the ambassador, the king's almoner, the chancellor of England, the archbishop of York, the cardinal. In lavish entertainment, in noble pageantry, the cardinal surpassed the king. His banquets 'with monks and mummers it was a heaven to behold.' The officers of his chapel and of his household were like the sands in number. He moved always in a procession. 'He rode like a cardinal, very sumptuously, on a mule trapped with crimson velvet upon velvet, his stirrups of copper and gilt; and his spare mule following him with like apparel.' Is it any wonder that fortune 'began to wax something wroth with his prosperous estate'? Almost at the outset, the note of warning is struck. The sinister influence of Anne Boleyn begins to be felt from the moment that the cardinal comes between her and the love of lord Percy. In other words, fortune 'procured Venus, the insatiate goddess, to be her instrument.' The king's displeasure at the slow process of divorce is heightened by the whisperings of Mistress Anne. And then, at Grafton, the blow falls. The cardinal is ordered to give up the great seal and to retire to Esher. Henceforth, misfortunes are heaped upon him, as they were heaped upon Job, and he bears them with an equal resignation. He is stripped of wealth and state. His hopeless journey from town to town brings him nearer only to death. The omens are bad. A cross falls upon Bonner's head as he sits at meat. When the earl of Northumberland, charged to arrest him of high treason, visits him, 'Ye shall have such cheer,' says the cardinal, with the true irony of Sophocles, 'as I am able to make you, with a right good will... hoping hereafter to see you oftener, when I shall be more able and better provided to receive you with better fare.' So, at last, he dies at Leicester, dishonoured and disgraced, stripped of his splendour, abandoned by his train. And Cavendish, speaking with the voice of the tragic chorus, exhorts his readers to behold 'the wondrous mutability of vain honours, the brittle assurance of abundance, the uncertainty of dignities, the flattery of feigned friends, and the fickle trust to worldly princes.'

Talent and opportunity were given to the simple, unlettered Cavendish, and he made the fullest use of them. Sir John Hayward was a historian of another kind. He was not driven by accident or experience to the practice of his craft. He adopted it as a profession, and resembled the writers of a later age more nearly than any of his contemporaries. Born in Suffolk, about 1560, he was educated at the university of Cambridge, and devoted himself with a single mind to the study of history. He was in no sense a mere chronicler. He aimed far higher than the popular history, digested into annals. His mind was always intent upon the example of the ancients. He liked to trick out his narratives with appropriate speeches after the manner of Livy. He delighted in the moral generalisations which give an air of solemnity to the art of history as it was practised by the Greeks and Romans. His first work, in which are described the fall of Richard II and the first years of Henry IV, and which was dedicated to the earl of Essex, incurred the wrath of Elizabeth, and cost him some years of imprisonment. The queen asked Bacon if he could find any passages in the book which savoured of treason. 'For treason surely I find none,' said Bacon, 'but for felony very many.' And when the queen asked him 'Wherein?' he told her that 'the author had committed very apparent theft; for he had taken most of the sentences of Cornelius Tacitus, and translated them into English, and put them in his text.' This criticism is as true as it is witty. Hayward aims at sententiousness with an admirable success, and did his best to make himself the Tacitus of England.

In the 'Epistle Dedicatorie' to his *Lives of the Three Normans, Kings of England*, he declares that, though he had written of the past, he 'did principally bend and binde himself to the times wherein he should live.' His performance did not agree with his bent. Concerning the times near which he lived he has left but a fragment: *The beginning of the Reigne of Queene Elizabeth*, of which beginning he had no more personal knowledge than of the *Life and Reigne of King Edward the Sixt*, which, in some respects, is his masterpiece. But, whatever was the period of his choice, he treated it with the same knowledge and impartiality. He made a proper use of unpublished material. The journal of Edward VI gives an air of authenticity to his biography of that king, and, in treating of William I, he went back to sources of information which all the chroniclers had overlooked. In brief, he was a scholar who took a critical view of his task, who was more deeply interested in policies and their result than in the gossip of history and who was always quick to illustrate modern England by the examples of Greece and Rome. His pages are packed with literary and historical allusions. He was, moreover, always watchful of his style, intent ever upon producing a definite effect, and, if he errs, as he does especially in his *Henry IV*, on the side of elaboration, it is a fault of which he is perfectly conscious, and which he does not disdain. Thus, at last, with the author of *Richard III* and Sir John Hayward, England reverted to the ancient models, and it is from them and not from the chroniclers that our art of history must date its beginnings.

CHAPTER XVI

ELIZABETHAN PROSE FICTION

AMONG the prose compositions of the Elizabethan era are numerous works which, with many points of difference, have this in common, that they all aim at affording entertainment by means of prose narrative. They are variously styled *Phantasticall treatises, Pleasant histories, Lives, Tales* and *Pamphlets,* and the methods and material they employ are of corresponding variety; they are, moreover, obviously written in response to demands from different classes, and yet their common motive, as well as a common prose form, unmistakably suggest a single literary species.

Previous examples of the type will rarely be found in our literature, for medieval fiction had mostly assumed the form of verse. The general adoption of prose at this date is, therefore, an innovation, and, as such, it was due to more than one cause. It was the outcome, in the first place, of natural development, the result of that national awakening which led to the overthrow of Latin as the language of the learned; with its activities extended in the one direction, the vernacular was not long in recommending itself for use in another, and so it came about that prose joined verse in the service of delight. Then, again, Malory, Caxton and the translators of Boccaccio had shown that narrative might adopt prose form without disadvantage; through the Bible and the liturgy the use of vernacular prose was fast becoming familiar; while further possibilities of prose were being revealed from its place in the drama. And, lastly, with the departure of the minstrel and the appearance of the printing press, there ceased, naturally enough, that exclusive use of verse for narrative purposes, which, under earlier conditions, alone had made long narrative possible.

Prose fiction, therefore, is one of the gifts of the Elizabethans to our literature, and the gift is none the less valuable because unconsciously made. It was no special creation, fashioned upon a definite model, but, rather, the result of a variety of efforts which, indirectly, converged towards one literary type. Its elements were of various origin, being borrowed, in part, from medieval England, in part, from abroad, while much, also, was due to the initiative of the age. The material with which it dealt, varied in accordance with the immediate end in view. Its 'treatises' and its pamphlets embodied studies of manners and character-sketches; it comprised tales of adventure as well as romance; it dealt with contemporary life and events of the past, with life at the court, and life in the city; it was, by turns, humorous and didactic, realistic and fanciful, in short, it represented the first rough drafts of the later novel. The history of the novel had really begun, and, although the term was not, as yet, generally applied, the word itself had already entered the language.

The two main centres of influence around which Elizabethan prose fiction revolved were the court and the people. The court was easily the supreme element in national life, and one great aim of contemporary letters became that of supplying the courtier's needs, just as, in Rome, it was the orator, the typical figure of the classical age, who had won similar attention. At the same time, a strong and self-conscious middle class was emerging from the ruins of feudalism, and the commons were becoming alive to the interests of their class. Hence, now for the first time, they made their way into literature, and the treatment of their affairs became the secondary aim of this prose fiction.

A period of apprenticeship came first, in which the lines of translation were closely followed, and then, with skill acquired in the art of story-telling, a host of writers devoted themselves to the newly found craft. A series of moral treatises, in narrative form, were the first to appear. They aimed, for the most part, at courtly education, and, up to about 1584, instruction, often in sugared form, became the main concern of a body of writers, of whom Lyly was chief. Then the business became one of a more cheerful kind: Greene and Lodge wrote their romances for court entertainment, while Sidney sought distraction in the quiet shades of Arcadia. In the last decade of the century came the assertion of the *bourgeois* element. As an embodiment of realistic tendencies, it followed, naturally enough, upon the previous romancing; but social considerations had, also, made it inevitable. Greene, Nashe and Deloney laboured to present the dark and the fair side of the life of the people: they wrote to reform as well as to amuse.

Throughout the whole period, England, as is well known, was singularly sensitive to foreign influence: one foreign work or another seems to have been continually inspiring Elizabethan pens. Castiglione and Guevara, Montemayor and Mendoza, each in his different way, exercised influence, which was certainly stimulative, and was, to some extent, directive. But, while this is true, it is equally true that, in most cases, the actual production springs readily and naturally from English soil; southern influence, undoubtedly, helped to warm the seed into life, but the seed itself was of an earlier sowing.

First, with regard to the treatises: the enthusiasm inspired by North's translation (1557) of Guevara's *El Relox de Principes*, and Hoby's translation (1561) of Castiglione's *Il Cortegiano*, was as great as it was undoubted, but it does not altogether account for Lyly's great work. Courtesy books had been written in English before those works appeared. *The Babees' Boke* (1475) 'a lytyl reporte of how young people should behave,' and Hugh Rhodes's *Boke of Nurture* (1450, published 1577), had previously aimed at inculcating good manners; afterwards came Elyot's *Governour* (1531), Ascham's *Scholemaster* (published 1570) and Sir Humphrey Gilbert's *Queene Elizabethes Achademy* (written after 1562), all of which treated of instruction, not only in letters, but also in social and practical life[1]. Such works as these, together with the numerous *Mirrours*, aimed at pointing the way to higher social refinement, and thus the movement which culminated in Lyly had already begun in fifteenth century England, and had kept pace with the national development, of which it is, indeed, the logical outcome.

Secondly, the romance is an obvious continuation of a literary type familiar to medieval England. Sanazzaro and Montemayor modified, but did not supply the form, while the French and Spanish works of chivalry introduced by Paynel and Munday (1580—90) merely catered for a taste which had then become jaded. Medieval romances, it is true, had fallen by this time into a decrepit old age. They were cherished by antiquaries, sometimes reprinted, less frequently reread; they figured mainly with 'blind harpers and... taverne minstrels... at Christmasse diners and bride ales, in tavernes and ale-houses and such other places of base resort[2].' But their tradition lived on in the romantic works

[1] Note, also, *A lytle Booke of Good Maners for Chyldren* (1554) by Whittinton, R., *The Myrrour of Good Maners*, translated from the Latin by Alexander Barclay and printed by Pynson, and R. Peterson's translation of G. della Casa's *Galateo* (1576).

[2] Puttenham's *Arte of English Poesie*, reprint of 1811, pp. 36, 69.

of Greene, Sidney and Lodge, though in the form of their survival they owed something to foreign influence. The pastoral colouring, for instance, is caught from the fashions of Italy and Spain; but, for the rest, their differences from the earlier English forms may be fairly put down to changed aspects of national life. In a general awakening, something of the old wonder and awe had, naturally, been lost; the world of chivalry and enchantment had receded, leaving the heroes of romance in a setting less heroic, just as, in active life, the knight had turned courtier and castles had become palaces. Moreover, the medley of form which these romances exhibit corresponds to that medley of past and present which lingered in men's minds at masque and pageant. The Elizabethan romance is, in short, firmly rooted in Elizabethan life. Modifying influences came from abroad; but the animating tradition and guiding impulses were forces derived from the national life.

And, again, the immediate origin of the realistic work which followed must be sought for in English works of an earlier date. It is not necessary to ascribe Nashe's *Unfortunate Traveller*, any more than the other realistic works of 1590—1600, entirely to the influence of *Lazarillo de Tormes*. In part, all these works represented a reaction against those 'feyned-no-where acts' which had proved enchanting in the preceding decade. But the ultimate causes were yet more deeply rooted, being social changes, partly national, partly European. Agricultural depression, long years of militarism and the closing of the monasteries, had done much to reinforce those bands of 'broken men' that swarmed like plagues over England. Their existence began now more than ever to force itself upon the notice of their countrymen, while, at the same time, the tendency of the renascence in the direction of individualism urged attention to these human units, and the sombre conditions under which they lived. And yet the realistic literature of 1590—1600 was of no sudden growth. Humble life had been portrayed in the lay of *Havelok*, its laments had been voiced in the vision of *Piers the Plowman* and alongside the romances of earlier England had existed coarser *fabliaux* which related the tricks and intrigues of the lower reaches of society. It was only a more specialised form of these tastes and tendencies which sprang into being in the sixteenth century. To the popular mind, collections of jests, as we have seen[1], had become an acceptable form of literature, while, at the same time,

[1] See *ante*, chap. v.

material was being collected for English rogue-studies[1]; and, while the jest-collections had aimed at mere amusement, the rogue pamphlets were prompted by ideas of reform. It is this material which anticipates the realistic work of Greene, Nashe and Deloney. The social influences which produced the earlier and cruder type of work also produced the later.

The probationary period of translation enters but slightly into the present narrative; and yet, as it marks the first stage in the development of prose fiction, it must not be entirely forgotten. Painter and Pettie, Whetstone and Riche are the translators mainly concerned, and their efforts are characterised by an interesting chango from mere translation to bolder and more original treatment. Painter, in his *Palace of Pleasure* (1566—7), supplies versions of a hundred and one tales, some forty of which are taken from Boccaccio and Bandello; Fenton, in his *Tragicall Discourses* (1567), reproduces thirteen tales of Bandello; and both, for the most part, are content with simple, faithful translation. In the twelve stories, however, which constitute *The Petite Pallace of Pettie his Pleasure* (1576), an advance on the mere process of translation is plainly visible, and additions of an interesting kind are occasionally made. Not only has Pettie's style certain interesting features[2], but his narratives are somewhat modified as compared with his originals. Into the tragical stories of Tereus and Procne, Scylla and Minos, to mention only a couple, the translator has skilfully worked an erotic element, while around his classical figures he has thrown a contemporary colouring in such a way as to suggest personalities of his day. In Whetstone's *Rock of Regard* (1576), which consists, in part, of prose versions of Italian novels, the method is, once more, one of mere reproduction, but it is worthy of note that one story, vaguely credited to 'an unknowne [Italian] author,' is, in all probability, due to Whetstone himself. And, again, of the eight stories which make up *Riche his Farewell to the Militarie Profession* (1581), while three are taken from the Italian, the remaining five are frankly 'forged onely for delight,' though the writer is careful to make his forgeries reminiscent of Italian motives. In this way did mere translation merge into adaptation, and then into the process of actual invention[3].

[1] Cf. Awdeley's *Fraternitye of vacabones* and Harman's *Caveat*, *ante*, pp. 102 ff.

[2] See *post*, p. 348.

[3] See Koeppel, *Studien zur Geschichte der ital. Novelle in der engl. Litt. des XVI Jahrh.* (Strassburg, 1892).

But these pioneers did more than render easy access to Italian tales, though this was a service of no slight value; the avenue thus afforded to new and strange realms revealed new springs of human passion, and opened out on wide vistas of unfamiliar life. And, more than this, the secrets of successful narrative, its material and its methods, were silently imparted, while the feature of originality was being implicitly suggested. They did much, too, in the way of popularising prose as a medium of narrative. The merits of a simple prose had long been recognised in France and Italy; its more modest garb had been seen to impose no restraint on the progress of the story, while it was obviously free from that counter-attraction, inevitable in verse, to the narrative itself. English writers had yet to learn the charm of a plain and simple prose, devoid of tricks, but, in employing prose in fiction, they had begun to learn.

This marked development in the methods of narrative soon led to its employment in one of the main literary businesses of the time, that of supplying moral treatises for courtly reading. These works, which aimed at edifying by means of disquisitions on subjects like love and friendship, form a sort of intellectual counterpart to such works as *Vincentio Saviolo his Practise*, which 'intreated' of the use of rapier and dagger and was 'most necessarie for all gentlemen that had in regard their Honors.' They were a revival, in some sort, of the medieval discussions, though scarcely, on the whole, as trivial. Under an attractive narrative form, they contrived to disseminate southern culture after the fashion of Castiglione and Guevara.

The great outstanding figure in this line is that of John Lyly, a native of Kent, and, in his day, a noted son of Oxford. His career was one of strenuous effort, ill-requited because ill-directed. His nice, fastidious temperament, which marked him off from the roaring section of university wits, seems to have rendered him ineffective in actual life. At Oxford, he missed recognition; his ambition to succeed to the Mastership of the Revels was quietly ignored; while his closing years, passed in penury and neglect, form a saddening sequel to the efforts of one, who, in his time, had adorned the stage, had beautified the conversation of exquisites 'of learned tendency' and had been the fruitful occasion of much wit in others.

The work for which he is famous appeared in two instalments. *Euphues, the Anatomy of Wit* was 'lying bound on the stacioners stall' by the Christmas of 1578; *Euphues and his England*, the second part, appeared in 1580. Together, they form an extensive moral treatise, and, incidentally, our first English novel. The whole hangs together by the thinnest of plots, which is, indeed, more a means to an end than an end in itself. Each incident and situation is merely an opportunity for expounding some point of philosophy. Euphues, a young man of Athens, arrives at Naples, where he forms a friendship with young Philautus. He falls in love with Lucilla, the betrothed of Philautus, and is duly jilted by that fickle mistress. This is all the action of *The Anatomy of Wit*: but the moralising element is something more considerable. The ancient Eubulus discourses on the follies of youth; Euphues, himself, on the subject of friendship. The complications brought about by the action of Lucilla lead to much bitter moralising upon fickleness in general, while Euphues, jilted, discusses his soul and indites 'a Cooling Carde for all Fond Lovers.' Over and above all this, the work contains the hero's private papers, his essays and letters; and opportunities are seized for inveighing against dress, and for discoursing upon such diverse subjects as marriage and travel, education and atheism. In *Euphues and his England*, the scene changes from Italy to England. The two friends, now reconciled, proceed to Canterbury, where they are entertained by one Fidus, a pastoral figure of considerable attractiveness; Philautus soon becomes involved in the toils of love, while Euphues plays the part of a philosophical spectator. The former lays siege to the heart of one whose affections are already bestowed, and so, with philosophy for his comfort, he enters upon the wooing of another, with more auspicious result. This brings the action to a close, and Euphues leaves England, eulogising the country and the women it contains, and returns forthwith to nurse his melancholy within his cell at Silexedra.

The significance of the structure is best appreciated by remembering that the work is really a compilation, and is, in fact, entered as such in the Stationers' register. Reminiscences of Cicero occur, particularly of his *De Amicitia* and his *De Natura Deorum*: but the body of the work is drawn from North's *Diall of Princes* (1557), the English translation of Guevara's great treatise. *Euphues*, in short, is little more than a re-ordering of this material, and Lyly betrays his source when he introduces certain details which, in his work, are obvious anachronisms, but which, in the pages of Guevara, were in perfect keeping. Apart from this, the adaptation has been consistently made, and the works coincide in much of their detail. Dissertations on the same subjects—on love and ladies, on friendship and God, occur in each. Both have letters appended to their close, which letters treat of identical subjects; Lyly's names of Lucilla, Livia and Camilla are taken over from Guevara, while the 'Cooling Carde' of Euphues finds its counterpart in that letter of Marcus Aurelius against the frailty of women which is embodied in Guevara's work[1]. It is only in a few instances that Lyly, while obtaining his idea from the Spanish work, goes elsewhere for fuller details. This is, however, the case in his remarks on education, in the section *Euphues and his Ephoebus* (I, 264). Guevara, it is true, embodies this material but Lyly's rendering is more nearly suggestive of Plutarch's *De Educatione Puerorum*, though his indebtedness is but indirect, the actual source being Erasmus's *Colloquia Familiaria* (*Puerpera*).

The character of these sources indicates, clearly enough, Lyly's didactic aim, in undertaking his *Euphues*. But, in projecting a moral treatise, he stumbled on the novel, and, considered as such, the work, though with many defects, has, also, abundant merit. It foretells the day of the novel of manners, of the novel involving a detailed analysis of love. It moves away from the fanciful idealism of the medieval romance and suggests an interest in contemporary life. Love is no longer the medieval pastime of knights and ladies; its subtleties are analysed, its romance and glamour are seen to lurk within contemporary walls and beneath velvet doublets. The defects of *Euphues*, on the other hand, are those of a writer unconscious of his art. There is a want of action, for the story is, after all, of but secondary interest. A poverty of invention is apparent in the parallelism which exists between the action of the two parts. Again, proportion is wanting; important events are hurriedly treated; the characterisation is but slight; the attempt at realism unconvincing. And yet the writer acquires skill as he proceeds. In the second part, he shows a distinct advance in artistic conception; there is more action, less moralising; characters multiply, characterisation improves and variety is introduced by changes of scene[2].

Not the least striking feature of the work, however, is the peculiar style in which it is written. The style, known as Euphuistic, won a following in its day, and has since become one of the most familiar of literary phenomena. It is the least elusive of styles, being deliberately compounded and, therefore, easily

[1] See Landmann, *Transactions of the New Shak. Soc.* (1885), pp. 255 ff.

[2] See Bond, *Works of Lyly*, vol. I, pp. 141 ff.

analysed; but, while its grotesque exaggerations have met with more than appreciation, justice has not always been done to its real aims and effects. With all its flowers of fancy, it is nothing more than the 'painful' expression of a sober calculating scholar, and is the outcome of a desire to write with clearness and precision, with ornament and culture, at a time when Englishmen desired 'to heare finer speach then the language would allow.' Lyly aimed at precision and emphasis, in the first place, by carefully balancing his words and phrases, by using rhetorical questions and by repeating the same idea in different and striking forms. Alliteration, puns and further word-play were other devices employed to the same end. For ornament, in the second place, he looked mainly to allusions and similes of various kinds. He alludes to historical personages, found in Plutarch and Pliny, to mythological figures taken from Ovid and Vergil. But his most daring ornamentation lies in his wholesale introduction of recondite knowledge; he draws similes from folklore, medicine and magic, above all from the *Natural History* of Pliny, and this mixture of quaint device and naïve science resulted in a style which appealed irresistibly to his contemporaries[1]. It should here be added, however, that the acquaintance with Plutarch and Pliny, which the elements of Lyly's style suggest, was not, necessarily, first hand. On the contrary, it was, almost certainly, obtained through the writings of Erasmus, which were in the hands of most sixteenth century scholars and which had already penetrated into the schools. In them, Erasmus had presented the fruit of his classical reading. His *Similia Colloquia*, *Apophthegmata* and *Adagia* offered in a clear, coherent form much that was best in antiquity and they represented a storehouse of learning which would save Lyly much seeking in his quest for learned material. In some cases, where Erasmus reproduces Pliny or Plutarch *verbatim*, Lyly's indebtedness to the great humanist might be doubted; but when Erasmus takes over his classical material in a somewhat altered form, when he expands or explains a thought, or falls into slight error or confusion, the fact that these variations from the original are faithfully reproduced in Lyly makes the latter's source undoubted. And if this indebtedness be proved in the case of variations, a further debt may be inferred even where identity of expression appears in the classical writers, in Erasmus and Lyly[2].

But this elaborated style, this 'curtizan-like painted affectation'

[1] See Bond, *Works of Lyly*, vol. I, pp. 141 ff.

[2] See De Vocht, H., *De Invloed van Erasmus op de Engelsche Tooneelliteratuur der xvi*e *en xvii*e *eeuwen* (eerste deel), 1908.

of Euphuism, did not originate with Lyly himself; he only 'hatched the egges that his elder friendes laide.' Its immediate origin lay in a certain stylistic tendency then fashionable in England. An almost identical craze had existed, a little earlier, in Spain, namely, in Guevara's *alto estilo*, which, however, had lacked the English device of alliteration. But the English fashion did not come from Spain, though North's *Diall of Princes* has often been credited with having effected the introduction: while this translation may have increased the vogue, it cannot have set the fashion. In the first place, North had employed a French version of Guevara's work for the purposes of translation, and this was a medium likely to dissolve any peculiarities of style in the original. And, secondly, many of the features of Euphuism, its parallelism and repetitions, its rhetorical questions and classical allusions, had already appeared in Lord Berners's *Froissart* (1524), not only before North, but before Guevara had written[1]. This fashion, of which Berners is thus the first English representative, can, subsequently, be traced to some extent in Cheke and Ascham; while, in Pettie's *Petite Pallace*, already mentioned, all the structural, and most of the ornamental, characteristics of Euphuism are present. It only remained for Lyly to expand the recognised methods of simile-manufacture by adding to Pettie's collection, based on fact and personal observation, others invented by himself, and based on fancy.

The ultimate origin of the fashion lay yet further afield, and is to be traced to that widespread movement for improving the vernacular which left its mark on almost every European literature. The coincidence of its effects in the literary styles of England and Spain must be ascribed to the prevalence of similar national conditions in both those countries. In each case, it was the outcome of a perverted classical enthusiasm, which led to the imitation of late Latin stylists with their many extravagances. It was due, also, in part, to the necessity for a courtly diction which arose simultaneously in both countries, in consequence of the growing interest which centred round the person and court of the monarch. As a movement, it was by no means isolated; nor did its results assume merely one form. Arcadianism and Gongorism, the conceits of seventeenth century France, and the pedantic mannerisms of Hoffmanswaldau and Lohenstein in Germany, are merely the outcome of the same influences, working at different times on different soils.

Nor are the results of Euphuism on English prose style by any

[1] See Wilson, J. D., *John Lyly*, chap. I.

means a negligible quantity, though its 'cunning courtship of faire words,' its tedious redundancies and mass of ornaments, led to its abandonment, generally speaking, about 1590. Sidney, by that time, had lamented the fact that his contemporaries enamelled 'with py'd flowers their thoughts of gold,' and Warner perceived that in running 'on the letter we often runne from the matter.' But some good came of it all. An attempt had definitely been made to introduce design into prose; and balance and harmony were the fitting contributions of an age of poetry to the development of prose style. Prose diction, moreover, was encouraged to free itself from obsolescent words; and further devices for obtaining lucidity, such as the use of short sentences and paragraph divisions, were, henceforth, to be generally adopted by English writers.

Apart from its prose style, the *Euphues* of Lyly exercised considerable influence upon its author's contemporaries. On Shakespeare, to mention only one, its effect is marked. Some of the dramatist's characters, such as his pairs of friends, the sententious old man Polonius and the melancholy philosopher Jacques, recall *Euphues* in different ways. Verbal resemblances also exist: Shakespeare's utterances on friendship[1], and his famous bee-passage[2], place his indebtedness beyond all doubt, even supposing his numerous similes drawn from actual or supposed natural history to be but drafts made upon the common possessions of the age[3].

Lyly's success with *Euphues* was not slow in inspiring a number of followers, and, up to about 1584, works of the moral treatise kind were constantly appearing. But their authors, as a rule, were painful imitators, who seemed incapable of original effort. Some affected his style, others worked 'Euphues' into their title-page, while the majority wrote, as Lyly had claimed to write, for 'the onely delight of the Courteous Gentlewoemen.' Anthony Munday's *Zelauto* (1580) is the first of this school; it is a 'delicate disputation... given for a friendly entertainment of Euphues,' in which Zelauto's praise of England is in emulation of that of Euphues. In Barnabe Riche's *Don Simonides* (1581) Philautus reappears and English manners, once again, form part of the topics discussed. Melbancke's *Philotimus* (1583) is made up of philosophical discussions on 'the warre betwixt nature and

[1] *Midsummer Night's Dream*, Act III, sc. 2. 198; *As You Like It*, Act I, sc. 3. 69.
[2] *Henry V*, Act I, sc. 2. 183.
[3] See Bond, *Works of Lyly*, vol. I, pp. 169–175.

fortune,' and, in Warner's *Pan his Syrinx* (1584), woman is under debate, and, as in *Euphues*, a 'cooling carde' is drawn up against the sex. The most notable exponent of this fashionable type of work is, however, Robert Greene. His character, the date of his appearance and the attendant circumstances, all made it inevitable that he should follow the fashion, and work it for what it was worth. In his *Mamillia* (1580) he relates how a fickle Pharicles undeservedly wins Mamillia's hand, a circumstance which leads on, naturally enough, to questions of love and youthful folly. Upon these topics Greene, therefore, discourses, and duly recommends what he has to say, by means of zoological similes and classical precedents. These details of ornamentation he repeats in succeeding works, in his *Myrrour of Modestie* (1584), based upon the story of Susanna and the elders, and in *Morando* (1587), a series of dissertations upon the subject of love. In 1587, two companion works, characterised by the same style, appeared from his pen. The first, *Penelope's Web*, consists of a discussion in which the faithful Penelope, strangely enough, embodies the ideas of the Italian Platonists in her conception of love, and then goes on to portray the perfect wife. In *Euphues his Censure to Philautus*, on the other hand, the perfect warrior is sketched, Euphues supplying the picture for the benefit of his friend. But, in spite of this and other sequels to Lyly's original story, the enthusiasm aroused by Euphues and the love-pamphlets he engendered had already begun to subside. Greene was already working in another field; and Lodge's still more belated pamphlet *Euphues Shadow, the battaile of the sences*, 'wherein youthful folly is set down' (1592), is nothing more than a hardy survival[1]. It was a work born out of season; and, though its author was pleased to describe his *Rosalynde* as 'Euphues golden legacie found after his death in his cell at Silexedra,' such a description was little more than the whim of one 'who had his oare in every paper boat'—the work itself belonged to another genre.

Before the vigour of this edifying output had begun to abate, the literary current was already setting in the direction of the court romance. The study of codes of etiquette and morality, was, after all, an unsatisfying diversion, and, to those who looked back regretfully to the more substantial chivalry of an earlier day, the romance still made a definite appeal. The earlier romance, however, had fallen into disrepute by this time; and the Elizabethan type was drawn up on lines somewhat different, and more in

[1] Cf. also J. Dickenson's *Arisbas, Euphues amidst his slumbers* (1594).

keeping with the fashion of the age. With the retention of characters of a princely kind and the frequent addition of a pastoral setting, a fresh situation was devised, that of the nobly born in a simple life; and this, in its turn, brought about a change of motive, so that the general theme became that of the separation and reunion of royal kindred. Therefore, while the earlier chivalrous and supernatural elements are, for the most part, absent from the romances of Sidney, Greene and Lodge, in their Arcadias and Bohemias true nobility shines all the more clearly through the wrappings of humble pastoral circumstance. And this was a theme of which Shakespeare made good use in his romantic plays.

Of all the workers in the field of romance, Sir Philip Sidney stands out as best qualified by nature and circumstance to deal with the theme. Amid the shades of Penshurst, the golden past had entered his soul, and its gentle influence was shed over his remaining days. He travelled abroad and made friends with Languet; at home, his sympathies were divided between art and action. He began life as a courtier in 1575, but his idealistic temperament proved to be but ill-adapted for an atmosphere of intrigue. Bickerings with the earl of Oxford and a rebuff from Elizabeth drove him, in 1579, into rustic retreat at Wilton, whence he emerged to take up diplomatic work abroad, and to fall before Zutphen in 1586.

The Countess of Pembroke's Arcadia was begun in 1580, during Sidney's retreat at Wilton, and was posthumously published in 1590. It was primarily intended as merely an expression of some of the 'many fancies' that lurked in his 'young head'; it was 'a trifle, and that triflingly handled'; and as the author sent his sheets by instalments to his sister, the countess, it was on the understanding that they should proceed no further. The prime motive of the work was to indulge his fancy with ideal scenes and sentiments, such as he had sought for in vain in the debased chivalry of the court; and fancy leads him on to pastoral scenes, to the calm of a golden age, as it had led others before him in similar periods of unsettlement.

Earlier pastoral works existed in Sanazzaro's *Arcadia* (1504) and Montemayor's *Diana* (1552); and to each of these Sidney is somewhat indebted, while, for occasional incident, he goes to Heliodorus and others[1]. From Sanazzaro he obtains his

[1] Notably Achilles Tatius's *Clitophon and Leucippe* and Chariton's *Chereas and Callirrhoe*; see Brunhuber, *Sir P. Sidney's Arcadia und ihre Nachläufer*.

title, and, possibly, the trick of infusing something of a personal element into his work. Although the work of the Elizabethan is never autobiographical to the extent of the Italian's, yet, amidst his fancies, there stray some serious and personal thoughts on religion, philosophy and love, while the pastoral Philisides shadows forth the friend of Languet. Sidney's debt to Montemayor is, however, less uncertain, as is shown by the striking parallel which exists between the opening passages of their respective works. In *Diana*, Sidney found a precedent for his mixed pastoral, for his happy blend of eclogue and romance; by Sanazzaro, on the other hand, the chivalrous element had been left untouched. Montemayor's conception of romance, moreover, embodied nothing of the magical, and Sidney follows him in discarding this piece of medieval machinery. And, once again, the love-plot in Montemayor's hands having become more than ever complicated, Sidney, by the employment of bewildering disguises, and a multiplicity of incident, succeeds in effecting the same artistic confusion[1].

The main interest of Sidney's plot centres in love-intrigue. Two shipwrecked princes, Musidorus and Pyrocles, after preliminary adventure, fall in love with Pamēla and Philoclea, daughters of the king of Arcadia, who has taken up his abode in the depths of a forest. Exigencies of courtship compel the princes to assume rustic disguises; and Pyrocles, appearing as a shepherdess Zelmane, soon becomes involved in awkward entanglements. The king falls in love with the pretended shepherdess, while his queen is attracted by the man whom she recognises through his disguise. From this compromising position, Pyrocles is only rescued by the privileged skill of the novelist; explanations and pardons follow, and the sequel is of a felicitous kind. But the story, as thus outlined, fails to give any idea of the plot's endless involutions, of its untiring series of alarums and excursions. Subordinate romances are woven into the main structure; there are tournaments and fêtes, long-drawn love-scenes and unceasing adventure with both man and beast. And the movement is further retarded by numerous experiments in metre, due to Sidney the Areopagite. There are some choice insertions, like the ditty beginning 'My true-love hath my heart,' but, by the side of these, there are limping hexameters and elegiacs, experiments in *terza rima* and *ottava rima* and occasional exhibitions of the *sdrucciolo* or trisyllabic rimes.

[1] See Greg, W. W., *Pastoral Poetry and Pastoral Drama* (London, 1906).

As a romance, the work enshrines Sidney's noble ideals of medieval chivalry. The Grecian heroes embody true knightly qualities: they are simple and gentle, daring in action and devoted in love. And the pastoral element gives an ideal setting to this chivalrous action. Arcadia is a land where morning 'strows roses and violets on the heavenly floor,' a land of flowering meadows and quiet pastures, where 'shepherd boys pipe as though they should never be old.' But, while the romance is thus prodigal of beauty, it is not without many faults, both of form and style. Its characters, in the first place, are of a shadowy kind; a strong suggestion of sheer unreality is inevitable. As regards its structure, there is an obvious lack of order and restraint, and this is a feature which, while characteristic of the age, is, perhaps, exaggerated in the case of the romance with its traditions of amplitude. In drama and poetry, there existed compelling forces of law and order, to which the intensity of the one and the grace of the other were due. But the laws of the prose romance were yet to be evolved, and in the *Arcadia* will be found no very logical development, nor skilful handling of the threads of the narrative. Its discursive character has already been noted, and one result of this exhausting method lies in the fact that the work concludes without decent disposal of all the characters. Nor must humour be looked for in either situation or phrase. Though a few rustics like Dametas and Mopsa are introduced by way of an antimasque, the humorous result apparently desired is not obtained. Sidney's temperament was melancholy as well as idealistic; his vision did not include either the ludicrous or the grotesque. The work, however, has the qualities of an eclectic performance, reflecting the rich confusion of the renascence mind. Fancy ranges in the romance from Greece to England, and within its purview the three ages seem to meet. The landscape, in the first place, has the bright colouring of renascence paintings—something, too, of the quieter tones of an English country-side; its temples and its churches, its palaces and pavilions, suggest a medley collected from Greece, Italy and England. Then, again, the ancient and medieval worlds appear to meet the modern. While the pastoral colouring revives the ancient notion of a golden age, and the chivalrous element is a faint afterglow of medieval days, a modern touch is perceived in the confessed unreality of the nature of the romance. Romance, hitherto, had been speciously linked with the real and actual: now, frankly removed to fanciful realms, it is made to imply an escape from reality—the sense in which it is accepted by the modern mind.

The style of the *Arcadia* represents a successful attempt at a picturesque prose, for the result is picturesque if somewhat extravagant. Other contemporaries were engaged upon the same quest, but, while Sidney avoids their several extravagances, he indulges in others of his own making. He avoids, for instance, the devices of Euphuism, the more obvious absurdities of bombastic, pedantic phrase, as well as those 'tricks of alliteration' and other 'far-fetched helps' which 'do bewray a want of inward touch.' His excesses, on the other hand, are those of a poet who forgets that he is now committed to prose. He enters upon a pedestrian task, unprepared to forego poetical flight; and, freed from the restraints which verse imposes, he strains even the limits of a more willing prose. With coherence of structure he is not greatly concerned. His sentences, long and rambling, are yet incapable of expressing his wealth of thought, and are, therefore, expanded by frequent parentheses. When he aims at emphasis, he occasionally employs Lyly's trick of antithesis, or, perhaps, the epigrammatic effect of the oxymoron[1]: but his favourite artifice is that of a jingle of words[2], which lacks effect as it lacks dignity.

The same excess characterises his use of ornament, for which he depends, not upon erudite display, but, rather, upon a free use of clever conceits in which sentiment is ascribed to inanimate objects. Sparingly used as an accompaniment to highly-wrought verse, the device is capable of excellent results, but, when frequently employed in ordinary prose, it soon becomes smothered by its own sweetness. Sidney, in short, rides the 'pathetic fallacy' to death; he is for ever hearing 'tongues in trees'; and commonplace thought, arrayed in delicate fancy, often leads to grotesque effect[3].

Sidney's prose style is, however, not all extravagance, it contains much that suggests the happier moods of a cultured mind. The famous prayer of Pamela, for instance, reads with a noble liturgical ring; pregnant apophthegms, scattered here and there, gleam like jewels of thought[4], while even the writer's foibles could

[1] Thus, a bare house is said to be 'a picture of miserable happiness and rich beggary': maidenly charms are described as 'a wanton modesty, an enticing soberness.'

[2] Cf. 'in the dressing of her hair and apparel she might see neither a careful art nor an art of carefulness,...a neglected chance...could not imperfect her perfection' (see *Arcadia*, ed. 1674, p. 244).

[3] *E.g.* a sewing operation is described in the following terms: 'the needle itself would have been loth to have gone fromward such a mistress but that it hoped to return thitherward very quickly again, the cloth looking with many eyes upon her, and lovingly embracing the wounds she gave' (ed. 1674, p. 260).

[4] Cf. 'all is but lip-wisdom that wants experience': 'the journey of high Honor lies not in plain ways': 'a lamentable tune is the sweetest musick to a woful mind.'

produce, at times, distinctly virtuous results, when they enter into some of his most glowing descriptions[1]. Sidney's extravagances were, in fact, not altogether a vain display. Lyly, in an age of poetry, gave to prose the subtle effects of harmony and balance; Sidney incidentally showed how dull prose might be lit up with flowers of fancy; and his work is, for all time, a rich mine of poetic ore.

The popularity of the work may be gauged from its frequent reappearances, as well as from its subsequent influence upon various writers. Upon the drama, in particular, its influence was considerable. It popularised the new machinery of the disguise of the sexes; it also suggested fresh situations arising out of fanciful realms such as Arden and Bohemia; while its love-passages must also have induced greater interest in the characterisation of women. It furnished episodes for more than one type of work. It supplied *King Lear* with the under-plot of Gloucester and his sons; Quarles with the material for his metrical tale *Argalus and Parthenia* (1629). Dramatic works, like Day's *Ile of Guls* (1606), Beaumont and Fletcher's *Cupid's Revenge* (1615) and Shirley's *Arcadia*, are, in some sort, adaptations of its theme[2], while Webster's *Duchess of Malfi* is indebted to it for certain figures and phrases[3]. Moreover, it inspired Lodge's *Rosalynde*, and lady Wroth's *Urania* (1621), both of which are imitations in novel form; and, lastly, its style set the fashion which helped to ring out the reign of Lyly.

While Sidney thus dreamed of his golden world, there was one who, under less happy circumstances, was to traverse the same fields. Robert Greene is the second great romancer of the Elizabethan period, in which he appears as a picturesque but pathetic Bohemian, with 'wit lent from Heaven but vices sent from Hell.' Before he had finished with Cambridge, his moral nature was tainted, and, after that, his way lay perpetually over stormy seas. A glimpse of happier things seemed promised in 1586, but, once again, his evil genius led him astray, until, finally, he was rescued

[1] Cf. the oft-quoted description of the land of Arcadia (ed. 1674, p. 6), and the description of the field for shepherds' sports: 'through the midst [of the field] there ran a sweet brook which did both hold the eye open with her azure streams and yet seek to close the eye with the purling noise upon the pebbles it ran over: the field itself being set in some places with roses and in all the rest constantly preserving a flourishing green, the roses added such a ruddy shew unto it as though the field were bashful at its own beauty' (ed. 1674, p. 68).

[2] To these might be added Glapthorne's *Argalus and Parthenia*; Shirley's *Andromana*; *Mucedorus*; McNamara Morgan's *Philoclea* (1754).

[3] See *Notes and Queries*, 10 Ser. vol. II, pp. 221 ff.

by a poor shoemaker in 1592, under whose rough shelter he made a pathetic end. His life had been one of struggle and drift, a wayward course of frustrated good intentions; and these things left their impress upon what he wrote, and upon his manner of writing. In the first place, he wrote merely to sell, and, as a consequence, he resembles a sensitive barometer, indicating the literary vogue from day to day. When Lyly was popular, Greene adopted his methods; when romance was called for, he also complied; his attempt at the pastoral followed Sidney's success; while his realistic pamphlets responded to a yet later demand. Secondly, with numerous creditors ever driving him on, he resorts in his haste to plagiarism and repetition[1]. He repeats himself without a blush: about thirteen pages of his *Myrrour of Modestie* occur in his *Never too late*, and parts of *Planetomachia* reappear in *Perimedes the Blacksmith*; from *Euphues*, he abstracts numerous similes, while from T(homas) B(owes's) translation of Peter de la Primaudaye's *French Academy* (1586), he takes entire passages when they please his fancy. And yet, though in life he followed the worse, he approved the better; his work is free from licentiousness, he never 'gave the looser cause to laugh.' His better self is revealed when, in his earlier work, he writes as a 'Homer of women,' when he sings in *Menaphon* a tender cradle-song, or when he works into his verse the saddening refrain of his life's story.

Greene's chief romances are *Pandosto* (1588), *Perimedes the Blacksmith* (1588) and *Menaphon* (1589). The first deals with the story of Dorastus and Fawnia, which Shakespeare afterwards refined in his *Winter's Tale*, adding such characters as Autolycus and Paulina, and removing from those he adopted their puppet-like stiffness. *Perimedes* embodies an evening tale, told by the fireside of the idyllic blacksmith, the story being based upon one in the *Decameron* (Giorn. II, Nov. II); the motive is that of the separation and reunion of kindred, and the chief figure is the noble Mariana. In *Menaphon*, the scene is laid in the realm of Arcadia, where occur the adventures of the shipwrecked princess Sephestia, who is loved by the shepherd Menaphon, but is duly restored to her husband and son, disguised as shepherds. Sidney's influence is apparent here, primarily, in the pastoral background; but, when Menaphon promises Sephestia that 'the mountaine tops shall be thy mornings walke, and the shadie vallies thy evenings arbour,' it is further evident that Sidney, rather than Lyly, has become the model of style. The plot, apparently, is taken from

[1] Cf. Hart, H. C., *Notes and Queries*, 10 Ser. vol. IV.

the narrative of Curan and Argentile in Warner's *Albion's England*; and the *Thracian Wonder* by a later pen, is a dramatic adaptation of the pastoral romance[1].

Other romances of Greene, though of less importance, must also be mentioned. In 1584 appeared his *Gwydonius* and *Arbasto*, two romances of an earlier heroic type, which were followed, in 1592, by *Philomela*, an attractive story, in honour of lady Fitzwater. The central incident of this last romance consists of a wager, made by a jealous husband, concerning his wife's fidelity—a favourite theme of Boccaccio—and the work is confessedly 'penned to approve of women's chastity.'[2]

From the point of view of art, Greene's romantic fiction cannot be said to rank very high, though it comprises interesting narratives, of moral and learned tendency, which waft their readers into the pleasant but fanciful realms of Bohemia and Arcadia. There is, however, considerable lack of structural skill, of artistic restraint and verisimilitude, in dealing with the affairs of the heart; as with Sidney, the art of story-telling in prose was yet in its infancy. But one pleasing feature of these works is the skill with which women-portraits are drawn: for the romances embody such creations as Myrania and Fawnia, Mariana and Sephestia, women of the faithful and modest type. It was only after 1588 that the reverence and sympathy which these portraits betray on the part of their author was to change into the 'bitterest hate.' In *Alcida*, a love pamphlet of 1588, he first revealed 'woman's wanton ways'; and, subsequently, he depicted fascinating sirens such as Infida (*Never too late*) and Lamilia (*Groatsworth of Wit*), who form a marked contrast with his earlier types. Excellent occasional verse is another outstanding feature of these prose romances; it culminates in *Menaphon*, as, for instance, in the lines of Melicertus on the description of his mistress, while the cradle song beginning

> Weepe not my wanton! smile upon my knee!
> When thou art olde, ther's grief inough for thee!

is notable even among Elizabethan lyrics.

[1] See Brereton, J. le Gay, *Mod. Lang. Rev.* vol. II, pp. 34–38, and Adams, J. Q., Jr., *Mod. Phil.* III, Jan. 1906.

[2] He also wrote other prose pamphlets reminiscent of earlier types of composition: thus, in his *Planetomachia* (1585), a dispute between the planets Venus and Saturn as to their respective influences on mankind, are to be found traces of the old *débat*, together with reminiscences of the ancient faith in the 'misticall science of astronomie': *Orpharion* (1588), on the other hand, embodies an imaginary dream, while in the *Spanish Masquerado* (1588) Greene turns from love to politics and indulges in a fierce tirade against the affairs of Spain.

Less interesting, because less tragic, is the personality of Thomas Lodge, who also was responsible for certain romances. During his Oxford days, he fell under Lyly's influence, which accounts for the Euphuistic strain which pervades all his works. His restless, unsettled career was typical of his age. He began with law, took to literature and ended as a medical man, while, from time to time, he indulged in lengthy cruises abroad. His first romance, *Forbonius and Prisceria* (1584), is a slight performance, and consists of a story of blighted affection, the subject of which seeks refuge in a pastoral life. *Rosalynde, Euphues Golden Legacie* (1590) 'fetcht from the Canaries,' is, on the other hand, one of the most pleasing of all the romances, and, upon it, Shakespeare, as is well known, based his *As You Like It.* It is a fresh story, steeped in idyllic sentiment, the charm of which even a Euphuistic manner is unable to dull. Lodge claims to have written it on a cruise to the straits of Magellan, whence 'every line was wet with the surge'; but the environment worked only by way of contrast, for pastoral scenes and rural notes are the products of this pen at work on the high seas. The story itself is based on *The Tale of Gamelyn,* a fourteenth century ballad of the Robin Hood cycle, which relates how the hero, defrauded by his elder brother, takes to the forest and becomes an outlaw[1]. This story of earlier England is removed by Lodge into the region of pastoral romance, and the English outlaws become Arcadians of the Italian type, polished in speech and courtly in manner. A love element is woven into the tale; Rosalynde and Alinda, as well as Phoebe, appear on the scene; and the plot develops, as in the *Arcadia,* by means of disguisals of sex. The narrative is also varied by the insertion of occasional verse, though the variations lack subtlety and the inserted eclogues frequently drag. But where the treatment most suffers is in the handling of character, which reveals no development, and is, moreover, stiff and formal. Shakespeare appreciated the charm and freshness of the woodland scenes, and he appropriated the elements of a good love-tale; but he also detected the unreality of Lodge's creations, and, while he quickens them into life in his own incomparable way, through the humours of Touchstone he smiles at the inconsistencies and unrealities which he takes care to remove. Another of Lodge's romances, *Margarite of America,* written in the winter of 1592 and published 1596, was also claimed to have been written at sea, on a voyage to South America with Master Thomas Cavendish; and the story, apparently, was taken from a Spanish work in the

[1] Cf. vol. I, p. 298.

Jesuit library at Santos, Brazil. A number of Cavendish's men certainly stayed at that place, and some are known to have been lodged at the Jesuit college. But the Spanish element is easily overrated; and several of its sonnets are borrowed from Italian sources, more particularly from Lodovico Dolce and Paschale[1].

The remaining works of a romantic kind present nothing new. Emanuel Ford's *Parismus* (1598), and its sequel, *Parismenos* (1599), are obvious imitations of the works of Greene. The scene is placed in Bohemia, and the action is made up of the usual excitements of princely love and war; the general tone, however, is less scrupulously moral than is the case with Greene, whence Meres's censure of Ford's work as being 'hurtful to youth.' It should be added that the story thus handled by Ford is reminiscent of *Romeo and Juliet*, and it is more than probable that the writer owes an unacknowledged debt to that dramatic work. Nicholas Breton is another of Greene's successors, his chief romantic work consisting of *Strange Fortunes of two excellent princes* (1600). Like Ford, he manages to shake himself free of faded Euphuisms, but his methods of romance are the methods of Greene, stiffened, perhaps, by a sense of inartistic symmetry. Nor must the Spanish romances, popularised by Anthony Munday in his English translations, be entirely forgotten. Between 1580 and 1590, he produced those versions of the Amadis and Palmerin cycles which represent modifications of the Arthurian romance. The works were viewed with disfavour by the cultured classes, on account of their preposterous plots, and the crudeness and inaccuracy of their rendering. Munday achieved a popular success, but he added little to his reputation, or to the dignity of the Elizabethan romance.

Before the last decade of the century was well advanced, a marked change came over works of fiction. By a sort of normal reaction, idealism gave way to realism[2], the romance to the realistic pamphlet and story, and, from Arcadia and Bohemia with their courtly amenities, the scene moved to London and its everyday life. The chief writers of this type of work were Greene, Nashe and Deloney, who, however, differ somewhat in the methods they adopt. Greene relates his own life-story, a grim narrative, which reveals, incidentally, much of the seamier side of life; and this he follows up with a series of revelations as to the tricks and knaveries of London rogues. Nashe, on the other hand, while less gloomy,

[1] Cf. Kastner, L. E., *Mod. Lang. Rev.* vol. II, ii, 156–8.

[2] Note the song 'In Praise of a Beggar's life,' a variant on the earlier theme of the mean estate. See Davison's *Poetical Rapsody*, Collier's reprint, p. 161.

is more satirical in what he has to say. He deals with follies and quackeries, rather than vices, and, while his methods are sufficiently trenchant, he has an eye to the humorous side of things: in his picaresque novel, the rogue becomes a hero. Deloney, again, has neither the grim realism of the one nor the forceful satire of the other. He is content to depict citizen life with a proper regard for the dignity of the crafts, and with a quiet sense of humour, which is by no means inconsistent with his more serious intentions.

Greene's autobiographical work begins in his *Mourning Garment* (1590) and *Never too late* (1590). He does not, as yet, deal directly with London life, though his own experiences, lightly veiled, form the nucleus of the tales. The *Mourning Garment* is an adaptation of the story of the Prodigal Son, with the addition of pastoral details as reminders of his earlier craft. But Greene is no longer 'Love's Philosopher,' as, indeed, he confesses; Philador gets into difficulties through the society of women, 'those Panthers that allure, the syrens that entice,' and the succeeding details are those of the Biblical narrative. In *Never too late*, the author's career is more closely followed. Here, it is Francesco who impersonates Greene; and he relates how he had married a gentlewoman, whom he abandoned for one less worthy, and how he was helped in his distress by strolling actors. These are well-known incidents in the life of Greene; but, when Francesco subsequently becomes reconciled to his injured wife, Greene pathetically suggests an event which, unhappily, found no counterpart in his actual life. In 1592, further autobiographical work was penned by Greene on his death-bed, when the veil concealing the author's identity is deliberately lifted. The main facts of his life are again dealt with, and, in the *Groatsworth of Wit bought with a Million of Repentance*, the writer is careful to state that Roberto is himself. The other death-bed pamphlet, *The Repentance of Robert Greene*, is still more direct; its style is, perhaps, inferior to that of his earlier work, and the writer seems intent on painting his life in the most sombre colours.

More direct descriptions of London life appear in further pamphlets, in which Greene exposes rogues and depicts honest tradesmen. The former object underlies his *Notable Discovery of Coosnage* (1591). Awdeley and Harman, as has been seen, had dealt with the vagabond classes, and had specified for public benefit the various classes of knaves, while Copland's *Hye Way to the Spyttel Hous* gave the earliest account of the thievish cant known as 'pedlyng frenche.' Greene, however, is indebted to none of these, except, perhaps, for the general idea. He is concerned with neither pedlars, nor gypsies, nor itinerant rogues; his aim, rather, is to warn country people against the snares of London. It is the wiles of panders and courtesans, card-sharpers and swindlers, that he undertakes to reveal, and this the *Notable Discovery* accomplishes. So successful was he, in fact, that an attempt was made upon his life, and *A Defence of Conny-Catching* appeared as an impudent rejoinder. In 1592, Greene followed up the attack by *A Disputation between a He Conny-Catcher and a She Conny-Catcher*[1], a lurid description of the London *demimonde*, which concludes with a pathetic account of the reclaiming of a courtesan. And in *The Blacke Booke's Messenger* of the same year, Greene once more wages war with rascals, by sketching the grimy career of a celebrated rogue, one Ned Browne, whose belated repentance takes place in the neighbourhood of the scaffold.

Besides dealing in this way with roguery, Greene also gives some attention to the more respectable side of London life, in his *Quip for an Upstart Courtier or a Quaint Dispute between Velvet-Breeches and Cloth-Breeches* (1592). The dispute is as to whether the courtier (*i.e.* Velvet-Breeches), or the tradesman (Cloth-Breeches) is deserving of the greater respect, and the decision is duly referred to a jury of tradesmen. This brings together a body of typical citizens, and is thus a device which enables the author to introduce his projected class-descriptions. The work reveals Greene's democratic sympathies, for he not only finds much interest in his commonplace types, but he also takes care, while giving short shrift to his upstart courtier, to assign more flattering treatment to the London tradesman. And this democratic attitude is not devoid of a certain significance, especially when a similar sympathy appears in Deloney's work: it explains, in some measure, the impulse which originated this realistic section of Elizabethan fiction. The form of the work is that of the medieval dream-vision, the fundamental idea, apparently, being taken from an anonymous poem, *A Debate between Pride and Lowliness.*

All this work of Greene had meant a considerable contribution to the literature dealing with contemporary life. With the author

[1] Conny-catchers were London rogues who duped simple people by various tricks and who primarily obtained their name from those typical cheats, the pedlars—those

gaderers of cony skynnes
That chop with laces, poyntes, nedles and pyns (Copland);

quoted by Hart, H. S., see *Notes and Queries*, 10 Ser. vol. IV, p. 484.

we pass through tavern doors, enter haunts of iniquity and become witnesses to the low cunning, the sordidness and the violence of the society found there. Bohemian life is laid bare, various characters of low life are drawn; and, in the middle of it all, a notable youth is pointed out, as he, a veritable Shakescene, is engaged in patching up old plays for the stage.

The next great realist, Thomas Nashe, was another of those university wits who lived hard, wrote fiercely and died young. He seems to have travelled in Germany and Italy; by 1589, he had done with Cambridge, and was endeavouring, in the metropolis, to live by his pen. His description as 'a fellow... whose muse was armed with a gag tooth and his pen possessed with Hercules' furies' shows how he struck a contemporary[1], but his vigour was of the cheerful kind. With all his boisterousness, there is about him an unconquerable gaiety, and, in spite of hopes of patronage deferred, and an imprisonment on account of his unfortunate play, the *Isle of Dogs* (1597), it was the ludicrous, rather than the morbid, in life, that appealed to him.

Like his friend Greene, Nashe was responsible, in the first place, for certain pamphlets dealing with the social life of London; but he does not confine himself, as was the case with Greene, to the outcast and the pariah, nor, on the other hand, does he find much attraction in the steady-going citizen. His attack is directed against respectable roguery, against foolish affectations and empty superstition, and these things proved excellent whetstones for his satirical wit. His *Anatomie of Absurditie* (1589) is a characteristic study of contemporary manners. He plays with the theme of Stubbes's *Anatomy of Abuses* (1583); but, while he does not deny that much evil was abroad, he yet contrives to find much that is amusing in the 'licentious follies' assailed by the puritan. In *Pierce Pennilesse, his Supplication to the Divell* (1592), where he figures as Pierce, Nashe gives a fair taste of his quality. He pillories, among others, the travelled Englishman 'who would be humorous forsooth, and have a broode of fashions by himselfe'; the brainless politician who thought 'to be counted rare... by beeing solitarie'; and those inventors of religious sects who were a confusion to their age. The result is a gallery of contemporary portraits, faithfully reproduced, and tempered with wit. In 1593, he wrote *Christ's Teares over Jerusalem*, a pamphlet which throws light upon the morals of Elizabethan London, and, incidentally, depicts the gamester, the threadbare scholar and tavern life generally.

[1] For Nashe's share in the Marprelate controversy, see *post*, chap. XVII.

He rails against those who 'put all their felicity in going pompously and garishly,' and then he turns his attack upon 'dunce' preachers and usurers. The former he accuses of 'hotch-potching' Scripture, 'without use or edification'; the latter had drawn from Lodge his *Alarum against Usurers* (1584), while their evil practices were numbered among notorious crimes in the 109th canon of 1603. The object of his ridicule in his next pamphlet, *Terrors of the Night* (1594), is the superstition of the age, and here Nashe amuses himself by discoursing on dreams, devils and such like, in a way that must have proved entertaining to many of his contemporaries. But his merriest effort was reserved for his last: in *Lenten Stuffe* (1599), he writes in praise of the red herring after a visit to Yarmouth, and his wit runs riot, as he suggests the part which that homely fish had played in the history of the world.

All this pamphleteering work, however, was completely overshadowed by his picaresque novel *The Unfortunate Traveller or the life of Jack Wilton*, which appeared in 1594, and which was the most remarkable work of its kind before the time of Defoe. It relates the lively adventures of the rogue-hero, an English page, who wanders abroad, and comes into contact with many kinds of society. He enters taverns and palaces, makes acquaintance with people worthy and unworthy, and so passes in review the Germany and Italy of his day. The scene opens in the English camp before Tournay, where the page is engaged in his knavish tricks. He terrifies, for instance, a dull army victualler into distributing his stores, so that the army had 'syder in boules, in scuppets and in helmets... and if a man would have fild his bootes, there hee might have had it.' Such a humorist became, perforce, a traveller, and he first appears at Münster in time to enjoy the conflict between the emperor and the anabaptists; then, in the service of the earl of Surrey, he makes for Italy. Passing through Rotterdam, the two travellers meet with Erasmus and Sir Thomas More; they witness at Wittenberg an academic pageant and the old play *Acolastus*, besides solemn disputations between Luther and Carolostadius, and, finally, they strike up an acquaintance with the famous magician, Cornelius Agrippa. At Venice, Jack elopes with a magnifico's wife, but is overtaken once more by the earl at Florence, where the latter enters a tournament on behalf of his English lady-love Geraldine[1]. The page then moves on alone to

[1] The authenticity of the episodes relating to Surrey is discussed in Courthope, *History of English Poetry*, vol. II, p. 77.

Rome, where he remains for a short period in an atmosphere of plague, robbery and murder, and, having learned, both by experience and hearsay, the gruesome horrors of the place, he finally leaves the 'Sodom of Italy' for the less lively scenes of his own country.

The form of this work, in the first place, is of great interest, for it resembles the picaresque type indigenous to Spain. But this need not imply that Nashe was a mere imitator; on the contrary, though he may have derived a definite stimulus from *Lazarillo de Tormes,* the elements of his work represent a spontaneous English growth. The Spanish rogue-novel was the outcome of a widespread beggary brought about by the growth of militarism and the decline of industry, by the increase of gypsies and the indiscriminate charity of an all-powerful church. Similar social conditions prevailed in Elizabethan England, though from different causes, and the conditions which produced *Lazarillo* produced *The Unfortunate Traveller.* It has, moreover, been shown, that while Lyly and Sidney were indebted to Spain for certain elements in their works, yet the ultimate origins of English courtesy-books and of the Euphuistic manner, were wholly independent of Spanish influence. And so, in general, it may be said, that parallels existing between the Spanish and English literatures of the time were the result of similar national conditions, of influences which were common to both[1]. In each case, the English development was later than the Spanish but not due to it. Moreover, as regards Nashe in particular, the matter and design of his novel would be quite naturally suggested by the material of his pamphlets, and, possibly, by reminiscences of his travels; while his choice of the realistic form is partly accounted for by his strongly expressed scorn of romances in general, as 'the fantasticall dreams of those exiled Abbie lubbers [the monks].'

When compared with the Spanish picaresque type, *The Unfortunate Traveller* will be found to possess many points of similarity. There is the same firm grasp of the realities of life, the same penetrating observation and forceful expression; there are the same qualities of humour and satire, the same rough drafts of character-sketches; and the aim is that of entertainment rather than reform. From the picaresque novel, however, it diverges in its English mixture of tragedy with comedy, and, again, in the fact

[1] See Underhill, *Spanish Literature in the England of the Tudors*; Chandler, *Romances of Roguery* (Pt I, the Picaresque Novel in Spain); and Utter, 'The Beginnings of the Picaresque Novel in England,' *Harvard Monthly*, Apr. 1906.

that the animating impulse of its rogue-hero is not avarice but a malignant and insatiable love of mischief. The Spanish *picaro*, also, generally belonged to the lowest class and was wont to confine his attentions very largely to Spanish society, but Jack Wilton, a page, moves further afield and reviews no less expansive a scene than that of western Europe in the first half of the sixteenth century.

As regards its form in general, the work may be classified as a novel of manners, though, obviously, it deals with different material from that employed by Lyly in his *Euphues*. It also represents our first historical novel. Nashe had promised some 'varietie of mirth'; he had also proposed a 'reasonable conveyance of history'; and thus the great intellectual and religious movements of the preceding age are duly represented. They are represented, too, at their most significant moments, and by the most impressive personalities. Erasmus and Sir Thomas More are the representatives of the humanistic movement; Surrey the courtier stands for a vanishing chivalry; the militant Luther and the anabaptists represent religious thought; while the supernatural pretensions of Cornelius Agrippa point to a still active superstition[1]. In this device of mingling history with fiction, Nashe is practically original. In introducing a tragic element into his work, he probably aimed at presenting a more complete picture of actual life than was possible by means of comedy alone; but in this he is not altogether successful. His tragedy is apt to border upon the melodramatic, and he is much happier in the comic vein. For his comedy, he depends upon lively situation; he scorns Euphuistic wit, and futile word play, as well as those cruder conceits which 'clownage kept in pay.' He is alike successful in his large bold outlines, and in his detailed descriptions; his scenes are the more effective on account of their incidental detail, and he is fully alive to 'the effect of a pose, of the fold of a garment.' The action is one of uniform movement, retarded by no irrelevant episode or unnecessary description; the novelist is proof even against the attractions of Rome with its storied associations. The movements of the hero are never lost sight of, and, in view of these facts, the work is something more than a mere succession of scenes. It is true that the author occasionally allows himself some latitude in the matter of personal reflections, but they can never be said to become intrusive. For instance, he puts into the mouth of one of his characters at Rome certain words of warning on the evils of travel; his ardent enthusiasm for poetry is revealed when he writes,

[1] See Kollmann, 'Nash's Unfortunate Traveller,' etc., *Anglia*, XXII (X), 80–140.

concerning poets: 'None come so neere to God in wit, none more contemn the world... despised they are of the world because they are not of the world'; and, again, his orthodox spirit cannot forbear to point a moral to his story of the anabaptists: 'Heare what it is,' he writes, 'to be anabaptists, to be puritans, to be villains.'

The main characteristics of Nashe's mature prose are its naturalness and force. Most of his contemporaries had aimed at refinement rather than strength, they relied upon artifice which soon lost its power of appeal. But Nashe, dealing with plain things, writes in plain prose, and it was but natural for the satirist of contemporary affectations to dismiss from his practice the prose absurdities of the time. While he was at Cambridge, *Euphues* had appeared to him as beyond all praise, and considerable regard for Euphuistic effects appears in his earlier work. But, later, he discarded, and helped Greene to discard, the specious aid of 'counterfeit birds and hearbes and stones,' and his later 'vaine,' he took pride in stating, was of his 'own begetting' and called 'no man father in England.' In the novel, the hero occasionally makes use of Euphuistic similes and Latin tags, but a dramatic intention underlies this device, for the page has frequently to 'engage his dupes with silver-sounding tales.' From Nashe's later work, all this is absent; he successfully aims at a familiar style, and the result embodies the strength and weakness of actual conversation. In thus turning from books to life, Nashe, like later writers in dialect, produces a style fresh and picturesque, vivid, terse and droll: he avoids abstract terms, and discards what is hackneyed. But, on the other hand, not infrequently, he is faulty in his syntax, and inartistic, even vulgar, in his colloquialisms. Not merely content with the forcefulness of the ordinary conversational manner, he aims at heightening its effects in several ways; his scorn becomes more emphatic in such descriptions as 'piperly pickthanke' and 'burlybond butcher'; he is audacious in adaptation and coinage alike; he is a lover of 'boystrous compound words,' for 'no speech or wordes of any power or force... but must be swelling and boystrous.' He also appreciated the charm of Biblical phrase, for that stately diction occasionally slips from his 'teare-stubbed pen,' while his description of the anabaptists is the earliest example of Scott's happy manner of dealing with the covenanters. In general, the page's description of Aretino holds good of Nashe:

> His penne was sharpe pointed like ponyard.... With more then musket shot did he charge his quill where he meant to inveigh.... His sight pearst like lightning into the entrailes of al abuses.... He was no timorous, servile, flatterer of the common-wealth wherein he lived.

But, while the realistic type of work failed to attract as many writers as the romance, Greene and Nashe do not stand alone. Lodge's contribution consisted of *The Life and Death of William Longbeard* (1593), which dealt, in humorous and realistic fashion, with the story of a daring rogue. Breton wrote his *Miseries of Mavillia*, which betrayed some want of acquaintance, however, with the scenes of low life described; and, in 1595, appeared Chettle's *Piers Plainnes seaven yeres Prentiship*, in which the *picaro* Piers relates his life-story to Arcadian shepherds in Tempe. The work thus hesitated between the Arcadian, the romantic and the picaresque types, but its most successful passages are those which relate to the hero's life in London, and to the haunts of usurers and dealers in old clothes. Dickenson also adopted the same type in his *Greene in conceipt new raised from his grave* (1598), a work, which, following the methods of Greene, concerned itself, primarily, with the tragic story of a fair Valeria of London, and, incidentally, with low life in the metropolis.

More than ordinary interest is, however, attached to the realistic prose fiction of Thomas Deloney, for he is the last of the Elizabethans to come into his inheritance. As a novelist, he is, practically, a recent discovery, though his work of the pamphlet and ballad kind had previously been recognised. But, apart from this, his prose tales possess considerable interest in themselves, no less for their attractive narrative, their humour and colouring, than for the fact that they help to fill in that picture of contemporary life, which had been outlined, only in part, by the other writers. Elizabethan prose fiction had, hitherto, been mainly concerned with the wit and romance of rogues and gallants; Deloney as the painter of the trading classes, discovers the humour, and even the romance, of the prosaic citizen.

Born in 1543, Deloney seems to have worked for some time as a silk weaver at Norwich, but, by 1586, he had moved to London, and, before 1596, had written some fifty ballads. In this latter year, however, he incurred official anger for introducing the queen into one of his ballads in 'fond and indecent sort,' and was compelled, in consequence, to seek temporary hiding. With his ballads now silenced as well as his looms, he turned his attention to literary work of another kind, and, having produced, between 1596 and 1600, his three prose narratives, before the century closed he 'dyed poorely' and was 'honestly buried[1].'

His three works are built up on a common plan; a framework

[1] See Lange, A. F., 'The Gentle Craft,' *Palaestra*, XVIII.

is constructed out of historical or legendary material, and into this are then worked *bourgeois* descriptions of contemporary life; each narrative, moreover, is devoted to the glorification of a craft, and the craft is eulogised either by relating the story of some successful captain of industry, or by glorying in the less tangible forms of its earliest patrons.

Thomas of Reading is written to the honour and glory of the clothiers' craft; it is designed to portray their honourable estate under Henry I (thanks to a hint supplied by William of Malmesbury), and this it does by relating certain incidents in the lives of six master-clothiers of the west country, whose wealth is represented by long lines of wagons creaking their way to London, their importance by the ceremony paid them by royalty. To these main incidents is added much humorous and descriptive matter, as well as a somewhat tragic love-story concerning duke Robert. There is no attempt at historical verisimilitude, for, in describing Thomas and his fellows, the novelist is obviously sketching Elizabethans. The humour, which is plentiful, arises out of a clever reproduction of inn scenes and gossiping wives, but the love passages are somewhat ineffective, being conducted on lines which are strictly Euphuistic. The second novel, *Jack of Newbury*, perpetuates the fame of a wealthy Berkshire weaver, one John Winchcomb (1470—1514), and, at the same time, it commemorates the ancient glories of the company of weavers. The hero is an affable apprentice, who is wooed and won by his master's widow, and, thereby, is raised to affluent circumstances. Subsequently, he confounds his betters by his patriotism and philanthropy, entertains Henry VIII in his Newbury establishment and helps his fellow-weavers in Wolsey's despite. There is, in addition, the usual digression and comic interlude. The widow's wooing, the hero's fifteen pictures with their didactic intention, and the practical jokes played upon a jester and an Italian, are all characteristic of Deloney's vein of humour. The work is amusing, in spite of its crudity, while it also lights up the humbler but respectable spheres of Elizabethan life.

The Gentle Craft, the third work, consists of a series of tales, dedicated to the shoemaking cult. The first two stories, *Sir Hugh* and *Crispine and Crispinus*, relate to early and noble patrons of the gentle craft; but these works are not in Deloney's best style. They aim at romantic and Euphuistic effects, and the author, obviously, is uneasy under the greatness of his themes. The third story, *Simon Eyre*, moves into the actual, and relates the career of the philanthropic founder of Leadenhall (*c.* 1450), who, from a shoemaker's apprentice became lord mayor. A comic underplot is added, in which a Frenchman and a Dutchman clumsily intrigue in broken English for the hand of a serving-maid, and this forms an excellent counterpart to Simon's stately progress through ceremonies and banquets. The principal figure in the next story, *Richard Casteler*, is that of Long Meg of Westminster, a serving-maid, whose rattling deeds of 1540 or thereabouts had, before 1582, become the subject of both ballad and pamphlet[1]. The story consists of a series of attempts made by Meg and her rival, Gillian, to win the love of the hero-apprentice. A most effective situation is brought about when the two maids arrive at the same hour at the supposed trysting-place in Tuttle Fields. They each awkwardly offer an awkward explanation for their presence there, but each sturdily refuses to leave the field; and

in this humour, they sat them down, and sometimes they stalkt round about the field, till at last the watch met with them, who, contrary to Gillian's mind, took pains to bring them home together. At what time they gave one another such privie flouts that the watchmen took no little delight to hear it.

The upshot of it all is that the desirable Richard marries neither, whereupon Meg indulges in a soliloquy reminiscent of Falstaff:

'Wherefore is griefe good?' asks the disappointed maid, 'Can it recall folly past? No. Can it help a matter remediless? No. What then? Can grief make unkind men courteous? No. Then wherefore should I grieve? Nay, seeing it is so, hang sorrow! I will never care for them that care not for me.'

The next story, *Master Peachey and his men*, gives a breezy account of the cudgelling administered by the sturdy master-shoemaker to certain insolent court bullies, and then goes on to describe the rebuff experienced at the hands of a widow by the journeyman Tom Drum, who, previously, had been an unfailing diplomat in affairs of the heart. Tom's character is touched with exquisite humour, while he has a pretty turn of verse, which he exploits on his road to London, as follows:

The primrose in the grene forest,
The violets they be gay,
The double dazies and the rest
  That trimly deck the way,
Doth move the spirits with brave delight
  Who beauty's darlings be,
With hey tricksie, trim go tricksie
Under the greenwood tree.

[1] For an account of Long Meg and the contemporary allusions to her fame, see Chandler, *Literature of Roguery*, vol. I, pp. 144–5.

The last story is concerned with tavern-haunters and the decayed race of minstrels. In it appears the figure of Anthony Now-Now, one of the last of his tribe, from whose lips come the following lines with their significant burden:

> When should a man shew himself gentle and kind?
> When should a man comfort the sorrowful mind?
> O Anthony, now, now, now.
> . . . .
> When is the best time to drink with a friend?
> When is it meetest my money to spend?
> O Anthony, now, now, now.

In these works of Deloney, there is much that differs materially from all previous types. Deloney, obviously, is far removed from Lyly, though he, too, produces novels of manners, but it is the *bourgeois* type which he handles, the city, not the court; he writes to amuse rather than to instruct, and humour, not wit, is the main ingredient of his style. He has reminiscences of the romance and its peculiar style, but they form no real part of his production as a whole; he succumbs to Euphuism when he diverges from his real path, and these Euphuistic passages are precisely those which reveal his limitations, namely, an occasional want of taste and an inability to deal with certain situations which he creates. This is clearly seen in the stilted character of all the love-passages and in the unreal effect of the quasi-pathetic scene in *Thomas of Reading*. Romantic themes, moreover, are as uncongenial to him as is the romantic style. Passion lies outside his ken; to him, love is rather a matter of side-splitting laughter, a creator of absurd situations, a provoker of rough practical jokes. His characters, therefore, have but little in common with Greene's feminine creations, with Sidney's Arcadians, or with Lodge's sylvan lovers. Nor does his work stand much nearer to the rogue-novel of Nashe, though it deals abundantly in practical jokes; for, while in the picaresque type these jests form the narrative and are an end in themselves, in Deloney they aim at describing manners, at affording an insight into contemporary life, or they are a device for inserting light interlude into the body of the narrative. And, moreover, the hero, in Deloney, is by no means a rogue: he is endowed, on the contrary, with perhaps more than his share of virtue.

The influences which seem to have decided the actual form of Deloney's novels are of various kinds. In the first place, their *bourgeois* colouring was the result of circumstances; a life spent within hearing of the looms had brought him into close sympathy with crafts and craftsmen. Then, again, his earlier ballads, to some extent, suggest his material and shape his style: so that in Deloney the ballad-maker, the potential novelist is already visible. His themes in verse had been partly historical[1], partly romantic[2] and partly journalistic[3], and these elements, particularly the first and the last, enter into his novels. But his ballading days did more than suggest certain themes: the experience simplified his style and encouraged him to adopt a more self-effacing prose than even that of Nashe, for, in Nashe, the scholar and the theorist are still visible. Deloney's 'quaint and plain discourse,' with its lack of 'pickt words and choice phrases,' was, as he maintained, best fitted for 'matters of merriment,' especially as, for the most part, he treated of neither courtiers nor scholars. Deloney's debt to the contemporary stage is also considerable; that he had observed to some purpose is evident from the happy parody which he devises of Falstaff's famous soliloquy. From the stage, also, he borrows the idea of the comic underplot, which forms an effective feature in all three works. To the same source must, also, be ascribed his skilful dialogue, which is more natural, less stilted than any that had yet appeared: while his use of dialect and broken English in his attempts at verisimilitude, the skill with which he drops and resumes the thread of his narrative, must, again, have resulted from his observation of dramatic methods. When Greene and Lyly wrote, the stage was yet to develop; Deloney, writing at a later date, does not fail to profit by its rapid extension, and his story of Simon Eyre, under Dekker's hands, was to pass easily into comedy form, in *The Shoemaker's Holiday*[4].

Deloney's attraction for modern readers lies, to some extent, in his scenes of London life. Familiar places like Billingsgate and Islington, Fleet Street and Cheapside, appear in his works, though it is the varied humanity which throngs those scenes that most engages the attention. With great gusto, he portrays London tradesmen and their apprentices, dignified aldermen and bragging captains, stately city dames and rough serving-maids; dress is described with knowledge and relish; he appreciates both the gay

[1] Cf. the ballads, *Edgar*, *King John*, *Wat Tyler* and *Flodden*.

[2] Cf. also *Patient Grissel*, *Rosamund*, *Lancelot du Lake*.

[3] Cf. *Lamentation of Page's wife of Plymouth* and *The Execution of 14 Most Wickett Traitors*.

[4] Wm Rowley's play *The Shoemaker a Gentleman* (1610) was based upon the first two stories in *The Gentle Craft*. Henslowe also records a tragedy *The Six Yeomen of the West* founded on Deloney's *Thomas of Reading* (see Schelling, *Eliz. Drama*, 1908), vol. I, pp. 297—347.

and the gray colouring of a picturesque age; and, while he notes with precision and relates with effect, he is fully alive to the humour of it all. He also revives earlier interesting traditions: his work belongs, in the first instance, to the tradition represented by the lay of *Havelok*, to the literature which celebrates the deeds of ordinary folk. It belongs, also, to the traditions of the minstrel and jester: he takes up their tasks where their oral labours leave off. He witnesses to the passing of the old minstrel *régime*, for, in him, minstrelsy merges into the novelist's craft: and in like manner he absorbs the current jest-books, which were already foretelling the decay of the jester. It is in this way that he reflects, as does no other of his contemporaries, certain transitions which were taking place in Elizabethan society and art.

His contribution to the Elizabethan novel is, in some sense, the most interesting of all. Even in the best of contemporary novels, there is much that is irksome, however interesting historically: many of them are laboured, nearly all are affected and the story is frequently hard to grasp, on account of the profuse efforts to reveal the same. Deloney, on the other hand, tells his narrative with a simple directness: almost everywhere there is present a lightness of touch. He is a delightful humorist and an accurate painter; his prose runs easily into spirited dialogue, and, when he wishes to enliven the way, he is capable, like Tom Drum, of some cheerful songs. His limitations are those of a pioneer; one must not look for cunning structure or historical colouring, any more than for analysis of motive or character development. He is plying a craft as yet unformed; he uses a big brush to paint what lay before him and he is successful in presenting a broad picture of his age.

When all this prose fiction, however, has been placed in its proper perspective, it presents a record of experiment rather than of achievement; by the side of the drama, it is crude in form, almost futile in effect. But the greatness of the drama was closely bound up with temporary conditions, among which was a theatre liberally patronised, important in social life and standing in close touch with the life of the people. And then there was the public, intensely fond of 'shows,' and finding in them what they were unable to gather from the written word; a public, moreover, long accustomed to dramatic representation, and whose idealistic temperament demanded poetic form. These conditions were not to be permanent, and the future lay with a type of work which provided entertainment independent of these aids. It is in the prose fiction of the time that the beginnings of this type are found, and this historical interest is its first claim to recognition.

As to its actual achievement, one has to confess that this is comparatively small, for it worked from no model and was inspired by no tradition. It was wanting in coherent form and definite purpose; its plots lacked logical development, the threads of a story might be hopelessly confused; its characters were stiff and formal, and its style was not always adapted to the matter in hand. Nor can it be said to treat, as yet, the problems of life; it was content, for the most part, with simple narrative, with rough outlines of character and with studies of manners. But it improved its methods as it went on, it experimented in styles both simple and ornate, it made use of dialogue and it realised something of the wit and humour, as well as the descriptive power, of which prose was capable.

In its own age, it appealed to both the court and the people, and it was later social considerations which determined its future line of progress. The courtly and heroic elements were to pass with the Stuarts; but the more popular elements were to be taken up in Addison's day by the growing middle class, and, with ever-widening province and increasing art, were to result in the novel as we now know it.

CHAPTER XVII

THE MARPRELATE CONTROVERSY

The fashion of printed discussion did not become general in England before the reign of Elizabeth. Previous to her day, the chapbook and the broadside, vehicles of popular literature, had contained little beyond attractive romances or exciting pieces of news in ballad-form. Not until a great party, eager to proclaim and to defend its principles, arose in the nation, were the possibilities of the printing press, as an engine in the warfare of opinion, fully realised. The puritan movement cannot, of course, be held responsible for every one of those countless pamphlets in which the age of Shakespeare was rich, but it is not too much to say that, excluding purely personal squabbles, there is hardly a single controversy of the time which is not directly or indirectly traceable to it. The revolution of the seventeenth century was both religious and social, and it is important to bear in mind that the pamphlet campaign preceding it shared its double character. The religious and doctrinal tracts of the puritan controversialists lie, for the most part, outside the literary field. One series, however, wholly theological in intention, has won a place in the annals of literature by originality of style and pungency of satire, and by the fact that the first English novelist and the greatest Elizabethan pamphleteer took up the fallen gauntlet. These, the so-called Marprelate tracts, which gave rise to the most famous controversy of the period, form the topic of the present chapter.

The origin of the Marprelate controversy, interesting as it may be to the church historian, is far removed from the atmosphere of general literature, and must, therefore, be indicated as briefly as possible. Under the weak archbishop Grindal, the puritan[1], or, as it was later called, the presbyterian, doctrine had

[1] The term 'puritan,' at this early period of the movement, was of almost entirely doctrinal implication, and denoted one who supported the so-called 'church discipline.'

been making great strides among the clergy of the church of England. John Whitgift, long known as an uncompromising opponent of puritanism, was raised to the throne of Canterbury in 1583, only just in time to prevent the English reformation from following in the course already marked out by the Scottish. As it was, matters had gone so far that Whitgift found it necessary to adopt the most stringent measures, if the destinies of the church were to be taken out of puritan hands. The most important of these, from our present point of view, was the decree which he procured, in 1586, from the Star chamber[1], forbidding the publication of any book or pamphlet unless previously authorised by himself or the bishop of London, giving him full control over the Stationers' company, empowering him to determine the number of printing presses in use, and, finally, reviving a previous law imposing the severest penalties on the printing of seditious or slanderous books. In this way, he hoped to stem the ever-rising tide of puritan pamphlets, and so to prevent the spread of doctrines which he considered heretical. The Marprelate tracts were the direct outcome of the feeling of indignation at his relentless policy of repression, and they appeared in defiance of the newly created censorship. Episcopacy, as an institution, had always been obnoxious to the puritans; it became doubly so now, as the political instrument of their persecution. Elizabeth, while sanctioning, and heartily approving of, Whitgift's ecclesiastical policy, was well content to allow all the unpopularity resulting from it to light upon his shoulders; and the civil authorities, reluctant to persecute the puritans, withheld their support from the bishops, and so forced them to fall back upon the resources of their own prerogatives, and to strain these to the uttermost. Excuses may, therefore, be found for both sides. Defenders of the establishment were placed in an extremely difficult and disagreeable position, while puritans cannot be blamed for converting an attack on episcopacy in general into a diatribe against individual members of the episcopate. After ten years of struggle, so strong a reaction set in that parliament, formerly puritan in its sympathies, passed the famous anti-puritan statute of 1593, punishing those who attacked the ecclesiastical settlement with banishment or even death. The effect was magical. The violence of the puritans abated as suddenly as it had sprung up in 1583[2].

[1] See addenda.

[2] Prothero, *Select Statutes*, pp. xxxiii, lviii, 89, 169.

Thus was the vessel of puritanism wrecked on its first trial voyage, in the teeth of the winds of tradition and authority. But literature was the gainer by this storm of a decade, for the receding waves left upon the shores of time a little body of tracts which are, admittedly, the chief prose satires of the Elizabethan period. It was when the battle between bishop and sectarian waxed hottest, that the quaint and audacious personality calling himself 'Martin Marprelate, gentleman' first made his appearance; and, though his activity only lasted two years, he succeeded, during that short time, in thoroughly frightening the whole episcopal bench, in doing much to undermine its authority and prestige with the common people, and in providing the general public with food for laughter that has not even yet entirely lost its savour.

Martin took the field at the end of 1588; light skirmishers, however, had been there before him. A year after Whitgift's accession to power there appeared a small octavo volume entitled *A Dialogue concerning the strife of our Church*, from the press of the puritan printer Robert Waldegrave, and in black-letter[1]. This pamphlet is almost certainly by John Udall—so similar is it to other of his writings. The discussion is chiefly carried on between a puritan divine and a bishop's chaplain, and turns upon topics such as non-residency, dumb ministers and the pomp of bishops; but it contains no hint at all of the presbyterian discipline. Two years later, in 1586, a clever satirical attack upon episcopacy attempted to penetrate the archbishop's lines of defence by masquerading in the guise of anti-popery. The keen eye of Whitgift at once detected its real object, and arrested its progress so effectually that, had he not himself preserved a copy of it in his library at Lambeth, we might never have heard of it. The satire in question is an anonymous pamphlet, also in black-letter, styled *A Commission sente to the Pope, Cardynales, Bishops, Friers, Monkes, with all the rable of that Viperous Generation by the highe and mighty Prince, and King Sathanas, the Devill of Hell.* It purports to be an infernal despatch, instructing the officials mentioned on the title-page, and especially 'the great bishops our true messengers...whom we have constituted petty-popes under the great Archpope of Rome,' as to the measures to be adopted against the puritans. The constant allusions to

[1] Of this tract there is an interesting copy in Trinity College library, Cambridge, with marginal notes in the writing of two, if not three, different and, apparently, contemporary hands. Some of the remarks have a direct bearing upon the subject of the Marprelate tracts, Aylmer, bishop of London, being constantly referred to.

'petty-popes,' 'gatehouses,' 'clinks' and 'proctors' leave no doubt as to the sympathies and intentions of the author, who may, possibly, have been Martin himself, or his spiritual father John Field.

Among Martin's forerunners, two were concerned in the production of the famous tracts themselves. One of them, John Penry, who has been called the father of Welsh nonconformity, published, in March 1587[1], a petition, which, at the same time, was presented to parliament, calling attention to the deplorable state of religion in his native country, Wales. Five hundred copies of this *Treatise, containing the Aequity of an humble supplication*, were seized at once by Whitgift; and its author was summoned before the court of high commission. After being characteristically heckled by the archbishop, Penry was retained for a month in prison and then released. In reading his offending petition, it is difficult to find any justification for such treatment. It has been described as a bitter attack upon the church; but it contains nothing to support this description. There are, indeed, certain passages that might be construed as anti-episcopal; but we have evidence for believing that it was for treason rather than for heresy that Penry was arraigned[2]; and there is a paragraph in *The Aequity* which lends colour to this view. The puritans were loth, both from feelings of loyalty and from fear of coming under the law of treason, to associate Elizabeth with what they considered the evil practices of the bishops; yet it was difficult to avoid accusing her by implication, seeing that the bishops derived all the civil authority they possessed from her. Penry attempted to solve the problem by turning the tables upon his adversaries and accusing them of treason for laying the queen open to the possibility of such slanders. It was this that seems to have roused the archbishop's anger; though, as it was not in itself sufficient cause for conviction, the argument passed muster and reappears in the writings of Udall and in the Marprelate tracts.

John Udall's personal connection with Martin was much slighter than Penry's; but a small tractate of his, published anonymously and printed without authority in April 1588, holds a more important place in the history of the Marprelate controversy than anything Penry is known to have written. Even were it not so, *The State of the Church of Englande* or, as it is generally called, *Diotrephes*, would still be worthy of notice in

[1] 'The Date of Penry's Aequity,' *Cong. Hist. Soc. Trans.* II, No. 2.

[2] *Th' Appellation of John Penri*, pp. 3—5.

a history of literature. King James is said to have considered Udall 'the greatest scholar in Europe,' and *Diotrephes* shows him to have possessed humour as well as scholarship. The dialogue in which the tract is written is, at times, handled a little crudely; but the delineation of the time-serving publican, the cunning papist and the worldly bishop, tolerant to all save those who threaten his privileges, is a distinctly clever piece of work. There is no mistaking Udall's intentions. He puts a stern denunciation of bishops and a defence of the new presbyterian discipline into the mouth of Paul, a solemn and somewhat sententious 'preacher'; while the moral of the dialogue is that, while episcopacy is the root of all social and religious evils, popery is the root of episcopacy. A certain air of quietness and assurance about the whole contrasts favourably with the boisterous spirit of raillery in which Martin approaches the same topics. *Diotrephes* must take its place as the first and most thoughtful of the puritan pamphlets in the controversy.

If *The Aequity* was seized and its author cast into prison, mercy could certainly not be expected for *Diotrephes*, which was infinitely more outspoken and dangerous. For the time, Udall, who was a preacher at Kingston-on-Thames, preserved his anonymity; and the whole weight of Whitgift's wrath fell upon the printer, Robert Waldegrave. This man, who was to play an extremely important part in the struggle that followed, had already suffered several terms of imprisonment for printing puritan discipline tracts[1]. Early in 1588, he had again defied the authorities by publishing Penry's second Welsh tract, *An Exhortation*. On 16 April, his house was entered by the officers of the Stationers' Company; and, by virtue of Whitgift's Star chamber ordinance, a press, some pica type and many copies of *Diotrephes* were confiscated. Waldegrave[2] managed to escape and to carry with him some small roman and italic type; but his occupation was gone, and he had a wife and six children dependent upon him. His ruin, we shall see, was Martin's opportunity.

One more name must be mentioned before we come to close quarters with Martin himself—that of John Field, a famous puritan preacher, and part author of the first *Admonition to Parliament* (1572), which, in the violence of its language and in the secrecy of its production, reminds us forcibly of the Marprelate tracts. He died in February 1588, at least eight months before

[1] *Hay any worke for Cooper*, ed. Petheram (1845), p. 65.
[2] See addenda.

the publication of Martin's first pamphlet; but the Marprelate controversy was his legacy to his old enemies the bishops. 'We have used gentle words too long,' he had remarked to the archbishop's chaplain who visited him in prison, 'which have done us no good: the wound grows desperate and needs a corrosive.'[1] It was Martin who applied this corrosive; but Field, before his death, had prepared the ingredients. He is known to have collected certain notes, consisting of stories to the discredit of the most prominent bishops of the day[2]. These came into the hands of Martin and formed the basis of his earliest tract *The Epistle*. Had these notes been destroyed, as, it is said, Field, upon his death-bed, desired, there would perhaps have been no Marprelate controversy; certainly, without them, the first tract would have lost all its point and very much of its piquancy.

It is now time to turn to Martin himself, and consider the history of the secret printing press, which, like a masked gun, dropped shell after shell into the episcopal camp. The type that Waldegrave had rescued from the hands of the authorities was conveyed to the London house of a certain Mistress Crane, a well known puritan, where it remained, according to the evidence of her servant, for two or three months, that is, until midsummer. It is somewhat difficult to follow Waldegrave's movements after the raid in April, as the information we possess about the Marprelate press before November 1588 is very scanty and untrustworthy. The seizure of the copies of *Diotrephes* probably necessitated its reissue; and, as there are two distinct impressions extant, it is legitimate to suppose that the printer, for some of this time, was engaged upon this task[3]. A close examination of the lettering and workmanship of the tract, together with hints let fall by those examined by the authorities in their investigation of the affair, support the belief that it was printed by Waldegrave on a press and with type belonging to Penry and secreted at Kingston-on-Thames, of which town Udall was then parish priest. Hardby, at the village of East Molesey, was Mistress Crane's country-house,

[1] Neal, *Puritans* (ed. 1837), vol. I, p. 188.

[2] Arber, *Introductory Sketch to the Marprelate Controversy*, p. 94. Most of the facts relating to the Marprelate press are to be found in this collection of documents. Field's importance has, hitherto, escaped notice. Penry confessed that his notes formed the substance of *The Epistle*. Udall's notes, of which too much has been heard, appear to have concerned his own wrongs alone, the account of which covers little more than a page of the first tract.

[3] See addenda.

whither the rescued type was brought about midsummer, and, at the same time, or in September, the black-letter in which the first four Marprelate tracts were to be printed. On 10 June, the pursuivants had been at Kingston-on-Thames, looking for Waldegrave; but, as they had failed to find him, he had probably moved to East Molesey by that date. Anyhow, in July, he was probably hard at work there upon a fresh tract by Udall, entitled *A Demonstration of Discipline.* This pamphlet possesses none of the literary interest of *Diotrephes,* being little more than a bald summary of the puritan arguments against episcopacy. Its author, it may be noticed in passing, was, about this time, inhibited as a preacher because of his outspoken sermons, and is, for that reason, perhaps, much more bitter here than in the earlier tract. It soon, however, became evident that something besides arguments for church discipline and pleas for Wales was being hatched in this little nest of puritans in the Thames valley. The first Marprelate tract, commonly known as *The Epistle,* was printed by Waldegrave under Penry's supervision at Mistress Crane's house, and issued in October or at the beginning of the next month. It burst upon the world with surprising effect. Early in November, 'Martin' was a name in everyone's mouth. So great, indeed, was the stir that, on the 14th, we find Burghley, by royal command, writing an urgent letter to Whitgift, bidding him use all the means in his power to bring the authors to book. Penry had foreseen the coming storm, and the Thames valley had long been under the eye of the pursuivants. On 1 November, therefore, Waldegrave was already in Northamptonshire and his press on the road behind him.

It was natural that the press should gravitate into this district. Penry, on 8 September, had married a lady of Northampton and made his home there; and there was another and no less important reason for the direction taken. At a village, called Hasely, lying a little to the north-west of Warwick and, therefore, no very great distance from Northampton, dwelt a certain Job Throckmorton, who had much to do with the production of the tracts. The place to which the press and printer were removed was the house of Penry's friend, Sir Richard Knightley, at Fawsley, twelve miles from Northampton on the Warwick side and, therefore, easily accessible both to Penry and Throckmorton. Notwithstanding the strictest secrecy observed by all, it was found impossible to remain long there. During the stay, only one tract so far as we know, was printed—'the second Martin,' known as

The Epitome. This, the longest but one of Martin's productions, was printed, distributed and already in the archbishop's hands, before 6 December[1]: possibly, therefore, it had been partially printed before the move from Molesey. Its appearance led the authorities to redouble their efforts to discover the wandering press. On 29 January 1589, a pursuivant made a raid on Penry's house at Northampton, carrying off his papers; and, in February, a proclamation was issued against 'sundry schismatical and seditious bookes, diffamatorie Libels and other fantastical writings' that, of late, had been 'secretly published and dispersed.' Meanwhile, the press was again on its travels. At the end of 1588, or the beginning of 1589, it was carted to another house belonging to Sir Richard Knightley, situated at a little village near Daventry, called Norton. Here it remained idle for about a fortnight, when it was taken to Coventry and bestowed in the White Friars, a house belonging to John Hales, a relative of Sir Richard. From thence, two Marprelate tracts were issued, *The Minerall Conclusions*, at the end of February, and *Hay any worke for Cooper*, about the 20th of the following month, another of Penry's Welsh pamphlets, known as *A Supplication to the Parliament*, appearing between these two dates. At this juncture, a worse evil befell the Martinists than the compulsory nomadism they had hitherto endured. The man behind the gun began to tire of his task. At the beginning of April, Waldegrave informed a friend of his intention to quit the Marprelate cause. He was encouraged in this determination, not merely by personal fears, but, also, by the dislike of Martin's methods, openly expressed by the majority of puritan preachers. What happened to him immediately afterwards is not clear. We hear of him next at Rochelle, whither he probably found it safest to retire. He took away with him the black-letter in which the first four Marprelate tracts are printed, leaving it, perhaps, in London on his way through. Though no longer the Marprelate printer, he did not, therefore, sever all connection with Penry and Throckmorton. During the summer of 1589, he printed *Th' Appellation of John Penri*, and, about the same time, an anonymous book *M. Some laid open in his coulers*, said to be by Throckmorton and, therefore, of value as evidence for the identity of Martin. It is generally believed that Waldegrave also printed a little tract on the lines of Udall's *Diotrephes*, entitled *A Dialogue wherein is plainly laide open the tyrannicall*

[1] 'The Date of the second Marprelate Tract.' W. Pierce, *Journal Northants. Nat. Hist. Soc.* vol. XIII, p. 103. Brook's *Lives of the Puritans* (1813), vol. I, p. 423.

dealing of L. Bishopps against God's children. It is not certain, however, whether this was issued like the two others from Rochelle, though undoubtedly, it appeared in 1589[1].

Waldegrave's desertion was a sad blow for Martin and silenced his guns for a while. Another printer, one John Hodgkins, 'a salt-petre man,' was engaged in May or early in June; but he probably took some time in obtaining the necessary assistants, for he did not begin to print until midsummer or after. The press, or, perhaps we should say, one of the presses, had been removed from Coventry and was now concealed in the house of Mistress Wigston, at Wolston, a village some six miles to the south. Hodgkins's first task was to print the *Theses Martinianae* or *Martin Junior*, part of which, it is curious to notice, he had picked up in the road, outside Throckmorton's house, when returning with Penry from a visit there. He appears to have finished this about 22 July, and its sequel, *The just censure and reproofe of Martin Junior*, about a week later. He was then urged to take in hand another tract called *More worke for the Cooper.* Not liking Penry's press, however, he decided to take this manuscript away and print it on a second press, previously sent by him to the neighbourhood of Manchester, which, possibly, was his home. Here, while actually printing the new tract, he and two assistants, Symmes and Tomlyn, were arrested near the end of August by the earl of Derby. The press, type and manuscript were seized, with all the printed sheets of *More worke* that had already been struck off, and Hodgkins and his men were carried to London and examined under torture[2]. But this was not the *coup de grâce.* There was still the other press and Penry's original type at Mistress Wigston's. With the aid of these, the seventh and last Martin was produced, in the month of September 1589, at Throckmorton's house in Hasely, as is usually supposed, and issued under the title of *The Protestation.* An examination of the original reveals the fact that two different printers are responsible for it: one, the merest amateur, the other, an accomplished craftsman. The former, who only printed the first half sheet, we may conjecture to have been Penry, assisted, perhaps, by Throckmorton; the latter, who finished the tract, we believe from the printer's signatures to have been Waldegrave, who seems to have returned from Rochelle in the autumn of 1589 and to have delivered at Throckmorton's house his

[1] The dates of these three tracts, with Waldegrave's movements in 1589, are discussed in an article by the present writer in *The Library*, October 1907.

[2] *Yelverton MSS*, vol. LXX, fol. 146, *verso.* *Manchester Papers*, No. 123.

printed copies of *Th' Appellation* and *M. Some laid open*, before continuing his journey to Scotland, where, in 1590, he became royal printer to king James[1]. Soon after *The Protestation* appeared, Penry, also, fled to Scotland, possibly travelling in Waldegrave's company. Their departure was only just in time. Henry Sharpe, a bookbinder of Northampton, on 15 October, revealed to the lord chancellor the whole story of the Marprelate press, whereupon Sir Richard Knightley, Hales and the Wigstons were arrested[2]. At the end of the year, Udall, who had left Kingston for Newcastle in December 1588, was summoned to London and there cast into prison. Some two and a half years later, Penry returned to England and joined the separatists. Not long after, he was arrested, and, on 29 May 1593, was hanged on a trumped up charge of treason, thus paying with his life for the part he had taken in the Marprelate controversy. His partner, Job Throckmorton, who, probably, was far more guilty than he, swore, at the trial, that 'he was not Martin and knew not Martin'; and it was only in 1595, when the storm had blown over, that the real nature of his connection with the Marprelate press seems to have been realised.

Of the extant Marprelate tracts there are seven. Others, we know from contemporary evidence, had found their way into print or had been circulated in manuscript, but, unfortunately, they have not survived. Those we have, however, are quite sufficient to give a clear idea of Martin's methods and style. His chief aim was to cover the bishops with ridicule, but the first two tracts were, ostensibly, written in reply to a recent apologetic for the episcopal cause, entitled *A Defence of the Government established in the Church of England for ecclesiastical matters*, and 'very briefly comprehended,' as Martin puts it, 'in a portable book, if your horse be not too weake, of an hundred threescore and twelve sheets of good Demie paper,' running, that is, into more than fourteen hundred quarto pages of text. Written by the laborious, but worthy, John Bridges, dean of Sarum, in hope of preferment, as Martin asserts, it was a thorough and well-intentioned attempt to stem the flood of puritan discipline tracts by flinging a huge boulder into the stream. The rock-hurling Goliath from Salisbury was too ponderous for the ordinary carving process, and the only possible weapon to use against him was the stone and sling of ridicule. For such warfare, Martin was eminently qualified. A puritan who had been born a stage clown, he was a disciple both of Calvin and

[1] *The Library*, October 1907, pp. 337—359.

[2] An account of their trial is given in *State Trials*, vol. I, no. 67.

Dick Tarleton. His style is that of a stage monologue. It flows with charming spontaneity and naturalness. Now, with a great show of mock logic, he is proving that the bishops are petty popes; now, he is telling stories to their discredit; now, he is rallying 'masse Deane Bridges' on his 'sweet learning,' his arguments and his interminable sentences. All this is carried on with the utmost vivacity and embroidered with asides to the audience and a variety of 'patter' in the form of puns, ejaculations and references to current events and persons of popular rumour. Whether Martin were blasphemous or not, must be decided by each reader in the light of his own particular tenets. Certainly, he must be exculpated from any intention of the sort, the very nature of his plea precluding such a possibility. Personal, he undoubtedly was. He sets out with the object of lampooning the bishops of the day and frankly admits that such is his rôle in the general puritan campaign: 'you defend your legges against Martins strokes, while the Puritans by their Demonstration crushe the very braine of your Bishopdomes'—a remark which seems to indicate that the publication of Udall's *Demonstration of Discipline*, simultaneously with *The Epistle*, was no mere accident. Yet there is nothing that can be called definitely scurrilous in his treatment of the bishops, with the exception of his cruel reference to bishop Cooper's domestic misfortunes. They are 'pernicious,' 'pestilent,' 'wainscot-faced,' 'tyrannical,' sometimes 'beasts,' 'patches' and 'dunces,' occasionally, even, 'bishops of the devil,' but all this is part of the usual polemical vocabulary of the day; indeed, Barrow the separatist did not hesitate to use such expressions to Whitgift's very face. Martin's wit is a little coarse and homely, but never indecent, as the anti-Martinist pamphlets were. Speaking of the argumentative methods of Bridges, he says: 'He can now and then without any noyse alledge an author clean against himself, and I warrant you wipe his mouth cleanly and look another way as though it had not been he'—which may stand as a type of his peculiar vein of humour. His shafts are winged with zest, not with bitterness. 'Have at you!' he shouts, as he is about to make a sally, and, again, 'Hold my cloake there somebody that I may go roundly to worke'; for he evinces, throughout, the keenest delight in his sport among the 'catercaps.' This effect of boisterousness is enhanced by various tricks of expression and arrangement. The tracts present no appearance of any set plan, they are reeled off with the utmost volubility, at the top of the voice, as it were, and are scattered up and down with quaint marginal notes and parentheses. All this reveals a whimsical and original literary personality utterly unlike anything we find in the attested writings of Penry or Udall. Yet, it must not be supposed that the tracts are nothing but 'quips and quidities.' These are only baits to catch the reader and lure him on into the net of puritan argument. Most of them contain serious passages, sometimes of great length, expounding the new discipline.

Leaving general considerations, we may now turn and briefly observe the main characteristics of each tract. *The Epistle*, intended, as its lengthy and amusing title implies[1], as an introduction to a forthcoming epitome of the dean of Sarum's apologetic, was, as we have seen, largely based on John Field's notes. It consists, therefore, for the most part, of those anecdotes relating to the bishops' private lives which are usually considered Martin's chief stock-in-trade, but which appear, in reality, very rarely in the later tracts. Some of them were, no doubt, untrue, and many were exaggerations of innocent incidents unworthy of mention. Naturally enough, too, they principally concerned those prelates who had made themselves particularly obnoxious to the puritans, chief of whom were Whitgift of Canterbury, Aylmer of London and Cooper of Winchester. Besides this scandal, *The Epistle* contains many references to the grievances of the puritans, special attention being paid to the cases of Penry, Waldegrave and Udall, the last of whom admitted under examination, in 1590, that certain notes of his, concerning the archdeacon of Surrey and a usurer at Kingston, had found their way, without his knowledge, into the tract. Yet, whatever the origin of the materials, they are treated consistently throughout in one vein, and no one reading *The Epistle* can doubt that its author was a single individual and not a puritan syndicate.

It is not possible to speak with the same certainty of *The Epitome*, in which Martin undertakes the trouncing of Bridges promised in *The Epistle*. It contains some of those serious passages before mentioned, in which it is open for critics to see a second hand at work, though it would be difficult, on such a hypothesis, to decide in every case where Martin left off and his collaborator began. The tract sets out on its title-page, which is practically identical with that of *The Epistle*, to be an epitome of the first book of Bridges; but, as before suggested, it is doubtful whether Martin ever seriously intended to do more than play with the worthy dean. A few extracts are quoted from his book and

[1] See bibliography.

ridiculed, or, occasionally, answered, in the quasi-logical fashion that is one of the characteristics of Martin's style; but a larger portion of the tract is, in reality, devoted to Aylmer, bishop of London. This prelate was considered a renegade by the puritans and was, accordingly, even more in disfavour with them than Whitgift. As has been seen[1], Aylmer had written a book in reply to Knox's *First Blast of the Trumpet.* In this, he had found occasion to inveigh against the worldliness and wealth of the Marian bishops, and even to imply disapproval of their civil authority. It was easy to turn such words against their unlucky author, now comfortably ensconced in the see of London and wielding the civil authority against the puritans; and Martin made the most of his opportunity. For the rest, *The Epitome* exhibits the same characteristics as its predecessor, though it more frequently lapses into a serious vein. There is one fresh touch of humour that is worth notice. The tract contains on the last page some *errata*, the nature of which may best be gathered from the first, which begins 'Whersoever the prelates are called my Lords... in this Epitome, take that for a fault.'

Soon after the appearance of the second Marprelate tract, Thomas Cooper, bishop of Winchester, took up the cudgels for the episcopal side, in his *Admonition to the People of England.* Far from discouraging Martin by his grave condemnation, the worthy bishop played straight into the satirist's hands and merely provided fresh fuel for the fire of his wit. The old business of Bridges was growing somewhat stale, and Martin turned with alacrity towards a new antagonist. Just then, the Marprelate press was on its journey from Fawsley to Coventry; but, so soon as it was comfortably settled at the White Friars, a broadside appeared, known as *The Minerall Conclusions,* which was intended to keep the game in swing until a more weighty answer to Cooper's *Admonition* could be framed and printed. It contained thirty-seven 'Minerall and Metaphisicall Schoolpoints, to be defended by the reverende Bishops and the rest of my cleargie masters of the Convocation house.' These school-points are arguments or opinions of the most ludicrous description, each purporting to be held by an ecclesiastical dignitary who is named as its defender. Nearly half of them are quoted (or misquoted) from Cooper's book, and the whole concludes with a witty address to the reader, stating that, if anyone can be found ready and willing to withstand these arguments and their formidable supporters, 'the matters

[1] See *ante*, p. 145.

shall be, according unto order, quietly tried out between him and the bare walles in the Gatehouse, or some other prison.' While this was circulating from hand to hand, a more fitting reply to the *Admonition* was being prepared under the title of *Hay any worke for Cooper?* a familiar street-cry of the time. The bishop's name afforded an opportunity for an infinite amount of word-play, and the atmosphere of the tract is thick with tubs, barrels and hoops. *Hay any worke* is the longest of all Martin's productions and, except for *The Protestation*, contains the greatest quantity of serious writing. There is a little of the familiar frolicking at the outset; but Martin very soon puts off his cap and bells and sits down to a solemn confutation of Cooper's new defence of the civil authority of bishops. After about fifty pages, he recovers himself, and, with a whoop of 'Whau, whau, but where have I bin al this while!' he launches out into ridicule of various passages in the bishop's apologetic, rounding contemptuously on him for his deficiency in humour—'Are you not able to discern between a pleasant frump given you by a councellor and a spech used in good earnest?'

Martin Junior or *Theses Martinianae*, the next in the series, exhibits a change in method. Field's notes, which Martin had merely decorated with his drolleries, had formed the basis of *The Epistle*, while the apologetics of Bridges and Cooper had given substance and cohesion to the sallies of *The Epitome* and *Hay any worke*. In *Martin Junior*, our pamphleteer aims, for the first time, at what may be called literary form[1]. In a period when fiction, apart from drama, was in its earliest infancy, any piece of imaginative prose, however rudimentary, is interesting. The bulk of the tract, indeed, consists of a 'speech' by Martin Marprelate and a hundred and ten theses against the bishops, in which the familiar 'discipline' arguments are reasserted; but it is prefaced with a short epistle, ostensibly by Martin Junior, younger son of the old Martin, and concludes with a lengthy epilogue in the approved Tarleton style, dedicated 'To the worshipfull his very good neame maister John Canterburie,' and signed 'your worship's nephew Martin Junior.' In this epilogue, we are given to understand that old Martin has disappeared, possibly into the Gate House[2], and that his son, a 'prety stripling' Martin Junior, has discovered under a hedge a manuscript containing the aforesaid theses in his father's handwriting. It will be remembered that it was precisely in this fashion that part of *Martin Junior* actually

[1] See addenda.

[2] Possibly this is an allusion to the departure of Waldegrave.

came into the hands of the printer; so it is just possible that there is more in the tale than appears upon the surface. This manuscript, which breaks off in the middle of a sentence, Martin Junior gives to the world, adding a long defence of his father's methods, obviously addressed to the puritans, whose 'misliking' had been the cause of Waldegrave's defection. The imaginative setting of the *Theses Martinianae* is continued in *Martin Senior* or *The just censure and reproofe*, which came forth a week later. Martin Senior is the eldest son of 'Martin the Great' and is, seemingly, very indignant at his stripling brother's rashness and impertinence in printing his father's theses. After a little introductory playfulness in this vein, the tract goes on to give 'an oration of John Canturburie to the pursuivants when he directeth his warrants to them to post after Martin,' which is reminiscent of *A Commission sente to the Pope* and, at the same time, anticipates the method of the *Satyre Ménippée*. In addition to this, we have 'eleven points,' with a solemn diatribe, against episcopacy, a reference to the 'slackness of the Puritans,' a proposal to present a petition to the queen and privy council, and, lastly, an answer to the anti-Martinist rimes in *Mar-Martine*, doggerel for doggerel.

At this juncture, the bishops succeeded, at last, in silencing their voluble antagonist by seizing his press and arresting his printers at Manchester. Martin died with defiance on his lips. His last tract, *The Protestation*, plunges at once into the question of the late capture, declares that it can do Martin no harm as the printers do not know him and proceeds to rail against the bishops as inquisitors and butchers. It is noticeable that Martin has almost entirely dropped his comic tone; and, as if he realised that the time for such a tone had passed, he emphatically declares 'that reformation cannot well come to our church without blood'—a phrase which, while it ostensibly refers to the blood of the martyrs, leaves it open for the reader to understand the blood of the bishops. He bids his readers believe 'that by the grace of God the last yeare of "Martinisme"... shall not be till full two years after the last year of Lambethisme,' a prophecy which received a curious fulfilment in the appearance of a pamphlet in imitation of Martin a year after Laud's execution. The climax of the whole tract is reached in the 'protestation,' or challenge, to the bishops to hold a public disputation upon the points of disagreement between puritan and prelate, its author proclaiming his readiness to come forward as the public champion of the puritan cause, for which, should he fail, he is willing to forfeit his life.

The Protestation is, strictly speaking, the last of the seven Marprelate tracts that have come down to us. But there is an eighth, *A Dialogue*, printed by Waldegrave in the summer of 1589, which, obviously, is Martinist in sympathy and purpose, and which deserves mention even if it cannot claim a place among the other seven. In 1643, it is interesting to notice, it was reprinted under the title of *The Character of a Puritan... by Martin Marprelate*; so that there was evidently a tradition which assigned it to our jester-puritan. The style of the whole is quite unlike Martin's; but it may be that the dialogue form would put considerable restraint upon his natural exuberance. This very form suggests that maker of dialogues, John Udall[1]. He had spoken the prologue to the Marprelate drama in his *Diotrephes*; it would seem fitting, therefore, that the epilogue should be his also. But, however this may be, the tract, if not Martin's, is interesting as a proof that there was at least one puritan who sympathised with his methods. 'The Puritanes like of the matter I have handled but the forme they cannot brooke,' our tractarian writes in *Martin Junior*; and it is worthy of notice that, while he constituted himself the spokesman of puritanism, he was far from being in touch with its spirit. The 'preachers,' as we have seen, looked with great disfavour on his levity. Thomas Cartwright, the leader of the movement, was careful to dissociate himself at the very outset from any suggestion of sympathy with him. Richard Greenham, another celebrated puritan and tutor of the still more celebrated Browne, actually went so far as to preach against *The Epistle* in a sermon delivered at St Mary's, Cambridge. 'The tendency of this book is to make sin ridiculous, when it ought to be made odious'; so ran the text of his condemnation. These words lay bare the very springs of puritanism and teach us not only why Martin failed to win puritan support, but, also, why the whole movement, despite its many obvious excellences, did not succeed, in the long run, in winning over the most intellectual forces of the nation. The puritans banished the comic muse from England. She returned, in 1660, as the handmaid of Silenus.

Before turning to the answers that Martin evoked from the episcopalians, a few remarks may be hazarded as to the authorship of the series of pamphlets that bear his name. An attempt has been made to father them on Henry Barrow, the separatist, whom the congregationalists regard as one of the founders of their church, and who, at the time, was lying in the Fleet. The theory is ingenious, but quite untenable. The Marprelate tracts were the

[1] There is, however, nothing else about the tract to suggest Udall's authorship.

product of the presbyterian, and not of the independent, or separatist, movement. Udall, Field, Waldegrave, all who were known to have been connected with the production of the tracts, were 'church discipline' men, who wished to reform the church from within. True, Penry joined the separatists in 1592, but, by that time, Martin Marprelate was ancient history. Further than this, it has recently been pointed out that *Hay any worke* contains a passage in reference to the question of tithe-taking which could not possibly have been written by a separatist[1]. In point of fact, most authorities are now agreed that the choice lies between Throckmorton and Penry. Possibly, the tracts, which exhibited two styles, or, at least, two moods, were the result of their combined energies. Two critics, with a special knowledge of Penry's writings, have rejected the theory of his identity with 'Martin' in the strongest terms[2]; but, as they are here obviously alluding to Martin the humorist, their disclaimer does not really affect the possibility of Penry's responsibility for the theological passages, though there is absolutely no evidence involving him even to this limited extent. On the other hand, there seem to be very strong reasons, even if they do not amount to actual proof, for assigning at least the comic portions of the tracts to Job Throckmorton. In 1589, Waldegrave had printed a tract entitled *M. Some laid open in his coulers*, which, almost without doubt, is Throckmorton's[3], though the signature I. G. at the end has led many critics to attribute it to John Greenwood, Barrow's friend and fellow prisoner —a theory which, like that ascribing the Marprelate tracts to Barrow, collapses before the theological test. Dr Some was a busy controversialist on the Whitgiftian side, and this pamphlet against him was one link in another chain of polemical writings, the particulars of which it is not necessary to examine here. Suffice it to remark that Some attacked both Penry and Barrow; and, therefore, it is probable that the author of *M. Some laid open*, who had no desire to divulge his identity, intentionally adopted Greenwood's initials in order to throw dust into the eyes of the authorities. Style may be a doubtful touchstone for the test of authorship; but one cannot conceive that anyone familiar with the tracts of Martin could fail to see the same hand in *M. Some laid open*. In every way, it is similar, in that boisterous, rollicking, hustling

[1] Powicke, *Henry Barrow*, pp. 82—85, which contain valuable information in reference to this question of authorship.

[2] Waddington, *John Penry*, and Greive, *The Aequity*.

[3] Sutcliffe's *Answere to Job Throckmorton* (Arber, *Sketch*, p. 179). It should be admitted, however, that not all authorities are inclined to trust Sutcliffe's statements to the same extent as the present writer.

manner of speech which has won them a place in the literature of the nation, and it deserves to share that place with them. For the rest, if further information regarding Throckmorton's real position in this famous controversy should be needed, there remains the valuable, if *ex parte*, testimony of Matthew Sutcliffe.

This man was a *protégé* of Bancroft and became provost of his college at Chelsea for the training of theological controversialists. In 1592, appeared an interesting little tractate, under the title of *A Petition directed to her most excellent Majestie*, dealing with the legal aspect of the controversy between the bishops and the puritans, dwelling, at considerable length, on Udall's trial in 1590 and, incidentally, clearing Martin of certain charges of conspiracy and high treason which Bancroft had levelled against him. In the course of the argument, the author has occasion to refer to a publication by Sutcliffe. In December 1592, Sutcliffe replied in *An answere to a certaine libel supplicatorie*, in which he accuses Job Throckmorton of being implicated in the 'making of *Martin*.' This, in its turn, called forth an angry, but scarcely convincing, rejoinder by Throckmorton, which Sutcliffe, in 1595, reprinted with running comments of the most damaging nature in *An Answere unto a certaine calumnious letter published by M. Job Throkmorton.* The value of this book lies in the fact that Sutcliffe bases his indictment upon evidence which has since been lost. Wherever it is possible to check them, the facts brought forward cannot be invalidated; and an attentive reader of the tract will find it difficult to avoid agreeing with its author that 'Throkmorton was a Principal Agent' in the Marprelate business, 'and the man that principally deserveth the name of Martin[1].'

We must now leave the puritan lines, and, crossing over into the episcopal camp, discover how the forces of authority met Martin's fierce bombardment. A close examination of the bishops' counter-attack will reveal three distinct phases in their tactics, each involving a different section of their supporters. Martin found himself opposed, not only by the heavy battalions of theology, but, also, by the archery of dramatic lampoon and the light cavalry of literary mercenaries. The theological attack, which need not long detain us, was undertaken, it will be remembered, by Thomas Cooper, bishop of Winchester, in his *Admonition to the People of England*, published in January 1589, and written as a reply to Martin's *Epistle.* The book is of no value from the literary point of view. It answered Martin's raillery with serious rebuke, and

[1] But see Wilson, J. Dover, *Martin Marprelate and Shakespeare's Fluellen*, 1912, published since the above was written.

was so lacking in humour as to attempt to refute categorically every accusation against the bishops to be found in *The Epistle.* For all this, Cooper, alone of the controversialists, earned the approval of Bacon, in his *Advertisement touching the Controversies of the Church of England*, a short treatise written about this time[1] on the main points of the ecclesiastical dispute. Cooper won Bacon's praise because he remembered 'that a fool was to be answered, but not by becoming like unto him.' It is evident that the directors of the episcopal campaign did not agree with Bacon and Cooper, for theological argument was soon laid aside and the methods of defence readjusted to changed conditions. The only theological contribution to the controversy, after the *Admonition*, was the publication, in March 1589, of *A sermon preached at Paules crosse the* 9 *of Februrarie... by Richard Bancroft D. of Divinitie.* This sermon, which was revised and enlarged before being sent to the press, was an assertion of the divine right of episcopacy as against recent attacks upon it, Martin's being especially mentioned. Bancroft, who, later, was to succeed Whitgift in the primacy, was, at this time, a rising man in the church and found in the Marprelate controversy an excellent opportunity of proving his mettle. The energy of the pursuivants who rode up and down the country to find the Marprelate press, the vigorous detective measures that were resorted to for the discovery of Martin's identity and the crowning triumph in Newton's Lane, Manchester, may all be traced to his untiring exertions. But more than this may be laid to his charge. As Whitgift himself tells us, he was the moving spirit in the new phase into which the controversy now entered[2]. At his suggestion, the Bridges-cum-Cooper method was laid aside and certain writers of the day were retained, possibly at a fee, to serve the episcopal cause by pouring contempt upon its enemy. The result was a second series of tracts, none of which are of any great literary merit, being, for the most part, as Gabriel Harvey described one of them, 'ale-house and tinkerley stuff,' but which have acquired a certain amount of importance from the fact that John Lyly and Thomas Nashe are generally supposed to have been engaged in their production. The new policy began to take effect in the spring and summer of 1589, and its first fruits were some verses of very inferior quality and a Latin treatise. The possibility that the famous

[1] *A Petition directed to her most excellent Majestie*, 1592, refers (p. 6) to Bacon's *Advertisement*, but describes it as 'not printed.'

[2] Strype, *Life of Whitgift*, vol. II, cap. XXIII, p. 387.

Euphuist and his friend were, in part, responsible for these effusions, alone makes it necessary to record their titles. A rimed lampoon calling itself *A Whip for an Ape*, in reference to the fact that 'Martin' was a common name for a monkey, appeared in April, followed, shortly afterwards, by a second, similar, but slightly inferior in style, under the title *Mar-Martine*. These clumsy productions provoked a reply in verse no less clumsy from some worthy person, with the pseudonym Marre Mar-Martin, who points out that, while Martin and Mar-Martin are at loggerheads, the protestant religion is in danger from the papists. The impartial attitude maintained by this writer has led to the conjecture that he may be one of the Harvey brothers, but there is no evidence to support it[1]. Such thin verses, whether impartial or antagonistic, were not likely, in any way, to affect the Martinist cause; still less was the sententious pamphlet *Anti-Martinus*, signed A.L., and entered at Stationers' Hall, on 3 July 1589, which addresses itself to the youth of both universities and solemnly ransacks the stores of antiquity for parallels to, and arguments against, Martin.

The poverty of invention and execution displayed in this first period of the anti-Martinist attack may be attributed to the fact that the bishops' penmen were engaged upon other matters. There are many indications that the summer of 1589 saw the appearance of certain anti-Martinist plays upon the English stage. Unfortunately, none of these have come down to us, probably because they never found their way into print. We may, however, learn something of them from various references, chiefly retrospective, in the pamphlets issued on both sides[2]. These scattered hints lead us to infer that Martin had figured upon the London stage in at least two plays, if not more. In one of them, apparently a species of coarse morality, he appeared as an ape attempting to violate the lady Divinity. Another, which was played at the Theater, seems to have been more in the nature of a stage pageant than a regular drama. Other plays may have been acted; but the authorities, finding this public jesting with theological topics unseemly, appear to have refused to license any more after September, and, early in November, put a definite stop to those already

[1] It would appear that *Plaine Percevall* and *Marre Mar-Martin* could hardly be by the same hand, as the latter is expressly inveighed against in the dedication to the former.

[2] The following are the chief contemporary references to anti-Martinist plays: *Martin Junior*, sig. D ii; *The Protestation*, p. 24; McKerrow's *Nashe*, vol. I, pp. 59, 83, 92, 100, 107; vol. III, p. 354; Grosart's *Nashe*, vol. I, p. 175, and *Harvey*, vol. II, p. 213; Bond's *Lyly*, vol. III, pp. 398, 408; *Plaine Percevall* (Petheram's reprint, 1860), p. 16.

licensed and any others that may have defied the censor. But the suppression of the anti-Martinist plays could not banish the topic from the stage. Martin was the puritan of popular imagination, and the dramas of the time are full of references to him.

Meantime, there had been a renewed outburst of anti-Martinist pamphlets, this time in prose. The first of the new series, *A Countercuffe given to Martin Junior*, published under the pseudonym of Pasquill, on or about 8 August, was a direct answer to *Theses Martinianae* and, at the same time, served as a kind of introductory epistle to the tracts that followed, being but four pages in length. Pasquill announces that he is preparing two books for publication, *The Owles Almanack* and *The Lives of the Saints*. The latter is to consist of scandalous tales relating to prominent puritans, to collect which the author has 'posted very diligently all over the Realme.' Whether he ever thus turned the tables upon Martin, we do not know; but one promise made in this tract was certainly fulfilled. Before the conclusion, Martin Junior is warned to expect shortly a commentary upon his epilogue, with epitaphs for his father's hearse. This refers to *Martins Months Minde*, and it is worth noticing that the writer claims no responsibility for it as he does for the other two.

Martins Months Minde, by far the cleverest and most amusing of the anti-Martinist tracts, in all probability saw light soon after *A Countercuffe*. Its title refers to the old practice of holding a commemoration service, known as a 'month's mind,' four weeks after a funeral. The fresh vein of humour opened by Martin in *Theses Martinianae* is here further worked out by a writer of the opposite side. After discussing the various rumours to account for old Martin's disappearance, the tract proceeds to give 'a true account' of his death, describing his treatment by the physicians, his dying speech to his sons, the terrible diseases that led to his death, his will and, lastly, the revelations of a post-mortem examination of his corpse. The whole is rounded off by a number of epitaphs in English and Latin by his friends and acquaintances. All this is retailed with much humour and a little coarseness, and is prefaced by two dedicatory epistles, the first of which is addressed to Pasquine of England and signed Marphoreus[1].

The tracts just mentioned do not refer to the capture of Martin's press or to the printing of *The Protestation*, and it is probable, therefore, that they preceded both these events. *Pappe with a Hatchet* and *The Returne of Pasquill*, the two that follow,

[1] For the probable origin of these pen-names see Bond's *Lyly*, vol. I, p. 55.

were almost finished before *The Protestation* came into circulation, each containing, in a postscript, a brief reference to its appearance. An approximate date is fixed for all three tracts by the postscript of *The Returne*, dated '20 Octobris,' in which the author states that 'olde Martins Protestation' came into his hands 'yesternight late.' Of the two anti-Martinist tracts, *Pappe with a Hatchet* was, probably, the earlier, since an answer to it by Gabriel Harvey, which we shall notice later, was concluded before 5 November. This worthless production is the only hitherto undisputed contribution by John Lyly to the controversy. It essays to imitate the style which Martin had adopted; but the frequent ejaculations with which it is besprinkled do nothing to relieve the tediousness of the whole. For the rest, it is a compound of sheer nonsense and frank obscenity and must have disgusted more with the cause it upheld than it ever converted from Martinism. *The Returne of Pasquill* was superior in every way to Lyly's work, but, even so, it cannot rank very high. Pasquill, returning from abroad, meets Marphoreus on the Royal Exchange, and they discuss the inexhaustible topic of Martinism together. A description of a puritan service at Ashford, Kent, leads us to suppose that the author of *A Countercuffe* may, indeed, have carried out his intention of posting over England for news of the Martinists, and we have further references to the two books containing his experiences already promised. The tract concludes with a brief reply to *The Protestation*, containing, it is interesting to observe, a eulogy on Bancroft.

Two new writers now joined their voices to the general wrangle, Gabriel Harvey and his brother Richard, and their entry was the beginning of yet another controversy, to which the poet Greene contributed just before his death, and which was eventually fought out over his dead body by Nashe and Gabriel Harvey. A detailed description of this dispute would carry us too far from the present subject[1], and we must here confine our attention to its opening stage, which alone concerns the matter in hand. In order, we may conjecture, to add a little flavour to the somewhat thankless task Bancroft had imposed upon him, Lyly, in his *Pappe*, had deliberately challenged Harvey to enter the Marprelate lists. Harvey at once took up the gauntlet in his *Advertisement to Papp-Hatchet*; but the writing of it seems to have cooled his anger, for it was not published until 1593, when, in other ways, he had involved himself in a quarrel with the literary free-lances of London. His pamphlet, when it appeared, was found to be more of a personal attack than

[1] See bibliography.

a contribution to the general controversy, concerning which it assumes an air of academic impartiality, dealing out blows to both parties in that 'crab-tree cudgell style' which we associate with its author, and displaying as ostentatiously as may be his learning and wide knowledge of theology. His brother Richard, it may be at his suggestion, now followed suit, though scarcely with the same impartial spirit, in *A Theologicall Discourse of the Lamb of God and his enemies*, wherein the 'new Barbarisme' of Martin is shown to be nothing but an old heresy refurbished.

The *Theologicall Discourse* is mainly interesting for its 'Epistle to the Reader,' which contained a passage apparently vilifying the *littérateurs* of the day under the name of the 'make plaies and make bates' of London. This roused Greene, in his *Quip for an Upstart Courtier* (1592), to retaliate by some comments upon the Harvey family in general. The poet soon afterwards died; but Gabriel Harvey's pride had been seriously wounded and he would not allow the matter to rest there. His reply, heaping contempt and imputations upon the memory of the dead man, was answered by Nashe, and the dispute continued with unabated vigour for some five years, when, at last, a stop was put to it by the authorities. That Richard Harvey, whose words had led to this fiery quarrel, should be the same man who had just published *Plaine Percevall the Peace-maker of England*, is somewhat hard to credit, but so we are definitely assured by Nashe[1]. After *Martins Months Minde*, this is the most readable of the answers to Martin. Its style is original, shows faint traces of Euphuism, and is embroidered with homely proverbs and parenthetical anecdotes in the manner of Sam Weller. Plaine Percevall himself figures as a countryman of commonsense, an unsophisticated 'man in the street,' who, amazed at 'this surpernaturall art of wrangling,' bids all 'be husht and quiet a Godsname.'

The entry of the Harveys is an indication of the widespread interest taken in the controversy, and certain tracts noted in the Stationers' register, together with the list of 'hageling and profane' pamphleteers given in *Martin Junior*, shows us that there were many other writers, not necessarily supporting either side, who felt compelled to record their opinions upon the vexed topic of the day[2]. The tracts of two only have survived, and both voice the same desire for peace and quiet that *Plaine Percevall*

[1] McKerrow's *Nashe*, vol. I, p. 270.

[2] If we may judge from the pessimistic tone of *The Tears of the Muses*, this raging controversy seems to have exercised the most depressing effect upon the mind of Spenser.

had expressed. Their titles are ***A Myrror for Martinists*** by one T. T. and ***A Friendly Admonition to Martin Marprelate*** by Leonard Wright; they were entered at Stationers' Hall on 22 December 1589 and 19 January 1590 respectively.

The last shot fired on the Marprelate battlefield was *An Almond for a Parrat* which, begun as a reply to *The Protestation*, was delayed for some reason and did not appear until the following spring[1]. Its literary merits are small, but it is much more closely reasoned and well-informed than any other anti-Martinist production, and its author seems to have been at pains to collect much information about Penry, whom he declares to be 'Martin,' Udall, Wiggington and other famous puritans. Though *An Almond for a Parrat* is a companion to *Pappe with a Hatchet*, written in the same ejaculatory, swashbuckling style and replete with similar ribald stories, nevertheless, the attribution of it to Lyly does not find favour[2].

The honour of this battle of the books belongs, so far as literature is concerned, to Martin. The Marprelate tracts are part of English literature, the answers to them little more than materials for literary history. None of the pamphlets written to order on behalf of the bishops were entered at Stationers' Hall—a fact which seems to imply that, while Whitgift and Aylmer sanctioned them privately, they were ashamed to authorise them publicly. *Martins Months Minde* and *Plaine Percevall* are amusing; but the rest are very unprofitable to be read and most unworthy to be regarded, if we may parody a familiar Euphuism. The fact that Lyly and Nashe were responsible, in part, for their production, and the numerous references throwing light upon the whole controversy which they contain have alone rescued them from the oblivion into which they would otherwise have fallen. It is idle to suggest that they did anything to stop Martin's mouth: his silence was the work of the pursuivants. Doubtless, the growth and final triumph of the cause he advocated did much to secure immortality for the puritan pamphleteer. The opening years of the Long parliament saw a revival of Martinism. *Hay any worke* was reprinted in 1641 and *A Dialogue* in 1643, while, in 1645, four tracts appeared by a writer calling himself 'Yongue Martin Marpriest.' Qualities of style and not peculiarities of doctrine singled out these from

[1] See the concluding words of the epistle dedicatory (McKerrow's *Nashe*, vol. III, p. 343) and Penry's reference to it in his *Brief Discovery*, 1590, sig. A 4 *recto*.

[2] See note at end of bibliography.

among the countless other puritan tracts that the age produced for the admiration of posterity. Martin's freakish and audacious personality and his unusual vein of satire were something new and not easily forgotten. He was the most famous prose satirist of the Elizabethan period and may rightly be considered as the humble forerunner of that much greater satirist whose *Tale of a Tub* was a brilliant attack upon all forms of religious controversy. Martin's style exercised an immediate and appreciable influence upon his contemporaries—a point that has hitherto scarcely been noticed—for Nashe, at this period, was a young writer whose style was hardly formed; and, though he afterwards proudly boasted 'that the vaine which I have is of my owne begetting and cals no man father in England but myself[1],' yet it is impossible not to see that the most modern and most racy prose writer of the Elizabethan age owed a considerable debt to 'olde Martin Makebate,' in contest with whom he won his spurs. The famous *Epistolae Obscurorum Virorum* were some seventy years earlier than the Marprelate tracts and rank much higher as literature. It is not, however, fair to compare the deliberate creation of some of the protagonists of German humanism with hasty and ill-digested attacks upon episcopacy, struck off from a travelling printing press. Much the same may be said of the *Satyre Ménippée,* which is frequently quoted as a parallel to its English contemporary. It was a curious coincidence that remarkable satires should appear in England and France almost simultaneously, but there was no connection and very little similarity between the two. The *Satyre Ménippée* was political in intention, the Marprelate tracts religious. The group of *politiques* who were responsible for the French satire represented the commonsense of France tired of the tyranny of the League and the long unrest of past years. Their work was an epitaph on an already fallen foe, and the laugh it elicited was one of relief and of hope. To Martin, on the other hand, it was given to be one of the first to blow the trumpet against the episcopal Jericho which, when at last it fell, involved the monarchy in its ruins. Few, even of those of his own party, sympathised with him or understood him, but, when the hour of victory came, some were found to remember his service in the cause.

[1] McKerrow's *Nashe*, vol. I, p. 319.

CHAPTER XVIII

OF THE LAWS OF ECCLESIASTICAL POLITY

THE London of the early days of Elizabeth has been described as a city of ruins. On every side lay the wreck of some religious house which had perished in the days of the dissolution, and had not been supplanted by new edifices. This description of the capital may not inaptly be applied in a wider sense to the condition of England. For more than a generation, the work of destruction in every department of social and political life had been in progress; and, in religion, which then completely overshadowed all other human interests, the old order had collapsed, and the signs of its fall were on every side. The work before the statesmen and divines of the age was emphatically one of reconstruction, which had to be done in the midst of much turmoil and distraction, with foes on every side ready to criticise, to deride and, if possible, to destroy, whatever was being erected. Perhaps the most striking and courageous act of the government of Elizabeth was to face the religious problem, a task on which, though complete success was impossible and serious failure would have been disastrous, the fate of the country largely depended.

The destruction of the scholastic system of theology, built up during the middle ages, left the nations of Europe without a theory either of government or religion; and the first results of the reformation had been a series of disastrous experiments in both spheres. Anabaptism and socinianism alike showed the need for protestantism to formulate and define its teaching; and the result was the rise of a new scholasticism. But for this, the entire reformation must have failed in face of the Catholic revival, which was rapidly gaining ground throughout Europe; and it is due to the genius of Calvin that a strong barrier to its progress was erected. Calvin showed at Geneva that he possessed in an eminent degree the power of ruling men and of supplying the moral support for which they craved. He defined the limits of theological speculation; by his action in the matter of Servetus, he proclaimed to the world that he had no sympathy with any attempt to tamper with the fundamentals of Christianity; whilst his *Institutes*, as was truly said, took the place of the *Sentences* of Peter Lombard as the groundwork of protestant theology.

But the Genevan church showed itself every whit as masterful and dogmatic as its Roman rival, and its actions were equally justified by an appeal to Divine authority. If the papal dogma rested on the rock of church tradition as defined by the successors of St Peter, that of Geneva was based on the impregnable rock of Holy Scripture as interpreted by John Calvin. Both churches were agreed in demanding unquestioning obedience and in regarding the civil power as simply an instrument to carry out their decrees. In both, St Augustine's ideal *Civitas Dei* was to be made as real a factor in human politics as circumstances would permit. The nations had practically to choose between two theocracies: the one, venerable with the unbroken tradition of ages; the other, full of the vigour of youth, the inspiration of genius and the confidence that the future of humanity lay in its hands. Elizabeth and her advisers deliberately refused to put England under either.

What England needed most at the accession of Elizabeth was time. The nation was as yet unprepared to make its final decision in the matter of religion; it was exhausted by internal dissensions and a ruinous foreign policy; revolution and reckless experiments had rendered the church almost impotent. Lutheran protestantism, Genevan protestantism, Zwinglianism and the Catholic reaction had all been welcomed and found wanting; and the queen was resolved to have no more experiments. Rome meant Spain and the inquisition; Geneva, the repetition of the miseries and disorders of the reign of Edward VI; and the country was in equal dread of both. Moreover, it was not by any means certain that the divisions of the western church were yet permanent, or the breach between Rome and the northern nations irreparable. The council of Trent had not concluded its sessions and there was still a hope, albeit a faint one, that the Roman church would so reform itself that reunion might be possible. The country had not yet made up its mind between the old religion and the new; and which side it would adopt time and circumstances alone could show.

Accordingly, with the general approval of the nation, Elizabeth temporised; and the arrangement she made in ecclesiastical matters was essentially of the nature of a compromise. The queen and her advisers had the wisdom to recognise the vital necessity of peace both at home and abroad, to give England time to recover from the disasters of the last two reigns. To have precipitated matters would have meant either a foreign or a domestic war—perhaps both. If peace were to be preserved, it was essential to persuade Catholic and protestant alike that nothing final had been done; to allow Philip and Spain to look for the speedy reconciliation of England to the church without unduly damping the expectations of the reformers, on whose support Elizabeth mainly relied. The result was the settlement of 1559, by which the prayer book and the communion service were restored and episcopacy and such ancient ceremonies as were not absolutely incompatible with the new theology retained. No one believed, perhaps, that the religious policy of Elizabeth possessed any more elements of permanency than those of her predecessors; and the nation acquiesced in what had been done in confident expectation of further developments.

Regarded from the purely political aspect, no legislation could have been more beneficial in its effects than that of the first parliament of Elizabeth. It saved England from the tyranny of a Spanish inquisition and from the horrors of the French wars of religion. It gave the country nearly ten years' respite from dangerous religious controversy and enabled it to enter upon a new era of progress in almost every department of life. Seldom, if ever, has a religious policy animated by aims so secular as those of the government of Elizabeth proved so complete a success. But it could not do more than mitigate the evils it sought to avoid. It could save England from civil strife, but not from religious dissension. It was not to be expected that fervent enthusiasts on either side would be satisfied with what, after all, was little better than a compromise prompted by the wisdom of statesmen rather than by the spirituality of earnest seekers after the kingdom of God. Events, moreover, moved rapidly during the first years of Elizabeth. It soon became evident that the breach with Rome was final. The attitude of Paul IV towards the overtures made by Elizabeth, the rebellion of the northern earls, the excommunication of the queen by Pius V and the Ridolfi conspiracy showed that all attempts on the part of the queen's government to leave a door open for reconciliation had hitherto failed, as they were destined to do, despite the attempts to bring about an amicable understanding with Rome which were continued to the last days of the queen's reign. Abroad, the counter-reformation had begun and soon the massacre of St Bartholomew was to reveal the lengths to which the papal party was prepared to go. Protestantism had entered upon a struggle for existence with powerful and able opponents, united to crush it and guided with consummate strategy. Against its enemy, the reformation had forces courageous and resolute enough, but divided into almost hostile camps. Was, asked many an ardent reformer in England, his country to stand aside during the great contest, content with a lukewarm adherence to the new doctrines, intended to conciliate protestant and papist alike, and capable of satisfying neither? Such was the state of affairs when, in 1572, Mr Strickland, an aged gentleman, introduced a bill for the further reformation of the church. The queen promptly silenced interference in church matters in the House of Commons; but, henceforth, it became evident that a strong puritan party was coming forward with a well thought out scheme of church government in opposition to the Elizabethan settlement.

The life of Calvin reads like one of the romances of ecclesiastical history. Arriving at Geneva in 1536, in the twenty-fifth year of his age, the young French priest found the little state just emerging from the throes of a successful revolution. The Genevans adapted their constitution, consisting of an ecclesiastical superior, a lay vicegerent and the commonalty, to the new conditions by making a board of elders exercise the authority formerly in the hands of their bishop. The genius and firmness of Calvin caused a great moral, as well as social, revolution. Expelled by the citizens, who were exasperated by his severity, he returned in 1541 to carry on his work with renewed success. Holding at bay the papacy and the powerful house of Savoy, he raised Geneva to the position of the capital city of the reformed religion. Its university poured forth preachers of the new doctrines, men of learning animated with fiery zeal and undaunted by the fear of martyrdom. The city became the home of persecuted protestants from all parts of Europe. Calvin's writings formed the text book of reformed theology. Nowhere did the English exiles receive a more hospitable reception than at Geneva, and it is little to be wondered that John Calvin was regarded by them with enthusiastic admiration. To these, the godly, orderly and strictly governed Swiss community was all that a church should be and furnished an ideal which they longed passionately to realise in their own country. It is difficult for men in our day, with their preconceived notion of Calvinism, as represented by its theology, to understand the extraordinary fascination which the church of Geneva exercised on the minds of those who had made the city their place of refuge in the days of persecution, as well as upon those to whom the order, piety and devotion of the Genevese were known only by hearsay.

Hooker fully recognises this. To him, Calvin, the founder of the discipline of the church of Geneva, is 'incomparably the wisest man that ever the French church did enjoy, since the hour it enjoyed him.' There is, however, a touch of malice in his next sentences, characteristic alike of the author and of the profound scholar's attitude towards the learning of the man of affairs: 'His bringing up was in the study of the civil law. Divine knowledge he gathered, not by hearing or reading so much, as by teaching others.' Hooker, however, in his preface to *Ecclesiastical Polity*, does ample justice to the attractiveness of the Calvinian system, which the puritan party advocated in their *Admonition to Parliament*. When this was first published (1572), the Elizabethan church system had had thirteen years of trial and had not yet proved a conspicuous success. At least, it had not united Englishmen in a single church. The Roman Catholics had left off attendance at the parish churches; the Independents had set up congregations; and the puritan faction, which had, from the first, regarded the established church polity as a temporary expedient, felt justified both in expressing its grievances and in suggesting a remedy. The pamphlet in which this was done, supposed to be the work of two ministers, John Field and Thomas Wilcox, styled the *Admonition to Parliament*, is a document of singular ability, both in lucidity of statement and in vigour of language. It sets forth what is called 'a true platforme of a church reformed,' in order that all might behold 'the great unlikeness betwixt it and this our English Church.'

The *Admonition* is brief, well arranged and extremely trenchant. After declaring that the notes of a true church are 'preaching the word purely, ministering of the sacraments sincerely, and ecclesiastical discipline which consisteth in admonition and correction of faults severlie' it treats of these three points in detail. As regards the ministry of the word, the writers are of opinion that the old clergy, 'King Henries priests, king Edward's priests (omitted 2nd ed.), Queen Maries priests... (yf Gods worde were precisely followed) should... be utterly removed.' Parliament is exhorted to

remove Advowsons, Patronages, Impropriations, and bishoppes' authoritie, claiming to themselves therby right to ordaine ministers, and to bring in that old and true election, which was accustomed to be made by the congregation.

'You must,' it goes on to say, 'displace those ignorant and unable ministers already placed, and, in their rowmes, appoint such as both can, and will, by God's assistance, feed the flock.... Remove homilies, articles, injunctions, a prescript order of service made out of the masse booke. Take away the Lordship, the loytering, the pompe, the idlenes, and livings of Bishops, but yet employ them to such ends as they were in the old churche apointed for. Let a lawful and a godly Seignorie look that they preache, not quarterly or monthly, but continually: not for filthy lucre's sake but of a ready mynde.'

The paragraph regarding the sacraments contrasts the practice of the primitive church with that of the time. Of the Lord's Supper it says:

They took it with conscience, we with custume. They shut out men by reason of their sinne...we thruste them in their sinne to the Lord's supper. They ministered the Sacrament plainely. We pompously with singing, pypying, surplesse and cope wearyng.

The petition was that all irregular baptisms by deacons or midwives should be 'sharplie punished,' that communicants should be examined by elders, 'that the statute against waffer cakes may more prevaile then an Injunction,' that kneeling on reception of the sacrament should be abolished. But the most important demand was that, in true conformity with the Calvinian system, 'Excommunication be restored to his old former force,' and 'that papists or other, neither constrainedly nor customably, communicate in the misteries of salvation.'

Discipline, rigorous and impartial, was the chief aim of the petitioners. The bishops and all their officials must be removed and complete equality of ministers be established. The whole regiment of the church is to be placed in the hands of ministers, seniors and deacons. These are to punish the graver sins, blasphemy, usury (2nd ed. 'drunkennesse'), adultery, whoredom, by a severe sentence of excommunication, uncommutable by any money payment. In a vigorous apostrophe, parliament is exhorted to imitate the example of the Scottish and French churches and thoroughly to root out popery.

'Is,' ask the petitioners, 'a reformation good for France? and can it be evyl for England? Is discipline meete for Scotland? and is it unprofitable for this Realme? Surely God hath set these examples before your eyes to encourage you to go forward to a thorow and speedy reformation. Ye may not do as heretofore you have done, patch and piece, nay, rather, goe backward, and never labour or contend to perfection. But altogether remove whole Antichrist, both head, bodie and branch, and perfectly plant that puritie of the word, that simplicitie of the sacraments, that severitie of discipline, which Christ hath commanded and commended to his church.'

It has been necessary to dwell at some length on the subject of the *Admonition*, not only because it is an excellent specimen of the eloquence and vigour of prose composition during the early days of Elizabeth, but, also, because it practically states the whole case for the demands of the puritans during the period; and it is practically against these that Hooker is contending throughout his controversies with Cartwright and Travers. There is, it must with justice be admitted, much to be said for the puritan demands for church reform. The abuses of the church courts, owing to the multiplicity of jurisdictions, were great; the new clergy, who had been ordained by the Elizabethan bishops, left much to be desired in both conduct and capacity; nor have the denunciations of the puritans regarding the expense of the cathedral establishments, the system of patronage and the like lacked the justification of subsequent experience. But had parliament been allowed to legislate as the puritans desired, the result would have been to set up an ecclesiastical tyranny which, inevitably, would have succeeded in damping the rising spirit of England, and, almost certainly, would have provoked a civil war. The puritans, like some other politicians of our own time, were aiming at an ideal state of society and were ready to allow the country to run any risk to secure its establishment. Experience has shown that such an attempt always demands the sacrifice of personal liberty, and to this, Englishmen, especially under Elizabeth, were thoroughly averse. With the possibilities of life ever growing wider, with a country developing at a rate hitherto unprecedented, with a constantly expanding horizon of life and thought, England, then, despite her religious zeal, thoroughly humanistic, was not going to submit to a system which had only succeeded in a petty municipality like that of Geneva, and which was being experimentally adopted, with doubtful benefit to the country, by a nation so barbarous as the Scots were considered to be in the sixteenth century. Elizabeth understood her people far better than did parliament when she resolutely opposed the discussion of the grievances of the puritans.

Richard Hooker entered the lists almost a generation after the early puritans; and he did so, not so much as a churchman pleading the cause of ecclesiastical authority, as a representative of humanistic Christianity and of the love of intellectual freedom.

The facts of his life can be briefly related from Izaak Walton's biography—a curious mixture of artless simplicity and consummate art, making the virtues of its subject the more conspicuous by darkening the background of family life and surroundings. Born in 1553, at Heavitree, Exeter, Richard Hooker came of good, though not noble or wealthy, stock, for his uncle John Hooker was a man of some note and chamberlain of Chichester. By the influence of this relative, he obtained the patronage of another Devonian, John Jewel, bishop of Salisbury, and was enabled to enter Corpus Christi College, Oxford, becoming a fellow of the society in 1577. Sandys, then bishop of London, made Hooker tutor to his son Edwin, and he also had charge of George Cranmer, great nephew of the celebrated archbishop. In 1581, when appointed to preach at Paul's Cross, Hooker, according to his biographer, made the fatal mistake of marrying his landlady's daughter.

'"There is,"' to quote Walton's quaint words, '"a wheel within a wheel"; a secret sacred wheel of Providence (most visible in marriages), guided by His hand that "allows not the race to the swift" nor "bread to the wise," nor good wives to good men: and He that can bring good out of evil (for mortals are blind to this reason) only knows why this blessing was denied to patient Job, to meek Moses, and to our as meek and patient Mr Hooker.'

In justice to Mrs Hooker, it may be remarked that she and her family seem to have belonged to the puritan party and, consequently, were extremely obnoxious to the high church friends of her husband, who seems always to have treated her with respect and to have named her executrix in his will. In 1584, Hooker was presented to Drayton Beauchamp in Bucks., then in the diocese of Lincoln, and, in 1585, after some dispute, he was given the mastership of the Temple, where he had his famous controversy with Walter Travers, the reader, 'a disciplinarian in his judgment and practice,' who had received only presbyterian ordination at Antwerp. It was at the Temple that Hooker began to plan his great work; and, wearied by his contentions with Travers, whom he admired as a man whilst differing from him as a divine, he petitioned archbishop Whitgift to relieve him of the mastership in order that he might study to complete 'a Treatise in which I intend a justification of the Laws of our Ecclesiastical polity.' Accordingly, in 1591, Whitgift preferred him to the rectory of Boscombe, six miles from Salisbury; and, in 1595, queen Elizabeth gave him the living of Bishopsbourne, three miles from Canterbury. The first four books of the *Polity* were completed at Boscombe and printed in 1594; the fifth appeared in 1597. His health began to fail in the year 1600, in consequence of a cold contracted on a journey by water from London to Gravesend; his will bears date 26 October 1600, and he probably died in the same year. The sixth and eighth books did not appear till 1648 and 1651, and the seventh was first printed in Gauden's edition of Hooker's works in 1662.

The preface, which, in itself, is as long as the shorter books of the treatise, is of great importance as a survey of the whole field of discussion. Hooker begins by declaring to the puritans

I must plainly confess unto you, that before I examined your sundry declarations in that behalf, it could not settle in my head to think but that undoubtedly such numbers of otherwise right well affected and most religiously inclined minds had some marvellous reasonable inducements, which led them with so great earnestness that way.

But careful study, as he affirms, only convinced him that the change which churchmen are required to accept 'is only by error and misconceit named the ordinance of Jesus Christ, no one proof as yet brought forth whereby it may clearly appear to be so in very deed.' That he approached the discussion, not in the spirit of a partisan, but with a strong desire to deal with fairness and moderation and to think well of his opponents, is seen in the justice he does alike to the greatness of Calvin and to the attractiveness of his system.

After having spoken of Calvin in the most complimentary terms, Hooker instantly puts his finger on the weak point of the Swiss reformation, the extreme dogmatism with which each independent church ordained its government 'in so commanding a form,' that it was to be received 'as everlastingly required by the law of that Lord of lords, against whose statutes there is no commandment to be taken.' This assertion of final infallibility on the part of the newly constituted churches made all mutual accommodation impossible, and sapped the strength of the continental reformation at the close of the sixteenth century. Hooker, thoroughly English in temperament and, in some respects, far in advance of his age, accepts no system of government, either in church or state, as unalterable and is prepared to discuss all forms on their merits. His contention is always for liberty. With much skill, and not a little quiet satire, he traces the popularity of the Calvinian discipline in England to a craving to exercise the right of private judgment, to the democratic spirit of the age and to the influence of women, as well as to reliance upon Scripture and the high spiritual pretensions claimed by its advocates. He discusses the inconsistency of the attempt to restore the exact condition of the apostolic age, and insinuates the impossibility of proving the existence of the so-called 'discipline' of those days. 'Of this very thing ye fail even touching that which ye make most account of, as being matter of substance in discipline, I mean the power of your lay elders, and the difference of your doctors from the pastors in all churches.' As regards the existing law of England, Hooker points out that it must be obeyed without disputation; for, though a law may be changed, it is, he tells the puritans, 'the deed of the whole body politic, whereof if ye judge yourselves to be any part, then is the law your deed also'; and, on this account, he deems public discussion inadvisable under the circumstances of their age. After stating the subject of each book of his proposed work, he goes on to point out the dangers of the puritan movement. In the first place, he sees that it must necessarily cause a serious schism, and, indeed, though the puritans lamented the secession of the Barrowists, these only followed out logically the teaching of the 'disciplinarians' who, by their own admission, were continuing members of a church which they were continually denouncing as 'anti-christian.' As for the 'discipline' itself, Hooker believed that it could not be established without civil disturbance, as the nobility would never submit to the local tyranny of small parochial courts of spiritual jurisdiction, none of which acknowledged any superior judge on earth. Discipline at the universities would, necessarily, be at an end if puritan equality of ministers were to be established, and the secular courts would be completely superseded by the powers claimed by the new 'discipline.' Hooker, naturally, alludes to the dangers disclosed by the spread of anabaptism and concludes with an eloquent appeal to his opponents to consider their position:

The best and safest way for you therefore, my dear brethren, is, to call your deeds past to a new reckoning, to re-examine the case ye have taken in hand, and to try it even point by point, argument by argument, with all the diligent exactness ye can; to lay aside the gall of that bitterness wherein your minds have hitherto over abounded, and with meekness to search the truth. Think ye are men, deem it not impossible for you to err; sift unpartially your own hearts, whether it be force of reason or vehemency of affection, which hath bred and still doth feed these opinions in you. If truth do anywhere manifest itself, seek not to smother it with glosing delusions, acknowledge the greatness thereof, and think it your best victory when the same doth prevail over you.

This dignity of language, combined with singular moderation, is characteristic of Hooker, whose guiding principle in controversy may be summed up in his own words, 'There will come a time when three words uttered with charity and meekness shall receive a far more blessed reward than three thousand volumes written with disdainful sharpness of wit.'

The first book, in some ways, is the most important of the

whole work, because in it we see Hooker at his best in dealing broadly with principles. Before proceeding to discuss any matters of detail, he sets himself, with the aid of the philosophers of Greece, the Fathers and the medieval schoolmen and canonists, to consider the ground and origin of all law, the nature of that order which presides over the universe, over the external cosmos and human society, and to determine the principle which renders certain laws of permanent, and others of temporary, obligation. The first book, accordingly, is philosophical rather than theological: it presents a magnificent conception of the world as existing under a reign of law—law not arbitrary but an expression of the divine reason.

The literary power of Hooker is admirably displayed in his eloquent treatment of the subject of the angels, which played a far more important part in theological speculation then than it does in our time. It is related that, when on his death-bed, Hooker was asked by his friend Saravia the subject of his meditations, and replied: 'that he was meditating the number and nature of angels, and their blessed obedience and order, without which peace could not be in heaven; and oh that it might be so on earth.' After speaking of the natural laws, which, so to speak, work automatically, he says:

> God which moveth mere natural agents as an efficient only, doth otherwise move intellectual creatures, and especially his holy angels: for, beholding the face of God, in admiration of so great excellency they all adore him; and being wrapt with the love of his beauty, they cleave inseparably for ever unto him. Desire to resemble him in goodness maketh them unweariable and even unsatiable in their longing to do by all means all manner of good unto all the creatures of God, but especially unto the children of men: in the countenance of whose nature, looking downward, they behold themselves beneath themselves; even as upward, in God, beneath whom themselves are, they see that character which is nowhere but in themselves and us resembled. Thus far even the paynims have approached; thus far they have seen into the doings of the angels of God: Orpheus confessing that 'the fiery throne of God is attended on by those most industrious angels, careful how all things are performed among men'; and the mirror of human wisdom plainly teaching that God moveth angels, even as that thing doth stir man's heart, which is thereunto presented amiable.

Here we have an excellent example of Hooker's literary style: language suitable to the subject, the very construction of the somewhat involved sentences enhancing its dignity, evidences of wide, even if somewhat uncritical, reading as shown by the quotation from the Orphic hymn preserved in the *Stromateis* of Clement of Alexandria, and poetic feeling perhaps echoing the words of Spenser's almost contemporary *Faerie Queene*. The high place assigned to reason in this book strikes almost the keynote of the entire work, since the consensus of human opinion is, to Hooker, an evidence of revelation. 'The general and perpetual voice of men is as the sentence of God himself.' Yet, true to his principles, he declines to bind himself to any single theory of government by drawing a sharp distinction between the law of nature common to all men and 'laws positive' which do not bind mankind universally. Reason depends on freedom of the will, and nature, whilst prescribing government as necessary to all societies, 'leaveth the choice as a thing arbitrary.' It is this broad generalisation, this determination to lay down the principles on which he proposes to treat the subject, which renders the first book of great importance. We are tempted to forget that the author is engaged in one of the fiercest controversies of a controversial age when we peruse a book in which the philosophy is detached from the immediate present. Like other great Elizabethans, Hooker had the power of writing for all time. He enters the lists of controversy resolved to contend not with the weapons of dexterous argument but with those of a more solid character, drawn from the arsenal of philosophy. 'Is there,' he asks at the conclusion of the book, 'anything which can either be thoroughly understood or soundly judged of, till the very first causes and principles from whence it springeth be made manifest?'

In the second book, Hooker is still preparing the way for his argument with his opponents and, though dealing with one of their main axioms, he does not so much join issue with them as deal with general principles. The puritans maintained that Holy Scripture must be the sole guide of *every* action of a Christian's life. Hooker has little difficulty in showing that the passages of Scripture quoted are irrelevant, and that the opinions of the Fathers cited in support of the thesis are not really applicable to it. The chief interest of this short book, however, lies in the way in which it reverts to those divisions of law made in the first, and shows that, though revealed Scripture is an infallible guide, it is not the only one by which our actions must be determined. There is the same underlying appeal to commonsense that we find in the first book, the same dislike of mere hard logical theory as opposed to practice and experience, which makes Hooker a pre-eminently English theologian. It is worth observing how he sums up the results of accepting the puritan position:

> But admit this, and mark, I beseech you, what would follow. God in delivering Scripture to his Church should clean have abrogated amongst them the law of nature; which is an infallible knowledge imprinted in the minds of

all the children of men, whereby both general principles for directing of human actions are comprehended, and conclusions derived from them; upon which conclusions groweth in particularity the choice of good and evil in the daily affairs of this life. Admit this, and what shall the Scripture be but a snare and a torment to weak consciences, filling them with infinite perplexities, scrupulosities, doubts insoluble, and extreme despairs.... For in every action of common life to find out some sentence clearly and infallibly setting before our eyes what we ought to do (seem we in Scripture never so expert) would trouble us more than we are aware. In weak and tender minds we little know what misery this strict opinion would breed, besides the stops it would make in the whole course of all men's lives and actions.

It is this large view of matters, this broad and tolerant sympathy, which gives Hooker a unique place among theological writers.

When we reach the third book, dealing with the question whether a definite form of church polity is prescribed in Scripture, it may be well to bear in mind that the title of Hooker's work is not *The Laws of* but *Of the Laws of Ecclesiastical Polity*, it being no design of his to lay down definite laws of church government but, rather, to discuss the principles whereon they are based. Strong churchman as he was, Hooker's aim was not to set up the laws of the church to which he belonged as a third code claiming the same infallibility as that which the advocates of the Roman and puritan ecclesiastical systems claimed. He was, as his whole argument shows, fighting the battle of toleration and progress, to which the assertion of infallibility must oppose an unsurmountable barrier. Circumstances tended, in after days, to cause posterity, rightly or wrongly, to identify puritanism with civil and religious liberty; but the demand for the establishment of a discipline, rigidly defined and sanctioned by the unerring voice of Scripture, must, if granted, have meant ecclesiastical tyranny and stagnation.

The error of the puritans was, as Hooker points out, the same as that of the African church in the time of St Cyprian and the controversy on rebaptism, and was due to the failure to distinguish the visible from the mystical church. Even heretics are acknowledged to be 'though a maimed part, yet a part of the visible church.' For,

if an infidel should pursue to death an heretic professing Christianity, only for Christian profession's sake, could we deny unto him the honour of martyrdom? Yet this honour all men know to be proper unto the Church. Heretics therefore are not utterly cut off from the visible Church of Christ.

This generous sentiment was completely at variance with the tenets of Calvinism, which held that Romanism was a worse sin than idolatry, and Hooker considers Calvin's answer to Farel, regarding the baptism of the children of papists, 'crazed, because, in it, he says, "It is an absurd thing for us to baptise them which cannot be reckoned members of our body."' This large conception of the church as opposed to the narrower view of the puritans pervades the whole argument.

The principal contention in this third book is, naturally, that Scripture only lays down what is absolutely necessary for doctrine and practice, and that this does not include the externals of church worship or government. An ecclesiastical polity is as necessary to all societies of Christian men as a language, but it no more follows that all should adopt the same form of government in church matters than that they should use the same tongue. Episcopal government seems, however, to be more in consonance with Scripture than any other, though Hooker does not consider that a church ceases to be truly one because it lacks this advantage.

'In which respect for mine own part,' he remarks, 'although I see that certain reformed churches, the Scottish especially and French, have not that which best agreeth with the sacred Scripture, I mean the government that is by Bishops, inasmuch as both those churches are fallen under a different kind of regiment; which to remedy it is for the one altogether too late, and too soon for the other during their present affliction and trouble: this their defect and imperfection I had rather lament in such case than exagitate, considering that men oftentimes without any fault of their own may be driven to want that kind of polity or regiment which is best, and to content themselves with that, which either the irremediable error of former times, or the necessity of the present, hath cast upon them.'

In his fourth book, Hooker undertakes to defend the church of England against the charge of Romanism because certain ceremonies were retained which the other reformed churches had rejected. And here it may not be irrelevant to remark that the question of toleration never entered into the dispute. The object of the Elizabethan settlement was to establish a church on the broad basis of comprehension; that of the puritans to set up a procrustean institution and to force every Englishman to conform to it in all particulars. The point at issue between Anglican and puritan in the days of Elizabeth was which of two ideals of a national church should prevail. This was recognised generally in the country, and puritanism, discredited by the violent language of the Marprelate libels, was, when Hooker, in 1594, issued his fourth book, manifestly on the wane, while Anglicanism, after an unpromising beginning, was daily gaining strength, so that he was able to say:

That which especially concerneth ourselves, in the present matter we treat of, is the state of reformed religion, a thing at her [Elizabeth's] coming to the crown even raised as it were by a miracle from the dead; a thing which

we so little hoped to see, that even they which beheld it done, scarcely believed their own senses at the first beholding. Yet being then brought to pass, thus many years it hath continued, standing by no other worldly mean but that one only hand which erected it; that hand which as no kind of imminent danger could cause at the first to withhold itself, so neither have the practice of so many so bloody following since been ever able to make weary.... Which grace and favour of divine assistance having not in one thing or two shewed itself, nor for some few days or years appeared... what can we less thereupon conclude, than that God would at leastwise by tract of time teach the world, that the thing which he blesseth, defendeth, keepeth so strangely, cannot choose but be of him. Wherefore, if any refuse to believe us disputing for the verity of religion established, let them believe God himself thus miraculously working for it, and wish life even for ever and ever unto that glorious and sacred instrument whereby he worketh.

When we reach the fifth book, which, in itself, is almost as extensive as the rest of the work, we find ourselves at the very heart of the controversy and discover that the same master hand has the same capacity for dealing with detail as it exhibited in regard to general principles. It would be impossible to show here at length how Hooker defends the prayer book against the criticisms of Cartwright and Travers; and we must be content with a cursory examination of the chapters wherein Hooker rises to the highest point of excellence as a theologian, namely those dealing with the sacraments. With questions purely ritual in character, Hooker is not a little impatient; the controversies of his own day about 'rites and ceremonies of church action' appear, as he remarks in the dedication of this book to Whitgift, 'such silly things, that very easiness doth make them hard to be disputed of in serious manner.' But, in treating of sacramental grace, he feels himself to be engaged in a congenial occupation, and he lavishes on it all the treasures of his wide reading and erudition combined with skill and judgment. He takes us back to the great controversies of antiquity and, with masterly skill, unfolds the doctrine of the Divinity of the Word and the relation of the Divine and human natures in Christ. From the Person he goes on to speak of the Presence of Christ, and from Presence to the participation we have of Him. Thoroughly acquainted as he is with all the theories of sacramental grace prevalent in his day, especially in regard to the Eucharist, he recognises that here, if anywhere, all parties are fundamentally agreed, now that the theories of Zwingli and Oecolampadius were rejected 'concerning that alone is material, namely *the real participation* of Christ and of life in his body and blood *by means of this sacrament.*' 'I wish,' he adds, later, 'that men would more give themselves to meditate what we have by the sacrament and less to dispute of the manner how.'

Hooker went further on the path of conciliation than any other divine in seeing that a recognition of the fact of the presence of the Saviour, however defined, was the essential point to which all others were really subsidiary. A passage of remarkable beauty in the 67th chapter he brings to the following conclusion:

> What these elements are in themselves it skilleth not, it is enough that to me which take them they are the body and blood of Christ, his promise in witness hereof sufficeth, his word he knoweth which way to accomplish; why should any cogitation possess the mind of a faithful communicant but this,
>
> O my God thou art true, O my soul thou art happy!

The fifth book was, as we have seen, the last to be published in Hooker's lifetime; and the remaining three can only be mentioned in brief. The sixth deals with the question of church discipline and contains a valuable survey of the system of penance, not only of that in the early church, but, also, of that in vogue among the Jews. Hooker also discusses the Roman view of the subject as put forward by cardinal Bellarmine. The seventh book answers the puritan objections to episcopal government, and is remarkable for the temperate way in which each is stated and discussed as well as for the erudition displayed. While he professes his belief in the apostolical origin of episcopacy, Hooker does not consider the institution absolutely indispensable, though, when he speaks of cathedral establishments, his knowledge of history enables him to see in them the outlines of the primitive churches, and he gives way to a moment of enthusiasm foreign to his usual habit:

> For most certain truth it is that cathedral churches and the bishops of them are as glasses wherein the face and very countenance of apostolical antiquity remaineth even as yet to be seen.... For defence and maintenance of them we are most earnestly bound to strive, even as the Jews were for their temple... the overthrow and ruin of the one if ever the sacrilegious avarice of Atheists should prevail so far, which God of his infinite mercy forbid, ought no otherwise to move us than the people of God were moved... when they uttered from the bottom of their grieved spirits those voices of doleful supplication *Exsurge Domine et miserearis Sion, Servi tui diligunt lapides ejus, pulveris ejus miseret eos.*

Hooker, it may be remarked, insists on the necessity of episcopal ordination except 'when the exigence of necessity doth constrain to leave the usual ways of the church, which otherwise we would willingly keep.'

The eighth book treats of 'the power of supreme jurisdiction' and the relation of the civil magistrate to the church. To Hooker, a Christian church and state are identical; but an English monarch's power is strictly limited by law. 'The axioms of our regal government,' he says, 'are these, *lex facit regem*... and *rex nihil potest nisi quod jure potest.*' In all the king's proceedings 'law is itself the rule.'

Such, then, is the main outline of a great work which had an abiding influence on English history. It showed the strength of the argument in favour of the Elizabethan settlement of religion, and the real weakness, despite the moral fervour which it evoked, of the puritan position. But, though Hooker's work had no small influence on the subsequent development of the Anglican ideal, his position was not that of the Laudian, much less of the tractarian, school of clergy. He had the advantage of living at the time when the first bitterness of the conflict between puritanism and Anglicanism had spent itself and before the struggle had entered upon its second phase. He lived too early to witness the final breach between Anglicanism and continental protestantism, and too late to experience the predominance of the latter in the time of the Zurich letters. The result is that his views are broad, sympathetic and tolerant. His singularly calm and dispassionate intellect enables him to rise superior to the prejudices of his age and, like St Paul, he makes the problems of the hour turn on everlasting principles. The remark of Clement VIII on hearing the first book translated at sight into Latin by Stapleton, related by Walton, is as creditable to the judgment of the pontiff as to 'the poor obscure English priest who had writ... such books.'

> There is no learning that this man hath not searched into; nothing too hard for his understanding. This man indeed deserves the name of an author; his books will get reverence by age, for there is in them such seeds of eternity, that if the rest be like this, they shall last till the last fire shall consume all learning.

Of Hooker's style, perhaps the most remarkable feature is the singular calmness and dignity with which he deals with the burning questions of his time. It was an age of literary scurrility, employed on both sides without either scruple or blame and thoroughly appreciated even by the learned public. This is conspicuously absent from Hooker's published work, and rarely indeed does he allow his real humour and power of retort to display itself. Fortunately, however, his notes to the *Christian Letter*, preserved in the library of Corpus Christi College, Oxford, reveal the man in his private study, and show how extraordinary a self-restraint he must have exercised in curbing his natural powers of sarcasm. On a remark upon the 'moral virtues' by the puritans in the letter, Hooker's note is:

'A doctrine which would well have pleased Caligula, Nero, and other such monsters to heare. Had thapostles taught this it might have advanced them happily to honour.' Again he asks 'Have you been tampering so long with Pastors, Doctors, Elders, Deacons; that the first principles of your religion are new to learn?'

Hooker speaks of his age as a learned one, but his knowledge of books must have been pre-eminent at any time. Of the thousand and ninety-two pounds which he left at his death, we are not surprised to hear that 'a great part of it was in books.' It was not merely that Hooker was well read in the Scriptures and the Fathers: it is the range of his learning that is remarkable. In the first book, which is not primarily theological, but deals, as we have seen, with the general principles of law, we have quotations from Mercurius Trismegistus, Stobaeus, Aquinas, Theophrastus, Aristotle, Clement of Alexandria, Ramus, Sallust, Vergil, Plato, Nicholas of Cusa, Telesius, Augustine, Cicero, Tertullian, Josephus, Lactantius, Duns Scotus, Gratian, the *Carmina* of Orpheus, Eusebius of Emesa and several other authors. His knowledge of Hebrew is shown in the fourth book, where he rebuts the charge that the ceremonies of the church were Judaic, whilst his extensive acquaintance with patristic literature is most evident in the fifth and sixth books. How keenly he was alive to the importance, not of the popular controversies of the day but of those which, if they attracted less attention, revealed dangerous tendencies, is seen in his dealing with the ubiquitarian doctrine of some Lutherans, who taught that the human body of Christ by reason of its union with his Godhead, was everywhere present, and that, as the body of the Son of God, it had the property of ubiquity: an error which would have deprived it of the true and essential character of a human body. This opinion is discussed in the great section of the fifth book L—LVII which speaks of the sacraments.

His *Ecclesiastical Polity* is remarkable as being one of the few theological or philosophical works which have taken a high place in the literature of the language in which they were written, and also for its far-reaching importance. Like Plato, St Augustine, Pascal and Berkeley, Hooker combines the often discordant elements of a deep thinker and a consummate literary artist. But, in one respect, he rose above them all: by his power of elevating a dispute of a purely temporary interest into a discussion of the great principles on which all human society must be based. Hooker has been compared to 'a Knight of Romance among catiff brawlers,' and, if this description be unjust to his contemporary opponents and supporters, it indicates the immensity of the gap which parted him from them. As surely as Bacon pointed out the right method of investigation in natural philosophy, did Hooker prepare the way for the future by indicating the true lines on which theology ought to develop. He not only called into being the language of Anglican theology; he laid down the lines on which it should proceed. His style has won the commendation of so great a master of English prose as Swift, and of a historian like Hallam. He can be fluent, easy and straightforward at times, but is equally capable of rising to a majesty of eloquence or a severity of diction according to the requirements of his subject. His singular sensitiveness to the rhythm and musical expression of his sentences has been remarked; and, even where he appears to be most obscure or involved, close attention will reveal a purpose alike in his choice of words and in the arrangement of the clauses of his sentences. It is certainly true that 'such who would patiently attend and give him credit all the reading and hearing of his sentences, had their expectation ever paid at the close thereof.'

But he was far more than a great prose writer, a ripe scholar, a pioneer in bringing Greek philosophy into English literature. Hooker's greatest merit was that he showed Anglican theologians that their object must be, not to contend about trifles, but to hold up the highest ideal of a church rooted in antiquity, ever studious in Scriptural and primitive Christianity, and, at the same time, large minded, open and tolerant. In an age of partisanship, he was not in the least a party theologian, and he appealed to the understanding of those who had no sympathy with either Anglican or puritan. Hooker, it is true, struck the decisive blow in favour of the Anglican position in the sixteenth century: but he did a more lasting work. He indicated that Anglicanism meant freedom combined with reverence, the exercise of the reason with a simple faith, and that liberality towards all churches was compatible with loyalty to that of the nation. He was greater both than his contemporaries and than his followers, and whenever the church of England has failed it has been when she has not been true to the liberal principles of her greatest apologist.

CHAPTER XIX

ENGLISH UNIVERSITIES, SCHOOLS AND SCHOLARSHIP IN THE SIXTEENTH CENTURY

THE history of the English universities to the end, approximately, of the Middle Ages has been dealt with in a previous volume of this work. The period treated in the present chapter falls into two unequal sections. The dividing line may be best fixed at the visitation of 1559, when twelve years of perilous unrest give place to an era of constructive growth, uncertain at first, but keeping step uniformly with the increasing national stability.

It is not unreasonable to regard the foundation of Trinity College, Cambridge, and of the new regius professorships, as setting the seal to the transition from medieval to modern ideals in the universities and in learning. Just as the 'college' henceforth dominates the university, so humanism, nationalism and the reformation supersede the Catholic idea in theology, politics and law. When Henry VIII died, the noteworthy group of Cambridge humanists, headed by Smith and Cheke, gave promise of high distinction for English scholarship. The abortive Chantries Act of 1546, which included the universities, was of evil omen in days of financial urgency, but it expired with the king, and Somerset astutely omitted universities and colleges, including Eton and Winchester, from the purview of his new bill of 1547, to be dealt with separately. The governing power, whether Somerset, Gardiner or Elizabeth, realised that English universities, like Paris and Wittenberg, were not merely seats of learning, but that from them passed religious and political influences which profoundly affected the national life. From them, as seminaries of the ministry and nurseries of the civil service, the country drew increasingly its leaders and administrators in church and state, and moulded opinion through the parson, the schoolmaster and the justice of the peace. Hence, Oxford and Cambridge became objects of high policy in exact proportion as they intertwined themselves with the several strands of English life and thought. It was not by way of compliment that Somerset, Gardiner and Cecil were elected university chancellors.

The standing difficulty of the historian of the time confronts the enquirer in this field also. The bitter temper of the age makes it well nigh impossible to determine facts. To Ascham, the arch-enemy of English learning was the Catholic restoration. At Oxford, Anthony à Wood has no hesitation in ascribing the miserable decay of letters to the Edwardian visitors. Yet, if Cheke, Ridley and Smith formulated the eminently reasonable statutes and injunctions of 1549, militant reformers like Latimer and Lever agree in deploring the evil case of education—'the devilish drowning of youth in ignorance'—since protestant courtiers had the ear of the crown. A whole library, we know, was to be had at Oxford for forty shillings when visitors were about, so heavy was the hand that was laid upon 'superstition.' 'Purgings' of this college and that were followed by the forced intrusion of new zealots. To Oxford was sent, to teach divinity, Peter Martyr, the fighting Zwinglian, a far less attractive spirit than the wide-minded Bucer, disciple and friend of Melanchthon, who filled the corresponding chair at Cambridge.

Thus, controversial theology overshadowed all else and both universities were drawn into the whirlpool of politics. But political divinity has rarely stimulated learning. If, at Cambridge, for a year or two, undergraduates kept their numbers, in seriousness of temper they showed marked decline. At Oxford, in 1550, there were 'a bare thousand on the books,' and most of these were not in residence. The stream of benefactions dried up. Pluralism and sinecures abounded. Far-seeing men abandoned university life for service in church and state. Ascham, though public orator at Cambridge, spent years at court or abroad. Sir Thomas Smith, while professor of civil law, left the university for political life. At best, it was the function of the university to supply the professions; learning, as such, was ignored. The 'university' declined, the 'college' was not as yet systematised or disciplined. Disputations—the one test of proficiency—were neglected, the schools deserted; few graduated even as bachelors; the higher degrees were rarely sought. It is much that the old comity of learning did not entirely die. As Thomas Smith taught at Padua, and Caius at Montpellier, so German theologians, Dutch Hebraists, or Italian lawyers could hold English posts. It is of more weight still, that the Edwardian statutes mark a genuine advance in administration and in the concept of learning. They breathe the renascence spirit, they evince sound judgment and first-hand knowledge of the needs of the universities. Elizabeth's advisers found little to alter in them, and they stood till the Laudian era. Philosophy—in humanist fashion—was held specifically to include politics, ethics and *physica*: Plato and Pliny were prescribed alongside of Aristotle. Dialectic covered not merely the text of Aristotle, but, also, that of Hermogenes and of Quintilian—implying that interrelation of logic and rhetoric which was the very core of humanist doctrine. Mathematics included cosmography; Euclid, Strabo, Pomponius Mela and Cardan were the authorities. The Greek professor had to interpret Homer, Euripides, Demosthenes and 'Socrates.' To civil law, to be read, like medicine, in the original texts, was added a study of 'the Ecclesiastic Laws of this Kingdom.' For undergraduates, the first year course was mainly in mathematics (Elizabethan statutes substituted rhetoric); the second year in logic; the third in rhetoric and philosophy. The master's degree required three years' residence, with reading in Greek, philosophy, geometry and astronomy. To a doctor alone was complete freedom allowed. But, gradually, the colleges imposed their own courses. Thus, the first year man at Trinity began logic, read Cicero and Demosthenes, wrote prose and verse. He was probably, we remember, a boy of 12 to 15 years of age. Plato was added in his second year; after graduation, he took up Hebrew. Much, perhaps most, of all this was on paper only. Circumstances, whether fiscal, political or religious, were equally adverse. Greed, polemics, dynastic insecurity kept learning stagnant in schools and universities alike.

Not that Mary herself was indifferent to learning, any more than Northumberland had been. But it was inevitable that Gardiner should revoke the new statutes, and turn adrift heads and fellows 'to eat mice at Zurich.' Peter Martyr promptly crossed the seas. In Oxford, Magdalen was 'thoroughly purged,' but Thomas Pope founded Trinity (1556), and White, St John's (1555). Gardiner was hard on Trinity and St John's at Cambridge, but Caius re-founded Gonville (1558). Reginald Pole was no obscurantist; with Sadoleto, his ideal was a humanism suffused with the spirit of a finely tempered Catholicism. The statutes of the two Marian foundations at Oxford are such as the scholarly bishop of Carpentras himself might have settled. 'I remember,' says Sir Thomas Pope, 'when I was a young scholar at Eton, the Greek tongue was growing apace, the study of which is now much decayed.' St John's was built to serve 'sacred theology, philosophy, and good Arts,' including civil and canon law. At Cambridge, Caius, a devout Catholic, was, none the less, a friend of Melanchthon; a student and a teacher in many continental universities; a Grecian of distinction, yet a pupil of Vesalius. Like Smith and Savile, he represents the versatility and enthusiasm which marked the larger minds of the revival in England. Yet, to judge from Ascham's lament—and Caius confirms it—we must assume that Cambridge, already predominantly protestant, reached its lowest depths under the Catholic *régime*; that teachers and students alike forsook the university; that degrees were seldom conferred, and, too often, gained by dispensation: between 1555 and 1559, only 175 proceeded to the bachelor's standing at Cambridge, and 216 at Oxford, less hostile to the dominant powers. Of all the causes which reacted unfavourably upon the universities, none made so deep an impression on the country as the Oxford and Smithfield martyrdoms.

As in the field of religion and of affairs, so in that of education, with the accession of Elizabeth the national unrest began to abate. Recovery, however, was slow. In the last year of Mary, only 28 degrees in arts had been conferred at Oxford. In 1561, no senior proceeded to the degree of doctor in any of the faculties. But Cecil, chancellor of Cambridge (1558—98) guided the new queen's university policy. Leicester, a chancellor (1564—88) of a different type, was, none the less, keen to secure Oxford for protestantism, and to raise the standard of efficiency in teaching and learning. Elizabeth herself was a lover of learning and, perhaps, the best-read woman of her time, with a bias to national continuity, and an aversion to the foreigner whether pope or Calvin. The visitations of 1559 once more eliminated hostile influences. Such heads of houses and fellows as clung to the old faith either withdrew or were expelled. Dr Bill and Lawrence Humfrey, with many others, were restored. Disaffected societies, like St John's, Trinity, or New College at Oxford, were effectually 'purged.' But, this done, and Edward's statutes reimposed, the visitors held their hands. When the queen visited Cambridge in 1564, a new temper, hopeful and earnest, prevailed. The number of residents at Oxford rose steadily from one thousand to two. Benefactions were again freely offered. Two results of importance gradually emerge: the restoration of the universities to their function as safe seminaries of the clergy, and the final subordination of the university to the colleges and their heads. By the Act of Incorporation of both the universities (1571), parliament, for the first time, recognised and confirmed the franchises, privileges and jurisdictions hitherto enjoyed by Oxford and Cambridge under royal charters and by usage, and each attained the status of a corporation under the style of 'The Chancellor, Masters and Scholars.' Although tests were not by statute reimposed, convocation at Oxford, at Leicester's instance, passed decrees, requiring, from all undergraduates over 12 years of age, subscription to the articles of 1562, with special stress on the royal supremacy. Freedom of teaching and even of study was jealously watched from court; and, as Whitgift made plain, protestant orthodoxy and loyalty rather than learning were approved marks of university efficiency. By degrees, the concept of the church approved by Elizabeth and expounded by Hooker became dominant in Oxford, whilst Cambridge cultivated an enlightened puritanism. But, in both the universities alike, the keenest interests were those of controversy. Cambridge, however, sent out from St John's and Trinity not a few schoolmasters of merit.

After 1590, Catholic influences were ruthlessly ousted from English universities. Douay (1569), with its English college ruled by Allen, had, by 1576, not less than two hundred students of British origin, amongst them not a few notable ex-fellows and lecturers from Oxford and Cambridge. And other English scholars found refuge at St Omer, Valladolid, Seville and in the English college at Rome. In 1581, Leicester still complained that Oxford suffered 'secret lurking Papists,' and, though less freely, Catholic houses continued to send their sons to Caius, Pembroke or Trinity Hall, at Cambridge, in spite of the harder temper of the university, or to Oriel, Trinity or St John's at Oxford. Puritan families mainly affected Cambridge, especially St John's and the new foundations of Emmanuel (1584), the avowed centre of militant protestantism, and Sidney Sussex (1599). Robert Brown, John Smith, the baptist John Cotton and Cartwright were all at Cambridge. Lawrence Humfrey, president of Magdalen, Oxford, 'did so stock his college with such a generation of nonconformists as could not be rooted out in many years after his decease.' The strongest minds (Whitaker, master of St John's, Cambridge, may be taken as a conspicuous example) drifted to theology. The best careers open to unaided talent lay in the church. Hebrew had more students than Greek. Tremellius, who taught it at Cambridge, was a foreigner; so were most of his successors. Oxford learnt Calvinian divinity from Huguenots and other refugees, Spanish and Italian. It is not the least title to their place in the history of literature, that Oxford and Cambridge bred the men to whom we owe the Bishops' Bible, the prayer-book and the *Authorised Version*[1].

The place of civil law in the English universities needs brief mention. Sir Thomas Smith claimed it as a branch of humanism. In Elyot's vein, he will have it broadly based upon philosophy, ethics and history. This, the doctrine of Cujas and Alciati, he had imbibed at Padua and Bologna. For a short time, he succeeded in winning minds of distinction to study in this spirit a jurisprudence from which, in respect of precision and authority, English lawyers might learn much. But the uncertain professional demand for civilians, the academic temper of the Cambridge school, the suspicion attaching to the subject as Italian and, therefore, inevitably, papal, the growing sense of nationality and the unassailable place of English law which accompanied it, rendered Smith's hopes ultimately fruitless. Yet there was felt in high places some need for civil lawyers to advise upon international usages, to draft treaties and conduct diplomatic correspondence. In 1549, visitors were instructed to set apart, at both universities, colleges for the exclusive study of civil law, but the proposal had no countenance. Fellowships, specifically allotted to this subject, as at All Souls, were, in very many cases, held by theologians.

Oxford possessed, in Albericus Gentilis (1552—1608) a civilian of Perugia, elected regius professor of civil law in 1587, the most learned lawyer of the Elizabethan time. In his hands grew up a system of international law to serve the needs of a world in which church and empire alike had ceased to be the dominant powers. His chief works were *De Legationibus* (1584), in which he defined the basis and limits of diplomatic privilege, and *De Jure Belli* (1588—98). This standing monument of Oxford civil studies exhibits a masterly examination of international historical precedents of the sixteenth century, utilised to reconcile the Bible, the protestant doctrine of natural law and the essential principles of the imperial code. Grotius, a century later, was deeply indebted to Gentilis, from whom, indeed, international law, as a systematic body of doctrine, is, ultimately, derived. Gentilis, a man of wide interests and of great learning, exercised profound influence in the university and was highly regarded at court. His method of teaching differed from that of Smith and his successor Haddon, in that he concentrated attention upon the development

[1] See *ante*, chap. II.

of civil law in its direct application to modern use, with entire indifference to it as a branch of humanist study; for so to regard law could, in the England of the sixteenth and seventeenth centuries, only end in its relegation to 'polite learning.' The supremacy of English law was, indeed, already secured. The activity of the Inns of Court and the genius of Coke did but serve to enforce the inevitable trend of things. Trinity Hall, however (especially under its master, Cowell, 1598), All Souls and Broadgates were, more or less, frequented by civilians. But, to Stewart parliamentarians, Roman law was identified with absolutism and high prelacy.

The lines of classical study were, nominally, determined by requirements for degrees. But the colleges were already dominant in teaching and in administration. The more strenuous exacted entrance tests. Rhetoric, in the wider humanist sense, philosophy, ethical and 'natural,' and logic were the accepted subjects for the degree. Oxford logic was strictly Aristotelian. Elsewhere, as at Cambridge and St Andrews, it began to be taught on lines which Ramus elaborated from Agricola, and this, in turn, developed into the logic of Port Royal. Greek, as a university study, steadily declined from the standard set up by Cheke. None of his successors could arouse the old enthusiasm. Whitgift, the strongest force in the university, knew no Greek. Under Mary, it was reputed to have disappeared from Oxford. Sir Thomas Pope's lament concerns this. Leicester, as chancellor, complained, in 1582, that the Oxford professor 'read seldom or never.' Indeed, it may be affirmed that no work in classical scholarship was produced at Oxford or Cambridge during the period under review which is remotely worthy of comparison with that turned out by Scaliger, Estienne, Nizolius, Casaubon, Turnebus, or a hundred industrious, but now half forgotten, scholars in French and German lands. Nor can English learning show a scholar, unless it were Henry Savile, to rank with George Buchanan. In Greek, not one of the translators, Savile excepted, but works through a French version, like North. There was, on the other hand, a large output of Latin plays[1]—evidence, no doubt, of careful study in school and university of classical or neo-Latin models. Trinity (Cambridge) statutes (1560) contain clauses concerning the performance of college plays. Acting was the accepted mode of training youth in speaking Latin and in grace of gesture, wherever humanists controlled education. Shrewsbury, in this matter, held the preeminence amongst English schools; but at none of any pretension

[1] See vol. v of the present work.

was the practice neglected, though in Westminster alone has the tradition retained its vitality to our own day.

As the humanism of the sixteenth century became more strictly literary in its range, so surely did mathematics and natural philosophy sink to a lower place in English learning. Their affinity was with navigation, architecture or military science, not with the learned professions; a typical and very popular hand-book was *Blundeville His exercises... in Cosmographie....* Methods of observation and experiment, working to practical ends, superseded authoritative appeal to Aristotle or Ptolemy. Recorde's *The Castel of Knowledge* (1553) had a vogue for half a century as a manual of the new mathematic, harmonised to the Copernican astronomy. The English Euclid (1570) would seem to have had but a poor sale. Original work, like Gilbert's *De Magnete* (1600) kept its Latin dress, and, apart from this, nothing of first rate importance in the field of pure science was produced from an English press during the period under discussion.

It is an interesting, though difficult, task to realise the actual range and level of the work of a studious undergraduate coming up from Westminster or Shrewsbury to Christ Church at Oxford or St John's at Cambridge. Statutes, in effect, lend little or no help. Colleges ordered and gave the instruction and, apparently, were powerful enough to secure dispensation from the formal university exercises. A large, though varying, number in every college never graduated at all. Though the age at matriculation tended to rise, Bacon (who, himself, entered at twelve years and three months) complained, in the closing years of the century, that a prime cause of the futility of university education lay in the immaturity of the undergraduate. We may remember that Bentham, two centuries later, went up at twelve. Magdalen (Oxford) wisely put raw first year 'men' to the learning of rudiments in its own admirable grammar school. Yet, there is ample evidence that ambitious and well-prepared boys—precocious, perhaps, to our seeming—not only found helpful teaching in classical letters, but developed broad and abiding interests. Bodley, Wotton, Savile, Sidney and Hooker at Oxford, Spenser, Downes, Fraunce and Harington at Cambridge, are typical of different groups of men who owed much to the universities for the shaping of their bent. But that single-eyed devotion to scholarship which marked the circle of Cheke, Smith and Ascham at the outset of this period is far to seek as it draws to a close. Theology attracted the strongest intelligence as it has done at certain epochs since. The way to secular advance lay at court or in adventure. Wotton, indeed, wrote his Latin play like many another. But he found his enjoyment at Oxford in reading law with Gentilis, in learning Italian and in working at optics. Donne had read enough for graduation by the time he was thirteen: and he then left to spend four desultory years at Cambridge. Henry Savile, warden of Merton and, later, like Wotton, provost of Eton, whose rightful repute for scholarship even Scaliger allowed, translated the *Annals* of Tacitus (1592) wrote on Roman warfare, edited Xenophon (the *Cyropaedia*) and produced the first substantial work of English patristic learning since the revival. He stands for the 'courtier' as developed on English soil, a man of the world, versatile and travelled, 'the scholar gentleman.' Before the queen died, the English universities had already begun to realise their national function as the breeders of men of talent for affairs, of divines and schoolmasters, with here and there, as a 'sport,' a man of letters and, yet more rarely, a leader in scholarship.

Three other foundations call for mention: Edinburgh (1582) Trinity College, Dublin (1591) and Gresham College (1596). The reformation struggle had all but extinguished university teaching in Scotland, which sent students to Padua or Douay, or to the Collège de Guyenne, at Bordeaux, where we meet with many Scottish names, that of George Buchanan, as a teacher, among them. It is characteristic of the time that young Scotsmen very rarely found their way to Oxford or Cambridge. Andrew Melville, though as fanatic as Knox, was, however, a humanist and did something to restore learning at Glasgow and St Andrews. Edinburgh was too young to take effective part in building up the fabric of Scottish protestant humanism. Trinity College, Dublin, an outstanding product of the English reformation, was, as Fuller describes it, a plantation settled from Cambridge. The first suggestion for a foundation in Dublin had come from archbishop Browne, some forty years before, and was repeated after Elizabeth's accession. The temper of the founder was revealed in the two men who filled the office of provost, the first, archbishop Loftus, a fellow of Trinity, Cambridge—and admirer of Cartwright—and the second, Travers, of *Disciplina* fame, puritan and arch-separatist. The college was, of course, part and parcel of the English occupation. Sir Thomas Gresham designed his college (1596), in London, to be 'an epitome of a University.' Oxford chose the original seven professors, who included Henry Briggs, Napier's collaborator. The professor of law was expressly directed to treat of contracts, monopolies, shipping and the like. 'Medicine' covered not only the study of Galen and Hippocrates, but, also, modern theories of physiology, pathology and therapeutics. Geometry was to be both theoretical and practical. In divinity, the professor was charged specially to defend the Church of England. It was a notable attempt to adapt the widening knowledge of the day to the needs of 'the spacious time.'

It is significant that, in both universities, the art of printing ceased at some date between 1520—30, to be restored at Cambridge, in 1582, when Thomas was recognised as printer to the university, and at Oxford, in 1585, when Barnes set up a press. But the centre of English printing and publishing was London, where fifty presses were at work under strict surveillance of court and bishop. From 1586, licence to publish was granted by the archbishop of Canterbury and the bishop of London, and the only two presses authorised without the London area were those of Oxford and Cambridge. Little of the first order was produced, however, by the university printers. The mass of texts for school and college were not of English origin, but bear the imprint of Plantin, Aldus, or Gryphius and of the busy workshops of Basel and Paris.

The influence of Edwardian legislation on English schools is a subject for the general historian. It is, however, to be noted how large was the supply of small schools, elementary, 'song,' or grammar schools in England, as revealed by the chantry commission of 1548, particularly in the eastern half of the kingdom. Some half dozen school foundations, such as Sedbergh and Birmingham, are in debt to Northumberland. Mary could do as little for schools as for universities. Elizabeth's counsellors took up the task where Edward's death had left it. The queen's trained intelligence was on the side of knowledge. In church and in state, the men she trusted owed more to acquired gifts than to birth. Classical education was in favour at court; money from religious houses was—though sparingly, as always—accorded to school endowments on request. To restore the local grammar school became a fashion. Merchants, servants of the crown, country gentry, superior clergy, borough corporations, founded free grammar schools. Westminster was reconstructed; Eton and Winchester, which had the immunities of a college of the universities, widened studies and enlarged their numbers. The leaving age was advanced. A new type of scholar, sometimes, like

Ashton of Shrewsbury, a man of versatile gifts and standing at court, or a travelled historian like Camden, became headmaster. Savile and Wotton dignified the office of provost of Eton. Purely local schools, such as Peterborough or Colchester, made stringent requirements of attainment in their headmasters. Fellows of the best colleges took service in schools, and, though often incompetent as teachers, were but rarely ill-educated men. The best houses began to send boys to school. The tutor remained for the younger brothers, or piloted the promising graduate through the perils of the foreign tour. The burgher class adopted the new education. Colet's reformed school of St Paul's was copied in fifty towns. Borough councils were importunate to secure charters and grants. In order to keep a high level of efficiency, here and there a founder linked his school to one of the colleges of the university, after the fashion of Eton or Winchester. The lay spirit became dominant. Shrewsbury, indeed, was a civic school, but ecclesiastical foundations also, like Westminster and Winchester, now and again had lay heads. The licence to teach was granted by the bishop of the diocese, and, nominally at least, royal sanction gave its imprimatur to a Latin grammar or to a historical text-book like Ocland's *Anglorum Praelia.* Yet, in reality, instruction was unfettered within the limits of school statutes.

There were, in effect, two main types of school. The first was the great public boarding school: Eton, Winchester and Westminster, drawing pupils from the country at large, though Westminster was, largely, a London school; with these ranked Shrewsbury, which, of local origin and a day school, yet served a province, and was filled with sons of the gentry of north Wales, and the north-west midlands. The second type was the town day school, of diverse origin, such as St Paul's, Merchant Taylors', St Saviour's Southwark, Manchester, Guildford, Tonbridge, or Magdalen College school. Wolsey's school of Ipswich apart, there is no reason to assume imitation of French or German models in organisation. The statutes of Wykeham or of Colet were the standing guide. Compared with the superior clergy, headmasters, like heads of houses in the universities, were poorly paid. Ashton had £40 per annum at Shrewsbury. The Westminster headship was worth £27. 11*s.* 8*d.*, but 'presents' were expected from parents. Camden said he earned enough. Guildford could pay £24 in 1596. Bucer's stipend of £100, in Edward's reign, was magnificent, but unique. The usual pay of the one master of a small grammar school, in 1548, was six or seven pounds. Rotherham and Southwell, collegiate schools, could afford £10 or a little more. Shrewsbury was, about 1570, far the best paid headship in England, and the school numbers exceeded those of Eton or Winchester. The custom of taking 'private pupils,' however, grew rapidly towards the end of the century. As a Cambridge fellow rarely received so much as £6, including his allowance for commons, the new schools tended to attract promising material to their staff.

The practice of the better schools was to require that boys, on admission, should have had good grounding in accidence, know the concords and read and write English intelligibly. The curriculum was, almost exclusively, classical. A little mathematics, some smattering of astronomy, may have been added here and there; but neither logic nor English was taught, and history (Ocland, indeed, is an interesting phenomenon) simply as a comment on Livy or Plutarch. The four public schools followed a very similar order. At Westminster, apparently, Greek was carried further than elsewhere: for Xenophon, Isocrates, Demosthenes, Homer and Hesiod are expressly prescribed in the Elizabethan curriculum. Eton seems to have aimed no higher than the grammar. Shrewsbury makes no mention of any author harder than Isocrates. Thucydides and Euripides are never named. The grammar generally used was Clenard's, until Grant, at Westminster, introduced his *Spicilegium* and Eton adapted it to its own use as the Eton Greek grammar. Efforts at Greek composition were exceptional. Chief stress was laid in every school upon exercises in Latin prose and verse. To lay the foundations of prose style was the object of every master. To this end, he began with the *Colloquies* of Erasmus, Cordier and Vives, and passed to Sturm's selection of Cicero's *Letters*. As early as possible, the pupil was turned on to Terence, whose pure Roman diction every humanist, Catholic or puritan alike, upheld for imitation. Caesar, properly, was not regarded as an elementary text. Sallust was commonly read, but Tacitus very rarely. There was no reluctance to put Juvenal and Martial into boys' hands. The *Figurae* of Mosellanus, the *Epitome Troporum* of Susenbrotus, the grammars of Despauterius and Lily are commonly alluded to. At Ipswich, Wolsey prescribed the *Elegantiae* of Valla. Rhetoric, in the developed sense, was left to the university. The school-play took the place of the mystery, and the pageant competed with the play. Shrewsbury and Chester schools were famous for dramatic exhibitions. Henry Sidney, lord of the Welsh March, whose son Philip was a pupil of Ashton, was entertained, after a visit to the town, with a noteworthy river-pageant performed by the boys as he was rowed down the Severn on his journey home. In many schools, the performance of a scene from Terence or Seneca was a weekly exercise, the example of Melanchthon and John Sturm being herein followed. English writing was, probably, more cared for than directly appears. For the admirable training provided by exact construing, by essay-writing and by declamations, though these were never vernacular exercises, developed taste in words and some sense of the logical texture of speech. What natural history was imparted was given by way of notes to classical texts. Much attention was often given to singing. But the arts of writing and ciphering were relegated to separate and inferior schools. There was, inevitably, much repetition, and a harsh discipline enforced attention to uncongenial task-work. In the Elizabethan school, the hard edge of circumstance was never softened to the weak. The 'big school,' in which all classes were held together, carried with it the idea of corporate life. Monitors were always employed for discipline and for aid in teaching junior forms. As a rule, foundationers, and these alone, received education free of all charges, except for 'birch broom and candles.' The age of leaving for the university is hard to estimate; but the better taught schools tried to retain their promising pupils till their sixteenth year. In time of plague, a large school, like the colleges, had its retreat; Westminster had a house at Chiswick, Eton at Chippenham, Magdalen College, Oxford, at Brackley. Not a few schools began to acquire a library of merit, which, in the case of such a school as Shrewsbury, has, by happy neglect, survived intact to our own day.

The rapid growth of the revival in England may be illustrated by contrasting the position and attainments of Grocyn at Oxford (1491) and those of 'John Cheke who taught Cambridge Greek' as regius professor, in 1540. Admitted at St John's when twelve years of age, Cheke so proved his skill in the tongues as 'to have laid the very foundations of learning in his College.' The foundation of the royal chair of Greek gave him the pre-eminence, both titular and real, in Cambridge scholarship. His expositions of Euripides and Sophocles, Herodotus and the *Ethics* of Aristotle, are specially recorded. These, probably, were of far more importance in the history of learning in England than the controversy as to the right value of Greek vowel sounds, with which his name is usually associated. Cheke became public orator in 1544, and was appointed tutor to prince Edward. At heart a reformer, he had no scruple in accepting conventual lands, whereby he became a man of wealth and station. As provost of King's College, one of Somerset's visitors, a knight and intimate at court, he was familiar with the currents both of learning and of politics. For rashly embracing the cause of lady Jane Grey, he went, in due course, to the Tower; he was soon released, but, circumspectly, passed to the continent, where we hear of him teaching Greek at Padua and at Strassburg. He was arrested by order of Philip II, near Brussels, as an 'unlicensed' traveller and conveyed, once more, to the Tower. Under threat of torture, he abjured his convictions, and died (1557) within a year, a broken man. Cheke was unquestionably a scholar of distinction. Of his criticism on Sallust as quoted by Ascham, something has already been said[1]. He left behind a copious body of Latin translation from the Greek, patristic and classical. His bulky tracts of controversial divinity are chiefly noteworthy as exhibiting the temper of the time, especially as it affected Cambridge learning. He wrote nothing but a pamphlet or two in the vernacular, though he endeavoured, unsuccessfully, to reform English spelling on a phonetic method. His outstanding merit lies in his stimulating force as a teacher, and the respect which his learning won for English scholarship.

The contribution of Thomas Wilson, friend and disciple of Cheke, to the classical renascence in England has, also, already been mentioned[2]. The first book of *The Arte of Rhetorique* (1553) treats of the purpose of rhetoric, which is affirmed to be the art which perfects the natural gifts of speech and reason. The distinctions of several types of 'arguments,' and their constituent factors, are set out by means of examples shaped, indeed, on classical and Erasmian models, but with an added seriousness, born of the time, which lifts them above the Petrarchian commonplaces of the Italians. The second book treats, in the customary manner, of the fundamental qualities of style as an instrument of persuasion. The orator must be easily intelligible. He must secure the goodwill of his audience, must wind his way into the subject by suitable approaches, particularly if he be a preacher. Let the latter diligently seek his pattern in Chrysostom. The conditions of right eloquence, such as logical order, emphasis, repetition, climax, are as necessary in English speech as in Latin; nor can an English speaker neglect the art of stirring the emotions by the employment of humour, or pathos, by appeal to indignation or passion. The third book, ranging over a wide field, deals with

[1] See *ante*, p. 290. [2] See *ante*, p. 23.

the choice of words and the use of figure and ornament; with the functions of gesture; with the essential art of memory. It contains some of the sanest Elizabethan criticism of classical writers.

The marks of *The Arte of Rhetorique* are its clearness, its freedom from pedantry and its modern instances. It was several times reprinted during the century and even now repays a reading. Wilson's treatise should be read side by side with Guazzo's *Civile Conversation*, translated by Pettie twenty years later, with a preface in which he refers to Wilson and in which he urges the need for a liberal expansion of English vocabulary. A work far less attractive than either was Richard Sherry's *Treatise of Schemes and Tropes* (1555). The author was headmaster of Magdalen College school, at this time, perhaps, the best Latin school in England. His writing is crabbed and technical, and had small vogue outside lecture rooms. More popular were Richard Rainolde's *Foundation of Rhetorike* (1563), Henry Peacham's *Garden of Eloquence* (1577) and *The Arcadian Rhetorike* (1584) of Abraham Fraunce, who works in modern examples from poetry and prose, notably quoting Sidney and Tasso, and not overlooking the Spaniards.

Roger Ascham was entered at St John's, Cambridge, a little later than Cheke and, as he neared manhood, found himself drawn into his circle, which embraced Redman and Pember, Thomas Smith, Ridley and Wilson. Upon Cheke, Ascham looked back as upon his great master, counting him worthy to rank with John Sturm of Strassburg, the chief luminary of protestant scholarship in the middle of the sixteenth century.

In 1548, Ascham, perhaps the ablest Greek scholar in England, and public orator of the university, was called to court as tutor to princess Elizabeth. But, while he enjoyed his task of teaching a pupil of Elizabeth's acquisitive temper, his self-respect ill brooked a court position. Two years later, he made the tour of Germany, as secretary to a mission, touching Italy at Venice. He was alert to meet scholars, observe institutions and visit historic sites. Characteristically, the secretary taught his chief Greek grammar during their intervals of leisure. The *Report and Discourse of the affairs of Germany*, written in 1553, shows him a keen student of French and German politics. He has made Thucydides, Polybius and Livy his models. Commines has his favour, but, though he would not have allowed it, we may safely affirm that Macchiavelli's *Relazioni* had taught him more than the ancients. Queen Mary made him Latin secretary at court, where his own caution, aided by Gardiner's personal feeling for him, secured him from molestation on account of his opinions, and Elizabeth was glad to keep him in her service as Greek preceptor and courtier of the new style.

Much of Ascham's classical writing—translation from Sophocles, studies in Herodotus, a tract *de Imitatione*—has disappeared. Probably, the three works by which he is now known adequately represent his powers. *Toxophilus* (1545), a treatise on the art of shooting with the long-bow, treats, in the accepted dialogue form, of the function of bodily training in education, with the urgent prescription of practice with the bow as the national exercise. There is not a little of Plato and the Italians in his concept of the place of physical grace and vigour in personality. Plutarch and Epicharmus, Domitian and Galen, are all called in to defend his argument. This was inevitable, given the time and place; but, in spite of the fanciful play made with Jupiter and Minos in this connection, the skilled English archer for more than a hundred years has made *Toxophilus* his text-book, and 'Ascham's Five Points' are part of the lore today.

Ascham's nationalism, which inspires every paragraph of *Toxophilus*, is but characteristic of English humanism of the finer type. Elyot, Smith, Cheke and Hoby are Englishmen first and men of scholarship next. Learning, indeed, they win from every source; they are voracious readers, their interests are well-nigh universal. But, whatever the flowers, native or foreign, wholesome or poisonous, the sweetness drawn therefrom is the honey of English hives. *The Scholemaster* (1570) is essentially the work of a scholar who has no illusions on the subject of Erasmian cosmopolitanism. Like Elyot, he wrote in his own tongue—English matter, in English speech, for Englishmen, as he had said in his *Toxophilus*. He made, indeed, of a technical treatise a piece of literature, and that of no mean order. We may notice that writings upon education which were written or found welcome in this country had a note of reality which is often far to seek in German or, still more, in Italian pieces of similar character. The starting point of *The Scholemaster* is, essentially, that of Elyot's *Governour*. This is, that England loses much fruitful capacity through the ill-training of its youth of station. In the first book, Ascham considers the chief reasons of the ineffectiveness of the new education. From the text that news had reached court that Eton boys had broken school to escape the birch, he inveighs, in the vein of Erasmus, against the cruelty of school discipline, not realising that, given the curriculum and the mode of teaching it, harsh punishments were, in fact, inevitable. He next considers the differing nature of 'wits.' The schoolmaster is prone to hold precocity the singular mental and moral virtue: Ascham pleads for the slow but solid temper, and protests that, by contempt for late developed minds, Pedantius drives away many a fine intelligence from due opportunity of public service. He draws from Plato seven true 'notes of a good wit,' which 'he plainly declares in English': in essence, these are industry, interest, curiosity, a good will, but never premature gifts of acquisition. Now, these are qualities which the 'lewd and ignorant' teacher bars from their natural growth by his impatient pedantry. The second hindrance is the decay of home discipline. The youth of seventeen sent to court, left without a career, hanging idly about a great house, falls to gambling, and all licence, swelling that clan of the gentle unemployed for which relief was sought later in adventure and plantation. Travel, in the third place, has made shipwreck of many,

> not because I do contemn either the knowledge of strange and divers tongues, and namely the Italian tongue, which next the Greek and Latin tongue I do like and love above all others, or else because I do despise the learning that is gotten or the experience that is gathered in strange countries,

but travel meant a sojourn in Italy, and, in well remembered words, he proclaims his aversion to what he had seen in Venice, and the deep seated distrust with which he views the morals, the politics, the irreligion, the newer literature of the Italy of the Spaniard and the inquisition. Study will provide all the worthy fruits of travel, and manners can be learnt by all who care to read Castiglione's *Cortegiano*, in its new English dress. Let a young Englishman be proud of his England, and, if he will see other manners, other minds, Strassburg or Frankfort will give him what he seeks, with no danger to faith and morals. The second book is largely concerned with the teaching of Latin. The method of Ascham, according to which a classical language is taught by the process of re-translation of construes, is, at least, as old as Cicero and is of slight importance in the history of instruction. But this section of *The Scholemaster* is of interest as evidence of the thoroughness and breadth of Ascham's reading. He avows Greek to be the subject of his truest affection. He has a sound view of the function of historical writing, which far transcends the superficial aspect of it which confronts us in Italian humanists prior to the later Patrizi. Much space is given to the art of teaching rhetoric. Cicero is the accepted master; where Quintilian differs from him, he is to be disregarded. John Sturm he regards as unapproachable amongst neo-Latinists. Ascham pleads for style: 'ye know not what hurt ye do to learning that are not for words but for matter, and do make a divorce betwixt the tongue and the heart.' The secret of true imitation is to read exactly and, at the same time, to read widely. English will have its fruit of such right imitation of classic models, for in them alone are the 'true precepts and perfect examples' of sound writing. Upon poetic imitation only did Ascham lapse into pedantry[1]. He will recognise no English metres. Much as he admires Chaucer, he apologises for his riming, an inheritance from the Goth and Hun.

It seems that *The Scholemaster* was, for a time, accepted as the approved manual of method in instruction. The licence of *The Positions* (1581) of Richard Mulcaster runs thus: 'provided always that if this book contain anything prejudicial or hurtful to the Book of Master Ascham . . . called *The Scholemaster*, that then this licence shall be void.' In passing from Ascham to Mulcaster we step into a different world. For Mulcaster, though an Eton boy and a student of Christ Church, spent his life as a master of the two great day schools of the city of London—headmaster of Merchant Taylors' 1561—86; surmaster and, later, highmaster (1596) of St Paul's. The fruit of his experience is embodied in two books, *The Positions* (1581) and *The Elementarie* (1582), the latter an instalment of a larger work. Whilst Ascham was concerned with youth of station, destined to become landowners, courtiers or diplomatists, Mulcaster's subject is the education of the burgher class. Both, again, use English as their instrument; Ascham wrote good Tudor prose, whilst it is no gibe to say that Mulcaster's own example is enough to imperil his thesis that English speech is as harmonious and as precise as Latinity itself. He had Spenser for his pupil, and has often been identified with the caricature in *Love's Labour's Lost*. Mulcaster is, by training and by interests, a humanist, but of a temper little akin to that of Cheke or Ascham. The hard experience of twenty years had proved to him how different was the training in letters set out by the great writers from the realities of the schoolroom. It is a standing puzzle to us today that men of strong intelligence, knowing however little of boys, should assume, as without question, that a rigorous course of grammar, construing, composition and conversation in Latin, and that only, must appeal to youthful minds. They do not seem to have understood that, to

[1] See *ante*, chap. XIV.

win effective attention to arid and meaningless material, nothing less than the most harsh pressure could be expected to succeed with the average boy. Now, Mulcaster is the uncouth prophet of a new order. For he sees the problem in a modern way. He has shaken himself free of traditional platitudes. He is conscious of a new world, and of the need of a new education adapted to it. His two books, written in close succession, exhibit a consistent idea and may be viewed together. He writes in English, wishing to reach the vulgar; no fishmonger or tailor in London could touch it in Latin shape. The time has gone by, as he perceives, for illusions as to the place of Latin speech in Elizabethan England. He will have the elements of education for all; the grammar school and the university will provide for the select few of promising wit. But he boldly states that he sees loss to the community in alluring the unfit to the unpractical training of letters. 'I am tooth and nail for woman-kind' in matters of education, he declares. But their instruction must fit them for their station. Only such as are born to high place or to prospect of coming wealth should, in humanist fashion, be taught the learned tongues or history or logic. Mulcaster has a sound perception of the importance of physical training to mental efficiency, which he partly owes to Girolamo Mercuriale and other Italians. The growing custom of sending boys of every class to school has his goodwill: but, sympathising here with Ascham, he sets himself against the habit of travel for youth as bad for patriotism and religious constancy. He would have a training school for teachers set up in each university; he is the first English master to grasp the significance of what Vives had said on this head long before. Further, he would see with approval the colleges at Oxford and Cambridge specifically allotted to the study of the three subjects of general training, languages, mathematics and philosophy, and to the four professional disciplines of medicine, law, divinity and teaching. He is consistent in objecting to the study of Roman and of canon law for English youth. He sets out in detail his views of the function of English in the new education, advocating, in particular, that scholars should devote themselves to the settling of the orthography, accidence and syntax of the language, that, thereby, English may claim its place side by side with Latin, whose merits of precision and elaboration he is foremost to perceive. For 'I love Rome, but London better, I favour Italy, but England more, I honour Latin, but worship English.'

It would be impossible to enumerate the works of foreign

origin which affected the ideals of manners and instruction in England during Elizabeth's reign, but account may be taken of certain representative books which were popular enough to demand translation. *Il Cortegiano* of Castiglione[1], translated by Hoby as *The Courtier* (1561) is, of course, much more than a treatise on the up-bringing of youth, but, as presenting a picture of the 'perfect man' of the renascence, it had an undoubted, if indirect, effect on higher education in England. *Il Cortegiano* speedily became cosmopolitan in its vogue. High society in France, Spain and the Low Countries, not less than in Italy, revered it as an inspired guide, supplementing, according to choice, its obvious omissions with respect to the side of religion and the stalwart virtues. The concept of a complete personality constituted of physical gifts, learning, taste and grace of manner was the gift which the Italian revival at its noblest offered to the western peoples. Himself 'a perfect Castilio,' Sidney never stirred abroad without *The Courtier* in his pocket. To Cleland, writing for the new century (*The Institution of a Nobleman*, 1607), it is the final word on a gentleman's behaviour. Especially does its spirit breathe through such writers as La Primaudaye and Count Annibale Romei, whose books were in wide circulation at the time when this period was drawing to its close. *The French Academy*—so Bowes translates the title of La Primaudaye's work —is written (1577) in dialogue form, and dedicated to Henri III. It is less strictly confined to the courtly ideal than Castiglione's *Il Cortegiano*; its gentlemen of Anjou discourse together of the means by which all estates of men may live courteously, happily and with true dignity. The secret of the worthy life lies in the due ordering of home and commonwealth by parent and ruler, 'the grace of God working in them.' The best chapter is that on the rearing of children, based upon accepted humanist precedents, though with a vein of Huguenot piety running through it all. The author holds that civility comes not of arms, but of learning and virtue; and, of all means of training, historic studies are the most effective instruments: he bids youth ponder Cyrus, Charlemagne and Francis I. The power of education is such that it can change the temper of whole countries not less than the character of a man. Hence, the modern state should have concern to provide right teaching for all its sons. 'In every town of the realm' should be ordained the public teaching of grammar (Latin) to all comers. The popularity of this bulky work is proved by the number of its editions during twenty years. Though written in the Aristotelian

[1] Ed. pr. Aldus, 1528.

vein made familiar by Patrizi and Acontio, the dialogue is modelled on Castiglione, with, it must be said, but little of the grace of *Il Cortegiano*. *Il Galateo* (1545), a far better known book, was translated into English (1576) by Peterson. It is a frank handbook of manners, a manual for the schoolboy and the parvenu, and became popular in England under the titles of *Refined Courtier* and the like, given to it by later editors and adapters. *The Courtier's Academy,* a translation, by Kepers, of the *Discorsi* of Count Annibale Romei of Ferrara (1586), treats of the ideal of personality approved in cultivated society when the renascence was already on the verge of decline. The Elizabethan scholar or merchant was interested, we can believe, in the argument for learning and for wealth as titles to *gentilezza,* when birth or skill in arms could not be pleaded.

As the century draws to a close, we trace, on the one hand, a gradual enlargement of the concept of what is possible in the way of education for a youth of parts and opportunity, side by side with a process of ossification of school instruction. Sir Humphrey Gilbert's project of *Queene Elizabethes Achademy* (1572) was an anticipation of later 'academies' and, in a sense, of Milton's 'generous' dream. Gilbert's scheme of a training in which languages, modern no less than ancient, mathematics and law, are grouped with technical and military exercises is an attempt to bring education into immediate touch with actual life. In essence, it is a protest against the narrow humanism of the public school, the herald of a reaction which was to take one shape in Bacon, and another in Montaigne. Meanwhile, in spite of Ascham, men of the world sent their boys to complete their training abroad. The French court was accounted the best school of courtesy. Venice was the centre for art, and for such sciences as astronomy; Florence for letters. Politics, history, painting, building, scientific invention, the technique of war, drew the interest of Englishmen wherever they sojourned. And the finer minds returned with a deeper and more intelligent patriotism. Hakluyt's *Principal Navigations,* Stow's *Annales,* Camden's *Britannia,* Holinshed's *Chronicles* and its predecessors are evidence of a fuller national self-consciousness. More truly than works of scholarship do these represent the genius of Elizabethan England. For the end of a man's 'whole traine' lay in action rather than in the knowledge itself which equipped him for it. The universities had definitely recognised this as their principal function, and the temper of the English race responded readily to the call.

CHAPTER XX

THE LANGUAGE FROM CHAUCER TO SHAKESPEARE

THE all-important feature in the development of English during the pre-Chaucerian period consisted of those grammatical changes which entirely altered the organic character of the language. From being a highly inflected language, it became one partially stripped of inflections, whereas its changes in vocabulary during the same period, though important in themselves, were far less radical in their effects. After 1400, the order of importance is reversed. It was a change in the vocabulary, particularly in that of the sixteenth century, which made almost all the difference; the grammatical structure was modified in but a comparatively slight degree.

The causes of these differing tendencies are not far to seek. The period before Chaucer was one in which English was not, as yet, the literary language: it shared that dignity with Latin and Anglo-French, and, of its four main dialects, no one had become predominant. These were conditions which readily permitted grammatical change and led to attempts being made at removing ambiguities and irregularities from the inflectional system. After 1400, the restraining influences of a recognised literary dialect and a growing literature made themselves felt. Writers became more and more adverse to modifications of grammatical forms, which had already been simplified almost to their limit, while the vocabulary grew mechanically under varying but ever increasing influences.

The period (1400—1600) with which this chapter deals divides naturally into two centuries, the dividing point being, roughly, the date of Caxton's death (1491). The first of these two periods—the fifteenth century—though transitional and somewhat chaotic in character, was, nevertheless, responsible for certain marked developments. In it an increased importance was given to the vernacular, and a uniform written language was established, both of which effects were due to tendencies visible already in Chaucer's day. And the period is further characterised by some considerable changes in vocabulary, as well as by changes of a more gradual kind in grammatical structure and pronunciation, which may be said to culminate in the following century.

The increasing importance of the vernacular in the fifteenth century was due, in part, to the growing sense of nationality under Edward III. Although the use of English had never died out, and even Robert of Gloucester had been able to state that 'lowe men holdeþ to Engliss,' yet, in the thirteenth century and later, Anglo-French was the courtly language, Latin the language of learned and documentary writings. Under Edward III, the conditions began to change: in 1362, parliament was opened by an English speech, and, about the same time, English began to be used in the law courts and the schools[1]. It also came to be generally regarded as the language of literature, as is seen when Gower forsakes French and Latin to write in English, and when Capgrave (1462) compiles what was the first chronicle in English since the Conquest. Though the struggles of the vernacular for recognition were not completed in this century, the position it held was stronger than at any time since 1066, and its supremacy was to be assured by Caxton's work.

The causes which brought about the recognition of a standard dialect of English have already been treated. London furnished that dialect, just as the chief city of Attica furnished the language of literary Greek and Paris the language of literary French; and throughout the fifteenth century this London dialect was gaining ascendency. Various dialectal forms inserted in a text would still betray the district from which their writer hailed, even when he had deliberately adopted the standard dialect; and such provincialisms remained until the time of printed texts. But, from now onwards, the one dialect was to represent the spoken language of the educated, as well as the literary and official medium. The dialects of *Ormulum* and the *Ancren Riwle* lost caste, and remained, apart from literature, on the tongues of the people.

The most striking feature in connection with the fifteenth century vocabulary was the rapid manner in which old native words became obsolete. This is clearly seen from the following lists, taken, on the one hand, from fourteenth century texts, and, on the

[1] The oldest private records in English are dated 1375 and 1381; the oldest London documents in English, 1384, 1386; the earliest petition to parliament in English, 1386; the earliest English wills, 1387. See Morsbach: *Über den Ursprung der neuengl. Schriftsprache* (Heilbronn, 1888), *passim*.

other, from modernised versions of those texts, belonging to the fifteenth and early sixteenth centuries.

Trevisa's *Chron.* (1387)	Caxton's version (1482)	Wyclif's trans. (1380)	Tindale's version (1525)
icleped	called	heathens	gentyls
schulleþ fonge	shall resseyve	ȝeerd	rod
to eche	encrece	to meke	to humble
byneme	teke away	soure dowȝ	leven
buxom	obedient	bitake	delyver
hiȝt	was named	axe him	questen with him
as me troweþ	as men suppose	walow a stoon	roll a stone
steihe	ascended	abide it	wayte for it
ȝede	went	elde	olde age
nesche	soft	to hie hymself	to exalt hym selfe[1].

Literary diction is not always a true test as to the condition of the spoken language, but there can be little doubt that the changes here represented stand for changes of the language in common use; for the object in modernising the texts had been to bring them into conformity with the language of the day. And it is also interesting to note that the forms of the later texts are practically those of modern English: they were to be fixed by the printing press.

It is evident from the above lists that the obsolescent native words were being mainly superseded by words of French origin. French words had been borrowed during the preceding centuries, when Anglo-French represented the language of the official and governing classes; but, in the fifteenth century, as a result of different social and literary influences, the borrowings were mainly of the Parisian or Picardian type, and their use became more marked than ever. Already, in the first half of this century, a change is visible; in Lydgate, for instance, abstract words of Romance origin are being substituted for Chaucer's concrete native terms[2], and the proportion of this foreign element steadily increased as the century advanced.

Translation, no doubt, accounts for the presence of many of these French words in fifteenth century English, also for the many Latin words and constructions which were freely adopted. But it by no means represents the only influence. Trade relations with the Netherlands and the settlement of Flemish weavers in England during the fourteenth century led to the introduction of many

[1] See T. L. K. Oliphant's *New English*, I, pp. 336, 409–10.

[2] In the diction of Chaucer's *Prologue* there is 13 per cent. of foreign element; in Lydgate's *Assembly of Gods*, 23 per cent. (See O. T. Triggs, *Assembly of Gods*, E.E.T.S. Ex. Ser. LXIX.)

Low German words, which were supplemented at a later date, when relations with the Low Countries were renewed in connection with printing. Then, again, Italian words like 'pilgrim,' 'alarm' and 'brigand,' are found naturalised before 1500; and so, in a variety of ways, the character of the vocabulary changed, anticipating the more expansive movements of the following century[1].

It is also clear, from the above lists, that the decay of the earlier inflectional system was being gradually completed. Unnecessary adjuncts like the prefix *y*-, the negative particle in *nas* and endings like -*eþ* in '*schulleþ*' (present plural) and '*haveþ*' (imperative plural), where the plural idea was denoted by the context, were being discarded. Prepositional forms were increasing, as well as the periphrastic method of comparison by 'more' and 'most.' There was also a growing tendency to avoid impersonal constructions, while vowel-differences, due to earlier *ablaut* or *umlaut*, as in '*schulleþ*' and '*elde*,' in the list given above, were being rapidly levelled. The most important of these changes, however, was the loss of final syllabic -*e* (-*es*, -*en*). It is probable that Chaucer's systematic use of that vowel represented merely an archaism utilised for metrical purposes, and it was owing to his influence that its value was preserved in poetry during the early part of the fifteenth century. But already in Lydgate there are signs that it had really become mute[2], more frequently, perhaps, in Romance words, than in those of Teutonic origin; and this led to much confusion in both language and metre after the middle of the century. The secret of Chaucer's metrical methods seemed lost, and the confused metre, the halting gait and the unmusical combinations of words illustrate how misapprehension of this final syllabic -*e* had interfered with literary effects[3]. A change in the whole poetic phraseology was, moreover, involved; dissyllabic words became monosyllabic, and poetic formulas, received from the past, became mere prose. Lydgate was able to embody phrases such as Chaucer's 'the grene levės,' or 'oldė stories tellėn us'; but, to later poets, unconscious of the syllabic -*e*, the phrases were lacking in harmony and rhythm. Instead of Chaucer's 'my grenė yerės,' Surrey has to

[1] Wyclif's phrases 'the streit ȝate,' 'to be of good coumfort,' and such expressions as 'the pees that the world may not geve,' 'for better for warse,' 'tyl dethe us departe' (translation of *York Manual*, 1390) are early indications of the influence of 'makers of English' (see p. 455).

[2] See Lydgate's later works for *y*, *yĕ*, rimes.

[3] See vol. II, chap. IX, and Courthope's *History of English Poetry*, vol. II, pp. 87 ff. For its influence upon Spenser's accentual measures in the *Shepheards Calender* see Greg's *Pastoral Poetry and Pastoral Drama*, pp. 94, 95.

write 'my fresh green years'; for Chaucer's 'sootė flourės,' Sackville writes 'soot fresh flowers'[1].

Of changes in pronunciation during the fifteenth century, those of open and close ē and ō, are, perhaps, the most important. The open and close values had, apparently, been distinct in Chaucer's time, for he avoids riming the one with the other; but, in the fifteenth century, the open values began to approximate those of the close. This change gave to open ō what is practically its modern value, but the other sounds were to undergo further changes in the sixteenth and later centuries[2]. At the same time, medial *gh* ceased to be pronounced. Chaucer does not rime a vowel followed by *ght* with a vowel followed by *t*; but, in Lydgate, 'fought' rimes with 'about,' and there is ample evidence that the Old English sound of medial *h* was, by this time, lost.

The orthography during this century was somewhat confused. It was irregular in the sixteenth century, in spite of the influence of printed texts, but already it was assuming forms which, with slight changes, were destined to survive all later modifications of pronunciation, thus producing the anomalies of our modern spelling. After Caxton's day, old symbols like ȝ and þ were discarded, and final non-syllabic *-e* was often used, as in 'stone' (nom.), without any etymological warrant: its use, in such cases, being due to analogy with the oblique forms in which it normally occurred.

We pass now to the sixteenth century and there we see the vernacular duly established as the literary medium, so that the main interest lies in tracing the subsequent development of the language of Caxton and in noting how it became a fit vehicle for some of our greatest literature. Now, for the first time, we see scholars concerned for its welfare, and attempting to improve its powers of expression. We also see the renascence movement and general national activities increasing its vocabulary to an enormous extent. We see its grammatical structure and its syntax being slowly modified; and, while there are visible certain approaches to modern expression, we also notice certain characteristics which give to Elizabethan English something of its peculiar charm.

[1] See J. Schick, Lydgate's *Temple of Glas*, E.E.T.S., 1891.

[2] These changes might, roughly, be indicated as follows:

M. E.	*Example*	14th *cent. pronunciation*	15th *cent. pronunciation*
open ē	mele (meal)	sounded as in Pair	sounded as in Pail
close ē	demen (deem)	,, ,, Pail	,, ,, Pail
open ō	stoon (stone)	,, ,, Paul	,, ,, Paul, Pole
close ō	doom (doom)	,, ,, Pole	,, ,, Pole.

When Caxton died in 1491, he had fixed, in the rough, the character of modern English. The works subsequently issued from the printing press were to give to the vernacular a definite standing, and to suggest its adoption as the literary medium, with a force denied to rarely handled manuscripts. But there still remained many obstacles to be overcome, before the capabilities of English were completely recognised. It had never yet been the object of serious study. The grammar schools founded in the sixteenth and previous centuries existed mainly for the teaching of Latin; grammar meant Latin grammar, and it became a generic term only at the close of the Elizabethan age[1]. Moreover, the English-Latin dictionaries[2] which had appeared at intervals since 1440, though they afforded valuable collections of English words, were primarily designed to help Latin scholars; and so it is not strange to find that, in the first half of the sixteenth century, the idea of Latin as the language of scholarship and the necessary medium for attaining literary longevity was still a deeply-seated notion. Thus, we find bishop Gardiner advising that religious works should take either Greek or Latin form, because those languages were well fixed, whereas 'English had not continued in one form of understanding for 200 years.' And, again, Sir Thomas Hoby, though himself a translator, writes, in 1561, that 'oure learned menne for the most part, holde opinion that to have the sciences in the mother tunge, hurteth memorie and hindreth learning.' The vernacular, too, was constantly being made the subject of apology. Many still felt with Ascham, that to have written in a tongue other than English would have been more honest for their names; and the monotony of lament for the 'vile terms' of English, which had become almost conventional since the days of Chaucer, was, to some extent, maintained.

The second half of the century, however, witnessed a change of attitude. Literary criticism began with an enquiry into language, the outward and visible sign of literature; scholars began to consider what was correct in the pronunciation and

[1] Besides the *English Grammar* due to Ben Jonson, the works of Mulcaster and Bullokar ought to be noticed. The former wrote an *Elementarie*, Pt I. (1582), 'which entreateth chefely of the right Writing of the English Tung'; while Wm Bullokar's *Bref Grammar for English* (1586) was an 'abbreviation out of his grammar at larg,' which 'grammar at larg' he claimed to be 'the first grammar for Englishe that ever waz' (see Warton's *History of English Poetry*, vol. III, pp. 346—7). For an article on Richard Mulcaster as Elizabethan philologist see *Mod. Lang. Notes*, XII, No. 3, pp. 129—39. See also *ante*, pp. 311 and 435.

[2] See bibliography.

spelling of English, and to set themselves to the task of improving its powers of expression.

With the appearance of *Toxophilus* (1545), the prejudice in favour of Latin may be said to have begun to wane. Though journals of the guilds and important records and accounts were still couched in Latin, there was an occasional championing of the vernacular even in connection with recondite subjects. Elyot had already protested: 'If physicians be angry that I have written physicke in English, let them remember that the Grekes wrote in Greke, the Romains in Latin[1],' and the vernacular slowly asserted itself in religious and secular works, and even in those which issued from the citadels of science. A sort of compromise between the old and new traditions was visible when More's *Utopia* was translated into English in 1561, and when Lawrence Humphrey, having written his *Optimates* (1560) in Latin, three years later turned it into English. And, though Bacon was yet to fear that modern languages would 'play the bankrupt with books,' his timidity was far from being shared by the bulk of his contemporaries.

The causes of this change were, no doubt, complex; but one great driving force must have been the growing sense of nationalism, the new-born temper, which rejoiced in everything English. Then, again, the desire to disseminate renascence learning, and to open up easy avenues to the classical stores, induced scholars to make a further use of their mother tongue. The reformation movement, in itself an assertion of Teutonism against Latinism, led to numerous English versions of the Bible; and, when the English prayer-book had also accustomed the nation to daily reading of their mother tongue, English, instead of Latin, had become the language of religion. Moreover, the work inaugurated by Caxton was duly organised when the Stationers' company was formed in 1557, and growing facilities for the book industry in England ensured an increase in the appearance of English works.

With this gradual recognition of the literary claims of the vernacular, scholars began to perceive the urgency of fitting it for its new tasks. The situation was paralleled across the Channel, where Ronsard and *La Pléiade* were engaged upon the improvement of their mother tongue; and, at a still earlier date, Bembo, the foster-father of Italian, had undertaken a similar work in

[1] Elyot's *Castel of Helth* (1534). The interlude called *The Four Elements* (1520) had already discussed the use of English for scholarly purposes, and lamented that it had been employed hitherto only for idle stories of love and war.

Italy. In Italy, the end had been obtained by a dictatorship; in France, the reformers aimed at devising rules; but in England, the method adopted was the characteristic one of compromise. A middle way was chosen between two conflicting tendencies, one of which, being conservative, aimed at retaining the language in its purity and severity, while the other made for innovation, for the strengthening of the native growth with foreign material. These opposing tendencies represented an inevitable stage in linguistic development. Innovations had been made continuously since the time of the Romans, and the work of sixteenth century innovators, Latinists for the most part, was simply a continuation of this practice. But the opposite tendency, that of the purists, was now felt for the first time; conservatism was generated only when time had brought about a due consciousness of the past and a pride in the vernacular as a national possession.

The purists were notably Cheke, Ascham and Wilson, though their sympathies were shared by many others. Cheke, as a lover of 'old denisened words,' expressed himself in unequivocal terms. 'Our own tung,' he writes, 'should be written clean and pure, unmixt and unmangeled with borrowing of other tunges; wherein, if we take not heed by tym, ever borrowing and never payeng, she shall be fain to keep her house as bankrupt.' Ascham, too, adopted the same attitude, and Wilson decried all 'overflouryshing wyth superfluous speach.' And this love of the vernacular and confidence in its resources was present with others. Mulcaster honoured Latin but worshipped English; Sidney maintained that for 'uttering sweetly and properly the conceits of the mind...[English] hath it equally with any other tongue in the world,' and similar sentiments were uttered by Golding and Pettie, while, before the end of the century, Carew's *Epistle on the Excellency of the English Tongue* had appeared[1]. Under certain conditions, religious zeal might also account for a purist attitude, as when Fulke, in his attack of 1583 upon the Rheims translation of the Bible, complains of the number of Latin words used in that version, where they occur 'of purpose to darken the sense...[and that] it may be kept [by the Papists] from being understood.'

But there were not a few who held that the vernacular needed improvement if it was to respond to the demands which were obviously ahead. To refuse innovation was to neglect the very

[1] It is contained in the 2nd ed. of Camden's *Remains* (1605). See also the prophecy of the glorious destiny of the English language in Daniel's *Musophilus* (1599) (quoted by Courthope, *History of English Poetry*, vol. III, p. 23).

means by which it had prospered in the past; and it was felt that the jealous exclusiveness of the extreme purists threatened to blunt all literary expression and would turn the vernacular into a clumsy instrument. Many of those whose instincts were conservative were also alive to the necessity for a certain amount of innovation. Even Cheke made a proviso to the effect that, 'borrowing, if it needs must be, should be done with bashfulness,' and both Pettie and Wilson definitely proposed to improve their language by Latin borrowings. 'It is the way,' remarked the former, 'that all tongues have taken to enrich themselves.' Gascoigne, though disliking strange words in general, was bound to admit that, at times, they might 'draw attentive reading'; while Nashe, complaining of the way in which English swarmed with 'the single money of monosyllables,' proposed to make 'a royaler show,' by exchanging his 'small English . . . four into one . . . according to the Greek, French, Spanish and Italian.' Other reasons were elsewhere advanced to justify innovation; but what is of more importance is that, in actual practice, the main body of writers were fully in sympathy with the aims of the movement.

The result of these conflicting tendencies was twofold. The conservatism of the purists proved a useful drag upon the energies of the reformers; it tended to preserve from obsolescence the native element in the language, and was a wholesome reminder of the necessity for moving slowly in a period of rapid change and hot enthusiasm. The efforts of the innovators, on the other hand, made great things possible. The language under their treatment became more supple, more ornate and more responsive to new ideas and emotions; but this was only after a certain amount of licence had been frowned out of existence.

The conservative tendency is revealed, not only in a negative way, by the general discountenancing of rash innovation, but, also, by positive efforts made 'to restore such good and natural English words as had been long time out of use and almost clean disherited.' Obsolescent words, no doubt, persisted in the spoken language, for Ascham, who held 'that good writing involved the speech of the comon people,' makes use of forms like 'stoure' (fight) and 'freke' (man), while, in Foxe's *Actes and Monuments*, which appealed to provincial and cultured taste alike, are to be found words like 'spill' (destroy), 'dere' (injure), 'lin' (cease), 'spur' (ask), 'lese' (lose) and 'middle-earth' (world). Then, again, works written under the influence of earlier poetic tradition might, also, contain a certain amount of the archaic: thus, Wyatt and Surrey have forms like 'eyen' and 'durre' (door), while Gascoigne, who writes under the influence of *Piers the Plowman*, uses 'sakeless' (innocent), 'fearli' (wonder) and 'grete' (cry). Very frequently, too, there was deliberate archaising. Sir John Cheke, in his unfinished translation of the New Testament[1], took many liberties not always justifiable; for 'publican' he writes 'toller'; for 'crucify,' 'cross'; for 'centurion,' 'hundreder'; and, for 'lunatic,' 'moond.' In the translations of Phaer, Twyne, Golding and North, further archaisms appear; while Stanyhurst, who was a man of many devices, has old forms like 'sib,' 'gadling,' 'quernstone' and 'agryse'[2].

In some cases, a definite literary motive might occasion the use of these forms. Spenser, for instance, in his *Shepheards Calender* makes a most liberal use of the language of Lancashire peasants as well as of obsolete forms. To the former class, probably, belong such northern forms as 'wae' (woe), 'gate' (goat), 'sike' (such), 'mickle' and 'kirke,' and they effectively suggest 'the rusticall rudenesse of shepheards.' In his *Faerie Queene*, while he uses Chaucerisms like 'gan tel,' 'areed' and 'lustyhed,' to suggest a medieval tone in keeping with his subject, he also finds such forms as 'ycled,' 'passen' and 'wawes' of great assistance, not only in completing the requisite number of syllables in the line, but, also, in affording riming variants. And, again, in the drama, dialectal forms were frequently employed to obtain greater verisimilitude. The west country speech was the conventional form of utterance for rusticity on the stage; whence the forms 'chad,' 'ichotte,' 'vilthy,' 'zembletee' (semblance), in *Ralph Roister Doister*, with which may be compared Edgar's diction in *King Lear*.

But this use of obsolescent and dialectal forms added nothing to the permanent literary resources. It was an artificial restoration of words, honourable enough in the past, but which the language had naturally discarded; for words rapidly become obsolete in a period of swiftly advancing culture. Where such words appear, they add a picturesqueness to Elizabethan diction, but it was not until the close of the eighteenth century that the full capabilities of words racy of the soil became properly appreciated, when dialect added new effects to English expression. For the rest, the ancient words continued to linger in their rustic obscurity, regardless of the

[1] *The Gospel according to St Matthew...translated from the Greek, with original notes by Sir John Cheke...by James Goodwin.* London, 1843.

[2] The rogues' language then current still survives in modern slang; thus: 'bowse' (drink), 'dudes' (clothes), 'fylche' (rob), 'ken' (house), 'mounch' (eat), 'prygger' (thief), 'tiplinge-house' (ale-house), 'typ' (secret). See Awdeley's *Fraternitye*, Harman's *Caveat* and Chandler's *Literature of Roguery*, vol. I, pp. 119 ff.

attention or neglect of literary men. That they were already fast becoming unfamiliar in polite circles would appear from the fact that a glossary of obscure words was appended to Speght's edition of Chaucer (1602), a convenience which had not been deemed necessary in the editions of 1542 and 1561.

The case, however, was different when words, instead of being drawn from a dead past, were taken from a living present, as elements contributed to the language by the changing thoughts and movements of the time. English, in the nineteenth century, assimilated the respective vocabularies of German metaphysics, the pictorial art and science; and, in the same way, the language of the sixteenth century was assimilating the phraseology of renascence learning and reformation zeal, as well as the expressions of travel and adventure. And, although English, owing to its plastic state, accepted, for the time being, more of these elements than it was destined to retain, the ultimate result was linguistic expansion, and a considerable step was thus taken by the language towards its modern form.

The influence of the renascence is seen in the classical importations with which the language became inundated—an influence parallel to that which induced scholars to turn to the classics for assistance in remodelling and reforming their literary art. Just as attempts were made to introduce classical 'decorum' into the native drama, to substitute classical prosody for native forms, so free use was made of classical diction in the attempt to obtain increased power of literary expression. The beginning of this influence is seen in the translations, where numerous words of the originals were, perforce, retained; then, again, in the fashion of introducing classical quotations into works of various kinds. This latter procedure was less pedantic than would at first appear, for Latin was still, to some extent, the traditional language of the learned, and represented the great link between our own reformers and those of other lands. It was used by Elizabeth in conversation with foreign ambassadors, and 'latine ends,' as Chapman put it, 'were part of a gentleman and a good scholler.' The inevitable result was an almost reckless borrowing of classical words, an occasional use of Latin idiom and, in some cases, an imitation of classical style.

The process of adopting classical and, indeed, all foreign words, is plainly shown in the various texts. At first they are frankly inserted as foreign elements and appear in their alien form; but they are often followed by explanations added to such phrases as 'that is to saie' or 'as we terme it.' Then, later, they take their places without any explanation, though, as they appear not unfrequently in synonyms like 'synchroni or time-fellows,' 'accersed and called together,' their respective meanings may still be gathered from the context.

But all classical importations did not meet with the same fate. In the struggle for naturalisation, different words obtained different degrees of success, according to the dictates of that mysterious arbiter 'the genius of the language'; and, when Puttenham, for instance, objects to such words as 'audacious,' 'fecundity' and 'compatible,' he only shows the inability of contemporaries to anticipate the verdict of time. Some of the claimants for naturalisation were adopted with little or no change of form, as, for instance, 'epitome,' 'effigies,' 'spondee,' 'catastrophe'[1]. Others retained their original forms for a time, as '*subjectum*,' '*energia*,' '*aristocratia*' and '*statua*'[2], or, again, in the case of inflected forms, '*critici*,' '*sphinges*,' '*chori*,' '*ideae*,' '*misanthropi*' and '*musaea*.' But, in all cases, naturalisation ultimately meant the loss of foreign endings, or their assimilation with the endings and inflections of native origin. Other classical words never became really adopted; they appeared at the whim of an individual and then disappeared, as, for instance, '*acroame*' (lecture) and '*polypragmon*' (busybody)[3]. This class was fairly large, as almost every writer, in the absence of a standard literary diction, considered himself at liberty to make experiments.

But, if naturalisation in the case of Latin words meant, generally speaking, assimilation with native forms and the adoption of endings similar to those assumed by earlier Latin borrowings derived through the French, no such precedent offered itself in the case of Greek words; for now, for the first time, it became possible to borrow from the Greek direct. Greek words, however, had previously entered the language through the medium of Latin, and now, when technical or other words were taken from the Greek, they were transliterated into Latin forms, as if they had normally passed through Latin channels. It became recognised in England and elsewhere that the Greek *κ*, *αι*, *ει*, *οι*, *ου*, *υ* and *ῥ* should be represented in the vernaculars by *c*, *ae*, *i*, *oe*, *u*, *y* and *rh*; hence, forms like 'acme,' 'phaenomenon,' 'oeconomia,' 'enthusiasm' and 'rhythm'[4].

Each word thus naturalised was made to conform gradually with the English mode of accentuation, and to this general

[1] Also, 'caveat,' 'emphasis,' 'enigma,' 'opprobrium,' 'exterior' and 'parenthesis.'
[2] Also, '*scaene*,' '*epitheton*' and '*parallelon*.'
[3] '*Absonisme*' (solecism), '*charientism*' (euphemism), '*commorse*' (compassion).
[4] See Bradley, *Making of English*, p. 98.

rule Greek and Latin proper names formed no exception. They were adopted with or without inflection, and the accent was thrown as far back as possible, irrespective of quantities: this accounts for the accentuation of such forms as *Hypérion* and *Andrónicus.*

It was only natural that these classical borrowings should retain, at first, their original meanings; and so we find many words used in a sense from which they have since departed, as, for instance, 'fact' (deed), 'success' (sequel), 'sentence' (opinion), 'prevent' (go before)[1]. Such words as these, being more or less strange to the common idiom of that age, were well suited to form part of its literary material; whereas, to a later age, which assigns to them different meanings, they suggest an archaic flavour, which is one of the charms of Elizabethan diction. Not unfrequently, they would deteriorate in meaning; this is true of classical words to a greater extent than of native words, and of this depreciation, 'impertinent' and 'officious' are examples.

Sometimes, however, classical enthusiasm would distort word-forms, which had been derived at an earlier date from Latin through Romance, and, consequently, attempts were made to restore letters which had been normally lost in that passage. Thus, *b* was inserted in 'doubt' and 'debt,' *l* in 'vault' and 'fault,' *d* in 'advantage' and 'advance,' while 'apricock' was thus written probably in view of the Latin *in aprico coctus.* Then, again, the form 'amicable' appeared by the side of 'amiable,' 'absency' (Latin '*absentia*') together with the French '*absence*'; through the influence of Greek, 'queriste' became 'choriste,' while 'fantasy' varied with 'phantasy'; and, in other forms like 'fruict,' 'traditour' (traitor), 'feact' (fact), 'traictise' and 'conceipt,' are visible further pedantries not destined to be permanent. Occasionally, more audacious changes took place in attempts to suggest a fanciful etymology: as, for instance, when '*fere*' (O.E. '*gefera,*' companion) was written '*pheere,*' or when 'eclogues' appeared as 'aeglogues,' as if to connect it with the Greek *αἴξ* (goat). The frail foundation upon which most of such changes rested may be gathered from the statement of one writer that the words 'wind' and 'way' were derived from the Latin '*ventus*' and '*via,*' while the spelling 'abhominable,' as if from the Latin *ab homine,* was generally accepted. Indeed, even in the case of so worthy an antiquary as Camden, we find the paradox that 'the Old English...could call a Comet a Fixed Starre...which is all one with Stella Crinita'[2]. The result

[1] Also, 'expect' (wait), 'record' (remember), 'table' (picture), 'abrupt' (wicked).

[2] That is, '*crinita*' = 'fixed,' the latter being taken as a derivative of O.E. 'feax' (hair) (!).

of all this was the introduction of a number of artificial spellings, many of which, having been retained, have greatly contributed to the vagaries of our modern orthography.

The effect of this host of classical borrowings was to increase, in many ways, the capabilities of the language in the matter of expression. They formed the language of reasoning, of science and of philosophy; from them, mainly, were drawn artistic and abstract terms, whereas the language of emotion, particularly that of the drama, remained very largely Teutonic in kind. Not unseldom, a classical word was borrowed, though its equivalent already existed in English, and this usage gave rise to frequent synonyms. The use of synonyms was by no means abnormal in English, nor was it ineffective as a literary device. They had entered very largely into Old English verse, and were still a feature of Elizabethan English, as may be seen from combinations like 'acknowledge and confess,' 'humble and lowly,' 'assemble and meet together,' in the English liturgy, or such forms as 'limited and confined,' 'wonder and admiration,' to be found elsewhere. Their increased use, at this date, was due partly to the exuberant character of the age, partly to an increase in the material available for such forms and partly to the plastic condition of the language, which made it easy for an unfamiliar word to be supplemented by one of a more familiar kind. The result of this usage was to give to the prose style a greater flexibility of rhythm, while, in course of time, the double forms, having become 'desynonymised,' furnished abundant material for the expression of slight shades of meaning. Another important effect of a certain section of these classical borrowings was to give an impetus to the art of forming compounds, which, though much practised in the earliest English period, had been somewhat neglected in Middle English times. Chapman's translation of Homer, in particular, brought before the age many Homeric compounds, such as 'thunder-loving Jove,' 'the ever-shining eyes,' 'fresh-sprung herbs' and 'well-greaved Greeks.' Many of these forms were preserved in the language, and from this period date some of the happiest of Pope's compound epithets.

Besides these new words of classical origin, there were many Romance forms which were being tentatively used, and which ultimately went to enrich the English vocabulary. In general, it may be said that they are less abstract in character than those contributed by the classics. Being drawn from living languages, they stand in a closer relation to actual life; they represent new objects rather than new ideas; and so reflect something of the nature of the current intercourse between England and the Romance countries. There were, in the first place, many new words of French origin, and their number, undoubtedly, was increased by the fact that many classical, as well as Italian, works were translated into English from French versions. They consist, for the most part, of words of a general kind, though military terms figure somewhat largely. The following are instances of borrowings connected with the soldier's trade: 'accoutrement,' 'battery,' 'flank,' 'pioneer,' 'calibre,' 'cassock' (a military cloak) and 'colonel' (pronounced in three syllables). Phrases such as 'plaine force' and 'body politicke' were, occasionally, borrowed, besides such common words as 'chart,' 'gallimaufry' (mixture), 'baies' (baize) and 'bombast' (cotton wadding). The word 'essay' now, for the first time, became used in its modern sense owing to Montaigne; 'genteel' represented a re-adoption of the French '*gentil*' which, previously borrowed, had, by this date, become 'gentle'; 'collcaryour' (messenger) was a modification of the French '*colporteur*,' while 'horly borly' was due to the ingenuity of Rabelais. There were, of course, many instances of words which never became Anglicised, for example: '*bourreau*,' '*bruit*,' '*haut*,' '*sanglier*,' '*travise*,' '*sparple*' (scatter), '*mures*' (walls) and '*cassed*' (discharged). The word '*faubourg*' (suburb) and the phrase '*all amort*' (*à la mort*) were naturalised for a time, but only to be treated as foreign at a later date. French influence on the orthography was but slight: the strange forms '*doggue*,' '*pangue*,' '*publique*' are interesting in view of the modern spelling 'tongue'; '*eguall*' represents a blend of both Latin and French.

Of still greater importance were the additions to the vocabulary derived from the Spanish. They were very largely connected with ideas of the New World, more particularly of the West Indies, where Spain had large interests, and, unlike the classical importations, they are concerned with the spoken, rather than with the literary, language. They became familiar in various ways: through the numerous pamphlets which aimed at supplying information about Spain, through translations of Spanish works such as Oviedo's *History of the West Indies*, or, again, through accounts of English voyages. But more important than all was the influence of English adventurers who returned from the west with wondrous tales and strange new words. Many of the words thus introduced had been adopted by the Spaniards from the West Indian (Hayti) language: for example, 'canoe,' 'hurricane,' 'tobacco,' 'maize,' 'cannibal'; but, in the forms 'mosquito,' 'El Dorado,' 'cocoa' and 'alligator,' Romance roots had been employed to denote the new phenomena. Of the remaining words, which were largely bound up with war, commerce or religion, a certain number ended in *-o* (*-ado*), as, 'cargo,' 'embargo,' 'desperado,' 'renegado.' Hence, in numerous others, the *-ado* ending is affected where the Spanish equivalents had *-ada*: for example, '*armado*' (armada), '*ambuscado*,' '*bastinado*,' '*bravado*,' '*carbonado*,' '*palisado*,' '*strappado*.' Other adaptations are, '*Canary*,' '*Bilbo*' (sword), '*fico*' (fig), '*flamingo*' and '*grandee*'; sometimes phrases were borrowed as '*paucas palabris*'[1] (in short) and '*miching mallhecho*.'

A great number of Italian words, also, were introduced at this time, but, as they often came through French, for instance, 'gazette' and 'carnival,' their identification is not always easy. Much of the Italianate English of which Ascham complains never became naturalised; the use of the Italian adverb '*via*' (go on), and '*ben venuto*' (welcome), was merely temporary, while words like '*bona-roba*,' '*amoretti*' and '*borachio*,' which promised to become permanent, were soon regarded as foreign. But English travellers, English traders and English translators could not fail to add something to their native vocabulary, and such words as '*duello*,' '*complimento*' and '*bandetto*'; '*argosy*,' '*magnifico*' and '*Bergomask*' (rustic dance); '*canto*,' '*stanza*' and '*sonnet*,' were among the additions. Architectural terms, too, were borrowed from Italy, for, in Elizabeth's reign, the Tudor style was being modified by the Cinque-cento, English buildings were being constructed after Italian designs and Italian treatises were being turned into English; in consequence, such words as '*belvedere*,' '*antic*,' '*grotta*' and '*portico*' became familiar. The jargon of the Italian fencing-schools also became fashionable, as a result of the displacement of the old broadsword by the foreign rapier: the Bobadils of the day talked freely of the '*punto*,' '*reverso*,' '*stoccato*' and '*passado*[2].'

Dutch borrowings must also be mentioned, though not numerically large. They were introduced by English adventurers who had fought against Spain in the Netherlands, and who, on their return home, larded their conversation with Dutch phrases there acquired: '*easterling*,' '*beleaguer*,' '*burgomaster*,' '*domineer*' and '*forlorn hope*' are instances of such additions. Similarly, oriental words, such as '*caraway*,' '*garbled*,' '*gong*,' '*dervish*' and '*divan*,' witness to extended nautical enterprise; each account of a voyage contained a host of such words, which might or might not become naturalised.

While the language, so far as its vocabulary was concerned,

[1] Corruption of Span. *pocas palabras*. See *Taming of the Shrew*, Ind. 1. 5.

[2] For commercial terms derived from the Italian, see Einstein, L., *The Italian Renaissance in England* (1902), p. 284.

thus kept pace with the expansion of national life and thought, by means of borrowing from abroad, it was also subject to certain internal influences. Literary men, in general, extended the vocabulary by indulging in coinages; but more important than this was the vogue given to certain words and phrases in consequence of their happy use by some of the great writers. Such expressions were stamped with permanency and became current coin of the highest value.

In the first place, new formations, devised by contemporary writers out of material ready at hand, represent an appreciable extension of the normal vocabulary, though, in many cases, they were not to prove permanent. A host of newly-coined compounds are scattered in the works of the time and represent the operation of various devices upon a plastic stage of the language. A spirited style would produce sonorous compounds like 'sky-bred chirpers,' 'heart-scalding sighs,' 'home-keeping wits' and 'cloud-capt towers.' A satirical effect might be obtained by onomatopoeic reduplication such as 'rif-raf,' 'tag-rag' and 'hugger-mugger,' though this formation, being crude and mechanical, failed to maintain a literary rank. A word like 'find-fault' would be coined with an eye to alliterative effect, 'gravel-blind' with a view to a play upon the word 'sand-blind' (*i.e.* sam-blind); while other coinages, like 'ablesse' and 'idlesse,' 'goddise' (deity) and 'grandity,' 'mobocracy,' 'fathership,' 'foehood,' 'praecel' (excel) and 'Turkishness' (barbarism), though they represent a blending of material, intelligible then and now, were rendered unnecessary by forms otherwise constructed, which, in some way or other, have maintained themselves.

Then, again, literary influences at work on the elements of the native vocabulary often resulted in the formation of expressions and phrases to which their authors, indirectly, gave a wide currency and a permanent value. Many of them were to enter into daily conversation, while their innate beauty still renders them fit for the highest literary usage. The main sources of this influence were the works of Spenser and Shakespeare, and the English Bible. From Spenser, we get such forms as 'elfin,' 'Braggadochio,' 'blatant,' 'derring-do' and 'squire of dames'; from Shakespeare, such expressions as 'benedict,' 'the undiscovered country,' 'the primrose path,' 'single blessedness,' 'to die by inches,' 'to eat the leek,' 'this working-day world' and 'coign of vantage'; while from the English Bible come the forms, 'loving-kindness,' 'heavy-laden,' 'peacemaker,' 'scapegoat,' 'shibboleth,' 'mammon,' 'Babel' and 'helpmeet,' as well as the phrases, 'the fat of the land,' 'the eleventh hour,' 'the shadow of death,' 'a soft answer' and 'a labour of love'[1]. Many of these expressions have attained the dignity of unidentified quotations, but, nevertheless, they are contributions to the growth of the language, and, as such, are possessed of as much significance as separate additions to the vocabulary.

While these changes, due, largely, to external influences, were taking place in the vocabulary, the language was also undergoing further changes in its grammatical structure, its syntax and its pronunciation, such modifications being due to those internal influences continually at work upon a living language.

In the first place, it is only natural to find that, while Old English inflections had, for the most part, been levelled, traces of earlier constructions still remained, and in larger quantity than at a later date. Disregarding archaic forms such as 'perishen' (they perish) and 'killen' (they kill), which appear in *Pericles* as obsolete expressions, we find other constructions, which, while they preserve something of the archaic, are still legitimate survivals. For instance, the adverbial form 'moe' is distinguished from the adjectival 'more,' the one indicating 'more in number,' the other, 'greater in size.' 'Can' and 'may' are still capable of being used in their earlier senses[2]. As in Old English, a verb of motion is sometimes omitted after 'will' and 'shall,' 'must' and 'be,' while the old imperative is still in use in the expressions 'go we,' 'praise ye the Lord,' though periphrastic forms like 'let us go' are far more general. The subjunctive is still used in principal sentences to express a wish, also in conditional and concessive clauses, and in temporal clauses introduced by 'ere,' or 'before.' But already this use is obsolete in the spoken language, and, as a result, its appearance in literary English is somewhat irregular.

The pronominal inflections, as in modern English, are, for the most part, retained, owing to the monosyllabic character of the words. The *-s* of the old genitive, of course, survived, though the modern apostrophe was not employed as yet. With this inflection is found, occasionally, the older word-order, as in 'Yorick's skull the king's jester.' This construction, owing to the uninflected character of the word in apposition, in this case 'jester,' involved a certain ambiguity, which had been wanting in Old English, and the idiom, consequently, was not destined to survive. Of still greater interest, however, is the use of 'his,' instead of the genitive *-s*, in phrases like 'Sejanus his Fall,' 'Purchas his Pilgrimage,' 'Christ His sake'

[1] See Bradley's *Making of English*, ch. VI.

[2] Cf. 'they can well on horseback' and 'I may (can) never believe.'

and 'Pompey his preparation.' This construction, which appears, at first sight, to be a popular adaptation of the regular suffix *-s*, represents, in point of fact, the survival of an idiom found in Old English and other Germanic languages, and which can be traced in Middle English, in such phrases as 'Bevis is hed.' It was, doubtless, a form which had come down in colloquial speech, for its early use in literature is only occasional, and it still occurs in modern dialectal and colloquial expressions. Its more extended use in Elizabethan English points to the close connection which then existed between the spoken and literary languages. Another survival of an Old English form was that of participles in *-ed*, adjectival in their force and derived from nouns. In Old English, there had occurred occasional words such as 'hoferede' (hunchbacked), and, in Elizabethan times, the manufacture of such forms as 'high-minded' and 'barefaced' proceeded apace and added considerably to the power of expression.

The earlier loss of inflections had begun by this date, however, to produce certain marked effects. What had once been a synthetic language had now become analytic, and it was in process of developing its expression under the new conditions. The immediate result was a vast number of experiments which often led to confused expressions, more especially as the brevity and conciseness formerly obtained with inflectional aids was still sought. Thus, ellipses were frequent, and almost any word that could be supplied from the context might be omitted. Intransitive verbs were used as transitive[1], ordinary verbs as causal[2], and the infinitive was used with the utmost freedom, for it had to represent active, passive and gerundial constructions[3].

But if the loss of native inflections resulted in a certain freedom of expression, together with a corresponding amount of vagueness and confusion, it also led to some new and permanent usages. In consequence of the fact that final *-e* had now become mute, many of the distinctions formerly effected by that suffix were levelled, and the various parts of speech became interchangeable, as in modern English. Thus, adjectives could be used as adverbs[4], or, again, as nouns[5], and nouns could be used as verbs[6].

The old grammatical gender had, moreover, been lost, together

[1] Cf. 'depart the field,' 'moralise this spectacle.'

[2] Cf. 'to fear (to terrify) the valiant.'

[3] Cf. 'he is to teach' (=he is to be taught): 'why blame you me to love you' (for loving you).

[4] Cf. 'to run fast,' 'to rage fierce.'

[5] Cf. 'the good,' 'the just.'

[6] Cf. 'to man,' 'to paper.'

with the noun-suffixes upon which it was based, and, therefore, in addition to the modern gender based upon sex, poetic gender became possible, which meant, from the literary point of view, a more lively presentment of various phenomena. Flectionless words permitted any gender to be assigned to them, according to the imagination of the writer; thus, words which suggested strength, as, for instance, 'sun,' 'death,' 'war' and 'winter,' could be treated as masculine, while words like 'patience,' 'beauty,' 'church,' 'ship' and 'nightingale,' with more gentle associations, could be regarded as feminine. Although the basis of this personification was mainly psychological in character, it was sometimes influenced by other considerations. In some cases, old mythological notions directed the choice, as when 'Love' is treated as masculine, 'Fortune' as feminine. Ben Jonson, on the other hand, was wont to consider the etymology of the word. But, whatever the method of assigning poetic gender, it was a literary device that only became possible in consequence of levelled inflections[1].

Further changes, due, very largely, to the same cause, were the development of the passive forms characteristic of modern English, and of personal constructions in preference to impersonal. In older English, the passive had been rare, the usual form having been the active with the indefinite nominative 'man' (Mid. Eng. 'me')[2]. But, with the loss of inflections in the oblique cases of nouns, an earlier object was easily taken as the new subject; and, since the indefinite 'man' had become obsolete, and was not yet replaced by the modern form 'one,' the verb naturally assumed a passive form. The result of this change was to render the interest personal throughout; the psychological and the grammatical subjects fell together and the expression gained in directness.

Similarly, the number of impersonal verbs, which had figured largely in earlier constructions, became, during this period, considerably reduced. This was due, in part, to the levelling of case-forms in nouns; for an impersonal construction with an uninflected dative would thus readily pass into a personal construction with a direct nominative[3]. Other causes, no doubt, contributed to this change, one being the influence of analogy exercised by the numerous personal constructions upon the much rarer forms of an impersonal kind; and this influence would be inevitable

[1] See Franz, *Shakespeare-Grammatik*, § 50.

[2] Cf. 'his broðor Horsan man ofsloh' (his brother Horsa was slain), O.E. *Chron.* 455.

[3] Thus, the quarto reading of *Richard III*, Act III, sc. 2. 99 is 'that it please your lordship,' while, in the folio, it stands, 'that your lordship please to ask.' See Franz, *Shakespeare-Grammatik*, § 473.

in a sentence such as 'This aunswer Alexander both lyked and rewarded,' where the impersonal form 'lyked' is linked with a verb of the personal type.

The classical influence upon Elizabethan idiom was but slight, for grammars, unlike vocabularies, never mix: the borrowing of grammatical forms on any considerable scale would involve a change in the method of thought, which is an inconceivable step in the history of any language. Occasional traces of classical idiom, of course, exist in Elizabethan literary English. The Latin use of *quin* is seen in such a sentence as 'I do not deny but,' and the Latin participial construction in the phrase 'upon occasion offered.' Comparatives are sometimes used where no comparison is intended, as in 'a plainer (rather plain) sort,' while a phrase such as 'of all others[1] the greatest' (*i.e.* the greatest of all) is, plainly, a Grecism. Individual authors, such as Hooker, will, sometimes, be found to omit auxiliary forms, or to give to certain emphatic words a Latinised importance of position. But, in general, attempts to convey Latin idiom into Elizabethan English were few, and, where they existed, they added no new grace. Such attempts were, indeed, foredoomed to failure, for their object was to imitate, in a language almost stripped of inflections, certain constructions which, in their original language, had depended upon inflections as aids to clearness. And this was the reason why the *oratio obliqua* was a dangerous experiment, while the long Latin sentence, with its involved relative clauses, simply tended to create a confused and inelegant method of expression.

With regard to Elizabethan pronunciation, certain differences, as compared with the sound-values of earlier and later times, may, perhaps, be noted. By 1600, Caxton's pronunciation had undergone certain changes, but it has also to be remembered that the sound of a given word might vary even within one and the same period, and this was due not only to the existence of doublets and dialectal variants at an earlier date, but, also, to the survival of sounds which were becoming archaic alongside their later developments. The Middle English open ē (seen in 'leaf' and 'heat') retained the fifteenth century sound (heard in 'pail'), which prevailed down to the eighteenth century, but it was frequently shortened in closed syllables, particularly before dentals, though no change was made in the orthography (cf. 'bread' and 'death'). The Middle English close ē (seen in 'deep' and 'bleed') also retained its fifteenth century sound (heard in 'pail'), but, at the same time, it was adopting a more modern value, namely, the sound heard in 'peel': before *r*, however,

[1] See Bacon's *Essays*, ed. West, A. S., p. 293.

an open value might still be retained (cf. 'hear'). In the spellings 'indide' (indeed), 'quin' (queen), 'bin' (been)[1], the classical ī stands for this later sound of the Middle English close ē. Middle English open ō (seen in 'goad' and 'stone') also retained its fifteenth century value (heard in 'pole'), and, to this, the word 'one' is no exception. The modern pronunciation of this word, as if with an initial *w*, was certainly not usual in Elizabethan times, and this is plainly suggested by such forms as 'such an one,' 'th'one,' and, also, by Shakespeare's rime of 'one' with 'Scone.' It seems, however, to have been general in the seventeenth century and may have been a provincialism in the sixteenth: the form 'wholesome,' with the *w*, appears in 1550. The Middle English close ō (seen in 'doom'), while it retained its fifteenth century sound (heard in 'pole'), also approximated its modern value (heard in 'pool'); and, about this date, Middle English ī and ū (*ou*) seem to have developed diphthongal values. The earlier value ī (heard in 'he') moves on towards the modern sound heard in 'while'; and, similarly, the earlier sound of ū (heard in 'boot') approximated the modern diphthongal value heard in 'house'[2].

With regard to consonants, the differences between Elizabethan and modern pronunciation are comparatively slight. It would appear that *r* was strongly trilled, for 'fire' and 'hire' appear in Shakespeare as dissyllabic, 'Henry' and 'angry' as trisyllabic; and, again, the pronunciation of *gh* (as *f*) seems to have been more frequent than at a later date, when, however, we have it in words such as 'laugh' and 'draught.' In Chapman, 'wrought' and 'taught' appear with this sound-value; in Shakespeare, 'after' is found riming with 'daughter'[3].

The task of ascertaining these sixteenth century sound-values was one of some difficulty, owing to the fact that Caxton's spelling was no longer capable of representing any changes in pronunciation. Fortunately, however, these values were preserved as a result of a series of attempts made by certain scholars[4] to denote the current pronunciation with the help of phonetic symbols. The works proceeded from various motives: one aimed at amending English orthography, another at teaching the pronunciation of Greek; but,

[1] *Letters of Queen Elizabeth* (Ellis's collection 1553—76).

[2] Further differences between Elizabethan and modern pronunciation are suggested by the rimes 'all,' 'shall'; 'racks,' 'takes'; 'steel,' 'well'; 'concert,' 'right'; 'join,' 'shine'; 'seas,' 'press'; although rimes are not invariably correct tests of pronunciation.

[3] *The Taming of the Shrew*, Act I, sc. 1. 244—5.

[4] See bibliography.

whatever their objects, their phonetic systems have preserved sixteenth century sound-values. The most important of these contributions was due to William Salesbury, who, in 1547, compiled *A Dictionary of Englishe and Welshe*, and, subsequently, wrote a tract on the pronunciation of Welsh (1567). In the dictionary, he had transcribed into Welsh characters some 150 English words; and, since he had clearly denoted in his tract the sound-values of Welsh letters, the pronunciation of the transliterated English words may thus be easily inferred.

Some of the main points in the development of the language during the fifteenth and sixteenth centuries have now been touched upon: namely, the evolution and development of a standard literary dialect, the rapid extension of the vocabulary and the completion of the change from an inflected to an uninflected character. It now remains to attempt an estimate of Elizabethan English as a literary medium, so far as such an estimate is possible.

In the first place, the language, at this date, was in an eminently plastic condition, which made the utmost freedom of expression possible. Men wrote very much as they spoke; the literary language has probably never stood nearer to the colloquial, and, consequently, it was peculiarly adapted to express the exuberant thought and feeling of the age.

But, while this freedom gave to Elizabethan utterance a naturalness and a force which have never been surpassed, it also led to numerous structural anomalies, frequent and even natural in ordinary speech. Literary expression was now less hampered than ever by inflectional considerations, and writers, not cognisant as yet of the logic which was to underlie the new grammar, indulged in expressions which set rules of concord at defiance. Thus, the form of a verb might be determined by the character of the nearest substantive, or two constructions might be confused and merged into one: almost any arrangement seemed justified, provided the sense were reasonably well conveyed. And this irregularity, the inevitable concomitant of Elizabethan freedom of expression, is, also, one of its disabilities, for it introduced an element of vagueness and ambiguity into contemporary writing. But such irregularity was not wholly due to the influence of colloquial speech: it could arise out of the undeveloped condition of the grammatical machinery then in existence. The conjunctions often gave but slight indications of the relation of the sentences which they joined: a word like 'but' would have to convey numerous meanings and would be represented in modern English by 'if not,' 'except,' 'when,' 'that,' 'without that.' Prepositions, too, were used in a manner far from definite: 'in' and 'on,' 'of' and 'from,' 'with' and 'by,' were yet to be distinguished, while 'for' would have to do duty for the phrases 'as regards,' 'in spite of,' 'for want of.' Then, again, the subjective and objective genitives were not clearly distinguished; a phrase like 'your injuries' had to stand for either, and the same indefiniteness occurs in such phrases as 'distressful bread' (bread hardly-won) and 'feeling sorrows' (sorrows deeply felt). The context, in each case, had to correct what was ambiguous in the expression and to supply its actual meaning.

Some efforts, were, of course, made to obtain greater clearness and precision, for the uninflected language was beginning to work out its expression under the new conditions. For instance, the neuter form 'its,' which aimed at avoiding the confusion caused by the older use of 'his,' for both masculine and neuter, occurs as early as 1598, though it was not until the second half of the seventeenth century that it was fully recognised. The suffix 'self' was used more frequently to indicate reflexives, and a pronoun would often be inserted to help out an expression. But, generally speaking, clearness was not always the first aim, and, as often as not, writers were content with an expression which sacrificed precision to brevity and pregnancy of utterance.

With all its tendencies to run into confused expression, Elizabethan English was, however, pre-eminently the language of feeling, and it was such in virtue of its concrete and picturesque character and its various devices for increasing vividness of presentment. In the first place, it contained precisely the material for expressing thought with a concreteness and a force not since possible. Comparatively poor in abstract and learned words, though these were being rapidly acquired, it abounded in words which had a physical signification, and which conveyed their meaning with splendid strength and simplicity. And this accounts for the felicitous diction of the Bible translations. The Hebrew narratives were made up of simple concrete terms and objective facts, and the English of that time, from its very constitution, reproduced these elements with a success that would have been impossible for the more highly developed idiom of later times. Between the Hebrew idiom and that of the Elizabethan, in short, there existed certain clear affinities, which Tindale had fully appreciated.

Then, again, this absence of general and abstract terms gave to Elizabethan English a picturesqueness all its own. The description of the Psalmist's despair as a 'sinking in deep mire,' or a 'coming into deep waters,' is paralleled in character on almost every page of Elizabethan work; and it was this abundance of figurative language which favoured Euphuism, and which constituted something of the later charms of Fuller and Sir Thomas Browne. Nor can the effect of a number of picturesque intensives be overlooked, as seen in the phrases 'clean starved,' 'passing strange,' 'shrewdly vexed' and 'to strike home.' The discarding of these intensives and the substitution of eighteenth century forms like 'vastly' and 'prodigiously,' and the nineteenth century 'very' and 'quite,' have resulted in a distinct loss of vigour and colour[1].

Further, the Elizabethan writer had at his command certain means for heightening the emotional character of a passage and for increasing the vividness of presentment. Thus, the discriminating use of 'thou' and 'you' could depict a variety of feeling in a way, and with a subtlety, no longer possible. 'You' was the unimpassioned form which prevailed in ordinary speech among the educated classes, whereas 'thou' could express numerous emotions such as anger, contempt, familiarity, superiority, or love. The ethical dative[2], too, added to the vividness of expression, suggesting, as it did, the interest felt by either the speaker or the hearer; while even the illogical double negatives[3] and double comparatives[4] were capable of producing a heightening effect in the language of passion.

The freedom and brevity, the concrete and picturesque character, of Elizabethan English, were, therefore, among the qualities which rendered it an effective medium of literary thought. At the same time, the language is seen to lend itself easily to rhythmical and harmonious expression, and it is not improbable that the sixteenth century translators of the Bible were among the first to realise with any adequacy the musical resources of the vernacular, they themselves having been inspired by the harmonies of their Latin models. The language of the *Vulgate* was certainly familiar to sixteenth century readers, and the translators must have worked with its rhythm and its tones ringing in their ears; while the close resemblance between the constructions and word-order of the Latin text and those used in English would render it an easier task to reproduce other qualities of that text. At all events, in

[1] Cf., also, the substitution of 'certainly,' 'indeed,' for 'i'faith,' 'i'sooth,' 'iwis,' 'certes.'

[2] *E.g.* 'villain knock me this gate.' [3] *E.g.* 'nor no further in sport neither.'

[4] *E.g.* 'more elder.'

the Biblical translations and the liturgy of the sixteenth century we find the broad vowels, the musical rhythm and the tones which had been the glory of the *Vulgate*: the English ear had become attuned, for the first time, to the vocalic music of the vernacular. Consonantal effects, which were still more characteristic of English, had long been turned to account in the native alliteration.

For the purpose of working out these rhythmical effects and of heightening the natural harmonies of the spoken language, certain linguistic aids were available. In the unsettled state of the language, there were certain variant forms, some of which were obsolete, which could still be utilised in prose as well as in verse. For instance, verbal forms in *-eth* (3rd pers. pres. sing.) were seldom used in ordinary speech; but, in a line like 'It blesseth him that gives and him that takes,' both the archaic and the current forms appear, to the improvement of the rhythm. Similarly, final *-ed* could be pronounced or not according to the required rhythm, as in the line 'Thou changed and self-cover'd thing,' and these devices have since remained with the poets. Then, again, the particle 'the' could, if necessary, be omitted in archaic fashion, for its modern definitive character had not yet been assumed. Advantage might, also, be taken of the unsettled state of the accent in Latin words, like 'complete' and 'extreme,' to accentuate such words in accordance with metrical exigencies; while the unemphatic 'do,' though obsolescent at this date, might frequently help out the rhythm in both verse and prose[1].

As regards its musical resources, however, Elizabethan English, as well as later English, had certain marked limitations. It was a language overloaded with consonants, many of them harsh and dissonant in character; and it was the prevalence of consonantal endings that made the language poor in rimes, as contrasted with the Italian, which abounded in words with vowel terminations. It also possessed a great abundance of half-pronounced vowels, which were neither long nor short and which defeated the attempts of the Areopagites to make the language run into classical moulds. The choice of metrical forms, as a matter of fact, was largely determined by the native method of accentuation; the majority of words of more than one syllable developed, naturally, a trochaic, iambic, or dactylic rhythm, and these were the elements out of which the stately blank verse and the many lyrical forms were built. Another inherent disability under which

[1] *E.g.* 'Why should he stay, whom love *doth* press to go.' See Franz, *Shak.-Gram.* § 444.

Elizabethan English laboured was that its word-order was necessarily more fixed, and, therefore, less elastic, than was the case with the highly-inflected languages of antiquity, which required no such rigidity of position. Furthermore, its grammatical forms lacked variety and, while it abounded in monosyllabic words, it was short of the much-resounding polysyllabic words, so that a rhythmical grace was not so inevitable as in Latin or Greek.

In the centuries which have followed the age of Elizabeth, the language has undergone many changes, and these changes may be roughly summarised, first, as the extension of the vocabulary to keep pace with the ever-widening thought, and, secondly, as the adaptation of the structure of the language to clearer and more precise expression. In the course of time, the numerous national activities, the pursuits of science and art, of commerce and politics, have enriched its expression with their various terminologies. Literal uses have become metaphorical, concrete terms, abstract; many words have depreciated in meaning, and the line has been drawn more rigidly between words literary and non-literary. There has been in the language what Coleridge calls 'an instinct of growth ... working progressively to desynonymise those words of originally the same meaning,' and this division of labour has enabled the language to express finer shades of thought. The verbal conjugation has been enriched, the elements which made for vagueness have been removed and in every way the language has adapted itself to a scientific age, which requires, before all things, clear, accurate and precise expression.

But Elizabethan English, alone among the earlier stages of our language, still plays a part in modern intellectual life. Thanks to the English Bible, the prayer-book and Shakespeare, it has never become really obsolete. Its diction and its idioms are still familiar, endeared and consecrated by sacred association. It yet remains the inspiration of our noblest styles, for beyond its concrete strength, its picturesque simplicity and its forceful directness, English expression cannot go. And so, in moments of exaltation the old phrases are recalled, untainted by any mingling in the market place, and, with their rich suggestiveness, they heighten the passion or beauty which a more explicit idiom would destroy. Modern English is the fitting medium of an age which leaves little unexplained; while Elizabethan English stands for an age too hasty to analyse what it felt. The one has the virtues of maturity, a logic, uncompromising and clear: the other, a vigour and a felicity, the saving graces of youth.

CAMBRIDGE: PRINTED BY
W. LEWIS, M.A.
AT THE UNIVERSITY PRESS